DAYS OF GLORY

DAYS OF GLORY

THE ARMY OF THE CUMBERLAND

1861–1865

Larry J. Daniel

LOUISIANA STATE UNIVERSITY PRESS

BATON ROUGE

DESIGNER: Amanda McDonald Scallan
TYPEFACE: Minion
TYPESETTER: Coghill Composition Co., Inc.
PRINTER AND BINDER: Thomson-Shore, Inc.

Library of Congress Cataloging-in-Publication Data

Daniel, Larry J., 1947–
Days of glory : the Army of the Cumberland, 1861–1865 /
Larry J. Daniel.
    p.   cm.
    Includes bibliographical references and index.
    ISBN 0-8071-2931-3 (alk. paper)
1. United States. Army of the Cumberland.   2. United
States—History—Civil War, 1861–1865—Regimental
histories.   3. United States—History—Civil War,
1861–1865—Campaigns.   I. Title.
E470.5.D355   2004
973.7′41—dc22

                                        200400584

The paper in this book meets the guidelines for permanence
and durability of the Committee on Production Guidelines
for Book Longevity of the Council on Library Resources. ⊗

for Marilyn, Lauren, and Mark

CONTENTS

ILLUSTRATIONS

PREFACE

THE OVERALL HISTORY of the Army of the Cumberland has been neglected. This indifference is perhaps understandable in light of how the nation has chosen to view the Civil War, namely through the eyes of the eastern armies. Even in light of more-recent western revisionism, however, this neglect has strangely continued. The modern reader sees the army's history only in fragments, through battle mono-logues or biographies that do not deal with the totality.

The only serious history is Thomas B. Van Horne's two-volume *The Army of the Cumberland,* a postwar work that fails in a couple of respects. First, it ignores the intra-army bickering that so often wracked the command; indeed, the officer corps was neither solidified nor fraternal. Second, the volumes often read like the imper-sonal battle reports that appear in the *Official Records* of the war. Third, Van Horne was a George Thomas advocate and one of his chief biographers. It was his clear attempt to vindicate the general and have him emerge as the army's hero. Indeed, Thomas actually approached Van Horne about writing the history, furnished him with documents, and edited the manuscript. Thomas has enjoyed a recent resur-gence in popularity due to historians such as Thomas Buell and Richard McMurry. Albert Castel has pronounced him the second-greatest Northern general, behind only Ulysses S. Grant.

In the present volume, George Thomas emerges as the catalyst that gave the army its lethal edge, but he is a flawed character who does not mature until late 1863. Undoubtedly Thomas supporters (the general has two Web sites) will think me "too hard" on him. I did not begin with a set conclusion but simply followed the sources. Much of his reputation is grounded in postwar writings that cannot be substantiated in contemporary evidence. In 1882, as a part of the Scribner's cam-paign series, Henry M. Cist wrote a brief volume entitled *The Army of the Cumber-land,* which includes little new information and leaves out much. While exonerating the army's high command, he blames incompetent corps commanders for failures.

More recently, Gerald Prokopowicz's *All for the Regiment* documented the his-tory of the Cumberland's predecessor, the Army of the Ohio. While an excellent work, it concentrates less on strategy and politics and offers a somewhat different twist, in that its primary function is to document the influence of small units on the army's development. Prokopowicz asserts that the manner in which the army was recruited and organized proved to be the primary determiner of performance. The Army of the Cumberland's primary opponent, the Confederate Army of Tennessee, has had its history told in Thomas L. Connelly's iconoclastic two-volume work *Army of the Heartland* and *Autumn of Glory*. Amid modern western revisionism, it is time that the main Union army in the West receive its own full-length treatment.

The sheer volume of manuscript material in the National Archives and in the Don Carlos Buell and William Rosecrans collections has perhaps dissuaded serious researchers. Much of the material has been previously published in the *Official Records*, but still thousands of other documents, as might be suspected, had to be discarded as useless for a study of this type. Thus, weeks of tedious research had to be spent in ferreting out nuggets buried deep within old bound volumes, all of which leave a tan-colored dirt on everything that they touch. The effort, however, has uncovered previously ignored sources that shed light on significant areas. Additionally, several state archives, particularly those of Indiana and Ohio, proved invaluable.

Another problem relating to the Army of the Cumberland is the lack of colorful units and flamboyant officers. There were no "Iron Brigades" (although John Turchin's brigade perfunctorily carried that name), "Irish Brigades," or "Fighting 69th" regiments that have so captivated students of the Army of the Potomac. Strangely the western army possessed only one sharpshooter unit. That is not to suggest that the army lacked color. For sheer raunchiness, the Irishmen of Chicago's 19th and 24th Illinois Infantry could match any unit in the East. While Don Carlos Buell and William Rosecrans both have solid modern biographies and George Thomas several of them (and another on the way by Brian Wills), most of the officers at the corps and division level (with the notable exception of Phil Sheridan) have been ignored. Commanders such as Alexander McCook, Thomas L. Crittenden, Lovell Rousseau, Charles Gilbert, Richard Johnson, and Thomas Wood are known only to Civil War scholars who wander off well-beaten paths. Even more renowned characters such as the brutish William "Bull" Nelson have received only slight treatment. In the West it has been Ulysses S. Grant and William T. Sherman, both of whom came out of the Army of the Tennessee, who have been highlighted by historians. The Cumberland army does not deserve this neglect.

Certainly the baleful influence of its early commanders, Robert Anderson and Sherman, negatively influenced the army's formative period. Buell's war aims and lack of ruthlessness ultimately placed him at odds with Washington officials and the majority of his soldiers. Although certainly superior to Buell, Rosecrans's "them versus us" bias against the War Department; his inability to grasp the interconnectedness of strategy, politics, and the fragility of the war coalition; and his lack of restraint in expressing opinions created a poisonous atmosphere with Republican officials, western Democrats, and to a lesser degree his own officer corps. Thomas, even before assuming command, held the position of revered senior adviser. But he was not totally liberated from the pettiness and parochial thinking that hindered his predecessors, his apologists' views notwithstanding. Clearly he lost his respect for Buell and perhaps resented being superseded twice by juniors, Rosecrans and Sherman, the last whom he had personally seen fail both in Kentucky and at Missionary Ridge.

The picture that emerges is that of an army exasperated in achieving its potential due to command discord, feeble leadership, politics, and a War Department that often viewed it as a stepchild to the Army of the Potomac. Indeed, Castel has referred to the Army of the Cumberland as "Lincoln's other army." Yet the army was charged with the defense of the Ohio Valley, the very heart of the North, a three-hundred-mile front with both Louisville and Cincinnati to protect as well as hundreds of miles of railroad. Nevertheless, entire divisions were siphoned off, leaving the field army's strength at barely more than parity with the Confederates during the Kentucky campaign and at Stones River, while at Chickamauga it was outnumbered. Thus, the Cumberlanders had to defend five times the territory of the Army of the Potomac with typically one-third to one-half fewer men.

The army evolved as the war progressed. Its initial assignment, the occupation of Kentucky and the liberation of East Tennessee, became an obsession with Pres. Abraham Lincoln and swayed the choices for army and division command. The Kentucky bloc would continue to have disproportionate influence up to the beginning of 1863. By that time the tremendous influx of Indiana and Ohio regiments could no longer be trumped, especially in the fall of 1862, when an entire corps was added to the Army of the Ohio. This addition altered the army's persona—older, more urban and diverse, and strongly Buckeye and Hoosier. Views also began to change on emancipation, influenced by what the men saw and more-liberal upper midwestern regiments from Wisconsin, Michigan, and Minnesota.

Yet another change occurred in mid-1863 as the cavalry finally came of age. No longer could the enemy penetrate deep into Kentucky and strike at random at vital Federal communications. Their evolving organization, with the added power of modern carbines, enabled the blue troopers first to match, and later at times to excel, the vaunted Confederate cavalry.

One oddity of the army is the length of time that it took for it to solidify. The various divisions did not fight a battle as a cohesive unit until Stones River in late December 1862. At Mill Springs, Shiloh, and Perryville, only certain divisions were engaged, and not the same ones at that. None of the army's regiments, up until Stones River, could claim more than a single laurel on their flag.

The format of this book is based upon the model of Connelly's work, that is, an analysis that focuses primarily upon the command level—the personalities of the generals and the dynamics between them. I have stayed clear of battle minutiae that can easily be found in other works and have concentrated more on an analysis of the strategic campaigns and the epic struggle that unfolded. Information not known to army commanders at the time is usually relegated to footnotes. Unlike Connelly, I have attempted, at least on a small scale, to incorporate the thoughts of the men in the ranks, especially on significant issues such as morale, conscription, emancipation, the peace movement, and the 1864 presidential election.

A word on the Atlanta campaign. The Army of the Cumberland ceased to operate as a distinctive force after Sherman took command in the West. In order to maintain subject focus, I tell the story of the campaign as seen through the view of the Cumberland army, not the collective army group. Subjects not distinctive to the Army of the Cumberland, such as logistics and cavalry raids, are generally bypassed. Nor is Sherman as a commander analyzed to any degree but rather considered through his ambivalent relationship with George Thomas and his army.

Ending the book proved somewhat problematical. After Atlanta, the army was discontinued, the XIV and XX Corps going with Sherman in his March to the Sea, under the name Army of Georgia, and the IV going with Thomas to Tennessee, where it fought in the Battle of Nashville alongside other units. Van Horne, who desired to follow Thomas's career, resolved the issue by writing about both Nashville and the March to the Sea. Although the story largely ends in September 1864, I feel justified in giving an epilogue of Thomas and the IV Corps in the Tennessee campaign. If any unit represented the heart of the Army of the Cumberland, it was the IV, the successor to the old XX and XXI Corps, originally the Left Wing and Right Wing.

I initially determined to devote six years to this project; it took over seven. In a real sense, I feel as though I have lived in the ranks of the Army of the Cumberland. As I began my research on chapter 1, I saw personalities unfold and, through thousands of letters and diaries, witnessed the men themselves evolve from untrained volunteers to hardened soldiers. This evolutionary veteran character was especially apparent in their increasing hatred of the Rebels and, by the summer of 1862, their need to vent retaliation. It is an epic story that, for good or for bad, the men in their postwar army society meetings would remember with pride—their days of glory.

ACKNOWLEDGMENTS

I am deeply indebted to Albert Castel of Hillsdale, Michigan, and Steven Wood-worth of Fort Worth, Texas, for reading the manuscript in its entirety and offering valuable criticisms, suggestions, and encouragement. While I was doing research at the Ohio Historical Society, Albert drove down to Columbus to meet me and graciously took me out to dinner. Steven and I usually bump into each other at various speaking engagements or at the annual meeting of the Historians of the Civil War Western Theater. We always have a marvelous time "catching up." Both men are national-level Civil War historians and valued friends.

While the personnel at several national parks proved most helpful in my research, I must single out Jim Ogden of the Chickamauga-Chattanooga National Military Park for putting up with me on a couple of trips that spanned several days. Also I am indebted to another longtime friend, Nat Hughes of Chattanooga. Nat was concurrently working on his own project for LSU Press about Jefferson C. Davis of the Army of the Cumberland. He graciously shared information and served as a sounding board for ideas.

ABBREVIATIONS

B&L	Robert U. Johnson and Clarence C. Buel, eds., *Battles and Leaders of the Civil War*, 4 vols. (1887–88; reprint, New York, 1956)
BHLUM	Bentley Historical Library, University of Michigan, Ann Arbor
"Buell Statement"	"Statement of Maj. Gen. Buell in Review of the Evidence before the Military Commission" (Cincinnati: N.p., 1863)
CCNMP	Chickamauga-Chattanooga National Military Park, Chattanooga, Tenn.
CHS	Chicago Historical Society
CINHS	Cincinnati Historical Society
FC	Filson Club, Louisville, Ky.
ILSHL	Illinois State Historical Library, Springfield
INHS	Indiana Historical Society, Indianapolis
KC	Knox College, Galesburg, Ill.
KNMP	Kennesaw National Military Park, Marietta, Ga.
LC	Library of Congress, Washington, D.C.
MASS	*Papers of the Military Historical Society of Massachusetts*, 14 vols. (Boston: Military Historical Society of Massachusetts, 1910)
MOLLUS	Military Order of the Loyal Legion of the United States
N&S	*North and South*
NA	National Archives, Washington, D.C.
OHS	Ohio Historical Society, Columbus
OR	U.S. War Department, *The War of the Rebellion: A Compilation*

of the Official Records of the Union and Confederate Armies, 128 vols. (Washington, D.C., 1880–1902). All citations are from series 1 unless otherwise indicated.

PBSHP	Perryville Battlefield State Historic Park, Perryville, Ky.
RG	Record Group
SNMP	Shiloh National Military Park, Shiloh, Tenn.
SRNBP	Stones River National Battlefield Park, Murfreesboro, Tenn.
UCLA	University of California, Los Angeles
USAMHI	U.S. Army Military History Institute, Carlisle Barracks, Pa.
WRHS	Western Reserve Historical Society, Cleveland, Ohio

PART 1

THE ANDERSON-SHERMAN LEGACY

1

Birth of an Army
The Anderson Legacy

IN THE SUMMER of 1861, troops chiefly from the Ohio Valley formed the genesis of what would become the North's second-most-powerful army. Tough, hard-fighting, and sometimes undisciplined and atrocious, these rugged westerners were soldiers second to none in the Federal army. Although initially named the Army of the Ohio, this force would eventually be remembered as the Army of the Cumberland.

Bronze-complexioned, white-haired, fifty-seven-year-old Brig. Gen. Robert Anderson had been offered a leave of absence after his highly proclaimed, though futile, defense of Fort Sumter, South Carolina, in April 1861. He instead chose an active field command and in May was assigned to the newly organized Department of Kentucky. Anderson brought with him a distinguished service record, having taught at West Point and fought in the Seminole and Mexican Wars. He never completely recovered from a bullet that lodged in his shoulder during the Battle of Chapultepec. A Kentuckian by birth, he was a Federal loyalist of the proslavery but antisecession persuasion, declaring that he would go to Europe if his state seceded. Unfortunately, his heart was never in the prosecution of a total war against the Confederacy, and he proved a poor choice.[1]

Kentucky was of great political-strategic importance. The state provided a buffer from a Confederate attack upon the lower Midwest. Control of both the Ohio River

1. *OR*, 52:140, 147; Roy Merideth, *Storm over Sumter: The Opening Engagement of the Civil War* (New York: Simon and Schuster, 1957), 35–36; "General Robert Anderson," in *The Army Reunion: Reports of the Meetings of the Society of the Army of the Cumberland, Fifth Reunion* (Cincinnati: Robert Clark, 1871), 189; Abner Doubleday, *Reminiscences of Forts Sumter and Moultrie in 1860–61* (New York: Harper, 1876), 42; Carl Sandburg, *Abraham Lincoln: The War Years*, 4 vols. (New York: Harcourt, Brace, 1939), 3:237; Patricia L. Faust, ed., *Historical Times Illustrated Encyclopedia of the Civil War* (New York: Harper and Row, 1986), 15; Ezra J. Warner, *Generals in Blue: Lives of the Union Commanders* (Baton Rouge: Louisiana State University Press, 1964), 7; *Cincinnati Commercial*, May 11, 1861.

Secretary of War Salmon P. Chase noted that "nobody cd. [could] reasonably object to Anderson's appointment. His character, position, services and worth all made his appointment a necessity." Chase to Nelson, Aug. 29, 1861, *The Salmon P. Chase Papers*, 4 vols., ed. John Niven (Kent, Ohio: Kent State University Press, 1993–97), 3:90.

and the Cumberland Gap in the Appalachians was vital. Although iron ore production had declined, the state remained rich in coal, pork, corn, and horses. The strong pro-unionist vote in the congressional race of June 1861 and the August state-representative election revealed that Kentuckians understood that their loyalty and economic future lay with the North. The six-thousand-member Union Club of Louisville, a secret society pledging Federal loyalty, spread rapidly throughout Kentucky and eastern Tennessee. Yet the Bluegrass region, hardly a hotbed of secessionism, had no stomach for a war with the South. The western portion of the state, the old Jackson Purchase, openly espoused pro-Southern sentiments. The four-thousand-man state guard was virtually an armed Confederate brigade, and Gov. Beriah Magoffin conspired with Southern operatives. In short, the future of the state was by no means certain.[2]

The people of Indiana and Ohio hoped that Kentuckians would lean toward the North, thus preserving the unity of the Ohio Valley. The Ohio River, the geographic feature that connected the region, meandered past rich farmland, coal fields, and teeming smokestacks. Some 250 steamboats, one hundred freight barges, and two hundred coal barges plied the river daily, bringing vital commerce to Louisville and the "Queen City of the West," Cincinnati, Ohio. The Louisville and Nashville Railroad, completed in January 1860, served as a further economic glue. The people of the valley were homogenous—mostly white, mostly rural; only fifteen towns had a population of more than five thousand. Yet the Ohio River divided the valley culturally and politically and served as the boundary between the North and the South, its northern bank free, the southern bank slave.[3]

2. OR, 1:167–70; J. Winston Coleman Jr., "Old Kentucky Iron Furnaces," The Filson Club Historical Quarterly 31 (July 1957): 239; Manufacturers of the United States in 1860; Compiled from the Original Returns of the Eighth Census, under the Direction of the Secretary of the Interior (Washington, D.C.: Government Printing Office, 1865), clxxiv; Agriculture of the U.S. in 1860: Compiled from the Original Returns of the Eighth Census, under the Direction of the Secretary of the Interior (Washington, D.C.: Government Printing Office, 1864), 62–63; Thomas Speed, The Union Cause in Kentucky, 1860–1865 (New York: Knickerbocker, 1907), 89–90; Shelby Foote, The Civil War: A Narrative, 3 vols. (New York: Random House, 1958), 1:86; E. Merton Coulter, The Civil War and Readjustment in Kentucky (Chapel Hill: University of North Carolina Press, 1926), 123; Allan Nevins, Ordeal for the Union, 4 vols. (reprint, New York: Macmillan, 1992), 3(1):132; R. M. Kelly, "Holding Kentucky for the Union," in B&L, 1:375; William C. Davis, The Orphan Brigade: The Kentucky Confederates Who Couldn't Go Home (New York: Doubleday, 1980), 8–9; James M. McPherson, Battle Cry of Freedom: The Civil War Era (New York: Oxford University Press, 1988), 284.

3. Roy P. Basler, ed., The Collected Works of Abraham Lincoln, 9 vols. (New Brunswick, N.J.: Rutgers University Press, 1953–55), 4:532; Kenneth M. Stampp, "Kentucky's Influence upon Indiana in the Crisis of 1861," Indiana Magazine of History 39 (Sept. 1943): 264; OR, 52(1):164; Excursion Made by the Executive and Legislatures of the States of Kentucky and Tennessee to the State of Ohio, January 1860 (Cincinnati: Robert Clarke, 1860), 51; Carl Russell Fish, "The Decision of the Ohio Valley," in American Historical

Pres. Abraham Lincoln had a strong desire to prevent secessionists from gaining control of Kentucky, believing, "to lose Kentucky is nearly to lose the whole game." The declared neutrality of the state legislature thus proved politically sensitive. Despite war cries from the press and the governors of Illinois, Indiana, and Ohio, Lincoln recognized that Kentucky would be secure short of an overt mistake. Throughout the summer of 1861, the administration's nursing policy tolerated slavery, neutrality, and even state trade with the South. Lincoln banked on stealth, not threats. While James Russell Lowell sneered at his "Little Bo-Peep policy," the president continued to show restraint until he had the state squarely in the Union column.[4]

Anderson's command thus remained nominal. He had no army and only managed recruiting south of the Ohio River. Although his department comprised northern Kentucky, he diplomatically established his headquarters in Cincinnati. A scheduled trip to Louisville in mid-May 1861 was made quietly for fear of demonstrations.[5]

From the outset, Anderson was plagued with a degenerative brain disease ("softening of the brain," army surgeons called it) and nervous exhaustion. He became bedridden soon after his arrival in the West and recuperated at the mansion of his brother Larz in Cincinnati. Although briefly rallying, in mid-June Anderson nearly suffered a breakdown, this time convalescing in Altoona, Pennsylvania. Officials at the War Department were left in a quandary.[6]

On the advice of prominent Kentuckians James Speed, James Guthrie, Jeremiah Boyle, John Marshall Harlan, and others, the actual work of organizing unionist home-guard forces was surreptitiously done by state agents, several of whom would become key players in the Army of the Cumberland. William Nelson, a bombastic,

Association, Annual Report of 1910 (N.p., 1910), 155–56; John Y. Simon, "Lincoln, Grant, and Kentucky in 1861," in *The Civil War in Kentucky: Battle for the Bluegrass State,* ed. Kent Masterson Brown (Mason City, Iowa: Savas, 2000), 19. David Donald concludes, "Ties of kinship and commerce, along with the institution of slavery, linked Kentucky to the South, but a long tradition, personified by Henry Clay and John J. Crittenden, bound the state to the Union." *Lincoln* (New York: Simon and Schuster, 1995), 299. About 20 percent of Kentucky's population was enslaved. Randall M. Miller and John Davis Smith, *Dictionary of Afro-American Slavery* (Westport, Conn.: Praeger, 1997), 383.

4. Nevins, *Ordeal for the Union,* 1(1):135–36.

5. *OR,* 4:263; 52(1):146–48; Nevins, *Ordeal for the Union,* 3(1):133–36; Thomas B. Van Horne, *History of the Army of the Cumberland: Its Organization, Campaigns, and Battles,* 2 vols. (reprint, Wilmington, N.C.: Broadfoot, 1988), 1:20; *Cincinnati Commercial,* May 17, 1861.

6. Merideth, *Storm over Sumter,* 205; *Cincinnati Commercial,* May 20, 26, June 21, 1861; William T. Sherman, *Memoirs of William T. Sherman,* 2 vols. (reprint, in 1 vol., New York: Da Capo, 1984), 1:193, 199; William Sumner Dodge, *History of the Old Second Division, Army of the Cumberland* (Chicago: Church and Goodman, 1864), 64, 68; Foote, *Civil War,* 1:87; *OR,* 52(1):156–57.

six-foot, five-inch, three-hundred-pound former navy lieutenant, like Anderson a native Kentuckian, would become a brigadier general and command a division at Shiloh. Throughout the late spring of 1861, he smuggled arms, so-called Lincoln Guns, to loyalist Kentuckians and Tennesseans. In August 1861, with Lincoln's approval, he technically violated neutrality by establishing Camp Dick Robinson, twenty-seven miles south of Lexington, where four Kentucky and two Tennessee regiments trained. The last comprised two thousand exiled mountaineers who, though shabbily dressed, were fanatical about liberating East Tennessee. These regiments comprised the First Brigade of the Army of the Cumberland. As complaints of alcohol abuse and harsh discipline emerged, however, Nelson began to incur disfavor with the Kentuckians.[7]

Son of prominent Kentucky senator John J. Crittenden and a Mexican War veteran, Thomas L. Crittenden, "Tom" to his friends, would rise to the rank of major general and command the XXI Corps. Prior to the war he had considered running for Congress, but he thought Washington "too dissipated for me." To a friend he confided his faults: "I drink, sometimes, and sometimes I ———." (He warned his friend to be careful in his replies, for Crittenden's wife read his mail.) During the early months of the rebellion, he led the reorganized Kentucky Home Guard, the unionist counterpart to the pro-Southern Kentucky State Guard. The initial outfits, the 1st and 2d Kentucky, organized at Camp Clay, just above Cincinnati, but they were in fact "bogus regiments" comprised chiefly of Ohio and Indiana men. The government rushed both units to western Virginia, with Crittenden remaining behind to organize other units.[8]

Rising from his background as a common dirt farmer to become a successful attorney and Kentucky state senator, the blunt, bourbon-loving Lovell H. Rousseau

7. Nevins, *Ordeal for the Union*, 3(1):135; Foote, *Civil War*, 1:86; Richard N. Current, *Lincoln's Loyalists: Union Soldiers from the Confederacy* (Boston: Northeastern University Press, 1992), 30–33; Van Horne, *Army of the Cumberland*, 1:11–12, 16, 27; Daniel Stevenson, "General Nelson, Kentucky, and Lincoln Guns," *Magazine of American History* 10 (Aug. 1883): 118–21; David G. Farrelly, "John Marshall Harlan and the Union Cause in Kentucky in 1861," *Filson Club Historical Quarterly* 37 (Jan. 1963): 8, 10–11; *Indianapolis Daily Journal,* Sept. 21, Nov. 4, 1861. Lincoln insisted that neutrality had not been violated in the Camp Dick Robinson situation because the action had been undertaken by Kentuckians, not the War Department.

8. Faust, *Encyclopedia,* 192–93; Warner, *Generals in Blue,* 100; Crittenden to John Coyle, Apr. 12, 1860, Thomas L. Crittenden Letters, FC; Lowell H. Harrison, *The Civil War in Kentucky* (Lexington: University Press of Kentucky, 1975), 14; Van Horne, *Army of the Cumberland*, 1:9, 14–15; *OR,* 52(1):156, 161–62; John G. Nicolay, *The Outbreak of Rebellion* (reprint, New York: Jack Brussel, n.d.), 131. A soldier who later saw Mrs. Crittenden described her thus: "She is a brunette, rather handsome, but masculine in face, has considerable of a moustache in face, and has the appearance of a strong minded woman." George Landrum to sister, July 16, 1862, George W. Landrum Letters, OHS.

would command a brigade at Shiloh and a division at Perryville and Stones River. In the spring of 1861, he lobbied President Lincoln for prompt action in Kentucky. Subsequently commissioned to raise troops, Rousseau assisted in establishing Camp Joe Holt, on the north bank of the Ohio River in Indiana between Jeffersonville and New Albany, where three Kentucky regiments and a battery organized. When he proposed to march his brigade through the streets of Louisville, local leaders pleaded with him not to stir up the Rebel element and perhaps evoke an attack. "By heaven! The damned scoundrels shall have enough of it before I am done with them." He defiantly marched his troops through the city and uneventfully returned to camp.[9]

In August 1861 Anderson's command, renamed the Department of the Cumberland, was expanded to include all of Kentucky and Tennessee, though he temporarily maintained his headquarters in Cincinnati. In a midmonth conference at the Willard's Hotel in Louisville, Anderson met with several grim-faced politicians, including Sen. Andrew Johnson and Rep. Horace Maynard of Tennessee, Ohio congressman Carey A. Trimble, and a Kentucky congressman. They told pitiful tales of barn burnings and a campaign of terror in eastern Tennessee, from where hundreds of refugees had fled into Kentucky. Loyalist Tennessee representative Thomas Nelson had been jailed by the Rebels. A unionist cavalry company on its way to a training camp in Kentucky had been ambushed nineteen miles from Cumberland Gap and cut to pieces.[10]

Anderson discussed the appointment of three brigadiers for the department. He desired a former lieutenant who had served under him at Fort Moultrie, South Carolina, many years earlier: the red-haired, talkative William T. Sherman—"one of my boys," he called him. All approved the selection; indeed, Sherman was present in the room. Anderson also tapped Kentuckian Don Carlos Buell—"I must have him," he notified Secretary of the Treasury Salmon P. Chase. The appointment of Brig. Gen. George H. Thomas, another of Anderson's Moultrie officers, encountered resistance. Despite his two brevets in the Mexican War, Thomas was Virginia-born (his sisters would forever disavow him for choosing the Federal side), and he had been an officer in the 2d U.S. Cavalry, a regiment that had produced many Confederate officers. Anderson's nephew, Lt. Thomas Anderson, assured the politi-

9. Warner, *Generals in Blue,* 413; Faust, *Encyclopedia,* 645; Dodge, *Old Second Division,* 42–48, Van Horne, *Army of the Cumberland,* 1:15–16; *Louisville Daily Journal,* July 3, 1861; William F. G. Shanks, "Recollections of General Rousseau," *Harper's Magazine* 30 (Nov. 1865): 765, 767.

10. *OR,* 4:254; Van Horne, *Army of the Cumberland,* 1:22–23; Thomas H. Anderson, "General George H. Thomas," *Military Service Institution Journal* 56 (Jan.–Feb. 1915): 39; Sherman, *Memoirs,* 1:192; Freeman Cleaves, *Rock of Chickamauga: The Life of General George H. Thomas* (Norman: University of Oklahoma Press, 1948), 78; Current, *Lincoln's Loyalists,* 32–33.

cians of Thomas's loyalty, but they remained unconvinced. Sherman's persistent lobbying for his old West Point roommate ultimately prevailed, and all three officers were assigned to the department, although Buell was subsequently reassigned to Virginia. Thomas received a furlough to visit his wife in Connecticut and did not arrive at Camp Dick Robinson until September 15. Wearing the old buff-colored stripes of a cavalry colonel rather than a brigadier's star, he replaced Nelson and established his headquarters in a tavern.[11]

On September 1 Anderson entered Louisville, took up residence in the Louisville Hotel, and established headquarters in a local mansion. His professional but unspectacular staff included Capt. Oliver O. Greene, assistant adjutant general; Capt. H. C. Symonds, with eight years in the regular army, chief of subsistence; Capt. Walford Jenkins, quartermaster; Italian-born, stout, thirty-year-old Capt. F. E. Prime, chief engineer; Lt. Nathaniel Michler, topographical engineer; Surgeon Robert Murray of Maryland, with fifteen years in the regular army, chief surgeon; and Lt. C. B. Throckmorton, aide.[12]

That same day Anderson met in brother Larz's home with James Speed, John Marshall Harlan, and other prominent Kentucky loyalists. The general, already becoming unnerved, expressed his grave concerns over the possible loss of the Louisville and Nashville Railroad and even feared the Confederate occupation of Louisville. Press reports of fifteen thousand Rebels just north of Nashville, Tennessee, and five thousand Southerners at Cumberland Gap alarmed the Northern public. Anderson penned a note to Chase pleading for help.[13]

Sherman, meanwhile, proceeded on a tour of Indiana, Illinois, and Missouri, appealing for arms and men. He remained pessimistic about the situation in Kentucky, believing that most of the residents, despite the recent elections, favored the South. To his dismay he discovered that almost all of the Indiana and Ohio troops had been sent to the flanks—east to the trans-Alleghenies or west to Maj. Gen. John C. Frémont in St. Louis. Frémont's reputation had plummeted on the heels of the stinging defeats of his subordinates at Wilson's Creek and, on September 19–20, Lexington, Missouri. He was now on the defensive, facing what he believed to be superior forces. Frémont left little doubt that his priorities were the Missouri and

11. Anderson, "General George H. Thomas," 39; Sherman, *Memoirs*, 1:192–93; Cleaves, *Rock of Chickamauga*, 78; James E. Merrill, *William Tecumseh Sherman* (New York: Rand McNally, 1971), 182; Foote, *Civil War*, 1:89; Warner, *Generals in Blue*, 500; *OR*, 4:255–56; Gilbert C. Kniffen, "The Life and Services of Major General George H. Thomas," in *MOLLUS, District of Columbia*, 4 vols. (reprint, Wilmington, N.C.: Broadfoot, 1993), 2:21–22; "War in the West," *National Tribune*, June 14, 1883.

12. Van Horne, *Army of the Cumberland*, 1:23; *New York Times*, Oct. 6, 1861; Sherman, *Memoirs*, 1:197; *New York Herald*, Oct. 6, 1861.

13. *Cincinnati Enquirer*, Sept. 2, 1861; Sherman, *Memoirs*, 1:193; Van Horne, *Army of the Cumberland*, 1:23; *OR*, 4:255–56.

Mississippi Valleys, not the Ohio Valley. Sherman thus turned to the crucial state from which he might draw men—Ohio.[14]

Throughout the summer of 1861, Ohio governor William Dennison worked fever-ishly to mobilize his state's forces. Organizationally the finest north of the Ohio River, the Ohio militia was nonetheless a loose connection of a score or so of inde-pendent companies, altogether numbering less than 2,000 men. Within three weeks the governor had organized twenty-three infantry regiments. Utilizing his huge raw manpower reserves (the Buckeye State would eventually supply more men to the Federal army than Tennessee, Arkansas, Kentucky, and Mississippi combined would furnish the Confederacy), Dennison fielded 22,380 three-month militiamen and 77,844 three-year Federal volunteers by the end of 1861. If Kentucky gave birth to the Army of the Cumberland, Ohio constituted its backbone.[15]

Having no Federal arsenal within his state, Dennison's most pressing need was the procurement of arms and artillery. The state arsenal at Columbus housed a pa-thetic 1,480 rusted and damaged muskets, no cartridge boxes, three honeycombed old 6-pounder field guns, and a pile of mildewed artillery harness.[16]

Dennison's pleas brought some response. In April 1861 the Federal government rushed to Ohio 18,330 altered muskets from the Watervliet Arsenal in New York. The next month 10,000 percussion muskets arrived from the Springfield Arsenal and 200,000 cartridges from Watervliet. The governor claimed that many of the arms went to Kentucky and Tennessee volunteers and urgently requested an addi-tional 20,000 muskets. Not only was the request denied but the War Department also stipulated that arms from the national government could only be issued to twelve-month troops mustered into Federal service.[17]

14. Sherman, *Memoirs*, 1:196; *OR*, 3:439, 441; John F. Marszalek, *Sherman: A Soldier's Passion for Order* (New York: Free Press, 1993), 152; B. H. Liddell-Hart, *Sherman: Soldier, Realist, American* (reprint, New York: Frederick A. Praeger, 1958), 99–100; John C. Frémont, "In Command of Missouri," in *B&L*, 1:279, 286.

15. Whitelaw Reid, *Ohio in the War: Her Statesmen, Generals, and Soldiers,* 2 vols. (Columbus, Ohio: Electric, 1893), 1:16, 19, 25, 27; *OR*, ser. 3, 1:149, 166; Jacob D. Cox, "War Preparations in the North," in *B&L*, 1:89; Nevins, *Ordeal for the Union*, 3(1):174; Matthew Oyes, "The Mobilization of the Ohio Militia in the Civil War," *Ohio History* 98 (summer–autumn 1989): 156. Ohio provided about 350,000 men to the Federal forces, while Tennessee, Kentucky, Arkansas, and Mississippi together furnished about 327,000 troops to the Confederacy. *Encyclopedia Britannica*, 24 vols. (Chicago: Encyclopedia Britannica, 1972), 16:892; Faust, *Encyclopedia,* 414; Thomas L. Livermore, *Numbers and Losses in the Civil War in America: 1861–1865* (reprint, Bloomington: Indiana University Press, 1957), 21, 24, 25.

16. Cox, "War Preparations in the North," 90; "Message of the Governor of Ohio," *Cincinnati Commercial,* Jan. 7, 1862.

17. *OR*, ser. 3, 1:114, 147, 183; Dennison to Ripley, Aug. 11, 1861, Gov. Dennison's Military Correspon-dence Letter Book, Aug.–Nov. 1861, OHS; State of Ohio, Quartermaster General's Department, Ordnance and Ordnance Stores, 1860–61, OHS.

Dennison sought his state's share of the ordnance at the U.S. arsenal at St. Louis. Some 7,000 muskets went to Missouri volunteers, while Illinois received 14,000 muskets, 500 carbines, 110,000 cartridges, and several cannon. Illinois governor Richard Yates yielded only 5,000 muskets to Ohio, despite Dennison's envoy and personal telegram.[18]

What Dennison could not get through persuasion, he sought through purchase. The state bought 5,480 English-made Enfield rifles, but a search of the Justus Arms Factory of Philadelphia produced nothing. Dennison acquired 12,000 arms in New York, all in need of repair. State agents purchased twenty-four field guns, and by December 1861 orders had been placed with Greenwood and Company of Cincinnati for an additional seventy-three pieces. A state-run munitions laboratory in Columbus eventually fabricated 2.5 million cartridges and more than sixteen thousand artillery rounds.[19]

An undistinguished officer corps led the militia. Three state brigadier generals in command were Joshua H. Bates of Cincinnati, a West Pointer who had long been out of the army and was now practicing law, and Jacob D. Cox and Newton Schleich, both nominal political appointees who had never even worn a uniform. Dennison picked political hack H. B. Carrington as adjutant general, a man described by the press as a "weak, imprudent little humbug." Col. Joshua Sill of Chillicothe, who would one day command a division in the Army of the Ohio, served as assistant adjutant general; Capt. George W. Runyan as commissary; and Capt. D. L. Woods as quartermaster. By mid-May 1861 a state-house committee had undertaken an investigation of both Runyan and Woods for contract errors.[20]

George B. McClellan, an officer distinguished in both military and civilian pursuits, briefly commanded the Ohio forces. Since state law mandated that the militia could be commanded only by someone from within the organization, Dennison sent a bill to the legislature (easily passed) amending the law to include anyone residing within the state. McClellan thus accepted a major general's commission, intending to lead an all-Ohio division in the field, but circumstances dictated otherwise.[21]

18. *OR*, ser. 3, 1:147; Reid, *Ohio in the War*, 1:35; *Cincinnati Commercial*, May 1, 1861; Nevins, *Ordeal for the Union*, 3(1):346.

19. Reid, *Ohio in the War*, 1:35–36, 39; Carl M. Becker, "Miles Greenwood," in *Ohio Leaders in the Civil War*, ed. Kenneth W. Wheeler (Columbus: Ohio State University Press, 1968), 285; Noel C. Fisher, "Groping toward Victory: Ohio's Administration of the Civil War," *Ohio History* 105 (winter–spring 1996): 40.

20. Reid, *Ohio in the War*, 1:34; *Cincinnati Commercial*, Apr. 25, June 2, 14, 1861; *Cincinnati Enquirer*, June 7, 1861; Cox, "War Preparations in the North," 89, 95; Joshua H. Bates, "Ohio's Preparations for the War," in *MOLLUS, Ohio*, 9 vols. (reprint, Wilmington, N.C.: Broadfoot, 1991), 1:133.

21. *OR*, ser. 3, 1:97; Reid, *Ohio in the War*, 1:32–33; Jacob D. Cox, *Military Reminiscences of the Civil War*, 2 vols. (New York: Charles Scribner's Sons, 1900), 1:106; Cox, "War Preparations in the North," 89, 95; George B. McClellan, *McClellan's Own Story* (New York: Charles L. Webster, 1887), 40–41.

The structure quickly fell apart. After commanding for only a few weeks, Mc-Clellan accepted a commission in the Federal army and went to western Virginia. Bates could not physically withstand the rigors of field service and resigned. Schleich later quit the militia and declined a Federal commission, hoping to get a staff position under McClellan; he failed to get it. Among the state brigadiers, only Cox would claim distinction, rising to major general of volunteers and commanding a corps in both the eastern and western theaters.[22]

Dennison faced a host of other problems. He established a chain of nineteen camps of instruction, Camp Dennison outside Cincinnati being the most prominent. Some seven hundred acres were leased and cabins constructed to accommodate a dozen regiments. Civilians daily visited this camp by railroad, carriages, and omnibuses. Despite the festive facade, serious problems existed. Overcrowding and exposure resulted in an outbreak of disease. Journalists reported leaky roofs and insufficient blankets at Camp Harrison. The deplorable conditions eventually resulted in a soldier insurrection in which several men fell wounded. In addition, complaints of wretched provisions surfaced at Camp Morrison.[23]

As quickly as regiments organized and trained, Dennison rushed them to the Kanawha Valley of western Virginia. Politics as much as strategy prompted the move; Republicans viewed western Virginia as a model for reconstruction. Exactly how many Buckeye regiments could be rapidly returned to the Ohio Valley in the event the Confederates broke the tenuous Kentucky neutrality remained an open question. Ohioans anxiously awaited word from their southern neighbor.[24]

"Invasion of Kentucky by Rebels" headlined the *New York Tribune* on September 6, 1861. Three days earlier, Confederates forces under Maj. Gen. Leonidas Polk, wildly estimated at between nine thousand and thirty thousand men, crossed into Kentucky and occupied Columbus along the Mississippi River, claiming that the Yankees were about to do the same thing. The Federals reciprocated by moving into Smithland and Paducah, towns at the mouths of the crucial Cumberland and Ten-

22. Reid, *Ohio in the War*, 1:133; Cox, *Military Reminiscences*, 1:28–29; Cox, "War Preparations in the North," 95–96.

23. *(Columbus) Ohio Statesman*, Aug. 10, 1861; Reid, *Ohio in the War*, 1:55; *Cincinnati Commercial*, May 4, 6, 8, 13, June 2, 1861; Mary Rahn Sloan, *History of Camp Dennison, 1796–1956* (Cincinnati: Joseph Berning, 1956), 29–30; *Cincinnati Enquirer*, June 9, 1861; Stephen Z. Starr, "Camp Dennison, 1861–1865," *Bulletin of the Historical and Philosophical Society of Ohio* 18 (July 1960): 176, 180–81; Cox, *Military Reminiscences*, 1:21–23.

24. McPherson, *Battle Cry of Freedom*, 299–301, 304; Faust, *Encyclopedia*, 633; Jacob D. Cox, "McClellan in West Virginia," in *B&L*, 1:126–30, 148; Francis F. McKinney, *Education in Violence: The Life of George H. Thomas and the History of the Army of the Cumberland* (Detroit: Wayne State University Press, 1961), 107. By October 3 Ohio had sent twenty-one regiments, two batteries, and two cavalry companies to West Virginia. *Indianapolis Daily Journal*, Oct. 3, 1861.

nessee Rivers. Although both sides had now invaded, the Kentucky legislature branded the Confederacy as the aggressor and took an openly pro-Union stance. On September 18 the Stars and Stripes waved over the capital; the veil of neutrality had been lifted.[25]

The immediate result of this turn of events meant that the troops promised to Anderson were instead redirected to Frémont. Secretary of War Simon Cameron ordered five Indiana regiments west to Cairo, Illinois, rather than south to Kentucky. "I am very uneasy about Kentucky, but I suppose the government is not, as orders to send troops to the border are countermanded," Indiana governor Oliver P. Morton noted on September 7. Secretary of State William H. Seward wrote plainly that the administration felt no apprehension for Kentucky. Although known to be in force in north-central Tennessee, the enemy had yet to make a thrust for the Bluegrass State. But a loyalist surgeon residing in the vicinity of Confederate Camp Boone along the Louisville and Nashville Railroad reported to Anderson on September 15 that an invasion was imminent. Felix Zollicoffer and a Rebel force of reportedly six thousand men also threatened Cumberland Gap. Throughout mid-September, at least in Anderson's mind, the Ohio Valley lay ripe for the picking.[26]

Although an enemy advance was anticipated, several incidents on September 17 raised no immediate suspicion at department headquarters. The morning train from Nashville to Louisville failed to arrive and telegraph wires went dead. Believing that an accident had occurred, officials sent a second train south. When it too failed to return, a locomotive was sent. A fireman on the last managed to escape and spread the alarm of the approach of the Rebels.[27]

That night Anderson summoned his second in command. Sherman arrived at department headquarters to learn that a Confederate force under Simon Buckner, estimated at eight thousand strong, had crossed the Kentucky line and that a detachment had penetrated as far north as the Rolling Fork of Salt Creek (thirty-three miles from Louisville), where a bridge of the Louisville and Nashville Railroad had been torched. A nearby ninety-foot trestle and a tunnel would, if destroyed, require months to repair. Sherman was to hasten to the bridge and Muldraugh's Hill, a strategic position near Elizabethtown ("a rather old and dilapidated town," according to one journalist) and secure the area before the Rebels arrived. His ad hoc force comprised one thousand nondescript home guards, even then assembling in Louis-

25. *New York Tribune*, Sept. 6, 1861; *New York Times*, Sept. 6, 1861; *OR*, 3:712; McPherson, *Battle Cry of Freedom*, 296; Albert Castel, "The War Moves West," in *Shadows of the Storm*, ed. William C. Davis (Garden City, N.Y.: Doubleday, 1981), 265.

26. *OR*, 3:425; ser. 3, 1:487, 490; *Cincinnati Enquirer*, Sept. 14, 1861; *Indianapolis Daily Journal*, Sept. 28, 1861.

27. Van Horne, *Army of the Cumberland*, 1:28.

ville, and Rousseau's two thousand half-trained troops at Camp Joe Holt. The latter, transported by ferry boats, did not arrive at the Louisville train depot until 2:00 A.M. on September 18, by which time word of the supposed Confederate advance had leaked out, inciting terror and chaos in the city.[28]

The trains proceeded slowly and did not arrive at Lebanon Junction, twenty-six miles out, until daybreak. There the troops unloaded and cautiously advanced to the burnt bridge. The 5th Kentucky (the "Louisville Legion") forded the stream and marched to the trestle, which they found intact. The Southerners in fact had not crossed the Green River in force but were concentrated seventy miles to the south at Bowling Green. The brigade crossed at a three-foot-deep ford, with Sherman proclaiming to the cheers of the men, "We cross this ford never to retreat again to this side." The troops chased off the few Rebels at Muldraugh's Hill and deployed. The "hill" was actually a 150-foot step off, where the land sloped down to a plain. Once on the summit, there was no reverse slope but an escarpment. The next day Col. Richard W. Johnson arrived with the 2d Kentucky Cavalry and a few additional home-guard companies.[29]

Anderson's fears were not allayed. On September 19 he met in conference with Governor Morton, an official as active as Dennison in Ohio. Morton, who had thirteen state regiments in various stages of readiness, promised immediate help, and Hoosiers soon streamed through the streets of Louisville. The 6th Indiana arrived on September 20, the first Federal regiment to enter the city. Although lacking uniforms, the troops boarded cars at the Louisville and Nashville depot and proceeded south. Over the next two days, the 750 men of Col. Benjamin F. Scribner's 38th Indiana from New Albany (the troops having to carry ammunition in their pockets) and the 39th Indiana from Indianapolis arrived. Told that Anderson's three thousand Federals faced an approaching ten thousand Confederates, Morton hysterically telegraphed Lincoln on September 25 that enemy pickets were within sight of Muldraugh's Hill. The War Department immediately shipped 3,500 muskets, with a promise of more to come.[30]

28. Sherman, *Memoirs*, 1:197–98; *New York Times*, Sept. 24, 1861. Van Horne placed Sherman's numbers at 1,800 home guards and 1,200 of Rousseau's command. *Army of the Cumberland*, 1:28–29. The *New York Tribune*, Sept. 26, 1861, gave the precise numbers: Rousseau's command—5th Kentucky, 946; 4th Kentucky, 600; Stone's battery, 117; four cavalry companies, 300; home guards, 1,000.

29. Sherman, *Memoirs*, 1:198–99; Kelly, "Holding Kentucky," 381; *New York Herald*, Oct. 6, 1861; *Chicago Tribune*, Sept. 26, 1861; *New York Times*, Oct. 3, 1861; *Indianapolis Daily Journal*, Sept. 19, Oct. 7, 1861; Richard J. Reid, *The Army That Buell Built* (Fordsville, Ky.: Wendell Sandefur, 1994), 7. A Confederate detachment also seized Hopkinsville after a brief skirmish with home-guard units.

30. William D. Foulke, *Life of Oliver P. Morton* (Indianapolis: Bowen-Merrill, 1899), 145; *OR*, 4:266, ser. 3, 1:520, 539, 542–43; *New York Times*, Sept. 21, 1861; Benjamin F. Scribner, *How Soldiers Were Made, Or the War as I Saw It* (New Albany, Ind.: Chicago, Donohue, and Henneberry, 1887), 20–21; F. A.

The department commander also appealed to Brig. Gen. Ormsby Mitchel, commanding a second defensive line north of the Ohio River, "with the urgency of despair." The 49th Ohio, which had not even elected field officers, boarded transports and arrived at Louisville on September 22, where Anderson personally addressed the men. Once at Muldraugh's Hill, Sherman pronounced it to be the best regiment in the West. In late September the 33d Indiana arrived, and Mitchel dispatched the 14th, 17th, and 35th Ohio, all being assigned to Brigadier General Thomas in eastern Kentucky. "Affairs in this quarter are looking much better," the Virginian informed Horatio Wright.[31]

Frantic appeals nonetheless clicked over the wires to Washington. A detachment of two hundred men of the 15th U.S. Infantry from Newport Barracks near Cincinnati arrived in Louisville on September 21. They manned several field guns in fixed positions on Muldraugh's Hill. The next day Secretary of War Cameron redirected two Illinois regiments en route to Washington to Kentucky. One of these outfits, the 19th Illinois, had been delayed by a terrible train accident 140 miles west of Cincinnati, which killed 26 soldiers and injured 114 others. On September 27 the 24th Illinois and Company A, 1st Ohio Light Artillery, paraded through Louisville to the electrifying cheers of thousands of civilians. The battery and the two Illinois regiments went to Thomas.[32]

Anderson and Sherman continued to feed one another's fears. Although Muldraugh's Hill was geographically strong, Sherman fretted that Buckner would get in his rear, cut the railroad, and bag his command—"I am to be sacrificed," he wrote on September 27. By October 4 his eight thousand men (five thousand on Muldraugh's Hill and three thousand guarding the railroad) faced, by Sherman's estimates, fifteen thousand Rebels. Although the main force of the enemy had remained at Bowling Green, a two-thousand-man contingent (or so reported) had probed to within eight miles of Elizabethtown. The citizens of Louisville remained in a panic, and Sherman detected that Anderson was cracking under the pressure.[33]

Mitchel, *Ormsby Macknight Mitchel: Astronomer and General, a Biographical Narrative* (Boston: Houghton, Mifflin, 1887), 220–21; Dodge, *Old Second Division,* 67; Frederick H. Dyer, *A Compendium of the War of the Rebellion,* 3 vols. (reprint, New York: Thomas Yoseloff, 1959), 2:220–21; *Indianapolis Daily Journal,* Sept. 21, 23, 24, 1861; Morton to Lincoln, Sept. 25, 1861, Morton Dispatch Book, INHS; Basler, *Collected Works of Abraham Lincoln,* 4:537.

31. Mitchel, *Ormsby Macknight Mitchel,* 220; Dick Chamberlain and Judy Chamberlain, eds., *Civil War Letters of an Ohio Soldier: S. O. Chamberlain and the 49th Ohio Volunteer Infantry* (Flournoy, Calif.: Walker Lithograph, 1990), 7; *New York Times,* Sept. 23, 1861; *OR,* 4:280–81, 282, 283, 284–85, 291, 294, 334; *Indianapolis Daily Journal,* Oct. 5, 1861.

32. *OR,* 4:266, 281–82; J. Henry Haynie, *The Nineteenth Illinois* (Chicago: M. A. Donahue, 1912), 144; *Cincinnati Enquirer,* Sept. 18, 19, Oct. 5, 1861; *New York Tribune,* Oct. 2, 1861; Dyer, *Compendium,* 2:1504, 1513.

33. *OR,* 4:278–79; *New York Times,* Sept. 23, Oct. 3, 1861; Lloyd Lewis, *Sherman: Fighting Prophet* (New York: Harcourt Brace, 1932), 184, 190; Marszalek, *Sherman,* 158–59; Sherman, *Memoirs,* 1:199.

The situation seemed to improve somewhat in early October as more troops streamed into the department. Four fresh Buckeye regiments, the 2d, 15th, 21st, and 38th Infantry, paraded through the streets of Cincinnati on the fourth. That night the men boarded railroad cars for the journey south. By October 7 the 32d Indiana, armed with four hundred Enfield and five hundred Springfield rifles, had reported to the lines at Muldraugh's Hill. The next day the 34th Illinois, armed with Enfields, crossed the Ohio River at Cincinnati after giving three cheers for the city. On the tenth the 29th and 30th Indiana, along with Batteries B and C, 1st Ohio Light Artillery, arrived in Louisville. Yet Sherman still complained that the War Department had focused on Frémont in Missouri and was largely ignoring the Ohio Valley.[34]

The brigadier based his assessment of enemy troop strength upon bits and pieces of information, none of it conclusive. Even normally hysterical news correspondents reported that Buckner's strength had been greatly exaggerated. On October 2 the *New York Times* accurately stated that the Bowling Green force did not exceed five thousand to six thousand secessionists. The *New York Herald* placed the number at ten thousand, perhaps as few as seven thousand. One report claimed that Sherman had evidence as early as the end of September that Buckner had only five thousand men.[35]

Throughout the summer and fall, the leadership of the Department of the Cumberland remained paralyzed, not only by fear and well-placed rumor but also by discord and intrigue. Anderson and Mitchel bickered over the defenses across the Ohio River from Cincinnati. "General Anderson believes in moral suasion, and deeply regrets the works on the Kentucky Hills, opposite this city. I can get nothing from him by telegraph, or by letter," Mitchel groused to Governor Dennison.[36]

Brig. Gen. Alexander McCook arrived in Cincinnati in early September and immediately scrapped with Anderson over a matter of minor military etiquette. According to the rumor, McCook, who had recently met with Lincoln in Washington, attempted to wrestle command from the ailing Kentuckian but was frustrated by Anderson's political allies. The *New York Times,* meanwhile, attacked the department commander as being "fatally impaired" in his vigor. On October 7, 1861, a broken and disheartened General Anderson submitted his resignation, citing "mental torture."[37]

34. *Chicago Tribune,* Oct. 4, 11, 1861; *New York Tribune,* Oct. 14, 1861; *National Intelligencer,* Oct. 16, 1861; *Indianapolis Daily Journal,* Sept. 28, 30, Oct. 7, 1861; *OR,* 4:298.

35. *New York Times,* Sept. 25, Oct. 2, 1861; *New York Herald,* Oct. 17, 19, 1861. As late as October 17, 1861, a *New York Tribune* journalist stated that Buckner had no more than 10,000 men. Buckner, in fact, believed that his 6,000 troops faced 14,000 under Sherman. *OR,* 3:437.

36. Mitchel, *Ormsby Macknight Mitchel,* 222.

37. *OR,* 4:296–97; *Louisville Journal,* Oct. 14, 1861; *New York Herald,* Oct. 8, 1861; *New York Times,* Sept. 30, 1861; Van Horne, *Army of the Cumberland,* 1:31, 35. For additional criticism of Anderson, see *New York Tribune,* Sept. 7, 1861.

2

Sherman Takes Command
A Baleful Sway

WITH ANDERSON GONE, command of the department devolved upon forty-one-year-old Sherman, an officer as psychologically unprepared for the post as his predecessor. Indeed, the Ohio brigadier had accepted his assignment upon the explicit promise that he would not be called upon to command. "I don't think I ever felt so much a desire to hide myself in some obscure place," he wrote his wife Ellen. Inexperienced (he had not fought in the Mexican War) and raked with feelings of personal inadequacies, he reminded one officer of a "splendid piece of machinery with all of the screws a little loose." Sherman's eccentricities had not gone unnoticed at Muldraugh's Hill; he nervously paced about in civilian clothes and a stovepipe hat. The Kentucky Home Guard despised his gruff methods and labeled him "Old Pills," for he was a "bitter pill to swallow." Later warming up to him slightly, the sobriquet changed to "Old Sugar Coated." An ordnance officer, seeing Sherman for the first time at Camp Dick Robinson, described him as "very crabid & nervice," a "perfect bundle of nerves."[1]

The strain of command quickly took its toll. Sherman went without food much of the day, drank, chain smoked, and paced about until the early hours in his quarters at the Galt House. Rumors began to spread of his mental instability; he suffered from depression and headaches. A curt letter that he sent to Lincoln went unanswered, causing him even greater depression.[2]

Sherman's eccentric mannerisms continued. As Thomas Crittenden, now a brigadier, awaited a train to assume command of home-guard units assembled at Henderson, Sherman glared at him with either scrutiny or scorn—it was difficult to tell

1. *Cincinnati Commercial*, Sept. 24, 1861; Marszalek, *Sherman*, 158, 160; Kelly, "Holding Kentucky," 381; *New York Herald*, Oct. 6, 1861; Perry McCandless, ed., "Civil War Journal of Stephen Keyes Fletcher," *Indiana Magazine of History* 54 (June 1958): 144–45; Albert Castel, *Decision in the West: The Atlanta Campaign of 1864* (Lawrence: University Press of Kansas, 1992), 42.

2. Henry Villard, *Memoirs of Henry Villard: Journalist and Financer, 1835–1900*, 2 vols. (Boston: Houghton, Mifflin, 1904), 1:210–11; Charles Royster, *The Destructive War: William Tecumseh Sherman, Stonewall Jackson, and the Americans* (New York: Alfred A. Knopf, 1991), 96; John Marszalek, *Sherman's Other War: The General and the Civil War Press* (Memphis: Memphis State University Press, 1981), 57.

which. He briefly questioned Crittenden about his eligibility to command and then turned around, stroked his short beard, and muttered, "He'll do." Capt. John Harlan recalled that while he stayed at Sherman's Lebanon headquarters, the general constantly had a cigar in his mouth, usually unlit. He would use Harlan's cigar to light his own and then, without a second thought, would throw Harlan's away.[3]

Political intrigue now added to Sherman's woes. In late September Senator Johnson and Congressman Maynard conspired with Secretary of War Cameron to replace George Thomas, whom they considered too listless about moving into eastern Tennessee and liberating their constituents. The politicians had also been in communication with Ormsby Mitchel, who slyly coveted command of Thomas's division. Mitchel advocated an immediate advance into eastern Tennessee—precisely what Johnson and Maynard wanted to hear. He wrote the War Department about the expedition, suggesting that it be placed under the command of one who held the complete confidence of the government—perhaps a veiled reference to Thomas's perceived questionable loyalty.[4]

On October 11, 1861, Johnson and Maynard appeared at Camp Dick Robinson with a War Department order stating that Thomas had been replaced by Mitchel. The news came as a shock; an incensed Thomas submitted his resignation. In truth, the Virginian had been the one bright spot in an otherwise gloomy picture. Amid Anderson's and Sherman's sniveling and lethargy, Thomas had remained cool and worked diligently toward an offensive, although he was hampered by a lack of funds. For his part, Mitchel feigned innocence—"My surprise was great." Within hours of receiving his new command, however, he was funneling orders to Thomas and pretentiously attempting to organize his own staff.[5]

Sherman resented the political and War Department interference and, in typical fashion, voiced his views openly at headquarters. Mitchel had been a professor and astronomer, and correspondents suggested that a "star gazer" would never suit the blunt and pragmatic Sherman. The problem went much deeper; Sherman had never felt comfortable with an East Tennessee offensive. The department commander assured Thomas that he would continue to work on his behalf, though he made no

3. *Chicago Tribune*, Oct. 15, 1861; Farrelly, "John Marshall Harlan," 16–17.

4. McKinney, *Education in Violence*, 113, 115.

5. *OR*, 4:300, 303; Cleaves, *Rock of Chickamauga*, 85–87; Thomas B. Van Horne, *The Life of Major General George H. Thomas* (New York: Charles Scribner's Sons, 1882), 43–44. Kenneth Williams discounts Mitchel's scheming and Cameron's distrust of Thomas. If Mitchel arrived with reinforcements, he argued, it would merely be a merger of commands, with the senior officer (Mitchel) assuming command. Yet there was never any mention of reinforcements. Williams nonetheless concluded that Thomas was being "unduly touchy" and that Cameron simply chose the better officer. *Grant Rises in the West: The First Year of the War, 1861–1862* (reprint, Lincoln: University of Nebraska Press, 1997), 445–46.

promise of a reversal. Until he sorted out the matter, Sherman simply ignored Mitchel. The two finally decided to meet in Lexington, but Sherman was detained and never arrived. For two weeks Mitchel awaited some word from him, while friends daily asked why the commander was not in Kentucky. On October 26 Mitchel received word from the War Department that the original order had been reversed and that Thomas would retain command of the division. Mitchel now submitted his resignation—"[it was] the only thing I could do to preserve my self-respect." The *Cincinnati Commercial* declared that the resignation resulted from his "unsatisfactory relations with Sherman." Mitchel later reversed his decision when offered a new command.[6]

Although Thomas remained in charge at Camp Dick Robinson, organizing what would become the First Division, he proved irritable and annoyed. Despite his stoic reputation, he now hated the East Tennessee politicians, a fact that he made no pretense of hiding when they ventured to camp one day and made speeches to the troops. The Virginian promptly withdrew to his office and paced in anger. When the troops called upon Thomas for a speech, he refused, stormed from his office, slammed the door, and did not emerge from his quarters until the next day.[7]

Sherman accomplished little in the way of organization beyond a few staff changes. Col. Thomas Sword arrived in Louisville on October 13, replacing Captain Jenkins as quartermaster. Maintaining Anderson's staff, Sherman added only a paymaster and ordnance officer.[8]

Brigadier General McCook arrived on October 14 to assume command of what would become the Second Division. Lovell Rousseau, under orders, had previously advanced his troops from Muldraugh's Hill to Nolin Creek, fifty-two miles from Louisville, where he established Camp Nevin, named after an old friend. McCook came from a distinguished military family (the famous seventeen "Fighting McCooks") and had graduated from West Point, where he later taught tactics. Despite his background and battlefield experience (he had led the 1st Ohio with distinction at the Battle of Bull Run in Virginia earlier that year), he could also be irritating and egotistical; Sherman would later brand him "a juvenile."[9]

6. *Chicago Tribune*, Oct. 16, 1861; Mitchel, *Ormsby Macknight Mitchel*, 229; *OR*, 4:306; Cleaves, *Rock of Chickamauga*, 87; *Cincinnati Commercial*, Nov. 4, Oct. 19, 1861.

7. Susan Lyons Hughes, *Camp Dick Robinson: Holding Kentucky for the Union* (Frankfort: Kentucky Historical Society, 1990), 8–10; Kelly, "Holding Kentucky," 382.

8. Sherman, *Memoirs*, 1:200.

9. *OR*, 4:303, 306; Warner, *Generals in Blue*, 294; "The War in the West," *National Tribune*, May 31, 1883; William F. G. Shanks, *Personal Recollections of Distinguished Generals* (New York: Harper and Brothers, 1866), 249; Robert G. Athearn, ed., *Soldier in the West: The Civil War Letters of Alfred Lacey Hough* (Philadelphia: University of Pennsylvania Press, 1957), 63.

Initial plans to organize the assembled regiments were delayed when Rousseau became gravely ill and had to recuperate in Louisville. It was left to McCook to form three provisional brigades, each commanded by a Kentucky general. Rousseau led the First Brigade, which, with the exception of a detachment of regulars, was composed entirely of Kentuckians. Thirty-nine-year-old Brig. Gen. Thomas J. Wood, a West Point graduate with eighteen years' experience in the regular army, commanded the all-Indiana Second Brigade, this assignment due largely to the lobbying efforts of Governor Morton. Wood's rugged western style meshed well with McCook, and together, commented a fellow officer, the two generals "swore like pirates." The Third Brigade consisted of Indiana, Illinois, and Ohio troops and was led by thirty-four-year-old Brig. Gen. Richard W. Johnson, a bland but genteel West Pointer with extensive regular-army experience. The three brigades, together with a regiment of cavalry and two batteries, mustered ten thousand men by mid-October.[10]

Secretary of War Cameron had been in St. Louis, attempting to straighten out the mess in Frémont's department. On the morning of October 14, he took a train to Indianapolis and the next day conferred with Governor Morton. He also toured the new state arsenal, which employed three hundred workers and turned out one hundred thousand cartridges daily, many destined for the Hoosier soldiers now streaming into the Department of the Cumberland.[11]

On October 16 Cameron, accompanied by Maj. Gen. Lorenzo Thomas and a half-dozen other men, arrived in Louisville. Although intending to merely pass through the city, Cameron remained at Sherman's urging. The party proceeded to Sherman's room at the Galt House. Cameron, not feeling well, lay in bed and griped about Frémont, but he eventually inquired, "Now, General Sherman, tell us of your problems." Sherman seemed hesitant to speak of department matters in the company of so many strangers, but he was rather tersely assured by Cameron that all present could be trusted. Closing and locking the door, the commander unwisely began reciting a depressing litany of concerns: Kentuckians had not sufficiently rallied to the flag; his two divisions sat impotent, encouraging the Confederates to attack; at least twenty thousand Kentuckians would flock to the enemy when the inevitable advance began. While McClellan, now commanding Federal forces in

10. Faust, *Encyclopedia*, 841; Warner, *Generals in Blue*, 253–54; John Beatty, *The Citizen Soldier* (Cincinnati: Wilstach, Baldwin, 1879), 235; *New York Herald*, Oct. 6, 1861; *Chicago Tribune*, Oct. 16, 1861; Richard W. Johnson, *A Soldier's Reminiscences* (Philadelphia: J. B. Lippincott, 1886), 180; *OR*, 4:300, 307, 308; *Cincinnati Commercial*, Oct. 12, 1861.

11. *OR*, 4:313; *Indianapolis Daily Journal*, Sept. 23, 1861; *Report of the Adjutant General of the State of Indiana*, 2 vols. (Indianapolis: Alexander H. Corner, 1869), 1:414–15.

Virginia, had one hundred thousand men to cover a front of a hundred miles, and Frémont had sixty thousand to cover a like area, Sherman had only McCook's ten thousand and Thomas's nine thousand to defend the entire center of the nation— over three hundred miles. He insisted that he needed sixty thousand men to remain on the defensive and an incredible two hundred thousand to assume the offensive. A startled Cameron, taken aback by Sherman's blathering, pledged immediate Federal support, with the understanding that an East Tennessee invasion must be forth-coming.[12]

Although Sherman felt good about the conversation (a "friendly spirit," as he termed it), the meeting in fact had been a disaster. The strangers present turned out to be journalists, one of whom, Sam Wilkeson of the *New York Tribune*, planned to submit an article detailing the meeting. He confided to Henry Villard, another correspondent present, that Cameron considered the general unbalanced and planned to replace him.[13]

Sherman remained unaware of his pending doom, as a new wave of Federal troops poured into Kentucky. A three-thousand-man Pennsylvania brigade under Brig. Gen. James Negley departed Pittsburgh on six transports, arriving at Louisville on October 22. The troops proceeded to Camp Nevin, giving McCook a fourth brigade. Several upper midwestern regiments also arrived: the 2d Minnesota, the unarmed 9th Michigan from Detroit, and the 1st Wisconsin from Milwaukee (which had gotten as far as Pittsburgh before being diverted), all going to Thomas. A new Indiana regiment, the 37th Infantry, was assigned to the mouth of Salt River. Despite this influx of manpower, Sherman believed that the Kentucky situation remained essentially unchanged. He had information that Gen. Albert Sidney Johnston, now commanding Confederate forces in Kentucky and Tennessee, had twenty thousand men at Bowling Green and the railroad cars to move them rapidly. On October 26 Sherman related to his brother, Ohio senator John Sherman, that the Rebels had sufficient strength to capture southern Indiana, southern Illinois, and St. Louis.[14]

12. Sherman, *Memoirs*, 1:201–3, 210–14; *OR*, 4:313–14; Stanley P. Hirshson, *The White Tecumseh: A Biography of General William T. Sherman* (New York: John Wiley and Sons, 1997), 99. Cameron appears to have been greatly alarmed by Sherman's assessment. He wired Lincoln that the situation was "much worse" than he anticipated and that more troops were needed "immediately." *OR*, 4:308.

13. Sherman, *Memoirs*, 1:203; J. Cutler Andrews, *The North Reports the Civil War* (reprint, Pittsburgh: University of Pittsburgh Press, 1985), 116; Marszalek, *Sherman's Other War*, 59–60.

14. Sherman, *Memoirs*, 1:203–4; *OR*, 4:308, 309, 314, 316, 318, ser. 3, 1:577, 582, 588; *Chicago Tribune*, Oct. 4, 11, 25, 1861; Dyer, *Compendium*, 2:1130, 1285, 1296, 1673; *New York Tribune*, Oct. 25, 1861; *Indianapolis Daily Journal*, Oct. 20, 28, 1861; William DeLoss Love, *Wisconsin in the War of the Rebellion; A History of All Regiments and Batteries* (Chicago: Church and Goodmen, 1866), 449; William Bircher, *A Drummer Boy's Diary: Comprising Four Years of Service with the Second Regiment Minnesota Veteran Volunteers, 1861 to 1865* (St. Paul: St. Paul Book and Stationary, 1889), 13–14; Albertson to wife, Oct. 24, 1861, in Joan W.

The supply of arms remained a serious problem. Sherman complained that Anderson had been promised 40,000 Springfield rifles but instead received 12,000 Belgian rifles, which had been previously rejected by the governor of Pennsylvania. The commander of the 9th Michigan flatly refused them, but the colonel of the 37th Indiana accepted the Belgian rifles for six of his unarmed companies. He later grumbled that bullets fired from them would not go sixty yards before striking the ground—"they are the poorest and meanest shooting irons I ever saw." Cameron did send 6,200 Enfield rifles to the West—3,000 for Indiana (purchased under state contract) and the balance for Sherman. Some of these rifles went to replace the muskets of the 37th Indiana at Salt River and the 38th and 39th Indiana in McCook's division.[15]

Wilkeson's article appeared on October 30. The department commander was characterized as panicked and Cameron as calm and deliberate. A startled Sherman gasped, both at the press leak and that his "200,000" projection had been ridiculed. He considered barring all reporters; both McCook and Thomas subsequently did eject journalists from their camps for leaking information. These actions prompted the *New York Times* to declare that "the only energy exhibited thus far by the Kentucky generals has been in hunting newspaper correspondents."[16]

Sherman plunged into a deep depression, brooded for much of the day, paid little attention to his staff, and would scarcely even answer a question. The Louisville and Nashville Railroad, he wrote Ellen on November 1, was guarded by "Volunteers who cannot appreciate the true State of the Case, and who are off their Guard & might be surprised and taken any night. This thought alone disturbs my sleep, and I cannot rest. Every night I fear this RR may be broken and 12,000 men left to fight their way back before & behind enemies more ruthless than Indians."[17]

McClellan assumed command of all the Federal armies on November 1, replacing the aged Winfield Scott. Sherman's subsequent reports to him croaked with pessimism. McCook's thirteen thousand men received supplies from Louisville by railroad (vulnerable at all times), and they had virtually no wagon transportation.

Albertson, *Letters Home to Minnesota* (Spokane, Wash.: P. D. Enterprises, 1993), letter 3, [18–19]; *National Intelligencer*, Oct. 23, 1861. Although the return for November 4, 1861, does not show the 42d, 43d, and 59th Ohio as present, other records reveal that these regiments were at Henderson, Calhoun, and Olympia Springs respectively. Dyer, *Compendium*, 2:1135, 1136, 1524.

15. *OR*, 4:314, 316; Reid, *Army That Buell Built*, 12; *Chicago Tribune*, Nov. 8, 1861; *Indianapolis Daily Journal*, Nov. 4, 9, 1861.

16. Lewis, *Sherman*, 192; Marszalek, *Sherman*, 162; Marszalek, *Sherman's Other War*, 60; Andrews, *North Reports the Civil War*, 116–17. Later newspaper reports declaring that Sherman had gone insane did not appear until the general had left the department.

17. Hirshson, *White Tecumseh*, 100–101.

Numerically superior (or so believed) Rebel forces hovered only twenty-three miles away, and rumors claimed that additional Southern troops would arrive from Virginia. Sherman cried that his forces were too few to do any good and too many to sacrifice.[18]

Such a gloomy assessment raised McClellan's eyebrows. Sherman suggested retreat across the Ohio River and desired to be returned to his old brigade in Washington, D.C. The general in chief sent his personal envoy, Col. Thomas M. Key, to ascertain the true state of affairs. After spending several hours with the department commander, Key reported that Sherman was on the verge of nervous exhaustion. The word around Washington, according to Assistant Secretary of War Thomas Scott, was that "Sherman's gone in the head, he's luny." The general's career hung by a thread.[19]

Thomas found affairs at Camp Dick Robinson (Camp Dick to the men) in an appalling state. Profiteering contractors had delivered shoddy materials, millions of dollars had been expended with no accounting, and he had not a single staff officer. John W. Scully, a civilian clerk who later reported for duty, noted: "It would astonish you to see the Volunteer officers. [They] bother the life out of the general." Thomas considered resigning several times. Desperate to supply his men, he ventured to large clothing manufacturers in Lexington and invited them to make sealed bids. Unfortunately, he had neither government authorization nor money. A staff officer dashed to a bank in Lexington and pleaded for an advance loan, stating bluntly that a bad check had been written to the low bidder. The banker surprisingly complied.[20]

Barely a week after Thomas's arrival, Confederate general Zollicoffer made a division-size incursion into eastern Kentucky, easily chasing off the 150 home guards at Barbourville and burning several houses. Col. Frank Wolford's 1st Kentucky Cavalry (U.S.), sent to scout the enemy positions, crossed Rockcastle Hills and established camp in a place so wild and foreboding that Wolford called it Camp Wild Cat. As some of the men began digging in, the colonel proceeded with his regiment to London, a mountain hamlet with a courthouse and four taverns along a mud road. Advancing Rebels brushed aside his troopers, together with 500 home guards, on September 29; Manchester, nineteen miles east of London, fell the next day. Home-guard units began frantically obstructing the road to Mount Vernon and fortifying Big Hill to protect the Richmond Road.[21]

---

18. OR, 4:332–33; Sherman, *Memoirs*, 1:206–10; Marszalek, *Sherman*, 163; Marszalek, *Sherman's Other War*, 61–62, 63.

19. Marszalek, *Sherman*, 163; Marszalek, *Sherman's Other War*, 61–62; McClellan, *McClellan's Own Story*, 201.

20. John Scully to wife, Nov. 10, 1861, John W. Scully Letters, DU; *Cincinnati Times*, Oct. 24, 1861; Cleaves, *Rock of Chickamauga*, 81; "War in the West," *National Tribune*, June 14, 1883.

21. OR, 4:272, 280–85; E. Tarrant, *The Wild Riders of the First Kentucky Cavalry* (Louisville: R. H. Carothers, 1894), 36–37.

Zollicoffer, as it turned out, was merely on a marauding expedition for salt and supplies and soon withdrew. Afterward, Thomas believed that the time was now right for the long-anticipated advance into eastern Tennessee. On September 30 Rev. William Blount Carter, a leader in the East Tennessee separatist movement and brother to Col. Samuel P. Carter, met with Sherman, Thomas, Andrew Johnson, and Horace Maynard at Camp Dick Robinson. He presented a sabotage scheme, whereby nine railroad bridges would be simultaneously burned in eastern Tennessee and northern Alabama and Georgia, to coincide with Thomas's advance upon Cumberland Gap. All agreed except Sherman, but he was eventually converted by Thomas's forceful support. The plan (with Lincoln's subsequent approval) would be executed on the night of November 8.[22]

Thomas envisioned a move through Cumberland Gap to Knoxville, striking the East Tennessee and Virginia Railroad (the only direct rail link connecting Richmond, Virginia, with the western Confederacy) and then turning on Zollicoffer's division. Given four more regiments and a battery, he wrote on October 4, the expedition could begin within ten days. But between October 11 and 26, before the proposed campaign could begin, Thomas maintained a very tenuous command over his division due to the scheming of the East Tennessee political bloc.[23]

Unexpectedly, on October 17, W. T. Ward, commanding the fifteen hundred home guards at Camp Andy Johnson at Greensburg, reported that two thousand to three thousand secessionists, perhaps as many as six thousand, were rapidly advancing upon his position, coming to within twelve miles. He hurriedly withdrew his force to Campbellsville. Fearing that a part of Johnston's Bowling Green army was attempting to get between him and Thomas, McCook dispatched fifteen hundred reinforcements. It turned out to be a false alarm, but the fear of an enemy incursion between the two divisions was thus planted in Sherman's mind.[24]

In mid-October Zollicoffer ("Snollegoster" to the unionists locals) again moved into eastern Kentucky along the old Wilderness Road, although this time it appeared as though he meant business. His division, estimated by scouts to number six thou-

22. *OR*, 4:284, 286, 289, 294, 321; Current, *Lincoln's Loyalists*, 34; David Madden, "Union Resistance to Confederate Occupation: The Bridge Burners of East Tennessee," *East Tennessee Historical Society's Publication* 53 (1981): 109; Oliver P. Temple, *East Tennessee and the Civil War* (Cincinnati: Robert Clarke, 1899), 375–76. Thomas apparently persuaded Sherman by suggesting an alternative route to the Wilderness Road. The column would march south through Somerset to Huntsville, Tennessee, and thence to Knoxville, thus avoiding the Cumberland Gap. Kenneth A. Hafendorfer, *Mill Springs: Campaign and Battle of Mill Springs, Kentucky* (Louisville: KH Press, 2001), 41–41. William Blount Carter subsequently met with Lincoln, McClellan, and Cameron in Washington, where the plan was approved and money advanced for expenses.

23. *OR*, 4:294; Temple, *East Tennessee and the Civil War*, 371; Van Horne, *Army of the Cumberland*, 1:37.

24. *New York Tribune*, Oct. 19, 30, 1861; *Chicago Tribune*, Oct. 22, 25, 1861; *OR*, 4:312, 316.

sand men, a number later raised to twelve thousand, marched forty miles from Cumberland Gap to London. Col. Theophilus T. Garrand's 3d Kentucky Infantry, occupying the lone outpost at Camp Wild Cat, felt imminently threatened. Garrand vowed that he would pull his regiment back if not immediately reinforced—"I have no idea of having my men butchered up here." Thomas rushed forward a brigade from Camp Dick Robinson under the newly arrived forty-nine-year-old Brig. Gen. Albin Schoepf, formerly of the Austrian army and on the losing side of the Hungarian independence movement (which resulted in his move to the United States).[25]

The relief column struck out on the morning of October 19, traversing the twenty-five-mile macadamized road past Crab Orchard. The final twenty miles to Camp Wild Cat was over a horrid mountain road. On October 20 a message arrived from Garrand to "push on for God's sake," resulting in a forced march through mud that brought half of the 33d Indiana to Rockcastle River by noon. The troops crossed over and arrived at Camp Wild Cat on the afternoon of October 20. Part of the 1st Kentucky Cavalry (U.S.) galloped in later that night.[26]

At 7:00 A.M. on October 21, Schoepf rode pell-mell into the camp of the 33d Indiana, ordering Col. John Coburn to immediately turn out his men—"The enemy are right on us." Shrouded by darkness and thick woods, Zollicoffer's Southerners had approached nearly to the base of the mountain. The 3d Kentucky held Wild Cat Mountain, while the 350 men of the 33d Indiana, reinforced with 250 troopers of the 1st Kentucky Cavalry, deployed on a knob eight hundred yards to the southwest. The Hoosiers had not been in position a half hour when two Tennessee regiments began clawing up the rocky gorge. A scattering fire for the next hour and a half came close to breaking the dismounted Kentucky horsemen, but the Rebels were eventually repulsed after closing to within fifty yards. At 2:00 P.M. a battalion of the 17th Ohio arrived on the main ridge, just in time to assist in repulsing a second attack.[27]

During the early hours of October 22, Zollicoffer called it quits and withdrew his division. A sizeable battle might have been fought but for the rugged terrain. Although limited in scope (the Federals sustained twenty-four casualties, the Confed-

25. *New York Tribune*, Oct. 18, 1862; *New York Herald*, Oct. 27, 1861; *New York Times*, Oct. 1, 1861; *OR*, 4:309, 310, 311, 312; Warner, *Generals in Blue*, 424, 657 n. 560; Kniffen, "Life and Service of Major General George H. Thomas," 23; *Cincinnati Commercial*, Oct. 24, 1861.

26. *Chicago Tribune*, Oct. 24, 1861; McCandless, "Civil War Journal of Stephen Keyes Fletcher," 146; Reid, *Army That Buell Built*, 13; Van Horne, *Army of the Cumberland*, 1:38. Schoepf's brigade was composed of the 33d Indiana; 14th, 17th, 31st Ohio; and Battery B, 1st Ohio Light Artillery.

27. *New York Herald*, Nov. 9, 1861; Kelly, "Holding Kentucky," 382–83; *Chicago Tribune*, Oct. 25, 1861; *OR*, 4:208–9, 210; Tarrant, *Wild Riders*, 45–46; Reid, *Army That Buell Built*, 12; McCandless, "Civil War Journal of Stephen Keyes Fletcher," 146.

erates fifty-three), the engagement at Wild Cat Mountain had been the largest in the department to date, and more important, Zollicoffer's advance had been blunted. An elated Thomas rushed to the battlefield for a personal inspection.[28]

By October 23 the Rebels had retreated to Laurel Bridge, nine miles south of London, and they did not stop until reaching Cumberland Gap. Responding to Thomas's order for a limited pursuit, Schoepf marched his brigade to within three miles of London, while Col. Samuel P. Carter's East Tennessee demi-brigade occupied the town and areas slightly beyond. Thomas moved division headquarters from Camp Dick Robinson to Crab Orchard, preparatory to an East Tennessee offensive. Wishing to avoid the rugged Rockcastle Hills, he planned to move by way of Somerset, which had a useable road all winter long. The expedition would require reinforcements (four more regiments), cash, and additional transportation, for the Cincinnati quartermaster had diverted four hundred wagons from Thomas for use in western Virginia.[29]

Reality quickly replaced momentary jubilation. By October 25 Sherman had reversed the Camp Dick Robinson conference and had decided not to move into eastern Tennessee. Until Thomas's supply line could be secured, he was not to advance his division beyond Crab Orchard. Sherman could "hardly sleep" for fear that an enemy incursion from Prestonsburg (reportedly occupied by an enemy brigade) might sever the railroad north of Nicholasville or seize the Kentucky River bridge south of town. Any advance would place Thomas's and McCook's divisions on divergent lines, thus drawing them farther apart. Until Columbus and Bowling Green could be retaken, Sherman considered an eastern Tennessee move impractical.[30]

Thomas also grew jittery. His requested four regiments had not arrived, and Sherman had warned that McCook could not send reinforcements. Schoepf needed forage for his mules and shoes for his men. The remaining secessionists in eastern Kentucky could easily be driven off, but more of everything was needed for an offensive. Still, he remained more resolute than his superior.[31]

The slight threat from Prestonsburg was eliminated on November 5 when Briga-

28. *OR*, 4:205, 210, 319, 321.

29. Ibid., 206, 207, 294, 318, 319, 321, 322, 338; McKinney, *Education in Violence*, 118; *Cincinnati Commercial*, Nov. 5, 1861.

30. *OR*, 4:310, 312, 319, 335; Sherman, *Memoirs*, 1:199; Van Horne, *Army of the Cumberland*, 1:40; Temple, *East Tennessee and the Civil War*, 378. By October 12 Sherman had expressed that he did not believe it possible to enter Cumberland Gap "this year." *OR*, 4:305. The Kentucky River bridge was located on what today is U.S. Highway 27.

31. *OR*, 4:319, 321; Noel C. Fisher, *War at Every Door: Partisan Politics and Guerilla Violence in East Tennessee, 1860–1869* (Chapel Hill: University of North Carolina Press, 1997), 53–54. Van Horne attempted to place the change of plans entirely upon Sherman, but such was not the case. *Army of the Cumberland*, 1:46.

dier General Nelson successfully drove out Confederate forces under Brig. Gen. John S. Williams. Three days later he sent a demi-brigade on a wide swing to the left of Piketon while he personally led a brigade on the direct road to that town. The Southerners retreated through Pound Gap into Virginia. Wild rumors claimed that one thousand Rebels had been killed and two thousand captured, but in truth there had been few casualties and fewer than fifty prisoners taken. Nevertheless, Thomas's supply line had been secured from the east.[32]

But Sherman still refused to allow his subordinate to budge. Officers in the division grumbled that Knoxville could be occupied within a week. The press portrayed Brigadier General Schoepf as the eager warrior, anxious to forge ahead but held in check by the bureaucrat Thomas. A New York journalist cried that the immigrant commander was "stopped, checkmated, fretted, worried, tormented, and annoyed every hour by Thomas."[33]

The issue was fast coming to a head. If Thomas did not advance soon, William Blount Carter's bridge saboteurs, not realizing the delay, would execute their operation. According to the plan, Thomas was already supposed to be in possession of Cumberland Gap. On November 6, with only two days remaining before the strike, Senator Johnson heard a rumor that the East Tennessee brigade, still at London, would be withdrawn. He warned Thomas that the chafing mountaineers might disobey orders and strike out on their own. The general bluntly replied that they must then go and risk disaster.[34]

Thomas and Johnson by now hated each other. The division commander exploded to Schoepf that an immediate advance was out of the question and that "all discontented persons" should be silenced. Schoepf, embarrassed by recent press reports that he too had been grousing, pledged his full support—"I have never urged it [forward movement]; do not now urge it." Johnson continued to receive reports that confirmed his suspicions that Thomas was the problem. Elijah Smith, an attorney closely aligned with the senator, admonished him not to let the Virginian command the expedition: "the troops have no confidence with him. I am not alone in the belief he [Thomas] is not in the right place."[35]

On the night of November 8, Carter's bridge burners struck. Five eastern Ten-

32. OR, 4:225, 228, 345; New York Herald, Nov. 13, 1861; New York Times, Nov. 13, 15, 20, 1861; Cincinnati Enquirer, Nov. 16, 1861; Kelly, "Holding Kentucky," 383–84; Edward O. Guerrant, "Marshall and Garfield in Eastern Kentucky," in B&L, 1:393.

33. New York Times, Nov. 9, 1861.

34. OR, 4:342–43.

35. Ibid., 343, 347–48; Leroy P. Graf, Ralph W. Haskins, and Paul H. Bergeron, eds., The Papers of Andrew Johnson, 13 vols. (Knoxville: University of Tennessee Press, 1979), 5:62; McKinney, Education in Violence, 118.

nessee and northern Georgia trestles were destroyed, but the other four on the list remained intact. As the news of the sabotage spread, loyal mountaineers made impromptu gatherings in Carter, Johnson, and Sevier Counties in East Tennessee, joyously believing that Thomas was coming and that their time of liberation was at hand. Some one thousand mountaineers gathered at Strawberry Plains, three hundred in Sevier County, and five hundred in Hamilton County, prepared to burn additional bridges in the belief that the Union army was even then coming to their relief. The overly alarmed Confederates, fearing a general uprising, rushed reinforcements into the area. Hundreds of unionists fled; at least four hundred were arrested and sent to Tuscaloosa, Alabama; and several of the saboteurs were caught and hanged, their bodies left to dangle. Sherman, of course, was not on the way, a fact that soon became apparent. A livid Andrew Johnson denounced the department commander's "shameless desertion of East Tennessee."[36]

The inability of Union intelligence efforts to penetrate south of Green River continued to hamper Sherman. Although William Blount Carter's spies reported that fifteen thousand Confederates were at Bowling Green and six thousand with Zollicoffer (including one thousand sick), Sherman placed the numbers at forty-five thousand and twenty thousand respectively. Despite these exaggerations, the commander was in no position to assume the offensive, Senator Johnson's views to the contrary. McCook's twelve thousand Federals faced an equal number of Confederates at Bowling Green, while Thomas's five thousand men confronted Zollicoffer's division of equal strength. Sherman maintained many troops in the rear, but even if he reduced that number by half, it probably would not have added five thousand soldiers to the front line. No invasion of eastern Tennessee could come until the Ohio units in western Virginia were released—twenty-three regiments remained in the area as late as November 21.[37]

Sherman remained fixated on the idea that Albert Sidney Johnston would unite Zollicoffer and Buckner and fall upon either McCook at Nolin or Thomas at Crab Orchard, then march into Louisville as deliverer. Governor Morton had previously apprised Lincoln of such a potential move, but the president considered the threat amounted to but little. If Zollicoffer reinforced Buckner, thought Lincoln, then

36. Temple, *East Tennessee and the Civil War*, 377–80, 388–90, 393–94, 397, 418; Thomas William Hume, *The Loyal Mountaineers of East Tennessee* (Knoxville: Ogden Brothers, 1888), 151–62; *OR*, 4:241, 243, 359–60; Current, *Lincoln's Loyalists*, 38–39; *Chicago Tribune*, Nov. 30, 1861.

37. *OR*, 4:337, 349, 350–51, 353, 360; *Cincinnati Enquirer*, Nov. 21, 1861. Nelson had a 3,000-man brigade in eastern Kentucky, and another 3,000 troops were stationed along the railroad between Lebanon Junction and Elizabethtown. W. T. Ward's 1,500 Kentuckians were not properly armed and organized and could not be relied upon. Other regiments were scattered about at Bardstown, Colesburg, Paris, and the mouth of Salt River.

Thomas would simply do the same for McCook, "and the thing is essentially the same." Indeed, McCook could be reinforced faster from Kentucky and Indiana than Buckner from Zollicoffer, leaving Thomas unopposed to march into eastern Tennessee. Sherman nonetheless believed his suspicions confirmed on November 11, when he received word of a twenty-seven-hundred-man enemy force attempting to get between his two divisions. The panicked department commander immediately ordered Thomas to fall back to the Green River; Carter's East Tennessee brigade would remain near Rockcastle River, while Nelson's brigade would withdraw to Lexington.[38]

Thomas realized that Sherman had overreacted to the point of embarrassment. He did his best to calm him and present a realistic assessment of the enemy's potential. The so-called Confederate advance in fact was nothing more than a single brigade (Patrick Cleburne's) on a feint/reconnaissance toward Tompkinsville. Sherman had two thousand troops at Columbia and Campbellsville, a force sufficient to slow the Rebels should they choose to advance, which they had no intention of doing. As late as November 14, a deluded Sherman still insisted that Thomas withdraw, even though there was not a secessionist within forty miles and the Rebel brigade at Tompkinsville had already begun to withdraw to Bowling Green.[39]

Thomas dutifully ordered Carter's brigade at London and Schoepf's brigade at Wild Cat Mountain to retire; a near debacle ensued. Mutiny broke out in Carter's camp, with entire platoons refusing to obey. Many bearded men wept and smashed their muskets in disgust, and a number of Tennesseans deserted, though most returned within a few days. An enraged Andrew Johnson added fuel to the mountaineers discontent. The order was soon countermanded and the brigade returned to London, but not before the sick had been sent to Mount Vernon in a driving rain.[40]

Schoepf received orders to withdraw to Mount Vernon on November 13. In a near farcical episode, Thomas's dispatch stated to move out at "8:00," referring to the morning of the fourteenth. With no "A.M." added, however, Schoepf understood that he was to break camp and be on the road within five hours that evening. Some six hundred of the sick were left behind. The night march, humorously labeled by the Confederates as the "Wild Cat Stampede," proved so horrid that a hundred horses and four wagons broke down in the thick mud and three men died. The three Ohio colonels in the brigade were all sick, and Col. James Steedman nearly fell off his horse in delirium. Large amounts of supplies were strewn along the road-

38. *OR*, 4:336, 350–51, 353, 357; Basler, *Collected Works of Abraham Lincoln*, 4:542.

39. *OR*, 4:350–51, 354, 357–58, 531, 545–46.

40. Kelly, "Holding Kentucky," 383; *New York Times*, Nov. 25, 1861; *Cincinnati Commercial*, Sept. 18, 18, 1861; Graf, Haskins, and Bergeron, *Papers of Andrew Johnson*, 5:48.

side. All this occurred to the musical backdrop of the "Dead March," played by the 14th Ohio's band. The next morning the men had to wade the three-foot-deep Duck River, which resulted in nearly the entire command coming down with fever. By Christmas Day 541 men of the 33d Indiana were in the hospital; only 125 answered roll. The press criticized Schoepf for riding ahead of the column to division headquarters at Crab Orchard and sitting in comfort rather than supervising the construction of a foot bridge over Duck River.[41]

Senator Johnson arrived at First Division headquarters in a rage. He specifically channeled his anger at Schoepf and his handling of the withdrawal, but he also rambled on about the general lack of leadership. The general threatened to have the senator removed from camp, which incited an on-looking crowd. Johnson dared Schoepf to lay a hand on him. Thomas, hearing the commotion, calmly walked out of the hotel, took Schoepf by the arm, and, without uttering a word, escorted him inside, thus ending the exchange.[42]

On November 15 Sherman, as broken down and overwhelmed as his predecessor, was notified by the War Department that he had been relived of command. The decision proved correct, even merciful. Sherman later admitted that only the thought of his children had stayed his hand from committing suicide. The *Chicago Tribune* took one final jab, denouncing the departing commander as a "do-nothing" general and bidding him good riddance.[43]

The Army of the Cumberland cannot be understood apart from the dynamics of the summer and fall of 1861. It was Lincoln's obsession with holding Kentucky and liberating East Tennessee that brought the force into being. Additionally, many of the Kentucky officers present during this formative period were to become corps and division commanders in the army. As late as January 1863, fully half of the army's top infantry officers hailed from the Bluegrass State. As for Anderson and Sherman, they had bequeathed an embryonic command that had little organization and less cohesion. Intra-army bickering and political interference, coupled with a muddled strategic vision, resulted in an impotent command with no offensive edge. Neither man had been physically or mentally up to the task at hand. It would prove an inauspicious beginning for an army entrusted with the protection of the Ohio Valley.

41. *New York Times,* Nov. 25, Dec. 7, 1861; *Cincinnati Commercial,* Nov. 19, 1861; *Chicago Tribune,* Dec. 4, 1861.

42. John R. McBride, *History of the Thirty-Third Indiana Veteran Volunteer Infantry* (Indianapolis: William B. Burford, 1900), 32.

43. *OR,* 4:358; Marszalek, *Sherman,* 163; *Chicago Tribune,* Nov. 23, 25, 1861. The *Cincinnati Commercial* of November 12, 1861, concluded, "General Sherman has disappointed the expectations of his friends in office here."

PART 2

THE BUELL INFLUENCE

3

Organization and Strategy
The Arrival of Buell

ON THE NIGHT of November 14, 1861, the new commander of the enlarged and re-named Department of the Ohio arrived in Louisville on a delayed train. At eight o'clock the next morning, in company with Sherman, he walked from the Galt House to headquarters, where he was introduced to the staff. Brig. Gen. Don Carlos Buell announced, "Gentlemen, I have assumed the command."[1]

Sadness had struck early in the life of the Ohio-born general. His father had died of cholera when Buell was only five. When his mother remarried, Don Carlos was turned over to his uncle, George P. Buell, in Lawrenceburg, Indiana, for rearing. The loss of his father and the seeming desertion of his mother (with whom he lost close ties thereafter) clearly influenced his introverted, some would say antisocial, personality. Through his uncle's political connections, Buell entered West Point at age eighteen, and he struggled academically for the next four years. Only two years after graduation, he was court-martialed, though exonerated, for striking a soldier with the flat of his sword. Buell later married a widow and, although they had no children, he adopted his two stepdaughters. Besides considerable wealth, his wife, Margaret (Maggie), brought to the marriage eight slaves, although Buell had sold them by the time of the war.[2]

In deportment and appearance, the short forty-three-year-old general appeared well suited for his new assignment. Studious, robust, and austere, Buell stood erect and looked directly at people when speaking. He was thoroughly professional and possessed both combat and administrative experience, having fought in the Mexican War (being both wounded and brevetted) and having served for thirteen years in the Adjutant General's Office. Unfortunately, his lengthy bureaucratic tenure had smothered his creativity, making him systematic to a fault. A disciplinarian and organizer, and thus an improvement over his predecessors, he was not a bold or inspiring field commander. The *Chicago Tribune* nevertheless hailed his arrival:

1. *Chicago Tribune,* Nov. 23, 1861; *OR,* 4:358, 359; "Buell Statement," 2.

2. J. R. Chumney, "Don Carlos Buell: Gentleman General" (Ph.D. diss., Rice University, 1964), 3; Stephen D. Engle, *Don Carlos Buell: Most Promising of All* (Chapel Hill: University of North Carolina Press, 1999), 5–8, 11–15, 48; *Cincinnati Times,* Nov. 20, 1861.

"Anderson was a gentleman of no mind. Sherman is possessed of neither mind nor matter. We are thankful we have a man who combines both."[3]

Buell's ascendancy to department command was closely related to his prewar association with McClellan. The two men had become acquainted in October 1852 in Texas, and McClellan thought Buell to be "one of the best in the army." Prior to his arrival in Kentucky, the general had commanded a division in McClellan's Army of the Potomac. The Ohioan's letters to the general in chief began "Dear Friend," and the *New York Times* characterized the appointment as "McClellan's own work." Writing years later, McClellan insisted that the single best thing he had done for the West was to send Buell. Although his businesslike friend lacked McClellan's charm and charisma, in two areas they were similar: both favored preparation over movement and maneuvering over fighting.[4]

Some suspected that politics as well as friendship had played a role in the appointment. Buell, a Democrat, shared McClellan's anti-emancipation views on slavery. The issue first arose in December 1861, when Secretary of War Cameron pushed for emancipation of contraband slaves. Buell strongly opposed the idea, endearing him not only to his friend but also to many in the western states. Maj. Gen. David Hunter, a division commander who desired command of the Army of the Ohio, believed his own pro-emancipation views caused McClellan to overlook him for the post, a conviction shared by others.[5]

Thomas's supporters would later claim that he should have received the army command. Such a conclusion overlooks several facts, however. For one thing, Mitchel, not Thomas, was the senior brigadier in the department. Also, Thomas remained under a cloud because of his Virginia birth. More significantly, he had been recently raked by the press for the abortive East Tennessee offensive. The *Chicago Tribune* denounced his "wrong-headed blundering," and the Cincinnati papers hinted that Thomas had purposely failed to destroy Zollicoffer. Congressman Maynard wrote the general bluntly: "There is a shameful wrong. I have not satisfied myself

3. "Buell Statement," 2; *OR*, 4:349, 7:445, 450, 746; Chumney, "Don Carlos Buell," 1–2; Shanks, *Personal Recollections*, 246; Ulysses S. Grant, "The Battle of Shiloh," in *B&L*, 1:482; *Chicago Tribune*, Nov. 9, 1861.

4. Stephen D. Engle, "Don Carlos Buell: Military Philosophy and Command Problems in the West," *Civil War History* 41 (June 1995): 92 n. 15, 93; *New York Times*, Nov. 12, 1861, Feb. 23, 1862; Foote, *Civil War*, 1:145. Originally ordered from California for service in Kentucky, Buell was detained in Virginia after he reported to the War Department.

5. *New York Herald*, Dec. 10, 1861; T. Harry Williams, *Lincoln and the Radicals* (Madison: University of Wisconsin Press, 1941), 102; Gerald G. Prokopowicz, *All for the Regiment: The Army of the Ohio, 1861–1862* (Chapel Hill: University of North Carolina Press, 2001), 203 n. 26; *Cincinnati Enquirer*, Dec. 15, 25, 1861. The contraband slaves in question did not come under the Confiscation Act of August 1861, which established the freedom of slaves who had been employed to advance the cause of the Confederacy.

where." The fact that Thomas had only obeyed Sherman's orders failed to resonate. The loyal Virginian took the criticism stoically, but the fact remained that, despite his competency, Thomas remained largely unproven and highly unpopular in some influential political circles.[6]

One-third of Kentucky remained under Confederate occupation. Upon his arrival, Buell claimed two divisions with twenty-three thousand men, neither prepared for offensive operations, with an additional four thousand men along the Big Sandy River in northeastern Kentucky. He believed that opposing him were Johnston at Bowling Green with thirty-five thousand Rebels, Zollicoffer in eastern Kentucky with six thousand, and Humphrey Marshall at Pound Gap with twenty-five hundred. In reality, the Federals had slightly more troops in the region (thirty thousand) and the Confederates significantly less (twenty thousand).[7]

Buell set about the monumental task of organizing, equipping, and training an army. He quickly evicted the paymasters from their rooms, where they had been interfering with the work of the engineers. Although expressing discontent with the feeble Colonel Sword, he retained Sherman's staff, adding to it three aides as well as two additions to the Adjutant General's Office—Capts. James B. Fry and Nathaniel H. McClean. The forty-four-year-old Fry, an Illinois West Pointer who had served under Irvin McDowell in Virginia, would depose Captain Greene as the functional chief of staff. Buell labored long hours, rarely going to bed before 2:00 or 3:00 A.M., yet his plodding style struck one journalist as "sluggish."[8]

Early reaction to the new department commander proved favorable, though his grace period would be brief. Regimental and brigade commanders, accustomed to taking their problems directly to Sherman, soon discovered that they no longer had access to department headquarters. Buell dealt directly only with division commanders, and even they learned, much to their chagrin, that in matters of strategy he rarely took counsel and related no confidences. He was aloof to the point of iciness, held no close associations, and soon incurred disfavor. Writing on December 1, 1861, Maj. Joseph Keifer of the 3d Ohio informed his wife that he had never seen Buell: "He keeps to himself very closely and in no case consults with his officers not even his division commanders." Thomas admitted later that month that he knew nothing of his superior's plans.[9]

---

6. Cleaves, *Rock of Chickamauga*, 91–92; *Chicago Tribune*, Dec. 4, 11, 1861.

7. "Buell Statement," 2.

8. *Cincinnati Times*, Nov. 20, 23, 1861; *OR*, 7:482, 520, 548; *Cincinnati Enquirer*, Dec. 12, 1861; *Indianapolis Daily Journal*, Nov. 11, 1861; Warner, *Generals in Blue*, 162–63.

9. *Chicago Tribune*, Dec. 18, 1861; *Cincinnati Enquirer*, Dec. 12, 1861; Grant, "Shiloh," 482; Joseph Warren Keifer to wife, Dec. 1, 2, 11, 12, 31, 1861, Joseph Warren Keifer Papers, LC; "Reminiscences of C. E. Blivens," Don Carlos Buell Papers, FC, 3; *OR*, 7:509–10.

The department commander conducted a hurried inspection of his divisions. He arrived at Camp Nolin on November 16. The narrow forest openings prevented an entire division review, so Buell performed the task by brigade; Sherman, also present, betrayed no emotion. The next day he traveled to Crab Orchard for a review of Thomas's division.[10]

Buell, now suffering from a bad cold after having slept on the ground, discovered that many of the men, especially in Thomas's division, had been stricken with measles and mumps. A similar outbreak had occurred at Camp Nolin, where half of McCook's division had contracted measles, typhoid fever, and chills. Some one thousand of six thousand men at Calhoun, Kentucky, were on the sick roll.[11]

Attempting to establish a semblance of military regimen, Buell issued a series of general orders. He limited the escort company of each division commander to twenty-four men, barred all women and buggies from camp, limited the baggage of officers, established a drill schedule, and required written reports from quartermasters, commissaries, and hospitals. Although Buell was generally well received, one woman, forced to leave camp, suggested that he dined daily at the Galt House and suffered little himself.[12]

A dearth of wagon transportation presented serious problems, with no immediate prospects of resolution. Buell had wagons sufficient to supply twenty thousand men only two days' march from the railroad. He immediately issued orders that cooking utensils and tents could not exceed one wagon per company, with each wagon also required to haul four days' rations of forage for the mules and two days' rations for the men. Regimental trains would also include two ambulances and a medical-supply wagon.[13]

Buell found a glaring shortage of qualified officers, and he complained that some lower-grade officers went about barking orders like generals. He requested that McClellan send six to eight brigadiers. Buell hesitated to make nominations from within the army until he knew the men, although several parties had approached him on behalf of friends and relatives. In particular, he urged McClellan to use cau-

10. *New York Times,* Dec. 3, 1861; *Chicago Tribune,* Nov. 25, 1861; Almon F. Rockwell Diary, Nov. 15, 16, 1861, LC.

11. Buell to wife, Dec. 18, 1861, Buell Papers; *Indianapolis Daily Journal,* Oct. 14, 1861; *OR,* 7:472, 513; *Cincinnati Enquirer,* Dec. 8, 12, 1861; John Blackburn, *A Hundred Miles, a Hundred Heartbreaks* (Fordsville, Ky.: Nicholstone Book Bindery, 1972), 29–30. For further documentation of sickness during the first winter, see Prokopowicz, *All for the Regiment,* 64.

12. General Orders No. 2, Nov. 16, 1861; No. 4, Nov. 22, 1861; No. 8, Dec. 3, 1861; No. 10, Dec. 5, 1861; and No. 13, Dec. 9, 1861, General Orders, Department of the Ohio, by Command of Don Carlos Buell, Adjutant General's Office, RG 94, NA; *Cincinnati Enquirer,* Dec. 5, 12, 1861.

13. "Buell Statement," 3; General Orders No. 8, Dec. 3, 1861; No. 10, Dec. 5, 1861; and No. 13, Dec. 9, 1861, General Orders, Department of the Ohio, RG 94.

tion in approving state nominations from Kentucky—"We have had very poor ones already."[14]

The most formidable organizational task confronting the Ohioan was the mustering and equipping of the Kentucky regiments. Kentuckians had been slow in rallying to the flag—only fifteen thousand had joined the Federal ranks by the end of November 1861. Fragments of forty regiments had been called in from their remote recruiting districts by the State Military Board to several central locations and consolidated into twenty-two regiments. Some two thousand Enfield rifles ordered by the state arrived in Louisville on November 3, but ten thousand additional arms were now required. McClellan ordered their delivery in early December, but in the meantime, most Kentuckians sat in staging areas. Only 125 of 650 men in the 17th Kentucky at Camp Chesley Calloway at Hartford possessed muskets, and the 26th Kentucky Infantry and 3d Kentucky Cavalry together counted barely two hundred firearms, and those were inferior. Although several Kentucky units had been mustered into Federal service by the end of November 1861, Buell considered them, for the present, of little value.[15]

Artillery was especially needed. The general initially had on hand only one regular and nine volunteer batteries, all of the last in bad condition, three being entirely without training. Although unaware of any other units then being organized, he required ten more.[16]

Since Indiana, Ohio, and Michigan were now in the reorganized department, Buell did not have to compete with other commanders for regiments from these states. Governors continued to interfere, however, Dennison being the worst, with Morton running a close second. Both sent staff officers to look after the interests of their troops and, in some cases, had regiments now in Federal service continue to report to them. "I shall stop all this sort of thing," Buell assured McClellan.[17]

Several new outfits were forthcoming. Seven Indiana regiments at Indianapolis, reportedly ready for the field, proved so ill trained and undisciplined that Buell retained them in camps of instruction. On November 10 the 10th Wisconsin, armed with a mix of rifles, arrived in Louisville. On November 20–21 the 3d Minnesota, 943 strong; a 100-man Indiana cavalry company (supposed to be McCook's escort); the 10th Kentucky; an Indiana battery; and four Hoosier regiments, the 44th, 49th,

14. *OR,* 7:444, 482; *New York Herald,* Oct. 24, 1861; "Buell Statement," 3; Buell to McClellan, Dec. 5, 1861, Telegrams Received, Dec. 1861–Jan. 1862, Department of the Ohio, RG 393, NA.

15. *Chicago Tribune,* Dec. 5, 1861; *OR,* 4:333, 7:443, 451–52, 468, 482; "Buell Statement," 3–4; *Indianapolis Daily Journal,* Nov. 4, 1861; Reid, *Army That Buell Built,* 15, 18; McClellan to Buell, Dec. 9, 1861, Telegrams Received, Dec. 1861–Jan. 1862, Department of the Ohio, RG 393.

16. *OR,* 7:455, 549.

17. Kelly, "Holding Kentucky," 385; *OR,* 7:443, 482.

52d, and 58th (only the 44th was ready for the field), all passed through Louisville. A contingent of regulars also arrived—Capt. William R. Terrill's six-gun Battery H, 5th U.S. Artillery, from Newport Barracks and, on December 4, the 18th Infantry, 1,200 strong, and a battalion (500 men) of the 16th Infantry, the former having been recruited in Columbus and the latter in Chicago. Although essentially volunteer units, the officers were regular-army veterans, and the training and discipline of the troops was clearly more stringent. Further distinguishing the regulars were their Model 1858 U.S. Army hats, turned up and pinned on the left side.[18]

Exactly how long McClellan would allow Brig. Gen. William S. Rosecrans to retain large numbers of Indiana and Ohio troops in western Virginia became an ever increasing concern. In early November Governor Morton journeyed to Washington to lobby for the release of twenty thousand of Rosecrans's men for use in Kentucky. Although the Confederate effort to regain control of western Virginia had been checked at Carnifex Ferry and Cheat Mountain in September 1861, this was not immediately perceived by the Federals. "There they [Rosecrans's forces] stay in the mountains doing nothing but keeping their feet warm," railed the *Indianapolis Daily Journal*, "while the Kanawha Valley has been nearly abandoned by the Rebels, and one brigade can defend Cheat Mountain pass."[19]

In late November McClellan at long last released eight of Rosecrans's regiments for service in Kentucky, with four more to follow in December. The troops anticipated a stopover in Cincinnati, but orders directed that they proceed immediately to their new assignments. A general breakdown in discipline occurred, with one officer conceding that the men were greatly demoralized. At Jefferson, Indiana, across the river from Louisville, men of the 9th Ohio quickly filled local saloons.[20]

Buell, on November 20, organized his Army of the Ohio into five divisions with sixteen brigades numbered consecutively, a departure from other Northern armies, in which brigades were numbered within their divisions. Buell adopted the unique policy of brigading regiments from different states. The purpose, according to one soldier, was "to make a general thing of it." The downside of the new structure was that each brigade was seen as a self-contained unit, with its own battery and cavalry company. Theoretically, sixteen independent maneuver units existed.[21]

18. *OR*, 7:451–452; *Chicago Tribune*, Nov. 23, 27, 30, Dec. 7, 1861; *Cincinnati Times*, Nov. 22, 1861, Jan. 18, 1862; *Cincinnati Enquirer*, Dec. 5, 1861; Dyer, *Compendium*, 2:1136, 1297, 1714; Frederick Phisterer, *Association of Survivors, Regular Brigade, Fourteenth Corps, Army of the Cumberland* (N.p., n.d.), 12, 19; General Orders No. 9, Nov. 24, 1861, Buell Papers.

19. *Indianapolis Daily Journal*, Nov. 4, 19, 1861.

20. *OR*, 4:358, 7:447, 458; *Chicago Tribune*, Nov. 27, 30, Dec. 7, 1861; *Cincinnati Enquirer*, Dec. 6, 1861; Beatty, *Citizen Soldier*, 85–86.

21. *OR*, 7:460–61, 476; *Chicago Tribune*, Dec. 19, 1861; *Indianapolis Daily Journal*, Dec. 18, 21, 1861; "Buell Statement," 3–4; Henry M. Cist, *Army of the Cumberland* (reprint, Wilmington, N.C.: Broadfoot,

Thomas's First Division organization proved chaotic. Initially designated the First, Second, Third, and Twelfth Brigades, the latter (Samuel P. Carter's) was soon notified to report directly to army headquarters. In its place Thomas received the Eleventh Brigade, but by December 19 it also had been ordered to report directly to Louisville, leaving the general only three brigades. Included in his division, however, were three veteran Ohio regiments from western Virginia and the 18th U.S. Infantry.[22]

McCook's Second Division at Nolin Creek, the most historic of the divisions, comprised the Fourth, Fifth, Sixth, and Seventh Brigades. Over two months had been spent in preparing the command for the field, and it was moderately well armed and trained. Especially touted were the 32d Indiana and 49th Ohio and a thirteen-hundred-man regiment of regulars (companies of the 15th and 19th U.S. Infantry) under Maj. John H. King. The division camp spread over two large farms, and a high tableland served as the parade ground.[23]

Troops of Ormsby Mitchel's Third Division, consisting of the Eighth, Ninth, and later Seventeenth Brigades, assembled at Camp John Quincy Adams at Bacon Creek Station, eight miles north of Munfordville along the Louisville and Nashville Railroad. The ten thousand troops represented several regiments already in the department, including the nine-hundred-strong 15th Kentucky, organized back in August but only now coming into service, and four Ohio regiments recently transferred from western Virginia.[24]

Mitchel, "Old Stars" to his men, possessed the stern countenance of a professor, which he in fact had been for the past thirty-two years. He could be genial, but he was also self-promoting and temperamental. Eighth Brigade commander Col. John B. Turchin (Ivan Turchanoov in his native Russia) was a hot-tempered officer with experience in both the Hungarian and Crimean Wars. Colonel Sill, commanding the Ninth Brigade, was a competent Ohio West Pointer with service in West Virginia. Although it was widely rumored that Col. William Lytle of the 10th Ohio

1989), 22; Prokopowicz, *All for the Regiment*, 39–40. Although technically named the Department of the Ohio, Buell's force was functionally styled the "Army of the Ohio." Gerald Prokopowicz suggests that Buell's national policy was a political strategy to lessen the authority of governors. Ibid., 39–40.

22. *OR*, 7:460–61, 467, 476, 508; Cox, "McClellan in West Virginia," 130.

23. Van Horne, *Army of the Cumberland*, 1:65; *OR*, 7:467; Chamberlain and Chamberlain, *Civil War Letters of an Ohio Soldier*, 7; *Indianapolis Daily Journal*, Sept. 30, Oct. 23, 28, 1861; Dodge, *Old Second Division*, 74, 82–83. An article in the *Cincinnati Times* on January 18, 1862, gave the strength of the 15th U.S. Infantry as 725 and the 19th U.S. Infantry as 275.

24. Van Horne, *Army of the Cumberland*, 1:67–71; Beatty, *Citizen Soldier*, 85, 87; Mitchel, *Ormsby Macknight Mitchel*, 237–38; *OR*, 7:460–61, 468, 476; *New York Times*, Dec. 19, 1861; *Cincinnati Enquirer*, Dec. 12, 1861; William P. McDowell, "The 15th Kentucky," *Southern Bivouac* 5 (1886): 246–47. By the time Mitchel's division began to organize, McCook's division had advanced beyond Munfordville, making it the lead division.

would lead the Seventeenth Brigade, the position went to former Indiana state legis-lator and Mexican War veteran Col. Ebenezer Dumont, affable enough but drawn to intrigue and frequently sick.[25]

In late November Brig. Gen. William Nelson's reassigned brigade marched from eastern Kentucky to Cincinnati and thence to Louisville. Nelson reported to Camp Wickliffe at New Haven, eighteen miles east of Elizabethtown along the Lebanon Railroad, where the Fourth Division organized. On December 10 a column of eight regiments departed Louisville for New Haven. The new division established camp eleven miles south of that town, past Muldraugh's Hill. The command initially com-prised the Tenth and Fifteenth Brigades, with the heart of the division being newly arrived Indiana and Ohio regiments from western Virginia.[26]

Nelson, forever obnoxious and volatile, was denounced by both officers and men as a foul-mouthed tyrant. Prior to his arrival at Camp Wickliffe, he had wrangled with Kentucky militia officers and Col. Samuel P. Carter, and he had not been in Cincinnati a day before colliding with General Mitchel—"[Nelson] behaved very absurdly," noted Buell. On another occasion, the Kentucky general nearly got into a physical altercation with a drunken soldier. Nelson nonetheless had his supporters, enjoyed a reputation for getting things done, and could lay claim to a victory, albeit a small one, at Piketon. Col. Stanley Matthews, commanding the 51st Ohio, con-ceded that the soldiers saw the general as "no better than a brute. He is coarse, savage, tyrannical, and continually insulting everyone with bits of his blasphemy." Nonetheless, he concluded, "he is a good officer, is vigilant, industrious, cautious, and brave." Adding stability to the division were the two brigade commanders, Cols. Jacob Ammen and Milo Haskell, both West Pointers with service in West Virginia.[27]

The Indiana and Kentucky regiments organizing at Owensboro, Henderson, Cal-

25. P. C. Headley, *The Patriot Boy; or the Life and Career of Major-General Ormsby Mitchel* (New York: William H. Appleton, 1865), 61–67, 134; Beatty, *Citizen Soldier*, 87–88, 90; Ernest E. East, "Lincoln's Russian General," *Journal of the Illinois State Historical Society* 52 (spring 1959): 106–7, 111–12; Warner, *Generals in Blue*, 132, 448–49; *Cincinnati Enquirer*, Dec. 12, 1861; George Buell to D. C. Buell, Dec. 20, 1861, Buell Papers.

26. Cist, *Army of the Cumberland*, 23; Van Horne, *Army of the Cumberland*, 1:69–70; *New York Times*, Nov. 25, 29, Dec. 23, 1861; *Cincinnati Enquirer*, Dec. 11, 1861; W. B. Hazen, *A Narrative of Military Service* (Boston: Ticknor, 1885), 13; *OR*, 7:460–61, 468; Buell to Nelson, Dec. 13, 1861; and Purnell to Buell, Dec. 14, 1861, Telegrams Received, Dec. 1861–Jan. 1862, Department of the Ohio, RG 393.

27. *OR*, 4:318, 7:451; *New York Times*, Dec. 5, 1861; Current, *Lincoln's Loyalists*, 31; Warner, *Generals in Blue*, 7, 213–14; Faust, *Encyclopedia*, 348; *National Intelligencer*, Apr. 29, 1861; Kelly, "Holding Ken-tucky," 384–85; Stanley Matthews to wife, Dec. 14, 22, 1861, Stanley Matthews Letters, CINHS. For an-other example of Nelson clashing with his troops (in October 1861), see Frank Furlong Mathis, ed., *Incidents and Experiences in the Life of Thomas W. Parsons, from 1826 to 1900* (Frankfort: University Press of Kentucky, 1975), 78.

houn, and Columbia formed the core of Brig. Gen. Thomas Crittenden's Fifth Division, divided into the Thirteenth and Fourteenth Brigades. Because of its location, the Fifth would comprise the right wing of the army. There was little to distinguish the unit, including its hard-drinking and inexperienced commander. "I don't know what to think of [Crittenden]," Lt. Col. James Shanklin of the 42d Indiana admitted to his wife on December 10. "He is a very fine man in his manners, easy and makes you at home at once; he possesses a great deal of pluk and courage I have no doubt, but whether he is the man for the place is the question—that is the question."[28]

Typical of the arriving regiments was the 33d Indiana, comprised almost entirely of native-born farmers, with only forty-two foreigners in the regiment. Yet the perception of a largely homogenous army leaves much unsaid. While most of the troops came from rural communities, there was a notable urban presence. Louisville and vicinity supplied the 5th, 6th, and 15th Kentucky Infantry; 2d Kentucky Cavalry; and Stone's battery. The 19th and 24th Illinois hailed from Chicago, while the 6th, 9th, and 10th Ohio originated in Cincinnati. The 41st, 42d, and 65th Ohio came (mostly) from Cleveland, as did Batteries B, C, and G, First Ohio Light Artillery. Several companies came from Indianapolis, while Detroit and Minneapolis likewise supplied individual companies. The 51st Indiana, consisting of railroad men and mechanics, remained in a camp of instruction during December 1861 but would soon join the others in the field.[29]

Several ethnic units added a cosmopolitan flair to the army. There were four all-German regiments—Col. Robert L. McCook's 9th Ohio, Col. August Willich's 32d Indiana, Col. Geza Mihalotzy's 24th Illinois, and Col. Henry A. Hambright's 79th Pennsylvania. The Irish claimed three regiments—the 10th Ohio; the "green caps" of the 35th Indiana, who carried a large green regimental flag with harp and shamrock; and the Zouaves of the 19th Illinois. Fully one-half of the 5th and 6th Kentucky

28. Van Horne, *Army of the Cumberland*, 1:70; *OR*, 4:305, 307, 315, 7:460–61, 468; *Cincinnati Enquirer*, Dec. 12, 1861; Kenneth W. Noe, ed., *A Southern Boy in Blue: The Memoir of Marcus Woodcock, 9th Kentucky Infantry (U.S.A.)* (Knoxville: University of Tennessee Press, 1996), 41; Beatty, *Citizen Soldier*, 235; *New York Times*, Nov. 29, 1861; Blackburn, *A Hundred Miles*, 27–28; Kenneth P. McCutchan, ed., *"Dearest Lizzie": The Civil War As Seen through the Eyes of Lieutenant Colonel James Maynard Shanklin* (Evansville, Ind.: Friends of Willard Library Press, 1908), 40–41.

29. McBride, *History of the Thirty-Third Indiana*, 12; J. Stoddard Johnson, *Memorial History of Louisville: From Its Settlement to the Year 1896*, 2 vols. (Chicago: American Biographical Publishing, 1896), 1:168–69, 171, 173, 179, 183; J. N. Reece, *Report of the Adjutant General of the State of Illinois*, 2 vols. (Springfield: Phillips Brothers, 1900), 2:276; Henry Howe, *Historical Collections of Ohio*, 3 vols. (Cincinnati: Henry Howe and Son, 1891), 2:44; David D. Van Tassell, ed., *The Encyclopedia of Cleveland History* (Bloomington: Indiana University Press, 1996), 194; James Barnett, "History of Company G, Ohio Light Artillery," James Barnett Papers, WRHS; *Indianapolis Daily Journal*, Sept. 10, Oct. 31, 1861; *National Intelligencer*, Oct. 15, 1861.

comprised Germans, and a company of Swedes was counted among the ranks of the 3d Minnesota. A company from Scranton in the 77th Pennsylvania comprised Welsh immigrants or men of Welsh descent.[30]

New regiments continued to arrive throughout December at a staging area (Camp Buell) five miles south of Louisville. Indiana and Ohio regiments anywhere near full compliment were ordered up, although this was done at the urging of Morton and Dennison for morale and discipline purposes and not through any encouragement from Buell. By the twenty-first, fourteen additional infantry regiments, two cavalry regiments, and three batteries from those states, as well as the 11th Michigan, had passed through Louisville. Three additional brigades, the Seventeenth, Eighteenth, and Nineteenth, were organized. A December inspection found many of the outfits in a deplorable condition: the discipline of Battery H, 5th U.S. Artillery, was "nothing to the proud of"; Col. Jesse Bayle's Kentucky cavalry regiment had men "under no restraint"; the company officers of the 43d Indiana were "careless and ignorant"; and the troops of Colonel Hawkins's Kentucky regiment acted "much like a herd of wild animals." Buell insisted that after discounting his unfit troops and guards for rear positions, he had a movable column of only fifty thousand men. His own end-of-the-year report, however, revealed seventy-two thousand present for duty. With such an impressive array, a Chicago newspaper questioned, "Shall we have something done in Kentucky?"[31]

30. Ella Lonn, *Foreigners in the Union Army and Navy* (Baton Rouge: Louisiana State University Press, 1951), 667, 668, 671, 673, 674; William L. Burton, *Melting Pot Soldiers: The Union's Ethnic Regiments* (Ames: Iowa State University Press, 1988), 80–85, 92–97; Emma Lou Thornbrough, *Indiana in the Civil War Era, 1850–1880* (Indianapolis: Indiana Historical Bureau and Indiana Historical Society, 1965), 126; Catherine Merrill, *The Soldiers of Indiana in the War for the Union* (Indianapolis: Merrill, 1866), 271; George W. Skinner, *Pennsylvania at Chickamauga and Chattanooga* (Harrisburg, Pa.: William Stanley Ray, 1900), 202; E. Eugene Miller, "The Contribution of German Immigrants to the Union Cause in the Civil War in Kentucky," *Filson Club Historical Quarterly* 64 (Oct. 1990): 466; Carl Wittle, "The Ninth Ohio Volunteers," *Ohio Archaeological and Historical Publications* 35 (1927): 408–13; Cox, "War Preparations in the North," 97–98; Constantine Grebner, *"We Were the Ninth": A History of the Ninth Regiment, Ohio Volunteer Infantry, Apr. 17, 1861, to June 7, 1864* (reprint, Kent, Ohio: Kent State University Press, 1987), 6–7; Kenneth W. Noe, *Perryville: The Grand Havoc of War* (Lexington: University Press of Kentucky, 2001), 190.

31. *Indianapolis Daily Journal,* Dec. 16, 23, 31, 1861; *Chicago Tribune,* Nov. 30, Dec. 9, 10,12,14, 16, 1861, Jan. 1, 1862; *Cincinnati Enquirer,* Dec. 12, 15, 1861; Daniel B. Weber, ed., *The Diary of Ira Gillaspie of the Eleventh Michigan Infantry* (Mount Pleasant: Central Michigan University Press, 1965), 13; *OR,* 7:468, 476, 503, 511, ser. 3, 1:775; inspection reports, quoted in Prokopowicz, *All for the Regiment,* 37; Otto F. Bond, ed., *Under the Flag of the Nation: Diaries and Letters of a Yankee Volunteer in the Civil War* (Columbus: Ohio State University Press, 1961), 12–13. New Indiana regiments were the 43d, 46th, 47th, 49th, 50th, 51st, and 58th. Ohio units included, among others, the 40th and 42d Infantry and the 6th Artillery.

By the time of Buell's arrival, the loyalist Tennessee uprising had become public knowledge. When the subsequent Confederate backlash became known in early December, pressure from the East Tennessee political bloc became intense. "If something is not done, and that speedily, our people will be cut up and ruined," implored Colonel Carter. Senator Johnson and Congressman Maynard made frantic appeals to Lincoln, eliciting his sympathies. McClellan urged an immediate advance and questioned why so many troops had been allowed to accumulate at Louisville. A political-strategic mission, the liberation of East Tennessee was being reserved for the Army of the Ohio.[32]

Although grasping the military significance of the East Tennessee and Virginia Railroad, Lincoln's goal was primarily humanitarian and political. In order to eliminate the main obstacle to a mountain offensive, the lack of a secure line of communications, the president proposed to Congress in early December the construction of an eastern Kentucky railroad that would link up with the existing railhead at either Lebanon or Nicholasville. The idea, born more out of desperation than insight, was soon abandoned.[33]

Although Buell had been sent to the West under McClellan's explicit orders to move rapidly on Knoxville via Cumberland Gap or Walker's Gap, the department commander failed to connect with the administration's urgency. He saw only the obvious—eastern Kentucky had neither a river nor a railroad. To launch an overland winter offensive with a two-hundred-mile supply line over rugged mountainous terrain would be risky. Additionally, the diagonal supply line (from Louisville to Knoxville) would subject the right flank to a Confederate attack from Bowling Green. Buell saw three options: first, pin Albert Sidney Johnston down at Bowling Green and move into eastern Kentucky via Somerset; second, move toward Nashville by way of Glasgow, Kentucky, and Gallatin, Tennessee, in conjunction with a joint army-navy operation up the Tennessee and Cumberland Rivers by Maj. Gen. Henry W. Halleck, Frémont's successor; or third, a combination of the two, that is, dual offensives. Buell clearly favored the second alternative.[34]

Although giving lip service to the plight of poor mountaineers, McClellan shared Buell's military logic. So strong were the political imperatives, however, that the

32. *OR,* 4:359–60, 7:447, 450, 469–70, 480, 485; *New York Times,* Nov. 15, Dec. 1, 1861; *Cincinnati Commercial,* Nov. 17, Dec. 6, 1861. Lincoln had actually proposed an East Tennessee offensive in early October 1861, but nothing came of the idea. Basler, *Collected Works of Abraham Lincoln,* 4:544–45.

33. Herman Hattaway and Archer Jones, *How the North Won* (Urbana: University of Illinois Press, 1983), 56; John G. Nicolay and John Hay, *Abraham Lincoln: A History,* 10 vols. (New York: Century, 1917), 5:66–67; McKinney, *Education in Violence,* 123.

34. McClellan, *McClellan's Own Story,* 202; Chumney, "Don Carlos Buell," 45–46; "Buell Statement," 4–5; *OR,* 7:450–51; Buell to McClellan, Dec. 10, 1861, Don Carlos Buell Papers.

general in chief, on November 29, insisted that East Tennessee take precedence over Nashville. He also counted on the East Tennessee and Virginia Railroad's being severed before he began operations with his own Army of the Potomac. In an effort to placate both Buell and Lincoln, however, McClellan agreed to dual offensives—a march on Nashville with fifty thousand men and a simultaneous fifteen-thousand-man attack column for East Tennessee.[35]

Despite McClellan's continued pleas throughout early December, Buell refused to budge. Nor did he fear, as expressed in a letter to his wife, that McClellan would override him. Buell never dismissed a winter offensive as impossible, and he even gave hints throughout mid-December that such an option was very much alive. It is highly doubtful if by that time, however, he seriously contemplated such a move, although he would not reveal his intentions until early January 1862. Buell did not desire to fight for Cumberland Gap but rather to outmaneuver the enemy by using Pound Gap, Looney's Gap, or Kyle's Gap. He also adamantly maintained that the main attack should be on Nashville, the occupation of which would assist in the capture of East Tennessee. It is difficult not to conclude that Buell intended to stall McClellan throughout the winter in an attempt to carry out his desired spring offensive against Nashville.[36]

In stark contrast to both Anderson and Sherman, Buell remained convinced that the Confederates posed no true offensive threat in Kentucky. He conservatively placed enemy strength at Bowling Green at twenty-five thousand, with an additional ten thousand advanced toward Hopkinsville, and considered the odds of their moving north almost nil—"I should almost as soon expect to see the Army of the Potomac moving up the road," he wryly suggested to McClellan. Buell dismissed reports of Rebel incursions ("roving bugbears," he called them) and focused on organization.[37]

He soon discovered, however, that raiding parties could not be completely ignored. The one-hundred-foot bridge of the Louisville and Nashville Railroad spanning Bacon Creek had been previously destroyed but rebuilt in advance of the army. On December 6 a small raiding party under John Hunt Morgan crossed north of the Green River and again destroyed the bridge. Buell appeared unmoved by this rather glaring breach of security, declaring that the structure could be rebuilt within four days. Morgan's men in fact had been up to more mischief. Although the superstructure of the Louisville and Nashville trestle at Green River had been previously destroyed, the four stone piers remained intact. The raiders attempted to blow them

35. OR, 7:457, 468.

36. Ibid., 468, 473, 487, 531; Kenneth P. Williams, Lincoln Finds a General: A Military Study of the Civil War, 5 vols. (New York: Macmillan, 1949–58), 3:145; Buell to wife, Dec. 10, 1861, Buell Papers.

37. OR, 7:444, 483; "Buell Statement," 2.

up but only succeeded with one. The Federals counted on these piers being in place as they constructed a replacement bridge. Even Buell conceded that their destruction would have been a serious setback. He belatedly ordered McCook's division forward fourteen miles to Bacon Creek and advanced Richard Johnson's Sixth Brigade to Munfordville, at Green River. "Yesterday was our first trial in marching any distance, and when it comes to marching fourteen miles and carrying a heavy knapsack it is a little like work[,] especially to the city boys," Sgt. Michael S. Bright of the 78th Pennsylvania wrote on December 8. By the twelfth, troops of the 32d Indiana occupied abandoned Confederate trenches on the south bank of Green River.[38]

At noon on December 17, an enemy brigade suddenly approached the picket line of the 32d Indiana, posted on a ridge one mile south of the river at Rowlett's Station. A sharp half-hour engagement over cultivated fields ensued, and the Rebels were repulsed in sporadic attacks. The 32d sustained thirty-eight casualties, the Southerners fourteen, but Buell and the Northern press hailed the action as a great victory.[39]

In truth, the Federals had been taking unnecessary risks by advancing lone infantry regiments as outpost garrisons. At Wild Cat Mountain, the 3d Kentucky had been spared only by the timely arrival of reinforcements. At Rowlett's Station, Richard Johnson immediately sent two regiments across Green River in support, but by the time they arrived, the fighting had ceased. McCook, hearing gunshots to the south, dispatched two brigades for Bacon Creek, but they could not cross without the express orders of Buell in Louisville. Telegraphic permission eventually arrived, though far too late to matter. The scenario was a recipe for disaster, and the 32d Indiana had escaped only by hard fighting.[40]

Buell nonetheless continued to ignore incursions. By November 25 a secessionist force estimated at eight thousand was reportedly advancing from Hopkinsville to Greenville to destroy the locks on the Lower Green River. Four locks on the Green River and one on the Barren River made these waterways navigable year round and provided the interior a direct link with the Ohio River. While Crittenden fretted, the department commander calmly placed enemy strength at twenty-five hundred to three thousand men and sloughed off the episode.[41]

38. *OR*, 7:12–13, 19, 483; *Cincinnati Enquirer*, Dec. 14, 15, 1861; *Chicago Tribune*, Dec. 11, 14, 1861; McCook to Fry, Dec. 6, 7, 1861, Telegrams Received, Dec. 1861–Jan. 1862, Department of the Ohio, RG 393; Maury Klein, *History of the Louisville & Nashville Railroad* (New York: Macmillan, 1972), 30; Aida Craig Truxall, ed., *"Respects to All": Letters of Two Pennsylvania Boys in the War of the Rebellion* (Pittsburgh: University of Pittsburgh Press, 1962), 63.

39. Dodge, *Old Second Division*, 89–91; *OR*, 7:15–20, 511; *New York Tribune*, Dec. 26, 1861.

40. *Chicago Tribune*, Dec. 27, 1861; *OR*, 7:19; *New York Tribune*, Dec. 26, 1861; *Cincinnati Commercial*, Nov. 4, 1861.

41. *OR*, 7:447, 449, 451; *New York Times*, Nov. 27, 1861; W. P. Greene, *The Greene River Country from Bowling Green to Evansville* (Evansville, Ind.: J. S. Reilly, 1898), 14.

Reports now began to surface that Zollicoffer had abandoned Cumberland Gap and was shifting his forces toward Gainesville, Tennessee. Buell nonchalantly took the opportunity to shorten General Thomas's supply line. He retained Carter's Twelfth Brigade (two thousand effectives) at London to observe the gap, while the First Division drew back and concentrated at Columbia and Lebanon. Louisville would thus be Thomas's main supply depot rather than Cincinnati, reducing his supply line by half and eliminating reliance upon the Kentucky River bridge. The roads proved so wretched, however, that the Virginian did not complete his concentration until November 26. As for Zollicoffer's reappearance in Kentucky, Buell appeared uninterested. The reported ten thousand Rebels he believed were closer to four or five thousand, the Southerners probably on another raid to interrupt coal trade on the Cumberland River.[42]

Col. W. A. Hoskins, on outpost duty with his 12th Kentucky, held a decidedly different view. His command represented the only organized force standing between Zollicoffer's division (eight thousand strong, according to Hoskins's scouting reports) and the north bank of the Cumberland River. A small force of the enemy had already crossed on November 26 and skirmished with the picket post opposite Mill Springs, twelve miles southwest of the Federal position. The situation appeared to be another Wild Cat Mountain/Rowlett's Station scenario, only this time no reinforcements were in the vicinity. A panicked Hoskins requested help from the nearest unit, Samuel Carter's Twelfth Brigade at London, a hard two-days' march distant, but Carter was under direct orders from Buell to maintain his position, and the colonel refused compliance.[43]

Buell did send reinforcements, but his response proved restrained. Brigadier General Schoepf marched from the vicinity of Lebanon with two regiments and a battery, while Frank Walford's 1st Kentucky Cavalry proceeded from Columbia. For an agonizing three days, until the evening of December 1, the isolated 12th Kentucky held firm. Fortunately, the Confederates made no attempt at a crossing. Upon his arrival, Schoepf began entrenching at Fishing Creek.[44]

The Southerners opened a brisk but harmless shelling upon Schoepf's camp on

42. *OR*, 4:360–61, 362, 7:439, 442–43, 451, 471, 477. The idea of concentrating the First Division in a more central position occurred to Thomas as early as November 17. Van Horne declared that the November 26 march was a "hurried one" over bad roads, even though Lebanon and Columbia were not threatened as Buell suspected. He denounced the general's decision as "costly and fruitless." *Army of the Cumberland*, 1:47. I have found no other evidence to support such a conclusion.

43. *OR*, 7:453–54; Van Horne, *Army of the Cumberland*, 1:48.

44. Van Horne, *Army of the Cumberland*, 1:48. Schoepf arrived in advance of his main column on the afternoon of December 1, with a detachment of cavalry and two guns. *New York Herald*, Dec. 10, 1861.

December 2, then shifted toward Mill Springs, on the south bank of the Cumberland River. Best estimates placed their numbers at one thousand cavalry and eight thousand infantry. Thomas quickly ordered two additional regiments and a battery to Somerset, but Buell just as quickly remanded the orders for one of the regiments. Buell's listless and piecemeal response to Schoepf's plight so perturbed Thomas that his mouthpiece, Thomas Van Horne, could hardly veil his anger when writing of the episode thirteen years later. The department commander expressly forbade Thomas to send additional reinforcements to Somerset without his approval. From Buell's perspective, Zollicoffer was more nuisance than threat.[45]

Although seemingly as impotent as either Anderson or Sherman, Buell's inaction was not based upon panic but his inability to grasp more than a single issue at a time. He remained preoccupied with a spring offensive on Nashville, believing that if the center collapsed the Rebels would be cleared from Kentucky. The Ohio general refused to concede that the pressure from Washington was partially a problem of his own making. By organizing the First Division so far in the rear, in order to consolidate for the move on Nashville, he had created a vacuum in southeastern Kentucky, one quickly filled by the Confederates.[46]

It is doubtful that Schoepf's brigade could have kept Zollicoffer's division on the south bank of the Cumberland River indefinitely, but as it turned out, the Federals made matters relatively easy for the enemy. On December 4 Schoepf sent Capt. Boston Dillon with two companies of the 1st Kentucky Cavalry to scout the crossing (Grinder's Ferry) opposite Mill Springs. Trailing the blue troopers would be the 17th Ohio and three pieces of artillery. Dillon never made it to the crossing; perceiving danger, he stopped well short of his destination. The Confederates, having built flatboats, crossed to the north bank not only unopposed but also without Dillon's knowledge. By the time the 17th Ohio arrived on December 4, the stunned Buckeyes found a sizeable enemy force on their side of the river. The regiment withdrew under cover of darkness. Believing his position at Fishing Creek now untenable, Schoepf pulled his brigade back three miles north of Somerset.[47]

Schoepf anxiously called upon Carter for help, much as Hoskins had unsuccessfully done days earlier. This time Carter, without orders, left his Kentucky regiment in place and hastened with his two East Tennessee regiments, reaching Schoepf on December 9. Thomas's other reinforcements (sent on December 3) also arrived, bolstering Schoepf's strength to six thousand. Thomas inquired of Buell if he should

45. *OR,* 7:471; Van Horne, *Army of the Cumberland,* 1:49–50; *New York Herald,* Dec. 10, 1861; *Louisville Journal,* Dec. 10, 1861.

46. *OR,* 7:501; Thomas B. Buell, *The Warrior Generals: Combat Leadership in the Civil War* (New York: Crown, 1997), 144–45.

47. *OR,* 7:474–75, 476–77; Van Horne, *Army of the Cumberland,* 1:49; *New York Herald,* Dec. 10, 1861.

rush additional troops from Lebanon, but the department commander dismissed the entire affair as "annoying" and made it clear that he would not be diverted from "more important purposes." He also began to express qualms about Schoepf.[48]

The Rebels had crossed the Cumberland River in force by December 6, entrenching on the north bank opposite Mill Springs in the junction formed by Fishing Creek and the Cumberland River. So formidable was the position that Schoepf admitted he could not get his artillery in a commanding location. Brig. Gen. Jeremiah "Jerry" T. Boyle, the outspoken former Kentucky slaveholder now commanding the Eleventh Brigade at Columbia, believed that ten thousand men would be required to dislodge Zollicoffer.[49]

At least three alternatives were available to Buell. The balance of Thomas's First Division could march to Somerset via Columbia, with Boyle's brigade protecting the left flank. If Zollicoffer attempted to get in between Thomas and Schoepf, as Boyle feared and Zollicoffer in fact planned to do, a pincers movement could be attempted. If the junction was successfully completed, the Federals could either make a direct assault or pin the Confederates down in the hopes of drawing them out of their works.[50]

A second option for Thomas was to distract Zollicoffer in front while Schoepf took one of his two brigades and crossed the Cumberland River at Waitsboro, twelve miles from Mill Springs, which the Confederates had conveniently left unguarded. Once on the south bank, Schoepf could destroy the sizeable wagon train at Mill Springs and shell the enemy from the opposite bank.[51]

A third approach was to send troops from Columbia across the Cumberland River and strike Zollicoffer from the rear, in conjunction with Thomas and Schoepf's pincers movement. The idea had been floated by Col. Thomas Bramlette of the 3d Kentucky at Columbia. He requested that his and three additional Kentucky regiments make the attempt. In truth, the headstrong and crotchety Bramlette would have done almost anything to get out of Boyle's Eleventh Brigade. His clannish eastern Kentuckians saw Boyle as a "Bluegrass" man and a politician, and they

48. OR, 7:474, 478–79, 481, 486, 512, 520; Van Horne, Army of the Cumberland, 1:50; Louisville Journal, Dec. 21, 1861. Although Buell recalled one regiment, it somehow got sent anyway, giving Schoepf five infantry regiments, two batteries, and a cavalry regiment.

49. OR, 7:480, 487, 506–7; Gerald McMurtry, "Zollicoffer—Battle of Mill Springs," Filson Club Historical Quarterly 29 (Oct. 1955): 306; Thomas to Buell, Dec. 11, 1861, Telegrams Received, Dec. 1861–Jan. 1862, Department of the Ohio, RG 393.

50. OR, 7:489–90; Williams, Lincoln Finds a General, 3:146.

51. OR, 7:496, 506; Edward Hagerman, The American Civil War and the Origins of Modern Warfare: Ideas, Organization, and Field Command (Bloomington: Indiana University Press, 1988), 156. Having heard from spies that only 6,500 Rebels (not 10,000) had entrenched at Beach Grove, Schoepf eagerly suggested this plan of action.

disliked him from the outset. The two officers had exchanged words when Boyle demanded that Bramlette extinguish a cigar. Thereafter they were barely civil to one another. Buell, not surprisingly, brushed aside the scheme.[52]

Although the general considered the destruction of the Rebel division at Mill Springs "too much to calculate upon," he actually had been presented a golden opportunity. Zollicoffer had made a serious blunder by camping with his back to a major river at high water with reinforcements far to the rear. It seemed incredible that Buell could pass up an opportunity to annihilate an enemy division. He nonetheless remained fixated on the master plan of capturing a place rather than the destruction of a portion of Johnston's army.[53]

To assist in the placement of earthworks and intelligence gathering, Buell dispatched his chief engineer, Captain Prime, to Somerset. Prime had a reputation of being adventuresome—too adventuresome. Early in the war, while in the vicinity of Manassas, Virginia, he had mistakenly ridden into the camp of a Georgia regiment and barely escaped. On December 14, near Somerset, his luck ran out; he stumbled into a Confederate picket post and was captured.[54]

The War Department politely suggested on December 17 that the Sandy Valley of northeastern Kentucky be placed in William Rosecrans's Department of Ohio, which included West Virginia. That department's rugged mountainous terrain presented the same logistical problems as confronted by Thomas. Buell, however, broke all speed records in dispatching Col. John A. Garfield's three-thousand-man Eighteenth Brigade to the area, thus forestalling realignment.[55]

Meanwhile, during the early morning hours of December 20, Schoepf moved out from Somerset with a detachment comprised of the two East Tennessee regiments, four cavalry companies, and a battery in an attempt to see if Zollicoffer could be lured from his works. The task proved fruitless; the secessionists were going nowhere. Maj. James T. Shelly of the 1st East Tennessee Infantry was of a mind that "Genl Zolly [Zollicoffer] is not going to fight us here [Somerset]. His is only a foraging party, etc."[56]

Faced with continued pressure, Buell finally ordered Thomas forward on December 29. His plan, often misunderstood by historians, was simply to maneuver Zollicoffer back across the Cumberland River. Even as the First Division broke

52. Hambleton Tapp and John W. Tuttle, *The Union, the Civil War, and John W. Tuttle: A Kentucky Captain's Account* (Frankfort: Kentucky Historical Society, 1980), 46, 66–69.

53. *OR*, 7:522; Buell, *Warrior Generals*, 153.

54. *OR*, 7:500; Van Horne, *Army of the Cumberland*, 1:52; *New York Herald*, Dec. 19, 1861; *Cincinnati Commercial*, Dec. 17, 1861.

55. *OR*, 7:501; Guerrant, "Marshall and Garfield in Eastern Kentucky," 395.

56. *Louisville Journal*, Dec. 21, 1861; Graf, Haskins, and Bergeron, *Papers of Andrew Johnson*, 5:84–85.

camp, Buell continued to insist that logistics prevented a full-scale mountain offensive. A column of twelve thousand men would require twelve hundred teams and would stretch along the road for miles. By the second week of January 1862, McClellan had sent an additional four hundred wagons from the quartermaster depot in Philadelphia, thus partially undercutting Buell's argument. The Ohio general now had a generous twenty-nine wagons per one thousand men in the First Division. But now the ever elusive Buell insisted that he needed more men, at least three divisions, for an East Tennessee campaign.[57]

By early January the troops of the ad hoc division near Somerset began to show signs of impatience. "We are under the command of Brig. Gen. Thomas who is as I think something like McClelland [sic] never in a hurry," Capt. S. R. Mott of the 31st Ohio wrote on January 5. "We have been here three weeks with some 5000 of a force and very willing to attack if we were permitted. But are not[.] . . . By some strange cause here we are compelled to remain idle spectators whilst Zollicoffer is raveageing [sic] and laying waste the country."[58]

In the end, it may have been Buell's own candor that forced a tactical confrontation. In an uncharacteristically forthright letter to Lincoln in early January, he characterized East Tennessee as of "little or no importance." Doubtless this had been his view from the beginning, but now he had been honest enough, or foolish enough, to put it in writing. The letter brought a predictably swift response from Washington. McClellan expressed shock over the "radical difference" between his and Buell's positions. Again, on January 13, the general in chief wrote of the "absolute necessity" of an East Tennessee offensive.[59]

Thomas, meanwhile, had departed Lebanon on the Columbia Pike with the balance of the First Division—Col. Mahlon D. Manson's Second Brigade and Col. Robert L. McCook's Third Brigade—on December 31, 1861. Despite the good turnpike between Campbellsville and Columbia, the march proved horrid. The rain at times was blinding, and the mud churned six to eight inches deep. Russell's Creek, just north of Columbia, was so swollen that a pontoon bridge had to be constructed. The column finally arrived at Logan's Cross Roads (near present-day Nancy, Kentucky), some ten miles north of Zollicoffer's encampment at Beech Grove. The division was strung out for miles in what one Hoosier described as "an ocean of mud." The sixty-five-mile march required eighteen days.[60]

---

57. *OR*, 7:522, 548–49; "Buell Statement," 4.

58. S. R. Mott to Johnson, Jan. 5, 1862, in Graf, Haskins, and Bergeron, *Papers of Andrew Johnson,* 5:92.

59. *OR*, 7:530–31, 547.

60. McMurtry, "Zollicoffer," 307, 317 n. 24; *Louisville Journal,* Jan. 15, 18, 1862; Raymond E. Myers, *The Zollie Tree* (Louisville: Filson Club, 1964), 82; *OR*, 7:79, 550; Van Horne, *Army of the Cumberland,* 1:54.

The march proved so laborious and barren of forage that Thomas began to have second thoughts about his linkup with Schoepf. He had mistakenly believed that there were sufficient wagons to immediately transport one hundred thousand rations from Lebanon to Columbia. Even by using every vehicle he could get his hands on, he was still two days behind schedule. On January 13, 1862, Thomas recommended to Buell that he instead proceed to Jamestown and thence to Burkesville, where he could cut off Zollicoffer's supply boats on the Cumberland River and be in a position to operate against the Rebels at Bowling Green. Actually, Boyle had already sent an expedition from Columbia a few days earlier for just such a purpose. Thomas's request proved moot, though, for Buell had already touted a direct confrontation with Zollicoffer to McClellan in an effort to placate Washington authorities. The Confederate division at Beech Grove could no longer simply be checked or chased back across the river—it had to be dispersed or destroyed.[61]

Exactly how Thomas planned to jar the Confederates loose from their den was not fully developed. Buell initially did not favor crossing the swollen Cumberland River to attack the enemy's rear, preferring instead that Thomas drive Zollicoffer's left flank away from the river crossing while Schoepf attacked in front. The Pole, in courier communication with Thomas, insisted that he had no chance to maneuver in front of the enemy earthworks. He suggested that they shell the Rebels from the west bank of White Oak Creek in an attempt to force them into the open for a fight. On January 13 Buell reconsidered the idea of a river crossing and left the decision to Thomas.[62]

On the morning of January 17, Thomas established his headquarters on the Columbia Pike, three-quarters of a mile west of Logan's Cross Roads. Portions of the Second and Third Brigades were still far in the rear, slowed by mud. Until his division closed up, Thomas ordered one of Schoepf's brigades (Carter's Twelfth) at Somerset to report to him. This left Schoepf with two regiments and a section of artillery at the Hudson's Ferry Road crossing at Fishing Creek and a like contingent at Somerset. His mission was to prevent the enemy from escaping to the east along the northern bank of the Cumberland River. As it turned out, Fishing Creek was so swollen with backwater from the Cumberland River that fording would prove difficult at best. Carter's brigade had gotten across downriver only by having the men jump in waist-deep water and cling hand over hand on a stretched rope. A regiment,

61. *OR,* 7:548, 550, 558; Hafendorfer, *Mill Springs,* 145–46; Thomas to Buell, Jan. 14, 1862, Letters and Telegrams Sent, Dec. 1861–May 1862, Generals' Papers, Don Carlos Buell, Entry 159, RG 94; *Louisville Journal,* Jan. 10, 24, 1862. The expedition to the Cumberland River was composed of the 3d Kentucky, 19th Ohio, a portion of the 5th Kentucky Cavalry, and later several guns of Bradley's battery.

62. *OR,* 7:542, 545, 548.

battery, and a battalion of Michigan engineers arrived at Thomas's camp on January 18, swelling his force to about five thousand.[63]

A cold rain marked the early morning hours of January 19. At 6:30 A.M. the distant crack of musketry suddenly sounded about a mile south of the Mill Springs and Columbia-Somerset intersection. Pickets of Frank Wolford's 1st Kentucky Cavalry fell back upon their infantry support, two companies of the 10th Indiana. A courier hastily reported to Colonel Manson that they were under attack by a large enemy force. What Thomas did not then know, but would soon find out, was that the Confederates were attempting the very thing he feared—a preemptive strike before the Federal concentration had been completed. Maj. Gen. George B. Crittenden, the Confederate brother of Fifth Division commander Thomas Crittenden, had arrived and superseded Zollicoffer in command. At midnight on January 19, he struck out north with his entire division in a desperate attack upon a portion of Thomas's scattered force. The Battle of Mill Springs had been joined.[64]

Colonel Manson immediately directed the balance of the 10th Indiana to the picket line. He then galloped to the camp of the 4th Kentucky, where he awakened Col. Speed S. Fry and ordered his regiment to turn out. After alerting Colonel McCook at Third Brigade headquarters, Manson, a Mexican War veteran but druggist in civilian life, acted the amateur that he was and proceeded personally to report to division headquarters. An irritated Thomas interrupted the hatless and disheveled brigade commander and snapped, "Damn you sir, go back to your command and fight it."[65]

The 10th Indiana and Wolford's dismounted troopers conducted a disordered retreat back to camp. Fry's shivering Kentuckians filled in the void as they stumbled ahead in the rain and fog, coming into line behind a fence fronting a field east of the Mill Springs Road. The Rebels, fighting from a ravine 250 yards distant, raked them. The action caused Colonel Fry, a usually mild-mannered former country judge, to mount the fence and shout defiance. In the brief lull that followed, Fry scouted the dense woods to his right. He bumped into an unknown general, and the two men began conversing. A Confederate aide suddenly rode up and fired upon Fry. Realizing that he had ridden into the enemy, the colonel returned fire, killing the general with whom he had been talking. His victim turned out to be none other than Felix Zollicoffer.[66]

The Southerners now brought up a second brigade and launched a fierce frontal

63. Ibid., 79, 96, 98; Kelly, "Holding Kentucky," 387, 392; *National Intelligencer*, Jan. 27, 1862.

64. *OR*, 7:79, 84, 90; Myers, *Zollie Tree*, 91–94.

65. *OR*, 7:84, 87, 93, 95; Warner, *Generals in Blue*, 310; Shanks, *Personal Recollections*, 66.

66. *OR*, 7:84, 87; Kelly, "Holding Kentucky," 389; Warner, *Generals in Blue*, 163; Prokopowicz, *All for the Regiment*, 74.

assault on the 4th Kentucky. Thomas finally made his appearance on the battlefield, slowed (or so reported) by his inability to get into his uniform. Seeing the 4th Kentucky in danger of being flanked, he called up McCook's Third Brigade. The 2d Minnesota and the Cincinnati Germans of the 9th Ohio advanced on either side of the Mill Springs Road, their arrival stabilizing the line. Capt. Dennis Kelly wheeled one section of his Ohio battery to within sixty yards of the enemy. The 2d Minnesota, passing through the retiring Union line in front, literally collided into the 20th Tennessee at a rail fence. A vicious half-hour fight ensued, with hand-to-hand combat. Col. Robert McCook, older brother of the Second Division commander, fell badly wounded in the leg.[67]

The climax came at ten o'clock, when the 9th Ohio made a screaming bayonet charge on the right, enveloping the enemy's flank. Almost simultaneously, Thomas ordered Carter's brigade to attack on the left. The Confederates could not resist these twin hammer blows, and their withdrawal quickly degenerated into a rout.[68]

Thomas again seized the moment. After replenishing ammunition supplies, he ordered a general advance south down the Mill Springs Road. "The line was kept up as uniform as I ever saw a drill," observed John Scully, with "every regiment and battery in its proper place, [so] that one would imagine he was at a grand review instead of a terific [sic] battle. All through [the fighting] the General [Thomas] was 'Cool as a Cucumber!'" A small enemy rearguard was easily brushed aside by a section of Standart's battery.[69]

Following a ten-mile chase along a road strewn with debris, Thomas's division, reinforced with two recently arrived regiments, deployed in front of the Confederate works at Beech Grove at 4:00 P.M. Two batteries were positioned on strategic Moulden's Hill, high ground commanding the camp, and a third battery unlimbered at the Russell house in order to prevent a river crossing. At this crucial moment Thomas stumbled. An immediate assault might well have broken the Southerners' precarious position, thus trapping them on the north bank, but the division commander contented himself with an artillery barrage and deferred the attack until morning. Colonel Fry noted to his wife: "We saw their little steam boat crossing back and forth all night but did not know whether they were falling back or bringing new regiments to this side." He later questioned Thomas as to why he did not at

67. OR,7:80, 93, 94, 96, 97; Buell, *Warrior Generals*, 157; Myers, *Zollie Tree*, 97–100; *New York Times*, Jan. 24, 25, 26, 1862.

68. OR, 7:94, 96, 97, 84; Judson W. Bishop, "Narrative of the Second Regiment," in *Minnesota in the Civil and Indiana Wars, 1861–1865*, by Minnesota Board of Commissioners (St. Paul: Pioneer, 1890), 83–84; Van Horne, *Army of the Cumberland*, 1:55–56; Kelly, "Holding Kentucky," 389.

69. OR, 7:80; Scully to wife, Jan. 17, 19, 1862, John W. Scully Letters, DU.

least send a demand for surrender that evening. The startled Virginian, momentarily hesitating, replied: "Hang it all Fry. I never once thought about it."[70]

At dawn amid a rainstorm, the Federals assaulted the works, only to find the one-hundred-acre camp abandoned. The Southerners had escaped during the night, burning their steamboat and ferry on the final crossing. The list of captured property during the two-day action totaled an impressive six flags, twelve field guns, one thousand arms (mostly antiquated flintlocks), 150 wagons, one thousand horses and mules, and a large amount of commissary and camp equipment. The Northerners sustained 262 casualties, the Confederates nearly 600.[71]

The numbers fail to convey the magnitude of this small, but significant, engagement. The Rebel division, which had terrorized loyalist citizens in southeastern Kentucky for nearly five months, had now scattered in panic. East Tennessee lay open to invasion, while Bowling Green and Nashville were vulnerable from the east. Additionally, the myth of the vaunted Confederate offensive capability, which had so paralyzed Anderson and Sherman, had been shattered.[72]

The battle also marked the emergence of George Thomas. Although the superior muskets of the Federals clearly played a role, it was superior leadership that had won the day. After the war Thomas had his critics. Thomas L. Livermore denounced him for his excessively slow march from Lebanon. He further claimed that the Virginian should have concentrated Schoepf's entire force at Logan's Cross Roads on January 17 and immediately advanced upon Beech Grove. Such disparaging hindsight, perhaps justified, was lost in the exuberance of the first significant Federal victory in the West. Although not all that it could have been, success was enough. After receiving his battle report, Lincoln nominated Thomas for the rank of major general, which was confirmed by the Senate on April 25.[73]

After the Battle of Mill Springs, however, Thomas hardly acted like a caged tiger ready to pounce into East Tennessee. One present-day historian claims that Buell, like Sherman before him, recalled the First Division and ordered it to turn its back upon victory: "Thomas would always remember the campaign with a smoldering rage. Twice he had had East Tennessee in his grasp. Twice he had been recalled." In fact, just the opposite was true. It was Buell who pushed for a limited pursuit and Thomas who argued against it. From the Virginian's perspective, the enemy was too

70. *OR*, 7:80; Myers, *Zollie Tree*, 106; Speed Fry to wife, Jan. 20, 1862, Speed Fry Letters, CHS; Buell, *Warrior Generals*, 157–58. Schoepf's brigade, which did not participate in the battle, arrived that night.

71. Myers, *Zollie Tree*, 108–9; *OR*, 7:81–82, 108. Although the Confederates claimed 99 missing, the Federals counted 157 prisoners.

72. Buell, *Warrior Generals*, 158; Hagerman, *American Civil War*, 160; McKinney, *Education in Violence*, 70.

73. McKinney, *Education in Violence*, 129–30.

dispersed to follow, no forage existed at Monticello (the next town after Somerset), the roads were impassable, and no enemy existed in East Tennessee. Carter's mountaineer brigade could be sent to Cumberland Gap and Knoxville, he asserted, but the First Division should be sent down the Cumberland River on flats to cooperate in the move on Bowling Green.[74]

Thomas continued to dally throughout January. "He never enjoyed the reputation of being a quick, dashing strategist," remarked a journalist. Some of the general's concerns were legitimate. The road from Lebanon to Somerset, over which 126 wagons passed daily to supply the First Division, had to be corduroyed for two-way traffic. Five regiments were put to work on the forty-mile route. The road south, from Somerset to Monticello, proved virtually impassable. Yet the problems in getting from the Cumberland River to the Cumberland Gap were no more than the Confederates had faced (and overcome) in getting from the Cumberland Gap to the Cumberland River. Thomas seemed to lose his aggressive edge. Manson's brigade wasted nearly a week at Mill Springs, tallying captured ordnance, while the engineers leisurely went about the task of putting up a bridge at Waitsboro, using four coal barges in lieu of pontoon boats. Carter's brigade, now reinforced, did not depart for the Cumberland Gap until January 29, and Schoepf's brigade did not proceed to Monticello until the thirtieth. Thomas retained the lion's share of the First Division at Somerset.[75]

Buell never challenged his subordinate for these delays; indeed, Thomas was telling the department commander precisely what he wanted to hear. Buell's priority remained Nashville, not Knoxville. His explanation to McClellan for why he did not wish to follow up on the Mill Springs victory, despite a total rout of the enemy, proved awkward. Previously he had stated that he required two divisions in the rear to advance one division to Knoxville. On February 1 Buell increased the number of necessary rear divisions to three—thirty thousand men. Some one thousand wagons would be required to supply ten thousand men advancing. The entire route would have to be corduroyed, he argued, and forage on either side of the road would be exhausted in a day or two.[76]

Despite an obvious lack of enthusiasm, Buell continued with his promise of an

74. Buell, *Warrior Generals,* 159. Steven Woodworth likewise concluded that Thomas desired to exploit his success "but was not allowed to." *Jefferson Davis and His Generals* (Lawrence: University Press of Kansas, 1990), 57.

75. *OR,* 7:562, 563–64; Thomas to Buell, Jan. 25, 1862, Letters and Telegrams Sent, Dec. 1861–May 1862, Generals' Papers, Don Carlos Buell, Entry 159, RG 94; *OR,* 7:564–65; *New York Tribune,* Jan. 20, Feb. 7, 1862; *Cincinnati Enquirer,* Jan. 30, 1862.

76. Buell to McClellan, Feb. 1, 1862, Letters and Telegrams Sent, Dec. 1861–May 1862, Generals' Papers, Don Carlos Buell, Entry 159, RG 94.

eastern Tennessee invasion. "How soon could you march and how long do you suppose it would take you to reach Knoxville?" he asked Thomas on February 2. Indeed, the press even announced the supposed plan of action—at Monticello, Schoepf's brigade would go left and Thomas's division right, while Carter's brigade occupied Cumberland Gap. Developments elsewhere would soon cause a major change of plans.[77]

In stark contrast to Anderson and Sherman, Buell brought a badly needed aura of calm to the Department of the Ohio. He received strong reinforcements, and by the end of 1861, an impressive army had been formed and equipped. Unlike his predecessors, the Ohio general also projected a creditable offensive plan, though it differed markedly from that of the administration. Almost in spite of himself, he had scored the first significant Federal victory in the West at Mill Springs and stood poised to carry the war to the enemy. Yet something was missing. Buell lacked charisma, flexibility, and a bold aggressiveness. His army, though massive, had not yet coalesced. But the long-awaited offensive would come—sooner than even Buell anticipated.

77. OR, 7:580; New York Tribune, Feb. 7, 1862.

4

The Drive South
The Buell-Halleck Feud

IN MID-JANUARY 1862 an unknown correspondent of the *New York Tribune* toured several of the divisions of the Army of the Ohio. Having just come from Virginia and an unofficial inspection of the Army of the Potomac, he was in a position to make a cursory comparison. He showed restraint in his initial article, noting the western soldiers' intelligence, physical vigor, and moral standards. "Nine-tenths consists of the high-spirited and self-reliant sons of the Northwest," he described, "the flower of the land." In subsequent articles the correspondent wrote with candor. Four-fifths of Buell's army was still limited to battalion drill, and many regiments had not progressed beyond company drill. The troops were a full three months behind the Army of the Potomac in training. Only ten of nineteen batteries performed good service, the others being more apt to "scare than to kill the rebels." A laxness in discipline and sanitary conditions had resulted in a much higher sick rate than in Virginia, and many medical officers, especially those from Indiana, the writer denounced as a "shame to their profession." Even though general orders had excluded women from camp, this was routinely ignored in McCook's division, the one closest to the enemy. The most serious concern related to the officer corps. The Army of the Ohio had only a dozen West Pointers, most of whom had held subordinate positions in the regular army. Not a half-dozen could handle a brigade, the reporter noted, much less a division. Crittenden had little military background, and McCook looked "rather youthful," although he did seem to have the confidence of his peers. At the regimental level it was even worse: of the twenty-eight Kentucky regiments, not one officer in a hundred had a military education.[1]

Buell would have agreed with the assessment. Although he conceded in mid-January that his aggregate strength had "suddenly risen" from 70,000 to 90,000 with the inclusion of the recently organized Kentucky regiments and fresh units from Indiana and Ohio, many of his men were unprepared for the field. His movable force included 41,563 infantry, 2,549 cavalry, and 2,038 artillery with 108 guns. He

---

1. *New York Tribune,* Jan. 13, 18, 25, 1862. The Confederates came into possession of these articles and printed portions of them in the *Richmond Examiner,* Jan. 31, 1862.

thus claimed fewer effectives than he had the previous month, even though he had 20,000 more men in the department.[2]

With few diversions and rampant sickness, morale plummeted throughout late December 1861 and early January 1862. The 38th Indiana, riddled with measles, had only 300 men report for duty. The 37th Indiana, in Mitchel's division, counted 563 present, with another 383 on the sick roll. For several weeks the rain and the snow kept the men in their quarters. "The poor soldiers do nothing but stay in their tents," wrote John Hardesty of the 34th Indiana at Camp Wickliffe. A regimental riot over a petty matter erupted in the Seventeenth Brigade. When Buell made division inspections in late December, many understood it to be the prelude of a general advance. Instead of marching orders, however, large teepee-shaped Sibley tents began to arrive, seemingly indicating that the army was going into winter quarters. The weather remained miserable. "We have had considerable of wet weather for the last two weeks," Sgt. Michael Bright of the 77th Pennsylvania (McCook's division) wrote on January 20. "It is raining today, the mud is nearly six inches deep in camp, and it is warm enough for a May day."[3]

New regiments continued to arrive throughout January, including the 64th and 65th Ohio; the 40th, 51st, 57th, and 58th Indiana; and in mid-February the 13th Michigan, all of which went to Bardstown. There the new Sixth Division formed under former Fifth Brigade commander Thomas J. Wood. The recent arrivals, coupled with two Kentucky regiments, formed the Twentieth and Twentieth-First Brigades under Cols. Charles G. Harker and George D. Wagner, the former a West Pointer, the latter a politician. Topping off the division was a transfer brigade, Milo Haskell's Fifteenth, from Nelson's division.[4]

In place of Haskell's brigade, Nelson received Col. William B. Hazen's Nineteenth Brigade. Although religious and polite, Hazen, a West Pointer, could be stern to the point of tyrannical. Lt. Col. Nicholas Anderson of the 6th Ohio wrote in his journal: "Hate Hazen heartily and hope to get out of his brigade soon; he is very severe to our regiment." The Fifteenth's three regimental commanders had only prominence and politics to recommend them. Another correspondent, visiting Nel-

2. *OR*, 7:511, 548–49, 563.

3. *Indianapolis Daily Journal*, Jan. 6, 14, 16, 1862; Scribner, *How Soldiers Were Made*, 36–37; Beatty, *Citizen Soldier*, 92–93; *Cincinnati Enquirer*, Feb. 11, 1862; *New York Times*, Jan. 19, 1862; Keifer to wife, Dec. 30, 1861, Joseph Warren Keifer Papers, LC; Weber, *Diary of Ira Gillaspie*, 14.

4. *Indianapolis Daily Journal*, Jan. 7, 16, Feb. 3, 5, 14, 20, 1862; *New York Herald*, Feb. 25, 1862; Wilbur F. Hinman, *The Story of the Sherman Brigade: The Camp, the Bivouac, the Battle, and How 'the Boys' Lived and Died during Four Years of Active Field Service* (Alliance, Ohio: privately printed, 1897), 60–64; *OR*, 7:539; Van Horne, *Army of the Cumberland*, 1:72–73; Warner, *Generals in Blue*, 207, 533–34; Faust, *Encyclopedia*, 795.

son's division in early January, found the burly Kentucky general to be "abrupt and repulsive," while Tenth Brigade commander Jacob Ammen was a "stickler for Army Regulations and a rigid disciplinarian." The division had been raked with measles, and over one thousand remained in camp hospitals.[5]

New artillery units continued to arrive. By mid-February the army included twenty-two field batteries, with five others and two siege batteries organizing. Buell anticipated two regular batteries from Missouri, but he received instead two under-strength companies (Batteries H and M, 4th U.S. Artillery), which together mustered only one officer, seventy men, and no guns. Capt. James Barnett's Battery G, 1st Ohio Light Artillery, a Cleveland outfit, arrived in Kentucky in February. The bulk of the men, including Barnett, had just recovered from the measles. Their six new Wiard rifles elicited great curiosity while passing through Cincinnati and Louisville. Initially assigned to Thomas's division, the battery eventually ended up in Crittenden's division in the frequent reshuffling of units that took place.[6]

Cavalry, the branch most difficult to equip and train, arrived slowly. In mid-February two companies of regulars, eighty-eight men, came in from Fort Leavenworth, Kansas. The heart of the fledgling cavalry corps, however, comprised ten volunteer regiments, six of which were raw and uninstructed. Regiments such as the 1st Ohio Cavalry and the 2d Indiana Cavalry, though mounted and partially armed, would be largely ineffective until spring.[7]

An inspector that February found many of the units in a deplorable state of discipline, including the "ignorant" company officers of the 43d Indiana, the longhaired men of a Kentucky cavalry regiment who showed "no restraint," and a Kentucky infantry regiment whose men acted "like a herd of wild animals." Even the regulars of Battery H, 5th U.S. Artillery, were "nothing to be proud of." As for the drills of the 5th Ohio Cavalry, they were "more suitable for 4th of July occasions."[8]

Buell pressured Washington for more arms. He protested that the muskets sent to Kentucky were so unsafe as to demoralize the troops. Officials at the Ordnance Department quickly declared as "good arms" the ten thousand Austrian rifles sent the previous November. Between the last week in January and the middle of February, some 5,517 revolvers and two thousand carbines were shipped to Louisville for

5. *OR,* 7:529; Hazen, *Narrative,* 15, 18; Warner, *Generals in Blue,* 225–26; Faust, *Encyclopedia,* 355; Isabel Anderson, ed., *The Letters and Journal of General Nicholas Longworth Anderson* (New York: Fleming H. Revell, 1942), 140; *Cincinnati Commercial,* Jan. 7, 1862.

6. *OR,* 7:611; "Buell Statement," 3; Barnett, "History of Battery G, Ohio Light Artillery," James Barnett Papers, WRHS.

7. "Buell Statement," 3; W. L. Curry, *Four Years in the Saddle* (reprint, Jonesboro, Ga.: Freedom Hill, 1984), 26–29; *Indianapolis Daily Journal,* Jan. 6, 7, 16, Feb. 17, Mar. 6, 1862.

8. Quoted in Prokopowicz, *All for the Regiment,* 37.

use by the cavalry. More arms arrived in mid-February, including sixteen thousand Prussian muskets and five thousand Springfield rifles.[9]

Buell also had to deal with officers bent on making proclamations. Col. Ebenezer Dumont, commanding the Seventeenth Brigade, issued just such an edict to local citizens in his area, stating that while their property rights would be respected, treachery would not be tolerated. In an order clearly aimed at the colonel, the department commander put an end to such bluster, despite the fact that Dumont received press support.[10]

Although initially conservative in his estimates of enemy strength, Buell began to fall prey to the same wild speculation that had so paralyzed his predecessors. He now placed the number of Rebels at Bowling Green at 40,000—an overestimate of 15,000. Although portraying himself as outnumbered, he in fact held a vast numerical superiority. Upon his arrival in Kentucky, Buell had caustically commented that he could get the job done with far less than 200,000 men (a reference to Sherman's widely published number), but he now pleaded to McClellan for a department strength of 120,000, and the number seemed to be rising. A Chicago correspondent could not fathom why, with 60,000 men in the central column, Buell could not advance against Johnston, who had half that number at Bowling Green.[11]

George Landrum of the 33d Ohio, encamped at Bacon Creek, was of a like mind. Writing to his sister, he confided: "There are as yet no signs of an advance. Gen. Mitchel said today that he had not the least idea when we would move. The [Bacon Creek] bridge is done, and the cars are running over it, so we are not waiting for that. The railroad, ten miles beyond Green River, is completely destroyed. If we have to wait until that is rebuilt we will have to be here a year. The fact is that we are all getting impatient and want to work. We feel that we are losing time. The fine weather has passed away, the roads are in a horrible condition, and an advance now would be very hard to make, if not impossible."[12]

Before any advance could be made by Buell's center, the 1,040-foot-long Green River railroad trestle had to be rebuilt. General McCook boasted that he could have the bridge in operation within seven days; it would take fourteen. He claimed circumstances beyond his control—two snowstorms and almost daily rain—caused this delay. The enormous undertaking was turned over to Col. W. P. Innes and three companies of his 1st Michigan Mechanics and Engineers (the balance of the companies having been distributed to the other divisions), supplemented by Willich's 32d Indiana, which possessed a fair number of skilled mechanics and carpenters in its

9. OR, 7:601–2, 606, 622.
10. Indianapolis Daily Journal, Jan. 13, 1862.
11. OR, 7:529, 549, 563; Chicago Tribune, Jan. 29, 1862.
12. Landrum to sister, Jan. [?], 1862, George W. Landrum Letters, OHS.

ranks. As the work progressed, Willich's Hoosiers and a company of the 1st Wisconsin, supplied with watertight wagons, constructed a pontoon bridge over the river. Work on the trestle hastened in early January as the river rose to fifteen feet. On the eighth, at 5:45 P.M., the first train creaked slowly over the span, to the cheers of thousands of soldiers who watched in anticipation.[13]

Extensive track damage existed beyond Green River. Beginning a few miles south of Munfordville and extending for five miles, the Rebels had quite literally removed the railroad—rails being carried off and ties burned. The tunnel at Horse Cave had been destroyed. The main turnpike to Nashville was blocked by felled trees and destroyed culverts, while the creeks and ponds along the road had reportedly been filled with dead cattle and pigs, thus poisoning the water.[14]

Although Buell had revealed no plan of action, even journalists could figure out the obvious move. McCook's Second and Mitchel's Third Divisions would proceed down the main turnpike to Bowling Green. Crittenden's Fifth Division would brush aside the Rebels at Hopkinsville and menace Albert Sidney Johnston's left. Nelson's Fourth Division would march down the good turnpike from Bardstown to Glasgow, where only a small enemy force remained. Conventional wisdom claimed that the Confederate would retreat rather than make a fight of it at Bowling Green.[15]

Maj. Gen. Henry W. "Old Brains" Halleck had succeeded Frémont in command of the troubled Department of Missouri. He was an odd sort: brilliant but personally uninspiring, essentially a bureaucrat, stubbornly fixated on his own ideas, and intense and unapproachable. Perhaps it was their similarities that ultimately led him and Buell to detest each other. Each had met his match.[16]

It was a shared boundary, the Cumberland River, that eventually forced the two men to deal with each other. Buell emphatically believed that the Rebels at Bowling Green must not be reinforced by the Columbus garrison as the Army of the Ohio made its big push south. Halleck must, therefore, pin down Johnston's left wing with simultaneous moves on Columbus and a joint army-navy operation upon Forts Henry and Donelson along the Tennessee and Cumberland Rivers. In short, the Federals should make a coordinated attack along a 150-mile front.[17]

13. Dodge, *Old Second Division,* 114; *Cincinnati Commercial,* Dec. 30, 1861, Jan. 6, 10, 13, 1862; Pennsylvania Battlefield Commission, *The Seventy-Seventh Pennsylvania at Shiloh* (Harrisburg, Pa., 1909), 72; *New York Times,* Jan. 15, 1862; *Chicago Tribune,* Jan. 5, 8, 9, 31, 1862.

14. Dodge, *Old Second Division,* 116–17; *Chicago Tribune,* Jan. 4, 8, 1862; *New York Herald,* Jan. 4, 1862.

15. *New York Tribune,* Jan. 18, 1862.

16. Nevins, *Ordeal for the Union,* 3(2):12–13; Williams, *Lincoln Finds a General,* 3:104–5; Hattaway and Jones, *How the North Won,* 54–55; Andrews, *North Reports the Civil War,* 158, 160.

17. *OR,* 7:528–29.

Halleck agreed neither with the strategy nor the priorities. He had to get Missouri in hand before supporting Buell. Besides, he insisted, simultaneous assaults on Columbus and Bowling Green would be hauntingly similar to the scenario that Maj. Gen. Irwin McDowell had attempted in Virginia back in July 1861, resulting in the disaster at Bull Run. Operating on exterior lines would lead to defeat ninety-nine times out of one hundred, he lectured.[18]

On January 7 a disgusted Lincoln telegraphed both Halleck and Buell, demanding to know exactly when they could cooperate in a move south. "Delay is ruining us, and it is indispensable for me to have something definite." What the president got was Halleck's vague promise that he would do something in February and Buell's continued complaints.[19]

Sensing that nothing would happen unless he intervened, Lincoln, most likely influenced by his new secretary of war, Edwin M. Stanton, issued a startling order on January 29, 1862. There would be a forward movement by all armies of the United States, from the Potomac to the Mississippi Rivers, to commence no later than February 22 (Washington's Birthday). The issue for Buell and Halleck came down to whose army would be attacking and whose supporting. Buell, of course, desired a direct advance upon Nashville, with Halleck giving demonstrations at Columbus and the twin rivers, the narrow neck of land between the Tennessee and Cumberland Rivers. Yet dual western command discouraged cooperation since both commanders desired direct lines of advance—Halleck the rivers, Buell the railroad. "I am not ready to cooperate with him [Buell]," cried Halleck. "Too much haste will ruin everything."[20]

It was false intelligence, not Lincoln's directive, that finally jogged Halleck (recovering from a bout with measles) into action. A January 29 message from McClellan alerted the Missouri department commander that Gen. P. G. T. Beauregard was on his way to the West from Virginia with fifteen regiments. Although Beauregard in fact was not bringing anyone but himself, Halleck had to take the information seriously. Buell's most recent biographer has suggested that Halleck not only desired to beat Beauregard but also to steal a march on Buell.[21]

On January 30 Buell learned that Halleck had already commenced a move on Fort Henry along the Tennessee River. Having had no prior consultation, Buell was

18. Ibid., 532–33.

19. Ibid., 535, 539–40, 568; Buell to Stanton, Feb. 1, 1862, Edwin M. Stanton Papers, LC; Benjamin P. Thomas and Harold M. Hyman, *Stanton: The Life and Times of Lincoln's Secretary of War* (New York: Knopf, 1962), 146.

20. Basler, *Collected Works of Abraham Lincoln*, 5:111–12; OR, 7:521, 527–28, 529, 587, 591; Stephen Ambrose, *Halleck: Lincoln's Chief of Staff* (Baton Rouge: Louisiana State University Press, 1962), 18.

21. OR, 7:571; Ambrose, *Halleck*, 22.

now being pressured to advance upon Bowling Green in order to pin down the Rebels at that place. He was neither logistically nor psychologically prepared for such a move. Further, although he conceded that the gunboats could probably pass the fort, Buell saw Fort Henry as a possible trap. He calculated that ten thousand secessionists would break away from Bowling Green to support the fort's garrison, in addition to Beauregard's (mythical) fifteen regiments. Halleck's land force, under Brig. Gen. Ulysses S. Grant, counted only fifteen thousand men.[22]

Although Halleck assured Buell on February 2 that his assistance would not be required, within days his pride gave in to near panic. "Old Brains" now pleaded for Buell to make a diversionary move on Bowling Green. Insisting that "my position does not admit of diversion," Buell did pledge to march in force upon the town. There was a catch, though—it would be at least February 17 before his army would be in position, far too late to help the Fort Henry operation. Halleck's subsequent appeal to McClellan brought a response. The War Department directed two Indiana and six Ohio regiments, which ordinarily would have gone to Buell, to report to Halleck; the regiments, fresh from camps of instruction, had not even been brigaded. Under pressure, Buell perfunctorily chose to reinforce Halleck, sending Charles Cruft's Thirteenth Brigade of Crittenden's Fifth Division.[23]

Halleck had gone out on a limb, and it is difficult not to conclude that Buell took some perverse pleasure in letting him squirm. The two generals, never close friends, now hated one another. Buell grudgingly notified Halleck on the night of February 6 that he would start the Thirteenth Brigade. The only advantage to this predicament was that it gave Buell a fresh excuse to postpone the East Tennessee expedition.[24]

In the midst of this crisis, Thomas A. Scott, assistant secretary of war, arrived in Louisville. Scott, sent to the West on a fact-finding mission, quickly fell in line with the Ohio general. He notified Stanton that the projected East Tennessee offensive was logistically impossible, that forty thousand to fifty thousand troops should be sent to Kentucky from the Army of the Potomac, and that Halleck must cooperate with Buell. Stanton, who actually favored Halleck's plan, notified Scott that he had gone beyond the scope of his mission.[25]

22. *OR,* 7:574, 580; Engle, *Buell,* 152–53. Buell became livid at Sherman's suggestion that Halleck had devised the concept of a river operation and had casually revealed it while Sherman visited him at the Planter's House. Buell insisted that he had initiated the idea, neglecting to mention that he had a very different strategic goal. Don Carlos Buell, "Major General W. T. Sherman and the Spring Campaign of 1862 in the West," *Historical Magazine* 8 (Aug. 1870): 74–82 [article initially written Sept. 4, 1865].

23. *OR,* 7:576, 578–79, 583–84, 597; Van Horne, *Army of the Cumberland,* 1:84.

24. *OR,* 7:584–85, 587–88, 589–600; Van Horne, *Army of the Cumberland,* 1:83; Ambrose, *Halleck,* 27.

25. Scott to Stanton, "Private and Confidential," Feb. 7, 1862, Stanton Papers, LC; Samuel H. Kamm, *The Civil War Career of Thomas A. Scott* (Philadelphia: University of Pennsylvania Press, 1940), 93–96.

While Scott and Buell conferred, Halleck took action. On February 6 a Union flotilla under Flag Officer Andrew H. Foote pounded Fort Henry into submission within two hours, the small Confederate garrison escaping to Fort Donelson. The gunboats proceeded eighteen miles south and destroyed the Memphis, Clarksville, and Louisville Railroad trestle, severing Johnston's east-west rail link. The Tennessee River was now opened all the way to Muscle Shoals, Alabama, where the rapids prevented further ascent. Halleck moved quickly to follow this success. Grant's army marched twelve miles to Fort Donelson, but he needed more men to take that post. Halleck pleaded to McClellan for reinforcements from either the Army of the Ohio or the Army of the Potomac. Failing that, he urged a complete western reorganization, ostensibly with him at the head of a unified command. "It is the crisis of the war in the West," Halleck asserted to Stanton on February 7. If Buell remained intractable about an overland approach, "why not direct him to Clarksville [on the Cumberland River]."[26]

Halleck buttressed Grant's army to thirty thousand men with troops from within his own department, but he believed the Rebels, heavily reinforced from Bowling Green (apparently due to Buell's inaction) had a like number at Fort Donelson. His fear was that the Confederates at Bowling Green would move by rail to Nashville in a single day and then proceed by transports to Fort Donelson, striking Grant's rear and then returning to Nashville before Buell could be halfway there. The logic proved somewhat strained. The enemy had nowhere near the rolling stock for such a lightning move, and even so, Grant could simply withdraw to the safety of the gunboats if threatened. The Confederates would then have to disengage or split their forces in order to hold Nashville. In a thinly veiled bribery attempt, Halleck even proposed to Buell that he should command the Cumberland River operation in the hopes that he would bring his army with him.[27]

Buell bristled at the thought of being forced into action. No longer could he use muddy roads as an excuse for not advancing upon Bowling Green. Already McClellan was adopting Halleck's suggestion that the Army of the Ohio abandon an overland approach and move to the Cumberland River to reinforce Grant. Buell had to make a decision soon. He must either march on Bowling Green or reinforce Grant. By February 13 he had decided to do both. Nelson's, Crittenden's, and McCook's divisions would depart by river to support Grant, resulting in towns between Cincinnati and Evansville being scoured for all available steamers. Thomas would leave a brigade of observation at Somerset and march with the balance of his division to

26. *OR*, 7:590–91; Hattaway and Jones, *How the North Won*, 66–67.
27. *OR*, 7:606, 607, 609, 621-22; Ambrose, *Halleck*, 32; Hattaway and Jones, *How the North Won*, 68.

Lebanon to await orders. Mitchel would take his division on the direct turnpike to
Bowling Green.[28]

Ormsby Mitchel had been chafing for a fight. Twice in January 1862 he had been to
Louisville, urging both a forward movement and that his division should spearhead
the march. Two problems existed. First, the nasty weather continued to make a mess
of the roads. "It rains, then snows a little, then freezes a little, then thaws a good
deal and finally everything on the surface of the ground seems liquid earth, and our
cavalry horses have the scratches to such a degree that half of them are this day unfit
for service," Mitchel related to his wife. Second, the Halleck-Buell stalemate forced
further delays. "Buell gives me to understand that no immediate cooperation could
be expected from Halleck, and that is one reason why we are mud-bound," the brig-
adier confided.[29]

In early February Buell summoned General McCook to Louisville. When asked
when the division commander could move on Bowling Green, McCook estimated
eight to ten days. On February 8 Mitchel was asked the same question, but he gave
the answer that Buell wanted to hear—"Tomorrow morning." He got the job. The
Army of the Ohio would begin its long anticipated advance in two days, with the
Third Division in the lead. "I am at last in the position [on the march] to which my
rank entitles me," he declared. Mitchel's brigades broke camp at Bacon Creek on
February 10, passing through the camps of the Second Division at Munfordville.
McCook's men were mortified to learn that the bridge they had labored so long to
construct would be crossed first by another division. That evening Mitchel's troops
crossed over the Green River. A bright halo glowed around the moon—a good
omen, thought many of the men.[30]

Mitchel's division took up the march at sunrise on February 13, with a dozen
bands providing martial music. The column made eighteen miles, stopping at Bell's
Tavern on the Louisville and Nashville Railroad. A light snow fell that night, at-
tended by a piercing wind. The 4th Ohio Cavalry, John B. Turchin's Eighth Brigade,
and Loomis's Michigan battery spearheaded the advance. The Chicago Irish Zou-
aves of the 19th Illinois went into a near frenzy of excitement when told that they
would lead the brigade. Their band struck up "Dixie" as the regiment marched out.
In a splendid forced march, Turchin's brigade arrived on the north bank of the
Barren River at 11:00 A.M., though still not in time to save the bridges, which were

28. *OR,* 7:590–91, 592, 593; "Buell Statement," 7; *New York Herald,* Feb. 25, 1862.

29. Mitchel, *Ormsby Macknight Mitchel,* 242.

30. Ibid., 244–45; Beatty, *Citizen Soldier,* 104; Angus L. Waddle, *Three Years in the Army of the Ohio
and Cumberland* (Chillicothe, Ohio: Scioto Gazette Book and Job Office, 1889), 9; Scribner, *How Soldiers
Were Made,* 37.

found in flames. Loomis's gunners unlimbered on a hill near the north bank and fired a few shots across the river, destroying an escaping locomotive. According to locals, a Rebel rear guard of four thousand was five miles south of town, but the garrison had escaped to Clarksville. Seizing a small ferryboat, the Federals occupied the town at 5:00 A.M. on the fifteenth.[31]

The weather soon turned mild, and the troops took up residence in local houses. Col. John Beatty believed that "this sort of life, however pleasant it may be, has a demoralizing effect upon the soldier." Although a huge amount of stores had been destroyed by the Confederates, sufficient meat rations remained to supply the division for a month. A sturdy pontoon bridge was constructed between three steamboats, but a raging current made for a tenuous crossing.[32]

Ever since February 13, Buell, under great pressure, had essentially decided to abandon the overland route to Nashville and, as Halleck urged and McClellan suggested, move toward the Cumberland River to reinforce Grant. Even Lincoln expressed the opinion that a small Confederate rear guard could break up the railroad as it retreated from Bowling Green and thus manage to keep Buell out of the Tennessee capital for three weeks. Having occupied Bowling Green two days earlier than anticipated, however, Buell's confidence was so buoyed that he now reverted to his original plan. McCook's division, after a twenty-one-mile forced march through a snowstorm, was now recalled and ordered to join Mitchel at Bowling Green. The men, totally jaded from marching and countermarching, arrived at Munfordville on February 15.[33]

Precisely why Buell so stubbornly resisted using the river, despite its obvious speed over a destroyed railroad with limited rolling stock, is not known. One historian has suggested that the general, like his antagonist Albert Sidney Johnston, was mesmerized with the modern technology of the railroad. James Guthrie, president of the Louisville and Nashville, also exhibited some influence over Buell. He advocated the use of his railroad, the only one (except for the Mobile and Ohio) that traversed both North and South, in the drive toward Nashville. Additionally, Buell may have rejected the river simply because it was Halleck's idea and he was too inflexible to alter his three-month-old plan.[34]

31. *Cincinnati Enquirer,* Feb. 22, 1862; *Chicago Tribune,* Feb. 26, 1862; Beatty, *Citizen Soldier,* 106; T. M. Eddy, *The Patriotism of Illinois,* 2 vols. (Chicago: Clarke, 1865), 1:211; *OR,* 7:615, 621, 622, 623; "Buell Statement," 7; Cist, *Army of the Cumberland,* 24; Captain Wood to Buell, Feb. 14, 1864, Generals' Papers, Don Carlos Buell, Entry 159, RG 94, NA.

32. Beatty, *Citizen Soldier,* 108; *OR,* 7:634–35; *Indianapolis Daily Journal,* Mar. 6, 19, 1862.

33. "Buell Statement," 7; *Cleveland Plain Dealer,* Feb. 18, 1862; *OR,* 7:621.

34. Klein, *Louisville & Nashville Railroad,* 27; Engle, *Buell,* 168.

An incredulous Halleck protested to McClellan that it was "bad strategy"; Buell should move his army by transports up the Tennessee River to Florence and Decatur, Alabama, thus turning Nashville. McClellan decided otherwise. He wired his friend Buell that he was "exactly right" to proceed to Nashville; with that city occupied, Fort Donelson would be turned. The general in chief largely ignored Halleck's ideas, considering the capture of Nashville "very important." Further, he did not agree that the occupation of Decatur would cause the abandonment of Nashville; Stevenson, Alabama, would also have to be threatened. While a division of the Army of the Ohio could be sent to Grant if necessary, McClellan believed that it could be better utilized in the advance on Nashville.[35]

Modern historians have debated why McClellan so quickly changed his mind about an overland approach. Perhaps, as has been suggested, the general in chief desired Buell to have a share in the Cumberland River victory. Buell's most recent biographer has concluded that McClellan simply could not resist the "sure capture" of Nashville. The reason may be darker, though. McClellan and Halleck deeply disliked one another. It is possible that the general in chief rebelled at the strategy lectures from his subordinate and was determined to show him who was boss. If so, Halleck's subsequent messages only served to agitate further. He maintained that Fort Donelson and Clarksville were the key points and that, with the capture of Bowling Green, Nashville was no longer of military value. "We shall regret it [the present course]," he warned. Fort Donelson should be the main attack and Nashville the diversion, not vice versa.[36]

Halleck's subsequent pleas for reinforcements did bring some response; McClellan directed Buell to send a division to Grant. On the night of February 15, two brigades of "Bull" Nelson's division departed Camp Wickliffe in the snow and sleet for the Ohio River, where they boarded steamboats on the sixteenth. Along with Cruft's Thirteenth Brigade of Crittenden's division, previously sent, some ten thousand troops from the Army of the Ohio had been dispatched to reinforce Grant.[37]

McClellan also urged Buell to keep pressure on the Confederates by pushing past Bowling Green. Even Ormsby Mitchel, who by February 16 had moved one cavalry and five infantry regiments across the Barren River by the use of two ferries, pleaded for an "immediate demonstration" upon Nashville. Yet Buell would not be budged. Nothing could be done until the railroad to Bowling Green had been repaired, he reasoned, and that would take up to ten days. To McClellan's suggestion that the

35. *OR,* 7:617, 621–22.

36. Williams, *Grant Rises in the West,* 250; *OR,* 7:624; Engle, *Buell,* 169.

37. *OR,* 7:620, 621, 622, 623; Cist, *Army of the Cumberland,* 25; Henry M. Davidson, *History of Battery A, First Regiment of Ohio Vol. Light Artillery* (Milwaukee: Daily Wisconsin Printing House, 1865), 23.

troops carry their bread rations, drive beef herds overland, and temporarily discarded all baggage, the department commander was noticeably silent.[38]

On February 17 Buell learned of the incredible news of the capture of Fort Donelson the previous day, along with fifteen thousand Rebel prisoners. In a letter penned to Halleck the same day, he could not bring himself to offer congratulations. Instead of racing past Bowling Green for the coup de grâce, Buell requested that Halleck return his borrowed troops and that the generals "stop until we understand each other." He maintained his determination to push toward Nashville, which he believed would now be heavily reinforced from across the Confederacy. Halleck vainly pleaded that Buell rapidly march to Clarksville: "You will not regret it. There will be no battle at Nashville."[39]

Meanwhile at Bowling Green, Mitchel moved with all haste to cross the Barren River, but the crossing proved both treacherous and logistically complicated. By February 18 his supply train had nearly all arrived—forty wagons with two days' rations, thirty ordnance wagons, and a 120-vehicle baggage train. Information received from civilians indicated that the Confederates were rapidly abandoning Clarksville and falling back on Nashville. Rain that day and snow on the next caused further delay.[40]

Buell arrived at Bowling Green on February 20, placing him forty miles beyond telegraphic communication. He learned by messenger of the capture of Clarksville by Foote's gunboats. An agitated McClellan, placing friendship aside, demanded that Buell either push immediately on Nashville or proceed to the Cumberland River. His perturbed mood was captured in his closing remarks: "I repeat, both Halleck and yourself keep me too much in the dark. Your reports are not sufficiently numerous or explicit."[41]

The Union high command now blundered. Halleck received information that panic had erupted in Nashville and that the Confederates would offer little resistance. Flag Officer Foote, on February 21, pleaded for permission to use his gunboats anchored at Clarksville. Had the order been given, the Tennessee capital doubtless would have fallen the next day, too late to catch Johnston on the north bank of the Cumberland River but in time to capture tons of supplies. But Nashville was in Buell's jurisdiction, and "Old Brains" was hesitant to proceed without first hearing "from Kentucky and Washington." Foote thus sat and fumed as the Southerners were granted an additional seventy-two hours to remove invaluable ordnance and

38. *OR*, 7:626, 627, 634.
39. "Buell Statement," 7; *OR*, 7:630, 632–33.
40. *OR*, 7:634; Mitchel, *Ormsby Macknight Mitchel*, 250.
41. *OR*, 7:642, 643, 646, "Buell Statement," 7.

commissary supplies. "It [the decision to wait] was jealousy on the part of Mc-Clellan and Halleck," Foote disgustedly related to his wife. He was right; McClellan had reserved Nashville for Buell.[42]

Yet Buell appeared to be in no rush. On February 21 a chagrined Mitchel wrote his wife: "We hope to advance every day on Nashville, but General Buell holds back and remains undecided, as he did in Louisville. . . . The railroad from here to Nashville is now uninjured, and I am begging General Buell to permit me to advance for its protection." Mitchel remained particularly concerned about a tunnel forty miles south of Bowling Green. Lined with timber, it could be easily destroyed within hours, but with boldness it might be taken intact.[43]

That evening the order finally came. The Third Division would move out on the Nashville Turnpike early the next morning, February 22, with three days' rations in the haversacks and no tents or wagons. Fifteen boxcars and two locomotives had been recovered south of town, and twelve hundred men, along with a section of artillery, were jammed aboard. The train slowly rumbled out of Bowling Green on schedule. Buell believed that his "express" would be within nine miles of Nashville that night. A handcar was sent in advance to watch for removed rails—only one was found. But the rains accomplished what the Rebels could not; four bridges were washed out, and the train came to a standstill. Buell needed luck, and none was coming his way.[44]

Nor were his divisions quickly concentrating. The army remained largely scattered on the twenty-second. At that time Mitchel's division, fifteen thousand strong, was marching toward Nashville. McCook's ten thousand men, who had been laboring on the railroad, were closing up on Bowling Green but still not within sight. Thomas's First Division, ten thousand fighting men, unable to come by the ordinary roads due to the rains, marched to Louisville to board steamers for the Cumberland River. Wood's raw Sixth Division, also ten thousand strong, remained at Munfordville, an estimated four days' march from Bowling Green. Two independent brigades would stay in Kentucky—Carter's Twelfth, to watch the Cumberland Gap, and Garfield's Eighteenth, to keep an eye on Pound Gap. Jerry Boyle's Eleventh Brigade (twenty-eight hundred men), at Glasgow, and Col. Sanders D. Bruce's newly organized Twenty-Second Brigade (two thousand), at Franklin, both unattached, pro-

42. OR, 7:648, 649, 650; Official Records of the Union and Confederate Navies in the War of the Rebellion, 30 vols. (Washington, D.C.: Government Printing Office, 1894–1922), 22:624, 626. Ironically, on February 21 Buell had written Halleck, "Move up the river with your gunboats, but without exposing them unnecessarily." Halleck may not have received the message until the twenty-third.

43. Mitchel, Ormsby Macknight Mitchel, 249.

44. Ibid., 250–51; "Buell Statement," 7.

ceeded under orders toward the Louisville and Nashville Railroad and would soon be incorporated into existing divisions.[45]

Two of Buell's divisions, Nelson's Fourth and Crittenden's Fifth, were now in Halleck's department, where Grant brazenly incorporated them into his Army of the Tennessee despite loud outcries from Nelson. As events ultimately developed, Cruft's Thirteenth Brigade of Crittenden's division would never return to the Army of the Ohio, nor would four other regiments (one of Crittenden's and three of Nelson's).[46]

Meanwhile, Buell's special troop train, with him on board, was turning out to be the slowest express of the war. It did not arrive opposite Nashville until the evening of February 24, about the same time as Mitchel's division, which had taken the turnpike. To Buell's astonishment, Nelson's division already occupied the city, and the Stars and Stripes waved atop the capitol. What had happened?[47]

The remains of the Fourth and Fifth Divisions (six thousand troops) had arrived after the fall of Fort Donelson. Grant, ignoring department lines, promptly sent the troops upriver on transports to Nashville. Finding the city evacuated, Nelson put ashore on the south bank. After struggling for ten days with mud, washed-out bridges, and sabotaged rails, Buell had been beaten to the prize by Grant—and with troops from his own department.[48]

Nelson, of course, was in no real danger. The Confederates, hanging on for dear life, had retreated to Murfreesboro, Tennessee. Even if he had been threatened, Nelson could simply have used the transports to cross his men to the safety of the north bank or, upon arrival of Mitchel's command, the Third Division could have crossed to the south bank. Instead, Buell, livid at Grant's interference, reciprocated by returning the transports to Clarksville and demanding that C. F. Smith's division of the Army of the Tennessee be rushed to Nashville. Smith considered the order total nonsense but felt compelled to obey. His division no sooner arrived at the capital than it was returned to Clarksville the same day.[49]

Buell entered the nearly deserted city on February 25, riding at the head of his column. A woman came rushing out of her house on High Street as the general passed, defiantly shouting, "Jeff Davis!" Buell promptly ordered her home confis-

45. *OR*, 7:656, 657; *Indianapolis Daily Journal*, Feb. 20, 1862.

46. *OR*, 7:651, 654.

47. "Buell Statement," 8; *OR*, 7:424.

48. Ulysses S. Grant, *Personal Memoirs of U. S. Grant* (reprint, 2 vols. in 1, New York: Library of America, 1990), 215–16; *Cincinnati Commercial*, Mar. 1, 1862; Matthews to wife, Feb. 26, 1862, Stanley Matthews Letters, CINHS.

49. Grant, *Memoirs*, 216–17; *OR*, 7:642, 652, 662, 671; "Buell Statement," 8.

cated and used as a hospital. He then conducted a two-hour meeting with the mayor.[50]

There is no evidence that the general had any plans to pursue the demoralized Confederates south of Nashville, but even had he done so, he would not have gotten far; Johnston had effectively felled trees and burned bridges behind him. Inflated enemy-troop figures also caused Buell to hesitate before plunging ahead. Despite the fact that the Northern press placed Confederate strength at no more than twenty thousand men, probably closer to twelve thousand, the department commander insisted that thirty thousand Rebels awaited him at Murfreesboro. He therefore chose to stop, consolidate his army, bring up supplies, and coordinate his next move with Halleck.[51]

Buell initially maintained his headquarters on the north bank of the Cumberland River in Edgefield for security reasons, according to a journalist. On February 27 Grant made an unannounced and totally unauthorized visit to Nashville. Accompanied by a bevy of correspondents, the victor of Fort Donelson boldly toured the city, making Buell appear foolishly timid. Grant sent him a rather terse note stating that Johnston was not far from the Tennessee line, the implication being that it was now sufficiently safe for Buell to enter the city. He signed his note, "U. S. Grant, Major General," as though he was writing to a junior rather than a department head.

At the end of the day, the two generals met at the wharf; the exchange proved formal and cool. Buell stated that the Rebels were still in the vicinity, a presence dismissed by Grant as nothing more than a rear-guard action. When Buell insisted that he knew his information was correct, Grant retorted, "Well, I do not know." Upon the heels of his great victory, Grant acted cocky. The incident unquestionably resulted in strained relations between the two generals, and even Halleck was angered by Grant's blatant crossing of jurisdictional lines.[52]

The work of crossing the Cumberland River pontoon bridge proved tedious. Mitchel's command passed over on February 25–26, but the other divisions had not crossed until March 5. By the first week in March, Buell had amassed three thousand wagons and fifteen thousand to eighteen thousand horses and mules at Nashville. With the arrival of Thomas's division by water on March 2, all six of his divisions, 55,800 troops, had assembled. The Confederate telegraph office, which had been left conveniently intact, was commandeered and communications established. Throughout early March, trains from Bowling Green came only as far as Edgefield

50. Mitchel, *Ormsby Macknight Mitchel,* 254; Robert L. Kimberly and Ephraim S. Holloway, *The Forty-First Ohio Veteran Volunteer Infantry* (Cleveland: W. R. Smellie, 1897), 17.

51. "Buell Statement," 8; *New York Times,* Feb. 24, Mar. 2, 1864.

52. Bruce Catton, *Grant Moves South* (Boston: Little, Brown, 1960), 192; *Chicago Tribune,* Mar. 8, 12, 1862; *New York Times,* Mar. 5, 1862; *OR,* 7:670, 675; Grant, *Memoirs,* 217.

Junction, nine miles from Nashville. It would be March 26 before the Louisville and Nashville bridge over the Cumberland River reopened for traffic.[53]

The men in the ranks offered mixed reactions about the Tennessee capital. "The city looked deserted. There were a great many fine buildings, particularly the capitol, a very grand and elegant structure, built entirely of marble," a Minnesota drummer boy noted in his diary. Hoosier Thomas Harrison wrote his wife on March 5: "Nashville is not so pretty a town as Indianapolis. The grounds are very uneven and the streets look like alleys. They are narrow." Harold Bartlett, a Michigan cannoneer, thought Nashville a "desolate looking city. All is to be seen is soldiers by the thousands coming in all the time." A Kentucky soldier noted that the city was "very different from Louisville . . . although there are many good, as well as fine buildings."[54]

The respite offered an opportunity for a quick reorganization. Buell desired to rebuild the depleted Fourth and Fifth Divisions, which had had four thousand men pinched by Halleck. He thus gave them his two independent brigades, the Eleventh going to Crittenden and the Twenty-Second to Nelson. The two remaining brigades in eastern Kentucky, Carter's and Garfield's, were organized into a new division, the Seventh, under Brig. Gen. George W. Morgan.

Minor reshuffling and additions also occurred. The 9th Indiana, newly arrived from duty in western Virginia, went to Hazen's Nineteenth Brigade. Since its colonel, Gideon C. Moody, had previously been a captain in the regular army, Hazen expected the 9th to be his premier regiment; it turned out to be his worst. Col. Thomas Bramlette of the 3d Kentucky continued his carping about being in the Eleventh Brigade, for its commander, Jerry Boyle, was ostensibly his junior. The outfit was thus transferred to the Nineteenth Brigade, where the seniority issue would be unquestioned. Capt. A. F. Bidwell's newly arrived four-gun 4th Michigan Artillery went to Thomas's division.[55]

In early March, Dumont's brigade marched out on the Murfreesboro Road to the village of La Vergne. There Colonel Beatty encountered a Mrs. Harris, who insisted that, unlike the Yankees, Confederate soldiers were all gentlemen. Beatty quickly replied that he did not doubt the truth of her statement but that he "had not been

53. "Buell Statement," 8–9; OR, 10(2):68; Cincinnati Commercial, Mar. 15, 18, 1862; William R. Plum, The Military Telegraph during the Civil War in the United States, 2 vols. (Chicago: Jansen, McClung, 1882), 1:204; Thomas Scott to Stanton, Mar. 1, 1862, Stanton Papers.

54. Bircher, Drummer Boy's Diary, 31; Thomas Harrison to wife, Mar. 5, 1862, Thomas Harrison Letters, INHS; James F. Mohr to brother, Mar. 5, 1862, James F. Mohr Letters, FC; James G. Genco, ed., To the Sound of Musketry and Tap of the Drum (Detroit: Detroit Book, 1990), 24.

55. Hazen, Narrative, 20–21; Tapp and Klotter, Tuttle, 57, 64; Genco, To the Sound of Musketry, 22–23.

able to get near enough to them [the Rebels] to obtain any personal knowledge on the subject."[56]

The men of the Army of the Ohio would have echoed his sentiments. Buell had been in command for nearly five months, yet with the exception of the First Division, scarcely a Rebel had been seen. Nashville had been captured, a prize sufficient to win Buell a major general's commission, but Johnston's army at Bowling Green had easily slipped away. It was the Ohio Valley's sister command, Grant's Army of the Tennessee, that was doing the fighting—and winning the laurels.

56. Beatty, *Citizen Soldier,* 113.

5

The Mettle Tested
The Battle of Shiloh

BY EARLY MARCH 1862, the strategic situation in the West had dramatically changed. Johnston's army at Murfreesboro had withdrawn south to Shelbyville. Leonidas Polk's corps at Columbus, Kentucky, also fell back, partly down the Mississippi River to Island No. 10 and partly to middle-western Tennessee. Halleck had "reliable information" that another fifteen thousand to twenty thousand enemy troops had concentrated at Corinth, Mississippi. Eager to repeat his river-turning movement, he desired to send Grant's army up the Tennessee River to Savannah, where a raid could be launched upon the Memphis and Charleston and Mobile and Ohio Railroads. Grant's twenty-seven thousand men would be deep into enemy territory and facing as many as thirty-eight thousand Confederates by best estimates, yet Thomas Scott assured Halleck that Buell would cooperate by sending ten thousand to twenty thousand troops. "I know he wishes to aid any important movement," he wrote.[1]

Scott was wrong. Buell's intelligence indicated that Johnston planned to withdraw from Shelbyville to Fayetteville, Tennessee, where twenty-five thousand reinforcements would join him from Virginia and South Carolina. An agitated Halleck wrote on March 8: "Do you propose to send any troops to the Tennessee, and, if so, how many and when? My own movements are delayed for this information." To Halleck's chagrin, Buell merely repeated an earlier suggestion that Grant occupy Florence, Alabama. Reminiscent of the previous winter's feud, Buell wrote on March 10 that Halleck should be crossing to the east bank of the Tennessee River (his jurisdiction) and not vice versa. Although there might be enemy concentrations at several points, including Corinth, "Decatur seems to be the main point."[2]

Out of all patience and perhaps hoping that Buell would not leave him out on a limb, Halleck started his river expeditionary force. Even though reinforced with a new division under the command of the back-in-action William T. Sherman, Halleck fretted as Buell continued to rebuff all requests for reinforcements. On March 9, affairs took a dramatic turn. Washington advised Halleck that his long-sought unified western command had been granted. His new Department of the Mississippi

1. *OR*, 10(2):7, 8, 12, 16, 18.
2. Ibid., 10, 11, 20, 22–23, 27, 33.

would combine the former Missouri and Ohio departments. Initially, "Old Brains" was sensitive in his dealings with Buell, assuring him that the "new arrangement" would not interfere with his plans. Buell, apparently believing that he would continue de facto independent command, proposed a strike upon the Memphis and Charleston at Florence. Upon receiving positive evidence of a growing enemy concentration at Corinth (a fact confirmed by Buell), Halleck dropped his forced cordiality. He promptly ordered Buell to move with his army to reinforce Grant at Savannah. The move south along the Tennessee was no longer a raid but a full-scale penetration. "Don't fail to carry out my instructions. I know I am right," admonished the theater commander.[3]

Halleck's strategy was debatable. By diverting Buell to Savannah, he chose the Mississippi Valley over the Tennessee Valley. Although Grant's army alone might not have been able to capture Corinth, John Pope's eighteen-thousand-man Army of the Mississippi could have been sent in place of the Army of the Ohio. Instead, it wasted weeks in capturing Island No. 10, with its garrison of four thousand troops, a post that would have fallen anyway once Halleck turned the position. Indeed, Grant's and Pope's armies would not necessarily have to besiege Corinth, only keep the Confederates pinned down. This would have left Buell free to march into East Tennessee, which at that time was held by only ten thousand Confederates.[4]

Buell advanced his army on March 15, leaving an eighteen-thousand-man garrison in Nashville and Middle Tennessee under James Negley. The main column of five divisions, thirty-seven thousand troops, marched forty-two miles southwest to Columbia, Tennessee, a town of thirty-five hundred residents on the south bank of the Duck River. George Botkin, in Nelson's division, frankly did not know how many men were moving out, but he noticed, "as far as we can see back of us it is a continual dark column of men." Protecting the flank would be Mitchel's eight-thousand-man division supported by a brigade at Murfreesboro. Mitchel would proceed southeast, then south to Fayetteville. If he encountered no resistance, he would continue into northern Alabama to strike the Memphis and Charleston Railroad and cooperate with the main column. Entering Murfreesboro on March 20, an Ohioan noted to his wife, "I saw no Union flags nor any other sign of love for the Union or joy at our arrival."[5]

3. Larry J. Daniel, *Shiloh: The Battle That Changed the Civil War* (New York: Simon and Schuster, 1997), 74–75; *OR*, 10(2):44, 60.

4. *OR*, 10(1):476. For my views concerning the strategy involved in taking Island No. 10, see Larry J. Daniel and Lynn N. Bock, *Island No. 10: Struggle for the Mississippi Valley* (Tuscaloosa: University of Alabama Press, 1996).

5. "Buell Statement," 9; George Botkin to friend, Mar. 19, 1862, Sidney Botkin Papers, OHS; *OR*, 10(2):37, 60; William E. Eamers to wife, Mar. 20, 1862, William E. Eamers Letters, SRNBP; *National Intelligencer*, Mar. 31, 1862; *Indianapolis Daily Journal*, Mar. 31, 1862; *New York Tribune*, Apr. 3, 1862.

Buell planned to make a cavalry dash on Columbia, securing the two 180-foot-long Duck River bridges before the Rebels had a chance to torch them. In the early morning hours of March 16, the 1st Ohio Cavalry galloped wildly into Franklin, terrifying the local citizens before continuing south. The plan soon went awry. Aware of their coming, the Confederates burned the two 60-foot-long Rutherford Creek bridges four miles north of Columbia. By the time the Ohio troopers got to the town, they found both bridges aflame and a rain-swollen river forty feet deep. Some of the Buckeyes foolishly swam their horses across to claim the town, but as at the Barren River, Buell had again been effectively checked.[6]

Snow mixed with rain fell as the infantry column tramped into Franklin on the sixteenth, a "smart little town with a good courthouse and . . . surrounded with a good country," according to 10th Indiana member Samuel McIlvaine. When Mc-Cook's division, in the van, finally arrived at the Duck River on the eighteenth, there was little that could be done but stop and build a bridge. An engineer battalion, assisted by the 32d Indiana, which had a fair number of mechanics, went to work on the project. From his headquarters in Nashville, Buell informed Halleck that he would be delayed only four or five days, meaning his force would arrive on the twenty-third or twenty-fourth. He subsequently moved the date back to the twenty-seventh. Incredibly, Buell had sent his newly completed pontoons by steamboat from Cincinnati to Savannah. Thus, as the Army of the Ohio sat, the pontoons went to Grant's army, which had (unknown to Buell) already crossed to the west bank.[7]

While the troops waited, many wondered if they would ever get into the war. Michigan artilleryman Harold Bartlett feared that the Southerners would "keep us chasing them around all summer, but we will corner them by & by." Cpl. Alexander Varian of the 1st Ohio wrote: "They say there are some Rebels [at Decatur]. I am sure I'd like to see them. I hope they won't run for I am tired of running after them." Writing from Columbia, A. S. Bloomfield commented to his sister that the Rebels might offer one more fight, "but I guess they will conclude the old way of fighting is the best, that is running and burning all they leave behind."[8]

6. Curry, *Four Years in the Saddle*, 30; *New York Tribune*, Apr. 3, 1862; Don Carlos Buell, "Shiloh Reviewed," in *B&L*, 1:491; "Buell Statement," 9.

7. Clayton E. Crummer, ed., *By the Dim and Flaring Lamps: The Civil War Diaries of Samuel McIlvaine* (Monroe, N.Y.: Library Research Associates, 1990), 77; Edwin Hannaford, *Story of a Regiment: A History of the Campaigns and Association in the Field of the Sixth Regiment Ohio Volunteer Infantry* (Cincinnati: privately printed, 1868), 228; Edwin W. Payne, *History of the Thirty-Fourth Regiment of Illinois Volunteer Infantry* (Clinton, Iowa: Allen, 1902), 15; Van Horne, *Army of the Cumberland*, 1:100; *OR*, 10(2):48, 58, 60–61, 82, 86, 92; "Buell Statement," 9. The army marched with a day's interval between divisions. Thomas's division, trailing the column, did not depart until April 1.

8. Genco, *To the Sound of Musketry*, 27; Alexander Varian to wife, Mar. 28, 1862, Alexander Varian Letters, WRHS; Bloomfield to sister, Mar. 27, 1862, A. S. Bloomfield Letters, LC.

A late snow dusted Middle Tennessee between March 21 and 24, hampering the work of engineers. Buell arrived on the twenty-sixth, expecting the bridge to be complete. He embarrassingly conceded to Halleck that the project had been far more complicated than anticipated and, for a second time, revised his completion date to March 31. Meanwhile, he also began a pontoon bridge; exactly where he got the pontoons is unknown. The theater commander had anticipated the two armies to juncture during the last week in March, but he showed no apprehension at the two-week Columbia delay. Indeed, Grant had wired him that "the temper of the rebel troops is such that there is but little doubt but that Corinth will fall much more easily than Donelson did." Nonetheless, Halleck urged Buell to press ahead: "Don't fail in this, as it is all-important to have an overwhelming force there."[9]

Although previously advised that Grant's army was on the west (enemy) side of the Tennessee at Pittsburg Landing, it was not until Buell received a dispatch on the twenty-seventh that the information apparently sank in. T. J. Bush, a staff officer, remembered the surprised look on the general's face. Upon hearing the news, Nelson exclaimed: "By God, we must cross the river [Duck] at once, or Grant will be whipped!" Later that day Buell gave his consent for Nelson to attempt a fording on the twenty-ninth. When the Kentucky general announced the crossing, Colonel Ammen asked if the bridge had been completed. "No," barked Nelson, "but the river is falling and, damn you, get over, for we must advance and get the glory." Ammen noted in his journal that evening: "He [Nelson] enjoined secrecy, lest we be prevented from taking the advance [by McCook]."[10]

On the cold dawn of March 29, Nelson's men, stripped to their drawers, jumped waist-deep into the frigid water. "It was fun to see the men jump into the water. All of them would take off the greater part of their clothing. Some all of them," noted a spectator. Maurice Williams of the 36th Indiana was one of the ones who took the plunge. "The water was about waist deep and very swift and most awful cold and still it was only sport for us," he jotted in his diary. By sunset the entire division had crossed, followed the next day by Crittenden's men. By the thirty-first, both bridges had been completed. The Army of the Ohio was at last on the move.[11]

9. Henry Carman, ed., "Diary of Amos Glover," *The Ohio State Archaeological and Historical Quarterly* 44 (Apr. 1935): 265; Payne, *Thirty-Fourth Illinois*, 15; *OR*, 10(2):44, 47, 50–51, 59, 65, 70, 77; Buell, "Shiloh Reviewed," 491; Hannaford, *Story of a Regiment*, 231; Chumney, "Don Carlos Buell," 68, 90–91 n.; Dodge, *Old Second Division*, 31.

10. *OR*, 10(2):44, 47, 59, 10(1):329–30; Hannaford, *Story of a Regiment*, 231; *National Intelligencer*, Apr. 29, 1862.

11. *OR*, 10(1):329–30; A. S. Bloomfield to sister, Mar. 31, 1862, Bloomfield Letters, LC; Prokopowicz, *All for the Regiment*, 98; Hannaford, *Story of a Regiment*, 232–33; Ralph E. Kiene Jr., *A Civil War Diary: The Journal of Francis A. Kiene, 1861–1865* (N.p.: privately printed, 1974), 83. Buell, "Shiloh Reviewed," 491; Archiblad Stinson to cousin, Mar. 31, 1862, Archibald Stinson Letters, INHS.

Nelson's men kept a steady pace, marching fourteen miles on April 1 and sixteen on the second, placing the division at Proctor's Furnace, five miles from Waynesboro. The next day a pro-Union crowd greeted the troops as they marched into town—a "union village" with several American flags waving, some inscribed "Peace and Union." "Women asked to let the band play some old tunes—Yankee Doodle, etc. The music makes them weep for joy," noted Colonel Ammen. At Waynesboro the army filed off onto a torturous eighty-two-mile country road leading to Savannah, with Nelson's division a day's march in the lead, followed by Crittenden's, McCook's, Wood's, and Thomas's, the last forty miles in the rear.[12]

Despite a drenching rain and mud-choked road, Nelson's forty-five hundred men pressed on during April 4, although Grant advised that there was "no need of haste; come on by easy marches." The column sloshed into Savannah the next morning. At 1:00 P.M. Nelson reported to Grant, wanting to proceed directly to Pittsburg Landing. When told instead to make camp, the Kentuckian impulsively asked Grant if he was not concerned about a possible enemy attack upon his beachhead. "The wonder to me is that he has not done so before," he quipped. Grant casually answered, "They're [enemy] all back at Corinth, and, when our transportation arrives, we have got to go there and draw them out, as you would draw a badger out of a hole."[13]

About 3:00 P.M. Grant and Nelson rode to the tent of Colonel Ammen. The colonel remarked that his men could well march on to Pittsburg Landing if necessary. Grant, declining to dismount, answered: "You cannot march through the swamps; make the troops comfortable; I will send boats for you Monday or Tuesday, or some time early in the week. There will be no fight at Pittsburg Landing; we will have to go to Corinth, where the rebels are fortified. If they come to attack us we can whip them, as I have more than twice as many troops as I had at Fort Donelson." A surgeon who overheard the conversation related in his journal: "Genl Grant called to see us. Did not give no orders to go on to Pitts[;] said he had plenty of men to relief them. Genl Nelson was anxious to be within sight of Pittsburg—Genl Grant seemed indifferent." That evening Buell arrived after a grueling day's ride, accompa-

12. William R. Hartpence, *History of the Fifty-First Indiana Veteran Volunteer Infantry* (Cincinnati: Robert Clarke, 1894), 34, 36; Almon F. Rockwell Diary, Apr. 14, 1862, LC; F. W. Keil, *Thirty-Fifth Ohio: A Narrative of Service from August 1861–1864* (Fort Wayne: Archer, Housh, 1894), 61; Carman, "Diary of Amos Glover," 265; *OR*, 10(1):330; Harold Bartlett Diary, Apr. 1, 1862, LC; Jacob H. Smith, "Personal Reminiscences—Battle of Shiloh," in *War Papers, Michigan Commandery, MOLLUS* (N.p., 1894), 8; Kiene, *Civil War Diary*, 83.

13. Hannaford, *Story of a Regiment*, 236; Cecil H. Fisher, ed., *A Staff Officer's Story: The Personal Experiences of Colonel Horace Newton Fisher in the Civil War* (Boston: Todd, 1960), 10; Buell, "Shiloh Reviewed," 492–93.

nied only by Fry, an aide, and an orderly. Perhaps exhausted, he did not inform Grant of his arrival.[14]

At precisely 5:20 A.M. on Sunday, April 6, according to a Nelson staff officer, a distant "poom, poom" could be heard upriver—the distinct sound of artillery. The fire, at first sporadic, became first more regular and then a continuous roar. Buell, having breakfast in Nelson's camp, feared that the Army of the Tennessee had been attacked. He immediately dispatched riders to the nearest divisions with orders to leave their wagons in the rear and force march to Savannah. He then proceeded to Grant's headquarters, the Cherry Mansion, where he learned that the general had already departed for Pittsburg Landing on *Tigress,* leaving an order for Nelson to proceed upriver along the east bank to that location.[15]

Nelson's men had been preparing for a scheduled review and inspection when the sounds of fighting became audible. A naval officer visiting the 2d Kentucky assured the men it was simply the gunboats routinely clearing the riverbanks of Rebels. But the pace quickened as Nelson rode rapidly into the camp of Ammen's brigade, ordering the men to fall in. They were to proceed to Pittsburg Landing either by boat or by foot—the decision had not yet been made. Rumors soon spread in camp of a defeat. As the minutes ticked away and no further orders arrived, Ammen hastened to the Cherry Mansion, where he found Buell and Nelson impatiently waiting for boats to transport them. Meanwhile, Capt. J. Miles Kendrick, commanding a company of the 3d Indiana Cavalry (Nelson's escort), had been sent to explore for a river trail. He returned at noon, reporting that the main road was impassable but that a higher trail back from the river would permit the passage of infantry. Throughout it all, Buell remained characteristically cool and controlled. Indeed, a captain perceived him as indifferent to the events going on and, within forty feet of him, characterized him as a Rebel; if Buell heard him, he made no response. When a small steamer finally arrived, the general determined to proceed to the scene of action, while Nelson took the road.[16]

On the way to Pittsburg Landing, Buell viewed a downriver steamer that came alongside, delivering a message from Grant. His army was under a full-scale attack

---

14. *OR,* 10(2):330–31; Joshua T. Bradford Diary, Apr. 5, 1862, LC.

15. Horace N. Fisher, "Memorandum of September 5, 1904, Buell's Army at Shiloh, April 6 and 7, 1862," SNMP; *OR,* 10(1):184–85, 292, 331; Buell, "Shiloh Reviewed," 492.

16. *OR,* 10(1):184–85, 292; Hannaford, *Story of a Regiment,* 246, 248–49; James E. Stewart, "Fighting Them Over," *National Tribune,* Feb. 19, 1885; Hartpence, *Fifty-First Indiana,* 36; Fisher, *Staff Officer's Story,* 10–11; William Grose, *The Story of the Marches, Battles and Incidents of the Thirty-Sixth Regiment Indiana Volunteer Infantry* (New Castle, Ind.: Courier, 1891), 102.

by an estimated one hundred thousand Rebels, and the arrival of Buell's army "might possibly save the day to us." The Ohio general soon got a firsthand view of the desperate nature of the conflict. As his steamer passed the mouth of Snake Creek, he saw a stream of fugitives wading through the backwater. What he found at the landing proved shocking—at least four thousand to five thousand men huddled beneath the bluffs like so many sheep.[17]

The two commanding generals met aboard *Tigress* shortly after 1:00 P.M. It was the first time they had seen one another since their last unpleasant encounter in Nashville. The conference proved to be as brief as it was icy. Grant had just returned from the front and showed his sword scabbard, which had been struck by an artillery fragment. "I did not particularly notice it," Buell contemptuously wrote; perhaps he took a perverse pleasure in seeing Grant, whom he clearly disliked, in his present predicament. They spoke briefly of the battle, and Buell requested transports for Crittenden's division. The conference concluded and Grant departed. Buell, in a foul mood, toured the landing, showing his obvious disgust at the frightened soldiers.[18]

Meanwhile, Nelson's men trudged through six miles of black-mud bottomland, marching four abreast, at times two abreast. The general, riding ahead, sent back a dispatch, "Hurry up or all will be lost; the enemy is driving our men." A second message arrived, then a third. As Ammen's troops, in the van, approached the bank opposite Pittsburg Landing, a shocking panorama of chaos greeted them—ten thousand of Grant's men cowering beneath the bluffs. "I blush to describe it," a member of the 6th Ohio wrote. "The entire bank of the river, for a mile up and down, was crowded with cowardly poltroons who were crowding down to be out of harm's way." Frantic signals were sent to cross the column over, though Ammen noted that the mass at the landing far outnumbered his own force.[19]

A small sutler's boat ferried across 200 men of the 36th Indiana and a mounted party, which included Nelson. As the boat touched shore, the general shouted: "Gentlemen, draw your sabers and trample these ——— into the mud! Charge!" As the riders barged their way ashore, the general angrily shouted to the huddled fugitives, "Damn your souls, if you won't fight, get out of the way, and let men come here who will!" He then had the infantry shout "Buell! Buell!" as they came ashore. Nelson led the 36th to the far left of the Union line to the deep ravine of Dill Branch. Three companies of the 6th Ohio came ashore next, filing to the left of

17. Buell, "Shiloh Reviewed," 492–93; *OR*, 10(1):292.
18. Buell, "Shiloh Reviewed," 493; Daniel, *Shiloh*, 244.
19. *OR*, 10(1):332–33; Grose, *Thirty-Sixth Indiana*, 102; Fisher, *Staff Officer's Story*, 11; Hannaford, *Story of a Regiment*, 566–67; Gary L. Ecelbarger, ed., "Shiloh," *Civil War Times Illustrated* (Apr. 1995): 66.

the 36th. By the time the Rebels attacked this last Federal position, Ammen had about 550 men on line.[20]

The subsequent two-brigade Confederate assault was easily repulsed. Buell would insist that it was the climactic moment of the battle. Had the attack been made before Nelson's arrival, "it would have succeeded beyond all question." "These two regiments [the 36th Indiana and the 6th Ohio] hurled the miscreants back and chased them down the ridge and saved the day—10 minutes later—only 10 minutes later, think of it sir, this army [Grant's] was gone—gone hook and line," Nelson explained to Secretary of the Treasury Chase. In postwar years veterans of the Ohio army would forever tout that they had saved Grant's command. In truth, the Confederate attack had simply sputtered out, and despite Buell's insistence, Grant did have troops of his own on the line. Nevertheless, the near superhuman efforts of Nelson's men to arrive on the field in time to receive the closing assault (spasmodic though it was), would stand as one of the army's finest hours.[21]

In the midst of a downpour, a steady stream of Federal reinforcements continued to arrive at Pittsburg Landing that night. Nelson's entire division was across by 9:00 P.M., and Crittenden's, having come by steamboats from Savannah, by eleven o'clock. Wood's division, at one point forced to cease marching by the driving rain, arrived early on the morning of the seventh, wet, tired, but full of fight. McCook's division marched the six miles to the landing only to find no boats awaiting them. "I ordered my staff aboard boats at the Landing, compelling the captains to get out of their beds and prepare their boats for my use," he reported. Lovell Rousseau's brigade filed ashore at 5:00 A.M. So strained were the relations between Grant and Buell that the two commanders never even consulted about the morning's counterattack. Buell assumed that the movements "would be in accord" with his army on the left and Grant's the right.[22]

Nelson, a black plume in his hat, advanced his division at dawn, the Tenth Brigade on the left, the Second in the center, and the Nineteenth on the right. "Now, boys, keep cool; given 'em the best you've got," Ammen calmly stated as he rode up and

20. Grose, *Thirty-Sixth Indiana*, 104; Hannaford, *Story of a Regiment*, 281, 568, 569, 577, 587; Fisher, *Staff Officer's Story*, 12–13; *OR*, 10(1):333–34; *Cincinnati Commercial*, Apr. 22, 1862; Ecelbarger, "Shiloh," 50, 66; Paul Hubbard and Christine Lewis, eds., "Give Yourself No Trouble about Me: The Shiloh Letters of George W. Lennard," *Indiana Magazine of History* 76 (Mar. 1980): 31.

21. Buell, "Shiloh Reviewed," 507; Nelson to Chase, Apr. 10, 1862, in Niven, *Chase Papers*, 3:169.

22. *OR*, 10(1):302–3, 324, 334, 354, 355, 359, 365, 372; Buell, "Shiloh Reviewed," 519–20. Sherman wrote in his memoirs that in a meeting with Buell that evening, the Ohio army commander "seemed to mistrust us" and repeatedly said that "he did not like the looks of things," causing fear that he might not land his army. Buell adamantly denied such statements. Sherman, *Memoirs*, 1:245–46.

down his line. Crittenden's division, led personally by Buell, using the Pittsburg-Corinth Road as its line of advance, slowly came up on Nelson's right at 8:00 A.M. McCook formed Rousseau's brigade in Stacy field. Riding to his old 1st Ohio, the general declared that if any man ran, he would personally "blow his brains out." After sporadic firing, the Ohio army emerged along a one-mile front from the timber along the Sunken Road, site of the heaviest fighting from the previous day. There they sighted the main Confederate line, formed along the Purdy-Hamburg Road to their front.[23]

Despite the disparity in numbers, perhaps forty thousand Federal effectives (Brig. Gen. Lew Wallace's division of Grant's army had also arrived during the night) against twenty thousand Confederates, many of the last having already headed back to Corinth, resistance proved surprisingly tough. Indeed, at 9:00 A.M. an advancing line of Rebels struck Hazen's brigade in the middle of the Sunken Road, placing Mendenhall's battery in jeopardy. Hazen personally led the 6th Kentucky in a splendid bayonet charge, with the balance of his brigade moving up in support, causing the Southerners to flee.[24]

Between eleven o'clock and noon, Nelson's division and Col. William Sooy Smith's brigade of Crittenden's division advanced through the Davis wheat field, temporarily overrunning the Louisiana Washington Artillery before being driven back in savage see-saw fighting. Hazen's brigade was shattered, the 41st Ohio losing 140 of 371 engaged. The same fate befell Col. Sanders D. Bruce's brigade to the east in the Sarah Bell field. The 13th Kentucky lost a third of its men. Bruce, who always kept a flask of whiskey by his side, had been in and out of arrest by Nelson, the officers detesting each other. The colonel would survive the battle only to have a temporarily paralyzing stroke two months later. Ammen's brigade held firm along the Hamburg-Savannah Road, supported by Terrill's Battery H, 5th U.S. Artillery. "Captain Tirrell's [sic] relatives are Secessionists. His father and three brothers hold high positions in the rebel army and he had been disinherited and disowned by them for his loyalty for the Union," an Ohio soldier wrote. Following the repulse of the enemy, Nelson rode along the line of the 6th Ohio and declared: "Men of the 6th Ohio, I'm proud of you. I *may* be mistaken, but I think I can depend upon you."[25]

23. *OR*, 10(1):241, 324, 328, 335, 337, 339, 340, 341, 342, 343, 357, 372; Hannaford, *Story of a Regiment*, 572; Hazen, *Narrative*, 25; Daniel, *Shiloh*, 268.

24. *OR*, 10(1):342, 343, 344–45, 347–48, 373–74; Hazen, *Narrative*, 26, 41; Alexander S. Johnstone, "Scenes at Shiloh," in *Camp-Fire Sketches and Battle-Field Echoes*, ed. W. C. King and W. P. Derby (Cleveland: N. G. Hamilton, 1888), 50.

25. *OR*, 10(1):339, 342, 343, 345, 348, 349, 350, 351, 366, 367, 368–69, 370, 372; Smith, "Personal Reminiscences," 13; Fisher, *Staff Officer's Story*, 15–16; *Louisville Daily Journal*, Apr. 25, 1862; Hannaford, *Story*

On Buell's far right, McCook advanced Rousseau's brigade, the Fifth and Sixth Brigades not yet having come up from the landing. Rousseau's right was in the air since Grant's line had not yet come abreast. A spirited attack drove the Rebels back through Duncan field. "You ought to have seen the Rebels run," noted an Ohioan. "They were in the woods and we charged across the open field with an awful yell; they only waited to give us a couple of vollics [sic] when they broke and ran for dear life."[26]

At Water Oaks Pond the enemy put up stiff resistance, even causing Grant's men to waver. Shortly after 1:30 Col. August Willich's 32d Indiana of the Sixth Brigade moved up in support. Willich complained that the ambulances had been left behind at Savannah, causing him to detach a number of his men to assist the wounded back at the landing. For the first time, Sherman saw his old Ohio army in action. He noted that the "well-ordered and compact columns . . . at once gave confidence to our newer and less-disciplined forces." Rousseau's brigade, following in the rear of the 32d Indiana, came up and penetrated as far as the pond. Buell's right and Grant's left had at last connected.[27]

Around two o'clock the Federals resumed the offensive, soon taking the Purdy-Hamburg Road. Brig. Gen. Jeremiah Boyle's and Sooy Smith's brigades took the intersection of the Eastern Corinth and Purdy-Hamburg Roads, partially capturing a Mississippi battery in the process. The Rebels began to withdraw from the field, with a rear-guard action south of Shiloh Church at three o'clock. Brigadier General Garfield's Twentieth Brigade of Wood's division came on the field just as the enemy retreated. Neither Grant nor Buell ordered a pursuit. Both generals would later point fingers at each other, but it appears that all communication between them had simply collapsed.[28]

The Army of the Ohio had only 17,918 men engaged at the Battle of Shiloh. Losses proved relatively light—241 killed, 1,807 wounded, and 55 missing, a total of 2,103, or 12 percent, mostly from McCook's and Nelson's divisions. (Grant's Army

of a Regiment, 574; Ecelbarger, "Shiloh," 68; "Account by a Participant," in The Rebellion Record, ed. Frank Moore (New York: G. P. Putnam, 1862), 415.

26. OR, 10(1):308, 311; Lewis M. Hosea, "The Second Day at Shiloh," in MOLLUS, Ohio, 9 vols. (reprint, Wilmington, N.C.: Broadfoot, 1991), 6:202; D. McCook, "The Second Day at Shiloh," Harper's New Monthly Magazine 28 (1863–64): 831; W. to King, Apr. 14, 1862, in Union Reader, ed. Richard B. Harewell (Secaucus, N.J.: Blue and Grey, 1958), 119.

27. OR, 10(1):120, 251, 307 10, 317 18; Hosea, "Second Day at Shiloh," 204–5; Payne, Thirty-Fourth Illinois, 17, 20.

28. Daniel, Shiloh, 291–94; OR, 10(1):291, 358, 360, 365, 372–73, 429, 431; Stephen E. Ambrose, ed., A Wisconsin Boy in Dixie: The Selected Letters of James K. Newton (Madison: University of Wisconsin Press, 1961), 15; James D. Norris and James K. Martin, eds., "Three Civil War Letters of James A. Garfield," Ohio History 74 (autumn 1965): 250.

of the Tennessee sustained a 22 percent loss.) Buell's army continued to arrive at Pittsburg Landing for the next several days. "We traveled two days and one night and only stopped to feed our men and horses but once," wrote an artilleryman in Thomas's division. "We were in hearing of the cannon all through the fight. We got within four miles of here [Savannah] that night it all ended. We only got three miles in the whole night we marched, the mud was so deep." The troops became sickened at the sight of the carnage. An officer of the 3d Kentucky observed two or three wagonloads of amputated legs, hands, and feet.[29]

The men of the Ohio army jubilantly wrote home that they had saved the day at Shiloh. "I suppose they [the press] will give all the glory to Grant, but I assure you, there never was a worse whipped army on the face of the earth than Grant's was on Sunday night, and were it not for the timely arrival of Buell, [it] would be utterly annihilated," insisted one staff officer. Surgeon Bradford likewise believed that, but for the arrival of the Army of the Ohio, Grant's "whole army would have gone up." Samuel Buford, a Nelson aide, remarked, "Grant was badly whipped and if we hadn't have come to his relief when we did his entire army would have been taken prisoners."[30]

Buell reached the pinnacle of his popularity. It became, according to one officer, "very difficult to suppress cheers as General Buell passed the men." In a letter to Chase, Nelson wrote: "The labors of Genl Buell all the long [winter] bore ripe fruit. Discipline held—the difference between our army and the Mob here is such that our soldiers sneer at them on all occasions." Rousseau, writing to Chase in a like manner, stated: "I do not know Buell very well, but I do know him well enough, to know that he is a just, a sensible, a discreet and an able man, and devoted to his country, though he may be, as is alleged, a cold man. We have entire confidence in him, in all things. . . . A part of Buell's army from 17,000 to 20,000 strong almost *alone* whipt the rebels on the second day, and Buell was with them and aided them."[31]

In a letter to his wife, Buell expressed privately what others openly stated. His troops "saved the army of General Halleck, commanded by General Grant, which otherwise was doomed to destruction. It is the voice of his [Grant's] entire army, as far as I know, that they were lost." Again he wrote, "I shall not speak boastfully to anyone, unless it is to you, my wife, of the part the 'Kentucky Army' has acted in it

29. *OR*, 10(1):322; Prokopowicz, *All for the Regiment*, 111; Genco, *To the Sound of Musketry*, 28–29. See also Henry M. Osborn Diary, Apr. 9, 1862, OHS.

30. John Scully to wife, Apr. 13, 1862, John Scully Letters, DU; Bradford Diary, Apr. 7, 1862; Samuel Buford to "Charlie," Apr. 21, 1862, in Charles Buford Letters, LC.

31. Engle, *Buell*, 235; Niven, *Chase Papers*, 3:169, 175.

[battle]." Forgotten in the self-praise was Buell's neglect in throwing a pontoon bridge across the Duck River days before he did.[32]

Halleck arrived at Pittsburg Landing on April 11 to assume personal command of the combined forces in the field. The day after the battle, Island No. 10 on the Mississippi River fell, along with forty-one hundred prisoners, thus freeing Brig. Gen. John Pope's Army of the Mississippi for further operations. Halleck thus forged his three armies (Grant's thirty-six thousand, Buell's thirty-two thousand, and Pope's eighteen thousand) of eighty-six thousand men into one massive Army of the West, with Buell, minus Thomas's division (which went to Grant), forming the Center, Grant the Right Wing, and Pope the Left Wing. With Mitchel's division in northern Alabama, Brig. Gen. George Morgan's newly organized Seventh Division at Cumberland Gap, Negley's at Nashville, and Thomas's with Grant, Buell had been reduced to only four divisions of twenty-five thousand infantry. Public opinion was heavily against Grant, and he was "promoted" to second in command, which in effect took away his field command. The Army of the Tennessee, for the time being, went to George Thomas.[33]

Halleck's tediously slow advance to Corinth took a month; there would be no more Shiloh surprises. By the time he arrived, the Rebels, now under the leadership of P. G. T. Beauregard (Albert Sidney Johnston having fallen during the first day at Shiloh), had also been reinforced by a corps from Arkansas, bringing their strength to fifty-one thousand, still leaving a large Northern advantage in numbers, but not the two-to-one disparity so often claimed by modern historians. As Halleck fought skirmishes and small engagements and prepared for siege operations, the Confederates, on the night of May 29, silently withdrew south to Tupelo.[34]

The Shiloh-Corinth campaign having concluded, Halleck had to determine his next move. A commitment had to be made soon, both to prevent the enemy from seizing the initiative and to dissuade the War Department from siphoning off troops to the Virginia front. He had essentially three options: pursue the Confederates south to Tupelo; march west to capture Vicksburg, Mississippi; or move east to take Chattanooga. In the end, politics as much as strategy would be the determining factor.

Halleck's first, and perhaps best, option was to drive fifty miles south en masse to Tupelo, relentlessly pushing the Rebels before him. John Pope, his army pursuing the enemy south of Corinth, sent back reports (all lies as it turned out) that the

32. Buell to wife, Apr. 8, 9, May 2, 1862, Don Carlos Buell Papers, FC.
33. *OR*, 10(2):146–51; Van Horne, *Army of the Cumberland*, 1:126–27.
34. *OR*, 10(1):523.

Southern army was breaking apart and that twenty thousand to thirty thousand secessionists had deserted. Yet there is no evidence that Halleck ever considered moving in for the kill, being deterred by the fears of using a vulnerable railroad for supplies and of the crippling effect of summer swamp fever upon his army. It would be his last opportunity to catch virtually the entire western Confederate army concentrated. Of course, the Rebels had already escaped once under his nose, and even if he did advance, they might succeed again.[35]

The second option would be to launch a joint army-navy expedition against Vicksburg, along the Mississippi River 240 miles from Corinth, the capture of which, according to Grant and Sherman, would have been invaluable and possibly have shortened the war. The town was then lightly defended by a small division. Halleck implied to Sherman that he preferred this option but that Washington blocked him. Such was not the case. With Memphis falling to the Federal navy on June 6, the theater commander naively hoped that the gunboats could quickly take the Mississippi town. Only after the first such attempt would he commit the army. Halleck could only see problems with a move west to Vicksburg: falling water levels that could make the rivers unnavigable and a railroad that could be severed at will by Rebel cavalry. Besides, the Confederates could reinforce Vicksburg by rail faster than an expedition could arrive from Memphis.[36]

Halleck, again focusing on the center of the Confederate line, selected his third option and sent Buell's army east to Chattanooga, taking advantage of Ormsby Mitchel's occupation of northern Alabama. The line of communications would be the Memphis and Charleston Railroad, one hundred miles of which were already in Federal possession. This move would also suit Lincoln's political obsession of liberating East Tennessee. If the town was evacuated by the time Buell arrived, he would move on to Atlanta. Vicksburg would belong to Grant (who resumed command of the Army of the Tennessee), while Corinth and vicinity went to the Army of the Mississippi. There would again be a two-front war in the West—the Mississippi Valley and the Tennessee Valley.[37]

35. Ibid., 669–71; Catton, *Grant Moves South*, 280; James Lee McDonough, *War in Kentucky: From Shiloh to Perryville* (Knoxville: University of Tennessee Press, 1994), 35–36; Nevins, *Ordeal for the Union*, 3(2):152–53. On several occasions I have heard historian Edwin C. Bearss declare Halleck's failure to pursue as one of the great missed opportunities of the war—the general should have "pushed them into the swamps." Past historians Bruce Catton and Allan Nevins have concurred. More recently, James Lee McDonough has expressed sympathy with Halleck's decision not to pursue. *War in Kentucky*, 35–36. I agree with Bearss.

36. McPherson, *Battle Cry of Freedom*, 512; Nevins, *Ordeal for the Union*, 3(2):152–53; McDonough, *War in Kentucky*, 33–34.

37. Archer Jones, *Civil War Command and Strategy: The Process of Victory and Defeat* (New York: Free Press, 1992), 85–86; Hagerman, *American Civil War*, 176.

On paper this looked good, but there were problems. The Confederates soon assembled a new army in Mississippi to confront Grant, comprised of the former New Orleans garrison, a transferred division from East Tennessee, a huge influx of volunteers hoping to avoid conscription, and exchanged Fort Donelson and Island No. 10 prisoners. As for Buell—there would be no bold push to Chattanooga.

PART 3

DECLINE OF THE BUELL INFLUENCE

6

The Chattanooga Campaign
Conservative War Aims

FROM THE OUTSET, Buell opposed approaching Chattanooga along the line of the Memphis and Charleston. The railroad crossed the Tennessee River at two points, and with both bridges down, the troops would have to be ferried across. The army would be strung out for miles, exposing its flank to attack. The railroad, due to disrepair and a lack of rolling stock, was "greatly overrated," Buell believed, while it made a "tempting object" for raiders. He desired to approach Chattanooga through Middle Tennessee via McMinnville, using Nashville, not Memphis, as his base. He was overruled. Halleck could see only the obvious—the shortest distance between two points is a straight line.[1]

Buell initially marched with only McCook's, Crittenden's, Wood's, and Nelson's divisions—twenty-five thousand infantry and artillery. To lighten the load he allowed only twelve wagons per regiment and five per battery, with an additional division train of about seventy-five wagons for food and forage. With such limited transportation, the army could get only five days' distance from a railroad source.[2]

On June 11 McCook's and Crittenden's divisions began their eastward march, the former from Corinth and the latter from Booneville. McCook arrived at Tuscumbia on the fifteenth, followed by Crittenden, whose troops picked up the line of march at Iuka. Wood's division entered Tuscumbia on the sixteenth and began repairs on the downed trestle there, leaving Nelson's division at Iuka. Engineers rigged an old steamer with two barges, and on this span Wood's troops crossed the river to Florence on the twenty-second. The balance of the army was to follow, but a false report of a threatened attack upon Nelson by ten thousand secessionists at Iuka suspended the movement.[3]

The lumbering pace of Buell's army began to worry Halleck. Realizing that Washington expected results in the West, he understood that at the first signs of

---

1. Cist, *Army of the Cumberland*, 41; *OR*, 16(2):33–34.

2. *OR*, 16(1):281, 16(2):5, 25.

3. Williams, *Grant Rises in the West*, 29, 467 n. 9; Van Horne, *Army of the Cumberland*, 1:142–43; *OR*, 16(1):486, 16(2):18–19, 27; *New York Times*, June 26, 1862. The troops at Tuscumbia crossed by boat at Jackson's Ford, three miles north of town, taking a full week to cross. *New York Tribune*, Aug. 23, 1862.

inactivity, troops would be ordered east to bolster McClellan. Hoping to forestall such action, Halleck attempted to entice the War Department with the thought of moving on to Atlanta after the capture of Chattanooga. It did not work. Some twenty-five thousand troops were ordered to Virginia with all possible haste. Halleck now played his trump card, stating that "under the circumstances, the Chattanooga expedition must be postponed." Fearful of letting East Tennessee slip from his grasp once again, Lincoln blinked. With the troop transfer canceled, Halleck revoked his order, at least for the time being.[4]

On June 21, with the bulk of the Army of the Ohio still in the Florence-Tuscumbia area, the western commander stepped up the pressure. "I am not satisfied with the progress which has been made," he wrote Buell. "There has been a negligence somewhere which I trust you to investigate and correct immediately. I repeat, the [rail] road to Decatur must be put in running order with all possible haste." The Ohioan replied the same day, noting his own frustration with the progress of affairs and repeating, "we have derived no benefit from the road [Memphis and Charleston] worth naming."[5]

Buell continued to fret about Rebel incursions. Despite rumors that a large portion of the western Confederate army was headed for Virginia (fully believed by the War Department), local unionists believed otherwise: as soon as the Army of the Ohio spread out, Beauregard would attack. Newspaper reports and intelligence received at army headquarters confirmed that the secessionists had a dangerous seventy thousand to eighty thousand men at or near Okolona and another fifteen thousand, under Earl Van Dorn and Sterling Price, at Fulton, twenty-five miles east of Okolona. As late as June 23, reports indicated that the Confederate army, now under Gen. Braxton Bragg, remained in position. Buell thus breathed a sigh of relief when, on June 25, McCook's and Crittenden's divisions crossed to the north bank at Tuscumbia, arriving at Florence on the twenty-eighth, while Nelson's division, with the army's wagon train, crossed at Eastport. Wood's division remained at Tuscumbia and vicinity, transporting supplies and repairing the track. In the meantime, Thomas had been relieved of his command of the Corinth garrison and returned to his division, which marched to Iuka, only to be detained there by Halleck until the end of July.[6]

The weakness of the Memphis and Charleston as a supply artery soon became

---

4. *OR*, 16(2):59, 62, 82, 88. Lincoln reduced his request to 10,000 men on July 5, but he again backed down. *OR*, 16(2):95, 100.

5. *OR*, 16(1):604, 16(2):44.

6. *New York Times*, June 22, July 5, 1862; Cist, *Army of the Cumberland*, 42; Van Horne, *Army of the Cumberland*, 1:143; *OR*, 16(2):25, 27, 53. Don Carlos Buell, "East Tennessee and the Campaign of Perryville," in *B&L*, 3:35. The combined strength of Beauregard's and Van Dorn's armies at that time (less a 3,000-man division that had been sent to Chattanooga) was only 45,000. *OR*, 10(2):604.

evident. Only two locomotives and a dozen boxcars operated between Corinth and Tuscumbia. In mid-June raiding guerillas burned the trestles at Bear Creek and Tuscumbia Creek, the last not being rebuilt until the end of the month. Poor management exacerbated the problem; a trip between Corinth and Decatur required three days. In an effort to increase the rolling stock, Buell directed Mitchel to ferry locomotives across from the north bank at Decatur, but he did nothing. Six locomotives were ordered from Louisville, to be floated by transport down the Tennessee River, but only two arrived, and one of those did not work.[7]

In order to avoid the destroyed Bear Creek trestle between Iuka and Corinth, four steamers shipped supplies up the Tennessee River to Eastport, the head of navigation, where laborers loaded them on wagons for the six-mile trip to Iuka. Thomas diverted two hundred wagons for this duty, but three thousand loads soon accumulated at Eastport. Buell attempted to acquire some of the quartermaster wagons at Pittsburg Landing for Eastport, but Halleck blocked the move.[8]

The Tennessee River was nearly impassable due to Culbert Shoals (only twenty-eight inches deep). In 1828 the Federal government had attempted to cut a canal around it, but the project ended in failure, and at the time of the war, the canal lay in ruins. Light-draught steamers could navigate the shoals with skilled pilots (forced to work under penalty of death), but even so the boats had to be dragged by laborers. Three steamers soon scraped bottom, leaving only one to make the trip, and that vessel could carry only thirty to forty tons at a time. When the water gauge continued to drop and river transportation ceased altogether, the Federals started an overland relay of wagons between Eastport and Florence.[9]

Buell began to consider alternatives, notably the Alabama Central Railroad and the Nashville and Chattanooga Railroad, which linked up with the Memphis and Charleston north of the Tennessee River at Decatur and Stevenson, respectively. These arteries, of course, had their own inviting targets. No fewer than thirteen bridges spanned the fifty-five-mile stretch of the Alabama Central between Nashville and Culleoka, Tennessee, including the six-hundred-foot-long Duck River bridge at Columbia and the eleven-hundred-foot-long trestle at Culleoka, ten miles below Columbia. Already the Rebels had struck the seven-hundred-foot-long Elk River bridge ten miles north of Pulaski, Tennessee, as well as a trestle a few miles to the south. Between Pulaski and Athens, Alabama, there was a highly vulnerable quarter-mile curving tunnel, which the Rebels had filled with debris, and another trestle stood south of Elkmont, Alabama.[10]

7. *OR*, 10(2):642, 16(1):249, 251, 280, 390–91, 604, 608, 610, 16(2):43, 82, 84, 89, 92–93.

8. *OR*, 16(1):339, 604, 16(2):22, 71, 73.

9. *OR*, 16(1):477, 602–3, 16(2):4.

10. McDonough, *War in Kentucky*, 43, 45; *OR*, 16(1):248.

Until engineer crews could repair the Elk River bridge, supplies would have to be hauled forty-five miles by ordinary road between Reynold's Station, Tennessee, and Athens. Since the army needed two hundred tons per day by this route, Buell committed all available wagons to the Reynold's Station relay—100 from Mitchel, 100 from Negley in Nashville, and 210 of his own vehicles from Florence, a total of 410. The number would eventually be raised to 500. This proved sufficient as long as Thomas's 150 wagons could forward one hundred tons daily from Eastport-Iuka via the Memphis and Charleston. By late June, however, the two remaining operating locomotives on that line broke down. The Alabama Central would now have to supply three hundred tons daily, exclusive of ammunition and quartermaster stores.[11]

Buell arrived in Athens on June 29, expecting to find 150,000 rations of forage for the horses and mules; he found none. The reasons were twofold. The supply base in Nashville was not getting three hundred tons daily from Louisville for reasons not yet understood by Buell. Also, insufficient wagons for the Reynold's Station relay caused delays. Since the army needed one hundred thousand pounds of food daily (sixty wagons), and a trip could not be made in less than five days, some 350 wagons were needed for commissary supplies alone. The quartermaster required (even for half rations) 700 wagons for forage but had only 150. In short, the expedition had come to a grinding halt, and the animals had to be immediately placed on half rations. There were simply too few wagons to cover the breaks in the railroad and continue the advance.[12]

By early July Halleck finally conceded the inevitable and abandoned the Memphis and Charleston. He remained adamant that the plan would have succeeded but for Mitchel's negligence in ferrying several locomotives across the Tennessee River from Decatur. On July 2 a staff officer wired that it would take three days to cross an engine, even if they had the proper rope, which they did not. A livid Halleck wrote Buell, "Had General Mitchel sent over locomotives and cars, as promised a month ago, it would have been of immense advantage." Although Buell had never been keen on transferring rolling stock to the south bank (he preferred to abandon the Memphis and Charleston altogether), he perfunctorily ordered a locomotive ferried across the river at Decatur.[13]

---

11. *OR*, 16(2):28–31, 39, 42, 44, 45, 68, 70, 71, 73, 79; Van Horne, *Army of the Cumberland*, 1:143. Thomas's wagons continued to haul freight overland from Eastport to Florence throughout July. Between July 10 and 23, steamers brought in 300,000 rations (at 3 1/4 pounds per ration). After that date the water gauge dropped so low that the river was eliminated as a supply source. *OR*, 16(1):339.

12. *OR*, 16(1):33, 516, 16(2):54, 73, 78, 79, 85, 101, 104, 123, 148.

13. *OR*, 16(1):82, 84, 89–90, 92–93. Kenneth Williams supports Halleck. He has asserted that Buell should have crossed his army at Eastport, not Tuscumbia. Despite Buell's claim that he was slowed by

According to Mitchel's biographer-son, the Third Division commander fumed at Buell's plodding pace. For four days the two generals conferred at Huntsville (the first meeting lasted over four hours), during which time Mitchel pleaded for an immediate advance to Chattanooga. Buell proved unyielding, at one time folding his map and walking away. Mitchel had had enough. He submitted his resignation and requested an immediate leave of absence. For his part, Buell, in postwar years, adamantly denied any such consultations occurred.[14]

The general became increasingly apprehensive of an attack upon Mitchel's advanced detachments at Battle Creek and along the Nashville and Chattanooga Railroad. On July 4 he belatedly ordered McCook's and Crittenden's divisions to Battle Creek, though the lead division would not arrive until the thirteenth. A brigade was also organized from some of Mitchel's scattered units and ordered to McMinnville and another sent to Murfreesboro. With Nelson's division at Athens, Wood's at Decatur, and Thomas's in the rear west of Athens, the Army of the Ohio now stretched a dangerous seventy-five miles.[15]

On July 8 Lincoln (through Halleck) expressed dissatisfaction with Buell's progress. "The long time taken by you to reach Chattanooga will enable the enemy to anticipate you by concentrating a large force to meet you," Halleck warned. Buell blamed the long march, hot weather, and, of course, the detested Mitchel. Until supplies could be stockpiled, the railroads repaired, and the pontoon bridge at Stevenson constructed, no advance could take place, although he added, "the dissatisfaction of the President pains me exceedingly."[16]

The situation worsened; between July 9 and 16, Buell received no provisions. His chief of staff, James B. Fry, sent a frenzied message to Col. Thomas Sword, in charge of supplies at Louisville: "the army will starve unless there is more activity and suc-

---

having to rebuild the track, McCook and Crittenden moved as rapidly as possible, and Nelson did only minor repair work at Iuka. Only Wood's division literally followed the track to Decatur, and it arrived only two days after the main column marched into Athens. Besides, Buell was initially just as optimistic about the use of the Memphis and Charleston as was the theater commander. *Grant Rises in the West,* 27–29, 467 n.9.

Halleck later bristled at the Buell Commission's conclusion that the use of the Memphis and Charleston as a supply artery had been faulty. "General Buell had no other line of supply than this road till he reached Decatur and connected with Nashville," he wrote. The problem lay in "too large supply trains and in not living more upon the country." *OR,* 16(1):12.

14. Mitchel, *Ormsby Macknight Mitchel,* 339–43; Engle, *Buell,* 264; Don Carlos Buell, "Operations in North Alabama," in *B&L,* 3:708.

15. Van Horne, *Army of the Cumberland,* 1:144–45; *OR,* 16(1):33–34, 16(2):87–88, 105. One of Wood's brigades did not finish work on the railroad until early July, and it did not cross the river until July 6. *OR,* 16(1):706.

16. *OR,* 16(2):104, 122–23.

cess in throwing forward supplies." Sword placed the blame upon Brigadier General Boyle, who was using the trains to transport troops in Kentucky, and upon two collisions, which had damaged four locomotives. Fry insisted that the Alabama Central could transport three hundred tons daily, only seventy-five of which were needed for food. The fault lay somewhere between Nashville and Louisville. On July 16 the Nashville commissary officer wrote that three steamers, loaded with one million rations, all of which should have come by rail, had recently started from Louisville. Horses continued to come by steamboat rather than being driven overland, and commissary supplies also came by river in order to use the Louisville and Nashville for sutler's stores and private freight.[17]

Buell foraged the countryside, but northern Alabama and the southern tier of Tennessee counties had been cultivated mainly in cotton, and the planters never kept stockpiles of corn and meat. The country east of Huntsville was bad, and that east of Stevenson even worse. No forage arrived by rail until August 1, meaning that the animals had to make do with the meager local supplies. The situation did not measurably improve until mid-August, when a new corn crop became available.[18]

Buell had counted upon the Alabama Central being operational by the end of June; it would be unavailable until the end of July. Four companies of Michigan engineers, along with a large infantry detail, worked rain or shine on the Elk River bridge. At the same time, two engineer companies toiled on the downed trestle near the tunnel, while other details labored on Richland Creek Bridge No. 2, repairing two miles of damaged track, and clearing out the tunnel. In mid-July two engineer companies moved up the track to repair the damaged Duck River bridge, which had been washed away by high water.[19]

Buell was becoming as fixated on the Alabama Central as Halleck was with the Memphis and Charleston. He unnecessarily committed six of his Michigan engineer companies to the Alabama Central, a line that would have to be abandoned as the army marched east anyway. Theoretically, freight could be hauled via the Alabama Central and transferred to the Memphis and Charleston north of the Tennessee River, thus giving two supply lines to Chattanooga. The choke point, however, was not south of Nashville but north of the city. Buell did not get three hundred tons daily because Nashville was not receiving that amount. Rather than squandering Wood's division on the Memphis and Charleston (south of the Tennessee River)

17. Ibid., 155, 165, 173; J. D. Bingham to J. F. Miller, Aug. 18, 1862, Letters Received, Jan.–Nov. 1862, Department of the Cumberland, 1821–1920, RG 393, NA.

18. *OR*, 16(1):32–33, 279, 280, 390, 473, 516, 517, 706.

19. Ibid., 33, 248, 297, 298; Charles R. Sligh, *History of the Service of the First Regiment Michigan Engineers and Mechanics during the Civil War, 1861–1865* (Grand Rapids: White, 1921), 50. A train stranded between two downed bridges south of the tunnel could not resume service until the end of August.

and the engineer companies on the Alabama Central, all available resources should have been concentrated on the Nashville and Chattanooga. True, Buell was now in the process of forwarding troops there, but would they arrive in time?[20]

As the Army of the Ohio penetrated into the heart of the Tennessee Valley, two issues increasingly emerged—the need for a policy toward the civilian population and what to do with fugitive slaves. The Lincoln administration had adopted a conciliatory policy based upon the belief that a large portion of the Southern population remained loyal unionists, silenced by an elitist-led opposition. Political reconstruction remained the goal, a policy that aligned Buell's "soft war" views with those of the administration. The army commander wished to restore the antebellum Union, not effect social change. But Buell failed to recognize the shifting attitudes of both the army and the government by the spring of 1862. The issue came to a head in the spring of 1862. Initially, Buell and Mitchel meshed, but the brigadier became increasingly exasperated and impatient with the army commander's slow pace and "extreme leniency." "His is the *slowest* person I have ever had the misfortune to be associated with, and [he] tries my patience in the severest manner almost every day," Mitchel wrote his family. Additionally, his longing for an independent command was not beyond intrigue (he commonly undercut the army commander in his letters to Chase), and he cringed at Buell's affinity with Nelson, an officer whom he despised.[21]

The feeling was reciprocated. "Gen. Mitchel has never been on very good terms with either the commander-in-chief [Buell] or the other division commanders of the Army of the Ohio," the New York press reported. The final issue appears to have been the destroyed Decatur bridge over the Tennessee River. Buell had given Mitchel permission to destroy it if he were threatened. Based solely upon a rumor that the Confederates might attack from Corinth, Mitchel ordered the trestle torched. Buell immediately complained to Washington, and Halleck denounced the move as "a most foolish operation." The trestle now had to be rebuilt, requiring three months.[22]

Precisely how much Tory sentiment existed in northern Alabama remained in dispute; few joined the Federal army that spring. An Ohio soldier remarked that Huntsville was "the worst Sesesh town we have had the fortune to go into; no attempt to disguise their sentiment, they boldly proclaim they are Secessionists." The

20. *OR*, 16(1):33, 279, 301, 342, 706, 16(2):104.

21. Engle, *Buell*, 182–84, 196–98; *OR*, 16(1):637; Mitchel, *Ormsby Macknight Mitchel*, 271.

22. *New York Tribune*, July 14, 1862; Buell, "Operations in North Alabama," 702, 705; Robert Dunnavant, *Decatur, Alabama: Yankee Foothold in Dixie, 1861–1865* (Athens, Ala.: Pea Ridge, 1995), 51.

women in town, according to Colonel Beatty, were "outspoken in their hostility, and marvelously bitter."[23]

During Mitchel's three-month occupation of the area, his troops increasingly came under bushwhacking attacks and small raids by partisans and irregular cavalry. Although the evidence suggests that these were spotty, the issue became magnified in camp. Mitchel's eight-thousand-man division was spread between Huntsville east toward Jasper and Battle Creek, Tennessee, and in Stevenson, Alabama, leaving large unprotected gaps. By July, guerrilla attacks had spread into Middle Tennessee, prompting Brigadier General Negley, commanding in Nashville, to fine citizens if telegraph wire had been cut on or near their property. Guerillas hanged two loyalist civilians near Pulaski. When the attacks continued, Mitchel increasingly began to turn a blind eye toward the retribution inflicted by his men. On May 2 the hamlet of Paint Rock, Alabama, widely known as a haunt for bushwhackers and bridge burners, was burned to the ground by Col. John Beatty, with Mitchel's express approval.[24]

The Paint Rock incident paled in significance next to another that occurred in Athens, Alabama, twelve miles north of the Tennessee River, that same day. Col. John B. Turchin's Eighth Brigade entered the town in a nasty mood. The 18th Ohio had been chased out by Confederate cavalry, with some local citizens taking sniping shots from their dwellings. Turchin, a former czarist officer, announced that he would shut his eyes for two hours, implying that the troops had free license in the town. His men took their cue, looting Athens, raping several black women, and so traumatizing one pregnant white woman that she later miscarried and died.[25]

The initial Northern response was one of outrage. It soon came out that Turchin's Eighth, which included two regiments of unruly Chicago Irish boys, had only months earlier plundered several houses in Bowling Green, Kentucky, but that incident had been "hushed up." The press generally denounced their actions, saying that traditional restraint against civilians had been violated. The Louisville papers demanded that Mitchel give an explanation. The division commander, himself shocked by the scale of the violence, issued only an implausible denial and did little

23. *OR*, 16(1):481, 16(2):124; McDonough, *War in Kentucky*, 90.

24. Mark Grimsley, *The Hard Hand of War: Union Military Policy toward Southern Civilians, 1861–1865* (New York: Cambridge University Press, 1995), 79; Beatty, *Citizen Soldier*, 138–39; Benjamin Franklin Cooling, *Fort Donelson's Legacy: War and Society in Kentucky and Tennessee, 1862–1863* (Knoxville: University of Tennessee Press, 1997), 73; *OR*, 16(1):636.

25. East, "Lincoln's Russian General," 112–13; Roy Morris Jr., "The Sack of Athens," *Civil War Times Illustrated* 24 (Feb. 1986): 26–32; *OR*, 10(2):212, 16(2):273–75; Spillard Horrall, *History of the Forty-Second Indiana Volunteer Infantry* (Chicago: Horrall, 1892), 128; Lawrence B. Pabst, "The Sack and Occupation of Athens, Alabama," *Bulletin of the North Alabama Historical Association* 4 (1959): 18–20.

more than rebuke Turchin. He refused to compensate the citizens who redressed him and declared that he certainly could not arrest an entire brigade.[26]

Mitchel ordered Col. John S. Norton of the 21st Ohio to initiate an investigation, but the plan backfired. Not only had full-scale plundering occurred, Norton discovered, but also Mitchel had been speculating in cotton, a fact the colonel revealed to the press. Buell now became involved. In early June 1862 he arrived in Huntsville, preferred charges against Turchin and three colonels, and ordered the breakup of the Eighth Brigade. Turchin protested that his brigade had seized two million dollars' worth of Rebel property in northern Alabama, but "instead of thanks I receive insults." Turchin and Col. Carter Gazlay were subsequently convicted and dismissed from the service.[27]

The tide of public and government opinion soon took a startling reversal. Norton had gone to Washington to prefer charges against Mitchel. He repeated his accusations before the Joint Committee for the Conduct of the War. While the committee took no action, Secretary of War Stanton did—against Norton. He ordered the colonel's arrest for leaving his command without approval and for violating military protocol. Norton went home in disgrace, and Mitchel was cleared of all charges.[28]

Turchin's dismissal at Buell's insistence (the court had urged leniency) generated sympathy for the colonel. Brig. Gen. James A. Garfield believed that Turchin had been cashiered "for not dealing quietly enough" with civilians. While Colonel Beatty did not sanction the wholesale plundering, he had less patience with Buell's conciliatory policy: "He [Buell] is inaugurating the dancing-master policy: 'By your leave, my dear sir, we will have a fight, that is, if you are sufficiently fortified; no hurry; take your own time.'" What the men wanted, Beatty concluded, was "an iron policy that will not tolerate treason, that will demand immediate and unconditional obedience as the price of protection." The Northern press soon claimed that Norton had exaggerated the entire episode. Even the Democratic *Cincinnati Gazette* condemned Buell for "guarding the property of secessionists, while his own soldiers are suffering." The War Department, under pressure from the governor of Illinois and others, soon overturned Turchin's dismissal; indeed, upon his return to Chicago, Turchin received a brigadier's commission. Mitchel subsequently transferred to South Caro-

26. *Cincinnati Enquirer,* July 15, 16, 1862; *OR,* 10(2):212–13. For soldier disapproval of Turchin's actions, see McDonough, *War in Kentucky,* 95. For pro-Mitchel reaction by his officers, see "Letter Submitted to the Louisville Journal," July 15, 1862, Box 9, George Thomas Papers, Misc. Papers, 1861–62, Generals' Papers, RG 94, NA.

27. Grimsley, *Hard Hand of War,* 82; *OR,* 16(1):637, 16(2):71, 92, 98–99.

28. Grimsley, *Hard Hand of War,* 82.

lina, where he contracted yellow fever and died in October 1862. Command of the division went to Brig. Gen. William Sooy Smith.[29]

The next incident of note occurred on August 5. A sick Brig. Gen. Robert Mc-Cook, commander of the Third Brigade and older brother to Maj. Gen. Alexander McCook, traveled in an ambulance near New Market, Alabama, in advance of his brigade. His escort rode ahead, leaving him with only four men. At that moment a hundred or so screaming irregulars burst from the woods. The driver turned the ambulance around in an attempt to make for the column but was soon overtaken. McCook, in a gown, shouted for the Rebels not to shoot, but one galloped up and put a bullet in his side, leaving him mortally wounded. When word reached the nearby brigade, the troops initiated a fruitless search. Out of control with rage over the murder, some of the men torched five nearby farms before being restrained by superiors. When Col. Dan McCook heard of his brother's death, he vowed that he would never take another Rebel prisoner "as long as God gives me breath." Unable to catch the guerrillas, the Federals targeted those upon whom they could get their hands—nearby civilians.[30]

Buell did not want soldier conduct to undercut reconciliation, believing that the war should be waged against the Southern army and not its people. The end result, however, was a decline in his credibility and polarization within the army. Due to the changing nature of the war, patience was wearing thin with the solicitous treatment of the populace. Although not true, the soldiers perceived Buell as coddling civilians who aided the enemy. "The citizens say to us," wrote Maj. Joseph W. Keifer on July 14, "that Buell is as good a secessionist as they want in our ranks." Garfield believed that it was "better in this country, occupied by our troops, for a citizen to be a rebel than to be a Union man." A soldier disgustedly wrote of civilian response: "'Mr. Buell is a gentleman, we will speak to him.' 'Mr. Buell pays us our prices, not the low rates of your government.' 'Mr. Buell hunts up our niggers.' 'Mr. Buell will make you find our horses.'"[31]

In truth, Mitchel had been more lenient to civilians than credited and Buell more firm than popularly perceived. In later testimony unionist civilians suggested that both officers had adopted a conciliatory policy, believing that loyalist sentiment in the area remained strong. It should be noted that neither Buell nor Mitchel opposed foraging, though they typically limited it to corn for the horses and mules. On one occasion, when under duress, Buell ordered the countryside scoured for everything

29. Ibid., 83–85; East, "Lincoln's Russian General," 116; McDonough, *War in Kentucky*, 98.

30. *OR*, 16(1):838–41; McDonough, *War in Kentucky*, 96. Thereafter, Dan McCook had inscribed on the flag of the 52d Ohio, "McCook's Avengers." Nixon B. Stewart, *Dan McCook's Regiment, 52nd O.V.I.: A History of the Regiment, Its Campaigns, and Battles* (Alliance, Ohio: Review Print, 1900), 23.

31. Engle, *Buell*, 271–72; *Chicago Tribune*, Sept. 6, 1862.

short of starving the people out, but only a few old cows and sheep were collected, hardly worth the effort.[32]

The Buell Commission later implied that a harsher policy would have prevented raiding. The country should have been laid waste on either side of the railroad where destruction occurred. The Tory population strongly rejected such a conclusion, however, insisting that the raiders were sent for the specific purpose of destruction and that the local population had virtually no control over the matter. Besides, when raids occurred, Union foraging in fact did increase, creating additional hardships for civilians anyway. If any breakdown in the conciliatory policy occurred, it was in making no distinction between secessionists and loyalists. Secessionists, therefore, enjoyed the benefit of Union protection, while loyalists had their supplies taken along with everyone else.[33]

Buell's policy regarding fugitive slaves further exacerbated the situation. He wanted to have as little to do with them as possible, considered them property, and ordered them returned to their owners. He turned out of camp those blacks not absolutely necessary for the work of the army. Thousands of fugitive slaves were coldheartedly left on the south bank of the Tennessee River when the army marched toward Chattanooga.[34]

Racism was endemic in the Army of the Ohio. Talk of national emancipation led two hundred men of the 2d Kentucky (Fourth Division) to desert en masse to the Rebels in early August 1862. Yet there were growing signs of abolitionist sympathy, especially among upper midwestern regiments such as the 21st Wisconsin and the Chicago 24th Illinois. Ohioan George Landrum believed that the Third Division was becoming increasingly abolitionist. Jack F. Pase of the 29th Indiana wrote contemptuously that in his company there were "some of the rankest kind of Abolitionists." Colonel Beatty expressed disgust at the treatment given slaves: "We worm out these poor creatures a knowledge of the places where stores are secreted, or compel them to serve as guides, and then turn them out to be scourged or murdered." He believed, "there must be a change in this regard before we shall be worthy of success." Garfield observed that many former anti-abolitionists in his brigade had begun to link "slavery and the rebellion together."[35]

A reporter of the *Cincinnati Gazette* observed: "Buell . . . cares more for guarding

32. *OR*, 16(1):351, 474, 481, 482, 603, 16(2):124.

33. *OR*, 16(1):256–57, 269, 350, 479, 480, 495.

34. *OR*, 16(1):351, 617, 16(2):44, 303.

35. *Mobile Advertiser & Register*, Aug. 15, 1862; Prokopowicz, *All for the Regiment*, 124–25; McDonough, *War in Kentucky*, 92–93; Engle, *Buell*, 249. See also D. B. Griffin to wife, Aug. 13, 1862, in Albertson, *Letters Home to Minnesota*, letter 52; and Norris and Martin, "Three Civil War Letters of James A. Garfield," 250.

a rebel cabbage patch, or enslaving a liberated Negro, than he does for gaining a triumph over the enemy. . . . General Buell is so intensely pro-slavery that I have no doubt he would sacrifice every officer in his District, for the sake of returning to bondage a single slave." Buell persisted in his policy of returning fugitive slaves, even after Congress enacted a law to the contrary. Several officers of the 2d Minnesota openly refused to return loyal blacks despite Buell's order. Writing to a friend on July 15, George Landrum concluded: "I wish we had fewer pro-slavery Gen[-eral]s."[36]

On July 12 Buell's run of bad luck appeared to be over. That day he received notification that the Nashville and Chattanooga Railroad was at last operational. It had not been easy; engineer and civilian mechanic crews had labored on the Elk Creek bridge for a month. Fortunately, the Rebels had not attacked the most vulnerable target on the road—the twenty-two-hundred-foot tunnel two miles south of Cowan, Tennessee.[37]

But the very next day, July 13, before a single train made it through to Stevenson, Alabama, Rebel raiders struck. At 4:00 A.M. a brigade led by the increasingly notorious Nathan Bedford Forrest attacked the garrison at Murfreesboro. The Federals made victory relatively easy for him: the troops slept soundly, no defenses had been erected, and because of bad blood between the colonels of the 3d Minnesota and 9th Michigan, which had spilt over to the troops, the infantry had been scattered in and about town for two miles. The debacle cost Buell one thousand men killed and captured as well as significant damage to the Nashville and Chattanooga track and the destruction of the Stones River bridge. Eight days later Forrest appeared at Mill Creek, near Nashville, destroying the bridges at that place.[38]

Buell immediately diverted troops from his army in northern Alabama to secure the railroad south of Nashville. Nelson's division was ordered to Murfreesboro. One brigade went by rail through Nashville, but due to the washed-out Duck River bridge, it did not arrive at Murfreesboro until July 18. Two brigades of Wood's division proceeded by forced marches from Decatur to Shelbyville, Tennessee, and subsequently to Decherd. Wood's remaining brigade went to Stevenson. One of McCook's brigades at Battle Creek went to work on the Nashville and Chattanooga between Stevenson and Decherd. Two units of the Third Division, the 18th Ohio and five companies of the 24th Illinois, concentrated at Cowan to beef up security at

36. Engle, *Buell*, 201–3, 248, 273; Landrum quoted in Prokopowicz, *All for the Regiment*, 125; *Chicago Tribune*, Sept. 12, 1862.

37. *OR*, 16(1):33, 35, 16(2):83, 93; McDonough, *War in Kentucky*, 43.

38. *OR*, 16(1):298, 794–807, 16(2):154; Prokopowicz, *All for the Regiment*, 129–33; Van Horne, *Army of the Cumberland*, 1:147.

the vital tunnel. A garrison of fourteen hundred men was assembled at Tullahoma, Tennessee. Engineers constructed blockhouses, sufficient to resist field artillery, along the Nashville and Chattanooga and stockades nine feet high and twelve inches thick along the Huntsville track.[39]

While repair crews labored on the Stones River bridge, supplies had to be hauled by wagon to Murfreesboro. The bridge was completed on July 28, and the next day the first train arrived at Stevenson with 210,000 rations. A second train arrived the next day with an additional 160,000 rations.[40]

It had taken the Army of the Ohio six weeks to edge toward Chattanooga and secure lines of communication. Since the Confederate army in Mississippi was hardly pinned down, Buell relied upon Bragg to simply sit passively while he methodically maneuvered. But the Confederate general had other ideas. On July 30 a dismayed Buell learned that the secessionist army was on the move, with the vanguard already in Chattanooga. Not only had the prize been lost, but the enemy could soon be on the offensive as well. "You can judge yourself of the probability of the concentrating of a heavy force against Middle Tennessee, now that they have nothing to apprehend in Mississippi," Buell wrote Halleck (recently promoted to general in chief in Washington) in an obvious swipe aimed at Grant, again commanding the Army of the Tennessee. He was partially correct. The Federals had not yet developed cavalry capable of intercepting the Confederates and making penetrating raids of their own.[41]

The president hoped that Halleck would coordinate an offensive by George McClellan's recently defeated Army of the Potomac and John Pope's Army of Virginia, poised north of Richmond. Halleck also detected a hidden agenda. Lincoln and Stanton wanted him to be the point man in firing McClellan; he refused to bite.[42]

In a cabinet meeting on August 3, Chase went on a tear about both McClellan

39. *OR*, 16(1):33, 35, 16(2):149; Charles C. Gilbert, "Bragg's Invasion of Kentucky," *Southern Bivouac* 1 (Aug. 1885): 218. Colonel Beatty derided Buell's "insane effort to garrison the whole country." *Citizen Soldier,* 161. Lt. Col. Nicholas Anderson wrote of Nelson's forced march: "Up at 2 A.M. and off immediately. Nelson a fool. Horrible march of 19 miles to Pulaski in terrible heat. No rations, many reported dying. Damnable shame. Reached Pulaski at 1 P.M. with only 40 men in the regiment." Anderson to wife, July 15, 1862, in Anderson, *Letters and Journals of General Nicholas Longworth Anderson,* 155.

40. *OR*, 16(1):608–9, 16(2):230.

41. *OR*, 16(2):236–37. The closest attempt at a penetration raid was James J. Andrew's spy ring, which resulted in the "Great Locomotive Chase" of April 1862. The Grierson raid in Mississippi in April 1863 was an example of how the Confederates were forced to tie down troops in an effort to defend territory. In defense of Buell, he had long lobbied for more cavalry, though with few results. See *OR*, 10(2):183, 203–4.

42. Donald, *Lincoln,* 369–70.

and Buell. The president himself had declared that "a McClellan in the army was lamentable, but a combination of McClellan and Buell was deplorable." According to Chase, Buell should "be replaced [by] a more active *fearless* and energetic leader in the [present] emergency." Besides, his limited goals on slavery proved unacceptable. When asked by Secretary of State William Seward whom he preferred over Buell, Chase deferred the issue to Halleck. The general in chief argued to retain them both, characterizing Buell as "slow but safe." Stanton held no faith in either McClellan or Buell.[43]

Three days later Halleck warned Buell, "there is a great dissatisfaction here at the slow movement of your army toward Chattanooga." The question was simple, the answer confused. Was the Army of the Ohio on the defensive or the offensive? At 5:45 P.M. on August 7, Buell telegraphed assurance to Halleck that, despite the large force of Confederates under Maj. Gen. Edmund Kirby Smith moving into East Tennessee, "I shall march upon Chattanooga at the earliest possible day."[44]

Reading between the lines, however, Halleck perceived a different story. First, Buell conceded that work on the fourteen-hundred-foot pontoon bridge at Bridgeport had not even begun. The nails and pitch ordered in mid-July sat unused in a Nashville warehouse. Only one mill in the area could cut the long boards necessary, and it was worked night and day, despite the constant threat of guerrilla raids. The pontoons also still had to be built, so it would be the end of August before the bridge would be operational.[45]

Second, if Buell was actually on the offensive, he would have made every effort to close up on the Sequatchie Valley and come within sight of Chattanooga in order to prevent Bragg from crossing the Tennessee River. But Buell seemed unconcerned, being aware that the secessionists had limited means of ferrying (one small boat and several flats as it turned out) and that it would consume a great deal of time in crossing a river one-half to three-quarters of a mile wide. Further, he could concentrate only thirty thousand men against what he believed to be sixty thousand Rebels. Buell, therefore, had no intention of opposing a crossing, thus effectively yielding the offensive to Bragg. Indeed, information received on August 4 indicated that the Confederates had already crossed "in heavy force" on July 30 and would soon be threatening McCook and Crittenden at Battle Creek. The information proved false, but it indicated the army's true defensive posture.[46]

It was Buell's dispositions, however, that tipped his hand. He had formed a defensive perimeter from Battle Creek (McCook's and Crittenden's divisions) to De-

43. Nevin, *Chase Papers,* 3:244; Engle, *Buell,* 277–79; David Donald, ed., *Inside Lincoln's Cabinet: The Civil War Diaries of Salmon P. Chase* (reprint, New York: Kraus, 1970), 103, 107, 109.

44. *OR,* 16(2):265–66, 278.

45. *OR,* 16(1):109, 248, 16(2):278–79, 302.

46. *OR,* 16(2):259, 271, 278, 296, 334.

cherd (Thomas's and a portion of Wood's divisions) to McMinnville (Nelson's division), with a possible concentration point of Altamont. He clearly was thinking about blocking Bragg's army, not marching against it.[47]

Lincoln had not withdrawn troops from the Army of the Ohio based upon Halleck's assurance of the capture of Chattanooga. What he got was the worst of both worlds—defeat in the East and inactivity in the West. Halleck wrote bluntly to Buell on August 12: "General, I deem it my duty to write to you confidentially that the administration is greatly dissatisfied with the slowness of your operations. . . . So strong is this dissatisfaction that I have several times been asked to recommend some officer to take your place." The War Department perceived that "you were accomplishing nothing," and unless some action was taken, "the present dissatisfaction is so great your friends here will not be able to prevent a change being ordered."[48]

Complaints also came from within the army, the chief grousing concerning rations. "Buell's whole army are now living on half rations, or as our boys have been for the last half month, on nothing at all, and I don't see the necessity in it," a soldier wrote from Bridgeport in early August. "The companies drew half rations for one night last night, and each man got one cracker, half ration, to last him one day, together with bacon, which ain't fit to eat in this hot weather. I have known boys out of this regiment to go on picket guard, morning after morning, with nothing in their haversacks, and not a thing had they for breakfast. . . . We get some fresh pork sometimes, but what good is it without salt? It would kill men off faster than yellow fever. The men stand it without a word of complaint, but it won't last long."[49]

At the very moment when Buell faced his most intense pressure, the Rebels struck again. This time it was not just an embarrassment but a catastrophe. In the early morning hours of August 12, raiders under John Hunt Morgan swept into Gallatin, Tennessee, twenty-five miles north of Nashville, catching the 125-man garrison napping. Forty boxcars, two bridges, and six hundred feet of track were destroyed. Morgan had just gotten started. His troopers then galloped seven miles north of the town to the weakest link in the western rail network—the Big South Tunnel of the Louisville and Nashville Railroad. A locomotive and several flatcars loaded with wood were set ablaze and run into the tunnel. The locomotive boiler exploded, igniting a vein of coal, collapsing the rafters, and filling the tunnel with rocks and debris so hot that it was several weeks before anyone could even enter. For weeks

47. *OR*, 16(1):35, 16(2):279, 319.
48. *OR*, 16(2):314–15; Engle, *Buell*, 279.
49. *New York Tribune*, Aug. 7, 1862.

Buell had labored to repair the tracks south of Nashville, and now his main supply artery had been shut down with alarming ease north of that city by a mere six hundred raiders.[50]

Since the wagon road around the tunnel had such a steep grade, the Federals were forced to open a new railhead ten miles north of Mitchellville, Tennessee. Wagons then had to traverse the twenty-five-mile winding road through Tyree Springs to Goodletsville. Some of the damage could have been mitigated by simply diverting rail traffic south of Bowling Green to Memphis Junction. There a branch of the Memphis, Clarksville, and Louisville Railroad could have been used to transport supplies to Clarksville, Tennessee, and thence by the Cumberland River to Nashville. In yet another debacle, however, a diminutive but ferocious-looking raider by the name of Tom Woodward hit Clarksville with his battalion on August 18, capturing its garrison of six companies of the 71st Ohio with near farcical ease. Col. Rodney Mason, the Union commander, who many witnesses claimed had panicked and run at Shiloh, amusingly had his photograph taken with the raider.[51]

Buell's failure to capture Chattanooga was due neither to an ineffective organization nor his attempts to pacify the population.[52] Logistics and aggressive Rebel raiders proved insurmountable barriers. This is not to suggest that he could not have moved faster. The general was clearly too conservative, both strategically and politically, a factor that not only kept him out of Chattanooga but also undercut his support base both in the army and in Washington. Even had Buell thrown caution to the wind and beaten Bragg to Chattanooga, he might well have found himself in a scenario similar to what in fact happened in the fall of 1863. At that time the Federals occupied the city and the Rebels the heights, thus besieging the Union army. That future situation was resolved when an uncommitted Army of the Tennessee (the Confederate Army of Vicksburg had surrendered by then) and troops from the Army of the Potomac made a rescue. In the summer of 1862, however, Grant's army faced a Confederate force of twenty-two thousand and McClellan was engaged on the Peninsula. Buell, if he could not open a supply line, would have had little option but to withdraw from the city and concentrate southwest of Nashville. The only way his campaign to take Chattanooga could have succeeded was for Halleck to keep Bragg's army pinned down in Mississippi, something that he failed to do at Corinth and refused to do at Tupelo.[53]

50. McDonough, *War in Kentucky*, 57–58.

51. Cooling, *Fort Donelson's Legacy*, 94–98.

52. Prokopowicz, *All for the Regiment*, 133; Engle, *Buell*, 284.

53. I concur with McDonough's assessment of the campaign. Doubtless, after Shiloh Grant would have relished the opportunity to reverse roles and rescue the Army of the Ohio. See *War in Kentucky*, 102–4.

7

Retreat to Kentucky
A Season of Blunders

ON AUGUST 8 a routine night patrol in the Sequatchie Valley by several companies of the 2d Indiana Cavalry collided with a squad of twenty or so Rebel cavalry. Shots were exchanged, and the enemy quickly disappeared into the pitch-black darkness. The incident would have been of little note but for the body of a dead Confederate officer discovered at dawn. In his bloodstained jacket troopers found a suspicious letter that they quickly forwarded to Major General McCook at Battle Creek.[1]

The confidential letter was written by Tennessee governor Isham G. Harris to Alfred J. Ewing, a Confederate congressman, and dated July 28. Several pages in length, the crux of the missive stated: "I shall return to Tupelo in a few days, to accompany General Bragg in his forward movement. He assures me that he will carry me to Nashville before the last of August, and I have every confidence in his assurance. . . . If General Bragg succeeds in crossing the Tennessee River and marching rapidly through Middle Tennessee it places him in rear of Buell's force, now threatening Chattanooga, and compels Buell to fall back, if indeed we do not cut him off. When he falls back General [Kirby] Smith will probably concentrate and pursue him."[2]

Could it be that the Federals had stumbled upon Bragg's ultimate target? McCook, Crittenden, and Capt. Horace Fisher, a staff member, discussed the letter's credibility at length. "I lit my pipe and we three smoked and thought for all we were worth," recalled Fisher. He remembered reading about an 1860 forgery case in Paris in which a handwriting expert testified that a letter was genuine when written naturally and without effort, unlike a forgery. They at last concurred as to its authenticity and forwarded the letter to Buell. It may not have been as important as the famed "Lost Order" of the Antietam campaign, but it was at least a clue to the Confederates' intentions.[3]

Buell, at Huntsville, received the document on August 9, forwarded it to Halleck

---

1. Fisher, *Staff Officer's Story*, 26; Horace Fisher, "Alexander McD. McCook," *Boston Transcript*, June 13, 1903, in folder 12, Alexander McCook Papers, McCook Family Papers, LC.

2. *OR*, 16(1):710–11.

3. Fisher, *Staff Officer's Story*, 27–30; *OR*, 16(1):121.

in Washington, and immediately departed for Battle Creek. In session with Mc-
Cook, Crittenden, Fisher, and Colonel Fry, he discussed the Harris letter at length.
According to Fisher, the Ohio commander decided to concentrate his forces at Bat-
tle Creek and McMinnville, avoiding a general engagement until within reach of
Nashville. Buell advised that he would personally apprise Major General Thomas of
the letter and that the officers present were never to speak of it again, even to one
another. The significance of the Harris letter, as matters developed, was in the seed
that it planted in Buell's mind. Henceforth, he became convinced that Nashville,
not Kentucky, was Bragg's destination.[4]

Although convinced that Middle Tennessee was Bragg's destination, Buell remained
unclear upon which route the Confederates would take. Bragg's crossing of the Ten-
nessee River could not be accomplished without "surprising us completely," so the
main attack must be coming from Smith in East Tennessee; "indeed there are al-
ready indications that it is about to be attempted." Halleck had received news that
Morgan's cavalry brigade also roved in East Tennessee (actually Kentucky by that
time). He admonished Buell on September 12: "If the enemy are concentrating in
East Tennessee, you must move there and break them up. Go wherever the enemy
is." Buell, of course, did not have to go to the enemy, for the Rebels were obligingly
coming to him—according to his best sources, lots of them.[5]
    By allowing Bragg to cross the Tennessee uncontested and enter the sixty-mile-
long, one-to-five-mile-wide Sequatchie Valley, Buell had given his opponent several
alternatives. The Confederates could march up the valley to Pikeville and then west
to Spencer, where they could turn either due west to McMinnville or north to
Sparta. Thomas strongly suspected this route. Another possibility was to march
down the valley to Dunlap, where a road (known locally as the Grassy Cove Road)
led directly to McMinnville. Early on, Nelson declared that Bragg would "come
straight here [McMinnville] and on to Nashville." South of Dunlap was the "rather
rough" Therman Road, which went to Altamont, from where four roads radiated.
Just outside Jasper, the Higginbotham Trace passed through Tracy City, where it
continued north to Altamont. Bragg could also veer onto the old Nashville and
Chattanooga Stage Road, winding through Pelham, Hillsboro, and ultimately Man-
chester. If the Rebels captured the Battle Creek bridge intact, they had a clear path
to Stevenson, Alabama, or could divert at Bolivar, Alabama, on a road that paral-
leled Big Crow Creek and led directly to Decherd. Buell took the northern Alabama

    4. Fisher, *Staff Officer's Story*, 30; *OR*, 16(2):296–97.
    5. *OR*, 16(2):302–3; Halleck to Buell, Aug. 12, 1862; and Nelson to Buell, Aug. 12, 1862, Letters and
Telegrams Sent and Received, June–Aug. 1862, Generals' Papers, Don Carlos Buell, Entry 159, RG 94, NA.

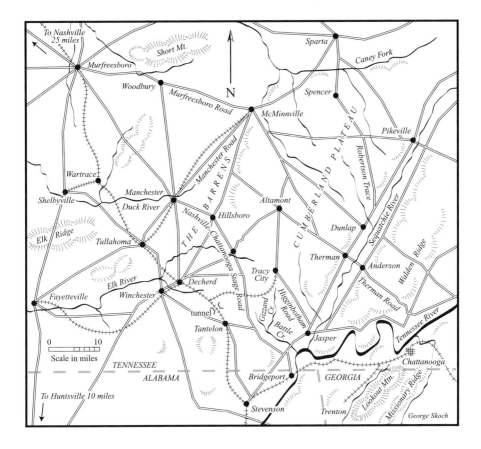

route seriously, although McCook and Crittenden had themselves experienced terrible difficulties in getting over the mountains to Battle Creek.[6]

Buell devised his plan. McCook, upon first intelligence of Bragg's advancing into the Sequatchie Valley, would march to the Therman Road and attempt to check him. If pressed, he would retire across Cumberland Mountain via the road to Altamont, with Crittenden's division moving up in support . If McCook retired, Crittenden would withdraw up the Higginbotham Road to Tracy City and Altamont, where a junction would be formed.[7]

Reports confirmed on August 19 that Bragg had crossed the Tennessee River in force. Buell notified McCook to put his plan into action. In marching up the valley, McCook, minus a brigade on outpost duty but brandishing four dummy cannon to

6. *OR,* 16(1):39, 43, 154, 180, 260, 263, 398, 520, 16(2):270.
7. *OR,* 16(1):38–39.

enhance his two batteries, received unconfirmed information from spies that Bragg's advance had already reached the Therman Road. Fearful of tangling with a force of unknown size and of losing his wagon train, the division commander prematurely withdrew. Instead of retiring by the Higginbotham Road, however, which he found impassable for artillery, McCook, along with Crittenden, went back past Jasper and all the way to Battle Creek. He notified Buell that the enemy were moving on McMinnville.[8]

The next day, August 20, Buell received additional information that Thomas, at McMinnville with the Fourth and Sixth Divisions, would be attacked by Bragg's main army in the valley, while a column of perhaps ten thousand would swing around by way of Sparta. Thomas remained nervous about the army's left flank being turned, but he too thought that Bragg was headed for McMinnville. He had "just heard that the rebels are repairing the Chattanooga and McMinnville road prepatory to advancing in this [McMinnville] direction." Buell, however, could "hardly credit" the McMinnville report. He remained convinced that the Confederates would march on Altamont, where he would then veer toward Decherd. Why? Because that is what Buell would have done had he been Bragg. He could not fathom that Bragg would consider otherwise. If the concentration occurred at Mc-Minnville, Decherd might be lost. McCook and Thomas must move on Altamont.[9]

Whether or not Bragg would think as Buell did remained to be seen, but Thomas clearly did not. "By all means concentrate here [McMinnville]," the Virginian urged on August 22. Altamont was a poor defensive position, void of forage and water. To get to Nashville Bragg would have to pass either McMinnville or Sparta. McMinnville should be the point of concentration, he argued, with only a division retained at Decherd.[10]

By August 23 matters had become more muddled. McCook now admitted that he did not actually know for sure that Bragg's army was in the valley in force. Buell could hardly restrain his anger. The next day he ordered Crittenden and McCook to Altamont, with scolding words to the latter: "As it turns out it was unfortunate that you did not move to the Therman Road as ordered. Let us not fail again." Writing of the incident years later, Buell still fumed. "The failure of McCook's movement up the Sequatchie Valley was unfortunate. It gave a false impression of the enemy's progress, and the route he was to pursue." The Rebels now had free rein in the valley, with their movements totally screened by the Cumberland Mountains.[11]

8. Ibid., 39, 87, 149, 708, 16(2):389, 397; *Louisville Daily Democrat*, Sept. 4, 1862; Noe, *Southern Boy in Blue*, 89; Fisher, "Alexander McD. McCook."

9. *OR*, 16(2):381, 389, 392.

10. Ibid., 392.

11. Ibid., 396, 397, 406–8.

Maintaining his headquarters at Decherd, a town of a single hotel and a depot, Buell ordered Thomas to proceed with two brigades of the Fourth Division (one brigade remaining at McMinnville) and two brigades of the Sixth Division to Altamont, despite Thomas's advice to the contrary. There he would juncture with the First, Second, and Fifth Divisions on August 25. Alarmed by false reports, Buell fretted that Bragg would appear at the all-important crossroad first. Thomas arrived at Altamont in the late afternoon of the twenty-fifth. The Rebels were not there (reports placed them no closer than Dunlap), and Thomas wished that he were not. As he had warned, Altamont could not support ten thousand men for even a week, the summit of the mountain being five miles from the town. Two brigades and a battery made it to the top after a grueling day's work, but Thomas called off the operation before the wagons got started. On his own judgment and without orders, he abandoned Altamont and withdrew his column to McMinnville. Buell had no choice but to stop his other three divisions at Pelham. For a second time his plans had been thwarted by a junior who had altered orders, though, unlike McCook, Thomas was not rebuked.[12]

Still relying on unsubstantiated citizen reports, Buell remained convinced that Bragg would take the Therman Road for Altamont and then on to Decherd. On August 27 he personally visited McCook at Pelham and ordered his division in advance of Altamont. He apparently hoped that McCook would somehow find the water and forage that had eluded Thomas. He did not. It took sixteen hours for McCook to get his wagons up the mountain, and he complained that the nearest water was three and a half miles away. As it turned out, Bragg appeared to remain passive in the valley. Some officers speculated that he was merely demonstrating in order to tie down Buell, thus giving free reign to Smith's corps at Knoxville.[13]

The problem, as always, was Buell's weak intelligence-gathering network. He had only five cavalry regiments with his immediate army, and these he kept scattered—two near Murfreesboro, two at McMinnville, and one at Decherd. They scouted in small groups and could never penetrate Bragg's cavalry screen. Indeed, most of his information he derived from civilian reports. Despite Buell's frantic shuffling of troops, by August 27 Bragg's infantry had not even entered the Sequatchie Valley.[14]

Buell's divisions remained scattered on August 28—the First at Decherd, the Second at Altamont, the Fourth and Sixth at McMinnville, and the Fifth at Pelham. The Third had already departed northern Alabama for Nashville, Huntsville having

---

12. *OR*, 16(1):44, 16(2):399–400, 406–7, 410, 420–21, 426, 439; *Chicago Tribune*, Sept. 6, 1862.

13. *OR*, 16(1):42, 88, 110, 156, 168–69, 16(2):426, 429, 439, 443, 444.

14. Kenneth A. Hafendorfer, *They Died by Twos and Tens: The Confederate Cavalry in the Kentucky Campaign of 1862* (Louisville: KH Press, 1995), 234–35, 238–39. Buell's cavalry units were the 1st and 2d Kentucky Cavalry, 3d and 4th Ohio Cavalry, and 7th Pennsylvania Cavalry.

been abandoned on the twenty-sixth. Two small divisions, led by Brig. Gens. Jefferson C. Davis and John Palmer, some nine thousand troops, had already been sent from Grant's army in northern Mississippi and would soon be in Nashville. Buell now only vaguely suspected that Bragg's army was even in the Sequatchie Valley. Reports stated that Forrest, with an estimated one thousand troopers, had attacked the wagon train of the Fourth Division at Woodbury, halfway between McMinnville and Murfreesboro, but had been chased off by Col. William Grose's Tenth Brigade.[15]

As early as August 28, Buell began considering a withdrawal from the McMinnville-Altamont-Decherd line. If the latter fell to the secessionists, it would give them a direct rail link to Bridgeport and Chattanooga. On the twenty-ninth Confederate cavalry attacked McCook's outposts at Altamont. The engagement, though only a skirmish, convinced Buell that Bragg was marching on Altamont and then on to Decherd. That afternoon he made his decision to withdraw to Murfreesboro—"it would be criminal to delay any longer," Buell wrote. Bragg had "at least" fifty thousand men who would soon emerge from the valley. (He discounted Col. Thomas Harrison, who from atop his lookout station on a mountain had actually watched Bragg's army file out of Chattanooga and placed their number at thirty thousand.) The Army of the Ohio could muster only thirty thousand bayonets to oppose them, but if the army withdrew to Nashville, Buell could raise his field strength by ten thousand. The Federals, down to ten days' supplies, had to get closer to their base. McMinnville could not be easily defended; nearby knobs made it vulnerable to artillery fire, and shallow Hickory Creek would not retard an enemy's progress. Finally, and more to the point, there were simply too many roads leading out of the valley, making it anyone's guess as to which one Bragg would take.[16]

Months later, before a court of inquiry, Thomas insisted that he had urged Buell to concentrate at Sparta, which he considered the obvious point of passage, whether Bragg was bound for Kentucky or Nashville. By the time the Rebels arrived, they would have been fatigued and could not have fought more than a day. Sparta offered a good defensive position and a source of water at Caney Fork. He only needed four divisions (twenty-four thousand troops) to check the Confederates, for probably no more than thirty thousand of the enemy's forty-five thousand would be brought to the point of contact. (The Buell Commission would later imply that fifteen thousand Federals could have kept the Rebels at bay.) Since Bragg's army subsequently did go by way of Sparta, Thomas's testimony proved compelling.[17]

15. OR, 16(1):709, 16(2):303, 333, 369, 438–39, 468–69, 17(2):144; Hafendorfer, They Died by Twos and Tens, 256–59; Chicago Tribune, Sept. 13, 1862.

16. OR, 16(2):439, 441–42, 451, 454–55; Cleveland Plain Dealer, Oct. 4, 1862.

17. OR, 16(1):182–83, 189, 203.

Buell bristled. He insisted that Thomas, mesmerized with a mere flanking column, refused to admit that the real danger was in the center. Under cross-examination, Thomas conceded that his suggested point of concentration in fact had been McMinnville, but, he insisted, it was with a view of marching toward Sparta if necessary. Thomas Van Horne declared that the Virginian advised rushing Wood's division to Sparta to intercept and slow the Confederate advance while maintaining three divisions at McMinnville and one at Decherd, but no such contemporary evidence exists.[18]

Thomas did himself no credit. He was not as committed to a Sparta concentration as he later claimed (and as historians have accepted without question). Van Horne's suggestion that the general merely went along with Buell's retreat decision is simply not true. There were reports that the Confederates might turn the Federals left at Sparta. In response, Thomas wrote Buell on August 30: "If he [Bragg] is moving on Murfreesboro by Sparta I think the sooner we concentrate to meet him the better and Murfreesboro seems to be the point from which we should operate." He concluded this, although admitting that he had not interviewed anyone who had actually seen Bragg's army. On September 1 he remained very concerned about the center. A spy had advised him that Bragg's forty-five thousand troops would be divided into two columns, one approaching by Sparta and the other by the Therman Road to Altamont.[19]

Even if Thomas had given more than passing support for Sparta, Buell would have rejected it for several reasons. First, the Confederates could approach to within twenty miles of McMinnville before committing to that place or Sparta. If they veered to Sparta, it would take two days (even by Thomas's estimate) for the Federal divisions to march the twenty-two miles to that place, cross the formidable Caney Fork at Rock Island, and get into position. Whether or not Thomas could have beaten the Rebels to Sparta was problematical—he claimed that he could have because he had the better road. Second, even if Thomas had arrived at Sparta first and dug in with four divisions, the Southern army would not necessarily have been "blocked." Indeed, Bragg could have taken a position between Sparta and Nashville, thereby cutting Thomas's communications and throwing Gov. Andrew Johnson into a panic. Third, if Thomas had concentrated at Sparta, he might have been caught in a pincers movement between Smith, believed to still be at Knoxville, and Bragg from Pikeville, something that even the mediocre Thomas Crittenden

18. Ibid., 42, 203; Don Piatt, *General George H. Thomas: A Critical Biography* (Cincinnati: Robert Clarke, 1893), 180; Van Horne, *Army of the Cumberland*, 1:155.

19. *OR*, 16(1):43–44, 16(2):452–53; Van Horne, *Army of the Cumberland*, 1:158. See Earl J. Hess, *Banners to the Breeze: The Kentucky Campaign, Corinth, and Stones River* (Lincoln: University of Nebraska Press, 2000), 60. Hess also believed that Thomas spoke from hindsight.

grasped. Fourth, if the Pikeville force developed to be only a column, while the main Confederate army was indeed approaching from McMinnville, could Thomas get to Nashville before Bragg got there? Crittenden surmised that the Rebels would arrive first.[20]

Virtually the entire army high command considered Murfreesboro a more practicable concentration point than either McMinnville or Sparta. Precisely what to do once at Murfreesboro, however, proved to be a point of contention. Thomas saw an opportunity to push Bragg's Therman Road force, which in fact did not exist, back upon Sparta while attacking his rear at Dunlap with a sizable force of infantry and cavalry. Wood agreed; indeed, he believed that Buell should have concentrated at Murfreesboro from the outset. An early massing there, he theorized, would have forced Bragg to march through the broken and unproductive area east of Sparta. Barring that, Buell could have given battle at Sparta just as easily from Murfreesboro as McMinnville. The Federal commander rejected the argument, stating that the Confederate army would have to "wait seven or eight days at that place to be attacked, which he [Bragg] did not do." The point was well taken—it would have required four and a half days' marching time from Murfreesboro just to get to Sparta even after obtaining definite confirmation that Bragg was there.[21]

In one of the most blundering decisions of his career, Buell reneged on his promise to "move against the enemy" and instead withdrew to Nashville. He claimed that dwindling supplies prompted the move. Thomas did not buy it, nor did the court of inquiry. The court concluded that twenty days' rations remained (Buell claimed ten), which could have been stretched to forty days' half rations—enough for the immediate emergency.[22]

As early as September 1, Buell had received word from Thomas that the Confederates were reportedly "on their way to Kentucky." In a telegram to Halleck the next day, the army commander admitted that Bragg appeared to be "moving up the valley, with the object of going to Kentucky." Why then did Buell withdraw to Nashville, leaving the road to the Bluegrass State open?[23]

The Buell Commission concluded that the general had no intention of defending Nashville. Indeed, Buell admitted as much to Governor Johnson, at which time a heated exchange ensued and the general backed down. The court suggested that Buell intended "to abandon both Tennessee and Kentucky and continue or rather

---

20. *OR*, 16(1):43, 190–91, 562, 560, 643. Engle concluded that the Buell Commission "considered only fighting Bragg and not the vulnerability of the Union army and limited supplies as justification for going to Sparta." *Buell*, 331.

21. *OR*, 16(1):45, 169, 174, 16(2):471.

22. *OR*, 16(1):9, 17, 182–83, 202, 16(2):439; Buell, "East Tennessee," 41; McDonough, *War in Kentucky*, 113; Van Horne, *Army of the Cumberland*, 1:158–59.

23. *OR*, 16(2):469, 470–71.

renew the contest on the banks of the Ohio." The truth may not have been so elaborate. It is certainly possible that Buell simply assumed that Bragg would oblige him and follow his army to Nashville, which he thought remained the prime danger spot. If so, it was wishful thinking.[24]

The commission would later argue that the general could, and should, have simultaneously covered both Nashville and the crossings on the north bank of the Cumberland River. Wood stated that if he had commanded the army, he would have placed some units at Lebanon and the balance at Gallatin, both within supporting distance of each other. There is no indication that he ever made such a suggestion to Buell, however, and when pressed he conceded that Bragg could still have skirted Lebanon farther to the east. On September 7 it was confirmed that a column of Bragg's army had already crossed the Cumberland River at Carthage. Thinking its destination to be Bowling Green, Buell immediately ordered Wood's division to Gallatin, where it arrived on the eighth, just before an enemy cavalry brigade. On the tenth additional information indicated that yet another column (apparently the bulk of Bragg's army) had crossed at Gainesboro. At that time, Buell began moving his army north. Despite the conclusion of the Buell Commission, the march to Bowling Green thus appears to have been more evolutionary than planned. Nonetheless, the failure to contest the crossings of the Cumberland proved to be the finale to a season of blunders. The contest for Middle Tennessee was now over; the struggle for Kentucky had begun.[25]

There was general outrage. "It seems incredible that Bragg has succeeded in scaring so powerful a body as the Army of the Ohio into seeking refuge behind the works around Nashville," a Cincinnati journalist wrote. A soldier phrased it in a more homely fashion: "Bragg deliberately threw sand in Buell's eyes and then ran away from him, before Buell could see what was up."[26]

Even as Buell stumbled strategically, he also struggled organizationally. Thomas Wood had gotten into trouble when an anonymous soldier wrote a letter, subsequently printed in New York papers, to the Committee for the Conduct of the War. He denounced Wood as being "the most profane man in the service, regardless of all moral obligation." Brig. Gen. Milo S. Hascall came to Wood's defense. He admitted that the division commander cursed freely, as did everyone in the army, chaplains included, but said Wood could not hold a candle to "Bull" Nelson in that regard. Nelson, meanwhile, went north to Kentucky to take charge of the newly

24. *OR*, 16(1):17; Cooling, *Fort Donelson's Legacy,* 126.
25. *OR*, 16(1):9, 17, 45, 160, 170, 183, 185, 196.
26. *Cincinnati Enquirer*, Sept. 20, 1862; soldier quoted in Engle, *Buell,* 286.

organized Army of Kentucky, with command of the Fourth Division, for the time being, going to Brigadier General Ammen. Thomas, temporarily handling affairs at McMinnville, had left the First Division in the care of Schoepf.[27]

Changes also occurred at the brigade level. Brig. Gen. Richard Johnson headed an ad hoc cavalry command of 750 troopers in search of Morgan, boldly vowing to bring the Rebel raider back in a band box. When he found him, the Federals were routed and 150 captured, Johnson included. Replacing him would be Brig. Gen. August Willich, which promptly resulted in the resignation of Col. Moses R. Dickey of the 15th Ohio, three weeks his senior. Brig. Gen. James B. Steedman assumed command of the Third Brigade upon Robert McCook's death.[28]

With his army at long last united, Buell took the opportunity to form his cavalry into two brigades, one under Col. Edward McCook (first cousin to the Second Division commander) and the other under forty-two-year-old, Bavarian-born Col. Lewis Zahm, altogether 3,100 sabers. Clearly, the most rugged of the regiments remained the mountain men of Frank Wolford's 1st Kentucky Cavalry. When Buell viewed a trooper donning a slouch hat, hickory shirt, immense Texas-style spurs, two pistols, and a carbine slung on his back, he correctly uttered: "I'll bet fifty dollars that he is one of Wolford's cavalry." Although Col. John Kennett commanded the mounted division, the brigades never operated as a cohesive unit and essentially served in the traditional role of wagon escorts and scouts. No counterforce existed to Forrest or Morgan, who continued to strike with near impunity.[29]

Unknown to Buell, the situation in Kentucky had begun to deteriorate. Nelson arrived in Louisville on August 15 only to discover that he had no legal authority there. Maj. Gen. Horatio G. Wright's newly created Department of the Ohio claimed all troops in Kentucky. Even though Nelson was senior, he uncharacteristically desired to avoid a row and agreed to serve under Wright. In mid-August Smith's Rebel corps swept into southeastern Kentucky, side-stepping to the west George Morgan's Seventh Division in Cumberland Gap. On the seventeenth gray cavalry swooped down on London, inflicting 138 Federal casualties and capturing forty-five supply wagons. Barbourville fell the next day, with fifty wagons seized. Another 120 men and twenty-seven wagons fell captive at Big Hill on the twenty-third.[30]

27. *New York Tribune*, Aug. 29, Sept. 10, 1862. For more on Wood's cursing proclivity, see Tapp and Klotler, *Tuttle*, 91.

28. *New York Tribune*, Aug. 24, 1862; Alexis Cope, *The Fifteenth Ohio Volunteers and Its Campaigns, War of 1861–1865* (Columbus, Ohio: Press of Edward T. Miller, 1916), 179, 799; *Cincinnati Enquirer*, Aug. 27, 1862.

29. *OR*, 16(2):484, 563; *Society of the Army of the Cumberland, 22nd Reunion, 1891* (Cincinnati: Robert Clarke, 1892), 170; Warner, *Generals in Blue*, 296; Tarrant, *Wild Riders*, 109.

30. Hafendorfer, *They Died by Twos and Tens*, 176, 189, 193–94, 217, 221.

On September 1, while at Murfreesboro, Buell received shocking news of a Federal disaster at Richmond, Kentucky. On August 30 a division-sized force of Smith's command attacked two brigades under Brig. Gen. Mahlon Manson. Rather than withdraw to Lancaster or the Kentucky River, Manson aggressively advanced his green levies against what he thought to be an inferior force; to do less, he later argued, would be disgraceful. When "Bull" Nelson, at Lancaster, received word of his advance, he attempted to recall Manson, though to no avail. In a series of flanking movements, the Federals were first driven, then routed—"the panic was well-nigh universal," conceded Col. Charles Cruft. Nelson arrived on the scene, slashing a half-dozen of his own panic-stricken men before falling wounded from a ball in his thigh. He made good his escape, but the ad hoc division was annihilated, losing 5,300 of 6,500 men. The road to Lexington was now open to the Rebels.[31]

Panic erupted in Cincinnati, which had been left nearly defenseless. Wright turned the defense of the city over to Maj. Gen. Lew Wallace, on leave in the state, and roused Gov. David Tod from his sickbed. Underscoring the Buckeye State's sheer ability to raise raw manpower, within days some forty-five thousand volunteers, including five thousand minutemen, or squirrel hunters, filled the trenches. By September 11, however, it had become apparent that the Rebels were not coming. The *New York Tribune* later railed at the "ludicrous sight of an army of 30,000 men drawn up in line of battle for days behind entrenchments waiting for an attack by a [single] Rebel brigade." Although actually a division, the point was made. Wallace soon requested permission to get rid of the troublesome squirrel hunters—"they are under no control."[32]

Brig. Gen. Jeremiah Boyle, commanding at Louisville, remained convinced that there was "too much nervousness about Cincinnati." He thought he knew exactly where Smith was headed—straight from Lexington toward him. Kentucky governor James Robinson concurred. Writing to Lincoln, he insisted that Wright was "creating a panic and will ruin the state. The enemy cannot be so foolish as to move on Cincinnati. . . . It is a trap in which General Wright will suffer us to be caught or suffer Buell's army to be cut off." On September 15 Boyle counted nearly nineteen thousand infantry and artillery and two thousand cavalry in Louisville, including

31. *Louisville Courier Journal*, Apr. 6, 1878; *OR*, 16(2):908, 913, 921; D. Warner Lambert, *When the Ripe Pears Fall: The Battle of Richmond, Kentucky* (Richmond, Ky.: Madison County Historical Society, 1995), 123, 126, 132, 135, 144, 189–91.

32. *OR*, 16(1):428–29, 16(2):499, 504, 506–7, 524; *Cincinnati Enquirer*, Sept. 10, 15, 1862; *New York Times*, Sept. 3, 8, 12, 1862. See also Chester F. Gleason, *One Moment of Glory in the Civil War: When Cincinnati Was Defended from the Hills of Northern Kentucky* (Newport, Ky.: Otto Printing, 1965). Cincinnati had a laboratory that turned out 80,000 rounds daily and a quartermaster depot fabricating 10,000 uniform suits monthly. *Cincinnati Enquirer*, Sept. 1, 1862, Jan. 28, 1863.

Jefferson C. Davis's division from Grant's army, but still he pleaded for more troops. They came—twenty-four infantry regiments, one cavalry regiment, and two batteries from Wright in Cincinnati, five infantry regiments from Illinois, and one cavalry regiment from Michigan. Yet Smith seemed content not to venture beyond Lexington.[33]

Nelson, in Louisville recovering from his wound, began molding his thirty-seven thousand levies into the rudiments of an organized force. This instant wave of fresh manpower, which would eventually be incorporated into the Army of the Ohio as a third corps, was more diverse, more urban, and generally older than the troops of '61. Ohio outfits included two new German Cincinnati regiments—the 106th and 109th Infantry. The 93d, 105th, and 111th Ohio were organized at Dayton, Cleveland, and Toledo respectively. The 23d Wisconsin, one thousand strong and armed with Enfields, formed within ten days, and the 21st Wisconsin comprised mostly laborers from the Northwestern Railroad. Two Chicago regiments, the 88th and 113th Illinois, became known as the 2d and 3d Board of Trade Regiments respectively. The Galena Railroad; the Chicago, Burlington, and Quincy Railroad; the Milwaukee Railroad; and others each furnished a company of the 89th Illinois, earning it the sobriquet of the "Railroad Regiment." The 73d Illinois became known as the "Preacher Regiment" due to a heavy infusion of Methodist ministers and members of prominent Methodist families. Another new Indiana regiment, the 70th, comprised working men and mechanics.[34]

The wagons brought off from Lexington, added to those collected by the quartermaster department, formed a commissary train for the new corps, providing supplies in addition to those kept in the regimental wagons. The train was divided into sections of ten wagons, each section capable of hauling twelve thousand rations. Discounting vehicles reloading, some two hundred wagons were thus kept constantly filled with a quarter-million rations.[35]

33. McDonough, *War in Kentucky*, 152–54; *OR*, 16(1):193, 663, 16(2):502, 506; 507–9, 518.

34. *Chicago Tribune*, Sept. 6, 16, Oct. 3, 15, 1862; *OR*, 16(1):428–29, 662; Gilbert R. Stormont, *History of the 58th Regiment Indiana Vol. Inf.* (Princeton, N.J.: Press of the Clarion, 1895), 95–96; Grebner, "We Were the Ninth," 114; Henry A. Castle, "Sheridan with the Army of the Cumberland," in *MOLLUS, District of Columbia*, 4 vols. (reprint, Wilmington, N.C.: Broadfoot, 1993), 2:162; Kenneth A. Hafendorfer, *Perryville: Battle for Kentucky* (Owensboro, Ky.: McDowell, 1981), 80; *Indianapolis Daily Journal*, Aug. 20, 1862; Leo M. Kaiser, ed., "Civil War Letters of Charles W. Carr of the 21st Wisconsin Volunteers," *Wisconsin Magazine of History* 43 (summer 1960): 265–66; Dyer, *Compendium*, 2:1084, 1537, 1542, 1544; Michael H. Fitch, *Echoes of the Civil War* (New York: R. F. Fenno, 1905), 41. Cincinnati alone had nearly seven regiments in the army at this time—the 2d, 6th, 9th, 10th, 106th, and 109th Ohio came from Hamilton County as well as part of the 50th Ohio. *Cincinnati Daily Commercial*, Aug. 27, 1862.

35. Gilbert, "Bragg's Invasion of Kentucky," 298–99.

On September 17 Morgan withdrew his Seventh Division from Cumberland Gap back through eastern Kentucky, not stopping until he reached the Ohio River. With Smith at his rear, a Confederate division investing his front, and supplies exhausted, he could do little else at the gap. The three-month Federal occupation of the gateway to East Tennessee thus came to an end. Additionally, a nine-thousand-man Rebel division was now freed to unite with Smith.[36]

On September 10 Wood, now in Kentucky, received a civilian report that thirty-five thousand Confederates had crossed the Cumberland River and were on their way to Glasgow and Munfordville. Buell remained skeptical, believing that the secessionists would either swing back and attack Nashville from the north or destroy his supply depot at Bowling Green. Similar to what he had done in North Alabama, he thus spread out his army for sixty miles. On the eleventh Wood's and Rousseau's divisions arrived at Bowling Green, while Ammen's, McCook's, and Crittenden's divisions remained midway between that town and Nashville, the last named anxiously awaiting an attack by Forrest's brigade on the night of September 13 that never developed. Thomas's, Negley's, and Paine's divisions guarded the Tennessee capital.[37]

Bragg's army in fact had headed toward Glasgow, placing him on a near parallel course with Buell. The Federal commander would later be criticized for not attacking the Confederates at Glasgow, but he claimed that the town was fifty miles from the Cumberland River and ninety-five miles from Nashville, meaning that Bragg could not have been intercepted unless "he tarried there." This was essentially the same rationale that he used for not attacking at Sparta. As long as Buell's defensive line ran north-south, the door to Kentucky would remain open. Too, Wood's and Rousseau's divisions were in Bowling Green a full twenty-four hours before the Confederate van arrived at Glasgow. They sat idle throughout September 12 and 13, waiting for the balance of the army to close up. Crittenden's division arrived on the thirteenth and McCook's on the fourteenth, along with Buell and his staff. Since the army commander understood that "the whole of Bragg's army . . . will be concentrated at Glasgow tomorrow [fourteenth]," he should have rushed troops to Prewitt's Knob, midway between Bowling Green and Munfordville. Indeed, Confederate infantry, some reports claimed in division-strength, had already been sighted at Proctors Station, north of Bowling Green. Preoccupied with Nashville, Buell failed to grasp that the greater danger was to the north, where Bragg could get between his army and Louisville.[38]

36. George W. Morgan, "Cumberland Gap," in *B&L*, 3:66–69; Buell, "East Tennessee," 46.

37. *OR*, 16(2):493, 501–2; Hafendorfer, *They Died by Twos and Tens*, 368–74; Crittenden to Buell, Sept. 13, 1862, Letters and Telegrams Sent and Received, June–Aug. 1862, Generals' Papers, Don Carlos Buell, Entry 159, RG 94.

38. *OR*, 16(1):10, 45, 171; Hafendorfer, *They Died by Twos and Tens*, 384–85; *New York Times*, Sept. 28, 1862.

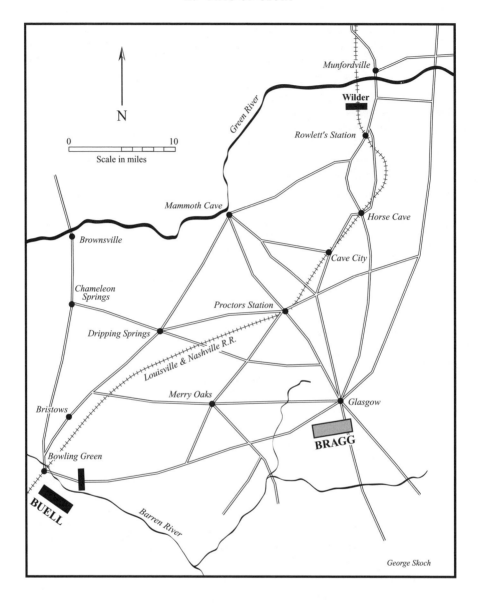

N

0 _____ 10
Scale in miles

Munfordville

Wilder

Rowlett's Station

Green River

Mammoth Cave

Horse Cave

Brownsville

Cave City

Chameleon
Springs

Proctors Station

Dripping Springs

Louisville & Nashville R.R.

Merry Oaks

Glasgow

Bristows

BRAGG

Bowling Green

BUELL

Barren River

George Skoch

On September 14 Buell received his first inkling that the Munfordville garrison might be in trouble, but even then he did not appear alarmed. His failure to appreciate the danger to the north could be blamed on inadequate cavalry, but to state the truth, it represented a reflection of his peculiar military personality. Buell based his movements upon preconceptions of what he thought the enemy would do. It made no sense for Bragg to move north of Glasgow, for he would "give up communications with Tennessee," be in a "much less productive region," and render communications "with Kirby Smith less secure against a force operating from the Ohio River." Since, from his view, Munfordville was "not essential to Bragg's army," he considered the garrison as Wright's problem, not his.[39]

Finally realizing that "if Bragg's army is defeated Nashville is safe," Buell belatedly ordered the First Division, once again under Thomas's command, to hasten to Bowling Green, leaving the defense of Nashville to Negley's and Paine's ten thousand troops and three thousand armed convalescents. Thomas linked up with the army north of Bowling Green on September 20. Buell would later lament, "I moved my army 65 miles while he [Bragg] was moving 50, and I was still 30 miles in rear of him."[40]

He spoke in hindsight. The Federal commander was not attempting to catch up to Bragg, as he implied, for he thought that the Confederates remained stationary at Glasgow, perhaps preparing to attack him at Bowling Green. For four days he dallied at the latter, claiming that he foraged for supplies. Yet his troops had been issued six days' rations at Nashville, which could have been stretched to twelve, and additional supplies from Louisville awaited him at the Salt River. Indeed, most of the foraged supplies went to the Nashville garrison. During this time, noted a colonel, Crittenden became "rather impatient to move" as did "particularly the Ohio and Indiana troops." The failure to move was not based upon logistics, however, but a tactical miscalculation.[41]

When Bragg did not march on Bowling Green, Buell made plans of his own. Instead of moving due east, he devised a complex scheme by which his army would get north of Glasgow and converge on the town by three separate roads. Slowed by Confederate cavalry and maddening inertia, by September 17 the forty-five-thousand-man Army of the Ohio had only arrived at Dripping Springs, eighteen miles from Glasgow. That night Buell received confirmation of a disaster. Bragg had slipped away from Glasgow, having stolen a march the day before, and gone to Munfordville while the Army of the Ohio trudged on back roads in a futile flanking attempt. The four-thousand-man Munfordville garrison under Col. John T. Wilder had surrendered that morning. When later asked what comments Buell made about the news, Thomas replied, "None at all."[42]

There was no real reason for the loss of the garrison, beyond the fact that Major

39. *OR,* 16(1):46.

40. Ibid., 45, 258–59, 16(2):511–12; Van Horne, *Army of the Cumberland,* 1:161.

41. *OR,* 16(1):47, 48, 79, 161, 168, 606–7.

42. Hafendorfer, *They Died by Twos and Tens,* 422–29; *OR,* 16(1):48, 78, 123, 209; Buell, "East Tennessee," 41.

General Wright had ordered Colonel Wilder to hold at all costs. Green River could be easily forded (the Confederates had actually surrounded the town from both banks) or the position bypassed on three roads to the east. The railroad bridge, if destroyed, could be rebuilt in ten days. Bragg would have skirted the position, Buell believed, "but for the bait which was offered him." Although held blameless by the court of inquiry, Buell suffered public scorn for the surrender. The *Indianapolis Daily Journal* denounced the general for being only a half-day's march away (actually nineteen miles) but failing to go to the rescue of brave men. A soldier-correspondent lamented, "He has allowed a vigorous and daring enemy to come between him and the threatened points north, and Louisville is now really in danger." A soldier in Crittenden's division decried the fact that "we just fooled along and did not get there soon enough." An Illinois soldier noted that every officer in the army had come to the conclusion that Buell was "either a Traitor or an imbecile."[43]

The capture of Munfordville did give Buell his best glimpse yet of the Confederate army, for several Federal officers, Wilder among them, had been paroled and allowed to pass through the lines. Indeed, Wilder had been magnanimously permitted to view the entire Confederate army before making his surrender decision. He placed Bragg's strength at 36,000 men and forty-five guns. Estimates from other officers and civilians ranged from as low as 30,000 to as high as 45,000 soldiers. Counting regimental flags and batteries and making average estimates, authorities derived the figure of 37,800. Thomas, Crittenden, and clearly Buell continued to believe 40,000 was closer to the truth.[44]

While the issue may appear pedantic, it would later become a major point of contention at the Buell inquiry. The commission accepted the figure 35,000, a number less than Buell's and far less than the 60,000 the Ohio general had earlier claimed while at Decherd. Bragg in fact never had more than 30,000 men, compared to Buell's six divisions and two cavalry brigades totaling 45,000. Even though the Federals held the numerical edge and superior ordnance, the Rebel army remained potentially decisive, their troops being battle hardened and better disciplined, a fact widely conceded. If Buell failed to keep his divisions within supporting distance, he could quickly find himself in trouble. His men also hardened to the rigors of campaigning. A photograph of a blue-clad regiment crossing the Big Barren River during this time shows all of the men wearing the wide-brimmed "slouch hat" so

43. *OR*, 16(1):9–10, 46–47, 163, 546; *Indianapolis Daily Journal*, Sept. 30, 1862; Noe, *Southern Boy in Blue*, 97; Prokopowicz, *All for the Regiment*, 232 n. 37; *Chicago Tribune*, Sept. 20, 1862.

44. For various perspectives on Confederate numbers, see *OR*, 16(1):12, 14, 15, 16, 37, 82, 85, 105, 121–22, 131, 132, 138, 149, 152–53, 208, 215, 216, 290, 320, 347, 403, 404, 427, 442, 522–23, 693. In postwar years Buell stated, "I supposed it [Confederate strength] to be from 30,000 to 40,000." Buell, "East Tennessee," 42.

popular in the West, some in shirt sleeves, others with a feather in their hat. But for the color of their uniforms, they could not be distinguished from their gray-clad counterparts.[45]

It took Buell five days to march the twenty-five miles through the cave country from Bowling Green to Munfordville. Halleck unleashed a salvo. "I fear here as elsewhere you move too slowly, and will permit the junction of Bragg and Smith before you open your line to Louisville." Historians have argued that the army commander should have gained the initiative and flanked Bragg out of position by marching to Elizabethtown, thirty-five miles to Bragg's rear. Even if the move had been detected by Rebel cavalry, as surely it would have been, it would still cause Bragg to withdraw. Yet Buell remained fearful that if he left no force in Bragg's front, the Confederates would then march back to Nashville. He thus never considered such a countermove, despite the fact that he had attempted just such a maneuver at Glasgow only days earlier. Besides, it was hardly likely that Bragg would have returned to Tennessee, leaving Smith isolated in the Bluegrass.[46]

Buell's dawdling pace to Munfordville has actually been misunderstood. Clearly, he was waiting for Thomas's division to come up, but he also did not want to give battle at the Green River, which he considered a strong position. McCook also opposed such a venture. By moving slowly, Buell hoped against hope that the secessionists would exhaust their supplies and abandon their position. When Bragg subsequently did evacuate Munfordville on the night of September 20, Buell breathed a sigh of relief. For once he had been lucky. He had gambled that Bragg would not entrench on the north bank and wait for Smith to link up with both additional men and supplies. Indeed, the Northern press had openly reported that this is what would probably happen. Meanwhile, Buell exhausted his own supplies, some divisions having rations only through September 25.[47]

If the Federal commander had been spared a battle, he now had to worry about the Rebels beating him to Louisville, his primary supply base and the symbol of Union authority in Kentucky. The thirty-six thousand new levies, he believed,

45. *OR*, 16(1):348, 16(2):527. Bragg had slightly over 27,800 infantry and artillery and about 2,200 cavalry. Considering losses in sickness and straggling along the way and casualties at an early attack on Munfordville, the 30,000 figure seems a fair estimate.

46. *OR*, 16(1):49, 16(2):527, 530; Hafendorfer, *They Died by Twos and Tens,* 431–33, 467–69, 471–77; Thomas L. Connelly, *Army of the Heartland: The Army of Tennessee: 1861–1862* (Baton Rouge: Louisiana State University Press, 1967), 233. Zahm's cavalry brigade rode to Glasgow, where they captured 200 Rebels, mostly sick.

47. *OR*, 16(1):48, 73, 78, 89, 163, 184, 16(2):527; *Cincinnati Enquirer,* Sept. 24, 1862; Buell, "East Tennessee," 42. McCook said that he knew of no officer who supported an attack upon Bragg at the Green River. *OR*, 16(1):113.

would not hold two hours in a serious engagement with the veteran Confederates. Nelson at Louisville concurred. All women and children were immediately ordered across the Ohio River on the two pontoon bridges constructed from coal barges. One of the Illinois recruits noted, "The city seems almost deserted except by soldiers and negroes." Indeed, Nelson planned to pull out his entire command and evacuate the city if driven from the trenches. A battle was expected during the day or night of September 23, but the New York Times denounced Nelson's "frenzied and absurd actions." With Buell's army only "hours behind," stated the paper, the threat to the city was more imagined than real. For Bragg to have had any serious chance of capturing the city, he would have had to bypass Munfordville and taken the direct route from Glasgow. Nonetheless, Buell believed that Louisville remained the target, though Bragg might attempt a stand at Muldraugh's Hill.[48]

Once again, the Ohio general had guessed wrong. On September 21 the Rebel army left the Louisville Road and veered toward Hodgeville, where it took the gravel road to Bardstown. Bragg's destination was no longer Louisville but the Bluegrass and a juncture with Smith. Buell force-marched his army to Louisville, with his van arriving on the twenty-fifth and the last division on the twenty-ninth. The march had been brutal, the daily fare being a slice of bacon or beef and a cracker and a half, with hundreds of men being entirely barefoot. The wagon train was kept well to the west, traveling under cavalry escort by way of Brownsville, Litchfield, and West Point. Historians would long tout the "race to Louisville"; it was a myth. Although jaded and exhausted (some divisions went a day without food), the men marched into the city with a sense of pride. In their view, they had saved Louisville, even as they had saved Grant's army on the banks of the Tennessee River. Civilians greeted the army with a near frantic demonstration of welcome from housetops, windows, and sidewalks, with flags waving and bands blaring. A veteran of the 15th Ohio could not help but feel a sense of contempt, however, as he viewed recent recruits cheering in new uniforms with white collars, "which we saw in great numbers along the sidewalks." More good news greeted them. McClellan had checked Lee's Maryland offensive at Antietam. The eyes of the nation now turned to the West.[49]

48. Chicago Tribune, Sept. 27, 1862; Barry Bingham, City of Conflict: Louisville in the Civil War (Louisville: Louisville Civil War Round Table, 1962), 85; New York Tribune, Sept. 23, 24, 1862; OR, 16(1):101, 16(2):527.

49. Buell, "East Tennessee," 48; New York Tribune, Sept. 28, 1862; Matthews to wife, Aug. 27, Sept. 28, 1862, Stanley Matthews Letters, CINHS; Chicago Tribune, Sept. 23, 25, 1862; Arnold Gates, ed., The Rough Side of War: The Civil War Journal of Chesley A. Mosman, 1st Lieutenant, Company D, 59th Illinois Volunteer Infantry Regiment (Garden City, N.Y.: Basin, 1987), 28; Cincinnati Daily Commercial, Oct. 1, 1862; OR, 16(1):48, 16(2):533, 540, 541, 542; Cope, Fifteenth Ohio, 201; Hinman, Sherman Brigade, 277–78;

The Army of the Ohio had come full circle. After nearly a year, it was back in the city of its birth. Buell had failed to act upon four opportunities to stop Bragg: containment in the Sequatchie Valley, a strike at Sparta, making a stand on the north bank of the Cumberland River, and moving quickly from Bowling Green. About all that could be said was that the army remained intact. Such was not the case for Buell's reputation.[50]

Paul M. Angle, ed., *Three Years in the Army of the Cumberland* (Bloomington: Indiana University Press, 1959), 16.

50. On September 27, 1862, a soldier in the Second Division wrote, "It is an open question in this army, whether this long march was a retreat or a pursuit." *Cincinnati Daily Commercial,* Sept. 30, 1862.

8

The Collapse of Command
The Anti-Buell Faction

THE EVENTS OF SEPTEMBER 25–30, 1862, became a microcosm of the problems that debilitated the Army of the Ohio. Buell allowed five days to reorganize and resupply his divisions and formulate an offensive plan, yet the time was squandered in bickering and intrigue. A chain of events on the twenty-ninth that bordered on the ludicrous left the high command in shambles. As a result, the army experienced an internal collapse before it even marched out to do battle with the Confederates.

Once in Louisville, Buell went about the task of reorganizing his army. He first had to deal with Horatio Wright in Cincinnati, who, the army commander explained to Halleck on September 27, stood in the way of a "homogenous command." General Wright did not resist the inevitable, recognizing both Buell's seniority and his own loss of control "of my own troops even." Buell got most of what he wanted—the merger of Nelson's corps into his command. His seventy-five-thousand-man army was now divided into the I, II, and III Corps, initially commanded by Major Generals Thomas, McCook, and Nelson, respectively. Thomas got the First, Third, and Fifth Divisions; McCook the Second, Sixth, and Ninth; and Nelson the Fourth, Tenth, and Eleventh.[1]

Precisely what to do with forty-one raw Indiana, Ohio, and Illinois infantry regiments ready for the field proved problematical. A score were placed in two newly formed divisions (the Tenth and Twelfth), and the balance scattered throughout the army, typically one to each veteran brigade. The eleven regiments received from Grant's army in Mississippi, which arrived by steamboat around September 25, were incorporated into the Ninth and Eleventh Divisions.[2]

---

1. "Organization of the Army of the Ohio," Don Carlos Buell Papers, FC; Hafendorfer, *Perryville*, 65, 67; James B. Fry, *Operations of the Army under Buell: From June 10th to October 30th, 1862, and the "Buell Commission"* (New York: Van Nostrand, 1884), 49–50; *OR*, 16(1):663.

2. "Buell Statement," 35; Clyde C. Walton, ed., *Behind the Guns: The History of Battery I, 2nd Regiment Illinois Light Artillery* (Carbondale: Southern Illinois University Press, 1965), 25; *OR*, 17(2):147–48, 200; Henry A. Castle, "Sheridan with the Army of the Cumberland," in *MOLLUS, District of Columbia*, 4 vols. (reprint, Wilmington, N.C.: Broadfoot, 1993), 2:162.

Buell reduced his baggage for better efficiency. Officers dispensed with trunks, and the men, much to their chagrin, received individual tin cooking utensils in lieu of company kettles and pans. Ammunition supplies varied, but most brigades averaged 120 rounds per man. In addition, a reserve ordnance train carried a massive 1,176,000 rounds. Generally, the artillery pieces averaged 180 rounds to the gun, but the long arm had only a small reserve train.[3]

Absenteeism and detachments drew thousands from the ranks. Between Nashville and Louisville, the forty-five-thousand-man Army of the Ohio had two thousand men collapse from sickness and exhaustion, none of whom were able to catch up before the command marched out of Louisville. Another twenty-five to thirty men per regiment were detached for extra duty—teamsters, clerks, musicians, hospital orderlies, and the like—over four thousand in all. An alarming number of desertions occurred while at Louisville (in the thousands, but no one knew for sure how many), a high percentage of whom turned out to be officers. They simply took the public ferry across the Ohio River, and their colonels continued to count them as present.[4]

The army's most serious problem was in the declining credibility of its commander. Republican papers, such as the *Cincinnati Times, New York Times, New York Tribune,* and the *Chicago Tribune,* held Buell's political views in disdain, but his poor military showing throughout September gave them fresh fodder for criticism. Noted the last, "Gen. Buell, after a year's campaign, has got back to his starting point [Louisville] one day ahead of the enemy." The attacks were both personal and bitter, with *Frank Leslie's Illustrated* being one of the most vicious. Not surprisingly, Democratic papers, such as the *Chicago Times* and *Cincinnati Enquirer,* came to his defense.[5]

Andrew Johnson bitterly complained to Lincoln in early September that Buell would never free East Tennessee, that his popularity with the Rebels was well known, and that he used his army as "a kind of body guard" to protect himself. Republicans also lined up in opposition. Michigan senator Zachariah Chandler visited the army and wrote on September 25 that the troops openly expressed exaspera-

3. Buell, "East Tennessee," 45; *OR,* 16(2):552; Theodore C. Blegen, ed., *The Civil War Letters of Colonel Hans Christian Heg* (Northfield, Minn.: Minnesota-Norwegian American Historical Association, 1936), 141; Noe, *Southern Boy in Blue,* 100–101; "Report of Ammunition, Sept. 15, 1862, Army of the Ohio," Don Carlos Buell Papers, FC.

4. *OR,* 16(1):664, 665, 714.

5. *Cincinnati Commercial,* Sept. 30, 1862; *New York Tribune,* Sept. 1, 2, 15, Oct. 4, 8, 1862; Villard, *Memoirs,* 1:304; Andrews, *North Reports the Civil War,* 292; *Chicago Tribune,* Sept. 25, 27, Oct. 1, 1862; *Chicago Times,* Oct. 10, 1862; Engle, *Buell,* 294; *Louisville Democrat,* quoted in *Cincinnati Enquirer,* Nov. 2, 1862.

tion and the need for a command change. Republican governors—David Tod of Ohio, Richard Yates of Illinois, and especially Oliver C. Morton of Indiana—joined in a chorus of denunciation. A united Republican front maintained pressure on Washington, where more than one cabinet member was willing to hear their complaints. Secretary of the Treasury (and former Ohio governor) Salmon P. Chase denounced Buell as "too slow."[6]

Criticism from within the ranks became widespread throughout mid-September. Threats of wholesale resignations surfaced when Buell failed to come to the rescue of the Munfordville garrison, many believing that he was unwilling to risk an engagement. Perhaps some of the animosity could have been mitigated had Buell simply made some visible effort to express concern for the men, but he remained coolly aloof. Since leaving Bowling Green back in January 1862, the general had never once reviewed his troops or visited a hospital or a camp kitchen. Indeed, few troops ever saw him. He rode about shabbily dressed, with a straw hat and in the uniform of a brigadier, looking at neither his staff nor the troops. "During the latter part of this march free use was made of epithets traitor, tyrant, fool, and coward," a captain of the 3d Kentucky jotted in his diary on September 25. According to one soldier, it was widely rumored that some of Buell's own men would murder him if they ever got the chance. A member of the 8th Kentucky disgustedly related, "That old poke-easy general of ours [Buell] has allowed the thieving rebels to overrun the best portion of the State and they are now in full possession of our homes." Minnesotan D. B. Griffin admitted, "it is thought that he [Buell] works for the South more than he does for us." Arthur B. Carpenter of the 19th U.S. Infantry, discouraged after a year of campaigning, wrote, "we are just where we started."[7]

Generally, however, the anti-Buell faction centered in three groups—the Indiana bloc, the general and field officers of the First Division, and the supporters of Alexander McCook. Precisely why Hoosiers took such a personal dislike to Buell was rooted in several factors. First, throughout September, Indiana soldiers had been captured in Kentucky almost as fast as they had been mustered into service—nearly

6. Graf, Haskins, and Bergeron, *Papers of Andrew Johnson,* 6:4–6; Williams, *Lincoln and the Radicals,* 194; Nevin, *Chase Papers,* 3:285.

7. *Cincinnati Commercial,* Sept. 30, 1862; *New York Tribune,* Oct. 8, 1862; Engle, *Buell,* 294; Tapp and Klotter, *Tuttle,* 125; T. J. Wright, *History of the Eighth Kentucky Vol. Inf. during Its Three Years Campaigns Embracing Organization, Marches, Skirmishes, and Battles of the Command, with Much of the History of the Old Reliable Third Brigade, Commanded by Hon. Stanley Matthews, and Containing Many Interesting Incidents of Army Life* (St. Joseph, Mo.: St. Joseph Steam Printing, 1880), 61; *OR,* 16(1):133; Griffin to wife and children, Sept. 28, 1862, in Albertson, *Letters Home to Minnesota,* letter 57; Thomas R. Bright, "Yankee in Arms: The Civil War as a Personal Experience," *Civil War History* 19 (Sept. 1973): 202; Hannaford, *Story of a Regiment,* 346. One Ohio newspaper referred to Buell as "the most reserved, distant and unsociable of the generals in the army." *Cincinnati Commercial,* Sept. 24, 30, 1862.

five thousand at Munfordville and two thousand at Richmond. On their way to Camp Chase, Ohio, to be properly exchanged, the captured Munfordville garrison passed through the lines of the Army of the Ohio. Humiliated and outraged to see their comrades being marched back unarmed, Hoosiers channeled their anger at Buell, who had failed (many thought purposely) to come to their relief. "Old Buell is a coward or a Rebel. Shoot him—let us go," declared one Indiana private. Alva C. Griest wrote on September 26: "I have just seen several boys of the 10th Indiana. Their opinion is that Buell is a traitor or a coward, or he might have whipped Bragg ere this." Some Indiana officers, such as Tenth Brigade commander Col. William Grose, a former Republican politician, disagreed both with Buell's strategy and his politics.[8]

Another factor consolidating the Indiana bloc was the *Indianapolis Daily Journal,* which kept up a barrage of ferocious attacks. During September, the paper denounced Buell's mismanagement of the campaign. "He richly deserves to be shot, and we hope he will be cashiered," the editor demanded. The paper again lashed out: "The salvation of the West depends upon the removal of so indifferent a general. The army despises him. . . . From the beginning he has been a laggard, and the longer he has retained his command the more useless he becomes."[9]

The primary source of the state's animosity came from the man at the top— Buell's archenemy Governor Morton. A letter to the secretary of war on September 26 hinted that the army commander was the source of "mismanagement and imbecility" that had led to the loss of seven thousand Hoosiers. The governor made numerous trips between Indianapolis and Louisville to visit (and virtually incite) his enlisted constituents. "Give soldiers less marching and more fighting," he declared. Buell believed that Morton's "habitual intervention in favor of Indiana troops against the rigidity of my control" resulted in the "seeds of mischief."[10]

A second anti-Buell faction came from within the general and field officers of Thomas's old First Division, now commanded by Brigadier General Schoepf. The Polish-born officer became the chief instigator of the friction, brazenly ranting, "If they [Rebels] admire him [Buell] so much he must sympathize with them at any

8. Thomas Small Diary, Sept. 22, 1862, INHS; Alva C. Griest Diary, Sept. 26, 1862, INHS. See also James B. Shaw, *History of the Tenth Regiment Indiana Volunteer Infantry* (Lafayette, Ind.: Burt-Haywood, 1912), 186; John H. Rerick, *Forty-Fourth Indiana Volunteer Infantry* (LaGrange, Ind.: privately printed, 1880), 69–70, 270–71; William Steele to "Dear Sir," Sept. 22, 1862, William N. Steele Letters, INSL; and Grose, *Thirty-Sixth Regiment,* 139.

9. *Indianapolis Daily Journal,* Sept. 19, 22, Oct. 1, 1862.

10. *OR,* ser. 2, 4:562, ser. 3, 2:590; Buell, "East Tennessee," 43; Noe, *Perryville,* 92. Between September 29 and October 1, Governor Morton remained in Louisville to personally inspect the army's forty-two Hoosier regiments. *New York Tribune,* Oct. 2, 1862.

rate." He added, "If all these stories are true I would not like to trust him a great deal, and I have not the utmost confidence in him anyhow." According to one account, Buell had threatened to arrest Schoepf for allowing his men to forage on the way to Louisville, at which time the hot-tempered division commander openly branded Buell a traitor, drew his revolver, and might have shot him but for the intervention of officers. Late one evening on the march to Louisville, Buell rode through a field and entered the camp of the First Division without being challenged by a sentinel. He had the division commander arrested, but he was later released. Schoepf laughingly commented that he might reciprocate and have Buell arrested "if he did not mend how he rode around the lines."[11]

Other First Division officers joined in near mutinous declarations. Col. George P. Este of the 14th Ohio, in the presence of several officers of his regiment, challenged Buell's loyalty; no action was taken. Col. Marc Munday remarked that he heard a major openly censure Buell's conduct within earshot of his brigade headquarters, the words being greeted with applause. Col. John M. Harlan, commanding a brigade in the First Division, advised fellow Kentuckian Thomas Crittenden that "there was great dissatisfaction in his command; the officers and men were unwilling to serve under Buell." Crittenden refused to engage in the conversation, but he failed to rebuke Harlan. Brig. Gens. Speed Fry and James Steedman openly spoke their minds.[12]

While at Bowling Green, Lt. Col. Charles D. Kerr, a newcomer to the Army of the Ohio, spent his first night in town in a hotel. Awakened by a conversation taking place in the next room, "mainly between generals and colonels," he related a plot to arrest Buell and replace him with Thomas. So detailed were the plans that the discussion bordered on a coup. Even though writing of the incident decades later, Kerr refused to divulge the participants, though he noted that Thomas was not among them. Buell later got wind of the meeting but could never determine who was present. In the light of subsequent events (explained below), it is probable that the conspirators were Schoepf and officers of the First Division.[13]

Alexander McCook and his supporters became a third anti-Buell bloc. Back at Pelham, Tennessee, McCook, sitting in Schoepf's headquarters and with several officers present, suddenly slapped his hand on his knee and uttered: "Don Carlos won't do; he won't do." General Steedman, commanding a brigade in the First Division, replied, "General, there is a considerable feeling in the army on the subject."

11. *OR*, 16(1):138, 545–46; Frederick Marion to sister, Sept. 12, 1862, Frederick Marion Letters, ILSHL.
12. *OR*, 16(1):135, 545–46, 641.
13. Charles D. Kerr, "An Episode in the Kentucky Campaign of Generals Buell and Bragg," in *MOL-LUS, Minnesota*, 6 vols. (reprint, Wilmington, N.C.: Broadfoot, 1992), 4:269–71, 273.

"Oh," replied McCook, "George Thomas is the man, and we must have him." Buell happened to be in another part of the house at the time, having a conversation with Crittenden.[14]

McCook himself privately coveted the job. On September 27 Major General Nelson held his own birthday party at the Galt House. Many high-ranking officers and politicians were present, though Buell declined to attend. At one point a toast was given to "General McCook, the coming leader of the Army of the Ohio." Colonel Hazen thought the words in poor taste, but he conceded that the statement met with the complete agreement of all present. Indeed, McCook's name frequently surfaced around the Galt House as a successor to Buell. Col. William P. Carlin thought it fair to say that "McCook's ambition accorded with the views of his friends." Col. Edwin A. Parrott, a former Republican politician and now commanding McCook's old 1st Ohio, was an outspoken Buell critic.[15]

Problems with the potentially troublesome Third Division (Mitchel's former command) had been averted in part by placing a strong Buell supporter (Rousseau) in command. Also, several regiments had been removed or exchanged with those in Negley's division in Nashville. The two Chicago Irish regiments were separated, the 19th Illinois going to Negley and the 24th Illinois remaining. The Eighth Brigade had been broken up and replaced with the newly organized Twenty-Eighth Brigade. These steps, along with the addition of several new regiments, gave the Third a new character.

Although numerically small, a pro-Buell faction did exist, comprised principally of high-ranking Kentuckians who held the general's political views. Rousseau and Jackson, commanding the Third and Tenth Divisions, supported him as did Crittenden of the Fifth Division and Wood of the Sixth. Colonel Hazen, commanding the Nineteenth Brigade; Colonel Harker, the Twentieth Brigade; and Colonel Carlin, the Thirty-First Brigade, likewise held him in high esteem.[16]

Festering tensions that had been mounting for some weeks broke out on September 29. Within eight hours, events left the army command in a chaotic and near dysfunctional state. The incredible chain of events occurred the day before the army was to begin its march.

14. *OR,* 16(1):134.

15. Hazen, *Narrative,* 54; Robert I. Girardi and Nathaniel C. Hughes, eds., *The Memoirs of Brigadier General William Passmore Carlin, U.S.A.* (Lincoln: University of Nebraska Press, 1999), 66. For McCook's lack of support of Buell, see *Cincinnati Enquirer,* Oct. 28, 1862; *OR,* 16(1):113; Dodge, *Old Second Division,* 457.

16. *New York Tribune,* Oct. 3, 1862; Beatty, *Citizen Soldier,* 237; Hazen, *Narrative,* 67; Girardi and Hughes, *Memoirs of Brigadier General William Passmore Carlin,* 41.

The first incident revolved around a simmering dispute between Nelson and Brig. Gen. Jefferson C. Davis, who had come with reinforcements from Grant's army in Mississippi. Still enraged about his humiliating defeat at Richmond, Nelson openly denounced Brigadier General Manson, a Morton appointee, and the Indiana regiments for their poor showing. He outrageously labeled Hoosiers "uncouth decedents of 'poor trash' from the mountains of Kentucky, Tennessee, and North Carolina." Rumors surfaced that some Indiana soldiers planned to shoot the Kentuckian during the next engagement. Morton openly lobbied for the general's removal.[17]

It did not take Nelson long to clash with Davis, another Morton protégé. The Indiana general had been on furlough but had left his sickbed to help in the present crisis. Aware of Davis's connections with Morton, Nelson ordered him to Louisville to assist in the defense of that place rather than giving him command of the Army of Kentucky. Two or three days after his arrival, the two officers encountered one another at the Galt House. Nelson posed several questions about the progress of the work, only to receive an answer of "I don't know" with each response. One source claimed that Davis disgustedly declared, "I am a regular army officer, and will not disgrace myself by mixing with a rabble of citizens." An agitated Nelson blurted: "But you should know. I am disappointed in you, General Davis. I selected you for this duty because you were an officer in the regular army, but I find I made a mistake." Words were exchanged, and Nelson ordered Davis back to Wright's headquarters in Cincinnati. When the fiery Indiana general protested, Nelson turned to his adjutant and uttered, "Captain, if General Davis does not leave this city by nine o'clock tonight, give instructions to the provost marshal to see that he shall be put across the Ohio."[18]

Davis did go to Cincinnati but did not stay long. Since Buell arrived in Louisville on the twenty-fifth, Wright, perhaps thinking that the department commander's presence would discourage further encounters, sent Davis back across the Ohio. It would prove a fatal mistake. Davis's hatred for Nelson had turned obsessive, perhaps fanned by Governor Morton, who accompanied him on the return trip. On the morning of September 29, Morton and Davis, along with Thomas W. Gibson, a Nashville attorney formerly of Indiana, entered the Galt House. Nelson had just come from the breakfast room and was leaning against the hotel counter. Davis, in short sleeves and without a hat, approached him and demanded an apology for his previous treatment. Nelson, hard of hearing, cupped his ear with his hand. Trying

17. Hazen, *Narrative*, 56; *Indianapolis Daily Journal*, Sept. 9, 1862; *Chicago Tribune*, Oct. 2, 1862; *Cincinnati Enquirer*, Oct. 1, 1862; Noe, *Perryville*, 92.

18. J. B. Fry, "Killed by a Brother Officer," quoted in J. Montgomery Wright, "Notes of a Staff-Officer at Perryville," in *B&L*, 3:60; Gilbert, "Bragg's Invasion of Kentucky," 338. For another version of the incident leading up to September 29, see *New York Times*, Oct. 6, 1862.

to ignore him, the Kentuckian walked away, but Davis persisted. Nelson then contemptuously dismissed him by snipping: "Go away you damn puppy. I don't want anything to do with you." Almost instinctively, the incensed Indianan crumpled a hotel desk card in his hand and flipped it in Nelson's face. An enraged Nelson slapped Davis with the back of his hand and then turned to Morton and demanded, "Did you come here, sir, to see me insulted?" "No," came the reply, whereupon the general began to walk away. To a reporter Nelson barked: "Did you hear that insolent scoundrel insult me, sir? I suppose he didn't know me, sir. I'll teach him a lesson, sir."[19]

Davis, both stunned and now out of control, called for a pistol, and Gibson quickly obliged. The general caught up to Nelson at the foot of the steps, called his name, and said, "Not another step, sir." As Nelson turned, Davis shot him just above the heart at a distance of three feet. Incredibly, the Kentuckian managed to stagger up the steps before collapsing in the second-floor hallway. He cried out: "Send for a clergyman. I want to be baptized. I have been basely murdered." Major General Crittenden rushed from the breakfast room to his side and asked, "Nelson, are you seriously hurt?" "Tom, I am murdered," he answered. By the time Surgeon Robert Murray arrived, the mortally wounded general lay unconscious. By 8:30 A.M., "Bull" Nelson lay dead.[20]

Colonel Fry, the army chief of staff, happened to be in the grand ballroom at the time. He approached Davis, took him by the arm, and placed him under arrest. He later remembered that, "though thoroughly agitated, [Davis] showed no signs of rage." Indeed, he appeared glad to be arrested and volunteered information. No trial was ever held, and incredibly, Davis was back commanding a division within weeks.[21]

Shockwaves reverberated throughout the army. Believing that some of Nelson's Kentuckians would seek revenge, Buell ordered extra provost guards in the city. Several Kentucky generals expressed outrage; it was rumored that Brigadier General Boyle and Morton exchanged blows. Brig. Gens. James Jackson and William R. Terrill vowed revenge on Davis. Adding an aura of intrigue to the entire affair was E. M. Ellis, a civilian friend of Nelson. Ellis claimed that the night before he had been approached by Col. Walter C. Whitaker of the 6th Kentucky. Whitaker said that he had heard a conversation between some Indiana officers and politicians who

19. Fry, "Killed by a Brother Officer," quoted in Wright, "Notes of a Staff-Officer at Perryville," 60–61; Andrews, *North Reports the Civil War*, 296; *New York Tribune*, Sept. 30, 1862.

20. Fry, "Killed by a Brother Officer," quoted in Wright, "Notes of a Staff-Officer at Perryville," 61.

21. Ibid.; "Orders for Gen. Jacob Ammen to Relieve Brig. Gen. Jefferson Columbus Davis of His Command," Oct. 29, 1862, Jacob Ammen Papers, CINHS.

planned to pick a fight with Nelson, knowing well that he would take the bait. The implication was that a quasi-assassination had taken place.[22]

Most of the men in the ranks appeared to support Davis. J. F. Culver stated that he had heard "no one express any regret. He [Nelson] was disliked by the whole army." Writing the day of the shooting, James I. Bingham informed his mother, "My sympathies are with Davis and I can hardly censure him for the deed." Another soldier jotted in his diary, "The soldiers as a general thing seem to be glad th[e] Gen. is shot, he was considered a great tyrant by his men." A Hoosier echoed the prevailing sentiment: "The general expression is that he served him right."[23]

Barely had the smoke cleared from the lobby of the Galt House than Col. Joseph C. McKibbon arrived from Washington with orders for Buell to turn command of the army over to Thomas. Incredibly, the news had already leaked out through an officer coming from Washington, D.C., who had seen the order and reported the news to an Indianapolis paper. By the morning of September 29, even before Buell had received the order, the *Chicago Tribune* was running three front-page articles on the story, suggesting that Maj. Gen. David Hunter would be the next commander. What McKibbon did not know was that Lincoln had already had a change of heart. Exactly why this occurred is not known—perhaps the president had been calmed by the knowledge that Louisville was safe, or perhaps it came through Halleck's influence. Two telegrams had been sent to the colonel telling him to stay the order, but he had not received them and carried out his original instructions. Indeed, McKibbon wired Halleck that it was fortunate that the command change had been made—"much dissatisfaction with General Buell."[24]

General Thomas was summoned to the Galt House from his headquarters out-

22. Buell, "East Tennessee," 43; A. M. Ellis, "Major General William Nelson," *Kentucky Historical Society Register* 7 (May 1906): 56–64; Arthur A. Griese, "A Louisville Tragedy—1862," *Filson Club Historical Quarterly* 26 (Apr. 1952): 142; Roy Morris Jr., *Sheridan: The Life and Wars of General Phil Sheridan* (reprint, New York: Vintage, 1992), 85; *Indianapolis Daily Journal*, Oct. 2, 1862. Kirk C. Jenkins examined the conspiracy accusations and found them groundless; "the murder was an impulse killing by a proud and angry man [Davis]." "A Shooting at the Galt House: The Death of General William Nelson," *Civil War History* 43 (June 1997): 102–3, 118.

23. Leslie W. Dunlap, ed., *"Your Affectionate Husband, J. F. Culver": Letters Written during the Civil War* (Iowa City: Friends of the University of Iowa Libraries, 1978), 9; Prokopowicz, *All for the Regiment,* 154–55; Arthur H. DeRosier Jr., ed., *Through the South with a Union Soldier* (Johnson City: Research Planning Center, East Tennessee State University, 1969), 23. See also Thomas C. James to "Dear John," Sept. 29, 1862, Jefferson C. Davis Papers, INHS. One regiment was read the news of Nelson's death at parade rest. After breaking ranks the men broke out in cheering. Jenkins, "Shooting at the Galt House," 111. Nelson's funeral was held on September 30, the pallbearers being Major Generals McCook, Crittenden, and Granger; Brigadier Generals Jackson and Johnson; and Captain Jenkins of army headquarters. For details of the procession, see *New York Tribune,* Oct. 1, 1862.

24. *OR,* 16(1):554; *Chicago Tribune,* Sept. 29, 1862.

side the city, but even before he arrived, the Kentucky bloc was at work in a desperate attempt to reverse the order. Sens. John J. Crittenden and Garrett Davis and Reps. Robert Mallory and George W. Dunlap wired Lincoln that it was imperative that Buell be retained. Kentucky generals Crittenden, Rousseau, Jackson, and Boyle all sent telegrams. A journalist noted the frenzied atmosphere: "There was caucusing in hotel parlors, mysterious interviews with General Thomas, and large disbursements of money at the telegraph office for dispatches addressed to 'His Excellency the President.' "[25]

Taken aback by the turn of events, Thomas promptly wired Halleck that the timing was wrong for a command change. Deposing a commander in the middle of a campaign would be fraught with danger. "My position is very embarrassing, not being as well informed as I should be as the commander of this army and in the assumption of such responsibility." He urged that Buell be retained.[26]

Precisely why Thomas refused the command has long been debated. Buell misconstrued that it was due to friendship. He later discovered during an inquiry that nothing could have been further from the truth; Thomas quietly opposed him just like everyone else in the First Division. Some historians have suggested that his refusal to assume command was a kind of courtesy, a *beau geste* on the part of the Virginian. Yet Thomas himself later stated: "I am not as modest as I have been represented to be. I did not request the retention of General Buell through modesty, but because his removal and my assignment were alike unjust to him and to me. It was unjust to relieve him on the eve of battle, and unjust to myself to impose upon me the command of an army at such a time." Had the government pressed the issue, Thomas admitted that he would have accepted.[27]

Some scholars have suggested a more calculating reason; the Virginian simply did not want to unscramble Buell's mess.[28] His reasons may actually have been more subtle. When Thomas had been given command of the Army of the Tennessee back in April, General Grant had suspected backstabbing. If Thomas now superseded yet another army commander, he would be opening himself to rumors and innuendo of undercutting a superior.

The appeals to Washington had their intended affect. Halleck remanded the order (which had already been canceled anyway) and Buell unashamedly resumed command. When word of the debacle leaked out to the army, there was a loud

25. *OR*, 16(1):557–58; *New York Tribune*, Oct. 3, 1862; *New York Times*, Oct. 10, 1862.

26. *OR*, 16(2):555.

27. Buell, "East Tennessee and the Campaign of Perryville," 44. Freeman Cleaves considered Thomas's rationale feeble and concluded that he should have accepted the command. *Rock of Chickamauga*, 112–13. See also Piatt, *Thomas*, 170–71; Engle, *Buell*, 302; and Chumney, "Don Carlos Buell," 166.

28. Engle, *Buell*, 300–302.

outcry. Brigadier General Garfield exploded with disgust: "Buell, removed one morning, for a year of unparalleled s[t]upidity and disaster, and reinstated the same evening at the request of a half dozen Kentuckians who misrepresent the army and the people of the whole West." A. A. Dunham, one of the new recruits in the 129th Illinois, wrote to his family of the army response. "The report is that Buell is superseded by Genl. Thomas, his men seam all glad of it. They say that if B[uell] had a mind he could have taken Br[agg] and his whole force at Green River, but Buell stopped them and let Bragg pass out (Buell is brother-in-law to Bragg). It is said that Thomas is a good genl." The field correspondent of the *Chicago Tribune* disagreed, believing that exchanging Thomas for Buell was "out of the frying pan into the fire, for Gen. Geo. H. Thomas is a slower man than Buell. It takes Thomas half an hour to say no."[29]

As if the situation could not be worse, within hours journalists had sent reports to newspapers across the North. On October 3 the headline of the *New York Tribune* read "Removal and Restoration of Gen. Buell." The correspondent gave his blunt assessment: "There can be no possible doubt that Buell has lost the confidence of the Army of the Ohio, with the exception of the Kentucky regiments. Three-fourths of the field and line officers and the whole rank and file openly denounce him." Although not named, the reporter intimated that "several division commanders" were dissatisfied. A later editorial claimed that Buell had been saved by "the Kentucky fossils," a pointed reference to Senator Crittenden. The *Cincinnati Enquirer* came to the defense of the beleaguered army commander, claiming that Oliver Morton and an abolitionist conspiracy were at the root of the discontent. "Governor Morton has permitted his zeal to carry him too far in this matter," declared the paper.[30]

The debacle further served to widen the gap between the Indiana and Kentucky blocs. Many Hoosiers resented protecting Kentuckians who, in numbers too large, refused to join the ranks. The *Indianapolis Daily Journal* implored that there be no quarrel between the two states. The paper nonetheless conceded, "General Buell, an Indiana man, though he has few admirers in his own state, has plenty of them in Kentucky."[31]

29. *OR*, 16(2):555; Frederick D. Williams, ed., *The Wild Life of the Army: Civil War Letters of James A. Garfield* (East Lansing: Michigan State University Press, 1964), 154; DeRosier, *Through the South with a Union Soldier*, 23; *Chicago Tribune*, Oct. 2, 1862.

30. *New York Tribune*, Oct. 3, 4, 18, 25, 1862; *Cincinnati Gazette*, Oct. 8, 1862.

31. *Indianapolis Daily Journal*, Aug. 20, Oct. 2, 1862. A private in the 87th Indiana observed on September 25, "Our boys hate Louisville and Kentucky in particular and if permitted would burn the secesh hole of Louisville." Jack K. Overmyer, *A Stupendous Effort: The 87th Indiana in the War of the Rebellion* (Bloomington: Indiana University Press, 1997), 26.

The death of Nelson and the removal and reinstatement of Buell had occurred before noon on September 29. Time remained for yet one more blunder. In a hurried reorganization, Thomas accepted appointment as second in command, a position that took away his field command and made him a de facto general's aide. Two corps vacancies now had to be filled. McCook received I Corps and Crittenden II Corps. Of the two, Crittenden had seniority, so the choice was not questioned. The fact that the Kentuckian had supported Buell in the decision to retreat from Murfreesboro and had lobbied for his reinstatement must surely have entered the commanding general's mind.[32]

Buell's choice to replace Nelson for III Corps came as more of a shock. After Nelson's wounding at the Battle of Richmond, Brigadier Generals Jackson and Cruft had petitioned Wright in Cincinnati to have Charles Gilbert promoted to major general and given command of the Army of Kentucky. Both officers ranked Gilbert in seniority, but they lacked professional army experience and admitted that they were not qualified for the position. Although Gilbert held only a staff position at the time (charged specifically with the protection of railroads), no one questioned his courage; he had been wounded at Wilson's Creek and brevetted for bravery at Shiloh. Premature graying made him appear much older than his forty years, but his regular-army service had been solid. Since the Kentucky "army" was now to be absorbed into the Army of the Ohio as a third corps, Buell reasoned that Gilbert's extension of command seemed logical.[33]

But a problem existed with seniority. Gilbert's commission as major general had never been confirmed and was bestowed by Wright entirely as provisional, something that he had no authority to do. Gilbert held only a brigadier's commission, having received it only three weeks earlier, and even that had not yet been confirmed by the Senate (nor would it be), so that technically he remained a captain. Buell later insisted that he did not know this, although it appears to have been general information to most everyone else. Virtually every brigadier in the Army of the Ohio was Gilbert's senior, a point not lost upon Schoepf, who by seniority should have gotten the command. The Pole suspected (and perhaps rightly so) that the retention of Gilbert had been a ploy to deny him corps command; he seethed with resentment.[34]

32. *OR*, 16(1):558, 562–63.

33. Henry Stone, "The Operations of General Buell in Kentucky and Tennessee," *MASS*, 7:272; *OR*, 16(1):375–77, 693; Warner, *Generals in Blue*, 173–74. Prokopowicz thought the promotion of Gilbert to be "startling and inappropriate." *All for the Regiment*, 155.

34. *OR*, 16(1):221, 601; F. J. James, "Perryville and the Kentucky Campaign of 1862," in *MOLLUS*, *Ohio*, 5:162–63.

The *Chicago Tribune* suggested a more sinister rationale for the appointment. During the Turchin affair back in Alabama, Gilbert served as Buell's "man Friday" in preparing charges against the colonel so that proceedings could begin against him. The assignment of Gilbert, therefore, smacked of a payoff for past services.[35]

Adding insult to injury, Buell promptly placed Schoepf's division in Gilbert's corps. A poisonous atmosphere permeated the entire First Division. Steedman admitted the animosity: "There was a feeling that he [Gilbert] was somebody's pet, and put where he had no right and for which he was not qualified. He quarreled with nearly all the officers of the First Division about unimportant and trifling things, and there was a general opinion that he gave his attention entirely to small things instead of attending to the important duties of his position."[36]

Gilbert's own display of stupidity fueled the hatred. All of the regiments in the First Division had been paid while in Louisville except for the 10th Kentucky and 10th Indiana. In protest the Hoosiers had fixed bayonets and stuck their muskets in the ground. On the very day that Gilbert assumed command, he called up Battery C, 1st Ohio Artillery, and ordered them to open fire on their comrades. They refused, and words were exchanged. Fortunately, General Thomas came over and quietly resolved the issue.[37]

Shortly after the army pulled out of Louisville, Gilbert again revealed a moronic display of power. Near midnight one evening, the exhausted men of the 10th Indiana fell asleep on either side of the road. Gilbert rode by with his escort and demanded that the Hoosiers properly greet him. Col. William C. Kise informed him that he would hold no midnight dress parade "for any damn fool" and that the general should move on. Gilbert rode over to the flag bearer and demanded the regimental colors, but the corporal refused to relinquish them and even threatened to shoot the officer. Some soldier in fact did fire a shot in the air, while another jabbed the corps commander's horse in the rear with a bayonet, causing the animal to rear and almost toss its rider. Gilbert quickly dashed off with his escort and charges were never filed.[38]

Buell likewise placed the Ninth and Eleventh Divisions in the III Corps, which brought an immediate protest from Brig. Gen. Philip Sheridan, newly arrived from Mississippi. "I considered it somewhat unfair that I should be relegated to a brigade, when men who held no commissions at all [Gilbert] were being made chiefs of corps," he wrote. In an effort at placation, Buell kept Jerry Boyle in Louisville to

35. *Chicago Tribune*, Nov. 15, 1862.
36. OR, 16(1):136.
37. Shaw, *Tenth Regiment Indiana Volunteer Infantry*, 171–72.
38. Ibid.

organize a new division and gave the Eleventh to Sheridan. Only weeks earlier Sheridan had been leading a cavalry regiment; he now commanded 6,500 infantry.[39]

About half of the Ninth and Eleventh Divisions comprised regiments recently received from Grant in Mississippi, including Davis's former division. Most of Davis's field officers quickly fell in line with the anti-Buell faction. Buell's reorganization had thus created a monster. The First Division anti-Buell bloc had now expanded to the entire III Corps.

The inevitable happened. Eight days later, on the night of October 7, with only hours remaining before the army would join battle at Perryville, officers from Gilbert's III Corps secretly gathered behind closed doors in a private residence some six or seven miles outside Lebanon along the Rolling Fork River. Schoepf appears to have been the ringleader, and the majority of officers present came from the First Division, including all three brigade commanders—Brigadier Generals Steedman and Fry and Col. M. B. Walker—in addition to eight other colonels, one lieutenant colonel, and a major. A few officers from Robert Mitchell's Ninth Division were also present, including Col. Sidney Post, commanding a brigade, and all of the regimental officers of Dan McCook's brigade of Sheridan's Eleventh Division. Col. Hans Heg of the 15th Wisconsin opposed Buell, but there is no indication he participated in the conspiracy. A document was drawn up, with all twenty-one officers present signing, requesting that the president remove Buell from command. Although the petition was never sent, the clandestine Rolling Fork meeting represented a startling no-confidence vote literally on the eve of battle.[40]

Beyond the colossal mess in III Corps, Buell faced a feeble, if not teetering, command structure. Thomas and the three corps commanders each had their distinctive personalities. The Virginian, though an excellent officer, lacked experience in his present assignment and, as time would develop, was evolving cool relations with Buell. As for McCook and Gilbert, both were undependable, the former having strained relations with the army commander and the latter never having worked with Buell. Crittenden, junior to McCook by three weeks, possessed western charisma but could offer the Ohio general only political support, not military genius.

The formation of four new divisions (the Ninth, Tenth, Eleventh, and Twelfth) meant that seven of the nine division commanders (Brig. Gens. Joshua Sill, William Sooy Smith, Horatio Van Cleve, James S. Jackson, Robert B. Mitchell, Philip Sheridan, and Ebenezer Dumont) were novices at that level. Army leadership brimmed

39. Philip H. Sheridan, *Personal Memoirs of P. H. Sheridan,* 2 vols. (New York: Charles L. Webster, 1888), 1:189–90; Morris, *Sheridan.* 86.

40. *OR,* 16(1):124, 135–36, 221, 560; Blegen, *Letters of Colonel Hans Christian Heg,* 142. Charles Kerr heard of another secret meeting that occurred in a farmhouse in Cave City a week after the Battle of Perryville. "Episode in the Kentucky Campaign," 274.

with individualists and divided loyalties. The *Chicago Tribune* claimed that the assignment of Jackson, the thirty-nine-year-old former Kentucky congressman, to the newly formed Tenth Division was nothing more than a payoff for his support of Buell. The inexperience of officers at the division and corps level, the lack of cohesion in the new structure, the low morale of the troops due to the retention of Buell, and the formation of two whole divisions of raw recruits all foreshadowed trouble.[41]

41. *Chicago Tribune,* Oct. 24, 1862. Buell attempted to reinstate Brigadier General Johnson, who had recently arrived in Louisville. He had not been formally exchanged from his capture, however, and Bragg would not agree to his early release. See *New York Times,* Oct. 4, 1862. Brig. Gen. Jacob Ammen had been relieved of command of the Fourth Division on September 27, 1862, due to ill health. He was confined to his room for two weeks and did not return until after Perryville. Hannaford, *Story of a Regiment,* 348; Jack D. Welsh, *Medical Histories of Union Generals* (Kent, Ohio: Kent State University Press, 1996), 3.

9

Faltering Communications
The Battle of Perryville

AT 9:00 P.M. ON SEPTEMBER 30, Buell summoned Thomas and all three corps commanders for a meeting at the Galt House. The army would move out early the next morning. Sill's veteran division (10,000 strong), along with Dumont's raw Twelfth Division (9,000 troops), would march along the Shelbyville Road in a feint toward Frankfort. Press reports placed Edmund Kirby Smith's army of 10,000 men there, with a 5,000-man division under Humphrey Marshall closing on the capital. Meanwhile, the Army of the Ohio, 58,000 strong, would approach Bragg's army at Bardstown, estimated at 35,000–40,000 men. McCook's two divisions (13,000 troops total) would proceed out the Taylorsville Road, followed by Crittenden's corps (22,000). A few miles outside of town, at a place called Doup's Point, Crittenden's column would veer off to the right onto the Bardstown Road. Gilbert's corps (22,000) would march south on the Shepherdsville Road. All three roads converged at Bardstown. The grand movement would force Bragg's army north toward the Kentucky River, thereby cutting off the retreat to Tennessee.[1]

The plan, if not brilliant, was at least logical, but it did present potential problems. First, although Smith initially did have 10,000 Rebels at Frankfort, the divisions of Humphrey Marshall (3,000) and Carter Stevenson (8,000) and Morgan's cavalry (1,500) soon joined him, bringing his total strength to 22,500. (Sill did not learn of this until late in the night of October 3.) That fact, coupled with the cautious, almost leisurely pace and divergent paths (from Frankfort) of Buell's march, meant that if Bragg acted boldly, he could use the Salt River as a shield and catch Sill's column in a pincers movement between the two Confederate forces. Even if Sill's two divisions retired to Louisville, Buell's left and rear would then be exposed. True, Buell could have continued on to Danville and cut off Bragg's retreat, but in so doing he would have exposed Louisville and his main supply line.[2]

---

1. *OR*, 16(1):559, 1028; Buell, "East Tennessee," 47; *New York Tribune,* Oct. 6, 1862; Hafendorfer, *Perryville,* 65–66.

2. *OR*, 16(1):572. Grady McWhiney, Herman Hattaway, and Archer Jones have all claimed that such a maneuver stood a good chance of working. Bragg did plan such a move, but it was foiled by Lt. Gen. Leonidas Polk, temporarily commanding the Confederate army at Bardstown. McWhiney, *Braxton Bragg*

The baggage train remained far in the rear on the morning of October 1. Indeed, the first of three sections did not arrive in Louisville until the night of the third. The seventeen-hundred-wagon train took up an incredible seventeen miles on the road. "I have never heard of a train moving in this large proportion," complained the half-sick Col. Lewis Zahm, whose escorting cavalry brigade took up yet another mile. Zahm pleaded never to be given such an assignment again. The reasons for delay were many: horrid roads, broken-down mules, and the fording of the Salt River.[3]

From the outset, the march bordered on the farcical. "The boys had been full of whiskey for three days, and fell out of the ranks by scores," noted Colonel Beatty. "The road [on October 1] for sixteen miles was lined with stragglers. The new men bore the march badly." John Bross of the 88th Illinois informed his wife that the march "seemed more like a parade than anything else." So jammed were the streets that it took some divisions six hours just to clear the city. A bumbled order created early havoc. "Light" marching meant that only a single ambulance and ammunition wagon could accompany each regiment as opposed to "half-baggage," which permitted an additional wagon for each regimental and brigade staff. "By some mistake the order 'light-baggage' was not received till the army was a mile on the march," related a soldier. "The staff wagons contained our provisions, blankets, etc., they being prepared without thinking the wagons would be left. They were not permitted to come on. The result is that we are here [twelve miles east of Louisville], and many of the regiments are without anything to eat." Stragglers lined the road for miles. At the end of the day, only thirty-six men of the raw 21st Wisconsin stacked arms, the rest drifting in for hours.[4]

The hot, dusty roads of October 1 turned into ribbons of mud on the second, the result of a steady downpour throughout the afternoon and evening. "Our rations on the march such as we had not eaten were saturated, so they were useless—and were emptied from the haversacks," lamented Capt. Robert Taylor of the 22d Kentucky. Since no commissary wagons accompanied the army, the men had to go out into

---

and Confederate Defeat (Tuscaloosa: University of Alabama Press, 1969), 299–305; Hattaway and Jones, How the North Won, 257.

3. OR, 16(2):567–68; New York Times, Oct. 16, 1862; Chicago Tribune, Oct. 4, 7, 1862; Society of the Army of the Cumberland, 22nd Reunion, 170.

4. Beatty, Citizen Soldier, 176; Bross quoted in Gerald Prokopowicz, "All for the Regiment: Unit Cohesion and Tactical Stalemate in the Army of the Ohio, 1861–1862" (Ph.D. diss., Harvard University, 1994), 300; Tapp and Klotter, Tuttle, 126; New York Times, Oct. 6, 1862; Kaiser, "Civil War Letters of Charles W. Carr," 266; John L. Berkley, ed., In Defense of This Flag: The Civil War Diary of Pvt. Ormond Hupp, 5th Indiana Light Artillery (Fredonia, N.Y.: n.p., 1992), 18. McCook later stated that his corps did have some staff wagons. OR, 16(1):89, 16(2):552.

the fields and eat parched corn—"live as the Rebels live," they were told. Straggling remained endemic, though mostly among the new recruits. During the first week of the march, between Louisville and Perryville, some six thousand men fell out of the ranks, some plunderers, but mostly those who could not keep up.[5]

Buell's cavalry remained in disarray. Commanding the newly organized Third Brigade was Brig. Gen. Ebenezer Gay, who actually held the rank of captain in the regular army. It was a situation similar to "Major General" Gilbert; indeed, Gilbert was the one who had provisionally (and illegally) given Gay his rank. Buell's other two cavalry brigades, McCook's and Zahm's, remained in the rear guarding the wagon train and railroads and would not link up until October 5, their horses totally jaded. In the meantime, Gay's brigade, composed of the 2d Michigan Cavalry and the 9th Pennsylvania Cavalry, some 900 men, spearheaded the march. The latter unit had only fifty-four carbines, the balance of the 450 troopers having revolvers. Preceding Crittenden's corps would be the 4th Indiana Cavalry (five companies) and the 6th Kentucky Cavalry, both, according to Gay, raw and totally undepend-able.[6]

The columns made steady progress despite frequent skirmishing with Confeder-ate cavalry. The 4th Indiana Cavalry got its nose bloodied in an ambush on the Bardstown Road the first day out. By October 3 Gilbert's corps had progressed to Shepherdsville, Crittenden's beyond the Salt River to High Grove, and McCook's to Taylorsville. Gay's cavalry, on the left flank, had penetrated eight miles south of the Salt River to Bloomfield. Convinced that the main Confederate force confronted Crittenden's corps in the center, Gilbert was ordered to send one of his divisions over to the Bardstown Road. Despite intelligence from a civilian on October 4 that the Confederate army remained in Bardstown and that "they intend to fight," the relatively uncontested crossing of the Salt River should have tipped off Buell other-wise. Indeed, after an ambush of Federal cavalry at the fairgrounds north of Bards-town, the town, along with eighty-six prisoners, fell easily. The Rebels, according to best information, had escaped east to Springfield.[7]

---

5. Hambleton Tapp, ed., "The Battle of Perryville, October 8, 1862, as Described in the Diary of Captain Robert B. Taylor," *Register of the Kentucky Historical Society* 60 (Oct. 1962): 258–59; *Cincinnati Enquirer*, Oct. 28, 1862; *OR*, 16(1):613, 655; Berkley, *In Defense of This Flag*, 18.

6. *OR*, 16(1):661–62, 16(2):552–53; James, "Perryville," 162–63; Hafendorfer, *They Died by Twos and Tens*, 565; John W. Rowell, *Yankee Artillerymen: Through the Civil War with Eli Lilly's Indiana Battery* (Knoxville: University of Tennessee Press, 1975), 85. Other units were the 1st Ohio Cavalry, 3d Ohio Cav-alry (four companies), and 2d Kentucky Cavalry (four companies). The total number of cavalry initially available to Buell probably did not exceed 2,200. Gay was replaced at the conclusion of the campaign.

7. *OR*, 16(1):1019, 1037, 16(2):571, 575; Hafendorfer, *They Died by Twos and Tens*, 576, 579, 600–601, 651–52; *New York Times*, Oct. 12, 1862; Curry, *Four Years in the Saddle*, 72; Tapp and Klotter, *Tuttle*, 126. At Bardstown Colonel Hascall formed the 100th Illinois in a skirmish line. Uncertain that the new regi-

Buell continued the march east, but past Bardstown the suffering became intense. Despite the rain on the second, the countryside remained in one of the worst droughts in years. The creek beds had dried up, and only stagnant pools remained. "A very little of it was all a man could drink at a time, and soon his thirst was more intense than ever before," Hoosier Jesse B. Connelly attested. Perry Hall of the 79th Indiana witnessed: "I never saw men suffer for *water* as we have done for a few days. We marched till *midnight* in search of it. It is horrible to think what we have been compelled to drink." Buckeye E. G. Wood notified his mother on October 5, "I have drank water from ponds which Northern horses wouldn't drink."[8]

By the sixth Sill, alert that the secessionists had abandoned Frankfort, advanced his division and occupied the town after a sharp fight with the enemy rear guard. The Army of the Ohio continued to cautiously creep ahead—McCook to Willisburg, Crittenden to Springfield, and Gilbert, in advance of that town, to Little Beech Fork. Up to this point Buell suspected that Bragg intended to concentrate his and Smith's armies north of Perryville, but scouts that day reported the latter marching toward Danville. McCook was promptly ordered to proceed to Harrodsburg, where Sill's division would join him by a forced march. During the night, additional intelligence indicated that Bragg would concentrate at or north of Perryville. Buell prepared for what might be the deciding battle of the campaign. McCook, whose troops camped along the Chaplin River on the night of the sixth, was redirected to Perryville via the Mackville Road, while Gilbert would proceed on the Springfield Road to Perryville. Crittenden would take a more circuitous route, marching south of Springfield to Lebanon and then northeast to Perryville, approaching the town from the southwest.[9]

October 7 delivered another unseasonably hot day. The three corps got under way early: Crittenden to Haynesville, McCook to Mackville, and Gilbert, preceded by Gay's brigade, reinforced with the 9th Kentucky Cavalry, on the Springfield Pike to Perryville. Six miles west of Perryville, at Brown's Hill, the inexperienced Kentucky troopers rode into a cavalry ambush, forcing them back upon Gay's two regiments, which in turn stampeded. Lead elements of Robert Mitchell's division—the 35th Illinois, 8th Kansas, and Pinney's battery—deployed astride the Springfield Road finally checked the embarrassing rout.[10]

ment would perform well, he had the 26th Ohio placed behind them, with orders to shoot shirkers. The irate colonel of the 100th assured Hascall that he had nothing to worry about, for the 100th was "from Illinois, not Ohio [Haskell's state]." George H. Woodruff, *Fifteen Years Ago; or, the Patriotism of Will County* (Joliet, Ill.: Joliet Republican and Job Steam Printing House, 1876), 232.

8. Jesse B. Connelly Diary, INHS; Perry Hall Diary, Oct. 7, 1862, INHS; Wood quoted in Prokopowicz, *All for the Regiment*, 162. See also McDonough, *War in Kentucky*, 210–12.

9. *OR*, 16(1):666, 670, 676–77, 682, 684, 686; Buell, "East Tennessee," 47.

10. *OR*, 16(1):526, 897, 1076; Hafendorfer, *They Died by Twos and Tens*, 694–97.

From a prominent ridge outside town, Buell used a long glass to scan the terrain ahead. He concluded that the Confederates had concentrated in his front. In truth, his sketchy intelligence offered little idea of what lay on the other side of the Chaplin River. Colonel Carlin—"Billy Carlin" to his friends—happened to be near Buell and his staff as they peered ahead and spoke confidently to him of having "all the fighting you want tomorrow." Yet Carlin looked at the same terrain and admitted that he "could see nothing but the woods and open fields that were in the lower lands along the creek [Doctor's]. . . . The town I could not see."[11]

If Carlin could have viewed the town, he would not have seen much. A hamlet of less than five hundred people, Perryville straddled the Chaplin River, with a merchant's row on the west side and residences and three churches on the east side. The river, the only appreciable supply of water in the area, was not running, portions of it being dry and other sections about two feet deep. A half-dozen pikes radiated from the town, leading into a rolling and wooded countryside.[12]

Gilbert's corps pressed the gray cavalrymen back toward Perryville. At this time, an accident occurred that would have far-reaching implications. Buell, ever the martinet, became angered when he saw some troops on the Springfield Pike who had broken ranks to forage at a farmhouse. When one soldier seemingly ignored his orders to get back in line, he rode over and shouted at him. The startled man instinctively jumped to his feet and grabbed the bridle of Buell's horse. The spooked animal reared, tossing the general and then falling backward on top of him. Staff officers immediately rushed to the army commander's aid, taking him to a tent three-quarters of a mile in the rear of Sheridan's headquarters. Buell was badly bruised and cut, and not being able to ride or even sit up for several days, he had to be transported in an ambulance.[13]

By the evening of the seventh, the III Corps, on the Springfield Pike, was three and a half miles outside Perryville; the I Corps, slowed by poor roads and frequent stops, at Mackville; and the II Corps at the Rolling Fork, having diverted several miles south off the Lebanon Pike in a desperate search for water but finding only a "succession of filthy ponds." Buell himself, now incapacitated, remained at the Dor-

11. Girardi and Hughes, *Memoirs of Brigadier General William Passmore Carlin,* 62; "Buell Statement," 36; Buell, "East Tennessee," 47; Frank J. Jones, "Personal Recollections of Some of the Generals in Our Army during the War," in *MOLLUS, Ohio,* 9 vols. (reprint, Wilmington, N.C.: Broadfoot, 1991), 6:76.

12. John E. Kleber, ed., *The Kentucky Encyclopedia* (Lexington: University Press of Kentucky, 1992), 110. Historic merchant's row is still present today. The depth of the Chaplin River is based upon a trip I made to Perryville in August 1999, when the surrounding region had undergone a six-week drought, thus making for similar conditions.

13. James Quinn, "General Buell at Perryville," Buell Papers, FC.

sey house, in the rear of III Corps. Precisely what battle plan he had developed for the next day he never revealed, either in his report or in postwar writings. Presumably, he would have attacked with the II Corps on the right in an attempt to roll up the Rebel left, a tactic he had attempted (unsuccessfully) throughout the campaign. At 7:00 P.M. he dispatched couriers to both flanking corps, ordering them to begin their march at 3:00 A.M. If all went as planned, the attack would begin at 7:00 or 8:00 A.M. on October 8.[14]

But everything did not go as planned. Thomas, with Crittenden's corps, and Mc-Cook for some unexplained reason did not receive their orders until 3:00 A.M. McCook got his men on the road by five o'clock, but in the darkness Jackson's division crossed the line of march of Rousseau's division, cutting off Col. John Starkweather's brigade and forcing it to bring up the rear. Crittenden's divisions, after only three hours' sleep, were ordered to march at 6:00 A.M. but, due to a signaling error, did not actually move out until seven o'clock.[15]

Two early morning actions on October 8 confirmed that the Confederates remained in close proximity in Gilbert's front. First, a midnight patrol by two companies of the 10th Indiana encountered resistance near the Sam Bottom house. Second, in an attempt to secure the few remaining available pools of water, Sheridan, under orders from Gilbert, advanced the brigade of Col. Dan McCook (the twenty-eight-year-old brother of Alexander McCook) at 2:00 A.M., with orders to seize Peters Hill, which overlooked Doctor's Creek to the north and Bull Run to the east. The Federals drove off a lone Confederate regiment, though not before losing thirty-three men.[16]

Around 5:00 A.M. Colonel McCook, from atop Peters Hill, saw what appeared to be two enemy brigades (actually only two regiments) and a battery getting into position on the far side of Bull Run Creek in the woods behind the Bottom house. For the next hour, Battery I, 2d Illinois Light Artillery, dueled with the Confederate guns. The secessionists then launched a determined assault upon McCook's position, which he easily checked at a range of two hundred yards. McCook nonetheless remained concerned. By six o'clock he could see distant swirls of dust, both on the right and his left, along the bottom of Chaplin River. Fearful of being flanked, he called for reinforcements. Sheridan soon arrived with his remaining two brigades. A lull now occurred, punctuated only by occasional sniping.[17]

14. OR, 16(1):526, 16(2):580–81; Hafendorfer, Perryville, 118, 121, 123; Noe, Southern Boy in Blue, 102–3; Tapp, "Battle of Perryville," 267; "Buell Statement," 37.

15. OR, 16(1):1038, 1045, 16(2):587; Hafendorfer, Perryville, 37; Kenneth Williams suggests that Buell's 4:00 A.M. follow-up dispatch ("You must get within supporting distance today [the eighth]") suggests that he was already thinking defensively, not offensively. Grant Rises in the West, 124.

16. OR, 16(2):581; McDonough, War in Kentucky, 225–26.

17. OR, 16(1):238–39, 1074, 1083; Hafendorfer, Perryville, 130–31; Sheridan, Memoirs, 1:194; Nixon, Dan McCook's Regiment, 26; Walton, Behind the Guns, 27–30.

Shortly after 7:00 A.M. Gilbert reported to Buell at the Dorsey house. Since nei-
ther flank corps had reported, the attack would obviously have to be postponed.
Buell had a more immediate problem on his hands. The thought began to occur to
him that the secessionists might attack "while the center corps was alone." But he
took no precautions such as ordering his men to erect makeshift barricades, though
he had personally witnessed what had happened to Grant's army at Shiloh for a
similar omission. Gilbert, who understood that the attack had been rescheduled for
about ten o'clock, was ordered to return to his corps and not bring on a premature
engagement.[18]

The III Corps commander returned to find that all in fact was not well. Despite
his specific orders not to advance beyond Peters Hill, he found that one of Sheri-
dan's brigades, the Thirty-Fifth, under Col. Bernard Laiboldt, was marching on the
Springfield Pike toward Perryville, while his remaining brigade, the Thirty-Seventh,
under Col. Nicholas Greusel, prepared to move out. What had gone wrong? In Gil-
bert's absence the eager Gay had gone to Colonel McCook at Peters Hill, revealing
his plans to advance his cavalry and root out the Rebels on Bottom Hill. He re-
quested infantry skirmishers to support him, but McCook refused. Undeterred, the
cavalryman proceeded on but soon came under heavy fire; seventeen troopers of
the 2d Michigan Cavalry fell within minutes. Seeing his old regiment in trouble, the
feisty Sheridan ignored orders to hold and advanced. When signaled by Gilbert not
to bring on an engagement, the diminutive young brigadier replied that he "was not
bringing on an engagement, but that the enemy evidently intended to do so" and
believed that he would "be shortly attacked." Gilbert sent a dispatch for the brigades
to immediately return and resume their positions. Sheridan shrugged off the matter
by claiming that it had been "a misunderstanding." He had gained possession of the
heights beyond the Bottom house, but his "misunderstanding" had cost him 154
men.[19]

At 10:30 Buell's luck appeared to change. The van of McCook's corps had been
sighted on the Mackville Pike. At least part of his plan appeared to be working. With
the arrival of the I Corps, Buell now believed that "the time had passed" for an
enemy attack upon Gilbert. Additional information indicated that Bragg's entire
army was not at Perryville after all, only Maj. Gen. William Hardee and two divi-
sions. McCook, who reported at noon, received orders to return to his corps, secure
his front, and make a reconnaissance for water toward the Chaplin River.[20]

Throughout the morning, Buell heard nothing from Crittenden or Thomas. He

18. Buell, "East Tennessee," 47; Charles C. Gilbert, "On the Field of Perryville," in *B&L*, 3:53.

19. *OR*, 16(1):90, 1025, 1039.

20. Morris, *Sheridan*, 91–92; Gilbert, "On the Field of Perryville," 53; *OR*, 16(1):239, 1037. The *New York Times* of October 15, 1862, gave a good account of Gay's encounter. Despite Dan McCook's assertion that he did not assist Gay, the news report indicated that skirmishers of the 52d Ohio did offer support.

had no intention of advancing until he was at full strength and the II Corps covered his right, even if it meant that the Confederates escaped. Maj. J. Montgomery Wright, the assistant adjutant general, noted, "we [army staff] all knew that the subject of attention that morning was the whereabouts of Crittenden's corps." At the very moment when Buell, both physically and emotionally, needed Thomas the most, the Virginian sulked. The night before, Buell had injudiciously written Thomas that he had not heard from him throughout the day and that he should report to army headquarters upon his arrival. It was a rebuke, a gentle one, but a rebuke nonetheless. Having turned down army command only a week earlier, Thomas perhaps now saw himself more as a co-commander than a junior. The net result was that, in a passive-aggressive gesture, Thomas did not report. At 1:30 Capt. O. A. Mack, a staff officer, arrived at Buell's headquarters and feebly explained that Thomas could not report in person since skirmishing had commenced. It strained logic, of course, that a lone Rebel cavalry brigade required his personal attention. Mack stated that as of noon two of Crittenden's divisions had deployed on the right and the third was moving up. (The last division did not actually get into position until 4:00 P.M.) Yet Buell made no attempt to advance, nor did he intend to. With only a few hours of light remaining, he reasoned that the attack should be postponed until the ninth. Thomas, as methodical as Buell, would probably not have advised differently even had he been present. It mattered not; the Confederates had plans of their own.[21]

About 11:30, forty-four-year-old Capt. Cyrus O. Loomis unlimbered the six rifled guns of his 1st Michigan Artillery on a ridge just north of the Mackville Road and southwest of the Bottom house. He had no time to think of his six-year-old son or his wife, who had died three years before the war. Spotting dust swirls along the Chaplin River bottoms, he asked: "General, what is that away up that pike across yonder?" "Well, I should say it is dust," Rousseau replied. The captain concurred and moments later added: "General, that's a large body of troops and that's—yes, Harrodsburg Pike. I guess we have tread on the tail of Mr. Bragg." Rousseau responded: "Well, Loomis, you are right. You can give them a small sized hell right here."[22]

At 12:30 Rebel artillery opened fire, prompting Rousseau to utter, "Now they

21. "Buell Statement," 37; Buell, "East Tennessee," 48; J. Montgomery Wright, "Notes of a Staff-Officer at Perryville," in B&L, 3:60; OR, 16(1):556, 16(2):581. McDonough has suggested that a "subtle tension" was developing between Buell and Thomas. War in Kentucky, 225–26.

22. Marshall P. Thatcher, A Hundred Battles in the West (Detroit: privately printed, 1884), 81–82. Matthew C. Swittik, "Loomis Battery: First Michigan Artillery, 1859–1865" (master's thesis, Wayne State University, 1975), 4–5.

show themselves." Loomis's guns and those of Capt. Peter Simonson's 5th Indiana Artillery replied. A vicious one-hour duel ensued between the twelve Union guns and a like number of enemy pieces. Neither side dominated; it was mutual destruction. The blue gunners made a direct hit on a limber and disabled a piece at the range of a mile, but counterbattery fire exploded one of Simonson's caissons, causing a huge explosion and killing and wounding a number of men and horses.[23]

McCook returned to his command shortly after 1:00 P.M. to find that Rousseau had advanced the I Corps eight hundred yards toward the Chaplin River in order to get water for his men. The 42d Indiana had gone down to Doctor's Creek to fill their canteens, though little water could be found. Col. William Lytle's Seventeenth Brigade straddled the Mackville Pike, with Col. Leonard Harris's Ninth Brigade to their left. Starkweather's brigade was belatedly deployed on the Benton Road behind Jackson's division, supported by two batteries on commanding hills west of the road.[24]

After approving Rousseau's position, McCook rode to confer with Jackson, the brusque, overbearing political general commanding the rookie 5,500-man Tenth Division. Col. George Webster's Thirty-Fourth Brigade formed to the left and rear of Harris's brigade. To the north of Harris, along a ridge, stood the Thirty-Third Brigade, led by twenty-eight-year-old William R. Terrill, a tyrannical, heavy-drinking Virginian whose Confederate-sympathizing family refused to have anything to do with him. McCook ordered Terrill to send skirmishers six hundred yards to his front to gain possession of the Chaplin River. "I'll do it, and that's my water," he replied. He promptly occupied a bald hill to the north of Starkweather's artillery, where he placed the wearied and frazzled 123d Illinois, backed by Lt. Charles C. Parson's eight-gun battery manned by infantry recruits of the division. The hill thus represented the extreme left of the Union line.[25]

At two o'clock the men of the 33d Ohio, far in advance of Harris's left flank, suddenly came under attack by Confederates in brigade strength (Daniel Donelson's Tennesseans). The Buckeyes hurriedly fell back, leaving old Lt. Col. Oscar F. Moore, a former congressman, wounded and in the hands of the enemy. The advancing Southerners came under the enfilade fire of Parson's battery as well as the direct frontal fire of the 19th Indiana Light Artillery. The 33d Ohio made a stand east of the Widow Gibson house, where the 2d Ohio of Harris's brigade and the 24th Illinois of

23. *Louisville Journal,* Oct. 13, 1862; *OR,* 16(1):70, 345, 1041, 1045, 1133.

24. *OR,* 16(1):90, 343, 1039, 1044–45, 1049, 1055.

25. Ibid., 90, 1039, 1059–60, 1062; *New York Times,* Oct. 11, 1862; McDonough, *War in Kentucky,* 239, 279; Ecelbarger, "Shiloh," 68; Loren J. Morse, *Civil War Diaries and Letters of Bliss Morse* (Wagoner, Okla.: privately printed, 1985), 29. One of Jackson's regiments was in the rear guarding wagons and is not included in the 5,500 figure.

Starkweather's brigade reinforced it. A galling fire checked the enemy advance within fifteen minutes. Although under orders not to initiate an attack, McCook, behind Harris's brigade, turned to a captain and uttered that if Buell supposed "Alex McCook was coming in sight of the enemy without fighting him, he was much mistaken in his man."[26]

At 2:30, as the initial enemy brigade retired, McCook's men stared in disbelief as thousands of Rebels suddenly emerged from the woods in attack formation, stretching the entire length of the I Corps. From atop a bald hill, Jackson watched stunned as a line of gray, barely three hundred yards distant, advanced due east of his position. He ordered Parson's battery to change front and load for canister. The 105th Ohio, behind the battery, laid prone as Terrill directed the 750-man 123d Illinois to charge the enemy, perhaps attempting to buy time for Parson's men. More than one report claimed that Terrill, an artilleryman in the old army, acted more like a cannoneer than a brigadier. Whatever the reason, the regiment was totally outmatched by the veteran Rebels, who raked their ranks, dropping a quarter of the Illinoisans within minutes. Watching this, Jackson remarked, "Well, I'll be damned if this is not getting rather particular." The thud of two bullets could suddenly be heard striking his chest; in moments, Jackson lay dead. Terrill attempted to rally the 123d, but it, the 105th Ohio, and Parson's battery disintegrated, the last saving only one gun. Seeing Terrill's brigade break apart, Colonel Webster dispatched the 121st Ohio in support, but it arrived in time only to get caught in the melee. Lieutenant Parsons, who at West Point had been knocked down seven times by a bigger man only to get up each time, had to be dragged from his guns. McCook's left was in shambles.[27]

Only the determined stand of thirty-two-year-old (and former Milwaukee lawyer) John C. Starkweather's brigade prevented a rout on the left. At three o'clock the 21st Wisconsin, hiding in ambush in an advanced cornfield, the stalks ten to twelve feet high, delivered two point-blank volleys that staggered, but failed to check, the enemy advance. A final stand was made on what would become known

26. *OR,* 16(1):1040–45, 1060; Andrews, *North Reports the Civil War,* 299; Hafendorfer, *Perryville,* 222. Like Buell, Bragg labored under faulty intelligence. He thus launched an attack believing that he faced only a portion of the Union army.

27. *OR,* 16(1):1034, 1040, 1060–63, 1066–67; Samuel M. Starling to "Dear Daughters," Nov. 16, 1862, James Jackson File, PBSHP; Thomas T. Haven, *Forty-Eight Days: The 105th Ohio Volunteer Infantry, Camp Cleveland, Ohio to Perryville, Kentucky* (Vista, Calif.: n.p., 1997), 34–39; Wright, "Notes of a Staff-Officer at Perryville," 61; Kenneth W. Noe, "Grand Havoc: The Climactic Battle of Perryville," in *The Civil War in Kentucky: Battle for the Bluegrass State,* ed. Kent Masterson Brown (Mason City, Iowa: Savas, 2000), 189. The Confederates hauled off Parson's two 12-pounder Napoleon guns, but the other pieces were recovered after the battle.

as Starkweather's Hill. Riding up and down the line, Rousseau shouted, "Now boys, you will stand by me, and I will stand by you, and we will whip ——— out of them!" The twelve guns of Asahel Bush's 4th Indiana Artillery and David Stone's 1st Kentucky Artillery could not be sufficiently depressed as the Rebels clambered up the slope. Twice the guns were taken, only for the enemy to be driven back by the massed fire (six ranks deep in places) of Starkweather's men and the remnants of Jackson's division. Terrill fell mortally wounded as he attended the artillery. The secessionists eventually broke off the attack, but not before Starkweather had suffered 736 casualties, one-third of his brigade.[28]

By 2:45 McCook's right had also come under attack. Swarming across the dry bed of Doctor's Creek, Rebels in division strength drove Lytle's and Harris's brigades back up the Mackville Pike. "The blue flag with a single star waved all along their line," noted a reporter. As Bushrod Johnson's Tennessee brigade swarmed past the Bottom house, it encountered Col. John Beatty's 3d Ohio of Lytle's brigade crouched behind a rail fence on the hill above. Some of the most intense fighting of the day occurred here. A shell struck the Bottom barn, setting it ablaze and creating consternation on the Federal right flank; to Beatty it "seemed as if all hell had broken loose." A Cincinnati reporter noted that many wounded men had crawled into the barn, and sadly, "several of our poor wounded boys perished in the flames." Having exhausted their ammunition, the Buckeyes withdrew, being replaced by Col. Curran Pope's 15th Kentucky. Patrick Cleburne's Rebel brigade also relieved Johnson's Tennesseans at this time. The Kentuckians now found themselves in the meat grinder and fell back along with Beatty's 3d. Of the one thousand men in the two regiments, nearly four hundred lay dead or wounded.[29]

Colonel Lytle, planning a shock bayonet charge, ordered the 10th Ohio to lie down and wait for his order. His line suddenly became enveloped on the right, however, causing the Ohioans to retire; a correspondent noted that they walked, not ran, to the rear. Amid the confusion Lytle fell wounded and was captured. Rousseau, riding along the line, his hat on the point of his sword, attempted to form a patchwork line near the Russell house with Lytle's and Harris's brigades. He galloped over to Loomis's battery and implored his support, only to be told by the captain that he had been ordered by McCook to save his ammunition for "close work." Excitedly

28. *Cincinnati Enquirer*, Oct. 14, 1862; *OR*, 16(1):1033, 1046, 1155–56; Warner, *Generals in Blue*, 472; "The Fight for Starkweather's Hill," Post No. 7, PBSHP; Kaiser, "Civil War Letters of Charles W. Carr," 269–90; Albion W. Tourgée, *Story of a Thousand, Being a Story of the Service of the 105th Ohio Volunteer Infantry, in the War for the Union from August 21, 1862, to June 6, 1865* (Buffalo: S. McGerald and Son, 1896), 124–26; Noe, *Perryville*, 250–51; Angle, *Three Years in the Army of the Cumberland*, 21.

29. *OR*, 16(1):1128–32; Beatty, *Citizen Soldier*, 178–79; Stuart W. Sanders, "Buckeye Warriors at Perryville," *American's Civil War* (Jan. 2001): 41–44.

pointing to the enemy, Rousseau exclaimed that they were "close enough, and would be even closer in a moment." A 4:30 attack was checked, but with no thanks to Gilbert, who, though only four hundred yards away, sent no reinforcements from his corps. "He [Gilbert] was certainly near enough to render us assistance had he been inclined to do so," Rousseau bitterly testified months later.[30]

Webster's brigade of Jackson's division fought doggedly as Harris's men to their right fell back in disorder. McCook rode over to the brigade and found Webster's flank hard pressed. "He [McCook] and all of us then saw the progress of the enemy on Colonel Webster's right, as evidenced by the steady approach through the corn of a flag with a black ball in the center of a white ground; and he had hardly time to change the front of Colonel Webster's command . . . when the enemy's infantry, arriving on the edge of the corn, opened fire upon them," a staff officer reported. The brigade held, despite the actions of Col. J. R. Taylor of the 50th Ohio, who hid behind stumps. The troops eventually withdrew under pressure, with Webster falling mortally wounded. The night before, Webster, Terrill, and Jackson had discussed the possibility of being killed in the upcoming battle, but they had dismissed the idea as remote. All three now lay dead.[31]

By 3:45 McCook's corps had been under attack for an hour and forty-five minutes. On the left Terrill's brigade had been smashed, and Starkweather's, though intact and holding, was decimated. On the right Lytle's and Harris's brigades had been driven nearly half a mile, and Webster's brigade, though standing fast, was rapidly being flanked. Still, Gilbert sent no reinforcements. How could army communications have faltered so badly?

The fault, in large part, was due to McCook himself. He waited until 2:30 before he sent an aide, Lt. L. M. Hosea, to Sheridan, advising him to "look to [the] right and see that it is not turned." At three o'clock another aide, Capt. Horace Fisher, rode to the nearest commander in Gilbert's corps for reinforcements. At 3:30 two more aides, Capt. W. T. Hoblitzell and Maj. Caleb Bates, were dispatched, the first to Schoepf to plead for reinforcements and the latter to Buell. Why did McCook not immediately apprise army headquarters of his situation? His own answer, given during the Buell inquiry, stated that he waited to confirm that the battle would be "a general one." Yet that fact was undeniably known by 2:30. The truth is McCook thought that he could handle the situation on his own—at least that is the conclusion that Buell reached, and he would never forgive him.[32]

30. OR, 16(1):346, 1033, 1047; Landrum to Amanda, Oct. 12, 1862, George W. Landrum Letters, OHS; "The Battle of Perryville," Blue and Gray Magazine 1 (Oct.–Nov. 1983): 37; OR, 16(1):70, 1047, 1049–50, 1058, 1060; McDonough, War in Kentucky, 281–82; Beatty, Citizen Soldier, 178–79; Cincinnati Enquirer, Oct. 3, 14, 1862.

31. OR, 16(1):1060–62, 1066, 1069; Gilbert, "On the Field of Perryville," 57.

32. OR, 16(1):91, 1040. A reporter watching McCook came to the same conclusion: "He is not a man of decision; he is not a man of energy." New York Times, Oct. 19, 1862.

So little did Buell and Gilbert anticipate an attack that at two o'clock they lunched together back at the Dorsey house. At that time, distant cannonading could be heard, prompting Buell to send a dispatch to Sheridan ordering him to "stop that useless waste of powder." The shelling soon subsided. Due to a quirk of nature called an acoustic shadow, the roar of musketry off to the left could not be heard. Both generals thus talked casually as a battle raged not three miles away. At 3:30 more artillery thundered, this time of a serious nature. "That is more than shelling the woods; it sounds like a fight," Buell remarked. Gilbert rode to the front to investigate. It was not until four o'clock that one of McCook's aides, Captain Fisher, arrived at the Dorsey house and divulged that the I Corps had been driven. Buell gasped at the news, and he later conceded, "I was astonished."[33]

Around three o'clock Sheridan received the message that he should watch Mc-Cook's right. Actually, from atop his position on Peters Hill, "Little Phil" had observed the Southerners forming in line of battle on the east bank of the Chaplin River. He had attempted to warn McCook by use of signal flags, but to no avail. He now watched in dismay as the Rebels lacerated the I Corps. The situation had partly been of Sheridan's own making. He sat idly as a Louisiana brigade passed the length of his division's front and attacked Lytle's unprotected flank. Having been castigated twice already that day for doing too much, he now hesitated. Sheridan did order Capt. Henry Hescock's Battery G, 1st Missouri Artillery, on Peters Hill to turn their guns and open an enfilade fire on the advancing Rebels. The artillery engaged only a short time before the general himself came under artillery fire and, at four o'clock, was threatened by a brigade-sized enemy force (Col. Samuel Powell's command). He then became more concerned about what the Confederates could do to him than he could do to them. The brigadier redirected Hescock's guns for counterbattery fire.[34]

Col. Daniel McCook, commanding Sheridan's left brigade, was rankled that no help had been sent to his older brother's I Corps. It was he, so he claimed, who had implored Sheridan to turn artillery toward the Rebel left flank. If McCook had been allowed to march his Thirty-Sixth Brigade only "250 yards over an open plain corn field[,] I could have taken the rebels in rear and flank and had them between Lytle's battery [Loomis] and my own."[35]

33. *OR*, 16(1):11, 284; Buell, "East Tennessee," 48.

34. Sheridan, *Memoirs*, 1:195–96; Charles C. Gilbert to cousin, Nov. 10, 1886, Charles C. Gilbert File, PBSHP; L. G. Bennett and William M. Haigh, *History of the Thirty-Sixth Regiment Illinois Volunteers, during the War of the Rebellion* (Aurora, Ill.: Knickerbocker and Hodder, 1876), 260; Hafendorfer, *Perryville*, 276, 317; *OR*, 16(1):283, 1082. Some writers place the attack at three o'clock. Regarding Sheridan's failure to respond to McCook, Kenneth Noe has stated that the battle "was cascading from north to south, suggesting that the enemy would next assail Sheridan's lines. . . . The best way to protect Mc-Cook's right was to hold Peter's Hill." *Perryville*, 232–33.

35. *OR*, 16(1):240.

The more pertinent question is why Mitchell, in support of Sheridan, and Schoepf, whose division served as the corps reserve, did not send reinforcements. In Gilbert's absence a command vacuum developed. When Captain Fisher arrived at Schoepf's headquarters around 3:30 with a request for assistance, the First Division commander passed him on to Gilbert. Upon hearing Fisher's report, Gilbert reported that he immediately sent Schoepf's and Mitchell's divisions forward to support Sheridan's left and right respectively and then sent the captain on to the Dorsey house to report the "astonishing news." In another postwar writing, however, Gilbert claimed that the captain reported only "some skirmishing" on the Mackville Pike, "where McCook's troops were all new." He, therefore, did not become overly concerned, for similar skirmishing had been going on in Sheridan's front all morning. It is hardly creditable that Fisher underreported McCook's plight, for he was the same officer who subsequently went on the Dorsey house and so shocked Buell with his news. Yet there is evidence that Gilbert failed to initially grasp the seriousness of affairs on the left. At four o'clock, in response to a message from Crittenden inquiring as to what all the distant noise was about, Gilbert lightheartedly replied that "his children were all quiet and by sunset he would have them all in bed, nicely tucked in, as we used to do at Corinth."[36]

One reason why Gilbert may have downplayed Fisher's report was that it was soon trumped by Sheridan's medical director, a Doctor Griffith, who arrived on the scene and portrayed Sheridan as being "hard pressed." Captain Hoblitzell arrived shortly thereafter and reported in unmistakable terms that the entire I Corps line had given ground and was on the verge of being routed. Although claiming in his official report that he immediately dispatched a brigade in response to the urgent plea, Gilbert later admitted that he waited to see Sheridan's issue decided before taking action. Mitchell even urged that one of his brigades be sent to McCook, but Gilbert replied that he could not do so without express orders from Buell. Schoepf would later claim that he pleaded to the point of tears to be allowed to reinforce McCook, all to no avail. What had in fact held back Sheridan's and Mitchell's divisions was a single Confederate brigade, easily repulsed and suffering heavy losses (Sheridan boasted that "we whipped them like hell"). Carlin described the action as "brisk skirmishing." The two brigades that did most of the fighting, the Thirty-Fifth and Thirty-Seventh, suffered only 268 casualties. With his own front now secure, Gilbert at last sent a brigade to the left, but even then a debacle occurred. Col. Moses Walker's brigade of Schoepf's division, nearest to McCook and the logical choice,

36. Ibid., 187, 556–57, 1040, 1072; Gilbert, "On the Field of Perryville," 57–58; Gilbert to cousin, Nov. 10, 1886.

was so insufficiently drilled, according to Gilbert, that it could not respond rapidly; this despite the fact that all of the regiments, save one, were veteran. Col. Michael Gooding's Thirtieth Brigade of Mitchell's division and Pinney's Wisconsin battery were at last sent.[37]

In sum, McCook had squandered at least half an hour before dispatching a courier for help. Captain Fisher consumed another half hour in getting to Gilbert. Gilbert then took an hour to make a decision. It was now about 4:30, and forty-five minutes would be required for Gooding's infantry to arrive at their destination. Who was to blame? Sheridan and his unprofessional panic over a single Rebel brigade? Gilbert for being paralyzed in decision making? The sulking Thomas for his refusal to personally report at 1:30? The failure to utilize the signal corps, which had a direct line of communication between army headquarters and the I and III Corps? The matter would be sorted out later, but for the fighting at hand, reinforcements were at last on the way.[38]

About 5:15 McCook glanced down the Benton Road and viewed Col. Michael Gooding's column advancing at the double-quick. It came none too soon. McCook's line had been driven back to the X-shaped intersection of the Mackville Pike and Benton Road. Gooding brought with him only three regiments—the 22d Indiana, 59th Illinois, and 75th Illinois (his fourth regiment guarded wagons), in all some 1,325 infantry, and Pinney's Wisconsin battery. McCook threw the midwesterners into a pasture to the right of the Benton Road, replacing Harris's battered brigade. Gooding was soon slammed by what he estimated to be a division (actually two brigades). Although checking the first enemy brigade, a slugfest developed, during which the 22d Indiana's Lt. Col. Squire I. Keith, while flourishing his sword, fell mortally wounded. The Indianans made a bayonet charge, only to have their thrust parried

37. Gilbert to cousin, Nov. 10, 1886; *OR*, 16(1):38, 283, 556–57, 1040, 1073; Girardi and Hughes, *Memoirs of Brigadier General William Passmore Carlin*, 64; Gilbert, "On the Field of Perryville," 58–59; *Chicago Tribune*, Oct. 24, 1862.

38. The Buell investigation commission placed the blame upon Gilbert. "He [Gilbert] should have done it [reinforce McCook], if for no other reason than because McCook's discomfiture exposed his own flank. Nothing but positive orders fixing and holding him in his position can justify his failure." *OR*, 16(1):10. Gilbert, in postwar years, justified his hesitancy by writing, "A wing may be allowed to be forced, but one never risks the center being broken." Yet his entire corps never faced more than a brigade. According to Gilbert, the mistake was in McCook's failure to immediately notify Buell that he was engaged so that Crittenden's corps could be advanced. Gilbert to cousin, Nov. 10, 1886. When Buell did receive notification of McCook's situation, however, he not only ordered Crittenden forward but also ordered Gilbert to immediately reinforce McCook. The commission did censure McCook, though, for his failure to send "instant notice" of the attack. *OR*, 16(1):11. The issue of the signal corps is discussed in ibid., 11, 283, 284.

by a second Confederate brigade. Gooding's line wavered and then collapsed, leaving behind 546 fallen men as it withdrew back down the Benton Road. Gooding, his horse shot from under him, became a prisoner. Mutual exhaustion and darkness mercifully halted the carnage on the Federal left.[39]

While the Thirtieth Brigade was being chewed up, a second reinforcing column arrived—Col. James Steedman's brigade of Schoepf's division. Steedman rode ahead and saw Gooding's line in trouble. He doubled back to bring up his own troops, but by the time he arrived, General McCook had already ordered them off the Benton Road in a supporting position. The Confederate attack would thus have been checked even if it had not sputtered out sooner—little comfort to Gooding's smashed brigade.[40]

Time remained for yet one more Federal debacle. At 4:00 P.M., when Buell first received word of the battle, to his credit, he immediately recognized the possibility presented him. At 4:15 he gave instructions to his aide, Lt. C. L. Fitzhugh, to ride to Thomas and order him to "press the attack on the right." The aide departed at 4:30. Although it was only a three-and-a-half-mile ride from the Dorsey house, Fitzhugh did not locate the Virginian until 6:30, an hour after sunset. Immediately a problem arose. Was Buell ordering a night attack, or should Thomas wait until the morning? A bright moon illumined the sky that evening, making it almost as bright as day. Yet Thomas, despite only minor skirmishing, labored under the delusion that a strong enemy force blocked his front. Had he taken time to make a reconnaissance in force, he would have discovered that only a single Rebel cavalry brigade (Brig. Gen. Joseph Wheeler's twelve hundred troopers and a couple of artillery pieces) prevented the II Corps from marching directly into Perryville. Lieutenant Fitzhugh could not advise him and only repeated the order. The general would thus have to use his own discretion; he would wait until the morning. He and Fitzhugh then retired for supper.[41]

Despite Thomas's lethargic performance, the Federals did in fact reach the outskirts of Perryville that evening. Gilbert, in one of his few redeeming decisions that day, ordered Mitchell to advance one of the Ninth Division's brigades. The sun had set when Carlin's command reached the stonewalls of the town. In the darkness the 36th Illinois bagged a 170-man Confederate ammunition-and-water detail. The colonel would later lament that, with an additional 2,000–3,000 men, he could have rolled up Bragg's left and driven it "up against the Dodd's Fort, the high steep bluffs of which could have captured them all." Perhaps, perhaps not; it would be left for

39. *OR*, 16(1):98, 104, 1047, 1079–80.
40. Ibid., 99, 137, 1035.
41. Ibid., 187, 667–69, 676.

historians to speculate. As for Buell, when Mitchell later advised him he could have entered the town that night, the army commander "laughed and turned it off."[42]

During the first half of the evening, Buell remained in denial. Gilbert and Sheridan had dinner with him that evening, and they were convinced that he did not grasp the magnitude of the battle that had occurred. Rousseau, who arrived at headquarters at 9:00 P.M., came to the same conclusion, stating that Buell was "pretty cool" about the day's engagement. Rousseau must have enlightened him, for by 10:30, when Thomas reported at the Dorsey house, the army commander informed him that the I Corps had been "badly cut up."[43]

General McCook arrived at army headquarters at midnight, finding Buell and Thomas in conversation. Buell could hardly veil his anger at McCook's failure to give him timely notice of the battle. Picking up a map, the corps commander explained his plight. He had fought a very severe engagement, the Tenth Division could no longer be relied upon as a fighting unit, and from all appearances at the time, it seemed as though he was cut off and surrounded. He asked for the loan of two brigades for two hours in order to dress his lines, but Buell "positively refused." McCook then pleaded for a single brigade, only to be told that he "should not have another man." The corps commander admitted that he was "vexed and provoked." He thought that he would be attacked in the morning, but Buell disagreed without explanation.[44]

What was not in dispute was the condition of the I Corps. McCook had lost 3,387 men killed, wounded, and missing; Rousseau's division alone had contributed 2,181 to the total. The Tenth Division had sustained 1,106 casualties, divided almost evenly between its two brigades. The fighting around Starkweather's Hill had been savage. By contrast, the entire III Corps had lost only 885 men, almost all in Sheridan's and Mitchell's divisions. The total Union loss topped 4,200 men, or a quarter of those engaged. Water remained so scarce that some surgeons went two days without washing their hands. Along with this unsanitary measure, before leaving Louisville, the army had discarded old ambulances but new ones were not forthcoming, thus burdening the medical staffs with a shortage of vehicles. In a final note of incompetence, medical supplies ordered from Louisville for the 1,700 Federal and 900 Confederate wounded left in Perryville, were detained two weeks in Bardstown.[45]

42. Ibid., 96, 345; Sheridan, *Memoirs,* 1:199; Girardi and Hughes, *Memoirs of Brigadier General William Passmore Carlin,* 39. Dobb's Fort is a reference to a fort built by early settlers as a protection against Indians. Kenneth Noe has written: "In the end, it was Buell and Thomas who kept the bulk of II Corps out of the Battle of Perryville, not Wheeler's cavalry." *Perryville,* 237.

43. *OR,* 16(1):345; Sheridan, *Memoirs,* 1:199.

44. *OR,* 16(1):99, 102, 1027.

45. Ibid., 1033–36; U.S. Surgeon General's Office, *The Medical and Surgical History of the War of the Rebellion, 1861–1865,* 3 vols. in 6 pts. (Washington, D.C.: Government Printing Office, 1870–88), 1:254–55.

During the night of October 8, the Confederate army escaped; the battle for Kentucky had concluded. A lack of lateral communication would later be blamed for Buell's failure to detect the enemy's retreat. The assumption behind this is that Thomas and Crittenden would have struck a powerful blow from the Federal right had they received timely notification. Given their lackluster performance on October 8–9, however, such may not have been the case. As for Gilbert, even had he been on the front line, he would have received word of McCook's plight no sooner than he actually did (3:30). He could have sent reinforcements an hour earlier, but this would probably have accomplished no more than checking the Confederate advance sooner. Even with reinforcements, McCook was simply not in a position, nor did he have the inclination, to launch a late-afternoon counterattack. In short, there had been a complete breakdown in command.[46]

46. Hagerman, *American Civil War,* 182.

Maj. Gen. Don Carlos Buell *(USAMHI)*

Brig. Gen. William B. Hazen, hero of the Round Forest *(USAMHI)*

Maj. Gen. George "Old Pap" Thomas *(LC)*

Col. Robert H. G. Minty, a shining star of the cavalry corps *(USAMHI)*

Maj. Gen. Thomas L. Crittenden, who was relieved of command following the Battle of Chickamauga *(USAMHI)*

Brig. Gen. Alexander McCook, whose corps was routed in three separate battles *(USAMHI)*

Soldiers of the Army of the Ohio crossing the Big Barren River *(USAMHI)*

Brig. Gen. James Negley (hat in hand) posing with his staff only days before leading his division into McLemore's Cove *(USAMHI)*

The 1st Michigan Engineers and Mechanics finishing the Elk River railroad trestle in July 1862 *(USAMHI)*

Maj. Gen. William S. Rosecrans and his staff. Seated, left to right: Lt. Col. Charles Ducat, Maj. Calvin Goddard, Rosecrans, Brig. Gen. James A. Garfield, Capt. Horace Porter, Maj. Frank S. Bond, Lt. Charles R. Thompson, Brig. Gen. Philip Sheridan. *(Massachusetts Commandery, MOLLUS, USAMHI)*

Brig. Gens. Jefferson C. Davis, John M. Brannan, Richard Johnson, and John H. King (seated around table, left to right) and staff *(Massachusetts Commandery, MOLLUS, USAMHI)*

"Thomastown," the headquarters of Maj. Gen. George Thomas *(Massachusetts Commandery, MOLLUS, USAMHI)*

Standing, left to right, are Col. Ferdinand Van Derveer, Brig. Gen. Washington L. Elliott, Col. Luther P. Bradley, and Col. Emerson Opdycke. Seated are Brig. Gen. Samuel Beatty, Brig. Gen. Thomas Wood, Maj. Gen. David Stanley, and Brig. Gen. Nathan Kimball. *(Massachusetts Commandery, MOLLUS, USAMHI)*

10

A Failure to Perform
The Removal of Buell

HAVING DETERMINED THAT BRAGG had concentrated his forces at Harrodsburg, Buell moved both northeast after the Rebel army and east toward Danville to cut off the retreat route to Cumberland Gap. On October 10 Crittenden's corps advanced east beyond Salt River, screened by Edward McCook's cavalry brigade. Gilbert's corps marched out the Harrodsburg Pike, bivouacking at Nevada Station, while McCook's two divisions remained at Perryville. Convinced that Bragg was preparing for a decisive battle, Buell recalled Sill's veteran division to reunite with its parent corps and waited for its arrival before closing for battle. The Confederates were thus given an additional twenty-four hours to either continue their concentration or escape.[1]

On the morning of the eleventh, the III Corps continued its snaillike pace toward Harrodsburg. Initially, scouts reported the Confederates in line of battle three miles south of town, but by early afternoon Gay's cavalry discovered Harrodsburg abandoned, the enemy apparently having escaped east over Dick's River. The Rebels had abandoned some twelve hundred sick and wounded and had destroyed all the bridges over Salt River. Rather than fight the decisive battle for Kentucky, both army commanders appeared content to call it quits. Bragg, aware of the move on Danville, fretted that his escape route would be severed. As for Buell, he was a maneuverer, not a fighter. Indeed, Buell and Thomas were not even with Gilbert's corps

---

1. "Buell Statement," 40; Van Horne, *Army of the Cumberland,* 1:95; Hafendorfer, *They Died by Twos and Tens,* 750. Dumont's division remained at Frankfort, while Maj. Gen. Gordon Granger's Army of Kentucky (three divisions totaling 17,000 men) were rapidly boarding railroad cars of the Kentucky Central Railroad to rendezvous at that place. *OR,* 16(2):589, 599, 603; Edwin C. Bearss, "General Bragg Abandons Kentucky," *Register of the Kentucky Historical Society* 59 (July 1961): 223. J. R. Chumney defended Buell's decision to wait for Sill's division before moving on Harrodsburg. "Don Carlos Buell," 176–77. He may well be correct, for one-third of the Army of the Ohio was marching toward Danville. Even with Sill's division, Bragg would have had numerical superiority. I strongly suspect, however, that Buell never intended to attack at Harrodsburg, though he never admitted as much.

Sill's division became engaged in a half-day skirmish at Dog Run on the way to reunite with Buell. He lost seventeen government and fifteen sutlers' wagons and seventy-five men of the 77th Pennsylvania. *New York Tribune,* Oct. 13, 1862.

but with Crittenden's column. That corps continued its drive toward Danville, and after slight skirmishing at the fairgrounds, Hazen's brigade of Sooy Smith's division chased out the remaining enemy cavalry, taking thirty prisoners and four hundred sick. During the rear-guard action, according to a member of the 6th Kentucky, "a half dozen of the ladies and children came out waving flags and cheering us on in our fight." The townspeople, elated at the sight of the Stars and Stripes, told of how the Rebels had stripped the town and countryside of everything of value—horses, cattle, blankets, oats, and hay. Senator Crittenden, accompanying corps headquarters, joyfully reunited with a part of his family. McCook's corps, reunited with the arrival of Sill's division that night, remained in the Perryville vicinity, waiting for the ammunition wagons to come up.[2]

Throughout a rainy October 12, Buell received reports that Bragg had indeed crossed Dick's River and formed line of battle near Camp Dick Robinson. Yet one report indicated that a body of secessionists had moved north toward the Kentucky River. Buell spent the entire day verifying the intelligence, false as it turned out, as he cautiously advanced his corps in close, parallel columns toward Dick's River. In a grand pivot movement, using Danville as the base, McCook marched to Harrodsburg, Gilbert midway between Harrodsburg and Danville, and Crittenden north up the Danville-Harrodsburg Road and then cross-country due east. Wrote one of Crittenden's Kentuckians, "Marched 8 or 9 miles across roads and through fields; three columns of our troops moving parallel to each other frequently being visible at the same time." The troops came to within six miles of the ragged and precipitous banks of Dick's River before being recalled at 1:00 P.M. to the Danville-Harrodsburg Road.[3]

Buell's next decision would be all important. The Confederate position at Camp Dick Robinson he thought virtually impregnable; Dick's River protected one flank and the rugged country to the east the other. The only viable approach, from the southeast, meant that Bragg could merely fall back behind the Kentucky River, with its easily defendable banks and fords. Since there were no parallel roads on the south bank for the Federals to take, Bragg could move virtually at will. Buell, therefore, decided to force a crossing of Dick's River and gain the enemy's rear at Lancaster, ten miles from Danville, thus turning Bragg's left. It could be decisive, but was his army in a position for a foot race? His army stretched between Danville and Harrodsburg, and if the Rebels detected the move, which they surely would, they would attempt to gain the crossroads first. Once past Lancaster, the Army of the Ohio would be rapidly leaving the Bluegrass and getting into the rugged mountain terrain

2. Van Horne, *Army of the Cumberland,* 1:195; *OR,* 16(1):242–43, 1137, 16(2):604–6; *New York Times,* Oct. 25, 1862; Hazen, *Narrative,* 63; "Buell Statement," 41; Joseph R. Reinhart, *A History of the 6th Kentucky Volunteer Infantry U.S.* (Louisville: Beargrass, 2000), 125–26.

3. "Buell Statement," 42; Beatty, *Citizen Soldier,* 182; *OR,* 16(1):54, 16(2):607; Noe, *Southern Boy in Blue,* 106; Sheridan, *Memoirs,* 1:109; Hannaford, *Story of a Regiment,* 375; Van Horne, *Army of the Cumberland,* 1:195. Some units were not withdrawn until late afternoon.

of eastern Kentucky, where passages could be easily blocked. Yet Buell did not seem overly eager about his southward shift, which could, and should, have started at sunset of the twelfth. He instead ordered it for sunrise of the thirteenth.[4]

But Buell squandered even that day in tediously concentrating his army at Danville and clearing the nearby hills and roads of pesky Confederate cavalry, which seemed as hard to shake as Kentucky camp lice. In a quirky move Crittenden's corps, the first to pass through Danville, filed out not by the Lancaster Pike but along the Old Wilderness Road to the southeast. Gilbert would take the Lancaster Road, followed by McCook. What Buell did not then know, nor would he discover until late that night, was that Bragg's army had been on the march since 1:00 A.M. of the thirteenth. As Buell spent the day patiently supervising an orderly progression, Bragg's wagon train and two of his corps had cleared Lancaster, leaving Edmund Kirby Smith's corps behind as a rear guard. Finally realizing that the Confederates had stolen a march on him, Buell frantically ordered a midnight march by Crittenden's corps along the Old Wilderness Road, hoping against hope that he could yet catch the secessionists at Crab Orchard.[5]

Buell later attempted to rationalize the Lancaster debacle, essentially claiming that he had no real chance to catch the Confederates. He figured that a sixty-thousand-man Rebel army, with fifteen hundred wagons, marching in two columns could clear Lancaster from Camp Dick Robinson within ten hours. Since Bragg departed at 1:00 A.M. on the thirteenth, that meant that his army would have been at Lancaster by 11:00 A.M. In truth, Bragg's Army of the Mississippi passed through Lancaster at a late hour on the thirteenth, camping only a short distance from town. If Gilbert's corps had forced a crossing and struck out even by midafternoon, he would have caught the Rebels stretched out along the road.[6]

Gilbert's bumbling at Lancaster set him at odds with Ninth Division commander Robert Mitchell, who admitted that he had no use for his superior. When finally within sight of the Lancaster Road, Gilbert ordered Mitchell to retire. The general chafed as he openly blurted that a great error had been made. A large wagon train had been spotted, and had he been allowed to proceed, a number of wagons could have been captured. Gilbert feebly responded that there was no water ahead, to which Mitchell replied that the men could have "stood it for one night." The corps

4. *OR*, 16(1):54–55, 63–64, 16(2):607, 612; Hafendorfer, *They Died by Twos and Tens*, 711, 767; "Buell Statement," 43. One soldier described the terrain south of Stanford as "the roughest country I ever was in." DeRosier, *Through the South with a Union Soldier*, 27.

5. Cist, *Army of the Cumberland*, 1; *OR*, 16(1):54, 64, 1137, 16(2):620; Hazen Ledger Book, William B. Hazen Papers, USAMHI, 404–5; *New York Times*, Oct. 25, 1862; Hafendorfer, *They Died by Twos and Tens*, 774. Wood's division of Crittenden's corps marched only four miles on October 13. Tapp and Klotter, *Tuttle*, 129.

6. *OR*, 16(1):56; Bearss, "Bragg Abandons Kentucky," 221.

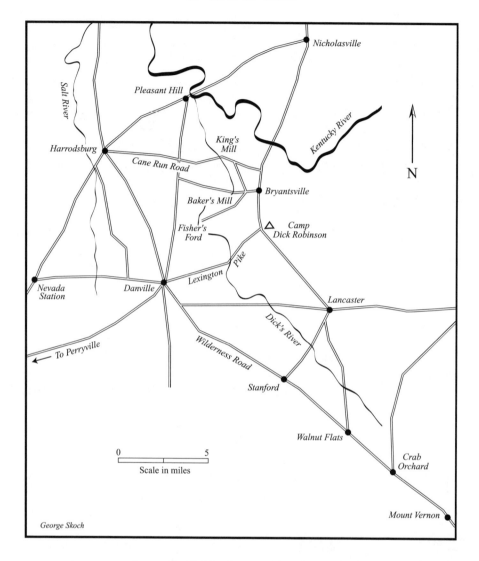

George Skoch

commander, attempting to justify his absence throughout the day, remarked, "You may think it strange that I was not in the front [of the column], but I remained in the rear for the purpose of supporting you." Mitchell fired back that he "preferred [Gilbert] would just let me alone and permit me to exercise my own judgment."[7]

Throughout the early morning hours of the fourteenth, Crittenden's corps,

7. OR, 16(1):95, 143. Col. Francis T. Sherman of the 88th Illinois wrote on October 16, 1862, "Gen. Gilbert, who commands the Third Army Corps (in which I am in), is not liked at all, and I have seen him take to the rear with his bodyguard at the discharge of two or three pieces of artillery." C. Knight

Wood's division in the van, continued its pursuit to Stanford, followed by McCook. After brief skirmishes at Hanging Fork and Hawkins Branch northwest of Stanford, Rebel cavalry withdrew through the town at 2:00 A.M., having lost fifty prisoners, twenty of them in hospitals. Wood's men encamped on a commanding hill overlooking the town. Gilbert again made slow progress, marching east on the Lexington Pike, not forcing a crossing of Dick's River until late afternoon, and halting late that night three miles west of Lancaster.[8]

Attempting to make up for lost time, Buell, accompanying Crittenden's column, directed Sooy Smith's and Horatio Van Cleve's divisions to continue the pursuit to Crab Orchard throughout the early morning hours of October 15, the latter in the van. Skirmishing continued throughout the cold, clear night. By early afternoon both divisions wearily trailed into Crab Orchard, which had been totally sacked by the Rebels. Upon entering the town, Buell exclaimed, "Bragg's army is mine!" The truth soon became known. Bragg had not veered toward Somerset on his way to Nashville, as the Ohio general had speculated, but rather had continued his retreat along the Old Wilderness Road toward Mount Vernon and London, ultimately leading to Cumberland Gap. The winding dirt road, neither macadamized nor graded, passed through rugged hills and deep gorges that could be easily blocked. The chase was over.[9]

Buell, not yet ready to admit failure, ordered Van Cleve and Wood toward Mount Vernon that afternoon. Four miles from town the road entered a deep gorge, which was totally blocked by felled trees. Sappers spent the balance of the afternoon cutting a new road rather than clearing the old. Realizing that the enemy could perform such delaying actions all the way to Cumberland Gap, Buell and Thomas could only stand "in dignified silence" while Crittenden futilely paced.[10]

Crittenden resumed the pursuit at daylight on October 16, passing through Mount Vernon, an "old dilapidated town" with a courthouse but no post office, before being stopped by skirmishing two miles beyond. Delaying actions and blocked gorges continued throughout the seventeenth, with Crittenden never gaining the enemy's rear. The Federals captured forty prisoners, some wagons, and twenty-five hundred barrels of pork at Wild Cat Mountain, but their advance was checked on the nineteenth at Little Rockcastle River, where the Confederates held their position throughout the day. Hazen's brigade entered London on the twentieth, collecting twenty-five Rebel stragglers. By then the Confederates had moved

---

Aldrich, ed., *Quest for a Star: The Civil War Letters and Diaries of Colonel Frances T. Sherman of the 88th Illinois* (Knoxville: University of Tennessee Press, 1999), 15.

8. Hafendorfer, *They Died by Twos and Tens*, 774–86, 790; Bearss, "Bragg Abandons Kentucky," 222–23; *New York Times*, Oct. 25, 1862.

9. Wright, *Eighth Kentucky*, 104; *New York Times*, Oct. 25, 1862; Hafendorfer, *They Died by Twos and Tens*, 796; "Buell Statement," 39; *OR*, 16(1):539.

10. *New York Times*, Oct. 26, 1862; *OR*, 16(1):57, 143.

past Big Laurel. The pursuit, by now more perfunctory than real, was formally hal-ted. On October 20 a soldier-correspondent of the *New York Times* wrote: "Affairs in Kentucky have ceased to be thrilling. The voice of the cloud has died away, and nothing is left for the present but a dull cold patter of rain."[11]

On the afternoon of October 18, Halleck received a dispatch from Buell via Lou-isville. Despite the army commander's declaration that "we are pressing upon him" and "[we] hope to gain some advantage," the truth could be seen by reading be-tween the lines. Buell's advance the previous morning reached Rockcastle River, al-though he conceded that Bragg's army had probably reached London the day before. On the nineteenth Halleck received yet another dispatch, this one detailing a litany of excuses—"obstructions placed in the road," "felled trees," "the absence of forage." Yet Halleck's eyes quickly focused on the operative sentence buried in the middle of the dispatch: "I shall direct my main force by the most direct route to Nashville."[12]

The only silver lining in Buell's failure to destroy Bragg's army was that it placed the Army of the Ohio in position to execute the administration's long-held pet proj-ect—the liberation of East Tennessee. Indeed, how much the government would have pressed the issue of Bragg's escape (which an investigative committee subse-quently did) if Buell had committed to entering East Tennessee is debatable. The Federal commander feared, however, that by following Bragg to Knoxville, the enemy could swing west and capture Nashville before he could be in a position to reinforce it. Besides, there was the old issue of inadequate food and forage, especially since the Rebels had fed on the countryside like ravishing locusts as they withdrew.[13]

Buell's announcement drew a prompt response. "If we cannot do it [liberate East Tennessee] now we need never hope for it," Halleck wrote in controlled anger at 3:50 A.M. on the eighteenth. Buell would not need to fall back to the Tennessee capi-tal but merely keep it between him and the enemy, while reinforcing Nashville by the glut of troops (thirty thousand) held in garrison in Kentucky. And, Halleck con-tinued, if Buell occupied Knoxville and Chattanooga, the secessionists could be pushed out of Kentucky and Tennessee and into Virginia or Georgia. After having consulted Lincoln on the nineteenth, the general in chief wrote that afternoon in unmistakable terms: "I am directed by the President to say to you that your army must enter East Tennessee this fall, and that it ought to move there while the roads are passable."[14]

Buell, showing that he also stayed up all night, answered at 1:00 A.M. on the

11. Bearss, "Bragg Abandons Kentucky," 230, 241, 244; *OR*, 16(1):1138–40; Hafendorfer, *They Died by Twos and Tens*, 808, 836; *New York Times*, Oct. 20, 26, 31, 1862.

12. *OR*, 16(2):621–22.

13. Ibid., 674, 677; Van Horne, *Army of the Cumberland*, 1:197.

14. *OR*, 16(2):623, 626–27.

twenty-second with a list of objections reminiscent of the previous autumn. Since Bragg had sixty thousand troops, he would have to have eighty thousand to seize and hold East Tennessee, with forty thousand in support in Middle Tennessee and Kentucky. Forage would have to come from Middle Tennessee, and the depot at Gainesboro, Tennessee, would not be operational for at least two months because of the low gauge of the Cumberland River. Even if he went into East Tennessee (which he had no intention of doing), the route through Cumberland Gap was "out of the question." Buell planned on moving first to Nashville and then turning Bragg's position by way of Jamestown and Montgomery.[15]

Halleck refused to blink. He replied emphatically, "It is the wish of the Government that your army proceed to and occupy East Tennessee with all possible dispatch." Exactly how Buell got there would be his decision, but the ultimate destination was not. To fall back upon Nashville would have a disastrous effect upon morale. Seemingly impervious to such directives, Buell, on October 26, ordered McCook and Gilbert to concentrate at Bowling Green and Crittenden at Glasgow. The die had been cast.[16]

Allowing Bragg's army to escape unmolested and the refusal to move into East Tennessee proved to be the final nails in the casket of Buell's tenure. "He must be removed or our army in Kentucky is ruined," clamored the *Indianapolis Daily Journal.* The *Chicago Tribune* declared, "Buell is a failure—a contemptible failure," and the *New York Times* denounced him as "a cock who wouldn't fight." The *Cleveland Plain Dealer* suggested that Buell had "too many Kentucky friends, if not relations, in the rebel army to wish to hurt them." Similar statements came from the *New York Tribune* and *Cincinnati Gazette.* The soldiers too had had enough. Tilghman Jones of the 59th Illinois believed Buell to be "a betrayer of the trust that his country has given him." Maj. James Connelly of the 123d Illinois remarked to his wife on October 24: "officers of every grade are flocking to him [Buell] with resignations. They are worn out . . . following a leader whose sole aim appears to be 'how not to do it.'" Ohio soldier Thaddeus Minshall labeled Buell "a great big limp fish . . . either a traitor or a failure." Col. Stanley Matthews denounced Buell for having forty thousand men in line of battle at Perryville who did not pull trigger. "If they had been advanced, Bragg's whole army would have surrendered," he wrote. A persistent rumor in the army, believed by many, claimed that the Ohio general had purposely held back two of his corps during the pursuit to allow Bragg to escape.[17]

15. Ibid., 636–37.

16. Ibid., 638; Van Horne, *Army of the Cumberland,* 1:196–97.

17. *Indianapolis Daily Journal,* Oct. 22, 1862; *New York Times,* Nov. 2, 6, 1862; *Cleveland Plain Dealer,* Oct. 23, 1862; Minshall quoted in Prokopowicz, *All for the Regiment,* 241; Andrews, *North Reports the Civil War,* 302; Cooling, *Fort Donelson's Legacy,* 138; Connelly Diary, 58, INHS; Matthews to wife, Oct. 31, 1862,

Even the Kentucky generals began to quietly concede that their confidence in the army commander had been misplaced. General Crittenden reportedly pronounced Buell "a hopeless case," and his father, the senator, expressed "profound disappointment." The *Chicago Tribune* claimed that Kentucky "is at last sick of Buell." Other members of the pro-Buell faction likewise expressed disenchantment. Sooy Smith spoke of the campaign as "a shame"; Wood remained silent. Only "Captain" Gilbert, as the press referred to the corps commander, held firm in his support.[18]

Schisms began to occur within the officer corps as recriminations for the Battle of Perryville were forthcoming. Buell's defenders claimed that McCook had prematurely engaged the enemy in an attempt to win a solo victory and steal army command. The Cincinnati press reported that the two generals no longer even spoke. Rousseau became so irate with McCook that Buell found it necessary to transfer him to another corps. McCook in turn pointed the finger at Gilbert and openly raised the question of his rank. The issue even came to the attention of Sen. Benjamin Wade. To his professed astonishment Buell discovered that Gilbert, although prancing around in the insignia of a major general, in fact did not even have Senate confirmation as a brigadier. Gilbert transferred back to Wright's department—"thrown out and left in the rear to guard railroad bridges," declared the *Chicago Tribune*. Crittenden also came under fire, and he was forced to publicly deny that he had received a request for reinforcements as early as 10:00 A.M. during the battle. Wrote a frustrated Colonel Beatty on October 13, "May it not be true that this butchery of men has resulted from the petty jealousies existing between the commanders of different army corps and divisions?"[19]

Most of the criticism, however, was reserved for Buell. Brigadier General Schoepf, back in Louisville a week after the battle, shot off his mouth to anyone who would listen. He declared Buell a traitor and insisted that there were "more brains in the Confederate army than there were in the Federal army." He boasted that he would be writing his political friends in Washington to apprise them of the situation. His public criticisms eventually got him arrested.[20]

Stanley Matthews Letters, CINHS. One officer later remarked that all the newspapers received in camp were anti-Buell. *OR*, 16(1):640. For additional soldier reaction to Buell, see Prokopowicz, *All for the Regiment*, 241 n. 3; and Angle, *Three Years in the Army of the Cumberland*, 25.

18. *New York Tribune*, Oct. 25, 1862; *Chicago Tribune*, Oct. 24, 31, 1862.

19. Hazen, *Narrative*, 54; Milo S. Hascall, "Personal Recollections and Experiences Concerning the Battle of Stones River," in *MOLLUS, Illinois*, 8 vols. (reprint, Wilmington, N.C.: Broadfoot, 1993), 4:152–53; Girardi and Hughes, *Memoirs of Brigadier General William Passmore Carlin*, 66–67; Beatty, *Citizen Soldier*, 183; *Chicago Tribune*, Nov. 15, 1862; *Cincinnati Enquirer*, Oct. 24, 28, 30, 1862; *Indianapolis Daily Journal*, Oct. 27, 1862; *New York Tribune*, Oct. 25, 28, 1862; *OR*, 16(1):95, 221, 16(2):662.

20. *OR*, 16(1):591–92, 600; *Chicago Tribune*, Oct. 24, 1862; Minshall quoted in Prokopowicz, *All for the Regiment*, 241. For other critical soldier statements, see McDonough, *War in Kentucky*, 297–98.

Certain officers conducted a routine court-martial at Crab Orchard. A very non-routine side discussion arose among the members of the judges' panel concerning Buell's performance at Perryville. Once again the instigators proved to be officers of the First Division and signers of the Rolling Fork declaration—General Steedman and Col. James George of the 2d Minnesota. A telegram, signed by all present except one, was sent to the president, indicating that the army had lost confidence in Buell. Colonel Carlin, the sole holdout, did not consider the dispatch instrumental, but merely "one of the drops that filled the bucket." He expressed disgust, however, that no action was taken against the signers for what he considered to be an unlawful and insubordinate act.[21]

The autumn congressional elections slated for late October and early November 1862 made time of the essence. Already, reports of low morale in Indiana and Ohio, due to the ineptitude of Buell many believed, had emerged. An Illinois Republican party official warned Lincoln that if the election went badly, McClellan and Buell were to blame. Governor Morton alerted the president that "nothing but success, speedily and decided, will save our cause from destruction." Governor Tod wrote in a similar vein. Stanton noted with remarkable candidness in his reply: "I have been urging his removal for two months, had it done once, when it was revoked by the President." Chase wrote caustically, "It just occurs to me that the Earth is a body of considerable magnitude—but moves faster than Buell."[22]

In early October 1862 Governor Morton had traveled to Washington, where he held a conference with Lincoln. Newspapers there speculated that the governor advocated for Buell's deposal, though the Indianapolis paper published a denial. Morton, it claimed, merely lobbied for the release of the recently captured Indiana soldiers. It was a half-truth. The governor did request that the prisoners be quickly exchanged and that Hoosier regiments in the army be furloughed so that they might be allowed to return home and vote (there was no provision for absentee ballots). While there, however, he denounced Buell as "utterly unfit for command of the great army under him—is slow, opposed to Emancipation, and had [a] bad influence in every way." By late October reporters leaked information about a reported western governors' conference with Lincoln, though David Tod was said to be lukewarm on the idea. During the last week in October, Morton and Yates scheduled a meeting in Louisville to gather the most recent facts on Buell, then proceed to a meeting with Governor Tod in Columbus, and then go on to Washington. In late October Senator Johnson pleaded with Lincoln for at least the return of the Seventh

21. Girardi and Hughes, *Memoirs of Brigadier General William Passmore Carlin,* 68.
22. *OR,* 16(2):634, 652; *Chicago Tribune,* Oct. 25, 1862; Engle, *Buell,* 314; Niven, *Chase Papers,* 3:295. See also Morton letters, Oct. 9, 27, 1862, Oliver C. Morton Papers, INHS.

Division (primarily a mountaineer division of Kentuckians and Tennesseans) from western Virginia. "Let them come and [they] will redeem East Tennessee before Christmas. East Tennessee must be redeemed."[23]

Beyond the upcoming election, there was the political sensitivity of Lincoln's recently released Preliminary Emancipation Proclamation, which received early opposition in the Army of the Ohio. Buell refused to raise black volunteers, and Stanton knew of his opposition to emancipation. Chase would later write, "It was Buell's pro-slaveryism I verily believe that caused more than half his halting."[24]

The president could wait no longer. With the congressional elections only days away, he could not alienate Democratic voters by removing McClellan (at least not for the time being), but Buell was expendable. The criticism of western politicians, the press, and officers within the army had grown to such avalanche proportions that even Buell seemed resigned to his fate; indeed, he almost prodded Halleck to relieve him.[25]

With the removal of Buell likely, rumors floated about his possible successor. After the Battle of Perryville, the Honorable George W. McCook, prominent Ohio politician, close associate of Stanton, and brother to the I Corps commander, visited the Army of the Ohio. Many speculated that his presence foreshadowed the ascendancy of Alexander McCook to army command. "There is hardly a doubt that if McCook had been entirely successful in his fight [at Perryville], he would have been appointed Buell's successor without loss of time," concluded Carlin. McCook had stumbled, however, and now appeared more a part of the problem.[26]

Although there had been talk around Washington about McClellan going west, only two officers appear to have been seriously considered—George Thomas and Maj. Gen. William S. Rosecrans, the recent victor of the Battle of Corinth. Thomas, as previously noted, had been offered the job weeks earlier but had begged off, a fact that now weighed heavily against him. Halleck preferred Rosecrans, as did

23. *Indianapolis Daily Journal,* Oct. 11, 1862; Donald, *Inside Lincoln's Cabinet,* 167; *New York Tribune,* Oct. 25, 1862; Graf, Haskins, and Bergeron, *Papers of Andrew Johnson,* 6:44.

24. Thomas and Hyman, *Stanton,* 260; Christopher Dell, *Lincoln and the War Democrats* (Cranbury, N.J.: Associated University Presses, 1975), 213; Niven, *Chase Papers,* 3:305. Chase had written on September 24, "I hear from all sources that nearly all the officers in Buell's army and Buell himself are proslavery to the last degree." Ibid., 3:278. Tennessee and Kentucky congressmen all denounced the Emancipation Proclamation. *Cincinnati Enquirer,* Oct. 21, 28, 1862. For army support of emancipation, see William Townsend, *Lincoln and the Bluegrass: Slavery and Civil War in Kentucky* (Lexington: University Press of Kentucky, 1955), 299–301. According to Maj. James Connelly, many in the army longed for a commander "from the free states! One who sees nothing sacred in negro slavery—one who can say to neutral Kentuckians 'Get thee behind me, Satan.'" Angle, *Three Years in the Army of the Cumberland,* 27.

25. *OR,* 16(2):619; Villard, *Memoirs,* 2:331.

26. Girardi and Hughes, *Memoirs of Brigadier General William Passmore Carlin,* 67.

Chase, but Stanton balked. He distrusted the general for having let the shattered Confederate army at Corinth escape. Lincoln finally decided the issue by reportedly proclaiming, "Let the Virginian wait; we will try Rosecrans."[27]

Halleck drafted the orders. Rosecrans would replace Buell and drive the enemy from Kentucky and Tennessee. He might receive help from Grant in Mississippi, with whom he was known to have bad relations, and in turn he might assist Grant if needed. A warning was also attached to Rosecrans's promotion: "I need not urge you [about] the necessity of giving active employment to your forces. Neither the country nor the government will much longer put up with the inactivity of some of our armies and generals."[28]

The North greeted Buell's dismissal with great enthusiasm. The *New York Times* expressed joy and took one last swipe by declaring, "Buell is a traitor." Speaking for Radical Republicans, Horace Greeley urged, "Be patient a very little while, and all the 'augers that won't bore' will be served as Buell has been," an obvious reference to McClellan and other Democratic generals. It was not the Radicals, however, who had been Buell's downfall, but more moderate Republicans such as Governors Morton, Tod, and Yates. Morton and Yates canceled their trip to Washington, stating that the removal had come just in time. Even the Democratically controlled *Cincinnati Enquirer,* long a Buell supporter, quietly noted that the Ohio general had done the best that he could, then gave a polite greeting to Rosecrans. The Kentucky generals continued their intractable support and warned that Buell's dismissal was untimely, for it would take Rosecrans months to formulate his own strategy. But no one was now listening.[29]

27. Tyler Dennett, ed., *Lincoln and the Civil War: In the Diaries and Letters of John Hay* (reprint, New York: Da Capo, 1988), 51–52; Thomas and Hyman, *Stanton,* 227; Cleve, *Rock of Chickamauga,* 117–18. David Donald has stated that Lincoln's selection of Rosecrans was "politically shrewd" because the general was "politically neutral," not "aligned with either the Moderate or the Radical faction of the Republican party," and he was known to "generally favor the President's policies." *Lincoln,* 390.

28. *OR,* 16(2):640–42.

29. *New York Times,* Nov. 2, 1862; *New York Tribune,* Oct. 25, 1862; *Cincinnati Enquirer,* Oct. 30, 1862.

PART 4

THE ROSECRANS ERA

11

Army of the Cumberland
The Rosecrans Influence

"I WILL LEAVE TOMORROW for General Buell's headquarters." Thus wrote Major General Rosecrans in response to the order dated October 24, 1862, directing him to report to Louisville and relieve Buell of command. He arrived at the Galt House on the thirtieth. Since the War Department failed to inform Buell of the impending change, Rosecrans felt in an awkward position, more "like a constable bearing a writ for the ejection of a tenant than like a general on his way to relieve a brother officer." Although arriving late, the new department commander, the fourth within seventeen months, was serenaded and addressed a large crowd.[1]

Rosecrans proceeded to Bowling Green, where he established his headquarters in a private residence on the thirtieth. The ungrateful, Southern-sympathizing hostess promptly tinctured his drinking water with soft soap, confining him to bed for a day. Although the forty-three-year-old, Ohio-born general considered himself deserving of command, there had been little in his background to prepare him for such an enormous responsibility. He had been an exceptional student at West Point (fifth in the class of 1842), where he earned the nickname "Old Rosy," but he had missed the Mexican War, and his eleven-year army career had been spent in teaching and routine engineering stints. By the time he resigned from the regular army in 1853 due to poor health, he had only risen to first lieutenant. The next several years Rosecrans devoted to the coal industry and attempts to keep his Cincinnati kerosene-refinery business afloat. During an experiment with odorless oil, a lamp exploded in his face, causing him to be bedridden for a year and a half and leaving a facial scar that resembled a smirk in a corner of his mouth.

Rosecrans came out of retirement at the beginning of the war and served with McClellan in western Virginia. Despite his significant role in the engagement at Rich Mountain, he was denied due credit by "that damned little cuss, McClellan." Reciprocating the ill feeling, McClellan viewed Rosecrans as "a silly, fussy goose." His next combat came in September 1862, when, with nine thousand men, he more than held

1. William M. Lamers, *Edge of Glory: A Biography of General William S. Rosecrans, U.S.A.* (New York: Harcourt, Brace, and World, 1961), 182; *Chicago Tribune*, Oct. 31, Nov. 3, 1862.

his own against Maj. Gen. Sterling Price's twelve thousand Rebels at Iuka, Mississippi. In early October he scored his most significant victory when he commanded four divisions that decimated a determined Confederate attack on Corinth by an army of similar size under Maj. Gen. Earl Van Dorn. Although the shattered enemy force had escaped, the victory was sufficient to catch Lincoln's attention.

One soldier described the general thus: "Gen. Rosecrans is with us, calm, cool, self-professed—a cigar in his mouth, not lighted—never is—never saw him without it; an old hat on, a common blue overcoat. His long, large hooked nose, sharp eyes, give him the appearance of a Jew peddler." Like Buell before him, Rosecrans appeared unflagging in energy (he rarely retired before 2:00 A.M.) and a perfectionist in planning. As often as not, he had his meals on horseback. Unlike Buell, who was cold and formally polite, Rosecrans proved boisterous, opinionated, and brusque. Like Sherman, he was talkative (sometimes to the point of astonishing indiscretion), excitable, and idiosyncratic. Under pressure he could become so rattled as to stutter. An adult convert to Catholicism, he carried a rosary and reveled in theological debate. Yet Rosecrans was western in character, both smoking cigars and drinking, and often erupting in profanity (he distinguished profanity from blasphemy). His penchant for argument and tactless outbursts was sometimes aimed at superiors, eliciting him the enmity of several powerful persons, notably Secretary of War Stanton. Despite his oddities, Rosecrans appeared to possess the one quality that the army desperately needed—he could fight.[2]

Soldiers and press alike hailed the new commander's arrival. "The army is well pleased with the change. The army in Kentucky will not remain idle long," declared a Cleveland paper. Correspondent A. D. Richardson noted, "it is wonderful how enthusiastically everybody believes in him." Colonel Heg of the 15th Wisconsin noted on November 2: "I have just been up to Rosencranses [sic] Head Quarters and had a shake of the old fellows hand. . . . You do not know how pleased everybody is at the change of Buell for him." Colonel Beatty proved harder to convince: "I predict that in twelve months Rosecrans will be as unpopular as Buell."[3]

At least one officer did not share the army's endorsement. Milo Hascall, commanding a brigade in Nelson's old division, had served with Rosecrans at Newport, Rhode Island, in 1852–53. Hascall remembered him as a fanatic on Catholicism, a

---

2. Lamers, *Edge of Glory*, 13, 16–18, 54–55, 79–80, 154; Stephen W. Sears, *George B. McClellan: The Young Napoleon* (New York: Ticknor and Fields, 1988), 86; Warner, *Generals in Blue*, 410; Reid, *Ohio in the War*, 1:312–27; Williams, *Wild Life of the Army*, 226–27; Gilbert C. Kniffen, "Army of the Cumberland at Stone River," in MOLLUS, *District of Columbia*, 4 vols. (reprint, Wilmington, N.C.: Broadfoot, 1993), 3:417.

3. Lamers, *Edge of Glory*, 183; Blegen, *Letters of Colonel Hans Christian Heg*, 152; Beatty, *Citizen Soldier*, 189; Louis M. Starr, *Bohemian Brigade: Civil War Newsmen in Action* (Madison: University of Wisconsin Press, 1987), 183–84.

true "crank on the subject." When he subsequently met the general again at Bowling Green, he remained unimpressed. "His [Rosecrans's] head seemed to have been completely turned by the greatness of his promotion," Hascall bitterly wrote years later. He caustically noted that army headquarters was soon overrun with priests and reporters, predicting that certain officers would win promotion simply because they were Catholic. When these officers did in fact advance, Hascall believed that his point had been made.[4]

The same order that had sent Rosecrans to Kentucky also renamed the department. For a second time, the jurisdiction (Tennessee east of the Ohio River and any area in northern Alabama and Georgia that could be occupied) would be styled the Department of the Cumberland. While the troops in the field would be designated the XIV Corps, by January 9, 1863, the army received the name by which it would be known both then and ever after—the Army of the Cumberland. With the name change would come an evolving persona. The army that had been created by Kentucky loyalists was beginning to expand beyond the Kentucky leadership bloc. Although the control of Kentucky and East Tennessee remained paramount in Lincoln's mind, the mission of the army would slowly expand beyond the Ohio and Cumberland Valleys.[5]

By early November 1862 Bragg had concentrated at Murfreesboro, his strength estimated at twenty-five thousand with thirty-five guns. Negley's division at Nashville, though low on rations, was in no real danger, newspaper hysteria to the contrary; Rosecrans could reinforce the city before a major attack could be organized. Morgan's and Forrest's cavalry brigades remained on the prowl, however, leaving Federal officers justifiably jittery. Morgan audaciously attempted to destroy the Cumberland River bridges on November 4, while Forrest feinted from the south, prompting the big guns at Fort Negley to open fire. Incredibly, due to a weather quirk, the booming artillery could be heard by the Federal army in Bowling Green. That same day Rosecrans ordered McCook's corps to relieve the city. The three divisions marched through Mitchellville, Tennessee, near the state line, and leaving Carlin's brigade at Edgefield Junction, reached Nashville on the morning of the ninth, having marched seventy-two miles in three days. The perceived danger, along with the lengthy process of assembling five thousand pack mules considered indispensable for mountain operations, also gave Rosecrans an excuse to ignore an East Tennessee move, for which he had no more enthusiasm than his predecessor.[6]

4. Hascall, "Personal Recollections and Experiences," 151–52.

5. Cist, *Army of the Cumberland*, 72, 77; Van Horne, *Army of the Cumberland*, 1:207.

6. Cooling, *Fort Donelson's Legacy*, 148, 150; *Chicago Tribune*, Nov. 8, 1862; William Bickham, *Rosecrans' Campaign with the Fourteenth Army Corps, or the Army of the Cumberland: A Narrative of Personal Observations* (Cincinnati: Moore, Wilstach, Keys, 1863), 19, 26, 35, 72, 86; Van Horne, *Army of the Cumberland*, 1:207–8; *OR*, 20(2):19, 22. See also John M. Palmer, *Personal Recollections of John M. Palmer: The Story of an Earnest Life* (Cincinnati: Robert Clarke, 1901), 138–39.

Leaving Sooy Smith's division at Glasgow, Crittenden's corps arrived at Gallatin on November 7. Zahm's cavalry brigade, supported by Harker's brigade, cleared the town of Morgan's rear guard, capturing twenty Confederates. The corps arrived at Silver Springs, where it remained until the eighteenth, when the troops marched leisurely into Nashville. Thomas's corps brought up the rear. Dumont's division relieved Smith's, Fry's occupied Gallatin, and Rousseau's forwarded supplies and assisted in railroad repair. Rosecrans had plans to move to Nashville on the eighth, but in deference to Sunday, he superstitiously canceled the move until the ninth. Each day he worked until 2:00 A.M., sometimes until 4:00 or 5:00 A.M., ignoring the pleadings of his staff to rest.[7]

The same problem that had so vexed Buell, a damaged Louisville and Nashville Railroad, now confronted Rosecrans. The Cumberland River remained too low for transports. Even the lightest-draft boats could not pass Harpeth Shoals, twenty-four miles below the city, meaning that the army's food had to come by way of the Louisville and Nashville. The tunnel south of Mitchellville remained badly damaged, so much so that the thirty-five miles to Edgefield Junction had to be covered by wagon. McCook hoped to repair the five bridges between Nashville and Gallatin by November 15 and then keep the twenty-two locomotives and three hundred cars in Nashville constantly running to that terminus. Repairs to the entire railroad would not completed until November 26.[8]

Meanwhile, Rosecrans began the task of army reorganization. He already had the core of a temporary staff, which had accompanied him from Mississippi. He preferred to be around bright young men who could keep pace with his slavish work habits. His chief of staff was thirty-year-old, Irish-born Lt. Col. Charles Ducat. Maj. Calvin Goddard, barely twenty-four and a former employee of Merchant's Loan and Trust Bank of Chicago, served as assistant adjutant general. Rosecrans's favorite aide was thirty-year-old former railroad executive Maj. Frank S. Bond, who was assisted by Lts. Bryan Kirby and Charles R. Thompson, the latter only twenty-two.[9]

The general soon assembled his permanent staff. Ducat, a "man of decidedly inferior ability," became inspector general, being replaced by Col. Julius "Jules" Garesché as chief of staff. A Cuban-born (to French parents) Catholic, forty-two-year-old Garesché had refused a major general's commission after Fort Sumter, de-

7. Van Horne, *Army of the Cumberland,* 1:210–11; Bickham, *Rosecrans' Campaign,* 44, 87; *OR,* 20(2):33; *New York Times,* Jan. 9, 1862.

8. Van Horne, *Army of the Cumberland,* 1:210–11; Cist, *Army of the Cumberland,* 81; *New York Times,* Dec. 15, 1862; *Nashville Union,* Nov. 12, 1862.

9. Bickham, *Rosecrans' Campaign,* 16–18; John Fitch, *Annals of the Army of the Cumberland* (Philadelphia: J. P. Lippincott, 1883), 47–48, 51, 53, 280; *Society of the Army of the Cumberland, 23rd Reunion, September 1892* (Cincinnati: Robert Clarke, 1892), 171.

claring that he would earn his stars on the battlefield. He arrived in mid-November 1862 and was received by Rosecrans "with open arms." The colonel related to his wife: "I get along most smoothly with Rosecrans. He is at most but little in advance of me in his Abolitionist views." The commanding general, Gareché believed, had changed dramatically since he knew him at West Point, being now utterly fearless and "quick as lightning."[10]

Other staff members included a mix of professionals and volunteers. Forty-two-year-old Col. James "Jim" Barnett, chief of artillery, had grown up in Cleveland, where he had operated a hardware store and served with the state militia. Thirty-six-year-old Lt. Col. Samuel Simmons, a former St. Louis attorney who had served with Rosecrans in Mississippi, was tapped as chief commissary. Lt. Col. John W. Taylor, chief quartermaster, was a former Iowa businessman and at age forty-five the senior of the staff. Capt. Horace Porter, a twenty-five-year-old West Pointer, became chief of ordnance. The brilliant, though peculiar, thirty-three-year-old Capt. James St. Clair Morton, a West Pointer, became chief engineer. Forty-year-old Grovin Perrin, with sixteen years in the regular army, served as medical director.[11]

Rosecrans found his new army in disarray—flagrant officer misbehavior, expiring enlistments, inexperienced levies, and war-weary veterans. He curbed applications for furloughs and returned invalids to duty rather than sending them home. Although impressive in size (seventy thousand infantry and artillery and four thousand cavalry), the army floundered along the banks of the Barren River like a beached whale. Absenteeism remained chronic—32,966 men absent to be exact, of whom 6,484 did not have permission—enough to fill a division. Lack of pay remained an ongoing problem. Many of the Kentucky troops had not been paid for eight or nine months, convincing Rosecrans that "the wants of their families is producing desertions." It would require one million dollars to pay the army through August 31, and he boldly requested that amount plus additional paymasters. This would result in the first sharp exchange between Rosecrans and Stanton; it would not be the last.[12]

The veteran regiments appeared in good shape, but a steady trickle of new outfits had appeared throughout the autumn. Unlike the South, which sent replacements to fill the depleted ranks of existing regiments, the North chose the ineffective policy

10. Bickham, *Rosecrans' Campaign*, 78–79; Beatty, *Citizen Soldier*, 224; Louis Gareché, *Biography of Lieut. Col. Julius P. Gareché* (Philadelphia: J. P. Lippincott, 1887), 35, 37, 388–89, 402, 411, 415.

11. Fitch, *Annals*, 49, 271, 280, 298–99, 301; Bickham, *Rosecrans' Campaign*, 76–78, 81–83; *Society of the Army of the Cumberland 31st Reunion, 1903* (Cincinnati: Robert Clarke, 1904), 178, 181.

12. Lamers, *Edge of Glory*, 187–88; *OR*, 20(2):7, 35; Bickham, *Rosecrans' Campaign*, 23–24, 47; Ducat to Larned, Nov. 14, 1862, Telegrams Received, Oct. 1862–Jan. 1865, Department of the Cumberland, Entry 916, RG 393, NA.

of creating new units. Such high-numbered regiments as the 100th and 110th Illinois, 99th and 101st Ohio, and 79th Indiana represented the new levies. Colonel Beatty expressed his disgust: "This [system] is ridiculous; nay, it is an outrage upon the tax-payers of the North. Worse yet, so long as such a skeleton is called a regiment, it is likely to bring discredit upon the State and Nation, for how can we perform the work of a regiment when it has but one-tenth of a regiment's strength? These [veteran] regiments should be consolidated, and the superfluous officers either sent home or put in the ranks." The system was one of patronage—the Republican governors could appoint new officers. The Democratically controlled *Cincinnati Enquirer* bluntly stated that the newly elected Ohio governor, David Tod, had appointed some of the poorest officers in the army.[13]

Rosecrans attempted to remedy the matter by having Governor Yates fill "the gallant 59th Illinois" with recent state draftees. The greatest appeal went to Governor Tod, however, who was petitioned for hundreds of draftees to fill the thirty-five Buckeye regiments in the army, many of which had been depleted at Perryville. Recruiting teams went to Ohio, but the overall results appear to have been minimal.[14]

Even for veteran officers, politics rather than performance often served as the basis for promotion. "The dispatches from Indianapolis speak of the probable promotion of Colonel [Fred] Jones, Forty-Second Indiana," noted Colonel Beatty. "This seems like a joke to those who know him. He cannot manage a regiment, and not even his best friends have any confidence in his military capacity. . . . [Robert] Milroy, Crittenden, and many others were promoted for inconsiderable service in engagements which have long since been forgotten by the public. Their promotions were not made for the benefit of the service, but for the political advancement of the men who caused them to be made."[15]

Division inspections remained high on the agenda. Rosecrans's visibility had an electrifying affect upon the troops, very few of whom had ever seen Buell. "All were anxious to see the general—the hero who has never lost a battle," observed an Illinois soldier. Surgeon John H. Rerick thought that he "made a most favorable impression on all officers and men." Nothing escaped the general's meticulous scrutiny. "Gens. Rosecrans, Crittenden, Van Cleve and their Staffs rode to the right of the Division," jotted a Kentuckian in Van Cleve's division, "and presently the smiling face of the Commanding General was seen coming up the lines, between

13. Beatty, *Citizen Soldier*, 194; *Cincinnati Enquirer*, Dec. 27, 1862.
14. Rosecrans to Tod, Nov. 3, 22, 1862; Rosecrans to Yates, Nov. 28, 1862; Rosecrans to Burke, Nov. 7, 1862; and Goodard to Thomas, Nov. 17, 1862, Telegrams Sent and Received, Oct. 1862–Jan. 1865, Department of the Cumberland, Entry 916, RG 393, NA.
15. Beatty, *Citizen Soldier*, 195–96.

the ranks, saying a word of kindness or instruction to almost every soldier he passed—asking one why he had no canteen, another 'where is your haversack?' and still another 'have you no blanket?' and thus he proceeded along the lines creating a good opinion among the troops." An unimpressed Hoosier in Crittenden's corps nonetheless thought the new army commander was "very common in appearanc[e], dress plain and rather homely." Joseph T. Smith of the 75th Indiana had his own opinion: "He is a fine looking man, dressed so plain and talked so common to the soldiers as he came along; he has [the] name of a fighter." Not all decisions were popularly received. The substitution of two-man shelter tents for the large Sibleys was hated, the men denouncing the former as "rags."[16]

Problems existed in all branches. Although most of the infantry had rifles rather than smoothbore muskets, there existed a lack of caliber uniformity within certain brigades. The Twenty-Ninth Brigade of Negley's division possessed fairly standard weapons: the 11th Michigan and 19th Illinois all Springfields; the 69th Ohio, Austrian rifles; and the 18th Ohio, Enfields. The Seventh Brigade of the same division, however, counted a hodgepodge of arms: 84 German rifles, 139 Springfields, 449 Prussian rifles, 50 Belgian rifles, 666 .69-caliber rifles, 583 Enfields, and 636 Austrian rifles. John Palmer's Fourth Division encountered a somewhat different problem. In Colonel Hazen's Nineteenth Brigade, the 9th Indiana was uniformly equipped with .58-caliber rifles and the 6th Kentucky with Enfields, but the 41st Ohio and newly arrived 110th Illinois still had old smoothbore .69-caliber muskets. "The arms of the 110th Illinois Reg't. are of the most nondescript character imaginable, of all calibers, dates and patterns," reported an inspector. Wood's Sixth Division was representative of the army as a whole. Of the fourteen regiments, seven had uniform weapons (one Austrian rifles, two Springfields, two Enfields, one Harpers Ferry rifles, and one .54-caliber rifles), four had a mix of Enfields and Springfields, and the remaining three a scattering of French, Austrian, Harpers Ferry, and .69-caliber rifles.[17]

Apart from several Pennsylvania and Missouri regiments, less than a dozen from the upper midwestern states, a score from Tennessee and Kentucky, and the U.S.

16. Phillip J. Reyburn and Terry L. Wilson, eds., *"Jottings from Dixie": The Civil War Dispatches of Sergeant Major Stephen F. Fleharty, U.S.A.* (Baton Rouge: Louisiana State University Press, 1999), 64; Noe, *Southern Boy in Blue*, 115; Scribner, *How Soldiers Were Made*, 64; Bickham, *Rosecrans' Campaign*, 29–30; Robert Wiley, *The Iron 44th* (n.p., n.d.), 74; Julie A. Doyle, John David Smith, and Richard McMurry, eds., *The Wilderness of War: The Civil War Letters of George W. Squier, Hoosier Volunteer* (Knoxville: University of Tennessee Press, 1998), 23; Joseph T. Smith to unknown, Nov. 9, [1862], Joseph T. Smith Letters, INHS; Dodge, *Old Second Division*, 383.

17. "Consolidated Semi-Monthly Report of Wings and Divisions, XIV Army Corps, December 12, 1862," Entry 1061, RG 393.

Regulars, the bulk of the infantry, some 76 percent, came from Ohio, Indiana, and Illinois. Despite the army's participation at Mill Springs, Shiloh, and Perryville, most of the veterans, though familiar with rugged campaigning, could not be called battle hardened. Thomas's old First Division, engaged at Mill Springs, did not participate at Shiloh or Perryville. Nelson's old Fourth and Wood's Sixth Divisions, both of which made a good showing at Shiloh, hardly pulled trigger at Perryville. Indeed, no regiment in the army could truly claim more than a single laurel on its banner, and Negley's division none. Despite the infusion of new regiments back in the early autumn, each of which averaged 800 men, the average infantry strength had significantly dwindled—a regiment comprising 388 soldiers; a brigade, 1,625; and a division, 4,722.[18]

The artillery armament badly needed modernizing. The army had thirty-two batteries totaling 164 guns. Among these units were thirty-eight outdated 6-pounders and twenty-four 12-pounder howitzers, 38 percent of the total. Effective weapons such as 12-pounder Napoleon guns and 3-inch rifles arrived slowly; there were only fifteen and nine respectively in the army. The backbone of the artillery was the 10-pounder Parrott rifle, thirty-nine being then in service. Most of the batteries had sufficient horses, ammunition, and men, although Hewitt's Kentucky battery and Battery I, 4th U.S. Artillery, remained badly depleted in all areas. Rosecrans desired to increase all thirteen of his four-gun batteries to the standard six guns.[19]

Securing arms and equipment for the depleted cavalry proved difficult. In early December 1862 there were only 3,038 troopers present for duty, armed with 1,966 carbines and 2,554 revolvers. An additional 2,883 horsemen were being assembled, but they had only 530 carbines. Ordnance officials rushed an order for 4,000 sets of cavalry equipment and 3,600 carbines and revolving rifles. The arms eventually arrived, accompanied by an unmistakable note from Stanton: "No effort shall be spared to supply what you ask for, but something is expected from you." Rosecrans requested an additional twelve hundred horses, and he explored the possibility of mounting some infantry regiments.[20]

The engineer corps also required expansion. The 1st Michigan Engineers and Mechanics, barely 550 strong, constantly worked on repairing bridges and railroad trestles. They had no experience with pontoons and stubbornly refused to drill as infantry. The 70th Indiana, known as the "Railroad Regiment," composed of working men and mechanics, went to work on the tracks at Tyree, Robinson County,

18. *OR*, 20(2):283–85, 303–5.

19. "Consolidated Semi-Monthly Report of Batteries, December 15, 1862," Entry 1062, RG 393; *OR*, 20(2):128.

20. *OR*, 20(2):60, 64, 135; Chandler to Jenkins, Nov. 4, 1862, Telegrams Sent and Received, Oct. 1862–Jan. 1865, Department of the Cumberland, Entry 916, RG 393.

Tennessee. Rosecrans, doubtless prompted by his own engineering background, ordered that 20 men (half laborers, half mechanics) from each regiment be placed under the command of an officer and two noncommissioned officers. Some 2,200 men were thus collected and organized into three pioneer battalions—the 1st, 2d, and 3d, with twelve, ten, and nine companies respectively. The men trained in bridge building, road repair, and fortifications. A new seven-hundred-foot-long pontoon train arrived from Cincinnati along with a company trained in its use. The battalions were brigaded together with an attached battery (the Chicago Board of Trade Battery) so that it could also serve as a fighting command.[21]

Securing skilled engineers proved problematical. Rosecrans pleaded, "The Army of the Potomac cannot possibly be in as much need of engineers as I am." Two additional officers were immediately dispatched, and a third sent the following spring. Rosecrans also ordered that every brigade and division detach an officer for topographical duty. These officers served as advisers and information gatherers, but Capt. Nathaniel Michler, the army's chief topographer, disapproved of the unorthodox idea.[22]

Rosecrans reversed Buell's policy of brigading the regulars with other units and assembled the battalions into a single brigade comprising the 1st Battalion, 15th U.S. Infantry; 1st Battalion, 16th U.S. Infantry; the all-Ohio 18th U.S. Infantry (three battalions); and the 1st Battalion, 19th U.S. Infantry. Forty-seven-year-old Lt. Col. Oliver L. "Blackjack" Shepard of New York led the brigade. Having lost his father at age fourteen, Shepard grew up on his uncle's farm and later graduated from West Point. Maj. John King, commanding the large 18th Infantry, had experience both in the Mexican War and on the frontier.[23]

A long-overdue army reorganization also came to the forefront. Rosecrans dispensed with the old system of consecutively numbering divisions and brigades. Several officer departures created vacancies. The inept Gilbert was banished to desk duty and the malcontent Schoepf sent to command a Federal prison in Delaware. Dumont departed (permanently as it turned out) on sick leave. Sooy Smith trans-

21. *OR*, 20(2):6, 38; Bickner, *Rosecrans' Campaign*, 34; "Consolidated Semi-Monthly Report of Wings and Divisions, XIV Army Corps, December 12, 1862"; Sligh, *First Regiment Michigan Engineers*, 7–10; Francis F. McKinney, "The First Regiment of Michigan Engineers and Mechanics," *Michigan Alumnus Quarterly Review* 62 (1956): 140–44; Phillip L. Shinman, "Engineering and Command: The Case of General William S. Rosecrans, 1862–1863," in *The Art of Command in the Civil War*, ed. Steven F. Woodworth (Lincoln: University of Nebraska Press, 1998), 88; *Indianapolis Daily Journal*, Aug. 20, 1862; *Chicago Tribune*, Nov. 21, 1862.

22. Shinman, "Engineering and Command," 90, 96.

23. Phisterer, *Association of Survivors, Regular Brigade*, 9, 12; Lewis Hosea, "The Regular Brigade of the Army of the Cumberland," in *MOLLUS, Ohio*, 9 vols. (reprint, Wilmington, N.C.: Broadfoot, 1991), 5:328–29; *Cincinnati Commercial*, Jan. 18, 30, 1862; *OR*, 20(2):285.

ferred to Mississippi—no great loss in and of itself other than another experienced division commander gone. Brigadier General Sill and Col. William E. Woodruff, temporarily in charge of divisions, reverted to brigade command. Lovell Rousseau, who had a predisposition to winter sickness, sought a way back to Louisville. Rosecrans requested the War Department for the assignment of Brig. Gen. Joseph Reynolds, saying that he had only twenty-one brigadiers for fifty-two openings.[24]

Robert Mitchell, commanding a division in Gilbert's former corps, arrived in Nashville to assume command of the capital's garrison. For the next two months, until a permanent replacement (Jefferson C. Davis) arrived, his division came under the authority of Colonel Woodruff, a Kentuckian "who for some reason claimed to be a brigadier general," declared Colonel Carlin, the true senior officer in the division. Carlin confronted him on the issue but failed to press the matter. Woodruff's claim turned out to be bogus.[25]

Rosecrans divided his infantry into three wings approximating corps. The blundering "Alex" McCook, known as "Gut" to his men for his portly profile, commanded the 21,667-man Right Wing. Colonel Beatty dismissed McCook as a "chucklehead" and "deficient in the upper story," while a journalist viewed him as "an overgrown schoolboy." Yet another reporter noted that no one could see McCook "without thinking of the biggest boy in school." A captain in the 93d Ohio believed that the corps commander "don't look to be equal to the position he holds; he seems to have drawn a lucky card." His three divisions were led by Jefferson C. Davis, Richard Johnson, and Phillip Sheridan (the old Ninth, Second, and Eleventh Divisions respectively). Both Davis and Johnson had been recently released from confinement—Davis for murdering "Bull" Nelson and Johnson from a Rebel prison camp, where he had been awaiting exchange since summer. The men of the newly redesignated Second Division preferred their temporary commander, Joshua Sill, to Johnson, and according to a soldier in the 49th Ohio, there was "a great dissatisfaction in camp on account of the change of generals." Sheridan, at age thirty-one, would be the youngest division commander in the army.[26]

24. Dodge, *Old Second Division*, 381; Van Horne, *Army of the Cumberland*, 1:210, 217; Warner, *Generals in Blue*, 133, 425, 464; Rosecrans to Halleck, Nov. 8, 1862; Rosecrans to Stanton, Nov. 8, 1862; and Rosecrans to Wright, Nov. 20, Dec. 24, 1862, Telegrams Sent and Received, Oct. 1862–Jan. 1865, Department of the Cumberland, Entry 916, RG 393.

25. Girardi and Hughes, *Memoirs of Brigadier General William Passmore Carlin*, 70–71.

26. Beatty, *Citizen Soldier*, 235; Shanks, *Personal Recollections*, 249; Warner, *Generals in Blue*, 116, 254; Kiene, *Civil War Diary*, 145; Bickham, *Rosecrans' Campaign*, 72–73; *Chicago Tribune*, Nov. 15, 1862; *Letters of Captain Henry Richards of the Ninety-Third Ohio Infantry* (Cincinnati: Wrightson, 1883), 14. Present-for-duty numbers for November 30, 1862, based upon "Rough Draft of a History of the Department of the Cumberland with Accompanying Notes and Consolidated Strength Reports, November 1861–June 1865," RG 393.

The Left Wing, 20,349 strong, would be led by the mediocre Thomas Crittenden, described by a journalist as a "country lawyer." He wore a felt hat turned up on the sides and, according to a fellow officer, was "a good drinker." Crittenden retained Wood and Van Cleve (now commanding the First and Third Divisions respectively) and inherited John Palmer. Colonel Beatty did not care for the profaning Wood, who knew how to "blow his own horn." The competent, though nonprofessional, Van Cleve, at age fifty-three, was the oldest division commander in the army. Brigadier General Palmer, the only division-level officer with neither regular-army nor Mexican War experience, led the Second Division. A highly ambitious former Republican politician and lawyer, he detested West Pointers nearly as much as the Rebels. A soldier described him as "the most common man, of his rank, that there is in the army." Much to Palmer's chagrin, his old division, the one he had brought with him from Mississippi back in September, was broken up and the regiments dispersed. He received Sooy Smith's former command, with the brigades of Brigadier General Cruft and Colonels Grose and Hazen, the last a "vain and selfish man," according to Palmer.[27]

Although the wing leadership proved weak, the oversized center, with 32,936 troops (two of the five divisions made up the Nashville garrison), would come under the reliable George Thomas. Handling the rebuffed Virginian would prove a thorny issue for Rosecrans. Thomas felt angry for being overlooked for army command, though he hinged his protest on the issue of seniority; Rosecrans's commission postdated his own. On a purely personal level, the two generals were friends. So impressed had "Old Rosy" been with Thomas at West Point that he frequently referred to him as "George Washington." The army commander now summoned him to headquarters and (in words that he later recalled) put the case to Thomas forthright. "General Thomas, without my seeking or the intervention of friends, influence, or otherwise, I have been ordered to this command by our common superior. You, McCook, and Crittenden have all been with it from the beginning. You and I have been friends for many years and I will especially need your support and advice."

Thomas made no effort to hide his feelings. "General, there is no man under whom I would rather serve than under you, but it seems to me improper that except in some real emergency, a senior should serve under a junior." He requested service in Texas, but when Thomas was informed that Rosecrans's commission predated his own, the Virginian appeared disarmed. "That removes the only objection to

<hr>

27. Beatty, *Citizen Soldier*, 235; John Palmer, *Personal Recollections*, 140–41; Castel, *Decision in the West*, 98. For Palmer's hatred of West Pointers, see Palmer to wife, Mar. 9, 1862, John Palmer Papers, ILHS.

serving under your command," he replied. Thomas was given the choice of being either second in command or leading the huge center corps. "You think it over and take your choice," Rosecrans directed. Thomas chose the latter.[28]

Halleck confirmed that Thomas was not senior to Rosecrans, but he sharply reminded the corps commander that the president had the right to ignore seniority at any rate and select whomever he wished. Thomas had previously turned down command of the army, and it had now gone to another. He replied, "I have no objection whatever to serving under General Rosecrans, now that I know that his commission dates prior to mine." Halleck and Rosecrans in fact had not been candid in their answers. The army commander belatedly admitted that upon coming to Kentucky, his commission had been backdated. Thomas again erupted to Halleck. "You may hereafter put a stick over me if you chose to do so. I will take care, however, to so manage my command, whatever it may be, as not to be involved in the mistakes of the stick."[29]

The four division commanders of the Center were Lovell Rousseau, Speed Fry, James Negley, and Joseph P. Reynolds. The coarse, nonprofessional, but highly popular Rousseau ("given to profanity somewhat, and blusters occasionally," according to Colonel Beatty) had been with the army since its fledgling organizational days in the summer of 1861. A journalist who knew him noted that the general genuinely "hated rebels like snakes." One admiring soldier believed Rousseau to be "just the man to command volunteers," though he admitted that "the Gen. can swear almost as well as Nelson." Pennsylvanian James Negley, well known in civilian life in the field of gardening, led the Second Division. Although unpopular among a certain clique of officers, he maintained the confidence of the army commander. The "mild-mannered" Brigadier General Fry, Buell's former chief of staff, was tapped for the Third Division (Schoepf's old First Division). Although he was a West Pointer, Fry's entire career, dating back to regular-army days, had been spent in staff service. Brigadier General Reynolds, a West Pointer with limited combat experience, led the Fourth Division.[30]

Nowhere were the leadership needs more apparent than in the cavalry. Rebel horsemen had been running rings around the blue troopers. Rosecrans needed someone to revamp the branch from top to bottom and he knew the exact person—

28. *The Army Reunion: Reports of the Meetings of the Society of the Army of the Cumberland, 1887 Reunion* (Cincinnati: Robert Clarke, 1888), 48. See also "Old Rosy," *National Tribune*, May 26, 1887.

29. Van Horne, *Thomas*, 88.

30. Warner, *Generals in Blue*, 163, 341–42, 397–98; Beatty, *Citizen Soldier*, 235; Landrum to sister, July 21, 1862, Jan. [?], 1863, George W. Landrum Letters, OHS; Bickham, *Rosecrans' Campaign*, 43; *Chicago Tribune*, Nov. 10, 1862. Rousseau compares favorably with Maj. Gen. Frank Cheatham in the Army of Tennessee.

Brig. Gen. David S. Stanley. Stanley had commanded an infantry division under Rosecrans in Mississippi, but he had extensive experience in the regular cavalry. "He can do more good . . . by commanding a cavalry than an infantry division," Rosecrans explained to Halleck. "I beg you . . . to send him to me. You know the expense of cavalry and what the Rebel cavalry has done. Stanley will double our forces without expense." The officer was subsequently transferred.[31]

Stanley set about the task of organizing brigades and drilling regiments in sizable formations, but he quickly encountered resistance from division commanders, who declared that they would never "give up their cavalry regiments." Rosecrans sustained his new chief, however, and a division was soon formed with three brigades, two under Cols. Robert Minty and Lewis Zahm and a reserve brigade under Stanley's control. The general had an antiquated quirk about the importance of saber drill, but most of the troopers hailed his leadership. By late December 1862 virtually all of the men were armed with a revolver and sword, and all carried a carbine of the Sharps or Burnside model. Some 5,208 troopers reported present for duty, an impressive number compared to past days, though still inferior to the Rebels in skill and experience.[32]

Perhaps the most startling aspect of the new army command was the underrepresentation of West Pointers and regulars, who now numbered only one of three corps commanders, six of ten division commanders, five of thirty-two brigade commanders, and one regimental commander. Except for Stanley and the officers of the 4th U.S. Cavalry, all of the field, staff, and line officers of the cavalry were volunteers. Only four officers in the artillery possessed regular-army experience, though the recently arrived forty-eight-year-old Capt. James H. Stokes, commanding the Chicago Board of Trade Battery, had graduated from West Point.[33]

The autumn 1862 elections had not gone well for the Republicans; indeed, the party had been trounced. In the area from which the Army of the Cumberland drew the lion's share of its strength—the border state of Kentucky, the middle and lower

31. *OR,* 16(2):655, 17(1):467, 468, 20(2):5, 6, 27, 31, 94; Warner, *Generals in Blue,* 470; Stephen Z. Starr, *The Union Cavalry in the Civil War,* 3 vols. (Baton Rouge: Louisiana State University Press, 1985), 3:110.

32. David Stanley, *Personal Memoirs of Major-General D. S. Stanley, U.S.A.* (Cambridge, Mass.: Harvard University Press, 1917), 120; Joseph G. Vale, *Minty and the Cavalry Campaigns in the Western Armies* (Harrisburg, Pa.: Edwin K. Meyers, 1886), 107–8; Thomas Crofts, ed., *History of the Service of the Third Ohio Veteran Volunteer Cavalry* (reprint, Huntington, W.Va.: Blue Acorn, 1997), 59; "Cavalry Returns, December 23, 1862, Department of the Cumberland," Entry 1062, RG 393.

33. Bickham, *Rosecrans' Campaign,* 129–30. Gerald A. Prokopowicz has written, "To its rank and file members, General Anderson/Sherman/Buell/Rosecrans' command, the great Army of Kentucky/the Cumberland/the Ohio/Fourteenth Army Corps/the Cumberland again, was little more than a bureaucratic abstraction." "Tactical Stalemate: The Battle of Stones River," *North and South* 2 (Sept. 1999): 26.

Midwest, and in the cities of Louisville, Cincinnati, and Chicago, which boasted large Irish-German populations—Democrats had proven especially strong. In Ohio, Indiana, and Illinois, Democrats had won eighteen House and three Senate seats. Fortunately for the Republicans, Governors Yates and Morton had not been up for reelection, and the Ohio governorship had been spared by a Union Party victory, the new name of the Republicans, meant to draw in pro-war Democrats. Yet antiwar feeling remained strong throughout the Ohio Valley.[34]

Opposition to the Emancipation Proclamation also intensified, both at home and in the army. "There is now no room to doubt that the President's proclamation of emancipation, though in itself right and intend[ed] for good, has come far short," observed Hoosier George Squires from Nashville. "Men are deserting every night by scores, mostly from the Kentucky regiment. There is now about 40,000 Kentucky troops in the field. On the first of Feb. [1863] there will not be 10,000 found willing to peril their lives to, as they say, free the 'Nigger,' and many, very many from the free states are very little better. Many in our regt. and in Company D [44th Indiana] say that if the Proclamation be put in force they will no longer carry a musket." Sgt. Maj. Stephen Fleharty conceded, "many of the Kentucky union troops have deserted and gone home, and the conviction is gaining ground that hereafter Tennessee and Kentucky troops will play a very insignificant part in suppressing the rebellion."[35]

Word reached Washington of a supposed anti-emancipation bloc among some of the high-ranking officers of the Army of the Cumberland, prompting Chase to express his concern to Rosecrans. He had been informed by a senator that "a good deal of hostility to the Admn. exists among the high officials of your army and that they are very liberal in denunciation of their abolitionism." McCook and the Kentucky generals, such as Rousseau, were in fact openly critical. Although the army as a whole remained polarized on the issue, a growing officer bloc favored emancipation (Colonels Beatty and Dan McCook). A few, such as Willich and Col. D. H. Gilmer of the 38th Illinois, had been antebellum abolitionists.[36]

34. James A. Rawley, *The Politics of Union: Northern Politics during the Civil War* (Lincoln: University of Nebraska Press, 1974), 89–92, 96–97, 121–22.

35. Doyle et al., *Wilderness of War*, 30; Reyburn and Wilson, *"Jottings from Dixie,"* 98. See also Prokopowicz, *All for the Regiment*, 123–24. For Ohio Valley civilian opposition to emancipation, see G. R. Tredway, *Democratic Opposition to the Lincoln Administration in Indiana* (Indianapolis: Indiana Historical Society, 1973), 9; Frank L. Klement, *The Copperheads of the Middle West* (Chicago: University of Chicago Press, 1960), 40; Richard L. Troutman, *The Heavens Are Weeping: The Diaries of George Richard Browder, 1852–1886* (Grand Rapids: Londervan, 1987), 141 (Dec. 25, 1862). In response to the threat that Kentucky troops might desert en masse, the Radical Republican *New York Tribune* on September 1, 1862, was emphatic: "Would it matter much if they laid down their arms? In spite of their numerous regimental organizations they do not number 5,000 in Gen. Buell's army. They are notoriously the worst drilled and disciplined troops in it."

36. Niven, *Chase Papers*, 3:331; *OR*, 16(1):107, 351; Beatty, *Citizen Soldier*, 194, 313; *New York Herald*, Feb. 21, 1862. See also Prokopowicz, *All for the Regiment*, 123–25.

Desiring to counteract political defeat with battlefield victory, President Lincoln needed Rosecrans to assume the offensive, a point not lost upon the general—"The Administration expects much of me," he wrote his wife on November 22. Yet like his predecessors, everywhere he looked he saw only problems, not opportunities. The country over which he had to advance was bad, and "there must be no failure." It was his final sentence that would put him in conflict with Washington—"I will not move until I am ready."[37]

Halleck clamored for action in early December. "The President is very impatient at your long stay in Nashville," he wrote Rosecrans on the fourth. Bragg had been resupplying his army from the very area that the Federals should have occupied by this time. "Twice have I been asked to designate some one else to command your army. If you remain one more week in Nashville, I cannot prevent your removal." The government demanded action, and if the Ohio general could not deliver, then "some one else will be tried." An agitated Rosecrans fired back a response. He insisted that no time had been lost and that the army was not prepared for a forward movement. If he attempted a winter offensive, a twenty-five-day food stockpile would have to be accumulated. Railroad officials had promised one hundred carloads a day at Nashville once the track was operational, but they had averaged only twenty-five. "If my superiors have lost confidence in me, they had better at once put some one in my place and let the future test the propriety of the change. . . . To threats of removal or the like I must be permitted to say that I am insensible." To W. D. Bickham, *Cincinnati Commercial* correspondent and aide at army headquarters, Rosecrans expressed his vehemence: "I will not budge until I am ready. I will not move for popular effect." The *Cincinnati Enquirer,* with a November 21 dateline, commented that in the three weeks that Buell had been removed, the army had not moved forty-five miles, with autumn rains soon threatening.[38]

His dispatch had not been intended as a threat, Halleck replied, but merely as a statement of facts. "The President is greatly dissatisfied with your delay, and has sent for me several times to account for it." The general in chief revealed that the urgency was diplomatic in nature. Great Britain and France, faced with an economic imperative, might within a few weeks intervene on the side of the Confederacy. "Tennessee is the only state that can be used as an argument in favor of intervention by England. You will thus perceive that your movements have an importance beyond mere military success. The whole Cabinet are anxious, inquiring almost daily, 'Why don't he move,' 'Can't you make him move,' 'Delay will be more fatal to us than anywhere else.'" Tennessee was characterized, albeit exaggeratedly, as the turn-

37. *Cincinnati Enquirer,* Nov. 23, 1862; Rosecrans to wife, Nov. 22, 1862, quoted in Lamers, *Edge of Glory,* 197.

38. *OR,* 20(2):117–18; Bickham, *Rosecrans' Campaign,* 87, 120; *New York Times,* Jan. 9, 1863.

ing point in foreign relations. It had been assumed, Halleck related, that Middle Tennessee would be recovered by mid-December, thus influencing the British Parliament convening in January 1863. No one doubted that Buell would eventually have succeeded, but he moved too slowly. "It was believed that you would move more rapidly. Hence the change."[39]

Republicans, such as Ohio senator Benjamin Wade, continued to express their support. So did Secretary of the Treasury Chase, but on December 11 he warned of mounting criticism: "I have heard a good deal of complaint about your long tarrying in Nashville. Perhaps there are those in high quarters who think you should not have gone to Nashville at all, but have pushed directly for East Tennessee through one of the many gaps. Again censure is bestowed on the many demands you make for many things."[40]

Preoccupied with his struggle with Washington officials, Rosecrans was stunned to learn on December 7 that Morgan's men had swept down on the Thirty-Ninth Brigade of Dumont's division at Hartsville, Tennessee, capturing all twenty-one hundred troops. The brigade, under Col. A. B. Moore, had been placed there by Thomas to guard the Cumberland River and watch the Lebanon Road. Before leaving the Galt House, the colonel had boasted that "Morgan was the only man that he wanted to have a brush with"; his desire had been met. The command had been taken by surprise, a fact that Rosecrans downplayed to the press by suggesting that Moore had been outnumbered three to one; in fact, Morgan had only thirteen hundred men. Two brigades at Castalian Springs, nine miles away, marched to the scene, but by the time they arrived, the raiders had long gone.[41]

Not wanting to significantly reach into his supply stockpile, Rosecrans foraged south and west of Nashville, but the expeditions were frequently harassed by Wheeler's cavalry. On December 10 Col. Stanley Matthew's brigade of Van Cleve's division, escorting fifty wagons five miles north of La Vergne, was suddenly struck. Matthews sustained forty-four casualties but lost no wagons. Stanley, in his first sortie, led Col. Edward McCook's cavalry brigade in a raid on Franklin, capturing or killing fifteen secessionists. It was a handsome little affair (the first time the troopers had ever used their new revolving rifles), but it paled next to the exploits of the gray horsemen.[42]

---

39. *OR*, 20(2):123–24.

40. Lamers, *Edge of Glory*, 197; Niven, *Chase Papers*, 3:331–32.

41. *New York Tribune*, Dec. 9, 1862; *New York Times*, Dec. 20, 1862; Cist, *Army of the Cumberland*, 82–83; *OR*, 20(1):45.

42. *Cincinnati Enquirer*, Dec. 27, 28, 31, 1862, Jan. 2, 1863; Cist, *Army of the Cumberland*, 216–17; *New York Times*, Dec. 21, 1862; *OR*, 20(1):34, 20(2):213, 296.

It now appeared as though Bragg planned to strike Federal communications be-tween Nashville and Gallatin. Beginning December 8 and extending for two weeks, persistent rumors floated of a phantom enemy force soon to arrive at Lebanon and strike at Gallatin. Wild estimates claimed that Morgan, with six thousand to twelve thousand men, would spearhead the assault, supported by Smith's corps, ten thou-sand to fifteen thousand strong. A reconnaissance by Minty's brigade, supported by Crittenden's corps, failed to shed any light on the so-called reports, hardly more than civilian tales. After the Hartsville disaster, however, no information, regardless of how unsubstantiated, could be dismissed out of hand.[43]

As if matters could not get worse, a string of Federal defeats now occurred in other theaters. On December 13 Maj. Gen. Ambrose Burnside's Army of the Poto-mac collided with Gen. Robert E. Lee's army at Fredericksburg, Virginia. Over thir-teen thousand blue troops were mowed down in a bloodbath. There was concern that some of Lee's units might move west to reinforce Bragg. "The news from Fred-ericksburg has cast a shadow over the army," admitted Colonel Beatty.[44]

Problems also occurred on Rosecrans's right flank. Forrest raided into West Ten-nessee, capturing twenty-five hundred men and ten guns, while Van Dorn's cavalry division struck Grant's supply depot at Holly Springs, Mississippi, capturing fifteen hundred men, destroying $1.5 million worth of supplies, and burning a new two-thousand-bed hospital. Grant's overland drive down the Mississippi Central Rail-road toward Vicksburg had to be aborted. On December 27–29 Major General Sher-man's expedition down the Mississippi River ended in failure. Attempts to storm the northern defense perimeter of Vicksburg at Chickasaw Bayou met with a bloody repulse, the Northerners losing nearly eighteen hundred men.

At the end of December, the exasperatingly bothersome Morgan raided into Kentucky. Rumors placed his strength at ten thousand horsemen (in fact, he had slightly over two thousand). He was everywhere; he was nowhere. A Christmas Eve report indicated the cavalryman would attack Gallatin. An eyewitness described the seriousness of the general's consultation at that place: "But few words were spoken. The disposition to meet the attack had been made. General Paine sat motionless as if wrapped in deep thought. Gen. Ward . . . seemed to be praying for a brush with the traitors. General Reynolds, a smooth-faced, business-like man, received and an-swered dispatches." But Morgan never showed.[45]

Christmas Eve found him at Glasgow, brushing aside three companies of the 2d

---

43. *OR*, 20(2):117–18, 139, 140, 144, 145, 150, 151, 155, 156, 157, 173, 176, 179, 180, 190, 196–97, 201, 204, 212, 226, 231, 232–33.

44. Bickham, *Rosecrans' Campaign*, 109–11; *OR*, 20(2):176; Beatty, *Citizen Soldier*, 193–94.

45. *OR*, 20(2):226, 231; Reyburn and Wilson, *"Jottings from Dixie,"* 87.

Michigan Cavalry. Nolin, with its garrison of 200 men, fell on December 26. The next day he struck for Elizabethtown, where the 91st Illinois, 652 strong, was captured and the Louisville and Nashville trestle burned. On the twenty-eighth Morgan made (predictably) for the two ninety-foot-high, five-hundred-foot-long trestles south of Muldraugh's Hill. The lower bridge was guarded by troops of the 63d Indiana, commanded by the regimental adjutant (the only field officer present), and the upper bridge by the 71st Indiana, whose colonel was still celebrating Christmas back in Louisville. All 900 men were captured and the trestles burned. It would take at least five weeks to repair the damage. After repairs had been made on the railroad first south of Nashville, then south of Bowling Green, the track was now down even farther north.[46]

The raid would have far-reaching implications. First, an entire supporting army (the thirty-two-thousand-man Department of the Ohio) was being kept in central Kentucky to prevent the very raid that was presently occurring with such ease. Two of Rosecrans's divisions (the old Tenth and Twelfth) had been siphoned off for this duty. Additionally, two of Thomas's divisions (Reynolds's and two brigades of Fry's command) had to be kept at Gallatin and vicinity lest the tunnel south of Mitchellville be destroyed again. Thomas's initially huge corps had thus dwindled to two divisions and a brigade.[47]

Food supplies began to run low. With the railroad down for weeks to come and the Cumberland River still unnavigable, there were only two transport possibilities. First, light transports could be sent through a series of locks via the Green River, where the stores would be transferred to trains for the trip to Nashville. One million rations were immediately sent by this route. Second, boats could be sent up the Cumberland River to Harpeth Shoals, where tons of supplies would have to be offloaded and put on wagons for the twenty-four-mile trip to Nashville. Either way, it would be tedious and time-consuming work.[48]

Quartermaster and ordnance needs also increased, as evidenced by the return of the Left Wing in late December 1862. The corps was short, among other items, 331 small arms, 19,415 rounds of small-arms ammunition, 657 bayonets, 1,592 cartridge boxes, 1,518 cap boxes, 788 knapsacks, 617 canteens, 2,554 haversacks, and 377 camp kettles. Clothing shortages included 4,326 pairs of pants, 4,778 shirts, 2,211 pairs of drawers, 12,892 pairs of socks, 1,350 pairs of shoes, 138 pairs of boots, 369 woolen blankets, 877 rubber blankets, 448 hats, and 567 caps.[49]

46. *New York Tribune*, Dec. 11, 15, 1862; Noe, *Southern Boy in Blue*, 118; OR, 20(1):34, 76, 77, 79, 153, 156, 158; Van Horne, *Army of the Cumberland*, 1:216.

47. OR, 16(2):658, 20(2):213, 237–38, 287.

48. OR, 20(2):275, 280–81; *New York Times*, Dec. 15, 1862.

49. Register of Inspection Reports, Dec. 30, 1862, Entry 1057, Vol. 139, RG 393, Pt. 1.

Christmas Eve proved miserable. "I am wet, muddy and in no amicable humor at the root of a giant oak solitary and alone," Hoosier Alva C. Griest wrote. The men attempted to celebrate, though not always successfully. The troops of the 19th Ohio gave up attempts at fun and broke into small groups to discuss friends and family. Several jokesters in the 6th Kentucky got their hands on musical instruments and went about camp blaring them, but the men were more concerned about a rumor that the army would soon be moving out.[50]

The rumors, for once, proved to be true. After continuous, mounting pressure from both Washington and the Rebels, Rosecrans's luck suddenly began to change. It was now confirmed that both Forrest's and Morgan's brigades were beyond supporting distance of Bragg's army. Better yet, ten thousand of Edmund Kirby Smith's men, instead of moving to support Morgan in Kentucky, had been confirmed on their way to Mississippi. Bragg, obviously not expecting an enemy offensive, had gone into winter quarters. Enough provisions had now been stockpiled in Nashville to sustain the army until February 1, and the Cumberland River, though not yet navigable, was rising. "We must therefore close in on them as rapidly as possible," concluded the army commander.[51]

Although the army would be traveling down a thirty-five-mile turnpike, communications might be tenuous. The wooded terrain made it impossible for the signal corps to maintain stations. Despite the fact that the Federals had been in Murfreesboro for over seven months, they had failed to adequately map the area. The wagon ratio was very low, and Confederate cavalry, even though reduced in numbers, remained dangerous. Since Stanley had been unable to penetrate Bragg's cavalry screen, most intelligence had to come by way of spies, civilians, and deserters. Estimates of Rebel strength thus ranged from forty thousand to sixty thousand men.[52]

The rumors notwithstanding, Christmas proved quite bleak. "I almost forgot this is Christmas. . . . It is the loneliest Christmas I ever seen," related 21st Ohio member Walter S. Burns to his wife. Sgt. George B. Ridenour of the 6th Ohio believed that he had never passed "a less merry Christmas." In a similar vein, artilleryman A. S. Bloomfield noted: "I do not see a soldier trying to put on any style. They are all going around as usual doing the regular camp duties."[53]

50. Alva C. Griest Diary, Dec. 24, 1862, INHS; Cope, *Fifteenth Ohio*, 106–7; Kiene, *Civil War Diary*, 147. See also Carrington T. Marshall and Leon C. Marshall, *Civil War Journal of John Wesley Marshall* (N.p.: privately printed, 1958), 41.

51. Bickham, *Rosecrans' Campaign*, 121; *OR*, 20(2):229, 258.

52. *OR*, 20(1):189, 223, 280; *New York Times*, Dec. 26, 1862; *Cincinnati Enquirer*, Dec. 19, 1862.

53. Walter S. Burns to wife, Dec. 25, 1862, Walter S. Burns Letters, 21st Ohio File, SRNBP; George B. Ridenour to unknown, Dec. 25, 1862, George B. Ridenour Letters, 6th Ohio File, SRNBP; A. S. Bloomfield to sister, Dec. 25, 1862, Battery A, 1st Ohio Artillery File, SRNBP.

On Christmas night an extended council of war was held in Rosecrans's head-quarters at 13 High Street—the George W. Cunningham mansion. Division commanders came and went, but the climax occurred at midnight. All three corps commanders were present as well as Stanley, Negley, Johnson, and Sheridan. The meeting took place in a bedroom that had been converted into an office, maps being pinned to the door and spread across the bed. The nearsighted Garesché sat at a table, rapidly writing orders and correspondence. Staff officers tiptoed about softly or lounged in easy chairs. Father Patrick Treacy slipped quietly in and out, as did Ducat—the "old man," as he was called.

The brass talked freely. "If the Rebels stand at all there'll be damned hard fighting," Crittenden muttered. Stanley walked about restlessly, his saber clanking as he moved. Phil Sheridan stood quietly. Thomas sat in between the bed and the front window, with Rosecrans pulling his chair up before him, getting almost in the Virginian's face as they conversed. The army commander spoke rapidly, almost nervously, and at times vehemently. Thomas mostly listened, occasionally nodding in approval, and every now and then giving an undertone suggestion. Rosecrans suddenly slammed his glass on Garesché's table and announced with animation: "We move tomorrow, gentlemen. . . . Drive them out of their nests! Make them fight or run! Strike hard and fast! Give them no rest! Fight, I say."[54]

54. Bickham, *Rosecrans' Campaign*, 137.

12

The Weight of Command
Clash at Stones River

ON THE MORNING of December 26, 1862, the Army of the Cumberland snaked out of Nashville in three columns. Jefferson C. Davis's division of McCook's corps, in a driving rain, slogged out the Edmonson Pike. At Prim's Blacksmith Shop, the column veered onto an old country road, made almost impassable by the consequent mud, to Nolensville. Despite the early hour, something had already gone wrong. Stanley's reserve cavalry brigade had allowed the infantry to get a head start, meaning that the road was hopelessly blocked for the horsemen. The only available cavalry was thus an escort company of Illinois infantry mounted for that purpose. The bluecoats nonetheless brushed aside token resistance by Confederate cavalry outside Nolensville and two miles beyond at Knob Gap. The Federals launched an assault at the latter place, with Billy Carlin's brigade crossing a field to the right of the pike (each man lifting "a square foot of mud three inches deep at every step") and Sidney Post's to the left. They chased off the Rebel cavalry and captured a gun, with Col. John W. C. Alexander of the 21st Illinois and Colonel Heg of the 15th Wisconsin gallantly riding to the summit in advance of their regiments.[1]

McCook's main column, Phil Sheridan's and Richard Johnson's divisions, encountered only slight resistance as they splashed down the Nolensville Pike, preceded by the raw 15th Pennsylvania Cavalry, in its debut combat mission, and four companies of the 3d Indiana Cavalry. On the right Thomas's corps (Rousseau's division and Moses Walker's brigade of Fry's division) filed out the Franklin Pike to link up with Negley's division at Brentwood. Negley was to halt at Owen's Store, south of Brentwood on the Wilson Pike, but hearing the sound of gunfire in the direction of Nolensville, he impetuously ordered his division down the same country road Davis had taken, arriving at Knob Gap after it had been secured. Zahm's 950 troopers continued south to Franklin, clearing out a regiment and a battalion of gray horsemen, taking fifty prisoners in the process. Minty's cavalry spearheaded

1. *OR*, 20(1):253, 262–63, 266, 269, 279, 295, 347; Bickham, *Rosecrans' Campaign*, 150–52; Girardi and Hughes, *Memoirs of Brigadier General William Passmore Carlin*, 73; Blegen, *Letters of Colonel Hans Christian Heg*, 160–61.

Crittenden's corps on the left along the Murfreesboro Pike. Due to a garbled order, Palmer's division, not Wood's, fell in line first, arriving at Hurricane Creek, just short of La Vergne, at dusk.[2]

Having heard nothing from McCook all day, Rosecrans made a late-night ride to Nolensville, accompanied by only a few staff officers. Getting lost more than once on back roads, the party finally found the corps commander. Prisoners had confirmed that only a brigade was in Triune, but McCook suspected that William Hardee's entire corps lay in wait. If true, Rosecrans directed that he give battle. If Hardee lost and fell back on Shelbyville, McCook would follow with a division, sending the other two on to Murfreesboro. If he simply retreated to Shelbyville, two divisions would be sent in pursuit. If he should proceed to Murfreesboro, the entire Right Wing would conform.[3]

A dense early morning fog on December 27 limited visibility to 150 yards. Stanley and three cavalry regiments, supported by Willich's brigade of Johnson's division, made a reconnaissance, but two miles out they collided with a mixture of infantry, cavalry, and artillery. With visibility now near zero, McCook thought it prudent to wait. The march did not continue until 1:00 P.M., and by that time only Confederate cavalry remained in Triune to contest the steep banks of Nelson's Creek. The Federals chased off the graycoats in a driving rain and spent the rest of the day rebuilding the destroyed bridge. Crittenden's corps, meanwhile, entered La Vergne shortly after noon and pressed on toward Stewart's Creek, where Milo Hascall's brigade captured a vital bridge. In like fashion William Hazen's brigade seized the bridge east of Smyrna, and with it thirty-five of Wheeler's men. Thomas was stuck in mud, with Negley's division taking nearly all day to march five miles.[4]

Rosecrans rejected a general movement on Sunday the twenty-eighth, owing less to mud than to religious considerations, a commendable and popular choice, but one that gave Bragg, who had no such aversions, an additional twenty-four hours to collect his scattered forces on this sunny day. Given the rugged terrain on the south bank of Stewart's Creek, many officers conjectured that the battle for Middle Tennessee would be fought as the army crossed, but Rosecrans surmised the site would be either Murfreesboro or Shelbyville. The Right Wing made a reconnaissance to determine Hardee's whereabouts. The Yankees of Willich's brigade impressed a dozen local farmers as guides, threatening to shoot them and leave their bodies along the roadside if they attempted any tricks. Circumstantial evidence

2. OR, 20(2):240, 372; Bickham, *Rosecrans' Campaign*, 152–55; Crofts, *Third Ohio Veteran Volunteer Cavalry*, 59, 62–63; Curry, *Four Years in the Saddle*, 91.

3. OR, 20(1):253; Bickham, *Rosecrans' Campaign*, 156–63.

4. OR, 20(1):253 54, 319, 372, 447, 458–59, 20(2):247; *New York Tribune*, Jan. 1, 1863.

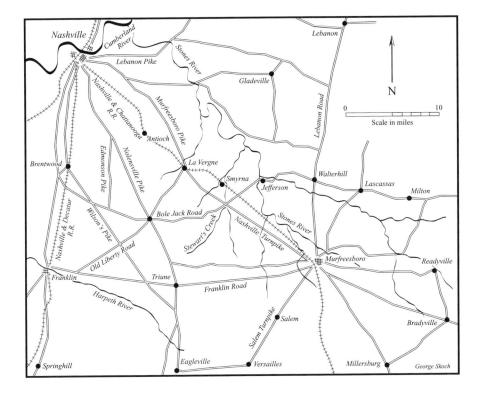

George Skoch

pointed toward Murfreesboro. At 10:45 P.M. McCook notified army headquarters that he would march in the morning along the Bole Jack Road, "doing everything mortal man can do to gain my position [Murfreesboro]."[5]

Crittenden pushed ahead on a sunny but cold December 29. At 10:00 A.M. a battery opened fire on the south bank of Stewart's Creek but received no response. The infantry plunged into waist-deep water and nearly impenetrable woods to discover that the Confederates had abandoned the position. Wood's and Palmer's divisions marched ahead, the two officers arguing over the proper marching order, and by 3:00 P.M. had closed to within two and a half miles of Murfreesboro. There they sighted the Rebels in what appeared to be substantial strength along both banks of Stones River. A battle line formed, with Wood east of the turnpike and Palmer west.[6]

Late in the afternoon Wood and Palmer rode to the front to observe the enemy, where they received a message through corps headquarters from Rosecrans: "Stanley

5. *OR*, 20(2):255–56; Bickham, *Rosecrans' Campaign*, 172–73; Fisher, *Staff Officer's Story*, 51–52.
6. Bickham, *Rosecrans' Campaign*, 175–76; *OR*, 20(1):448, 459; Ephraim A. Otis, "The Murfreesboro Campaign," *MASS*, 7:302.

reports from Triune that the people say that Bragg has abandoned Murfreesboro. You will therefore occupy the place with one division, and camp your others near them." Wood and Palmer knew better, though they hardly realized that the entire Confederate army had arrayed against them. The nearest supporting division, Negley's, was still seven miles in the rear, with Van Cleve's division of Crittenden's corps behind it. As the sun began to set, Wood went to Crittenden and pleaded that the order be canceled, arguing that the advance should wait until daylight. He refused, and Wood prepared to advance. A second time Wood came to corps headquarters, this time accompanied by Palmer. Both officers urged that the advance order be rescinded, but again Crittenden refused, although he did postpone it for one hour. Meanwhile, Rosecrans himself came up and, hearing of the circumstances, canceled the movement, though not before Harker's brigade had already engaged in skirmishing. The next morning Rosecrans surprisingly told Crittenden that Palmer had advised that the town had been abandoned. Palmer vehemently denied any involvement, but even so, in his after-action report, the army commander blamed the former Illinois politician for the near disaster. An enraged Palmer suspected a blatant coverup to protect Stanley, a regular and a Catholic.[7]

Actually, that day Rosecrans had been more concerned about the Right Wing, which had still not come up. Delayed by bad roads and Rebel cavalry, McCook wrote Crittenden at 4:25 P.M. "Dear Tom: I am up and ready for work . . . I have not heard of Thomas, Rousseau, or Negley today. The rebels, as far as my information goes, are in line of battle, their left on the Franklin road and extending to the Murfreesboro pike. . . . I have not heard from Rosecrans to know what to do. I suppose I will get instructions tonight. We all should meet and have a conference; don't you say so? . . . Was sick yesterday, but am well today. Would be glad to see you." His corps did not reach the Wilkinson Pike (five miles from Murfreesboro) until eight o'clock that night. At 1:00 A.M. McCook got a message to report to army headquarters, where he arrived at 3:30 A.M. He received instructions to link up with Negley's right at first light.[8]

Had Bragg fiercely contested McCook's crossing at Overall's Creek on the fog-shrouded morning of December 30, he would have been in position to knife between the center and left of Rosecrans's army, fighting the corps in detail. Yet McCook, who must have known that Bragg could get between him and Thomas, seemed not to grasp the gravity of the situation. He dallied much of the morning and did not leave until 9:30 A.M. By noon Sheridan's division had reached the Har-

7. John Palmer, *Personal Recollections*, 143–44; *OR*, 20(1):448, 459; George Thomas Palmer, *A Conscientious Turncoat: The Story of John M. Palmer, 1817–1900* (New Haven: Yale University Press, 1941), 103.

8. Bickham, *Rosecrans' Campaign*, 177–78; *OR*, 20(1):254, 295, 20(2):268–69.

ding house, where he sent a brigade to support Zahm's hard-pressed troopers on the Franklin Road. Indeed, both Sheridan's and Johnson's divisions encountered stiff resistance coming into line, losing 260 men. In charging an enemy battery a hundred yards west of the Smith house, the Chicago Irishmen of the 21st Illinois walked into an ambush and sustained severe casualties.[9]

At 2:00 P.M. Stanley sent a cooperative farmer to McCook's headquarters. The man lived on the Franklin Road, only a half mile from the Confederate position, and had visited their lines three times. According to him, Leonidas Polk's corps lay between the Wilkinson Pike and the Franklin Road. If true, McCook's right rested in the center of Bragg's army. An alarmed McCook immediately advanced Brig. Gen. Edmund Kirk's and General Willich's brigades of Johnson's division. Kirk came into line to the left of Post's brigade, while Willich re-fused to the right in the vicinity of the Franklin Road and Gresham Lane, not completing the deployment until after sunset. In an attempt to keep Bragg preoccupied with his left while Rosecrans massed on his right, McCook received written instructions to start large campfires hundreds of yards beyond his right (the far right of the army) to deceive the enemy. The Confederates fell for the ruse and, fearing that they had been overlapped, extended their left to meet this phantom threat, again overlapping McCook.[10]

With images of Perryville doubtless in his mind, McCook grew nervous. He unquestionably feared that he would be attacked in the morning "by the entire Rebel army," and he related such to Johnson. Yet he thought his position a strong one—a compact, double-line formation, generally along a wooded ridge fronted in places by rolling land and cultivated fields, and with a strong line of skirmishers deployed. His 15,700 troops in fact faced 20,000 Confederates—not impossible odds.[11]

Yet several glaring problems existed as the sun began to set. The battle lines were dangerously close at places—as little as three hundred yards. Enemy pickets could be distinctly heard mumbling in the distance. No attempt was made to construct rude barricades from rocks and trees. Col. Philemon Baldwin's large brigade of Johnson's division served as the corps reserve, yet McCook retained it in the center rear, a mile away from the extreme right. Kirk's brigade deployed in the cedar woods rather than advancing to the edge of the forest, where they would have a clear field of fire. Historians have long recognized these flaws, but in criticizing Mc-Cook, they have overlooked Rosecrans's far larger mistake. The army commander clustered five of his eight divisions between the Wilkinson Pike and Stones River.

9. *OR*, 20(1):254, 270, 279–80, 348. Bragg was actually more preoccupied with Crittenden that day and had Hardee's corps east of Stones River. At the approach of McCook, he shifted two divisions to the left flank.

10. Ibid., 254–55, 263, 303; Otis, "Murfreesboro Campaign," 304.

11. *OR*, 20(1):255, 295–96; Johnson, *Reminiscences,* 210.

Rousseau's reserve division on the left should more properly have been placed in the center by the Wilkinson Pike. Once it had been determined that McCook was secure, the division could have been shifted east toward the turnpike. As it was, McCook held back two (Baldwin's and Col. Frederick Schaefer's) of his nine brigades, allowing the Confederates to overlap his line by a quarter mile.[12]

Rosecrans planned to attack the Confederate right, east of Stones River, on the morning of December 31. Van Cleve's division would strike first, crossing at McFadden's Ford, with Wood's division on his right, crossing at the upper ford. These thirteen thousand troops would sweep aside Maj. Gen. John Breckinridge's division (sixty-five hundred) and proceed into Murfreesboro, cutting the railroad line and taking Bragg's center in reverse. Wood's artillery would unlimber on Wayne's Hill and open an enfilade fire across the river. Crittenden's remaining division, John Palmer's, along with Thomas's corps in the center (Negley's and Rousseau's divisions, the latter in reverse), would engage the enemy's center and continue the right-wheel movement.[13]

McCook's role would be crucial. On December 30 at 4:00 P.M., Capt. Horace Fisher, one of the general's aides, had been told at army headquarters by Rosecrans: "While he [McCook] holds Hardee, the Left, under Crittenden, will swing round and take Murfreesboro. Let Hardee attack if he wants to. It will suit us exactly." At 6:30 Capt. R. S. Thoms arrived at McCook's headquarters, bringing tersely written instructions for the following morning: McCook would slowly retire if attacked, contesting every inch of ground. If not attacked, he would make his own slight, but convincing, demonstration. No conference meeting occurred that evening, Rosecrans's statement to the contrary. At 9:00 P.M. McCook, accompanied by Stanley, rode to army headquarters. During the hour-and-a-half-long meeting, Rosecrans, according to Bickham, said: "General McCook, you know the ground; you have fought over it; you know its difficulties. Can you hold your present position [in the morning] for three hours?" When the Right Wing commander replied, "Yes, I think I can," Rosecrans added: "I don't like the facing so much to the east, but must confide that to you who knows the ground. If you don't think your present the best position, change it. It is only necessary to make things sure."[14]

McCook would later take issue with much of the above account. No meeting occurred, a fact substantiated by Thomas, who wrote that he was rather informally told

---

12. *OR*, 20(1):255, 278; Van Horne, *Army of the Cumberland*, 1:266; Peter Cozzens, *No Better Place to Die: The Battle of Stones River* (Urbana: University of Illinois Press, 1990), 82.

13. *OR*, 20(1):192, 20(2):284–85. Coincidentally, Bragg had in mind the exact same plan in reverse, that is, to attack the Union left. Whoever started the attack first would obviously have the edge.

14. *OR*, 20(1):120, 255, 23(2):383; Bickham, *Rosecrans' Campaign*, 188.

of the battle plan as he and Rosecrans rode together during the afternoon. McCook implausibly insisted that no plan was ever explained to him, nor did he know of it until he read it in the *Cincinnati Commercial* on February 28, 1863. (One must, of course, wonder what the two officers talked about for an hour and a half.) Rosecrans never gave him an option to change his position, nor was "three hours" ever mentioned. As to whether or not he could hold his position, McCook conceded that he answered, "Yes, I can." What he meant to say, he later explained, was that he could hold out against the same enemy force that he had encountered that afternoon.[15]

Rosecrans trusted that McCook would "make things sure" on the right and thus made no personal inspection. Whether or not a hurried night inspection would have uncovered the weaknesses on that flank is questionable, but given that both officers had been alerted to the possibility of an attack in that sector, an effort should have been made. Rosecrans counted on McCook to do what he had to do to hold the line—"it was a mistake," the army commander would later admit.[16]

About ten o'clock on the night of the thirtieth, Brigadier General Sill, commanding a brigade in Sheridan's division, became increasingly alarmed. Mounting enemy activity in his front caused him to suspect that the Rebels were marching around by way of Overall's Creek and massing on the Federal right for a night or early morning attack. He expressed his concerns to Sheridan, and both officers proceeded to corps headquarters. Finding McCook asleep on some straw near the Gresham house, Sheridan roused him and reported Sill's information. McCook replied: "General Rosecrans is fully advised of the fact that the enemy is massing troops in my front, but he explained to me his attack upon their right in the morning will be so vigorous that they will be compelled to withdraw their forces to support that portion of the line. I am only to hold my line, and wait for orders from headquarters."[17]

During the early morning hours of the thirty-first, McCook began to get nervous. He ordered all of his division commanders to get their men under arms. Sheridan had already reinforced Sill's brigade with two regiments, and by foot and unattended, he now began to personally inspect his entire line. Davis and Johnson did not take similar precautions, and McCook did not make a personal inspection. Brigadier General Willich, while eating breakfast, received a dispatch from Johnson: "Gen. McCook is apprehensive that an attack will be made upon your line at daybreak. See that your men are under arms and on the alert." Willich laughingly dismissed the warning and

15. *OR*, 23(2):382, 383.

16. *OR*, 20(1):192.

17. James H. Woodward, "Gen. A. McD. McCook at Stone River," in *MOLLUS, California/Oregon* (reprint, Wilmington, N.C.: Broadfoot, 1993), 154–55.

in his German accent muttered, "They are so quiet out there that I guess they are no more here." Nonetheless, he mounted his horse and began to ride along the line, at which time he received another message from McCook, expressing concern and admonishing him to be on the lookout. The tension built.[18]

Johnson's division roused at 5:00 A.M. on the thirty-first, but as late as 6:15 his brigades had not formed in line of battle. At 6:22 someone in Kirk's brigade shouted, "They're coming!" "All was so quiet, not a shot having been fired, I felt decidedly skeptical," admitted Sgt. Maj. Lyman Widney of the 34th Illinois. Col. J. B. Dodge of the 30th Indiana sprang up on a fence to see over the morning fog. "There they were! It was a magnificent but fearful sight. Their lines extended as far as we could see in the dim light," he recalled. Maj. Gen. John McCown's Rebel division smashed into the brigade. Kirk ordered the 34th forward into a cornfield in a fruitless attempt to blunt the juggernaut. Within minutes, 72 of 354 men had dropped, including General Kirk, a ball having lodged near his spine. The 29th and 30th Indiana fired a few volleys from a prone position before breaking to the rear. The 77th Pennsylvania was the only regiment that made a show of it, the unit actually driving back the enemy in its front 150 yards before becoming isolated and having to withdraw; only 66 of the 288 Keystone troops would answer roll at day's end. Capt. Warren P. Edgarton, a well-known professor of elocution, had the six guns of his Battery E, 1st Ohio Light Artillery, in park, with half the horses in the rear being watered. Within minutes, screaming Confederates engulfed his battery.[19]

Willich's brigade, on the far right, was even less prepared, the troops eating breakfast and their rifles stacked. Like Edgarton's company, the guns of Wilbur F. Goodspeed's Battery A, 1st Ohio Light Artillery, were unlimbered and the horses in the rear. The men looked up in horror at the gray wave bearing down upon them. All was chaos as the commanding officer of the 15th Ohio shouted nonsensical orders. The Confederates shattered the brigade and sent the troops reeling in disorder. Frantic, Willich blundered into the enemy lines, fell wounded, and was captured. Col. W. H. Gibson took command, but with his horse dead and most of the field officers down, little could be done. The 1st Ohio battery withdrew with the loss of two guns.[20]

18. Ibid., 155; Sheridan, *Memoirs*, 1:220–22. The number of troops available on the morning of December 31 has often been misstated. Rosecrans had 40,996 troops, not counting 1,600 wagon guards. During the course of the battle, he received three additional brigades numbering at least 5,032 men for a grand total of 46,028. The return of December 31 does not include Walker's brigade and two regiments of Spears's brigade. Bragg had 37,712 present for duty. *OR*, 20(1):200–201, 284, 674.

19. Lyman S Widney Diary, Dec. 31, 1862, SRNBP; J. B. Dodge, "What I Saw at Stones River," Dec. 31, 1862, 30th Indiana File, SRNBP; *OR*, 20(1):300, 321, 325, 327, 329–30, 334–36; Walsh, *Medical Histories*, 196; A. S. Bloomfield to parents, Jan. 16, 1863, Battery A, 1st Ohio Files, SRNBP.

20. *OR*, 20(1):296, 304–5, 310, 312, 314; Walsh, *Medical Histories*, 372, Cope, *Fifteenth Ohio*, 234–39.

Richard Johnson watched in dismay as his division disintegrated. Willich's and Kirk's 4,200 men streamed back to the northwest, shouting, "We are sold! Sold again!" They left behind eight guns, 750 prisoners, and a carpet of 900 killed and wounded. Who was to blame? Johnson? McCook? "The army is hostile to both at the present," a reporter would later write.[21]

As the Confederates continued en echelon, rolling up the Union right, they struck Colonel Post's brigade of Davis's division. Although a dense and near impenetrable thicket of cedars obstructed the view to the right, the former Illinois lawyer knew that the position had been flanked because of the Rebels' "advancing cheers." He deployed his brigade on either side of Gresham Lane, backed by Capt. Oscar Pinney's 5th Wisconsin Artillery. The line held for half an hour, even causing the Confederates in his front (Bushrod Johnson's Tennessee brigade) to momentarily recoil. The Yankees fixed bayonets in a desperate attempt to hold, but with Post's right flanked, "the position was already untenable." The colonel ordered a withdrawal, one gun being abandoned, and the infantry fell back in reasonably good order.[22]

At 7:30 A.M. Richard Johnson brought forward Colonel Baldwin's reserve brigade in an attempt to accomplish what three front-line brigades had failed to achieve—plugging a crumbling dike. Baldwin aligned his men behind a fence on the edge of wooded ground south of the Wilkinson Pike, but Johnson oddly ordered them into an open cornfield behind a split-rail fence. Scarcely had the deployment been completed when the enemy appeared in immense numbers and at short range. Fearful of being outflanked, Maj. Joab Stafford ordered his 1st Ohio to retreat, but in the process the Buckeyes became entangled with the 5th Kentucky and 93d Ohio in their rear. The Kentuckians came under a galling infantry and artillery fire, losing 99 of 320 men. Baldwin retired his troops to avoid annihilation.[23]

The battle now rippled toward Colonel Carlin's brigade to the left of Post. Their initial volleys staggered Brig. Gen. S. A. M. Wood's Mississippians and Alabamians, giving Carlin time to realign his four regiments. As the fighting renewed, bullets struck Carlin's horse in four places, one bullet violently jolting but not penetrating the colonel's right leg. The brigade began a disorderly withdrawal, with the Scandi-

---

21. *OR*, 20(1):296, 307, 324; *New York Times*, Jan. 9, 1863; W. D. Smith, *The Battle of Stones River, Tennessee, December 31, 1862–January 2, 1863* (n.p.), 26. "The feeling against Gen. Johnson is intense," wrote E. P. Sturges of Battery B, 1st Ohio Light Artillery, on January 8, 1863. "With an Artilleryman at Stones River," *Civil War Times Illustrated* 2 (Feb. 1964): 41. After the battle Capt. Jay Butler of the 101st Ohio wrote: "There was a great deal of carelessness somewhere and General Johnson is blamed very much." Watson Hubbard Butler, comp., *Letters Home: Jay Caldwell Butler* (Privately printed, 1930), 57.

22. *OR*, 20(1):270, 271, 273, 275, 278; David Lathrop, *The History of the Fifty-Ninth Regiment Illinois Volunteers* (Indianapolis: Hall and Hutchinson, 1865), 188; Sidney Post Diary, Dec. 31, 1862, KC.

23. *OR*, 20(1):337, 339, 341, 343; Alexander F. Stevenson, *The Battle of Stone's River near Murfreesboro, Tenn., December 30, 1862, to January 3, 1863* (reprint, Dayton: Morningside, 1983), 42–43; Johnson, *Reminiscences*, 213.

navians of Colonel Heg's 15th Wisconsin covering the retreat. The troops came under a flanking fire from Rebels shooting from behind trees and fences. Carlin, along with Generals Davis and McCook, was watching the withdrawal when "suddenly the thud of a bullet was heard and instantly a stream of blood spurted upwards from the left shoulder of McCook's horse," recalled Carlin. "McCook was a large fleshy man, but the agility he displayed in leaping from that wounded horse was truly wonderful to behold."[24]

The dominoes continued to topple. Colonel Woodruff's three-regiment brigade, backed by the 8th Wisconsin Artillery, initially stopped the enemy—"They were mowed down as grass beneath the sickle," he reported. The line eventually collapsed under heavy pressure, however, as the colonel vainly attempted to rally his men. Carlin later related that a brigade commander (probably Woodruff, whom he hated) attempted to desert and make his way back to Nashville that night but could not get through. To Woodruff's left was General Sill's brigade of Phil Sheridan's division. The blue infantry withheld their fire until the enemy closed to within fifty yards and then unleashed a wall of flame, supported by the direct and oblique artillery fire of three batteries (4th Indiana; G, 1st Missouri; and C, 1st Illinois), sending the Rebel line reeling. Seizing the moment, Sill led a counterattack, during which he fell with a bullet in his brain. A renewed Confederate onslaught forced the brigade to retreat, the 36th Illinois retiring with a staggering 60 percent loss. Sheridan withdrew Sill's regiments and ordered Col. George W. Roberts's Illinois brigade to change front. As a lull occurred, Roberts found Sheridan behind Hescock's Missouri battery and received permission to launch an audacious bayonet attack. The troops formed in a field facing south toward the Harding house. Advancing as if on dress parade, the 42d Illinois (the other front-line regiment had been stopped by a cedar thicket) dove into Brig. Gen. Arthur Manigault's unprepared and terrified Confederate brigade, driving it for some distance, before Roberts withdrew in good order, dangerously low on ammunition.[25]

McCook's corps, as at Perryville, lay in shambles. Johnson's and Davis's divisions had been driven from the field with terrifying speed, and Sheridan was conducting a fighting withdrawal. During a lull in the fighting, a reporter mingled with the ranks to gather information for a story. "Along the whole line there was an outcry

24. OR, 20(1):280–85; Blegen, Letters of Colonel Hans Christian Heg, 165–66; Lewis Day, Story of the One Hundred and First Ohio Infantry (Cleveland: W. M. Bayne, 1894), 84–87; Girardi and Hughes, Memoirs of Brigadier General William Passmore Carlin, 78–79.

25. Gilbert C. Kniffen, "The Battle of Stone's River," in B&L, 3:621; Stevenson, Battle of Stone's River, 55–57; John Mitchell, In Memoriam: Twenty-Fourth Wisconsin Infantry (n.p., 1906), 27; OR, 20(1):288–89, 348–49, 354–55, 357, 366, 370; Girardi and Hughes, Memoirs of Brigadier General William Passmore Carlin, 82.

against officers," he wrote. "The men said, despondently, 'We'll fight if they give us officers.' Imprecations were heaped upon the heads of McCook and Johnson. . . . The *esprit de corps* of the right wing appeared to me to be gone."[26]

The troops ran toward the Nashville Pike, soon discovering that Confederate cavalry had already gained the rear. McCook's seventy-six-wagon reserve ordnance train lay ripe for the picking. Zahm's cavalry brigade formed in line to receive the attack of Brig. Gen. John Wharton's fifteen hundred gray horsemen. Most of Zahm's men did not wait for the Rebels but bolted to the rear. Col. Minor Millikin led his 1st Ohio Cavalry in a desperate countercharge in column of fours, only to be killed and have a hundred of his troopers surrounded and captured. Six companies of the 4th U.S. Cavalry, many of whom had been infantrymen who had been mounted only five days earlier, opportunely arrived and, along with a still-intact battalion of the 3d Ohio Cavalry, managed in a dramatic old-fashioned saber charge to check a portion of Wharton's assault, taking a hundred prisoners, releasing many captured Federal infantrymen, and saving McCook's train. Wharton's shotgun- and pistol-wielding troopers now swung around, scattering the balance of Zahm's brigade "like sheep." Lt. Col. John G. Parkhurst, commanding the army's provost guard, the 9th Michigan, managed to collect the remains of Johnson's division and seven guns, placing them on a ridge overlooking Overall's Creek. Where was Stanley during all of this? At 5:30 A.M. the cavalry chief had been sent by Rosecrans to check the defense of the army's baggage train at Stewart's Creek. Finding all in order, he took time to indulge in some whiskey with both the colonel and chaplain of the 10th Ohio. A courier interrupted him with an order to "Hasten to the right and do your best to restore order."[27]

Under McCook's orders, Sheridan pulled his brigades back under heavy fire to the woods along the Wilkinson Pike. Roberts's brigade faced south and connected at right angles with Negley's division, while Colonel Schaefer's brigade and Colonel Greusel, now commanding the deceased Sill's brigade, faced west, at right angles to Roberts and protecting Negley's rear. After placing ten guns at the Roberts-Negley apex, Sheridan rode over to his right to find Davis and Carlin collecting squads of men, the latter calmly smoking a pipe and in stark contrast to the excited manner of Davis.[28]

26. *New York Herald,* Jan. 9, 1863.

27. Sheridan, *Memoirs,* 1:224; Edwin C. Bearss, "Cavalry Operations in the Battle of Stones River," *Tennessee Historical Quarterly* 19 (Mar. 1960): 120–21; Starr, *Union Cavalry,* 3:118; Gates P. Thurston, "Personal Recollections of the Battle in the Rear at Stones River, Tennessee" (Nashville: n.p., n.d.), 8–16; Curry, *Four Years in the Saddle,* 83–84.

28. Charles Bennett, *Historical Sketches of the Ninth Michigan Infantry (General Thomas Headquarters Guard) with an Account of the Battle of Murfreesboro, Tennessee, Sunday, July 13, 1862* (Coldwater, Mich.: Daily Courier, 1913), 28; *OR,* 20(1):349; Sheridan, *Memoirs,* 1:225.

* * *

From his position on the Union Left Wing, Rosecrans could hear the rising din of battle on McCook's front. The general assumed that the corps commander had engaged the enemy and the plan had proceeded as projected. When a staff officer appeared about 7:30 with McCook's misleading message that "the Right Wing was heavily pressed and needed assistance," the army commander remained calm. "All right, never mind, we will rectify it," he replied. "Tell General McCook to contest every inch of ground. If he holds them we will swing into Murfreesboro with our left, and cut them off." Rosecrans merely repeated his orders from the night before. To his staff he confidently murmured, "It is working right."[29]

Indeed, Crittenden's turning movement had already begun. Sam Beatty's and Samuel Price's brigades of Van Cleve's division had forded Stones River and formed a line of battle on a hill a mile and a half from the river. To Van Cleve's right Thomas Wood's division, its commander quite ill but nonetheless present, prepared to cross the lower ford. But something was not right. The sound of battle was, observed one of Wood's staff officers, "nearing too rapidly" and "curling around to our rear."[30]

A harried staff officer arrived and confirmed the awful truth rapidly becoming self-evident. "The Right Wing is broken, and the enemy is driving it back!" he exclaimed, telling of Sill's death, Kirk's wounding, and Willich's capture. "Never mind, we must win this battle," a stunned Rosecrans replied. Large numbers of stragglers began to emerge from the woods, revealing to all that a rout had occurred. Thomas, under orders, sent Rousseau's reserve division into the cedar brakes to the right and rear of Sheridan's division (where it should have been from the outset), while Crittenden suspended his movement and recalled Van Cleve's division. Van Cleve's thoroughly soaked troops recrossed Stones River and started toward Rousseau's right. Finding a brigade at McFadden's Ford, Rosecrans inquired who commanded it. "I do sir," replied Colonel Price. "Will you hold this ford?" the general asked. "I will try, sir," came the response. Unsatisfied, Rosecrans again asked, "Will you hold this ford?" "I will die right here," came the answer. The general thundered for a third time, "Will you hold this ford?" This time Price responded merely, "Yes sir." "That will do," said Rosecrans, and he rode away. The general then galloped to Wood's division, ordering Harker's and Hascall's brigades to the right, pointing toward the rear. The former got off well, but Hascall's infantry became entangled in a hapless mass of fleeing refugees and wagon teams. The Pioneer Brigade, bolstered by the

29. *OR*, 20(1):193; Bickham, *Rosecrans' Campaign*, 207.

30. *OR*, 20(1):449, 467, 574, 607; Bickham, *Rosecrans' Campaign*, 206; John Lee Yaryan, "Stone River," in *MOLLUS, Indiana* (reprint, Wilmington, N.C.: Broadfoot, 1993), 168.

Chicago Board of Trade Battery, was meanwhile positioned on a knoll west of the Nashville Pike and near army headquarters. Reinforcements were on the way.[31]

"I knew it was hell in there before I got in," Rousseau would later recall, "but I was convinced of it when I saw Phil Sheridan with hat in one hand and sword in the other, fighting as if he were the devil incarnate." Rosecrans rode up at one point and heard Little Phil swearing. "Hold on, Sheridan, omit the profanity. Remember, the first bullet may send you to eternity." "I can't help it, general," he replied. "We must hold this point and my men won't think I'm in earnest unless I swear at them like hell." Sheridan's infantry had been stubbornly resisting in the cedar brakes and limestone outcroppings, having repulsed three Confederate assaults, but they were now dangerously low on ammunition. He had little choice but to withdraw. Col. Fazilo A. Harrington of the 27th Illinois had his jaw ripped off by a shell. Colonel Roberts, in attempting to rally one of his regiments, had been killed. Likewise, in order to buy time, Colonel Schaeffer had led a failed two-regiment counterattack in which he fell dead. The Confederates captured Capt. Charles Houghtaling's six guns, the horses having been shot, and the barely living artillery commander. The men were down to three to four cartridges, and nearly sixteen hundred men had been lost.[32]

To Sheridan's right Rousseau's division (Col. John Beatty's Indiana and Ohio brigade on the left, Lieutenant Colonel Shepard's regulars on the right, and Colonel Scribner's five-regiment brigade in reserve) clawed through cedar thickets so dense that visibility beyond battalion length proved impossible. Barely had dispositions been completed before the secessionists launched a furious assault. Rousseau ordered Beatty to hold "till hell freezes over." Col. John Sanderson observed the "dashing courage and bravery of Rousseau and the gallant old Third [now the reorganized First Division] were sure to tell. Gen. Thomas, cool as marble, was there to hold Rousseau in check (as he is brave almost to rashness)." Rousseau repulsed the initial assault with terrible losses on both sides, but the enemy came back with even greater fury. James B. Forman, the boy colonel of the 15th Kentucky, fell dead. Shepard's regulars fell back under a murderous fire, with a third of the brigade either killed or wounded. With Sheridan's division withdrawing to the left, Rousseau ordered his three brigades back under the protective fire of Lt. George Van Pelt's Battery A, 1st Michigan, and Lt. F. L. Guenther's Battery H, 5th U.S. Artillery. In order

31. OR, 20(1):193, 467; Bickham, *Rosecrans' Campaign*, 209, 213; Kniffen, "Battle of Stone's River," 623.

32. Stevenson, *Battle of Stone's River*, 66–70; OR, 20(1):242, 349–50, 375; Reid, *Ohio in the War*, 1:505–6; James R. Gilmore, *Personal Recollections of Abraham Lincoln and the Civil War* (Boston: L. C. Page, 1898), 124.

to avoid sharpshooter and artillery fire, Scribner ordered his brigade to disperse and reform on the turnpike. Realizing that Thomas might think that they had been routed, the colonel hurriedly rode over to explain. "And now, General, you see, they are re-forming. Have you any further orders?" "No," the corps commander answered without expression, "reform on the pike."[33]

By 9:00 A.M. the Sheridan-Negley V-shaped formation had collapsed on the left, and the victorious grays came close to enveloping the far rear of Negley's position and John Palmer's division to his left. Fearing that possibility, Colonel Grose, with Palmer's permission, had earlier pulled his brigade out of line and formed his own V with Colonel Hazen's brigade. Capt. Charles Parson's eight-gun battery (H/M, 4th U.S. Artillery), along with Van Pelt's and Guenther's batteries, unlimbered on a rise that offered a sweeping trajectory across a cotton field. To Grose's astonishment Shepard's regulars suddenly fell back upon his men in utter confusion, closely followed by an advancing line of gray, consisting of Gen. James E. Rains's brigade of Georgians, North Carolinians, and Tennesseans. At nearly point-blank range, a galling fire from twenty guns, backed by Palmer's infantry, erupted. Within minutes it was over; when the smoke cleared, the Rebels had melted away.[34]

Negley's two brigades remained in trouble. With his front battered and rear threatened, he ordered his troops to make a dash for the Nashville Pike, joining the jackknifing movement of the entire Union right. The 21st Ohio and 19th Illinois, armed with Colt revolving rifles, performed a rear-guard action, Col. James Niebling shouting, "Give 'em hell by the acre boys." Together the two regiments made a bayonet charge that delayed the Confederates, albeit momentarily. Six guns of the division artillery had to be abandoned.[35]

By noon the Confederates had bent back the Federal right, which now paralleled the Nashville Pike. Here, a hundred yards in advance of the pike, they encountered Morton's sixteen hundred pioneers, supported by the Chicago Board of Trade Battery, on a slight rise west of the road. Rosecrans instructed the engineer officer that "if he could hold that place for one hour, he would save the day." A brigade of Texans burst from the cedar woods on the double-quick, preceded by a swarm of

33. Kniffen, "Battle of Stone's River," 624; *OR*, 20(1):373, 377–78. 383, 400; Beatty, *Citizen Soldier*, 153; Landrum to sister, Jan. [?], 15, 1863, George W. Landrum Letters, OHS; Scribner, *How Soldiers Were Made*, 78–79; Hosea, "Regular Brigade," 339–40; Phisterer, *Association of Survivors, Regular Brigade*, 5–6. Rousseau's Third Brigade, under Colonel Starkweather, was at Jefferson Crossing eight miles below Murfreesboro and would not arrive until late in the day.

34. *OR*, 20(1):378, 388, 405, 569–72, 565; John Palmer, *Personal Recollections*, 146; Stevenson, *Battle of Stone's River*, 79–80.

35. Cozzens, *No Better Place to Die*, 141–43; *OR*, 20(1):407–10, 421, 426, 432, 437; Van Horne, *Army of the Cumberland*, 1:238.

Union refugees that broke through Morton's ranks. Only the remnant of the 79th Indiana (Kirk's brigade) managed to rally. The pioneers, lying in a prone position, then rose at one command and delivered a murderous volley, together with canister charges from the Chicago battery.[36]

As the Texans began to curl around the Federal right, Sam Beatty's brigade of Van Cleve's division advanced to extend the line. As they dashed into position, Col. Lyne Starling, Crittenden's adjutant, threw up his hat and shouted, "Here comes the old gallant 11th Brigade, I know we will whip the Rebels now." Rosecrans, waving his sword above his head and with tears in his eyes, yelled, "Boys, you must drive them." So many demoralized Federals fled toward the pike that the "scene was one of disorder and panic," reported the colonel of the 19th Ohio. "Regiment after regiment swept through our lines in the greatest confusion; but through it all our men preserved an unbroken front." A destructive fire cleared the Rebels, followed by a bayonet charge by the 19th Ohio and 79th Indiana, which drove back the Texans a quarter of a mile.[37]

Beatty or Van Cleve (who by this time was suffering from a painful wound in his right leg) probably should have recalled the brigade. Instead, Col. James P. Fyffe's Indiana-Ohio brigade formed on Beatty's right near Asbury Church, with Colonel Harker's brigade of Wood's division coming up on their right, all three brigades in advance of the main line. To their astonishment the Federals now witnessed the lone Texas brigade replaced by thousands of Rebels, four brigades to be exact, that far overlapped Harker's right. In order to protect his flank, the colonel shifted farther right toward the Widow Burris house, thereby creating a gap between his left and Fyffe's right. At one o'clock the Southerners came pouring through the breach, cracking the Union line. Rosecrans personally formed a patchwork line by the pike, to the right of the Pioneer Brigade, backed by massed artillery, six batteries of thirty guns, that finally checked the enemy advance. Added to the line on McCook's right was Colonel Walker's brigade, which had opportunely arrived from the rear. After seven hours of murderous fighting, the Confederate assault had lost its momentum. The Yankee right had at last been secured.[38]

The Union line now resembled a narrow V, the right having jackknifed on the left. Palmer's division formed a sharp salient at the apex. Between the Nashville Pike and

36. John A. Noorse Diary, Dec. 31, 1862, SRNBP; *OR*, 20(1):245 49, 251; Henry V. Freeman, "Some Battle Recollections of Stones River," in *MOLLUS, Illinois*, 8 vols. (reprint, Wilmington, N.C.: Broadfoot, 1993), 3:234–36.

37. *OR*, 20(1):584, 585, 594; Noe, *Southern Boy in Blue*, 123.

38. *OR*, 20(1):502–3, 574, 597–98; Cozzens, *No Better Place to Die*, 146–49; Bickham, *Rosecrans' Campaign*, 252–56; Walsh, *Medical Histories*, 350.

the Chattanooga and Nashville Railroad stood a four-acre clump of cedar and oak timber known to the locals as the Round Forest; to the soldiers it would become Hell's Half-Acre. Holding the forest and astride the pike and railroad was the brigade of William B. Hazen, a man as skillful and courageous as he was arrogant and tyrannical. Wounded by a Comanche bullet in 1859, his arm remained in a sling at the beginning of the war. Before this day concluded, his shoulder would be bruised by a Minié ball. Colonel Wagner's brigade of Wood's division deployed to Hazen's left, between the forest and Stones River. General Hascall's brigade, also of Wood's division, roughly formed an obtuse angle on Hazen's right, parallel with the pike, railroad, and Colonel Grose's brigade of General Palmer's division. The remnant of Shepard's regulars formed parallel to the railroad.[39]

A series of afternoon piecemeal attacks astride the pike hammered the Round Forest, but none came close to cracking the salient. Rosecrans appeared at 1:30, ordering the 73d Illinois and 2d Missouri from Sheridan's division to assist in holding the position. The converging fire of four batteries—10th Indiana; F, 1st Ohio; 8th Indiana; and H/M, 4th U.S.—decimated assaults made at 2:00, 2:30, and 4:00 P.M., leaving (with two failed morning assaults) more than 1,000 dead and wounded Southerners strewn about the perimeter. In the two o'clock assault, Wagner's 15th and 57th Indiana Regiments made a sortie on the right of the attacking Confederate brigade, capturing the 13th Louisiana almost en masse. Hazen's compact ranks sustained serious losses too. In close proximity to where the Hazen Monument would later be built, the 9th Indiana suffered 113 killed and wounded. The colonel had his horse shot from under him, and an aide was killed while removing the saddle.[40]

Throughout the morning and afternoon, Rosecrans, chewing on a stumpy cigar that was long since extinguished, led from the front, at times almost recklessly exposing himself. His commanding presence and unflappable temperament proved his greatest contribution to the first day's battle. Trooper James H. Wiswell of the 4th U.S. Cavalry wrote his father: "As for 'Old Rosy' he is the only fighting genl. that I ever saw during the action. He was constantly riding up and down the line cheering on his men." Even Palmer, who would grow to detest the army commander, conceded, "if I was about to fight a battle for the domination of the universe, I would give Rosecrans command of as many men as he could see or who could see him."[41]

39. Cozzens, *No Better Place to Die*, 153–55; Walsh, *Medical Histories*, 165; Buell, *Warrior Generals*, 201.

40. Hazen, *Narrative*, 81–82, 92; Van Horne, *Army of the Cumberland*, 1:242–43; Stevenson, *Battle of Stone's River*, 104–15; John Palmer, *Personal Recollections*, 146.

41. Bickham, *Rosecrans' Campaign*, 365; Gilmore, *Recollections*, 131; James H. Wiswell to father, Jan. 8, 1863, James H. Wiswell Letters, DU; George Palmer, *Conscientious Turncoat*, 97–98.

Near the Round Forest, the commanding general and all three corps command-
ers clustered together near the turnpike. Fearful that they might become a tempting
target for Rebel artillery, McCook uttered, "This is a nice mark for shells. Can't you
thin out, men?" Rosecrans ignored him, and Thomas dismissed the remark by say-
ing that one side of the road was as good as the other, although he subsequently
moved, followed by McCook. But not everyone had been pleased with Rosecrans's
performance that day. In his later testimony before the Buell Commission, Critten-
den stated that he heard Rosecrans censured by many officers "for his impetuosity,
for his great excitement during the battle [Stones River]." The corps commander
made it evident that he concurred. He also remarked that officers complained that
"they could not turn their backs on their commands without his ordering a portion
of them away." It is difficult not to conclude that Crittenden also shared this
opinion.[42]

Riding in advance of the Round Forest by the tracks, Rosecrans and his staff
came into the sights of Confederate gunners on Wayne's Hill, across Stones River.
Gareschè, riding behind the general, suddenly received a direct hit squarely in the
face, blowing off the top of his head and leaving only the lower jaw intact. Grimly,
the headless rider continued on for about twenty paces before slumping to the
ground. Both brains and blood splattered Rosecrans's uniform, but he quickly re-
gained his composure. (The general later superstitiously expressed that Gareschè
had served as a Christlike sacrifice to help win the day's battle.) Major Bond rode
abreast of Rosecrans and implored, "General, do you have a right to expose yourself
so much?" only to be ignored. The army commander would later admit to feeling
"no sensations under fire that day."[43]

No celebrating occurred that New Year's Eve night. The army had been saved
(barely), but the losses were horrific—more than ten thousand casualties and
twenty-eight guns, compared to a Confederate loss of seventy-five hundred men.
They had only enough ammunition for one day's fight. Furthermore, Rebel cavalry
had struck at La Vergne and Nolensville during the day, capturing about 150 wagons
and seven hundred men. Fortunately, a fresh brigade—Colonel Starkweather's—
arrived from the rear and was placed in line. The troops, with no fires, endured a
hard freeze that night.[44]

During the night, the army constricted its lines. The center and right extended to

42. Lamers, *Edge of Glory*, 232; *OR*, 16(1):578.
43. Gilmore, *Recollections*, 130; Starr, *Bohemian Brigade*, 183–84.
44. Bearss, "Cavalry Operations," 131; *OR*, 20(1):194, 209, 960, 968. Arville L. Funk, ed., "A Hoosier
Regiment at Stone's River: An Account by Lt. Colonel Daniel F. Griffen," *Filson Club Historical Quarterly*
37 (Jan. 1963): 24–28.

218 DAYS OF GLORY

the northwest, with the extreme right re-fused on the Nashville Pike. From right to left were Davis's, Sheridan's, and Johnson's divisions; Walker's and Harker's brigades; Van Cleve's division, now under Samuel Beatty; the Pioneer Brigade; Rousseau's division; and astride the pike and railroad and extending to the river, Palmer's and Wood's divisions, the last now led by Hascall after Wood's wounding in the foot. Negley's division and Starkweather's brigade were held in reserve, the former in the center, the latter behind Sheridan's left. The cavalry remained on the flank at Overall's Creek. Just before dawn Crittenden retired his line five hundred yards to higher ground, yielding the hard-contested Round Forest to the Confederates.[45]

A midnight staff meeting occurred at army headquarters. All the generals sat on the floor of the cabin save Rosecrans, who used a camp stool. (He graciously offered it to Wood, who was on a crutch, but he declined.) Varying accounts emerged from the meeting. Rosecrans claimed that he polled the corps commanders as to whether or not the army should remain and fight it out or retire to Nashville. Crittenden and Thomas refused to commit; McCook and Stanley advised retreat. Rosecrans and Stanley then made a two-hour night reconnaissance and concluded (wrongly) that the Confederates had gained their rear. "Well, gentlemen, we shall not retreat, but fight it out here and to the front," the army commander announced. A staff officer later confirmed that Thomas was noncommittal, though another wrote that the Virginian dramatically rose and announced, "General, I know of no better place to die than right here." He then departed and the issue was decided. Still another version has Rosecrans returning from his night tour and awakening Thomas with the words, "Will you protect the rear or retreat to Overall's Creek?" "This army can't retreat," muttered Thomas, who then went back to sleep. Crittenden reportedly declared upon Rosecrans's return, "My corps is not whipped and we must not fall back." As for his part, Crittenden recalled that there was some talking about retreating, to which he responded that the men would be "very much discouraged." Clearly, the officers discussed a retreat, but who said exactly what cannot now be determined. More to the point, Rosecrans made the decision to stay and fight—there would be a second day's battle.[46]

45. Van Horne, *Army of the Cumberland*, 1:245, 247; Walsh, *Medical Histories*, 377; Stevenson, *Battle of Stone's River*, 122–23.

46. "Sketch of the Life of Gen'l. William Starke Rosecrans Intended to Give Some Facts, Incidents, and Personal Characteristics of his Civil and Military Supplementary to What Is Generally Contained in Popular Official Public Records," William S. Rosecrans Papers, UCLA, 36–38; Thomas L. Crittenden, "The Union Left at Stone's River," in *B&L*, 3:633. The best account of the night meeting is given in Cozzens, *No Better Place to Die*, 173–74.

Glenn Tucker and more recently Russell F. Weigley both have suggested that Thomas's greatest contribution to the battle was his insistence not to retreat on the night of December 31. Tucker, "George H.

* * *

At daybreak on January 1, 1863, Sam Beatty's division, under orders from army headquarters, crossed Stones River at McFadden's Ford. Price's and Fyffe's brigades gained the high ground a half-mile from the ford, though a gap separated the units. Beatty's former brigade, now led by Col. Benjamin "Ben" C. Grider (well known for his alcoholism), deployed in support. Worried that his left was in the air, Beatty requested, and received, an additional brigade, Grose's of Palmer's division, but it returned that night. A stalemate continued throughout the cold and overcast day. Rosecrans expected Bragg to attack, but the Confederates made only forays and artillery actions. It appeared as though the Rebel commander was either probing for weak spots or hoping that Rosecrans would quit the field.[47]

Nor did the Federal commander make his intentions clear. His supporters would later insist that by placing Beatty's division across the river, Rosecrans intended to renew his planned left-wing offensive into Murfreesboro. No evidence supports such a notion; indeed, the general himself never claimed such in his after-action report. Crittenden stated that Rosecrans never related a plan of battle to him. The most significant piece of evidence, however, was the disposition of troops; there was never a troop buildup on the left. Rosecrans clearly operated on the defensive.[48]

During the day, an anonymous division commander, probably Johnson or Davis, related to one of his brigade commanders that he would attempt a breakout the next day. "This army is whipped; the rebels are between us and Nashville, and the only thing to do now is to cut our way through. Someone has to take the lead, and I want you to do it tomorrow; otherwise we shall all be captured." The brigade commander vehemently argued the issue and inquired if his superior had expressed these thoughts to Rosecrans. "No," the general replied, "but be ready tomorrow to cut your way through to Nashville." Speaking privately with another brigade commander, the colonel learned that his comrade had been given the same message. "If he orders me to desert the balance of this army, and run away to Nashville, I'll arrest him as a traitor, and march him under guard to General Rosecrans's headquarters," the second colonel indignantly answered. This information reached the division commander, prompting him to drop the idea.[49]

Thomas—A Personality Profile," *Civil War Times Illustrated* 5 (Apr. 1966): 33; Weigley, *A Great Civil War: A Military and Political History, 1861–1865* (Bloomington: University of Indiana Press, 2000), 196. It is far from certain that Thomas was so adamant; he never made such a claim, nor did his supporter Van Horne.

47. Stevenson, *Battle of Stone's River*, 123; *OR*, 20(1):575–76, 587, 589, 601–2, 604–5, 608, 612–14; Van Horne, *Army of the Cumberland*, 1:604–5.

48. Bickham, *Rosecrans' Campaign*, 307; *OR*, 20(1):195, 450.

49. Stevenson, *Battle of Stone's River*, 125–26.

* * *

January 2 dawned cloudy and cold. At 8:00 A.M. the Rebel artillery unexpectedly opened a vicious half-hour barrage up the Nashville Pike. "They had our range perfectly," admitted Hascall. So many horses fell dead in Lt. George Estop's 8th Indiana Artillery that it had to withdraw, abandoning two guns. The fire also raked Capt. Cullen Bradley's 6th Ohio Artillery, which also took friendly fire from the Chicago Board of Trade Battery in the rear. The Ohio gunners pulled back, as did Battery B, Pennsylvania Light Artillery. Rarely were the Yankee cannoneers so dominated.[50]

Despite this diversionary barrage, attention focused on Samuel Beatty's isolated division on the east bank. Grose's brigade, accompanied by the 3d Wisconsin Artillery, followed orders to cross the river, where it deployed on Beatty's left behind an earthwork of rails, logs, and stones. There is no indication that Rosecrans or Crittenden appreciated the east bank for its true value. From an eminence shouldering the river (now occupied by Price's brigade), the Federals could plant artillery and enfilade the Confederate concentration in and to the north of the Round Forest. What Rosecrans failed to grasp, Bragg understood. He either had to vacate bloodstained land or occupy the sector Beatty held.[51]

The colonel remained anxious. Even reinforced, Beatty had only four thousand or so infantry and a battery to hold a very exposed position. Throughout the afternoon in a driving sleet, the Rebels had been placing artillery—a battery in his front and a two-gun section on his left. He also feared that enemy artillery across the river would rake Price's right and threaten McFadden's Ford in the event it became necessary to recross the river. For Beatty to maintain his position, the west bank absolutely had to be occupied. "You [Beatty] and we all were assured that this was attended to, and we rested on that assurance," Colonel Grider would write in his afteraction report, a not-so-veiled criticism of Crittenden, who in fact did not attend to the matter.[52]

Throughout the afternoon, Crittenden received reports of continued Confederate activity on Beatty's front. At 2:30 P.M. more gray artillery unlimbered; at three o'clock Confederate skirmishers tore down fences, obviously in preparation for an assault. Still, no additional infantry or artillery shifted to the east bank. By then sixteen enemy regiments had been counted crossing the river, where they concentrated in the forest's edge sixteen hundred yards distant. But the attack did not come. By four o'clock most officers thought that the assault had been canceled until daylight of the next day.[53]

50. Cozzens, *No Better Place to Die*, 180–81.

51. *OR*, 20(1):561, 567, 569; Crittenden, "Union Left at Stone's River," 633.

52. *OR*, 20(1):587; Stevenson, *Battle of Stone's River*, 130.

53. Stevenson, *Battle of Stone's River*, 131; *OR*, 20(1):587; Louis A. Simmons, *The History of the 84th Ill. Vols.* (Macomb, Ill.: Hampton Brothers, 1866), 34–35; Samuel Welch, "A Sketch of the Movements of the Fifty-First Ohio Volunteer Infantry," 51st Ohio File, SRNBP; Noe, *Southern Boy in Blue*, 134.

Then it happened. "[The Rebels] massed column emerged from the woods and moved forward rapidly, across the valley and up the hill on which we [Price's brigade] were situated. . . . Our pickets were soon driven in, and as they took their place in the line they would say: 'Boys, they are coming. The woods are full of them.'" Moving to the attack was Breckinridge's fifty-three-hundred-man division, supported by three thousand cavalry and twenty-six guns. The assault proved savage. Within ten minutes, Beatty realized that his two-brigade front would not hold, and he frantically called up Grider's reserve brigade. The three regiments—one Ohio, two Kentucky—momentarily caused the Confederate attack to sputter, but they were not enough. Beatty's broken division streamed toward McFadden's Ford. Grose's brigade watched in horror as Beatty's men ran toward them in full retreat. One of those doing the running was Lt. Marcus Woodcock of the 9th Kentucky, who later admitted in his diary that "every man [was] taking his own course and running at the top of his speed. The rebels followed so closely that the slightest stumble or accident insured the capture of the unfortunate."[54]

Rosecrans watched in dismay at the disaster unfolding. Although he had anticipated an attack all afternoon, the only support unit at McFadden's Ford was the 7th Indiana Artillery. Frantically, he dispatched the Pioneer Brigade and two brigades of Negley's division, Negley vowing to "pay them back for what they did on Wednesday." Along the way, Negley found the Chicago Board of Trade Battery and shouted, "For God's sake, Captain Stokes, come to the front, our men are giving way." Rosecrans summoned William Carlin to army headquarters, where the colonel found the army commander "pale" and in "deep excitement." "Carlin, I wish you to take your brigade over Stone's River at 'double-quick,' and if you find the enemy driving our men, form your troops in two lines, charge bayonets, and with a whoop and a yell go at them."[55]

Crittenden turned to thirty-four-year-old West Pointer Capt. John Mendenhall, his chief of artillery, and exclaimed, "Now, Mendenhall, you must cover my men with your cannon." Two batteries in the immediate vicinity were ordered up. The captain found two more nearby and directed them to the ford as well. Near the railroad he ordered two batteries to change front in order to deliver an enfilade fire across the river. Negley brought up parts or all of four batteries, totaling twelve guns. These pieces, along with the battery already at the ford and the one with Beatty's division, totaled fifty-seven guns, thirty-nine at the ford proper, hub to hub along a ridge about a hundred yards from the river. The scene was set for

54. Stevenson, *Battle of Stone's River*, 135; *OR*, 20(1):587. Van Cleve's losses for the day were placed at 450 killed and wounded. See *New York Tribune*, Jan. 6, 1863.

55. David R. Logsdon, ed., *Eyewitnesses at the Battle of Stones River* (Nashville: n.p., 1989), 59; Girardi and Hughes, *Memoirs of Brigadier General William Passmore Carlin*, 82–83; *OR*, 20(1):195, 455.

the most decisive and stupefying use of artillery in the western theater during the war.[56]

Sgt. Samuel Welch, part of Beatty's disordered mass, thought that the "Army of the Cumberland was rapidly passing out of existence." As he splashed across the two-foot-deep Stones River, he glanced up at the ridge ahead and was relieved to see massed artillery and "General Negley's division, lying in massed column in a cornfield, ready to move into action." As Breckinridge's Confederates crested the east bank, a sheet of flame lacerated their division. The ground literally shook. Confederate guns brought up for counterbattery fire proved helpless in matching the Federal firepower. The Union long arm rained shot and shell upon the attackers, which first staggered and then routed them. The slaughter was terrible, the results undeniable. "From a rapid advance they broke at once into a rapid retreat," reported Crittenden. A staff officer wrote that "not less than a hundred shots per minute were fired. As the mass of men swarmed down the slope they were mowed down by the score." One shell is documented to have killed or wounded eighteen to twenty men. Barely a dozen Rebels crossed the river.[57]

Realizing that the momentum had shifted, Col. John F. Miller, without receiving Negley's order, impatiently ordered his brigade across the river in hot pursuit (the orders of an unnamed general, presumably Crittenden, to the contrary), followed by Stanley's brigade. Negley himself never crossed. The spontaneous counterattack spread total consternation in the Rebel ranks as they dashed to the rear, abandoning three guns. Portions of other brigades—Carlin's, Hazen's, Cruft's, and Morton's—as well as Beatty's re-formed troops, which recrossed the river, joined in the frenzied chase. Night stopped the bloodletting; fifteen hundred secessionists had been killed and wounded. The entire affair had lasted but forty-five minutes. Some would later argue that an organized drive by Rosecrans could have pushed into Murfreesboro, but the general claimed that he was prevented by the rain. Regardless, the day had been a stunning victory, and that evening no one was second-guessing.[58]

56. *Society of the Army of the Cumberland, 24th Reunion, 1893,* (Cincinnati: Robert Clarke, 1894), 247; Francis B. Heitman, *Historical Register and Dictionary of the United States Army, from Its Organization, September 29, 1789, to March 2, 1903,* 2 vols. (Washington, D.C.: Government Printing Office, 1903), 1:703; OR, 20(1):451, 456; Edwin C. Bearss, "Stones River: The Artillery Fight at 4:45 P.M., January 2, 1863," *Civil War Times Illustrated* 2 (February 1964): 12–13.

57. Welch, "Sketch of Movements of the Fifty-First Ohio"; Crittenden, "Union Left at Stone's River," 633; OR, 20(1):451, 455–59; Kniffen, "Battle of Stone's River," 630–31; McDonough, *Stones River,* 195.

58. Kniffen, "Battle of Stone's River," 631; Stevenson, *Battle of Stone's River,* 142–43; Van Horne, *Army of the Cumberland,* 1:249–50; OR, 20(1):195, 408, 434, 451; Crittenden, "Union Left at Stone's River," 633.

*   *   *

The rain fell in torrents during the morning hours of January 3; there would be no letup all day. Despite a lack of shelter and food, Ebin Swift, the army's medical director, reported that "few were sick—none complaining." As on New Year's Day, the two battered armies mostly glared at each other, neither seemingly capable of delivering a knockout punch and both stubbornly refusing to quit the field. At daylight the 42d Indiana of Sheridan's division, having reoccupied the Round Forest, was suddenly driven back with heavy loss, including fourteen captured. Brig. Gen. James G. Spears's ad hoc brigade of fifteen hundred infantry, a battery, and three hundred cavalry arrived from Nashville at 10:00 A.M., escorting a godsend—303 mud-clogged wagons filled with food.[59]

Only slight action occurred throughout the afternoon. Annoyed by enemy snipers on Rousseau's front, Thomas unleashed four batteries to dislodge them. That night a sortie by Spears's brigade and two of John Beatty's regiments successfully reoccupied the Round Forest, driving the Rebels and capturing thirty. It was a handsome affair, although Spears's raw and excited East Tennesseans nearly fired into Beatty's men in the darkness. Back at army headquarters, a staff officer commented to Rosecrans that the men had been pleased with their leader's tenacity. "I suppose they have learned that Bragg is a good dog, but Holdfast is better," the general answered.[60]

Sunday, January 4, dawned clear. Dan McCook, with two and a half infantry regiments and some cavalry, arrived during the early morning hours with a hospital train, having beaten off an attack by Wheeler on the way down from Nashville. At 7:00A.M. Rosecrans received confirmed reports that Bragg had withdrawn from Murfreesboro during the night. The Federals occupied the town but made no pursuit. Rosecrans never gave an official reason, but in a conversation with Crittenden, the two generals decided it was best not to anger the Almighty with a Sunday march. The Sabbath notwithstanding, Crittenden "imbibed freely" with Rousseau and McCook that evening, the Kentuckian being "the merriest of the party" and singing "Mary Had a Little Lamb."[61]

On the heels of Burnside's disaster at Fredericksburg, the Northern press claimed a great victory at Stones River. Congratulatory messages came from all quarters— the White House, the War Department, the legislatures of Indiana and Ohio, but notably not from Grant. Rosecrans became the darling of the nation. Be-

59. Bickham, *Rosecrans' Campaign,* 322; *OR,* 20(1):195, 221, 374; Stevenson, *Battle of Stone's River,* 147.
60. Bickham, *Rosecrans' Campaign,* 321, 324; Beatty, *Citizen Soldier,* 209–10; *OR,* 20(1):196, 417.
61. Bickham, *Rosecrans' Campaign,* 322; Beatty, *Citizen Soldier,* 211–12; *OR,* 20(1):638.

yond exaggerated press accounts of 12,000–15,000 Rebel casualties (actually 10,000), the truth was that the battle had been a slugging match that had accomplished little. Indeed, Bragg merely fell back thirty-five miles to Tullahoma. Rosecrans wrote of defeating an overwhelming Confederate force estimated at 62,500, but in fact he had barely held his own with an army 17 percent smaller.[62]

Union casualties had been horrific, even for a nation that had become familiar with such startling numbers. There were 9,220 killed and wounded, with an additional 3,686 captured, for a total of 12,906. As at Perryville, McCook's corps had taken a severe hit—34 percent casualties. Van Cleve's tiny division received the worst blow—a staggering 44 percent of those engaged. A reporter viewing Samuel Beatty's brigade hospital "saw nearly a cord of amputated legs, arms, and feet, interspersed with slices of human flesh lacerated and torn by shells and cannonballs—it made the heart grow sick and faint." Most of the medical supplies of the Right Wing had been lost during the first day's battle. Fortunately, Ebin Swift had a reserve medical train with bedding for 2,500 patients, along with twenty ambulances, that arrived during the battle. Additionally, eleven other reserve medical wagons arrived, and the Left Wing also had a reserve train of ten wagons. The medical department had come of age.[63]

Rosecrans's assets during the battle—his commanding presence and timely shifting of troops—barely offset his mistakes before the battle—failing to secure the right flank, mispositioning his reserve division, and failing to deliver a timely assault on the left. Also, he did not sufficiently seek the destruction of the Confederate army after the battle, even as he had not (according to Grant) at Corinth. Yet if the War Department had sent him the reinforcements before the fighting that it did immediately afterward, the results might have been very different.

If the battle had not been strategically significant and offered what historian James M. McPherson has called only "a thin gleam of cheer to the North," it served to blunt the growing antiwar sentiment that had been making significant gains in Ohio, Illinois, and Indiana, the states from which the Army of the Cumberland drew most of its troops. "I can never forget, whilst I remember anything," Lincoln would later write Rosecrans, that "you gave us a hard earned victory which, had there been a defeat instead, the nation could hardly have lived over." The North breathed easier.[64]

62. *Chicago Tribune,* Jan. 6, 1863; *OR,* 20(1):186–88, 197.

63. Livermore, *Numbers and Losses,* 97; Surgeon General's Office, *Medical and Surgical History,* 1(2):256, 257, 259, 265; *Cincinnati Enquirer,* Jan. 23, 1863.

64. McPherson, *Battle Cry of Freedom,* 582–83. Rosecrans's name was briefly floated as a successor to Ambrose Burnside as commander of the Army of the Potomac, but officials considered it impolitic to place a "western man" in the position. Charles F. Benjamin, "Hooker's Appointment and Removal," in *B&L,* 3:239.

13

Interlude
The Business of War

THE BATTLE WON, Rosecrans found himself deep within enemy territory, some 212 railroad miles and 250 turnpike miles from his main base in Louisville. The winter rains, which began in late December 1862, continued throughout January 1863, punctuated with sleet and snow. Roads, except those macadamized, became impassable. The general arrived in Murfreesboro on January 5 and established headquarters at the Keeble house. Although sick and confined to bed, he continued to "hourly hurry up ammunition and supplies."[1]

The immediate problem was the Nashville and Chattanooga Railroad, which connected Murfreesboro to the Tennessee capital. Although it was presently not operational, Rosecrans believed that he could have it running by January 14. The larger problem remained the Louisville and Nashville, which had proven to be an inviting target to Rebel raiders in the past. Indeed, during the year that ended June 30, 1863, the Louisville and Nashville was completely open only seven months and twelve days. Every major bridge had been hit, some more than once, and the Gallatin tunnel destroyed. Fortunately, the Cumberland River began to rise in mid-January. "Forty foot rise in the Cumberland, now we'll have stores!" the general exclaimed. A convoy of supply transports soon docked at the Nashville wharf, bringing three thousand barrels of flour, ten thousand pounds of bacon, nine hundred sacks of oats, and two thousand bushels of corn. By mid-February the commissary depots in the city would be bulging with sixty days' rations, with an additional fifteen days' supply at Murfreesboro.[2]

The War Department, under pressure from Andrew Johnson and Horace Maynard, believed that it was time once again to revisit the issue of East Tennessee. On January 7 Stanton, in an obvious attempt at coaxing, sent a letter to General Grant, a copy of which went to Rosecrans, pronouncing the road to East Tennessee open,

---

1. *OR*, 20(2):318; 23(2):20, 60; Williams, *Wild Life of the Army*, 225, 227. Rosecrans's illness was described as "lung fever."

2. *OR*, 23(2):60; Cist, *Army of the Cumberland*, 138; *New York Tribune*, Jan. 6, 1863; *Chicago Tribune*, Jan. 20, 26, 1863.

"and if Rosecrans takes possession of it, 200,000 rebel troops cannot drive him out."[3]

The ploy failed. Rosecrans had no intention of marching on East Tennessee; indeed, he considered himself on the defensive. He remained convinced that Richmond would "strip everything they can" in an effort to reinforce Bragg and regain Middle Tennessee. Rumors claimed that troops from Savannah, Georgia, were already on their way. The general immediately drew in two of his divisions—Joseph Reynolds's five thousand infantry from Nashville to Murfreesboro and James Steedman's division from thirty miles to the southwest to near Nashville.[4]

An unconfirmed, though troubling, report that Lt. Gen. James Longstreet's corps from the Army of Northern Virginia was on its way to Tennessee and would arrive by the end of January further heightened Rosecrans's fears. Railroad experts assured the War Department that it would be utterly impossible for the Confederates to move twenty thousand troops by rail in that span of time, but Rosecrans persisted. By January 13 he was convinced that there was no longer any doubt of this report. A "reliable man" from Abington, Virginia, who appeared at Wright's headquarters on January 16, claimed that fifty-five secessionist regiments had passed that place on the way to join Bragg, with more to follow, thus adding credence to the idea. The *New York Tribune* reported on January 19 that Longstreet had already arrived in Shelbyville with thirteen brigades and had superseded Bragg in command.[5]

The rumors, as usual, turned out to be false, but they prompted Halleck to do what he should have done a month earlier. He ordered Major General Wright to concentrate his troops to defend Louisville and the Louisville and Nashville Railroad and to send the balance to Rosecrans. Accordingly, three divisions assembled at Louisville in late January and packed aboard fifty-four steamboats for the arduous journey to Nashville, where they would proceed to Brentwood and Franklin. They numbered twelve thousand troops, virtually all rookies—the veterans called them hundred-dollar soldiers because of the bounty they received at their enlistment. The corps commander, Maj. Gen. Gordon Granger, was a West Pointer and professional, but the soldiers had made up their minds about him, dismissing him as an "old granny" and a "red tape soldier." Leading his divisions were Brig. Gens. Absalom Baird, a thirty-nine-year-old West Pointer transferred from the East, whose receding gray-sprinkled hair and handlebar mustache made him appear older than his years; Charles C. Gilbert of Perryville infamy; and George Crook, another West Pointer transferred from the East. Despite Wright's pledge to "strip to the last man"

3. *OR*, 20(2):307, 313, 317.
4. Ibid., 317; Lamers, *Edge of Glory*, 249.
5. *OR*, 20(2):302–3, 310, 323, 333.

and his subsequent whining that Kentucky might have to be abandoned, the move was not as draconian as he implied. Wright maintained twenty-eight thousand troops in Kentucky as well as forty-four hundred in rear positions in Indiana and Ohio. That spring the inept Major General Burnside arrived in Kentucky, straight from the killing fields of Fredericksburg, bringing with him two divisions of the IX Corps. Although a step down for him, the West might be the only place where the former Army of the Potomac commander could redeem himself. He would soon take charge of the Department of the Ohio and its field force, now designated as the Army of the Ohio.[6]

Back at Murfreesboro, the soldiers huddled into hastily constructed winter quarters. "Jan. 15th opened with snowing, blowing, and freezing and everything wore a dreary aspect," a Kentuckian despondently wrote in his diary. That night the cannoneers of the 18th Indiana Light Artillery exercised their horses to keep them from freezing. A private in the 44th Indiana noted that his regiment had dwindled to 174 men. "We have nothing to eat but fat meat, hard crackers, and coffee, with not the least hope of even getting the sight of a potato," he groused. The regiment had inherited tents discarded by another outfit, and the army had not been paid in six months. Capt. William S. Mitchell noted that "the officers of the 24th [Wisconsin] are a lot of homesick fellows. The majority of them want to resign."[7]

Prior to Stones River, Rosecrans had only briefly touched upon the issues of administration and logistics. Stockpiles were now depleted and shortages existed in all areas. Some 20,307 artillery projectiles had been expended in the battle, and thirty-six field pieces and five thousand small arms had to be immediately replaced. The number of patients in the army's hospitals had swelled from thirteen thousand to twenty thousand almost overnight. Tents had to be ordered from Nashville. Quartermaster shortages in January included 1,762 camp kettles and 5,518 tools. Many of the men were short on shoes (4,391), blankets (5,750), coats (3,505), pants (16,215), shirts (18,645), canteens (3,818), haversacks (5,918), and knapsacks (4,628). The army's transportation totaled 1,659 wagons and 335 ambulances drawn by 4,421 horses and 12,223 mules. The three infantry corps, which had an exceedingly low 30

6. Ibid., 310, 333, 342–43, 23(2):41–42, 58, 147, 298–99; Claire E. Swedberg, ed., *Three Years with the 92d Illinois: The Civil War Diary of John M. King* (Mechanicsburg, Pa.: Stackpole, 1999), 64, 67, 68.

7. Noe, *Southern Boy in Blue,* 143; *Cincinnati Enquirer,* Feb. 21, 1863 (letter written Feb. 2); Rowell, *Yankee Artillerymen,* 58; William S. Mitchell to father, Jan. 11, 1863, 1st Wisconsin File, CCNMP.

It was during this time that a soldier requested a furlough from General Thomas, claiming that he had not seen his wife in three months. "Three months!" exclaimed Thomas. "Why my good man, I haven't seen my wife in ten months." Replied the soldier, "Well, you see, me and my wife ain't that kind."

wagons per thousand men, were short 93 wagons and 90 ambulances. The army commander had to momentarily turn his attention from strategy to the herculean task of the business of war—staff expansion, logistics, transportation, and mobility.[8]

The issue of corps renumbering came to the forefront that winter. By order of the War Department, the Center, Right, and Left Wings under Thomas, McCook, and Crittenden respectively were redesignated the XIV, XX, and XXI Corps. Although it represented nothing more than a new nomenclature, Sheridan thought it "a decided improvement over the [former] clumsy designations."[9]

In late January thirty-two-year-old brigadier general and current Ohio Republican congressman James A. Garfield arrived at Murfreesboro. Rosecrans kept him at general headquarters for three weeks, during which time he declared his intention: "I have now got a division ready for you, but I want to ask what you think of staying here with me and taking the place as my chief of staff. I am almost alone in regard to counsel and assistance in my plans, and I want a power concentrated here that can reach out through the entire army and give it unity and strength." The brigadier was taken aback—"I am considerably embarrassed by the proposition and hardly know what to say about it," he wrote his friend Salmon Chase on February 15. Although hesitant to connect his career to the general's fortunes, he subsequently accepted the position. Like Garesché before him, Garfield spent long hours at night mentally sparring with the army commander on issues of religion and politics. With Garfield possessing the political savvy that Rosecrans lacked, the partnership appeared to be complimentary. But Garfield was no "yes man," a quality that "Old Rosy" would interpret as personal disloyalty.[10]

Staff problems mounted. Rosecrans sought twenty-three-year-old R. S. Thoms, a Cincinnati lawyer who had served on the general staff voluntarily and with distinction at Stones River, as his permanent aide. He instead got Lt. Col. Joseph C. McKibbon, an officer already rejected due to alcoholism. Thoms was retained, but the War Department reassigned Maj. Charles Larned, the army's chief paymaster, leav-

8. Fitch, *Annals,* 297, 292; *OR,* 20(2):297, 299, 307, 23(2):77; Monthly Inspection Reports, 1863–64, Monthly Inspection Reports Received, 1863–65, Entry 1058, RG 393, Pt. 1, NA. Edward Hagerman apparently did not have access to the army inspection reports when he estimated that Rosecrans had seventy wagons per thousand men, the highest in the Union army. *American Civil War,* 212, 331–32.

9. *OR,* 23(2):36; Sheridan, *Memoirs,* 1:256.

10. Williams, *Wild Life of the Army,* 233, 234; Nevin, *Chase Papers,* 3:382–83; Faust, *Encyclopedia,* 299. On February 16, 1863, Garfield wrote a friend: "He [Rosecrans] wants me to stay with him as Chief of Staff instead of taking command of a Division. I am greatly in doubt which to choose." Mary L. Hinsdale, ed., *Garfield-Hinsdale Letters: Correspondence between James Abram Garfield and Burke Aaron Hinsdale* (reprint, New York: Kraus, 1969), 66. The division that Rosecrans had in mind for Garfield was Van Cleve's, he having been wounded at Stones River. Lieutenant Colonel Goddard, the former chief of staff and a "universally popular" officer, was made assistant adjutant general. *Chicago Tribune,* Mar. 11, 1863.

ing Rosecrans to angrily charge, "There must be a screw loose." Maj. W. D. Bick-ham, a volunteer aide and correspondent of the *Cincinnati Commercial,* also departed for home that spring.[11]

The officer corps had been wrecked in the late battle. Casualties included five brigadier generals (one killed, three wounded, and one captured) and twenty colo-nels (ten killed and ten wounded), two of whom had commanded brigades. Other field officers killed and wounded included ten lieutenant colonels and nine majors out of a total of 44 officers. Adding lower-grade officers, the number soared to 549. Rosecrans also dismissed sixty-six officers for incompetence, including Col. Benja-min C. Grider of the 9th Kentucky and Col. W. B. Cassidy of the 69th Ohio, both alcoholics. One journalist observed, "This command has been weeded out."[12]

Rosecrans requested both the assignment of three brigadiers for division com-mand and the promotion of officers who had proven themselves. In McCook's corps only sixteen of thirty-seven regiments were commanded by colonels, and six of the others by captains. There was only one brigadier, the other seven brigades being led by six colonels and one lieutenant colonel. These officers had no staffs, and their absence robbed their regiments of leadership. Rosecrans requested that Brigadier Generals Stanley, Sheridan, Negley, Palmer, Wood, and Van Cleve be ad-vanced to major general and Cols. John Beatty, Samuel Beatty, Carlin, Hazen, Gib-son, Grose, Lytle, and Starkweather to brigadier general. (It was no secret that the governor of Wisconsin hoped that the last would be promoted, therefore removing him as a potential gubernatorial candidate.) Rosecrans's request failed to budge Halleck. "I cannot take good generals away from armies in the field, and bad ones you do not want. . . . You already have your share of the best officers," he chided, later adding that too many of Rosecrans's officers had requested leaves of absence.[13]

Palmer, commanding the Second Division of the XXI Corps, did not mince words. Not yet knowing that he had been recommended for promotion, he in-formed his wife that Rosecrans preferred "regulars and Catholics." "Rosecrans swears and swallows more whiskey in a day than I do in a month, but his headquar-

11. Rosecrans to Fry, Apr. 15, 1863, Telegrams Sent and Received, Oct. 1862–Jan. 1865, Department of the Cumberland, Entry 916, RG 393; *New York Tribune,* Jan. 20, 1863; *OR,* 31(2):54, 23(2):146–47; *Chicago Tribune,* May 13, 1863. For McKibbon's alcoholism, see *OR,* 31(2):54, 64.

12. *New York Times,* Jan. 20, 26, Apr. 17, 1863; *OR,* 20(1):215–17; Rosecrans to Thomas, Feb. 8, 1863, Telegrams Sent and Received, Oct. 1862–Jan. 1865, Department of the Cumberland, Entry 916, RG 393; *Chicago Tribune,* Jan. 19, 26, 1863. Col. Albert S. Hall of the 105th Ohio was stricken with typhoid fever after the battle and died that summer. Dean H. Keller, "A Civil War Diary of Albion W. Tourgée," *Ohio History* 74 (spring 1965): 113.

13. *OR,* 23(2):19, 20, 83; Rosecrans to Lincoln, Jan. 28, 1863, Telegrams Sent and Received, Oct. 1862–Jan. 1865, Department of the Cumberland, Entry 916, RG 393.

ters are the resort of the priests. General Stanley is a Catholic and must go up. That fills one chance. General Negley is reported to be a Catholic. . . . That takes another. It makes no difference that Negley confessed the night of the fight [Stones River] that I saved him."[14]

Many officers failed to make the cut. Richard Johnson came under blistering criticism for his performance at Stones River, a false story even circulating that Rosecrans had angrily torn the straps from his shoulders. A Buckeye explained to his wife, "our division commander Genl. Johnson dislikes and is very much disliked by Genl. Rosecranz." Neither he nor Jefferson C. Davis received a recommendation for promotion. Davis, unaware of the situation, remained hopeful. To a friend he wrote on March 3: "You will observe a long list of brigadiers are recommended for Major Generals—do you think I can make the ripple? I have commanded the same Div. at Pea Ridge, Corinth & Stone River, all since my Brig. appointment—not one in that list can present such a claim to promotion. Can't you induce someone to undertake the job who has the desire and influence. . . . My friends are as good as anybody else's friends, but unfortunately they don't belong to the right political church right now."[15]

Those not being recommended for brigadier included twenty-seven-year-old Col. Charles Harker, who now feared that he might soon "have to go back to a regiment." Col. Charles Dodge, a "very industrious talker, chewer, spitter, and drinker," who spoke of himself in the third person ("Colonel Dodge knows what hot firing is, sir!"), also failed to get the nod. Col. Hans Heg, the Wisconsin Scandinavian, had hoped for a promotion (he wanted his wife to "sleep with a General") but was passed over, as was Col. Benjamin Scribner, though, as he wrote, "I was the senior officer in the First Division." Col. John Miller, whose brigade made such a valiant stand at Stones River, failed to be tapped, the *New York Tribune*'s report to the contrary and despite Thomas's declaration, "If anybody is made brigadier, it should be Colonel Miller."

Col. William E. Woodruff, commanding a brigade in Davis's division, failed to get a star, thus prompting his resignation—"I have waited sufficiently long for justice to be done me," he wrote a friend. Replacing him would be Brig. Gen. Thomas T. Crittenden (first cousin to Maj. Gen. Thomas L. Crittenden), though he remained under a cloud for having lost the Murfreesboro garrison to Forrest back in July 1862. Col. Stanley Matthews, who had been commanding a brigade, resigned his commission to accept a judgeship in Cincinnati and was succeeded by Colonel

14. George Palmer, *Conscientious Turncoat,* 100.

15. *OR,* 20(1):198; Dodge, *Old Second Division,* 471; *New York Herald,* Jan. 9, 1863; Hiram Strong to wife, Mar. 29, 1863, Hiram Strong Letters, 93d Ohio File, CCNMP.

Lytle, who had been exchanged from his capture at Perryville. Lytle's fair, "almost effeminate" complexion failed to cover the half-inch bullet scar that marred the left side of his face. One who made the list for brigadier was forty-three-year-old former Ohio sheriff Samuel Beatty, who briefly commanded the Third Division of the XXI Corps after Stones River. Life was going well for "Sam"—he would take a furlough in April to marry. Unfortunately, the newspapers got their Beattys confused and wrongly announced the marriage of John Beatty, much to his dismay.[16]

Confusion reigned in Sheridan's First Brigade. Upon the resignation of the able Colonel Greusel, Col. Francis Sherman took command. "Almost all of the regimental commanders are pleased at the change, so they say, and I take their words for it," Sherman expressed. The command change did not stand. Colonel of the 24th Wisconsin (and also former judge and U.S. congressman) Charles H. Larrabee, Sherman's senior by five days, went over Sheridan's head to his political contacts and had the decision reserved. "I am in the way of Colonel Larrabee and I am satisfied that he is in an underhanded way trying to injure me," Sherman concluded. When it was determined that Larrabee would not retain command, he ("by wire pulling," according to Sherman) got Brigadier General Lytle transferred to lead the brigade. A disgusted Sherman wrote that Larrabee "is drunk half of his time (and, I am sorry to say, our Brigadier is not entirely free from this vice)."[17]

Confidence in Rosecrans remained high. "I have the greatest confidence in Rosy, who is known to every man in this army," 34th Illinois soldier Lyman S. Widney related to his wife on February 20. "He never passes a soldier but what he has something to say—generally to give him a good-natured cursing in terms which only Rosy could utter. He professes to be a pious Catholic, but this habit of swearing is his greatest fault." Following a brigade inspection, a corporal in the 21st Wisconsin noted: "A speech from 'Old Starky' brought tears to many eyes unused to weep. . . . We love to hear 'Old Starkey's' thunder-voice; it stirs our souls."[18]

16. Beatty, *Citizen Soldier,* 219, 236, 249, 252–53, 254–55; Blegen, *Letters of Colonel Hans Christian Heg,* 199–200, 205–6; Scribner, *How Soldiers Were Made,* 112; *New York Tribune,* Jan. 20, 1863; Matthews to wife, Jan. 16, 29, Feb. 5, 8, 11, 21, Mar. 1, 7, Apr. 1, 7, 1863, Stanley Matthews Letters, CINHS; Nathaniel Cheairs Hughes Jr. and Gordon D. Whitney, *Jefferson Davis in Blue: The Life of Sherman's Relentless Warrior* (Baton Rouge: Louisiana State University Press, 2002), 149, 154, 156; Alfred Pirtle, "Leaves from My Journal: A Brief Sketch of the Last Campaigns of Brigadier General William H. Lytle," Lytle Family Papers, CHS; A. C. Kemper, "General W. H. Lytle," *National Tribune,* July 15, 1883; Welsh, *Medical Histories,* 207–8. Not surprisingly, only two of eleven promotions came from McCook's corps.

17. Aldrich, *Quest for a Star,* 27–28, 56; Ruth C. Carter, ed., *For Honor, Glory, and Union: The Mexican and Civil War Letters of Brig. Gen. William Haines Lytle* (Lexington: University Press of Kentucky, 1999), 169.

18. Lyman S. Widney to mother, Feb. 20, 1863, Lyman S. Widney Letters, 34th Illinois File, SRNBP; corporal quoted in Richard A. Baumgartner and Larry M. Strayer, *Echoes of Battle: The Struggle for Chattanooga* (Huntington, W.Va.: Blue Acorn, 1996), 9.

232 DAYS OF GLORY

At the heart of Rosecrans's reorganization program was the expansion of the cavalry corps. Ever since the previous summer, Rebel troopers had wrought havoc upon Federal communications, striking almost at will. On January 14 the army commander wired Secretary of War Stanton that the Rebel cavalry had done great mischief (three transports had recently been attacked below Nashville), outnumbered his own four to one, and that to match them he had to have something approaching parity in numbers. As if to emphasize this point, on the twenty-ninth a raiding party captured a train of thirty-four wagons and 164 men.[19]

Retaliatory expeditions were occasionally made, but they paled next to Confederate exploits. Colonel Beatty commented that "slight affairs" were "magnified into serious engagements." He noted the example of the colonel of the 123d Illinois, who claimed to have killed many secessionists and captured three hundred rifles. "The truth is," Beatty concluded, "that he did not take time to count the rebel dead, and the arms taken were one hundred old muskets found in a house by the roadside."[20]

Unable to wait for additional cavalry regiments, Rosecrans devised the idea of mounting an infantry brigade, perhaps a division. He requested five thousand horses, saddles, and revolving rifles for the troops; with such an outfit he could "drive the rebel cavalry to the wall." The unit selected was Col. John T. Wilder's two-thousand-man Second Brigade of J. J. Reynolds's division. At first a majority of the infantrymen balked at being mounted, but after a rugged three-day march, most changed their minds. Horses would simply be a means of mobility; the men in combat would dismount and fight as infantry. The brigade comprised the 17th and 72d Indiana and the 98th and 123d Illinois, the last replacing an Indiana regiment that voted to remain infantry. Capt. Eli Lilly, a twenty-four-year-old pharmacist and future founder of the pharmaceutical company that bears his name, commanded the attached 18th Indiana Artillery. The brigade would ultimately become the most renowned fighting unit in the Army of the Cumberland—the famed Lightning Brigade.[21]

The weapon of choice was the Spencer seven-shot repeater made in Boston. The rifle had an effective range of three hundred yards, but at fifty yards Colonel Wilder, who had been shown a demonstration by inventor Christopher Spencer, was convinced that no enemy line could "get away alive." Unfortunately, the weapons could be made at the rate of only three hundred per month, and the government was slow

19. *OR*, 20(2):322–23.

20. Beatty, *Citizen Soldier*, 221.

21. Ibid., 326; Richard A. Baumgartner, *Blue Lightning: Wilder's Mounted Infantry Brigade in the Battle of Chickamauga* (Huntington, W.Va.: Blue Acorn, 1997), 19, 25; Samuel C. Williams, *General John T. Wilder* (Bloomington: Indiana University Press, 1936), 1–6; Rowell, *Yankee Artillerymen*, 61, 62, 65, 66; William R. Jewell, ed., *History of the 72d Indiana Volunteer Infantry of the Mounted Lighting Brigade* (Lafayette, Ind.: S. Vater, 1882), 122.

in securing contracts. Wilder thus took the situation into his own hands and agreed to be a cosigner of a promissory note by every man in the brigade to buy his own Spencer at thirty-five dollars a gun. (The men would later be reimbursed by the government.) It would be spring before the weapons arrived.[22]

Mounting the brigade proved daunting. Quartermaster General Montgomery Meigs in Washington replied that no one had bothered to tell him about the plan, and with his department already in debt, it would take considerable time to procure the animals. To accelerate the process the War Department granted permission for the army quartermaster to purchase animals. In the meantime, the Ordnance Department forwarded twenty-five hundred sets of cavalry equipments from St. Louis with a promise of twenty-five hundred more to follow. As for the revolving rifles, there was little that the government could do.[23]

On January 15 Rosecrans, insisting to Meigs that the Rebel cavalry, eight thousand to ten thousand strong, "have things their own way," increased his order to eight thousand horses. Meigs replied that one thousand mounts had already been sent from Indianapolis and another thousand would be started from that station, but the balance must come from St. Louis and Louisville. Revealing his ignorance of western terrain, Meigs inquired if infantry could not be loaded aboard wagons to oppose the enemy cavalry, prompting Rosecrans to tartly reply that such an idea "would do well on Pennsylvania Avenue."[24]

Rosecrans's oft-repeated demands for more horses and arms soon began to peeve Washington officials. Having been granted permission to mount infantry, "you [Rosecrans] now bitterly complain of the want of better cavalry arms," Halleck testily replied. "You cannot expect the best of arms or anything else, to the exclusion of others, who need them as much as you." Never known for his diplomacy, Rosecrans merely answered that he did what he had to do, concluding that it was not for personal ambition but "the public interest."[25]

While Rosecrans sparred with Washington, he also reminded Major General Wright in Cincinnati that seven cavalry regiments then patrolling in Kentucky belonged to his department and that he wanted some of them back. Wright grudgingly complied, sending the 2d Michigan Cavalry and the 9th Pennsylvania Cavalry. Rosecrans also eyed two fresh outfits—the 2d Ohio Cavalry at Camp Chase and the 10th Ohio Cavalry in Cleveland. It was mid-February before the regiments left, however, neither fully mounted and the 2d Ohio unarmed.[26]

22. Baumgartner, *Blue Lightning*, 33–34.

23. *OR*, 20(2):328, 329, 330, 331, 23(2):155.

24. *OR*, 20(2):331, 332, 333.

25. *OR*, 23(2):31, 33–34, 38, 62.

26. *OR*, 20(2):333, 334, 342–43, 23(2):25, 41–42, 45, 58; Gerald J. Miller, "Middletown Yank's Journey to War and Back," 25th Illinois File, CCNMP.

During this time, the army commander investigated the unusual situation of the 15th Pennsylvania Cavalry. Originally an escort company for army headquarters, it was eventually recruited to a full regiment. The men soon began to complain of false recruiting promises and that their officers had never been properly sworn in, prompting the troopers to boycott. Complicating the matter was a bevy of Philadelphia lawyers who showed up in camp assuring the troops that they were within their rights. Rosecrans had no patience with the situation and desired to have the entire unit tried for mutiny. In a compromise agreement, the regiment was reorganized and new officers elected. This was sufficient to have four hundred of the men return to duty, leaving the balance of fifteen to be court-martialed. As an outfit, the regiment was of little value for the present, having no horses and a questionable record of reliability. Trouble also occurred in the 7th Pennsylvania Cavalry. On February 13 three men, convicted of rape, were lashed to an artillery wheel and given forty lashes each.[27]

The weather turned warm with intermittent rain that March. Depleted regiments remained a concern. Colonel Beatty lamented the number of skeleton units and the number of able-bodied men who, for one reason or another, were on furlough or otherwise not present. "There is a screw loose somewhere," he declared. Enos Bennett of the 101st Ohio lamented on the twelfth: "Our regiment has run down to nearly nothing. We left Monroeville with 980 men and now can't get more than two hundred fit for duty. And sometimes not more than 150. . . . The rest are in hospitals, convalescent homes, dead and diserted [sic]." While the veteran regiments dwindled, freshly recruited ones, such as the 124th (a Cleveland regiment) and 125th Ohio, arrived.[28]

Rosecrans began a series of inspections, which allowed him not only to see but also to be seen; the troops loved it. "Our Old Rosy keeps everything a moveing, and this Army is better disciplined than ever it was before although it is very much reduced," a Pennsylvanian told his uncle on March 1. After a grand review on the twenty-third, 39th Indiana soldier Winfield Scott Miller wrote his parents, "Old Rosy looks like he has not any sympathy for the secesh and is greatly beloved by all the boys in the army." James Crawford of the 80th Illinois was somewhat taken aback that Rosecrans "was the plainest and most common man of the whole lot of them [generals]. . . . He don't put on many airs. Thats so." A 37th Indiana soldier

27. OR, 23(2):345–80.

28. Beatty, Citizen Soldier, 218; William D. Dillon, ed., "The Civil War Letters of Enos Barret Lewis, 101st Ohio Volunteer Infantry—Part 2," Northwest Ohio Quarterly 57 (summer 1985): 84; Dyer, Compendium, 1:1548; Tassell, Encyclopedia of Cleveland History, 149.

remarked to a newspaper reporter that "no one who has been with the army for the past two months can fail to perceive the wonderful change and spirit." On St. Patrick's Day the 10th Ohio and 35th Indiana, both predominantly Irish regiments, proudly marched down the main street of Murfreesboro to the accompaniment of the 15th U.S. Infantry's band. Nonetheless, Surgeon Edward Blair, while watching the army commander play chess at Major General Crittenden's headquarters one evening, noted with some disgust, "I don't suppose he will be looking for Bragg very soon."[29]

Blair was right. Rosecrans had comfortably settled into the routine of daily life. His wife and one of her daughters arrived at Murfreesboro on March 13 (he had seen his wife only forty-eight hours over the past ten months), making for happier days. On one occasion Rosecrans rather ineptly engaged in a ten-pin-like game invented by Sheridan, causing Little Phil to roar with laughter. On a typical day he attended to requests and administrative matters until 2:00 P.M. He would then ride out to inspect the various corps ("General Rosecrans makes a fine display in his visits about the camps"), talk with officers, and view the progress of the fortifications under construction around the town. At four o'clock he took supper—he had a particular quirk about eating only twice daily—whereupon he would smoke a pipe and read the newspapers, followed by a brief nap. Throughout the evening he would tend to his correspondence and confer privately with his corps commanders.[30]

On March 17 the cavalry made a show. Lt. Henry Potter of the 4th Michigan Cavalry thought that the grand review "made a handsome show with the officers with their full uniforms and white gauntlets and red sashes. Gen. Stanley wore a yellow sash. The major general [Rosecrans] wore none at all." The army commander revealed his receding hairline as he tipped his hat; Potter thought he was near bald. "Good morning, gentlemen! I am glad to see you all out this morning. You are the hope of the army. Do you mind that?" Rosecrans declared. All in all, the young lieutenant suspected that his commander was "the most popular general in the army."[31]

29. Truxall, *"Respects to All,"* 88; Winfield Scott Miller to parents, Mar. 23, 1863, Winfield Scott Miller Letters, INHS; Elizabeth E. P. Bascom, ed., *"Dear Lizzie"* (N.p., n.d.), 87; William W. Blair to wife, May 18, 1863, William W. Blair Letters, INHS; *Cincinnati Commercial,* Mar. 26, 31, 1863.

30. Fitch, *Annals,* 257–62; Lamers, *Edge of Glory,* 256–57; Williams, *Wild Life of the Army,* 247; Beatty, *Citizen Soldier,* 235. See also W. W. Blair to wife, Mar. 18, 1863, W. W. Blair Letters, 58th Indiana File, SRNBP. Many officers' wives visited their husbands in Murfreesboro that spring. Fitch, *Echoes of the Civil War,* 114–15; Beatty, *Citizen Soldier,* 172, 245, 276. George Landrum wrote on March 19: "Gen. Rosecrans' wife is here and several of his staff have their wives here. Gen. McCook's wife is here with him. There are at least twenty-five or thirty ladies visiting their husbands. They ride on horseback and look very gay and happy." Landrum to sister, Mar. 19, 1863, George W. Landrum Letters, OHS.

31. Henry Potter to sister, Mar. 17, 1863, Henry Potter Letters, 4th Michigan Cavalry File, SRNBP.

Various intelligence reports filtered in throughout March, indicating that much dissatisfaction existed in the secessionist ranks. By midmonth Bragg's strength was placed at forty thousand infantry in six divisions and fifteen thousand cavalry under Joe Wheeler. Reported reinforcements from Chattanooga, however, soon bolstered the strength to an estimated fifty-five thousand infantry and a huge cavalry force of twenty thousand by the twenty-fourth. Earl Van Dorn's cavalry division from Mississippi had linked up, and rumors claimed that Bragg planned to mount as many as fifteen thousand infantry with horses stolen in Kentucky. His apparent idea was to essentially mobilize his infantry to operate on the Federal flanks and rear. Rosecrans became increasingly concerned about this spiraling growth of the Confederate cavalry.[32]

The threat posed by the gray troopers was underscored twice in March. With the arrival of Granger's corps from Kentucky, Gilbert's division advanced to Franklin. On the fourth Col. John Coburn's brigade marched south on a reconnoitering mission. Coburn, who had declared that "Wheeler and Forrest will not dare to attack me," soon collided with a sizable Rebel cavalry force coincidentally on a similar mission. The colonel did not properly feel his way and underestimated the enemy in his front (six thousand horsemen under Van Dorn and Forrest). Compounding the problem was Gilbert, who gave little direction and sent no reinforcements. It proved a recipe for disaster. The next day at Thompson's Station, Coburn walked into a trap—Forrest got in his rear and captured the entire two-thousand-man brigade. The troops pointed the finger at that "damned fool" Granger, who, according to an Illinois soldier, "is believed to be an incompetent man by everybody from colonels to privates." On the twenty-fifth Forrest swooped down on the Brentwood garrison, capturing the 19th Michigan and 22d Wisconsin, some eight hundred men. It would seem that there were many "damned fools."[33]

Back in Kentucky, a panicked Wright wired Rosecrans that rumors had reached Cincinnati that the state would be invaded by two mounted columns of seven thousand men each, one from the south and one from the east, between March 18–20. If invasion came, Wright noted, "I look to you." When additional intelligence "more than ordinarily reliable" claimed that John Pegram, with ten thousand to twelve thousand cavalry, would be raiding from Knoxville, Rosecrans notified Halleck that he anticipated a "serious raid" via Cumberland Gap. The army commander nonetheless refused to withdraw the Army of the Cumberland despite Wright's

32. Report of the Chief of Scouts, Mar. 18, 19, 24, 1863, Daily Summaries of the News Reaching the Headquarters of Gen. W. S. Rosecrans, 1863–64, Entry 986, RG 393.

33. Frank J. Welcher and Larry G. Ligget, *Coburn's Brigade* (Carmel, Ind.: Guild Press of Indiana, 1999), 51–80; *OR*, 23(1):176–94; John W. Rowell, *Yankee Cavalrymen: Through the Civil War with the Ninth Pennsylvania Cavalry* (Knoxville: University of Tennessee Press, 1971), 114–15, 118–20.

pleadings that Kentucky "will be overrun." "I think this 'pawn' ought not to move back," Rosecrans replied, declaring that enough troops remained in central and eastern Kentucky to handle the emergency. Pegram did in fact strike on March 22, though with only fifteen hundred men. The invasion turned out to be nothing but a beef raid and was soon ended.[34]

By April 10 Stanley had returned from Louisville on a horse-finding mission and resumed his command, which, with the addition of several East Tennessee and Kentucky regiments gathered in from rear positions, had been expanded to a corps of two divisions. Rosecrans planned an immediate expedition to crush Van Dorn. The cavalry would be backed by Granger's corps, but neither Granger nor Stanley showed any enthusiasm for the task. The former believed that the odds of catching the Mississippian by surprise were almost nil. As for Stanley, he wrote bluntly: "With one of our old divisions we could whip them out of their boots. I do not know whether or not it would be judicious to attack with this green force, but if you think the 'game is worth the candle' we will slap at them." Van Dorn ended the debate by attacking Franklin, and, although he drove back Stanley, the infantry garrison was more than he felt disposed to contend with. After extended skirmishing, which occasionally rose to the level of a sharp fight, the enemy withdrew south of Spring Hill.[35]

In response to these incursions, Rosecrans stepped up the pressure for more horses. Halleck responded by asserting that too many infantrymen were already being mounted—"mounted infantry are neither good infantry nor good cavalry." What he failed to understand was that by this time, Forrest's "cavalry" were essentially mounted infantry. Ignoring him, Rosecrans wired the quartermaster in Louisville on April 10, "I must have horses," claiming that he needed thirty-five hundred animals for the mounted infantry brigade. Undaunted, he also continued to nag Washington. The commander needed more horses (thirty-five hundred), Colt's revolvers (six thousand), and sabers (three thousand). An exasperated Halleck merely replied: "I have only to repeat what I have so often stated, that there is no more

34. *OR*, 23(2):106, 121, 126, 127, 143, 147, 149, 171.

35. Garfield to Stanley and Granger, Apr. 10, 1863; Garfield to Granger, Apr. 11, 1863 (two messages); Thompson to Granger, Apr. 11, 1863; Rosecrans to Granger, Apr. 11, 1863 (two messages); Rosecrans to Halleck, Apr. 11, 1863; Garfield to Granger, Apr. 12, 1863; and Rosecrans to Halleck, Apr. 12, 1863, Telegrams Sent and Received, Oct. 1862–Jan. 1865, Department of the Cumberland, Entry 916, RG 393; Stanley, *Personal Memoirs,* 132. Regiments brought down from Nashville and Kentucky include the 2d, 4th, 5th, 6th, and 7th Kentucky Cavalry and the 1st, 2d, and 3d East Tennessee Cavalry. See W. R. Carter, *History of the First Regiment of Tennessee Volunteer Cavalry in the Great War of the Rebellion* (Knoxville: Gaut-Ogden, 1902), 59–67. Of the 1st East Tennessee Cavalry, George Landrum wrote that they were "a perfect terror to the Sesech." Landrum to sister, May 6, 1863, Landrum Letters.

cavalry to send you. We have none, and can get none, until a draft is made." Meanwhile, the army commander tightened his own belt by replacing mounted orderlies with foot soldiers and by limiting escort companies to army and corps headquarters.[36]

An incident had occurred by this time (discussed in the next chapter) that had badly strained relations between Rosecrans and Halleck. On April 20 the general in chief, claiming to write as "your friend," sharply noted Rosecrans's excessive use of the telegraph for mundane issues, which "is really injuring you in the estimation of the Government." "The truth is, you repeat again and again the same thing by telegram . . . without the slightest necessity," Halleck remarked, noting that perhaps twenty telegrams had been received in the last few months asking for more cavalry. "The Government is fully aware of your wants, and has been doing all in its power to supply them."[37]

On April 28 Halleck, no longer feigning friendship, sent a telegram couched in unmistakable words. "I regret very much to notice the complaining tone of your telegram in regard to your supply of horses. You seem to think the Government does not do its duty toward your army. You have been repeatedly informed that every possible authority has been given to the quartermaster of your army, and to all the quartermasters in the West, to purchase all the animals they possibly can for you. . . . The authorities here have done all in their power to supply your wants. . . . You now have a larger number of animals in proportion to your forces than any other general in the field."[38]

The Army of the Cumberland's April report tallied 33,747 horses (11,478 cavalry mounts, 3,939 artillery horses, and 19,164 draught horses) and 23,859 mules. The cavalry mounts were consumed rapidly, and Rosecrans claimed that one-third of them were unserviceable (his own army quartermaster put the figure at one-fourth). The army received horses at the rate of only 29 per day, an insufficient number. Meigs bristled and questioned whether or not the horses were being needlessly worn out. As for Colonel Sword, the quartermaster in Louisville, he presented documentation that in the previous six months, horses had been delivered at the rate of 83 per day; mules, 66.[39]

Meigs also questioned the premise of Rosecrans's calculations. If the general had 11,478 cavalry, how was it possible for Bragg to have five times that number? "Have they 60,000 mounted men? How do they find food for them? . . . I cannot but think that you are mistaken in your estimate." Rosecrans insisted that he had nowhere

36. Rosecrans to Sword, Apr. 10, 1863, Telegrams Sent and Received, Oct. 1862–Jan. 1865, Department of the Cumberland, Entry 916, RG 393; OR, 23(2):154–55, 199, 245, 270–71, 336, 351.

37. OR, 23(2):255.

38. Ibid., 284.

39. Ibid., 282, 289–90.

near 11,000 cavalry, for 3,000 horses were used for orderlies and other duty. Actual cavalry mounts on hand numbered 8,475 (including 1,938 for mounted infantry), less one-fourth not serviceable, totaling 6,356. At any given time, however, not 5,000 animals could be relied upon.[40]

According to the April 30 return, the XIV, XX, and XXI Corps numbered 29,000, 14,000, and 13,500 men respectively. The average of the ten divisions was 5,700, similar in size to its Confederate counterpart. Besides the standard components, the Army of the Cumberland also contained two regiments and a battalion as provost guard, a 175-man signal detachment, an engineer regiment, and the 1,800-man Pioneer Brigade with attached battery. The weak link was Gordon Granger's raw corps; the Battles of Richmond and Perryville had exposed the vulnerability of such inexperienced units against veteran forces. Rosecrans addressed the issue by exchanging several of Granger's regiments with veteran ones from other corps. He also removed "Old Jim" Spears's troublesome East Tennessee brigade from the XIV Corps and placed it in the Reserve Corps, under the temporary management of Brig. Gen. George Crook. "These were the worst yet, perfectly lawless, and with little or no discipline. Because of my effort to discipline them, they accused me of disloyalty," recounted Crook.[41]

Turnovers occurred at the division level. Charles C. Gilbert, who briefly commanded a division in Granger's corps, was relieved, James B. Steedman being tapped as his successor. A civilian turned general, Steedman had the ability to inspire farm boys; indeed, to "hear and talk to him you would say he is a common farmer," described an Indiana artilleryman, adding that his voice was "mild but gruff." Steedman's transfer to Granger's corps left a vacancy at Third Division; XIV Corps. Brig. Gen. John M. Brannan, fresh from duty on the South Carolina coast, filled the position. Although a West Pointer, Brannan was essentially an artillery officer with limited experience in handling infantrymen; he now had eight thousand of them and would have to learn fast. The West offered him some anonymity from a personal trauma that had become public back East. His wife had disappeared, and fearing she had been murdered, he had hired investigators and had nearby lakes dragged. She eventually turned up in Italy with her lover, another Union army officer. The new commander was not well received by the troops. "Our new Gen. [Brannan] is not liked very well. So far he is not the man for the volunteers. He puts on too much style and goes too much upon formalities to suit us," 2d Minnesota member D. B. Griffin informed his wife.[42]

40. Ibid., 301, 320–21.

41. Ibid., 297–98, 398–400; Martin F. Schmitt, ed., *General George Crook: His Autobiography* (Norman: University of Oklahoma Press, 1960), 101–2.

42. "Chickamauga," *National Tribune,* Dec. 28, 1893; Warner, *Generals in Blue,* 42–43, 473; Faust, *Encyclopedia,* 76–77; Overmyer, *Stupendous Effort,* 29, 55; Griffin to wife, May 25, 1863, in Albertson, *Letters Home to Minnesota,* letter 84.

Officers nuzzling up to Rosecrans provided entertainment for General Palmer. "The humors of the army are ludicrous. I derive great amusement from the opinions, religious, political and social, of my various acquaintances. Rosecrans is a fervent Catholic and is sincerely devoted to that form of faith, yet he will swear and drink freely. Crittenden too is free and social, swears, drinks and, it is said, gambles a little; but he has a great deal of devotional about him. Rosecrans' preference for Catholics makes it the fashionable faith in the army. Stories are, in consequence, told of certain officers who were formerly somewhat ostentatious protestants, who, in their subservience to the general, are now said to agree with him. I told one of these stories to General Brannan, a deeply religious and pious man, and he said: 'I'll be damned if I will change my religion to suit anybody!' "[43]

Other changes were forthcoming that spring. Colonel Willich, having been exchanged, returned to assume command of his brigade. "He was very glad to see us and we to have him back with us once more," remarked Sgt. George Sinclair of the 89th Illinois, "for he is a fine gentleman and a splendid general. He is the illegitimate son of King Frederick of Prussia." Brigadier General Wood, commanding the First Division, XXI Corps, departed for home in April due to sickness. Some believed that Brannon would get his division. Indeed, upon his return, Wood was reassigned and given command of the Nashville garrison; his troops protested the veteran's departure from field command, however, and he was returned to his division. Rosecrans also snatched away Lieutenant Colonel Shepard's command of the regular-army brigade, stating that Shepard held insufficient rank to lead so important a body of troops. The officer landed a desk job back in Rhode Island. (In postwar years he would embezzle money that he had raised for a monument to the regulars at Stones River.) Maj. James H. King, though not a West Pointer, had been in the regulars for twenty-four years and, having recuperated from his recent wound, received promotion to general and given the brigade.[44]

Rosecrans's cavalry slowly became an asset rather than a liability. In late April, Wilder's and Minty's brigades, backed by infantry, struck a blow—a small one to be sure but a clear-cut victory. On the twenty-second the blue troopers dashed into McMinnville, destroyed sections of the McMinnville and Manchester Railroad, torched the depot and cotton mill, and captured 130 of the secessionist rear guard, all without the loss of a man. Even more impressive was the strike of the 6th and

43. George Palmer, *Conscientious Turncoat*, 105. One of those Palmer referred to may have been Garfield, who appears to have briefly taken up Catholicism due to Rosecrans's influence. See Williams, *Wild Life of the Army*, 250.

44. George W. Sinclair to wife, May 28, 1863, George W. Sinclair Letters, 89th Illinois File, SRNBP; *Chicago Tribune*, Apr. 30, May 20, 1863; The material on Sheppard may be found in Capt. Mark W. Johnson, U.S. Army. comp., 1st Battalion, 19th U.S. File, SRNBP; Warner, *Generals in Blue*, 268.

7th Kentucky Cavalry on the camp of the 1st Texas Legion eight miles south of Franklin on the twenty-seventh. The surprise attack ("the 'Johnnies' fled without firing a gun") captured 150 men and an equal number of horses and mules.[45]

Problems nonetheless persisted. Although the aggregate present on April 30 was 6,419 troopers, the present for duty strength totaled only 4,961 men, not counting Wilder's mounted infantry brigade. The difficulty was unmounted horsemen, a concern that caused Stanley to spend some of his time in Louisville that spring. Although better equipped with short-barreled Spencer and Burnside carbines, the blue troopers lacked the boldness and prestige of their gray counterparts. Stanley admitted that his divisions were green and not yet the equal of the vaunted and seemingly invincible Confederate cavalry, a perception also generally held by the Federals.[46]

The cavalry leadership remained feeble. Colonel Zahm had resigned after Stones River due to failing health. Only two of the four brigade commanders were effective—Colonel Minty, the thirty-seven-year-old former British officer ("He will get a star before long. . . . He is a rising man," predicted an officer), and Col. Eli Long, a twenty-seven-year-old bachelor and graduate of the Kentucky Military Institute with service in the regular cavalry. Col. Edward McCook, leading a brigade, was seen as capable but unstable and described by some as "pompous" and "a little absent minded." In a surprise turn of events, two former infantry officers, Brigadier Generals Mitchell and Turchin, were placed over the two divisions. Neither had an aptitude for cavalry, and Stanley detested them both. Mitchell he dismissed as a political general who "was always thinking of the votes he could win in Kansas," and Turchin he contemptuously saw as a "dumpy, fat, short-legged Russian, who could not ride a horse." When Turchin was later transferred back to the infantry at the cavalry chief's insistence, a staff member wrote: "Turchin was relieved this morning. Good!"[47]

A surprising number of Stanley's rank and file still lacked basic equipment. On May 1 there were 6,105 horses (853 of which were unserviceable), with 913 more required. Other items on hand included 7,344 saddles (short 370), 7,056 bridles

45. *OR*, 23(2):267–69; Fitch, *Annals*, 434–36; Angle, *Three Years in the Army of the Cumberland*, 69–72.

46. *OR*, 23(2):298; Stanley, *Personal Memoirs*, 132.

47. Fitch, *Annals*, 205, 210; *Society of the Army of the Cumberland, 22nd Reunion*, 171; Henry Potter to Father, Mar. 8, 1863, Potter Letters, 4th Michigan Cavalry File; "Synopsis of the Military Career of Brevet Maj. Gen. Eli Long," Eli Long Papers, Civil War Misc. Coll., USAMHI; Stanley, *Personal Memoirs*, 134–35; Peter Cozzens, *This Terrible Sound: The Battle of Chickamauga* (Urbana: University of Illinois Press, 1992), 177; David Evans, *Sherman's Horsemen: Union Cavalry Operations in the Atlanta Campaign* (Bloomington: Indiana University Press, 1996), 219–20.

(short 423), 6,638 carbines (short 371), 7,286 pistols (short 458), 6,290 sabers (short 232), 6,979 saddle blankets (short 522), and 6,447 curry combs (short 901).[48]

Camp rumors persisted throughout April. "The rebels are said to be gathered at Shelbyville in great strength, but so much is said here that you can't believe anything unless you see it," commented Iver Torkelson of the 15th Wisconsin. Ohioan Jay Butler remained complacent on the subject. "I see a great many rumors in the papers of the forward movements of the army of Cumber. They who got them up know no more about it than you or I do and I assure you that is very little."[49]

A raid undertaken by Col. Abel Streight that started from Tuscumbia ended in disaster in early May. In the first use of mounted infantry (on mules), the inept colonel proved no match for the notorious Nathan Bedford Forrest, who captured his fifteen-hundred-man brigade near Gaylesville, close to the Alabama-Georgia line. The expedition had been the brainchild of Garfield, who, fumed Stanley, "had no military ability, nor could he learn anything, yet he persuaded Rosecrans that with four regiments of mounted infantry, one could ride through the Confederacy."[50]

In early May the news from the Virginia front remained contradictory. Reports of a large battle had filtered out, and while many hoped for victory, there seemed to be little in the fragmentary dispatches received to sustain that hope. Ohioan Bliss Morse conceded that if the Army of the Potomac had been defeated, the depression would ripple all the way to the West. The news turned out to be the worst. Robert E. Lee had struck a powerful blow against a greatly superior Union army at Chancellorsville, and the troops of Maj. Gen. Joseph "Fighting Joe" Hooker were now reeling back. The Cumberlanders, however, did not "build largely on the Eastern army," which they considered good but "unfortunate." They simply assumed that in every instance defeat was a given, and thus "when the result is announced we feel sad enough, but not disappointed." Captain Mitchell of the 1st Wisconsin nonetheless wrote his father bluntly, "We are losing confidence in the Army of the Potomac."[51]

The work at Murfreesboro meanwhile continued, with strides being made in the artillery modernization program. On May 1 the thirty-five batteries counted 211 guns, including twenty-seven old 6-pounders and twenty 12-pounder howitzers, 22

48. Monthly Inspection Reports, 1863–64, Entry 1058, RG 393, Pt. 1.

49. Torkelson to parents, Apr. 3, 1863, in Anthony R. Torkelson, ed., "A Norwegian in Blue: Letters of Iver Torkelson, 15th Wisconsin," *Military Images* 9 (Jan.–Feb. 1988): 10; Butler to Mother, Apr. 23, 1863, in Butler, *Letters Home*, 68.

50. Starr, *Union Cavalry*, 3:217–20; Stanley, *Personal Memoirs*, 131–32.

51. Morse, *Diaries and Letters of Bliss Morse*, 62; Beatty, *Citizen Soldier*, 271; Mitchell to father, May 16, 1863, William S. Mitchell Letters, 1st Wisconsin File, CCNMP.

percent of the total. The ninety-eight rifles were about evenly divided between 10-pounder Parrotts, 3-inch rifles, and James rifles, the last being bronze pieces, which, because the lands and grooves of the rifling wore out more quickly, would have to be replaced. The backbone of the armament became the bronze 12-pounder Napoleon gun, a smoothbore with an effective range of twelve hundred yards. At Stones River there had been only eight; there were now fifty-six.[52]

The lack of small-arm uniformity continued to complicate ammunition supply. In Rousseau's division the 38th Indiana was equipped entirely with Austrian rifles and the 21st Wisconsin with Springfields. More typical, however, were the 1st Wisconsin, which shouldered Harpers Ferry rifles, .69-caliber rifles, and Austrian rifles, and the 33d Ohio, which had Enfields, Springfields, Austrians, and Greenwood rifles, the last having been altered from smoothbores. Other divisions faced a similar situation. Johnson's division of McCook's corps had eight regiments with uniform arms (three with Enfields, two with Springfields, one with .69-caliber rifles, and one with .69-caliber smoothbores) and six regiments with mixed arms.[53]

The troops received adequate, if monotonous, rations. Indeed, many of the soldiers never drew one-sixth of the week's rations, choosing instead to receive vouchers that could be exchanged for cash. About one hundred head of cattle were slaughtered daily, almost all coming from Chicago, while the bread came from Cincinnati, New Albany, Chicago, and St. Louis. Only rarely did vegetables, in the form of onions and potatoes, arrive, the latter being cut, scalded, and dried and having the appearance of coarse cornmeal. The meat ration was either 1 1/4 pounds of fresh beef or 3/4 pounds of salt pork per day to go with a bread ration and eight pounds of rice or beans per hundred men.[54]

The problem of the commissary paled next to that of the quartermaster, which had the responsibility of feeding the army's animals and the shipping of all supplies. At one point the army quartermaster had stockpiled twenty-four thousand bales of hay and two hundred thousand bushels of corn. Foraging expeditions had to be made in large parties and under heavy escort, but even so the Middle Tennessee countryside had been stripped. One expedition took four hundred wagons and came back with only forty filled. Rations, corn for the animals, ammunition, and medical supplies all had to come by rail.[55]

52. Monthly Inspection Reports, 1863–64, Entry 1058, RG 393, Pt. 1.

53. Ibid.; Fitch, *Annals,* 295.

54. *New York Times,* June 25, 1863; Fitch, *Annals,* 274–81. On May 3, John Morse, a 105th Ohio soldier, noted: "The Sanitary Commission gets 1 or 2 railroad cars a day in of vegetables—dried fruit, pickles & sour kraut. Yesterday they issued over sixty barrels of potatoes." Bianca M. Federico, ed., *Civil War: The Letters of John Holbrook Morse, 1861–1864* (Washington, D.C.: privately printed, 1975), 90.

55. *OR,* 23(2):601; Fitch, *Annals,* 274–88.

Wagon transportation increased slightly. By the first of May, 2,287 wagons and 280 ambulances, drawn by 4,421 horses and 12,223 mules, accompanied the infantry—thirty-eight wagons per thousand men. The cavalry claimed 356 wagons (short 25) and 27 ambulances. Henceforth, regiments would be limited to 12 wagons and batteries 1 per gun.[56]

Desertion remained an urgent, if somewhat sensitive, problem. Rosecrans fumed that forty thousand men were absent without leave, thirty thousand of them from Illinois, Ohio, and Indiana. He proposed to send officers after them, but Halleck denied permission. Stoppage of pay for the period of absence served as the usual punishment, a price that many considered acceptable. Rosecrans now upped the ante, and the crack of the firing squad was afterward heard. The execution of Julius Melika of the 10th Michigan, a repeat deserter, was widely reported. Marcus Woodcock of the 9th Kentucky thought that it was past time for such a harsh measure, though he admitted that he turned his eyes away at the moment of firing.[57]

With the coming of June, the men realized that the time to break camp and advance would soon be at hand—a welcome prospect to most of them. An Indiana artilleryman admitted that, apart from daily drills, he did little more than play chess and fight flies. A Michigan cannoneer wrote his mother on the third: "We are expecting to march from here [Triune] shortly. We have orders to be in readiness to move at a moments notice. . . . The most of the men are pleased—they have been in camp here so long it is getting to be an old story. They desire a change and more active service." The prospect of battle failed to dampen the mood in camp, which was almost festive in some regiments. "No sign of a forward movement," wrote R. S. Lackey of the 19th Indiana Artillery in mid-June, "but Old Rosy knows what he is about therefore his army is content and will go when he orders." On June 16 Thomas held a grand review of the XIV Corps, the troops stretching for over a mile. Although "the Corps was like a clumsy giant" and "hours were required to execute the simplest movement," it proved a good experience for the division commanders, if not for the men in the ranks, who sweltered in temperatures approaching one hundred degrees.[58]

The medical branch by now had been reshaped and fully supplied. There were less than a half-dozen regular-army medical officers, the balance of the surgeons

56. Monthly Inspection Reports, 1863–64, Entry 1058, RG 393, Pt. 1; *OR*, 23(2):41, 74, 116. Fitch stated that the army had 3,000 wagons and 600 ambulances, but official records do not support such high numbers. *Annals*, 267.

57. *OR*, 23(2):37, 60, 62, 75, 76, 77–79; Beatty, *Citizen Soldier*, 248; Noe, *Southern Boy in Blue*, 166–67; *Chicago Tribune*, May 21, 1863.

58. Rowell, *Yankee Artillerymen*, 73; Genco, *To the Sound of Musketry*, 93; Noe, *Southern Boy in Blue*, 168; R. S. Lackey to uncle, June 19, 1863, R. S. Lackey Letters, INHS; Beatty, *Citizen Soldier*, 281.

being volunteers with state commissions. The army counted 30 ambulances for each division of thirty-five hundred to five thousand men and an additional ambulance per regiment and battery, though the latter frequently carried officer's baggage. A supervisor led 10 ambulances, the whole under the division quartermaster. The three infantry corps would march with a total of 407 ambulances. Each regiment possessed a medical-supply wagon, yet by the end of the summer the XX Corps would reduce the supplies to five hundred pounds and eliminate the wagons. Additionally, each corps had a reserve medical train—19 wagons for the XIV Corps, 11 for the XX, and 14 for the XXI. These vehicles carried hospital tents, clothing, blankets, food, medicines, and dressings. An advance hospital at Murfreesboro held fifteen hundred patients (all in tents), but there were three thousand beds in hospitals in Nashville and twelve thousand at the army's base in Louisville.[59]

The men began to strip for action. Wall tents, except for officers, were already a thing of the past, the soldiers having been issued two-man shelter tents, or "dog tents," as the soldiers called them. Already having enough to carry, the men hated them (they made barking noises as officers rode by), though one Kentuckian thought it desirable to get away from the smells produced by twenty men in a Sibley. As for clothing, they were down to basics. "[We are] cut down to one hat or cap, two shirts (I have 4 and shal keep them), one coat jacket or blouse, 2 pr. drawers, 2 pr. socks (have got 4 pr.), one pr. pants, and one pr. shoes or boots. Allso one w[oo]len blanket, one rubber blanket, and one 'purp' tent," a Hoosier inventoried.[60]

A New York journalist arrived in Murfreesboro that June fresh from a visit in the Army of the Potomac. The difference between the two armies "strikes one at a glance," he informed his readers. He declared that the Army of the Cumberland was in "fine condition" with "great" morale. Although the western army had no crack regiments to compare with those in the East, the reporter did witness a division drill with bayonet and a skirmish practice that he pronounced as "excellent." After six months of strategic inactivity, the army was at long last ready to move.[61]

59. "The Great Battle of the West, Chickamauga," in Louis C. Duncan, *The Medical Department of the United States Army in the Civil War* (reprint, Gaithersburg, Md.: Olde Soldier, 1987), 276, 278–79; *OR,* 31(2):259, 619.

60. *OR,* 23(2):234; Federico, *Civil War,* 90; Noe, *Southern Boy in Blue,* 264; Correspondence with Units Relating to Inspection Reports, May 1, 1863, Third Brigade, Second Division, XX Corps, Entry 1054, RG 393. The report of the Third Brigade stated: "Men exclusively use shelter tents. Cloth is mostly flimsy and buttons badly put on. Men furnished with rubber blankets which serve as shelter tents. On march they are much preferred to shelter tents."

61. *New York Times,* June 25 [report submitted June 17], 1863.

14

The Politics of War
Rise of the Anti-Rosecrans Faction

DURING THE EXTENDED Murfreesboro encampment, Rosecrans strengthened the army's infrastructure and readiness. Morale remained high, numbers were bolstered, and discipline improved. Unfortunately, the army commander's personality quirks—enjoyment of verbal dominance, lack of discretion, hyperactivity, and intensity of opinions—inevitably drew him into clashes, both within the army and with Washington. The byproduct would be six months of distraction and strategic inertia for the North's second-largest army.

The popular concept that Rosecrans spent his time at Murfreesboro strengthening his army while his antagonist Bragg became absorbed with vendettas and recriminations against his generals leaves much unsaid. Clearly, Rosecrans held overwhelming support within the army officer corps. "Its [army] confidence in Rosecrans is boundless," appraised Colonel Beatty on March 4. Col. Morton C. Hunter of the 82d Indiana commented to a reporter: "I was all through the Mexican War, and have seen something of generals. Rosecrans is the ablest I ever saw." Garfield observed that the officers had "the most unbounded confidence in Rosy and are enthusiastic in his praise."[1]

Yet Rosecrans's volatile personality—genial and personable one moment, in a rage the next—unnecessarily alienated him from some officers and chipped away at his support. On April 28 Col. John Beatty found a battery and a regiment reporting to him in the evening. Not having received any orders, he thought it a mix-up and sent the units to Col. Samuel Beatty in Van Cleve's division. Orders belatedly came to him to march to Nashville with his brigade and a battery and regiment that would report to him. Realizing the misunderstanding, Beatty rode over to army headquarters to explain. Even as he spoke, Rosecrans interrupted him and went into a tirade: "Why in hell and damnation, did you not mount your horse and come to headquarters to inquire what it meant?" The general spoke "inflamed with anger, his rage uncontrollable, his language most ungentlemanly, abusive and insulting," described

1. *New York Tribune*, July 6, 1863; Beatty, *Citizen Soldier*, 25/; Williams, *Wild Life of the Army*, 225–26.

Beatty. The colonel momentarily thought about slapping him but had second thoughts. A week later, still seething, Beatty sent a written demand for an apology. He never got one; indeed, Rosecrans conceded, "some men I like to scold for I don't like them," but he did express fondness for the colonel and attempted to soothe the injured officer's feelings.[2]

Milo Hascall, commanding a brigade, requested a transfer following Stones River. The reason was not complicated—he detested Rosecrans. Furthermore, he resented the general's perceived favoritism toward Catholics. Hascall transferred to Indianapolis to round up deserters and thereafter had no connection with the Army of the Cumberland.[3]

Palmer also harbored grudges. "You perhaps have seen the official [Stones River] reports of Rosecrans and Crittenden," he explained to his wife on March 5. "You will see that Old Rosy pretends that I sent him a message that the rebels had evacuated Murfreesboro and makes that message an excuse for a foolish order which, if executed, would have sacrificed the whole left of the army. The truth is, I sent him no message whatever and, in his order, he states that he received the information from General Stanley. I have the dead on him. He selected me because he thought that as I was the only civilian, he might destroy me with impunity. He will find that a harder job than he imagines."[4]

In a subsequent letter on March 23, Palmer continued his denunciations. "My personal relations with the army officers are very pleasant except with Rosecrans," he declared. "He knows his [Stones River] report is false so far as I am concerned and he knows my opinion of him, no doubt, as a man of truth and honor. I never go about him and he never calls on me. I have seen him but three times as I came back [from Washington]. Our business is all done in writing. . . . Another weakness of his is the facility with which he listens to flattery and sycophants. Anybody may acquire his favor by telling him he is a great man. I don't believe it, and I don't say it to him."[5]

A breach also occurred between Alexander McCook and Rosecrans. The former was livid at reading the commanding general's Stones River report in the *Cincinnati Commercial.* He believed that he had been singled out as a scapegoat for the rout of his corps on December 31, even as Buell had blamed him for the rout at Perryville. In fact, he was to blame in both instances. Dodging that issue, however, he formally complained that he had never been told the battle plan, an assertion that (as pre-

2. Beatty, *Citizen Soldier,* 256–57, 260–63.

3. Hascall, "Personal Recollections and Experiences," 154, 169.

4. George Palmer, *Conscientious Turncoat,* 104.

5. Ibid.

viously discussed) was preposterous. Nevertheless, he did catch Rosecrans in a lie about calling a formal meeting of his corps commanders the night before the battle, which he had not convened. Rumors spread that "Genl. McCook dislikes and is very jealous of Rosecranz. One of [Richard] Johnson's staff officers said to me the other day that Rosecranz was very jealous of McCook. I nearly laughed in his face," wrote an officer.[6]

Lovell Rousseau, an ardent pro-Buell general, quite naturally fell in with the anti-Rosecrans minority. "The best of feeling has not existed between him and the commanding general for some time past," revealed Col. John Beatty. "Rousseau has had a good division, but probably thought he should have a corps. This, however, is not the cause of the breach. It has grown out of small matters—things too trifling to talk over, think of, or explain, and yet important enough to create a coldness, if not an open rupture."[7]

That summer while at Manchester, McCook complained to Rosecrans about the Pioneer Brigade—it had encumbered his way and given him no help when asked. When Brig. Gen. St. John Morton reported to army headquarters as ordered, Rosecrans unleashed a blistering lecture. "I have never been able to rid myself of the impression left upon me by the coarse and unjust language of General Rosecrans," recalled Hazen, who witnessed the event. Morton requested a transfer to the Army of the Potomac, but it was not forthcoming.[8]

Trouble loomed both within the army and without. Andrew Johnson had expressed relief when Rosecrans took command, but a recent rift with the governor's chief of police, William Truesdail, now tainted his relationship with the general. Stanton expressed weak support for Rosecrans from the outset, but Halleck had been a backer. The general in chief now became increasingly irritated at the army commander's litany of wants and irksome reasons for delaying an advance. On March 1 he attempted a new and somewhat crass tactic. Stanton sent a telegram to both Rosecrans and Grant stating, "There is a vacant major generalcy in the Regular Army, and I am authorized to say that it will be given to the general in the field who first wins an important and decisive victory." The message was clear. There would be a race between Grant for Vicksburg and Rosecrans for Chattanooga, with the winner getting the prize. Grant tucked the message away and said nothing, but Rosecrans characteristically erupted. A reporter heard him blurt out: "Does Stanton intend to regulate army promotions on the principals of a gift enterprise? Does he

6. OR, 20(2):381–83, 23(2):59; Hiram Strong to wife, Mar. 29, 1863, Hiram Strong Letters, 93d Ohio File, CCNMP.

7. Beatty, Citizen Soldier, 308.

8. Hazen, Narrative, 408.

suppose I will sacrifice my men to my personal ambition?" He at once dictated a reply. "As an officer and a citizen, I feel degraded to see such auctioneering of honor. Have we a general who would fight for his own personal benefit, when he would not for honor and the country? He would come by his commission basely in that case, and deserved to be despised by men of honor." An aide confided to a reporter, "I never saw him so angry as when he received that letter."[9]

Halleck waited a week to reply, but even then he had not cooled to Rosecrans's "indignant answer." "If this be so [auctioneering] the general orders of the President announcing that he would appoint brigadier and major generals only for distinguished services in the field is also 'auctioneering of honors,' and should have incited equal indignation. . . . When last summer, at your request, I urged the Government to promote you for success in the field, and, again at your request urged that your commission be back dated to your services in Western Virginia, I thought I was doing right in advocating your claim to honor for services rendered."[10]

Rosecrans now despised both Stanton and Halleck and believed, with good cause, that the feeling was reciprocated. In May *New York Tribune* journalist Henry Villard visited Murfreesboro. He quickly saw the general's excessive hospitality as nothing more than a veiled attempt at winning a favorable press; it did not work. "He [Rosecrans] criticized General Halleck and Secretary Stanton with such freedom—with such total disregard of official propriety—not once, but repeatedly, that it really embarrassed me to listen to him, although, fortunately, he was content to do the talking without expecting sympathetic echoes from me," the journalist later wrote.[11]

The subject of slavery remained bitterly divisive within the army. Racism was endemic, and Lincoln's Emancipation Proclamation evoked strong emotions. "We did not hire ourselves to the Government to *free* Negroes, and we do not wish to see thousands of our own race fall by disease and in battle to sustain that famous proclamation," a private in the 44th Indiana adamantly wrote on February 2. Days later John Morse of the 105th Ohio expressed his views. "You wish to know what I think of the Proclamation freeing all of the slaves. . . . They are a race that have always

9. Lamers, *Edge of Glory,* 246, 256. *OR,* 30(1):133, 23(2):95, 111; Gilmore, *Recollections,* 142; James R. Gilmore, "Why Rosecrans Was Removed," *Atlanta Constitution,* Dec. 22, 1895. Lamers stated that Stanton mildly supported Rosecrans until the general made an indiscreet comment about the Louis Benker affair, which occurred back in the spring of 1862 in West Virginia and for which Rosecrans blamed the secretary. *Edge of Glory,* 254.

10. *OR,* 23(2):138.

11. Villard, *Memoirs,* 2:65–67.

had someone to provide for them and are not used to looking out for themselves. Now turn such a horde loose upon the country and what would be the result?" The thought of elevating the "ebony-hued and thick-lipped race" sickened Pvt. Arthur B. Carpenter of the 19th U.S. Infantry. Azra Bartholomew of the 21st Michigan remained fearful "that the government will not settle the war unless they can free the Niggers. I would be satisfied if they [Southerners] would come back just as they were in the first place, but that will never satisfy the abolitionist." Although Hoosier William Clark opposed abolitionism "with all my might," he conceded that his views were in the minority. Eightieth Illinois member James Crawford held a different opinion. "It seems strange to me that we should try to cure anything and still preserve the thing which caused the evil. And it is plain to me that slavery caused the war." Sgt. Maj. Lyman Widney thought that "these Torys appear to have trouble in regard to the Negro. . . . They are afflicted with 'nigger on the brain.'" Ohioan George Landrum became convinced that "this army endorses the President's proclamation. . . . A few Kentucky troops are the only ones here who do not like the proclamation. As a general thing, they are not much to us, and might as well be home as here."[12]

Some officers openly expressed abolitionist views. Colonel Hunter of the 82d Indiana, a Democrat, noted, "A large majority of Rosecrans' men went into the war friendly to slavery; but now not one of them would consent to any peace that would not destroy it root and branch." Col. Emerson Opdycke revealed to his brother, "I am anxious for peace but [no] other basis than annihilation of rebellion and its black cause—slavery." Maj. H. F. Kalfus of the 15th Kentucky, however, "painfully and reluctantly" submitted his resignation on the grounds that the object of the war was now to elevate blacks. "The service cannot possibly suffer from my resignation," he concluded. John Beatty endorsed the request, adding caustically: "[I] cheerfully certify to the correctness of one statement which he makes herein, to-wit: 'The service can not possibly suffer by his resignation.'"[13]

12. *Cincinnati Enquirer*, Feb. 21, 1863; Federico, *Civil War*, 79; Carpenter to mother, May 30, 1863, quoted in Bright, "Yankee in Arms," 205; Azra Bartholomew to "Dear Frank," Jan. 10, 1863, Azra Bartholomew Letters, 21st Michigan File, SRNBP; Margaret Black Tatum, ed., "Please Send Stamps: The Civil War Letters of William Allen Clark," *Indiana Magazine of History* 91 (Mar. 1995): 202, 208; Bascom, *"Dear Lizzie,"* 24; Widney to wife, Mar. 17, 1863, Lyman S. Widney Letters, 34th Illinois File, SRNBP; Enos Lewis to parents, Apr. 21, 1863, Dillon, "Civil War Letters of Enos Barret Lewis," 90; Landrum to sister, Feb. 6, 1862, George W. Landrum Letters, OHS. For a positive reaction to the proclamation, see *Chicago Tribune*, Jan. 26, 1863.

13. *New York Tribune*, Jan. 24, 1862; Emerson Opdycke to brother, June 23, 1863, Emerson Opdycke Letters, OHS; Beatty, *Citizen Soldier*, 223, 225. Major Kalfus was arrested on March 4, 1863, "for using treasonable language in tendering his resignation. He was escorted outside the lines and turned loose. The Major is a cross-roads [small-town] politician, and will, I doubt not[,] be a lion among his half-loyal neighbors when he returns home," wrote Beatty.

The issue intensified that winter as the results of the congressional races became fully known. The Democrats, widely perceived as the "Peace Party" and obstructionists, trounced the Republicans. Democrats in Illinois, Ohio, and Indiana, states that Lincoln had carried in 1860, had gained eighteen seats in the House and three in the Senate. The vote, in part, resulted from the fact that there was not yet an absentee ballot (except in three small states), which disenfranchised soldiers in the army. The voice of the Copperheads, those advocating peace with the Confederacy, which was substantial in the West at any rate, thus became magnified.[14]

The antiwar surge on the home front initially caused grave concern in the army. "The action of the copperhead Democracy and the repeated rumor of the recall of McClellan, with the revival of his policy is making this fine army feel anxious," Garfield warned Chase. John Beatty also became jittery: "Surely the effort now being put forth by a great party in the North to convince the troops in the field that this is an unjust war, or abolition or nigger war, must have a tendency to injure the army, and, if persisted in, may finally ruin it." Colonel Heg believed that the only thing holding the Rebels together was the hope that "the Democrats up North are getting up a civil war amongst us at home."[15]

Far from damaging morale in the Army of the Cumberland, however, the troops actually became solidified against the peace movement as a great wave of war patriotism swept the army. Reflective of this attitude, Enoch Lewis of the 101st Ohio wrote on April 21: "I understand that the coperheads are beginning to cool down conciderable since the elections. Coperheadism has brought the soldiers together more than anything else. Some of the men that yoused to be almost willing to have the war settled any way are now among the strongest Union soldiers we got. So that the coperheads did not gain anything of the soldiers." Lyman S. Widney wrote bluntly: "We in the Army, consider them [Copperheads] the most contemptible creatures in the States, North or South. . . . They are traitors in the darkest sense of the word." In like tone Pvt. Abram Kipp related to his mother on April 5: "Mother, you nor any person else has the least idea of the soldiers' feelings in the army at present. I ain't only speaking of our regiment. I am speaking of the Army of the Cumberland! Every regiment wants to go home to fight the Copperheads. I never saw the like." Sgt. George G. Sinclair of the 89th Illinois detested the extremes on both ends and suggested that the army "be led back at the Canada line and exterminate 'Copperheads' and abolitionists together." George Landrum believed that if several regiments of the Army of the Cumberland could be sent North, "they will attend to

14. Rawley, *Politics of Union*, 96–97.

15. Garfield to Chase, Feb. 15, 1863, in Niven, *Chase Papers*, 3:383; Beatty, *Citizen Soldier*, 220–21; Blegen, *Letters of Colonel Hans Christian Heg*, 190.

their business thoroughly; hanging will become fashionable and a favorite amusement with us."[16]

The debate did not simply remain within the ranks. General and field officers also became engaged, and the issue soon became highly charged and politicized. Col. William W. Caldwell of the 81st Indiana in Davis's division was dismissed for "Copperheadism." John Beatty recognized the dynamics when he wrote on February 17: "The army is turning its attention to politics somewhat. Generals and colonels are ventilating their opinions through the press."[17]

When the Democratically controlled Indiana state legislature passed a peace pronouncement, reaction was swift. The Hoosier officers serving in the Army of the Cumberland called a meeting to denounce "the butternuts" in the state legislature and to support Republican Governor Morton. Colonel Hunter as well as Col. Michael Gooding, both Democrats, were outspoken in their denunciation of antiwar sentiment.[18]

When a similar resolution came from the Ohio legislature, Buckeye officers quickly followed suit by denouncing "incipient treason." "If some miserable demagogues amongst you must vomit forth their treason, let them keep it at home. We know for what we engaged in[,] an abolition war." The "Action of the Ohio Regiments at Murfreesboro Regarding the Copperheads" was drafted by Col. John M. Connell, a lifelong Democrat, who was assisted by Cols. W. B. Walker (71st Ohio), E. H. Phelps (38th Ohio), and J. M. Council (17th Ohio). Additional resolutions included the "Address of the Ohio Soldiers of the Western Army to the People of Ohio," in which virtually all Buckeye regiments—thirty infantry, three cavalry, and one artillery (though some units had not responded by February 1)—pledged "their support of the prosecution of the war" and their determination to "put down this rebellion." John Beatty was convinced that the declarations had "done a great deal of good."[19]

In one notable instance politics came close to dividing a family. The mayor of Chicago, Francis C. Sherman, a Democrat surrounded by antiwar associates, had a

16. Dillon, "Civil War Letters of Enos Barret Lewis," 90; Widney to wife, Mar. 17, 1863, Widney Letters, 34th Illinois File; Edward S. Osheskie, *Civil War Echoes* (N.p., n.d.), 35; Sinclair to wife, June 20, 1863, George S. Sinclair Letters, 89th Illinois File, SRNBP; Landrum to sister, Feb. 6, 1862, Landrum Letters.

17. Hughes and Whitney, *Jefferson Davis in Blue*, 149; Beatty, *Citizen Soldier*, 220–21. Several officers' names were floated as possible gubernatorial candidates that spring, including Garfield and Steedman for Ohio and Starkweather for Wisconsin. See Williams, *Wild Life in the Army*, 273.

18. *New York Tribune*, July 6, 1863; "The Indiana Officers on the Political Situation," *Chicago Tribune*, Jan. 27, 1863.

19. "Action of the Ohio Regiments at Murfreesboro Regarding the Copperheads," Sidney Botkin Papers, OHS; Beatty, *Citizen Soldier*, 249–50.

son in the Army of the Cumberland, Col. Francis T. Sherman of the 88th Illinois. The colonel made his feelings public by writing a pro-war letter for publication in a Chicago newspaper. "Best rest assured of one thing: the soldiers are loyal and will support the government, and they would as soon war on traitors in Illinois as in Tennessee," he wrote. Although never mentioning his father's name and not intending to start a rift, the Republican *Chicago Tribune* immediately recognized the propaganda value: "His [mayor's] own son, who is in the field, wrote an indignant rebuke of his father's apostasy." The colonel, in a letter to his parents, replied: "It seems that my letter . . . has made a great stir in the Chicago world. Well, let it. . . . As to having turned myself over to the abolitionists, that is not so. I only wrote my honest sentiments about this unhappy war and its consequences."[20]

Maj. James A. Connolly of the 123d Illinois, a self-avowed "conservative young Democrat," became a pragmatic abolitionist, he admitted to his wife on May 18. "Yes, while in the field I am an abolitionist; my government has decided to wipe out slavery, and I am for the government and its policy whether right or wrong, so long as its flag is confronted by the hostile guns of slavery."[21]

Most officers strongly advocated the prosecution of the war. "They [officers] detest Copperheadism, and the heartiest ones I find are from Ohio, the home of [Copperhead champion Clement L.] Vallandigham," observed Alfred Hough. Brigadier General Stanley was convinced that only the victory at Stones River saved the "Northwest from falling under the domination of the peace or coward's party." When Garfield heard of some antiwar students, he could hardly restrain his anger. "Tell all those Copperhead students for me that were I there in charge of the school I would not only dishonorably dismiss them from the school, but if they remained in the place and persisted in their cowardly treason, I would apply to Gen. Burnside to enforce General Order No. 38 [against giving comfort to the enemy] in their cases."[22]

The politics of slavery ignited sparks between some officers. Colonel Heg of Wisconsin noted to his wife on January 21: "Yesterday I had quite a spat with Jeff. C. Davis—our Division Commander—he is a proslavery General, and he is down on the Abolitionists. I had some plain talk with him, and told him what I thought of proslavery generals—I have no good feeling for them, and have made up my mind that I will not go into another battle under his command." Both he and Colonel Carlin requested transfers, though to no avail.[23]

20. Aldrich, *Quest for a Star*, 29–33.
21. Angle, *Three Years in the Army of the Cumberland*, 58.
22. Athearn, *Soldier in the West*, 97; *OR*, 23(2):412; Hinsdale, *Garfield-Hinsdale Letters*, 67.
23. Blegen, *Letters of Colonel Hans Christian Heg*, 178.

As for his part, Davis did not mince words about his anti-emancipation views. "What are the politicians doing?" he asked a friend on January 20. "Is there no one to oppose this fatal policy among our statesmen? The army will not stand it. It will divide as sure as fate. I see no hope for the country if this abolition policy is to continue to rule at Washington. It is making the South more and more bitter every day and at the same time disgusting the army. The whole scheme is visionary and absurd." To the same friend he wrote on June 11: "A book entitled Rosecrans Campaigns has just been published by one E. D. Biekhem [*sic*] formerly of his staff. He does not like me in the least because he is an Abolitionist and I ain't. I do not therefore come in for a very great share of his high standing adjectives."[24]

Palmer remained an adamant anti-abolitionist. While on a mission in Washington, D.C., he met with the president. When asked how the men of the Army of the Cumberland received the Emancipation Proclamation, Palmer responded that Lincoln might as well have said to the slaves, "Arise, Peter, slay and eat." Palmer admitted that he was strongly opposed to emancipation, prompting Lincoln to answer, "Well, don't you see that, on an average, I am about right?"[25]

Although creating further unrest back home, the impending passage of the Conscription Act pleased the soldiers. Wrote John Leanard to his father: "I am listening with patience to hear of the conscript law being put in force and I hope they will take every young man that is able bodied and fit to carry a gun and send him to the front. We will put them through on the double quick." Abram Kipp wryly suggested that the men of the Army of the Cumberland would be happy to "give them [conscripts] a grave in Tennessee." "The army is lying still now waiting for the Conscription Act to pass and be put in force," Wisconsin soldier Benjamin Boardner informed some friends on March 3. "I hope and pray that it will pass in less than two weeks and bring some of them young bubbers in."[26]

Amid this political volatility Rosecrans, a War Democrat, now interjected himself. In a couple of open letters, he assailed the peace pronouncements that had emanated from the Indiana and Ohio legislatures. "This is war for the maintenance of the Constitution and the laws. I am amazed that anyone could think of peace on any terms. He who entertains the sentiment is fit only to be a slave; he who utters it at this time is a traitor to his country." The enraged Ohio legislature refused to print Rosecrans's letter "on patriotism and home traitors," with twenty-two Demo-

24. Davis to TWG, Jan. 20, June 11, 1863, quoted in Hughes and Whitney, *Jefferson Davis in Blue,* 156, 157.

25. George Palmer, *Conscientious Turncoat,* 101.

26. Benjamin Boarner to friends, Mar. 3, 1863, Benjamin F. Boarner Letters, BHLUM; John C. Leanard to father, June 17, 1863, John C. Leanard Letters, 21st Ohio File, SRNBP; Osheskie, *Civil War Echoes,* 34. See also Hiram Russell to wife, Mar. 13, 1863, Hiram Russell Letters, 21st Wisconsin File, SRNBP.

crats voting no. The pro-Democratic *Cleveland Leader* denounced the letter: "No man in the Union army has more the confidence of the soldiers and the people than General Rosecrans. Of the contemptible acts of the Copperhead party we know not one as low and meanly partisan as this." Rosecrans promptly banned two Democratic organs from the army, the *Chicago Times* and the *Cincinnati Enquirer,* and admonished a Nashville editor for printing misinformation. He then went after four colonels who had made public antiwar statements, placing them in irons. Palmer was convinced that Rosecrans was "getting more and more in harmony with the radical men of the army each day." Adding its voice, the *Cincinnati Enquirer* declared that the general had made statements that could only be heard "from the lips of Abolitionists of the most radical stripe. It is not only a party [partisan] letter, but one of unusual bitterness."[27]

The result of Rosecrans's overt political expressions was that Stanton became even more suspicious of him, believing that the army commander was attempting to become the champion of the Radical Republicans. Concerning Rosecrans's public letters, the secretary of war blurted, "That man, Rosecrans, should drop letter writing." The *Cincinnati Times* even reported that Stanton "flew into a rage." In truth, Rosecrans was not a political ideologue. He was simply a man of strong opinions who never had an idea that he did not voice publicly.[28]

Ironically, though, Rosecrans did catch the eye of the Radical Republicans. Horace Greeley, editor of the *New York Tribune,* backed by powerful Republican associates, had lost confidence in Lincoln. Initially, he planned to campaign for an administration shakeup, with Lincoln being asked to resign (the president himself had twice suggested it) in favor of Vice Pres. Hannibal Hamlin. Among several planned cabinet turnovers, Rosecrans would replace Stanton. By the spring of 1863, Greeley was mulling grander ideas; Rosecrans would become the presidential candidate. The fact that he was a War Democrat would be a drawing card for the Union

27. William S. Rosecrans, *Letter from General Rosecrans to the Democracy of Indiana* (Philadelphia: Union League, 1863); Rosecrans, *A Savory Dish for Loyal Men* (Philadelphia: For Gratuitous Distribution, 1863); Rosecrans, "Letter from Rosecrans to the Ohio Legislature," Feb. 3, 1863, OHS; *Cincinnati Enquirer,* Mar. 4, 1863; Rosecrans, *The Patriot Soldier and Hero: General Rosecrans to the Legislatures of Ohio and Indiana* (Loyal Publication Society, 1863); *New York Tribune,* Apr. 17, 1863; *Cleveland Leader,* Apr. 10, 1863; "The War for the Union; What General Rosecrans Says of It; His Letter to Governor Tod of Ohio," *Chicago Tribune,* Feb. 12, 1863; "Rosecrans Letter to the Ohio Legislature and Cincinnati City Council," *Chicago Tribune,* Feb. 17, 1863; "Letter from General Rosecrans," *Chicago Tribune,* Feb. 28, 1863; George Palmer, *Conscientious Turncoat,* 109. See also *Chicago Tribune,* Feb. 16, 1863. Lyman Widney informed his wife: "The Chicago Times and Cincinnati Enquirer never reach us. Old Rosy wan't let them come within our lines. Everybody is satisfied with the arrangement." Widney to wife, Mar. 17, 1863, Widney Letters, 34th Illinois File.

28. *Cincinnati Times,* Oct. 21, 1863.

Party (the new bipartisan name of the Republicans), and his Catholicism would help deliver a block Irish vote. But was the general nonnegotiable on the subject of peace *without* slavery? James A. Gilmore, a wealthy merchant and newspaper writer, was sent to Murfreesboro ostensibly for a story but in reality to investigate Rosecrans's political views.[29]

As always, the army commander openly expressed himself. On the chief issue, Gilmore found him "sound in the goose"—an abolitionist, but not for racial equality. Before he made his move, however, he wanted to first test Garfield. The chief of staff was typically guarded about his views, but he was known to be thick with Chase and Sen. Benjamin Wade, both anti-Lincoln Republicans. When Palmer had earlier expressed support of Lincoln, Garfield remained quiet, and he thereafter became uncommunicative with the brigadier. Garfield proved more open with Gilmore. When the reporter confided his true mission, the brigadier/congressman replied, "If the country were canvassed, so fit a man could not be found." Having gotten the answer he sought, Gilmore now went directly to the army commander. Rosecrans was surprised but listened intently. He ultimately declined, however, stating: "My place is here. The country gave me an education, and so has a right to my military services. This and not the presidency is my post of duty, and I cannot, without violating my conscience, leave it."[30]

Exactly how much, if anything, Stanton knew of Rosecrans's presidential discussion is unknown. He clearly suspected him and his perceived identification with the Radical Republicans. Rosecrans's involvement with the politics of slavery thus further widened the breach with Stanton. The rudiments of an anti-Rosecrans bloc, both inside and outside the army, were beginning to emerge.

In late May ex-congressman Clement L. Vallandigham, a leading Copperhead advocate in Ohio, arrived in Murfreesboro. Exactly how he got there is a story in itself. Burnside had foolishly sentenced him to confinement for the duration of the war, making him a martyr for the antiwar movement and raising some sticky legal issues. To resolve the matter Lincoln ordered Burnside to send Vallandigham to Rosecrans, who would then place him beyond the Federal lines. When the Ohioan arrived, Rosecrans could not refrain from making a comment. "Why, sir! Do you know that unless I protect you with a guard my soldiers will tear you to pieces?" "That, sir, is because they are just as ignorant of my character as yourself. But draw your soldiers up in a hollow square tomorrow morning, and announce to them that Vallandigham desires to vindicate himself, and I will guarantee that when they hear

29. Gilmore, *Recollections*, 39–62, 92–102.

30. Ibid., 114–50. One story purported that Rosecrans was also approached by Ohio Democrats to run against Ohio governor Tod, but the general angrily declined. David Homer Bates, *Lincoln in the Telegraph Office: Recollections of the States Military Telegraph Corps during the Civil War* (reprint, Lincoln: University of Nebraska Press, 1995), 160–61.

me through they will be more willing to tear Lincoln and yourself to pieces!" Taken aback by his brashness, Rosecrans, shaking his finger, blasted back: "Vallandigham, don't you ever come back here. If you do, I'll be God damned—and may God forgive me for the expression—I'll be God damned if I don't hang you." The next morning the Copperhead was sent over to the Rebels, who scratched their heads as to what to do with him.[31]

Grant made his move against Vicksburg in May. Having successfully gotten ironclads and transports past the city's heavy batteries, he crossed his army over the Mississippi River to the south at Bruinsburg. Shortly afterward the Army of the Tennessee fought and won several battles, but details of these were sketchy in Tennessee. The Chattanooga paper of May 16, in Rosecrans's possession, admitted that Jackson, Mississippi, had fallen. Confederate theater commander Gen. Joseph E. Johnston was now attempting to piece together a relief army. Back at Murfreesboro, Lyman Widney wrote his parents, "everybody is engrossed in the operations of General Grant at Vicksburg. We look forward to the results with feverish anxiety."[32]

Washington authorities became concerned that the Confederates would take advantage of Rosecrans's inactivity to send reinforcements from Bragg's Army of Tennessee. Dispatches had been received at the War Department that some troops had already departed for Mississippi. By May 18 Rosecrans too had read accounts in Rebel newspapers that three brigades had been sent to Johnston from Charleston and Savannah. He also confirmed that it was possible that McCown's division from Tennessee had gone, yet he still thought it premature to advance. "I would not push you to any rashness," Lincoln wrote Rosecrans, "but I am very anxious that you do your utmost, short of rashness to keep Bragg from getting off to help Johnston against Grant." Rosecrans tersely replied, "I will attend to it."[33]

But he did not. Rosecrans ignored the president's attempt to prod him into offensive action, though by May 19, scout reports and deserter interrogations had confirmed that ten thousand to fifteen thousand Rebels had left Shelbyville for Mississippi. Other intelligence indicated that from three to seven brigades had passed Chattanooga for Jackson. Rosecrans related to Halleck that if he had six thousand cavalry and two thousand mounted infantry, he would advance, but as it was, all of his division and corps commanders opposed a move.[34]

31. Sandburg, *Lincoln*, 2:160–64; *New York Times*, June 4, 1863; "Vallandigham Sent Home," *Chicago Tribune*, May 27, 1863; Athearn, *Soldier in the West*, 96–97.

32. *OR*, 23(2):334; Widney to wife, May 29, 1863, Widney Letters, 34th Illinois File.

33. *OR*, 23(2):337–38, 351; Daily Summaries of News Reports, May 18, 19, 1863, Daily Summaries of the News Reaching the Headquarters of Gen. W. S. Rosecrans, 1863–64, Entry 986, RG 363, NA.

34. Henry Potter to John, May 26, 1863, Henry Potter Letters, 4th Michigan Cavalry File, SRNBP; Doyle et al., *Wilderness of War*, 56; Morse, *Diaries and Letters of Bliss Morse*, 65; Angle, *Three Years in the*

On Sunday, May 26, wild excitement swept the army. A rumor circulated that Vicksburg had fallen. Everywhere cheers went up. A Michigan cavalryman described the glee: "We are getting glorious news from Grant if it be only true. We have the word here today that Vicksburg is ours with 20 or 30,000 prisoners. I do hope it so." A skeptical Marcus Woodcock thought it sounded "too good to be true." He was right. After two failed attempts to breach the fortifications of the city, Grant had settled into a siege. Three days later Rosecrans informed the president of a report that Johnston had crossed the Big Black River to the north and rear of Grant with twenty thousand troops. He was quick to say, however, that probably only Breckinridge's Rebel division had gone from Tennessee, not McCown's as previously reported, and he personally suspected that both divisions were still in his front. Both were in fact already on their way to Mississippi.[35]

Rosecrans reasoned that by doing nothing he was doing something. To the journalist Villard he explained this paradox, which would become the basis of the general's entire strategic argument. He was holding Bragg in place and preventing troops from being siphoned off to Mississippi. Villard was not impressed. The "simple truth," he wrote, was that the sheer blunt force of the Confederate attack at Stones River "still exercised a deterrent influence on his mind," and Rosecrans "had not pluck enough to again undertake anything against him [Bragg]" until he held a numerical preponderance.[36]

The "simple truth," as Villard put it, was that Rosecrans was not preventing troops from reinforcing Johnston in Mississippi, a fact evident to War Department officials. "Much apprehension is felt in the North that the enemy would escape from your front and fall on Grant," Stanton advised the general on May 29. Rumors claimed that Forrest's cavalry had gone south and that Maj. Gen. D. H. Hill and eighteen thousand troops were coming from Virginia. As disturbing reports continued to filter in, Halleck offered a stern warning, "If you cannot hurt the enemy now, he will soon hurt you."[37]

As Washington officials fretted, Rosecrans sat. Reviews, frequently followed by parties, became the order of the day. At one such event, John Beatty admitted that

Army of the Cumberland, 68; *History of the Seventy-Ninth Regiment Indiana Volunteer Infantry in the Civil War of Eighteen Sixty-One in the United States* (Indianapolis: Hollenbeck, 1899), 74; Noe, *Southern Boy in Blue*, 162–63; OR, 23(2):366, 369.

35. Henry Potter to "Dear John," May 26, 1863, Potter Letters, 4th Michigan Cavalry File; Doyle et al., *Wilderness of War*, 56; Morse, *Diaries and Letters of Bliss Morse*, 65; Angle, *Three Years in the Army of the Cumberland*, 68; *History of the Seventy-Ninth Regiment Indiana*, 74; Noe, *Southern Boy in Blue*, 162–63; OR, 23(2):366, 369.

36. Villard, *Memoirs*, 2:68.

37. OR, 23(2):337–38, 371, 373, 383.

the officers imbibed freely: "General Rosecrans' face was as red as a beet; he had, however, been talking with ladies, and being a diffident man, was possibly blushing. . . . Lieutenant Colonel Ducat . . . insisted upon introducing me to the ladies but fortunately I was sober enough to decline the invitation. . . . General Thomas, after sitting at his wine an hour, conversing the while with a lady, arose from the table evidently very much refreshed, and proceeded to make himself exceedingly agreeable. I never knew the old gentleman to be so affable, cordial, and complimentary before."[38]

Rosecrans tinkered with the idea of an offensive, even going so far as to advise Burnside in Kentucky that he should advance the Army of the Ohio to cover his left flank against Maj. Gen. Simon Buckner's forces in East Tennessee, but marching orders never came. "Bragg is holding us by his nose which he has inserted between our teeth for that purpose. We shall keep our teeth closed on his nose by our attitude until we are assured that Vicksburg is within three weeks of its fall," Rosecrans revealed.[39]

Washington officials were not the only ones frustrated with Rosecrans's lethargy. As early as March, General Garfield believed that the army was ready to move. "This is a splendid army," he wrote, "not so much in its numbers as in its character. Nearly every man is a veteran, and has been tested in battle. It is in a fine state of health and discipline and it will make a terrible fight when it next meets the enemy." On April 12 he declared: "This army is in [a] most excellent condition. . . . The men are reduced to solid muscle and they have that esprit de corps which I have never yet known in any other army. The country has a right to expect great things from this army." To his wife Palmer wrote on June 1: "Of course, none of us knows what we will do or where we will go; but my impression is that the rebels are gathering all their spare forces to crush Grant and I am urging Rosecrans to press them here, though most of the officers are opposed to it. We ought to have attacked them a week ago."[40]

On Monday night, June 1, Rosecrans met with each corps and division commander individually by appointment. He carefully explained his plan to turn Bragg's right. Even then Burnside's corps was advancing from Kentucky to protect the army's left flank. On Wednesday, June 3, the troops received three days' rations in their haversacks and four in their knapsacks. The War Department now abruptly interceded. Halleck, frantic about the growing Confederate concentration in Grant's rear, ordered the IX Corps (eighty-seven hundred troops) from Kentucky to Missis-

38. Beatty, *Citizen Soldier*, 275–78.

39. *OR*, 32(2):373; Lamers, *Edge of Glory*, 264.

40. Williams, *Wild Life of the Army*, 251, 256–57, 263; George Palmer, *Conscientious Turncoat*, 109.

sippi. This took the heart out of Burnside's strike force and effectively put an end to Rosecrans's plans for simultaneous advances. Nor was Halleck finished. On June 2 the general in chief warned Rosecrans that a similar fate may await him. "If you can do nothing yourself, a portion of your troops must be sent to Grant's relief."[41]

An alarmed Rosecrans responded within hours. He shared Halleck's "anxiety about General Grant," and for the first time he admitted that Breckinridge's and McCown's divisions and W. H. Jackson's cavalry division had in fact left Tennessee for Mississippi. An advance by the Army of the Cumberland at this time, however, would merely cause Bragg to fall back, destroying bridges and railroads "which we would be obliged to repair," while he would "send much heavier detachments south." In his private conversations with his generals, all concurred in this view. Lincoln did not immediately press the issue, having received good news from Grant that momentarily "abated my anxiety for him."[42]

Facing a showdown with Halleck, Rosecrans determined to buttress his position by canvassing his seventeen generals. In a confidential memo dated June 8, he directed them to answer five questions. Rosecrans did not reveal that before the written summaries were presented, he held an officers' meeting at his headquarters to determine their positions. Not surprisingly, they sustained the army commander's views.[43]

The first question related to whether or not Bragg's army had been reduced by detachments to Johnston. Eleven of fourteen answered "no," and even those who believed that ten thousand or so troops had been detached suspected that the number had been partially, if not totally, offset by additions of conscripts and reinforcements. Revealing how astonishingly out of touch he was, Thomas even insisted that only a single brigade from Breckinridge's division had gone, even though Rosecrans had by now identified, and so reported to Washington, the names of three divisions. The army commander knew the answer to his own question, and he could not possibly have gleaned more information from division commanders who had fragmentary intelligence at best. For weeks now, the press had reported that Bragg had sixty thousand troops. If he accepted that number and deducted ten thousand (Stanley's estimate), he could have estimated Bragg's strength at fifty thousand. It actually would not have been a bad guess; Bragg had forty-seven thousand men.

41. *New York Tribune*, July 1, 1863; *OR*, 23(2):384, 24(3):376. Other reinforcements sent to Grant included Sooy Smith's 7,500-man division from West Tennessee and Maj. Gen. Francis J. Herron's 5,100-man division in Missouri.

42. *OR*, 24(3):376–77. An article datelined Murfreesboro, June 2, 1863, detailed the information of Breckinridge's, McCown's, and Jackson's divisions going to Mississippi. *Cincinnati Enquirer*, June 10, 1863.

43. Gilmore, *Recollections*, 125–36. See also Gilmore's article in *New York Tribune*, June 9, 1863.

The generals concurred that an immediate advance should not be undertaken. Indeed, most thought that the Confederates would not fight along the Duck River (Stanley and Sheridan proved exceptions) and that an advance would be merely a "fruitless stern chase." "There is no apparent advantage to be gained by simply drawing Bragg from our front, extending and weakening our own line," concluded Negley. Crittenden, very outspoken in the conference, remarked, "Beaten at Shelbyville, Bragg will fall back to Tullahoma, and having fought one bloody battle at Shelbyville, you will have to fight another to dislodge him, and the only result will be that you will be cooped up at Tullahoma, cut off from your communications, with only a wretched mountain country road, already devastated by Bragg, to depend upon for your supplies." Some thought that the Confederates might even abandon Middle Tennessee and withdraw to the south bank of the Tennessee River, thereby hastening reinforcements to Johnston.

Rosecrans explored the possibility of flanking Bragg out by taking a more easterly route to Chattanooga. "Then you might get there with less loss of life and only our cavalry cut to pieces, but you would have left behind to guard your communications one-fourth of your men and would appear before the formidable entrenchments of Chattanooga with a much smaller force than Bragg would have," concluded Crittenden. "General, you should not move a mile with less than 100,000 infantry and 6,000 to 10,000 cavalry. Mr. Stanton is either crazy or bent upon the destruction of this army." McCook concurred, adding: "I think him [Crittenden] wrong about Stanton. He is a natural born fool." "You are both wrong about the secretary," answered Rosecrans. "He is neither a knave nor a fool, but he fears the administration will go to pieces without victories, and he is so impatient for them that he doesn't stop to consider how they are to be won."

Thomas concurred. "We need 100,000 men, and a strong cavalry support besides, while we are on the way to Chattanooga. Bragg may, and probably will, receive strong reinforcements. We might get there with from 35,000 to 40,000 men, but I should expect Bragg already there with 75,000. I should want to know that General Meade would give such active employment to General Lee as would hold every one of his men in Virginia." There was consensus that the Army of the Cumberland should do nothing until the fate of Vicksburg had been sealed. Should Grant be defeated in Mississippi, coupled with Hooker's recent rout at Chancellorsville, the Army of the Cumberland would be the only reserve army for either force.[44]

Even after the war, knowing well that part of Johnston's army united with

44. *OR*, 23(2):403–15; Gilmore, "Why Rosecrans Was Removed." For Confederate strength, see *OR*, 23(2):873. Stanley's "10,000" estimate was quite close; the actual number was about 12,000. See *OR*, 20(2):500–501, 24(3):978.

Bragg's Army of Tennessee against him in September 1863, Rosecrans insisted that an advance that spring would have been a strategic mistake. The Union army would have been stuck six weeks to two months on the north bank of the Tennessee River repairing railroads and bridges, giving Bragg ample time to join Johnston. But if, say, Hardee's corps of the Army of Tennessee had gone to Mississippi, Rosecrans could have sent a corps as well, offsetting the numerical gain. Meanwhile, the lion's share of Rosecrans's army could have cut off Bragg's remaining corps, leaving Burnside free to brush aside Buckner's division in East Tennessee and march all the way to Chattanooga.[45]

Putting the issue to a vote proved the coup de grâce to the command morass that paralyzed the Army of the Cumberland that spring. Rosecrans almost gleefully reported the Buell-esque decision to Washington—"not one yes, seventeen no," for an advance. Little could be expected from the likes of Crittenden and McCook, but even Thomas, who had proven himself on the battlefields of Mill Springs and Stones River, remained strategically ambivalent even as he had in East Tennessee in 1861 and McMinnville in 1862.

Halleck chaffed that Rosecrans would neither drive Bragg toward Chattanooga nor, at the very least, prevent him from sending reinforcements to Mississippi. As to Rosecrans's meeting with his generals, he answered in disdain, "Councils of war never fight." Regarding Rosecrans's advice to counsel "caution and patience," the general in chief retorted, "I have done so very often; but after five or six months in inactivity, with your force all the time diminishing, and no hope of any immediate increase, you must not be surprised that their patience is pretty well exhausted." While not ordering an advance under the circumstances, Halleck warned that the army's prolonged inactivity was causing "much complaint and dissatisfaction, not only in Washington, but throughout the whole country." Forever getting in the last word, Rosecrans answered that he would advance only when he expected success.[46]

Meanwhile, correspondent James Gilmore, serving as Rosecrans's personal envoy, arrived in Washington for a conference with Lincoln. This was an attempt by the general to go around Stanton—"words are wasted upon him," he said. Gilmore reported, sometimes in verbatim detail, the contents of the meeting and the concerns of the army command. At the conclusion of the four-hour session, the president canceled Stanton's order.[47]

Lincoln nonetheless remained mystified at the Ohio general's conclusion. In later reviewing the record, the president remarked that when he "saw a dispatch of yours

45. William S. Rosecrans, "The Mistakes of Grant," *North American Review* (Dec. 1885): 581.

46. *OR*, 23(1):8–9.

47. Gilmore, "Why Rosecrans Was Removed."

arguing that the right time for you to attack Bragg was not before but would be after the fall of Vicksburg, it impressed me very strangely. . . . It seemed no other than the proposition that you could better fight *when* Johnston should be at liberty to return and assist him, than you could *before* he could so return to his assistance."[48]

Back at Murfreesboro, Garfield began to increasingly brood over Rosecrans's inaction. "I have been so distressed at the long delay of this army to move . . . that I could hardly write to anyone, more than to utter my disgust," he confided to his wife on June 11. To his friend Chase he complained that the commanding general had given no serious consideration to a move until June. Then, on the eve of the advance, there suddenly "seemed to fall down upon the leading officers of this army, as suddenly as a bolt from the blue, a most determined and decided opinion that there ought to be no immediate or early advance. Officers who . . . were restless and impatient for a forward movement became suddenly conservative and cautious and think masterly inactivity the chiefest of virtues."[49]

Garfield, present at the council but not a participant, compiled the responses. He urged Rosecrans for permission to express his opinion of the proposed move, and, though irritated at his persistence, the commanding general assented. What followed was a refutation as thorough as it was startling. According to Garfield's calculations, based upon an average estimate of regiments and batteries in Bragg's army (from prisoners), the Confederates could not possibly have more than 41,680 men, compared to Rosecrans's 67,717 sabers and bayonets supported by 292 guns. "Whatever be the result of Vicksburg, the determination of its fate will give large re-enforcements to Bragg," he continued. "If Grant is successful, his army will require many weeks to recover from the shock and strain of his late campaign, while Johnston will send back to Bragg a force sufficient to insure the safety of Tennessee. If Grant fails, the same result will follow, so far as Bragg's army is concerned." Besides, he argued, there would be political ramifications for postponing an advance, which was needed for "the success of the Government at the polls, and in the enforcement of the Conscription Act." The chief of staff concluded with a subtle suggestion that the failure to advance might lead to Rosecrans's replacement.[50]

The reaction was swift and decidedly one sided. Rosecrans chafed at "the indeli-

48. Nevins, *Ordeal for the Union*, 3(2):410.

49. Williams, *Wild Life of the Army*, 283, 289–90.

50. Manuscripts Relating to Rosecrans' Removal from Command of the Army of the Cumberland, Folder 17, Box 81, William S. Rosecrans Papers, UCLA. Garfield was wrong on two counts. First, he underestimated Confederate strength by 5,000 men. Second, he misjudged how quickly Grant would rebound after the fall of Vicksburg. Even before the capture of the city, Grant had Sherman's corps advance against Joseph Johnston.

cate tone" of the document and suspected that it was "intended for outsiders." Stanley, still annoyed at Garfield's role in the ill-fated Streight raid, contemptuously wrote, "as he [Garfield] had no command, and had no right to vote, and as he was not consulted I cannot see the propriety of his claim." When the campaign finally commenced, Major General Crittenden came to Garfield and angrily declared: "It is understood, sir, by the general officers of the army, that this movement is your work. I wish you to understand it is a rash and fatal move, for which you will be held responsible."[51]

Chief of Artillery Jim Barnett recalled that despite Garfield's views, which he never hid and with which many lower-grade officers agreed, he always remained cordial to the army commander, calling him "Rosy." Rosecrans appeared to turn on Garfield, however, for the chief of staff came to Barnett one day and said in a grieved tone: "What do you suppose is the matter with Rosy? Do you see how he is attacking me?"[52]

Halleck's patience had come to an end by June 16. His nudging attempts going nowhere, he telegraphed Rosecrans: "Is it your intention to make an immediate movement forward? A definite answer, yes or no, is required." Realizing the ultimatum nature of the dispatch, the general replied: "If immediate means tonight or tomorrow, no. If it means as soon as all things are ready, say five days [by the twenty-first], yes." The target date came and went with no movement. On the twenty-second, with the investment of Vicksburg certain to end in its capture, Rosecrans breathed a sigh of relief. "Thank God, Vicksburg is now within our grasp and the Army of the Cumberland can move," he said. Finally, at 2:10 A.M. on June 24, Rosecrans telegraphed Halleck, "The army begins to move at 3 o'clock this morning."[53]

51. Rosecrans to Francis Darr, Nov. 26, 1879, Rosecrans Papers; Stanley, *Personal Memoirs*, 142; Reid, *Ohio in the War*, 1:756.

52. "Garfield-Rosecrans," *National Tribune*, Mar. 18, 1882.

53. *OR*, 23(1):10; Montgomery Blair and Charles Dana, "Recollections of Circumstances Surrounding the Removal of William Starke Rosecrans from Command of the Army of the Cumberland," Folder 19, Box 81, Rosecrans Papers.

15

Tullahoma
Military Gain, Political Vexation

THE FALL OF VICKSBURG and the not-so-gentle prodding of Washington authorities finally prompted Rosecrans to move in late June 1863. The Army of the Cumberland had mass, but there were weaknesses. The XIV Corps, led by the revered George Thomas, had four divisions under the mixed competence of the popular but limited Lovell Rousseau, the generally reliable James Negley, the novice John Brannan, and the veteran Joseph Reynolds—23,166 men, with twelve batteries totaling 72 guns. The XX Corps, weakly led by the blundering Alexander McCook, comprised the divisions of the hot-tempered Jefferson C. Davis, the at-best-mediocre Richard Johnson, and the hard-fighting Philip Sheridan—14,096 men, with nine batteries totaling 54 guns. The XXI Corps, commanded by the highly affable but generally unstellar Thomas L. Crittenden, had three divisions under the crude, prickly, but seasoned Thomas Wood; the able and self-professed hater of West Pointers John Palmer; and the aging Horatio Van Cleve, recently covered from a battle wound—15,031 men, with nine batteries totaling 58 guns. The overrated and hard-drinking David Stanley led 9,960 horsemen with 9 guns. The infantry brigades had a mean strength of 1,635 soldiers; the regiments, 386. Absalom Baird's division (6,300 strong) of Gordon Granger's Reserve Corps brought total field-army strength to an impressive 68,560 troops "present for duty," with thirty-three batteries totaling 202 guns.[1]

Having accurate information about the enemy position throughout mid-June, Rosecrans knew that Bragg's line north of the Duck River would prove formidable. Polk's corps, believed to be 18,000 troops (actually 15,700), was at Shelbyville, protected by a redan line fronted with abatis, extending from Horse Mountain on the east to the Duck River on the west. The twenty-four-mile turnpike connecting Murfreesboro and Shelbyville ran through the Highland Rim at Guy's Gap. Hardee's

1. OR, 23(1):410–19; Robert G. Caldwell, *James A. Garfield: Party Chieftain* (Hamden, Conn.: Archon, 1965), 83. For Stanley's drinking problem, see *OR*, 31(2):63. Rosecrans canceled all mail coming and going for two weeks. Robert J. Snetsinger, *Kiss Clara for Me: The Story of Joseph Whitney and His Family: Early Days in the Midwest and Soldiering in the American Civil War* (State College, Penn.: Coronation, 1969), 96.

corps, supposedly 13,000 strong (in fact 16,400), was eight miles east at Wartrace along the Nashville and Chattanooga Railroad. The main road to Wartrace cut through Bellbuckle Gap, but the town could also be approached from the east via Liberty Gap. The Confederate cavalry protected the flanks, with Forrest at Columbia–Spring Hill and Wheeler in a wide arc from the Manchester Road to McMinnville. Throughout the spring and summer, Rosecrans had insisted that the Rebels had fifteen thousand horsemen, but realizing that John Hunt Morgan's brigade had departed on a raid, he lowered the estimate to eight thousand. His first guess was better.[2]

Although there were several approaches that Rosecrans could choose, each had its own unique problems. The broad turnpike to Shelbyville offered the most direct route, but a frontal assault against well-manned fieldworks would be playing into Bragg's hands. Rosecrans was not about to recklessly throw his men against fortified positions. Flanking Bragg's left offered some advantages, notably avoiding the narrow gaps of the Highland Rim and utilizing more-level terrain, making maneuver advantageous. The fertile countryside to the west of Shelbyville could furnish at least some food and forage, and the Nashville and Decatur Railroad, if made operational, could serve as an alternate supply line.

The disadvantages of this route were twofold. First, the Duck River, now at flood stage, had few fords and bridges. Second, the army would be marching south into northern Alabama rather than southeast toward Chattanooga. A march on Wartrace would be directly following the Nashville and Chattanooga Railroad, but the low hill country to the west meant that the Federal right flank would have little terrain protection. Indeed, unknown to Rosecrans, Bragg suspected that the Yankees would follow the railroad, and he had plans to swing Polk's corps around from Shelbyville on the Federal flank and rear. The most confounding difficulty, however, would be the gaps—Bellbuckle, Liberty, and Hoover's—in the chain of hills fronting Wartrace, which could neutralize the Northern numerical advantage. There were other approaches farther east toward McMinnville, but they led through the rocky and unfertile region known as the Barrens. Reports indicated only sparse Confederate outposts in that sector.

Rosecrans would play on his opponent's expectations. Baird's division of the Reserve Corps, reinforced by Brannan's division of the XIV Corps, would make a feint on Shelbyville. To magnify the appearance of the column, a train of three hundred wagons accompanied the infantry. R. B. Mitchell's First Cavalry Division (fifty-five

2. *OR*, 23(1):404, 585. For once Rosecrans would actually have a bit of luck regarding the Confederate cavalry. Forrest's 4,000-man division, its leader still recovering from a gunshot wound inflicted by a would-be assassin, failed to come up in time and would not play a significant role in the campaign.

hundred troopers), driving southwest of Murfreesboro toward Middleton and Unionville, would provide a cavalry screen. McCook's XX Corps would also make the appearance of moving on Shelbyville, with Sheridan's division marching down the pike for nine miles, then halting to allow Johnson's and Davis's divisions to veer east six miles to Liberty Gap. These movements (hopefully) would keep Bragg fixated on his left flank.[3]

In fact, Rosecrans planned a wide swing around Bragg's right. Two divisions of Crittenden's XXI Corps would march out the McMinnville Road, but once past Bradyville they would turn south and approach Manchester from the north. Historians have largely misunderstood Crittenden's role; his was not the primary flanking column. Rosecrans hoped that Bragg would think that Crittenden, not Granger, was the feint. Although never definitely stated, Thomas's XIV Corps, which proceeded directly down the Manchester Pike toward Hoover's Gap, the southern terminus of which lay only ten miles from Manchester, was probably the main flanking column. Whether or not the Virginian could force the gap quickly, however, was problematical. What is certain is that both the XIV and XXI Corps had the same destination—Manchester—it mattered not who got there first. From there, they could march twelve miles to get in the Confederate rear at Tullahoma, Bragg's main depot, before Hardee could arrive from Wartrace. A cavalry raid on the vital Duck River bridges southeast of Tullahoma would sever Bragg's line of communications, forcing him into a battle. It was a bold plan, but the key, and as it developed the flaw, was speed. Thomas and/or Crittenden had to gain the Confederate rear before the enemy detected the move and escaped. Even so, Bragg's flank would be turned, and he would have to withdraw, if not fight.[4]

Rosecrans never explained his master plan to his corps commanders. So secretive was the grand design that he gave only one day's instructions at a time, apparently so that his lieutenants could not divulge the big picture. Indeed, McCook apparently believed Shelbyville to be the main thrust. Too, despite the army commander's claim, there may not have been (and probably was not) an officers' meeting the evening of June 23. The evidence seems to suggest that, as with the supposed Stones River conference, Rosecrans lied. None of the corps commanders mentioned such a meeting in their reports, and some made it clear that they were not at army headquarters that night but received only written instructions.[5]

From the outset, Crittenden's column, consisting of Wood's and Palmer's divi-

3. Ibid., 404–5, 411; William S. Rosecrans, "Tullahoma Campaign," *National Tribune*, Mar. 11, 1882.

4. *OR*, 30(1):404–5, 521; Williams, *Lincoln Finds a General*, 5:220.

5. *OR*, 23(1):405; Williams, *Lincoln Finds a General*, 5:217–18; Thomas E. Griess, ed., *American Civil War* (Wayne, N.J.: Avery, 1987), 172.

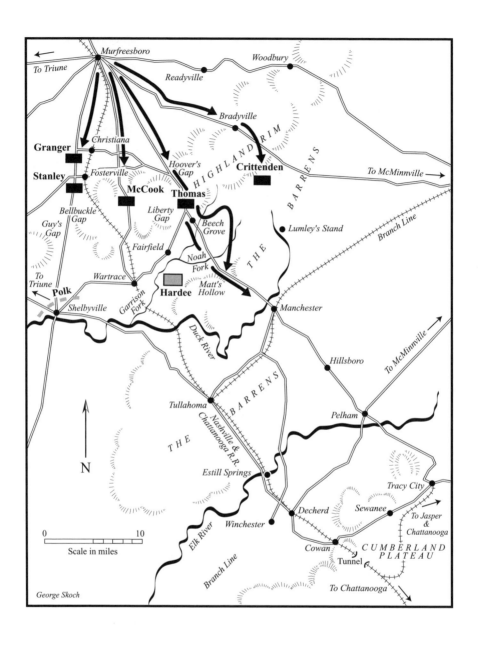

To Triune

Murfreesboro

Woodbury

Readyville

Bradyville

Granger

Christiana

Hoover's
Gap

HIGHLAND RIM

Crittenden

To McMinnville

Stanley

Fosterville

THE BARRENS

McCook

Thomas

Bellbuckle
Gap

Liberty
Gap

Beech
Grove

Lumley's Stand

Branch Line

Guy's
Gap

Fairfield

Noah
Fork

THE

To
Triune

Wartrace

Hardee

Matt's
Hollow

Polk

Shelbyville

Garrison
Fork

Manchester

Duck River

Hillsboro

To McMinnville

THE BARRENS

Tullahoma

Nashville & Chattanooga R.R.

Pelham

N

Estill Springs

Tracy City

Decherd

Sewanee

To Jasper
&
Chattanooga

0   10

Winchester

Elk River

Cowan

CUMBERLAND
PLATEAU

Scale in miles

Tunnel

Branch Line

To Chattanooga

George Skoch

sions and Eli Long's cavalry brigade, encountered problems. Palmer had posted two of his brigades at Cripple Creek, seven miles from Murfreesboro, and a third at Readyville. The division could not march until it had been issued the requisite rations, which had to come from Murfreesboro. Despite having six months to prepare, the commissary department was not ready, and the wagons did not reach Palmer until 7:00 A.M. on June 24. The division, therefore, did not move out until 10:00 A.M., four hours behind schedule. At 8:00 A.M. a "warm, soaking harvest rain" started, followed shortly by heavy rain, "no Presbyterian rain either, but a genuine Baptist downpour," recalled a soldier. When Wood's division, coming from Murfreesboro, arrived at the Bradyville–Cripple Creek intersection, he encountered Palmer, who still had not cleared the crossroads. Not particularly fond of Palmer anyway, Wood now had to sit in the rain and wait, noting with disgust in his report that Palmer had had only four miles to march to this place compared to Wood's ten.[6]

While Crittenden bogged down, Thomas marched along the macadamized Manchester Turnpike, Reynolds's division departing at 4:00 A.M., Rousseau's at 7:00, and Negley's at 11:30. Spearheading the column was Wilder's brigade of mounted infantry, much to the dismay of Stanley, who feared the "tadpole cavalry," as he referred to them, would get captured, giving the Rebels two thousand repeating rifles. The intrepid Wilder instead rushed Hoover's Gap, catching the enemy cavalry (a lone Kentucky regiment) totally unprepared. By 2:00 P.M. he had gained possession of the gap, posted his brigade and Lilly's battery at the southern exit, and waited for Reynolds's division. Later that afternoon gray-clad infantry appeared in brigade strength. The enemy attacked during a driving rain, only to be cut down by the rapid-fire Spencers and Lilly's double-shotted guns. In the middle of the action, Reynolds sent orders for Wilder to break off the engagement, which he refused to do. The troopers tenaciously held with a loss of 60, the Confederates 145. Thomas later rode up with an uncharacteristic look of glee on his face. Shaking Wilder's hand, he declared: "You have saved the lives of a thousand men by your gallant conduct today. I didn't expect to get this gap for three days."[7]

Meanwhile, the XX Corps started at daylight along the Shelbyville Pike, light skirmishing commencing three miles outside of Murfreesboro. At Lee's Knob, ten miles out, the corps deployed to drive off Rebel cavalry supported by artillery. Sheri-

6. *OR,* 23(1):523–24, 528; John Palmer, *Personal Recollections,* 162–63; Victor Hicken, *Illinois in the Civil War* (Urbana: University of Illinois Press, 1966), 188.

7. Baumgartner, *Blue Lightning,* 49–51; *OR,* 23(1):430, 442, 457–59; James A. Connolly, *Three Years in the Army of the Cumberland, the Letters and Diary of Major James A. Connolly* (Bloomington: Indiana University Press, 1959), 90–94; John T. Wilder, "The Battle of Hoover's Gap," in *MOLLUS, Ohio,* 9 vols. (reprint, Wilmington, N.C.: Broadfoot, 1991), 6:169–72; Roswell, *Yankee Artilleryman,* 130.

dan's and Davis's divisions deflected east toward Millersburg, while Johnson's advanced on Liberty Gap. Finding the position lightly defended (two small Arkansas regiments, according to prisoners), Willich's brigade pushed forward and seized the gap with remarkable ease. Beginning at four o'clock, Southern reinforcements attempted unsuccessfully to retake the passage in a sharp engagement that lasted an hour and a half. McCook, who accompanied Johnson, wrote Rosecrans at 5:15: "We are in the act of driving the enemy from the Liberty Gap. It is a strong place. We will have it in an hour and a half." Brannan's division, which had been on the right with Granger's corps, now passed behind the XX Corps to link up with the XIV Corps on the left. It marked the beginning of a subtle army shift east. On the right flank, R. B. Mitchell's First Cavalry Division chased off Confederate cavalry at Middleton and Unionville after brisk skirmishing.[8]

By the end of the day, Rosecrans, with headquarters at the Widow McGill house four miles north of Hoover's Gap, remained uncertain if the Confederates would take the bait. If so, Bragg could mass on his left at Shelbyville or possibly concentrate to pounce on Thomas's flank near Fairfield. The plan on June 25 was for the XX Corps to continue to feign an advance on Wartrace via Liberty Gap. Stanley's cavalry would further attract attention at Fosterville, near the Nashville and Chattanooga Railroad, with Granger supporting him at Christiana. Thomas would march toward Fairfield, driving the Rebels back on Wartrace. While Bragg remained occupied with the Shelbyville-Wartrace front, Crittenden would continue his right-flank swing by reaching Lumley's Stand, where he would turn south toward Manchester. Surgeon J. Dexter Cotton of the 92d Ohio wrote his wife on the night of the twenty-fourth: "We have orders to be ready to march at 4 A.M. The whole army is to move south to meet Bragg. There will be a fight soon or a footrace."[9]

The deluge continued throughout the twenty-fifth. All went as planned on the center and right, though the Confederates continued to give strong resistance to Willich's brigade at Liberty Gap. Late in the afternoon Johnson sent Colonel John Miller's brigade in support. The situation stabilized before dark, but not before Miller had an eye shot out. The primary problem remained Crittenden's corps, which continued to plod through the mud and rain while ascending the rugged Barrens. Despite placing fifty men to a wagon, it took Palmer all day to get his train over Gilley's Hill, meaning that only Eli Long's cavalry made it to Lumley's Stand. The big mistake of the day would be in retaining the XIV Corps at Hoover's Gap. Apparently, Rosecrans did not want to draw Bragg's attention away from the Shel-

8. *OR*, 23(1):405, 450, 462, 532, 535; *Chicago Tribune*, July 2, 1863.

9. *OR*, 23(1):406; James R. Furqueron, "A Fight Soon or a Footrace: The Tullahoma Campaign," *N&S* 1 (Jan. 1998): 83; *Chicago Tribune*, July 2, 1863.

byville sector, but in doing so he squandered the advantage gained by Wilder the previous day. The army commander would later write that Thomas arrived at Manchester thirty-six hours late, having been detained at Hoover's Gap. Twenty-four of those thirty-six hours were of Rosecrans's own doing and not because of Rebel resistance.[10]

The rain continued unremitting on Saturday, June 26. While Granger's single division near Shelbyville and Davis's division of the XX Corps at Liberty Gap maintained a show of force, McCook's other two divisions quietly shifted east toward Hoover's Gap. The XXI Corps continued to go nowhere, but the big break came when the regular brigade (absent Brigadier General Kirk, who was sick) of Rousseau's division and Walker's brigade of Brannan's division of the XIV Corps drove the secessionists back toward Fairfield, leaving the Manchester Road open. Thomas immediately advanced Reynolds's division through the extremely narrow Matt's Hollow and by night had closed to within six miles of Manchester.[11]

Wilder's cavalry dashed into Manchester on Sunday morning, June 27, capturing the forty-man picket post. Reynolds's division arrived at 8:30 A.M., but with the balance of the corps trailing far behind, little could be done but wait. Negley arrived at 8:00 P.M., Brannan at ten o'clock, and Rousseau at midnight. Thomas's wagons had so choked Matt's Hollow that McCook's lead division, Sheridan's, was forced to go around by way of the old Fairfield Road. The van of the XXI Corps came to within four miles of Manchester that night, but the column was strung out for miles. Overnight, Rosecrans received reports that the Rebels had discovered his plan and were withdrawing. Despite the day's frustrating delays, he remained hopeful that if his army could concentrate rapidly at Manchester, he could still get to Tullahoma before Bragg.[12]

On the Shelbyville front, Stanley remained out of sorts with Mitchell's division (Mitchell himself being sick), which had been in the lead but had been making slow progress. Minty, whose twenty-five hundred troopers later linked up, became so irritated at the delays that, according to one of his staff, he became as "a chained lion." A chagrined Stanley ordered Minty to take the van. A subsequent attack by two of his regiments, the 4th U.S. Cavalry and the 1st Middle Tennessee Cavalry, cleared Guy's Gap. Yet Granger refused to rush in with infantry and chose instead to deploy and slowly advance. Convinced that the Confederates, about eighteen

10. *OR*, 23(1):408, 430–31, 463, 464, 484, 521, 524; Walsh, *Medical Histories*, 230–31.

11. *OR*, 23(1):407, 430, 431, 435, 452, 456, 459, 463–64, 466, 471, 480; *Chicago Tribune*, July 1, 2, 1863; *New York Times*, July 1, 1863.

12. *OR*, 23(1):406, 431, 456, 459, 524, 23(2):470, 471, 472, 475; Thomas L. Connelly, *Autumn of Glory: The Army of Tennessee, 1862–1865* (Baton Rouge: Louisiana State University Press, 1971), 128–29; Griess, *American Civil War*, 1.

hundred strong (Will Martin's cavalry division), were evacuating, Minty received permission to press ahead.

In a tactic that would become standard for the western cavalry, Minty advanced five hundred dismounted skirmishers, backed by two thousand men in column of attack, against fortifications a mile north of Shelbyville. The position was quickly outflanked, and the "enemy's line wavered, the men huddled like sheep, broke and went at full speed towards Shelbyville." When the Confederate cavalry made a stand in the town square, two guns of the 18th Ohio Artillery unlimbered in the turnpike. After the Buckeyes discharged their pieces, the 7th Pennsylvania Cavalry made a spectacular charge in column of fours (hereafter, Minty's men became known as the "Saber Brigade") that cleared the town and captured three guns and three hundred men; Wheeler himself barely escaped. At a loss of fifty men during the day, Stanley's troopers had taken seven hundred prisoners, marking the continued ascent of the Union cavalry. Granger proudly noted that the Stars and Stripes waved from many windows in Shelbyville.[13]

Historian Steven Woodworth insists that throughout the twenty-seventh, Rosecrans exposed his own line of communications. Indeed, if Bragg had launched Polk's corps in a counteroffensive through Guy's Gap, he could have brushed aside Granger and Stanley and turned on Liberty Gap, where that morning only two Federal brigades remained. With Hardee in front and Polk in the rear, "the result would undoubtedly have been the destruction or rout of the Federals." Such a scenario would have placed Rosecrans "in a very bad situation." Even though the Army of the Cumberland "would probably have managed to extricate and escape back to Murfreesboro," the result would have been hailed as a Confederate victory. If Bragg captured Murfreesboro while Rosecrans detached a substantial number of troops to continue southeast to take Tullahoma, the exchange of bases "would not have been negative from the Confederate point of view."[14]

While it is difficult to comprehend that the two Yankee brigades in Liberty Gap would have sat passively while Polk's corps got in their rear, Woodworth's point is well taken. With Granger's force pushed aside and the bulk of the Federal army on Bragg's right, the gaps would be open for a Confederate strike east against Federal communications or north against Murfreesboro. At that point, however, the scenario becomes more complicated. Stanley's eight thousand troopers, Granger's

13. OR, 23(1):536–37, 539, 540, 557–60, 565; Vale, *Minty and the Cavalry*, 174–80; Stanley, *Personal Memoirs*, 147–49; George Steahlin, "Stanley's Cavalry: Colonel Minty's Sabre Brigade at Guy's Gap," *National Tribune*, May 27, 1882; Lawrence D. Schiller, "Two Tales of Tennessee: The Ups and Downs of Cavalry Command," *N&S* 4 (Apr. 2001): 82–86.

14. Steven E. Woodworth, "Braxton Bragg and the Tullahoma Campaign," in *The Art of Command in the Civil War* (Lincoln: University of Nebraska Press, 1998), 163–66.

sixty-three hundred infantrymen, Van Cleve's division (with some engineer troops) of perhaps forty-five hundred infantry, and probably the brigade at La Vergne, in all some twenty thousand troops, would have withdrawn inside massive Fort Rosecrans outside Murfreesboro—no easy steal, especially considering that the entire Army of the Cumberland would doubtless be coming up from the rear. Bragg could have bypassed the position, but for what—another failed attempt at Kentucky? Nonetheless, by turning Bragg's right and striking for his line of communications, Rosecrans had made little contingency for the fact that Bragg could do the same to him. In retrospect, the XX Corps was prematurely withdrawn to the Manchester Road.

The anticipated race to Tullahoma on June 28 never occurred. Perhaps it simply had been too much to expect the army to close up and march to Tullahoma before the Confederates arrived in force. Johnson's and Davis's divisions of the XX Corps did not enter Manchester until the early morning hours of the twenty-ninth, having been slowed by wretched roads and blocked by the pontoon train; Colonel Heg noted that the troops trudged "through mud that reached half ways to the mens knees" and did not go into camp until 1:00 A.M. Rosecrans fumed as he wrote the corps commanders about the "criminal neglect" in failing to reduce baggage in compliance with orders. If the army failed, he declared, it would "be mainly due to the fact that our wagons have been loaded down with unauthorized baggage." He ordered all wall tents sent to the rear and company ammunition turned over to the division ordnance trains, thus eliminating seven wagons per regiment. At the same time, he conceded that the incessant downpour had also played a significant role. The roads had become "so soft and spongy that wagons cut into it as [if] it were a swamp." If the general had undertaken his campaign earlier, as administration officials had pleaded, the torrential rains could have been avoided and the plan might have worked. As it was, Wood's division of the XXI Corps did not trail into Manchester until the thirtieth, having taken five days to march twenty-one miles.[15]

While the army closed up, Rosecrans unleashed Wilder's brigade on the Confederate rear in an attempt to disrupt rail communications. On June 28 the two thousand mounted infantry rode southeast from Manchester toward Pelham, where they crossed the still badly swollen Elk River at a bridge. From there they cut back sharply southwest toward Decherd, which they entered at 8:00 P.M. The garrison of eighty was captured, the depot burned, and three hundred yards of track torn up. Fearing detection, the column hurriedly returned to Manchester. The 123d Illinois had been earlier detached to burn the vital railroad bridge at Allisonia. They came upon the Tullahoma Road only to discover it filled "with rebel wagon trains, infantry and

15. *OR*, 23(1):407, 467, 521, 524, 529, 23(2):478–79; Blegen, *Letters of Colonel Hans Christian Heg*, 227.

batteries of artillery, moving southward rapidly. Bragg's army was slipping away and we didn't have the strength to stop it," observed a chagrined Maj. James Connelly. Back at Manchester on the morning of the thirtieth, Stanley rode into town, hearing of the raid for the first time. He angrily rode up to Rosecrans, wagering that the entire brigade would be captured by Forrest. Just as he made the bet, he looked up in amazement to see a mud-covered Wilder riding into town at the head of his jaded troops.[16]

The army continued to inch forward. By the morning of June 29, Rousseau's and Brannan's divisions of the XIV Corps had deployed along Crumpton's Creek, with Reynolds's division advanced to Concord Church and Negley's to Bobo's Crossroads. The XXI Corps began to take up the left at Hall's Chapel, along the Hillsboro-Shelbyville Road, and the XX Corps the right, astride and to the right of the Manchester Railroad. Scouts reported hearing train whistles at Tullahoma, leading some to speculate that Bragg was withdrawing. Rosecrans moved cautiously on the thirtieth, spending the day in dispatching reconnaissance patrols amid a downpour. With most of his strength in the center and left in an attempt to interpose his army between Tullahoma and the Elk River, Rosecrans remained concerned about his weaker right, suspecting that Bragg might attempt to get between his army and the route back to Murfreesboro. Thomas, learning from a civilian that Tullahoma had been evacuated, advanced Steedman's brigade to investigate. The troops entered the town around noon, finding it deserted except for a few stragglers. Rousseau's and Negley's divisions hurried forward in pursuit, skirmishing with the Confederate rear guard at Bethpage Bridge.[17]

The column pursued the Confederates on July 1 on a road that, according to Hazen, "seemed almost lost as we marched through woods and with almost bottomless mud." The pursuit continued toward Cowan on the second and third. Wrote Brigadier General Lytle to his wife on July 3: "As we approached [Cowan] we saw from a height plainly visible to the naked eye, the enemy's line of mounted skirmishers. Our cavalry (new troops) hesitated a little about going in and Sheridan ordered me to throw forward my skirmishers and drive the enemy out. The cavalry was finally brought to the scratch & charged driving the rebels from town." For all intents and purposes, the campaign had come to a close.[18]

16. *OR*, 23(1):460; Angle, *Three Years in the Army of the Cumberland*, 96–97; *New York Times*, July 10, 1863.

17. *OR*, 23(1):407–8, 431, 466–67; Michael R. Bradley, *Tullahoma: The 1863 Campaign for the Control of Middle Tennessee* (Shippensburg, Pa.: Burd Street, 2000), 85; *Chicago Tribune*, July 1, 1863; Keller, "Diary of Albion W. Tourgée," 111; Van Horne, *Army of the Cumberland*, 1:307.

18. Carter, *For Honor, Glory, and Union*, 177–78; Hazen Ledger Book, William B. Hazen Papers, USAMHI, 439. See also Hannaford, *Story of a Regiment*, 436.

The Army of the Cumberland had advanced eighty miles in eleven days, despite the extraordinary rain, sweeping the Confederates from Middle Tennessee, the state's breadbasket. At a cost of less than 600 men, Rosecrans had inflicted nearly 2,000 casualties, including taking 1,634 prisoners. Historians have generally conceded that it was Rosecrans's finest hour, a performance foiled only by the weather.[19]

But not all agree. Historian Keith Poulter, in a blistering, though convincing, revisionist article, has concluded that the campaign failed in both conception and execution. The only chance of bringing Bragg to battle was to destroy the Elk River bridge, the "critical target." This might have been accomplished by taking Turchin's division and Wilder's brigade, some seven thousand horsemen on the Union left, as a composite strike force to capture the bridge and hold it until the infantry came to their relief. Rosecrans never considered such a bold move. Nor was Thomas "the man to execute a rapid movement." Never known for speed, the Virginian initially sent only one division into Matt's Hollow, holding back the others at Fairfield "to guard against a single enemy brigade, defensively deployed." Indeed, a powerful thrust toward Fairfield and a threatened breakthrough toward Wartrace alarmed Bragg, thus causing the Federals to "prematurely spring their own trap." Instead of fighting north of the Duck River, Bragg immediately ordered a retreat to Tullahoma. The Southern general thereby avoided the destruction of his Army of Tennessee, the true object of the campaign, which thus was an utter failure.[20]

Would such a plan have been a "bridge too far"? What if Hardee had blocked the XIV Corps in Matt's Hollow while Polk's corps slipped away from Shelbyville to pounce on Turchin? Or, more likely, what if Thomas had moved the bulk of his corps on to Manchester, only to have Hardee launch an attack east from Wartrace on the right and rear of the XIV Corps? Even if Turchin could not hold the Elk River bridges, what effect would their destruction have had on events? There are so many complexities.

Rain continued on July 4, making for a miserable Independence Day. Alexander McCook nonetheless made the best of it and invited Rosecrans to a magnificent dinner at Winchester. Others at the table included Carlin, Garfield, Heg, and several staff officers. Heg related to his wife, "The Dinner was splendid and we had plenty of music—two brass bands being on hand." Word soon arrived of victories on other fields. "Heard the glorious news of the fall of Vicksburg & the defeat of Lee [Gettysburg] fully confirmed; all feel well over it & strong hope that it will soon close the war," a Hoosier noted in early July. Capt. Phillip Welshimer of the 21st Illinois jubi-

19. *OR*, 23(1):408–9, 425; Furqueron, "A Fight or a Footrace," 89; Bradley, *Tullahoma*, 94; Lamers, *Edge of Glory*, 290.

20. Keith Poulter, "But Then Again . . . ," *N&S* 1 (Jan. 1998): 36–38, 82–83.

lantly wrote on the sixteenth, "They are whipped to death now and I think will soon cry enough." Buckeye Albion Tourgée believed that "a few more successes and Rebellion will be a forgotten thing." James Wier of the 25th Illinois added on the sixteenth: "The news from the Army of the Potomac has created the greatest excitement for we did not expect much of them[,] but I have never doughted but they would thrash the rebels if they had a fair chance. . . . So the victory by Mead over Lee gives more encouragement than the surrender of Vicksburg[,] because we [expected] that would happen, and Lee's army will never be so hard to whip after this." There was much to celebrate, or so Rosecrans thought.[21]

Back in Washington, the authorities failed to be impressed with Rosecrans's campaign, which from their perspective was only the first step toward Chattanooga. Coming on the heels of the fall of Vicksburg (no thanks to Rosecrans) and the repulse of Lee's army in Pennsylvania, it appeared to Stanton as though the Army of the Cumberland had gained real estate but no great victory. "You and your noble army now have the chance to give the finishing blow to the rebellion. Will you neglect the chance?" the secretary wired on July 7. Rosecrans was stunned at both the lack of appreciation and the implied criticism that he had not pulled his weight. The sharpness of his reply could hardly be missed: "Just received your cheering dispatch announcing the fall of Vicksburg and confirming the defeat of Lee. You do not appear to observe the fact that this noble army has driven the rebels from Middle Tennessee. . . . I beg in behalf of this army that the War Department may not overlook so great an event because it is not written in letters of blood."[22]

Halleck then joined in, urging Rosecrans to finish the job he had begun. "You must not wait for Johnston to join Bragg, but must move forward immediately against the latter," he wrote on July 24. "There is great disappointment felt here at the slowness of your advance. Unless you move more rapidly, your whole campaign will prove a failure, and you will have both Bragg and Johnston against you." In a second note that day, this one labeled "Private and Confidential," Halleck warned of serious consequences if an immediate advance was not forthcoming. "The patience of the authorities here has been completely exhausted, and if I had not repeat-

21. Blegen, *Letters of Colonel Hans Christian Heg*, 227; Donald E. Reynolds and Max Hikele, eds., "With the Army of the Cumberland in the Chickamauga Campaign: The Diary of James W. Chapin, Thirty-Ninth Indiana Volunteers," *Georgia Historical Quarterly* 59 (summer 1975): 228; Keller, "Diary of Albion W. Tourgée," 114; Phillip Welshimer to wife, July 16, 1863, Phillip Welshimer Letters, 21st Illinois File, CCNMP. See also Thomas Frazee to sister, July 26, 1863, Thomas Frazee Letters, ILSHS; Keller, "Diary of Albion W. Tourgée," 113; Wier to mother, July 16, 1863, James Wier Letters, 25th Illinois, CCNMP; John Lynch to "Dear Friend," July 13, 1863, in Morris E. Fitch Papers, BHLUM.

22. *OR*, 23(2):518.

edly promised to urge you forward, and begged for delay, you would have been removed from the command. It has been said that you are as inactive as was General Buell, and the pressure for your removal has been almost as strong as it was in his case." The urgency for an East Tennessee offensive was now so great that "neither you nor I can resist it."[23]

Rosecrans went on the attack. A thorough knowledge of the tremendous obstacles that confronted him would, he thought, abate "any disappointment that may be felt at the apparent slowness of our movements," adding pointedly that he wished "to avoid such remarks and letters as I am receiving lately from Washington." He assured the general in chief that "the officers of this army [are] as anxious for success . . . as any member of the Government can be."[24]

Halleck, perhaps disingenuously, portrayed himself as caught in the middle. "I perceive from the tone of your dispatch today [July 25] that you are displeased at my urging you to move forward your army against Bragg. In other words, general, while I am blamed here for not urging you forward more rapidly, you are displeased at my doing so." Halleck assured him that he wrote out of "kindness and friendship," but the time for such familiarity had passed. Rosecrans no longer trusted his superior and perceived himself as fighting a two-front war—the Rebels to the front and the War Department to the rear. The army commander nonetheless managed, perhaps also disingenuously, a sigh of relief "that the injustice which I have experienced from the War Department" did not extend to Halleck. He added, nonetheless, "whenever the Government can replace me by a commander in whom they have more confidence, they ought to do so, and take the responsibility for the result."[25]

Therein lay the problem. If the War Department replaced Rosecrans, who would be his successor? The obvious choice, if they chose to give him a second chance, was Thomas, but there appeared to be no groundswell of enthusiasm for him. Thomas had missed Shiloh and played only a passive role at Perryville. His performance at Stones River had been competent, though not pervasive, and he had gone on record with his opposition to an advance after the battle. Would it do any good to replace Rosecrans with one of a like mind? As for McCook, he had been routed at both Perryville and Stones River. Rumors claimed that he anxiously hoped for a transfer to the Army of the Potomac. Crittenden was not a West Pointer, and Granger, in his Tennessee debut, had lost a brigade. The "short list" within the army was indeed short.

Rosecrans, meanwhile, deployed his army. Protecting the Nashville and Chatta-

23. Ibid., 552, 554–55.
24. Ibid., 555.
25. Ibid., 555–56, 585.

nooga Railroad north of Boiling Fork, from Cowan northwest to Decherd, were three divisions of the XIV Corps. The 1st Michigan Engineers and the Pioneer Brigade rebuilt the 450-foot Elk River trestle and repaired the Nashville and Chattanooga Railroad from Decherd to Stevenson, which had been damaged in many places, especially along the foot of the Cumberland Mountains and near Stevenson along Crow Creek. By July 25 the road was operational to Bridgeport. Sheridan's division guarded the track south of the Elk at the Cowan tunnel, Stevenson, and Bridgeport. Stanley's cavalry corps and a division each from the XIV and XX Corps occupied Winchester along the Fayetteville Railroad. A second line stretched along the rail spur from Tullahoma (Johnson's division), through Manchester (Cruft's brigade), to McMinnville (Van Cleve's division), with Wood's division in advance at Hillsboro. Granger's Reserve Corps held the far rear, at Shelbyville, Murfreesboro, and Nashville.[26]

The army had to be supplied by rail—sixty cars a day to be exact. Forage for forty-five thousand animals required 225 tons, or twenty-eight cars, and rations for seventy thousand men totaled 105 tons, or thirteen cars. Other items included quartermaster stores, 80 tons (ten cars); medical stores, 16 tons (two cars); and contingencies, 56 tons (seven cars). Incredibly, the principal delay was not in the Nashville and Chattanooga but in the spur track to Tracy City, where Rosecrans determined to establish a depot. The spur had been built for coal runs around the steep and curvy mountain grades, and the one-of-a-kind locomotive was nonfunctional. A somewhat similar engine came down from Nashville but was broken en route and had to be repaired. Rosecrans thus stubbornly held up the North's second-most-powerful army while waiting for the repair of a single locomotive.[27]

Almost as maddening as Rosecrans was Burnside, who refused to budge ("he seems tied fast to Cincinnati," wrote Halleck) to cover Rosecrans's left flank from the threat of General Buckner in East Tennessee, estimated to have fifteen thousand infantry and three thousand cavalry (actually only eight thousand men of all arms). When Halleck applied pressure, Burnside could hardly contain his rage. His cavalry had been chasing after Morgan in central Kentucky and southern Indiana and Ohio (the raider and his twenty-five-hundred-man brigade were eventually captured), and he waited for the return of the IX Corps, which had been promised by Grant after the fall of Vicksburg but never sent. He had concentrated a twelve-thousand-man force at Lebanon, half of the troops available in Kentucky, but he could not move until early August.[28]

26. Ibid., 529, 572–73, 30(1):50; Carter, *For Honor, Glory, and Union*, 187; William S. Rosecrans, "Rosecrans on Chattanooga," *National Tribune*, Mar. 25, 1882.

27. *OR*, 23(2):560, 601, 30(1):50.

28. *OR*, 23(2):531, 553, 560, 561, 581, 591 92, 593 94.

The thin veneer of cordiality dropped on August 4. At noon on that day, Rose-crans received another galling telegram from Halleck: "Your forces must move for-ward without further delay. You will daily report the movement of each corps till you cross the Tennessee River." "Old Brains" simply lacked the patience for ex-tended civility. If "friendship" failed to achieve the desired results, he was not averse to pulling rank. Five hours later Rosecrans replied by asking if the order was in-tended to take away his discretion. The curt response left little doubt; the order was peremptory.[29]

As at Tullahoma, Rosecrans promptly called together his corps commanders—Thomas, McCook, Crittenden, Granger, and Stanley—at Winchester Springs on August 6. McCook and Crittenden had just returned to the army, the former having attended the funeral of his father, a major and paymaster, who had been killed in Morgan's attack at Buffington, Kentucky; the latter to tend to his ill father, the sena-tor. Rosecrans showed them his orders and reviewed with them the complexities involved in crossing the Tennessee River with twenty days' rations and ammunition. "They all saw the danger," he recalled. The general proceeded to read them his reply. The army could not move "on narrow and difficult roads, destitute of pasture and forage, and short of water," and the order must either be modified or Rosecrans should "be relieved from the command." "That's right!" Thomas exclaimed. "Stand by that and we will stand by you to the last."[30]

In his reply, the general in chief repeated the desire of the government but left discretion to Rosecrans. "If you wish to promptly carry out the wishes of the Gov-ernment, you will not stop to discuss mere details. In such matters I do not inter-fere." Halleck had blinked. On August 9 he added conciliatory, but firm, words:

> If you suppose the Secretary of War has any personal hostility to you, or would not rejoice at your success as much as with any other general, I think you are mistaken. I do not think he would willingly do you any injustice; but, as I have before written, neither the President nor the Secretary have been satisfied with your long delays. . . . In your official dispatches, as well as your private notes, you seem to be laboring under the impression that the authori-ties here were making war on you. There never was a greater mistake. I know of no one here who has not the kindest and most friendly feelings for you.
>
> Nevertheless many of your dispatches have been exceedingly annoying to the War Department. No doubt such was not your intention, but they cer-

29. Ibid., 592.

30. *Chicago Tribune*, Aug. 1, 1863; Rosecrans to McCook, Nov. 8, 1879, William S. Rosecrans Papers, UCLA; *OR*, 23(2):594.

tainly have been calculated to convey the impression that you were not dis-
posed to carry out the wishes of the Department at least in the manner and
the time desired. It is said that you 'do not draw straight in the traces,' but
are continually kicking out or getting one leg over.[31]

Rosecrans did not mince words when he wrote of the contempt "apparent from
the War Department," which had "produced a feeling that the Secretary is unjust,"
adding, "The impression at the War Department that I do not 'draw straight in
the traces' is very unjust to me." He also forthrightly expressed his long-harbored
suspicions about Halleck. "As for myself, I am quite sure you, even you, wholly
misunderstand me. You take my remonstrances and importunities for complaints.
I know that from your dispatches last autumn." Rosecrans was open to a fault. If he
could not trust Halleck—and clearly he could not—he nonetheless needed a liaison.
The doors of communication were rapidly closing.[32]

Brigadier General Rousseau, accompanied by Col. John Sanderson of the 15th U.S.
Infantry, departed Tullahoma for Washington, D.C., in late July. As Rosecrans's per-
sonal emissaries, they were to persuade the War Department of a plan to organize
ten thousand veterans willing to reenlist as mounted infantry. Although a farfetched
idea, it had the backing of several western governors. Neither of the officers was
prepared, however, for the cold reception they received. "I would rather you would
come to ask the command of the Army of the Cumberland. He shall not have an-
other damned man," snarled Stanton. Rousseau came away convinced of Rose-
crans's certain downfall. Halleck proved even more chafed. "Halleck is violent
against granting our wishes, and Stanton but little better," Sanderson wrote his wife.
Several days later the officers called upon Lincoln, whom they found "decidedly
favorable. The prospects are that he will take the matter in his hands, and act ac-
cordingly giving us a triumph over the bull-headed general-in-chief and the bearish
and unmannerly Secretary of War," the colonel concluded. Recalled by Stanton,
Rousseau was informed that his division would be mounted on mules and repeating
rifles furnished. The elated officers departed for points east, but neither the animals
nor the rifles were forthcoming.[33]

Returning on August 1, Rousseau informed Rosecrans that Lincoln would not

31. *OR*, 23(2):597, 601–2.

32. *OR*, 30(3):110.

33. *OR*, 30(2):559–68; William S. Rosecrans, "The Campaign for Chattanooga," *Century Magazine*
(May 1887): 131; John Sanderson Letter Diary, Aug. 16, 23, 1863, John Sanderson Letters, OHS. The Rose-
crans article, for some unknown reason, did not appear in *B&L*.

consider a direct letter to him as breaking protocol. The Ohio general thus wrote a lengthy missive, expressing his oft-repeated difficulties with an advance. Lincoln patiently replied, assuring him, "I am not casting blame on you," and "I am not watching you with an evil eye." Rosecrans, seemingly blind to the president's expressed support, foolishly answered by refuting certain points mentioned in his letter. "You think Johnston was freed by the fall of Vicksburg. Was not Bragg set free by the evacuation of Middle Tennessee? You think we ought to have prevented Bragg from reinforcing Johnston. Why cannot Grant keep Johnston from reinforcing Bragg?" Lincoln must have been exasperated by the rather maddening suggestion that Grant should now get busy and do what Rosecrans for six months had refused to do. He nonetheless replied in a fatherly tone ("I repeat that my appreciation of you has not abated"), though adding that he did not wish "to engage in an argument with you." Unfortunately, that was the only way the general knew how to communicate.[34]

As vexations mounted in Washington, a voice of dissent now arose from within the army. James Garfield had been increasingly vocal about his dissatisfaction with Rosecrans's tactics, even loosely talking around reporters at army headquarters. His July 27 letter to Chase, though written in frustration and not intrigue, as some would later claim, clearly fanned the flames of the anti-Rosecrans bloc in Washington. While his personal relationship with the army commander was "all that I could desire," the army's chief of staff nonetheless remained adamant that "this delay is against my judgment and my every wish." The men stood idle while "golden moments are passing." If the inaction continued much longer, he concluded, "I shall ask to be relieved and sent somewhere where I can be part of a working army." Clearly not a political neophyte, Garfield was sufficiently sophisticated to realize the possible ramifications. Indeed, he encouraged the War Department to "allow no plea to keep this army back." The letter was passed about; John Hay, the president's secretary, denounced it as "one of the worst specimens of epistolary literature I have ever come across."[35]

Chase, in response, expressed his disappointment in Rosecrans. By halting his army, the general removed "from me the ability to defend him against the censures of the War Department—by which, I mean the Secretary [Stanton] & the Comg. General [Halleck]." He continued: "The Secretary feels most deeply the importance of activity and aggressive movement: and as his temper is not the most patient in the world, he expresses himself very decidedly against dilatoriness: and I saw with

34. Lamers, *Edge of Glory*, 293–94.
35. *Cincinnati Enquirer*, Mar. 16, 1863, Williams, *Wild Life of the Army*, 290; Hay quoted in Cozzens, *This Terrible Sound*, 26.

real pain his admiration of Rosecrans change to painful doubt and then to positive disapproval. As things stand now, I should not be surprised by some action which would be very disagreeable to him and all his friends. The President, who is always disposed to make great allowances and to admit the possibility of good reasons for action which disappoints & pains him, could not I think oppose what the Secretary & General agree on as necessary to be done."[36]

36. Niven, *Chase Papers,* 4:103.

PART 5

THE DECLINE OF ROSECRANS

16

An Aura of Vanity
The Road to Chattanooga

FOR SIX WEEKS the Army of the Cumberland remained in and around Tullahoma as the Federals repaired bridges, stockpiled supplies, and established forward depots. Rosecrans maintained frequent personal inspections, one of the hallmarks of his popularity with the troops. "He had a kind word with the boys in every regiment and shook hands with every commander. He is a very pleasant man," observed D. B. Griffin of the 2d Minnesota. Rosecrans's attempt to accumulate twenty days' rations proved unsuccessful. The rolling stock of the Nashville and Chattanooga Railroad was limited, and its track width did not permit the use of Northern engines. Authorities went in search of five locomotives of five-foot gauge and contracted for a hundred cars to be built, but this would take time. On August 14, the day before the army moved forward, the XX and XXI Corps had accumulated about eighteen days' rations and five or six of forage, but the XIV had only eight days' rations and five of forage. It had to do.[1]

The medical department organized a unique hospital train, with four passenger cars (two fitted with bunks) and a boxcar for cooking. In mid-September two specially built hospital cars also arrived, giving the train a total capacity of 120 patients. The hospital at Murfreesboro was broken up and all eighteen hundred beds sent to Stevenson, with a smaller hospital for the short-term ill at Bridgeport.[2]

While at Winchester, the Federals captured a young Confederate lieutenant in civilian clothes. Rosecrans became personally involved and offered the man a deal to escape certain hanging. He was to return to Bragg and tell him that the Army of the Cumberland would enter East Tennessee above Chattanooga. Rosecrans even went about giving phony orders so that the lieutenant could overhear and be convinced. The army commander placed great store in the scheme, but there is no indication that it in any way influenced Bragg, if indeed the officer ever got back to him.[3]

1. *OR,* 30(1):50, 30(3):28–29, 84, 171; Griffin to wife, Aug. 13, 1863, in Albertson, *Letters Home to Minnesota,* letter 98; Rosecrans, "Campaign for Chattanooga," 130; Rosecrans, "Mistakes of Grant," 583.

2. "Extracts from a Memorandum of Events in the Campaigns of the Army of the Cumberland about Chattanooga," Surgeon General's Office, *Medical and Surgical History,* 1(2):287, 289.

3. Rosecrans, "Rosecrans on Chattanooga," *National Tribune,* Mar. 25, 1882.

Several leadership changes occurred in the army. Rousseau, on a mission in Washington to mount his division, turned over command to newly promoted Brigadier General Starkweather, recently returned from furlough in Wisconsin. "This gentleman has been mourning over the ingratitude of Republics ever since the battle of Perryville; but, henceforth, he will, doubtless, feel better," noted John Beatty. Starkweather nonetheless remained physically broken, having been stricken with rheumatism, neuralgia, and diarrhea, from which he nearly died. Privately, he wished to run as a War Democrat in the Wisconsin's governor's race, but noted a member of the 1st Wisconsin, his past would be brought up, "and we all know what that is [drinking?]."[4]

Starkweather soon returned to his brigade, with the division going to Brigadier General Baird, formerly of Granger's corps. Brigadier General Steedman succeeded Baird, thus leaving a vacancy at Second Brigade in Brannan's division. The senior colonel, twenty-six-year-old Yale-educated John Croxton, described by George Thomas as "the best soldier Kentucky has furnished to the war," received the command. Turchin, removed from command of his cavalry division and "considerably cast down in spirit," accepted a brigade in Reynolds's division, swapping commands with Brigadier General Crook. James G. Spears, the brutal, hotheaded brigadier commanding the Third (East Tennessee) Brigade, Third Division, Granger's corps, returned to his command following his leave of absence, despite the petition of his officers to the contrary. To Beatty's dismay the inept McCook retained command of XX Corps—"he looks, if possible, more like a blockhead than ever, and it is astonishing to me that he should be permitted to retain command of a corps for a single hour."[5]

All was not business that August. One pleasant day McCook and his division commanders, along with their staffs, "sat out on the lawn on camp stools smoking and having a good time." Although initially subdued, the generals "soon broke out into jokes and funny stories." According to a staff officer, they "acted more like a lot of boys, and when you stop to think that the oldest of them had not yet reached forty, they weren't *very old* men." Soon the impulsive Sheridan jumped to his feet and shouted to Davis, " 'Jef,' haven't you got anything to drink around this camp. If you have trot it out. Baird here is so dry that he can't spit." The comment brought smiles, for Baird was the biggest teetotaler of the lot.[6]

Having achieved the two necessities needed to advance—rebuilding the Elk River

4. Beatty, *Citizen Soldier*, 270; Welsh, *Medical Histories*, 319; William S. Mitchell to father, June 13, 17, 1863, William S. Mitchell Letters, 1st Wisconsin File, CCNMP.

5. Beatty, *Citizen Soldier*, 295, 303–4, 306–7, 308; *OR*, 30(3):4, 266, 330–31; "General J. T. Croxton," *Society of the Army of the Cumberland, Eighth Reunion*, 1874 (Cincinnati: Robert Clarke, 1875), 172–74; Warner, *Generals in Blue*, 466–67; Schmitt, *General George Crook*, 103; Cozzens, *This Terrible Sound*, 125.

6. Quoted in Hughes and Whitney, *Jefferson Davis in Blue*, 162.

bridge and assuring that Joseph Johnston was pinned down in Mississippi—and though still woefully and inexplicably short of pontoons and the wagons to carry them, in mid-August Rosecrans finally resumed the offensive, determined to finish what Buell had failed to accomplish the previous summer—the capture of Chattanooga. The strategic value of the city of five thousand residents was obvious and undisputed. The railroads that had given the town its life provided vital links northeast to Virginia (Virginia and Tennessee Railroad), south to Atlanta (Western and Atlantic), and west to northern Alabama, where at Stevenson, the track both veered northwest to Nashville (Nashville and Chattanooga) and continued due west (Memphis and Charleston) to Corinth. In Union hands Chattanooga could become a massive staging center for waging war on the Deep South, the heart of the Confederacy's food and munitions production. The possession of Nashville, Chattanooga, and ultimately Atlanta meant that the western Confederacy would be fractured, even as the capture of Vicksburg had isolated the trans-Mississippi. "With the possession of Chattanooga, the whole complection of the war . . . undergoes a fundamental change," commented the *New York Times*.[7]

The formidable and complex East Tennessee terrain offered basically only two approaches to Chattanooga. First, the army could advance along a wide front from McMinnville, Tullahoma, and Decherd across the steep Cumberland Plateau; debouch into the Sequatchie Valley; ascend Walden's Ridge; and then descend into the Tennessee River gorge, where the river could be crossed at or above Chattanooga at one of twenty-five crossing sites. Once on the east bank, the ground there being comparatively level, the city could be approached from the northeast. The best advantage of this course was that Burnside's XXIII Corps (alias the Army of the Ohio), moving simultaneously from Kentucky toward Knoxville, would be in close support. Yet the logistics of traversing fifty miles of broken mountain terrain with no railroad, crossing dual ranges, and supplying a sixty-two-thousand-man army in such broken and drab countryside meant that, even if Rosecrans successfully crossed the Tennessee River and captured the city, he could not long sustain his army, especially if Bragg prepared for siege operations.

In a second scenario, the army might cross the Tennessee River southwest of Chattanooga beyond the Cumberland Range, turning Bragg's left and threatening his communications with Atlanta. The closest crossing sites would be at the mouth of Battle Creek, where a large Federal fort had been built the previous year, and

7. *OR*, 23(2):555; Steven E. Woodworth, *Six Armies in Tennessee: The Chickamauga and Chattanooga Campaigns* (Lincoln: University of Nebraska Press, 1998), 12–13; McDonough, *War in Kentucky*, 38; *New York Times*, Aug. 26, 1863. The Northern press reported in late July that Johnston had been driven out of Jackson, Mississippi; that he had lost 10,000 troops by desertion since the fall of Vicksburg; and that the balance of his force was "utterly demoralized." *New York Tribune*, July 23, 24, Aug. 1, 1863.

Bridgeport. To reach the latter the army would follow the Nashville and Chattanooga Railroad over the mountain plateau and down Big Crow Creek to Stevenson, Alabama, where the track linked with the Memphis and Charleston. From there it was eleven miles to Bridgeport, where a crossing could be attempted, though the river was wider by one-third than above Chattanooga. Between Bridgeport and Bellefonte, thirty-two miles southwest, six ferries and two fords could be used. East of the river were dual mountain ranges—the Raccoon Mountain–Sand Mountain Range, six hundred to seven hundred feet high, and the towering Lookout Mountain Range, which extended from Chattanooga through northwest Georgia and into Alabama, its heavily timbered escarpment varying from one to seven miles in width. The range culminated in the north with a two-thousand-foot-high panoramic view of Chattanooga and the valley below.[8]

The last option held obvious appeal to Rosecrans since it mirrored his recent and highly successful Tullahoma campaign. By hard marches he hoped to maneuver Bragg out of Chattanooga by feinting directly toward the city along a twenty-mile front with the XXI Corps (14,000 troops), threatening a crossing at or near Blythe's Ferry, forty-five miles above the city. Meanwhile, using the mountains as a shield, the XIV and XX Corps (34,500 strong) would make a wide, bold sweep southwest of Chattanooga. Thomas would send two of his divisions (Reynolds's and Brannan's) down Battle Creek Valley to the mouth of Battle Creek and the other two (Negley's and Baird's), followed by Davis's division of the XX Corps, along the railroad to Stevenson, where Sheridan's division had already taken position with a brigade advanced to Bridgeport. Baird's division would then march to Bridgeport, twenty-eight miles below Chattanooga, where a crossing would be made. Davis's and Johnson's divisions of the XX Corps and Negley's of the XIV Corps would march by way of Bellefonte, crossing at Caperton's Ferry, fifteen miles below Bridgeport. Stanley's cavalry patrolled throughout northern Alabama as far west as Decatur.[9]

By August 15 Rosecrans had established his headquarters in the deserted four-story Female Institute at Anderson, Tennessee. He lived with his wife and stepdaughters in a local residence. Lucius F. Brown, of the 2d Battalion, 18th U.S. Infan-

---

8. *OR*, 30(1):48–49; Michael H. Fitch, *The Chattanooga Campaign* (Madison: Wisconsin Historical Commission, 1911), 52–55; Connelly, *Autumn of Glory*, 146; Rosecrans, "Campaign for Chattanooga," 130; "Character and Condition of the Fords & Ferries on the Tennessee River, Intervening Knoxville and Chattanooga," [unidentified volume relating to roads in Tennessee, Georgia, and North Alabama,] Box 13, George Thomas Papers, Misc. Papers, 1861–62, Generals' Papers, RG 94, NA, 55–66. See also *Atlas to Accompany the Official Records of the Union and Confederate Armies* (Washington, D.C.: Government Printing Office, 1891–95), plate CXLIX.

9. *OR*, 30(1):50–51, 30(3):36–38, 276; Rosecrans, "Mistakes of Grant," 583–84.

try, was convinced of one thing: "I don't think the Army of the Cumberland is going to fight[,] not if we go to the ocean. Bragg has seen quite enough of this army."[10]

On a cloudy August 16 the army snaked forward over a fifty-mile front, the corps in their accustomed places—the XXI on the left, XIV in the center, and XX on the right, with Stanley's cavalry (three brigades) and Minty's and Wilder's brigades on the northern and southern flanks respectively. Wrote 44th Indiana soldier George Squier from McMinnville: "The Army of the Cumberland is again in motion, nor will it stop until the rebel stronghold, Chattanooga, is thronged with 'blue coats.' There may be many days hard fighting, though it is the general opinion that Brag will follow up his old System of fighting, which you know is running."[11]

Minty's brigade, twelve hundred sabers, galloped out of McMinnville, moving northeast to Sparta. As they approached the town on the afternoon of the seventeenth, the 8th Tennessee Cavalry, one of Forrest's regiments, lay in ambush. In the subsequent engagement and running skirmish, Minty sustained fifteen wounded and one dead, the last in a drowning accident while crossing a creek. Leaving a battalion at Sparta, the brigade veered southeast to Pikeville, crossing Walden's Ridge and proceeding to Washington on the Tennessee River, where, supported by Hazen's brigade, it protected the army's left flank. Forrest's division, estimated at four thousand troopers, was known to be thirty miles up the road at Kingston.[12]

Wilder's brigade, strengthened by a fifth regiment, left Decherd, camping the night of August 17 on the grounds of the University of the South at Sewanee. They arrived at Tracy City, three houses and a depot, the next morning. Although slowed by their battery, the brigade descended into the Sequatchie Valley at Therman's on the twentieth, surprising and capturing a fourteen-man picket post. The horsemen rode to Dunlap, arriving there only an hour before the van of Palmer's division. With Wagner's brigade in support, the mounted infantrymen reached the summit of Walden's Ridge at 1:00 P.M., descending at Poe's Tavern, fifteen miles north of Chattanooga, where another picket post surrendered.[13]

On the morning of August 21, Wilder split his forces, two regiments and a section of artillery going southeast to Harrison's Landing. The balance of the brigade headed due south for Stringer's Ridge, which it crested shortly after 9:00 A.M. In the valley below, in full panoramic view, lay the Tennessee River and Chattanooga. Captain Lilly's four 3-inch rifles opened fire at a range of two thousand yards at 10:30, targeting the two steamers at the dock, both of which were destroyed. "They were

10. Lucius F. Brown to sister, Aug. 15, 1863, Lucius F. Brown Letters, KNBP.

11. Doyle et al., *Wilderness of War*, 67.

12. *OR*, 30(1):51, 920, 921, 30(3):48, 70, 79, 90, 121; Vale, *Minty and the Cavalry*, 206–7, 210–15; Hazen, *Narrative*, 103.

13. *OR*, 30(1):445, 30(3):117; Baumgartner, *Blue Lighting*, 60–71; Rowell, *Yankee Artillerymen*, 93.

completely thunderstruck at our sudden appearance and audacity, and so great was their surprise that if it were not for the river over which there was no bridge, we could have ridden clear through the city," gloated Major Connolly. The gunners took great delight in seeing the consternation in the city as panicked citizens fled and Rebel gunners feebly returned fire.[14]

For the next several days, the XXI Corps made camp throughout the length of the Sequatchie Valley, with Van Cleve's division at Piketon, Wood's at Therman's, and Palmer's, along with Crittenden's headquarters, at Dunlap, with supplies coming via the railheads at McMinnville and Tracy City. Wilder's brigade feinted at several crossings up and down the river. At night large and numerous fires created the appearance of a phantom army—"we have made them believe our force is at least 10,000 strong," Wilder boasted. Constant hammering convinced enemy pickets that boats were being constructed for a crossing.[15]

Coupled with Crittenden's activity was that of Burnside's XXIII Corps, which finally began its East Tennessee advance on August 21. The column of three thousand cavalry and fifteen thousand infantry marched along a wide front from Columbia to Somerset, skirting Cumberland Gap by using four mountain passes to the west. Buckner's eight thousand troops withdrew along the line of the East Tennessee and Georgia Railroad. On September 1 a brigade of Federal cavalry dashed into Knoxville unopposed. Burnside entered on the third to cheering throngs of loyalist East Tennesseans. The two-thousand-man Rebel garrison at Cumberland Gap surrendered a week later.[16]

Rosecrans's charade on his left has been touted by historians as a masterpiece of deception. The case has been overstated. Bragg clearly feared a juncture of Rosecrans and Burnside, which would have been overwhelming and virtually unstoppable, and he deployed his army heavily to the northeast of Chattanooga. He knew, however, that the force in the Sequatchie Valley was not Rosecrans's entire army, having been aware since late August that at least one Union corps had arrived at Bridgeport. If he desired to know the general locations of all four Union corps, all he had to do was read the September 3 edition of the *Appeal*, which conveniently lifted the information from Northern newspapers. Crittenden's corps would attempt a crossing thirty miles above Chattanooga, the article claimed, and swing into

14. Baumgartner, *Blue Lighting*, 73–75; OR, 30(1):445, 30(3):90, 103, 123; Angle, *Three Years in the Army of the Cumberland*, 116.

15. OR, 30(1):51, 445–46, 601, 625–26, 30(3):78, 119, 121, 164; John Palmer, *Personal Recollections*, 168; Noe, *Southern Boy in Blue*, 181; Rosecrans, "Chattanooga Campaign," 131.

16. OR, 23(1):593–94, 30(3):94–95, 107; *Cincinnati Enquirer*, Sept. 4, 5, 1863; *Cincinnati Commercial*, Sept. 16, 1863; Mary U. Rothrock, ed., *The French Broad-Holston Country: A History of Knox County, Tennessee* (Knoxville: East Tennessee Historical Society, 1946), 138; *New York Times*, Sept. 11, 1863.

the rear of the city. If he did not need reinforcements, Thomas's and McCook's corps in northern Alabama would move rapidly on Rome, Georgia. Bragg, outnumbered by half and with his cavalry spread over 150 miles, believed that the more immediate threat lay to the north. He determined to deal with Crittenden first and then, presumably, respond to the threat to the southwest. Concluded historian Steven Woodworth: "Bragg had almost no choice but to take Crittenden's fake seriously. A Federal move upstream on the Tennessee River was simply too dangerous to ignore." Indeed, if the downriver crossing stalled, so Rosecrans informed Burnside, the feint might become the actual thrust.[17]

The XIV and XX Corps, meanwhile, took up their respective positions below Chattanooga, with army headquarters established at Stevenson, a town of a few miserable buildings and the three-story Alabama House, on August 18. Rosecrans remained in an agitated mood, openly denouncing the antiwar movement as "the peace party," "white-rag faction," and "not-another-man-or-dollar conspiracy." Colonel Carlin arrived at army headquarters and found Rosecrans "discouraged or oppressed with anxiety. Garfield looked angry. I was not pleased with the appearance of men and things at headquarters of the Army of the Cumberland."[18]

The men expressed more optimism. Capt. Horace Porter, army chief of ordnance, remained convinced that once the army had crossed the Tennessee River, "half of Bragg's army will desert." A trooper in the First Cavalry Division shared the exuberance, noting that not since he had been recruited had he "witnessed so much enthusiasm and confidence as now animates the Army of the Cumberland." Intelligence reports from civilians and Confederate deserters seemed to justify the optimism. Having sent three divisions to Mississippi, Bragg's army, according to sources, had dwindled to thirty thousand men, perhaps as few as twenty thousand, with Hardee's entire corps having gone to Johnston. Hardee's corps had in fact gone nowhere (only its corps commander), and Bragg actually had thirty-three thousand infantry and artillery and eleven thousand cavalry, a weakened, though potentially lethal, force, especially if the Southerners correctly divined the exact crossing points.[19]

Troubling signs were on the horizon, though not initially self-evident. Grant,

17. Judith Hallock, *Braxton Bragg and Confederate Defeat* (Tuscaloosa: University of Alabama Press, 1991), 40, 44–45, 49; *OR*, 30(1):560–61, 30(3):126–27, 202, 30(4):600; *Memphis Appeal*, Aug. 22, Sept. 3, 1863; Andrews, *North Reports the Civil War*, 446–47; Steven Woodworth, *Chickamauga: A Battlefield Guide* (Lincoln: University of Nebraska Press, 1999), 4; Cozzens, *This Terrible Sound*, 49.

18. *New York Tribune*, Sept. 18, 1863; Horace Porter quoted in Cozzens, *This Terrible Sound*, 39; Girardi and Hughes, *Memoirs of Brigadier General William Passmore Carlin*, 94.

19. Rosecrans quoted in Cozzens, *This Terrible Sound*, 39; *New York Times*, Sept. 9, 1863; *OR*, 30(3):48–49, 136, 162–63, 187, 30(4):518–19.

languishing in pain from a riding accident that occurred in New Orleans, did not appear to be keeping Johnston's five divisions pinned down in Mississippi. Indeed, when Rosecrans questioned Grant's seeming inactivity in early August, Halleck tersely replied, "Grant's movements at present have no connection with yours." In a decision that would have far-reaching implications for the Army of the Cumberland, Washington authorities dispersed Grant's army to other theaters of operation—ten thousand troops to Texas, five thousand to Missouri, the IX Corps returned to Kentucky, and a brigade to Natchez, Mississippi. Two Union corps, commanded by Sherman in Grant's absence, remained huddled around the Vicksburg environs. Already reports, in truth little more than rumors, claimed that twenty thousand of Johnston's men would soon be on the way to Chattanooga. One statement, from a Rebel deserter, stated that ten thousand had already arrived.[20]

Bridgeport, Alabama, proved to be a disappointment. Brigadier General Lytle wrote of the miserably hot days and heavy fog and mist at night, which saturated all clothing. The troops found no town, not even a station house, only the twenty-seven-hundred-foot-long Memphis and Charleston Railroad trestle, the Howe Turn Bridge, over the Tennessee River. Unfortunately, six of the nine spans had long since been destroyed, with only the stone supports remaining. A small portion of the bridge remained intact on the south (Confederate) side, but on the night of August 14, much to Sheridan's embarrassment, the Rebels set it on fire.[21]

The trestle, at least for the time being, was of secondary importance. It would require two months for two civilian building companies, Fletcher and Company of Cleveland and Boomer and Company of Chicago, to complete the new spans. For now, Sheridan had his Third Brigade, along with Colonel Innes's Michigan engineers, construct a temporary wooden bridge to Long Island in the middle of the river, from where a pontoon bridge would be built to the south bank. During a two-day period, the troops cut fifteen hundred logs and stripped local homes of flooring for use as planks. Despite an August 25 statement from a Rebel deserter that two enemy brigades lay in wait on the opposite bank, scouting reports indicated little activity. Two companies of infantry on Long Island, plus artillery on the north bank, preventing Rebel sniping.[22]

The crossing at Caperton's, scheduled for dawn of August 29, proved largely un-

20. *OR*, 30(3):102, 136, 147, 162; Grant, *Memoirs*, 387–88.

21. *OR*, 30(3):32–33; Aldrich, *Quest for a Star*, 57; Carter, *For Honor, Glory, and Union*, 191; Rosecrans, "Mistakes of Grant," 581.

22. Sheridan, *Memoirs*, 1:272–73; Luther Bradley to mother, Sept. 3, 1863, Luther Bradley File, CCNMP; *OR*, 30(1):51–52, 203, 30(3):279, ser. 3, 5:934; Rosecrans, "Mistakes of Grant," 586; *New York Times*, Aug. 28, 1863.

eventful. The advance of Colonel Heg's brigade, Davis's division, quietly slipped into pontoon boats and seized the south bank of the Tennessee River without a shot being fired. "We went over expecting every minute to be shot at, but all went well," Heg explained to his wife. Work immediately began on a pontoon bridge. By afternoon Heg's entire brigade had crossed and ascended Sand Mountain to the fork of the Trenton and Winston Roads, five miles from the river, where Rosecrans and McCook visited them. The balance of the division arrived the next day, with Johnson's and Negley's divisions crossing in succeeding days. John Beatty, among the last to cross, saw Rosecrans on the twenty-ninth, noting that he "checked up, shook hands, and said, 'How d'ye do?' Garfield gave us a grip which suggested 'vote right, vote early.'" McCook's cavalry took both the bridge and a downriver ford.[23]

The upriver crossing proved slightly more unconventional, but no less uneventful. The men of Reynolds's division had earlier captured Shellmound, finding seven flatboats capable of transporting four hundred men per hour. Brannan's division at Battle Creek was ferried across by means of rafts built of cedar logs from local houses. Mules swam to the other side with a guide rope for the ferry that stretched five hundred yards across the river. By the late afternoon of September 1, both Reynolds's and Brannan's divisions had essentially crossed. Crittenden's corps soon moved down the valley and began ferrying at Battle Creek on the second.[24]

Engineers completed the pontoon bridge at Bridgeport on August 29. The canvas-covered pontoons (a modification made by Rosecrans) soon gave way, however, sending five wagons splashing into the river, drowning two men and five mules. Other breaks occurred, and the repair work was not completed until September 2. That night Rosecrans held a consultation with Thomas, McCook, and Crittenden at Bridgeport.[25]

With his army scattered forty miles on either side of Chattanooga and on a divergent line with Burnside, Rosecrans had to move quickly. Bragg's and Buckner's forces, now concentrated between Chattanooga and the Hiwassee River, were in position to strike the XXIII Corps. Crittenden expressed no undue alarm, however, writing on September 2, "If Bragg should make a dash at Burnside and Burnside retire slowly, declining to fight, I think we can destroy his (Bragg's) army." In addi-

23. Blegen, *Letters of Colonel Hans Christian Heg*, 238–39, 247–48; *OR*, 30(1):52, 496–97, 52(3):219; Girardi and Hughes, *Memoirs of Brigadier General William Passmore Carlin*, 94; Beatty, *Citizen Soldier*, 323. By September 20 the Caperton's Ferry pontoon bridge had been removed to Battle Creek. DeWayne Kellogg to parents, Sept. 20, 1863, 34th Illinois File, CCNMP.

24. *OR*, 52(3):214, 215–16, 232, 233, 236, 251, 279, 284, 601–2; John Palmer, *Personal Recollections*, 169; Noe, *Southern Boy in Blue*, 184–85; Woodworth, *Six Armies in Tennessee*, 58.

25. *OR*, 30(1):50, 30(3):303, 304, 305; Genco, *To the Sound of Musketry*, 113; Shiman, "Engineering and Command," 100–101.

tion, all reports continued to indicate that Bragg would evacuate Chattanooga and withdraw to Atlanta. "Deserters are coming in constantly, and confirm that Polk's and Buckner's armies [corps] will be dissolved by desertion," noted a *New York Times* correspondent. Rosecrans, giddy with optimism, immediately ordered up Granger's Reserve Corps from the rear to Bridgeport and Stevenson.[26]

Once across the Tennessee River and the broad plateau of Sand Mountain, the Federals faced an even more daunting task—Lookout Mountain. It could not be crossed with wagons and artillery save at the gaps, only four of which existed: the Tennessee River gorge to the north, through which ran the Memphis and Charleston Railroad; Cooper's and Steven's Gaps, sixteen and eighteen miles southwest of Chattanooga respectively; and Winston's Gap in Alabama, forty-two miles from Chattanooga.[27]

During the early morning hours of September 3, Garfield drafted Rosecrans's plan. Davis's and Johnson's divisions of McCook's Corps would strike out through Winston's Gap to Valley Head, Alabama, preceded by Stanley's cavalry (three brigades) moving southwest to Rawlingsville, Alabama, with an advance pushed toward Alpine, Georgia. Sheridan's division, crossing at Bridgeport, would march by way of Trenton down Lookout Valley (sometimes called Will's Valley) to reunite with the parent corps at Winston's Gap. Thomas's XIV corps would concentrate at Trenton, a town of "a couple of churches, stores and taverns, and a number of old dilapidated buildings," sending an advance to secure Stevens's Gap. The XXI Corps, minus Minty's and Wilder's brigades and their infantry supports, in all some seven thousand troops left to maintain the ruse against Chattanooga, was to essentially follow the Memphis and Charleston Railroad through the Tennessee River gorge that separated Sand Mountain from Raccoon Mountain to Wauhatchie, taking post on the Murphy's Hollow Road and penetrating as close to Chattanooga as practicable.[28]

The shaky component of the Federal strategy remained Rosecrans's advance over a broad thirty-two-mile front, with his corps not within supporting distance of one another. He may not have realized exactly how risky this was, however, since he thought that Winston's Gap was only ten miles from the XIV Corps at Trenton—it was actually twenty-three miles. The commander gauged his strategy to avoid bottlenecks at the gaps and thereby to trap Bragg's army between Chattanooga and

26. *OR*, 30(3):187, 202, 234, 242, 305, 351, 362, 381; *New York Times*, Sept. 5, 1863.

27. Woodworth, *Six Armies in Tennessee*, 59.

28. *OR*, 52(3):322–23, 331, 357; *New York Tribune*, Sept. 18, 1863; Bridges to wife, Sept. 11, 1863, in Albertson, *Letters Home to Minnesota*, letter 104; Woodworth, *Six Armies in Tennessee*, 59–60. Rosecrans never designated a precise "blocking point" but merely stated "between him [Bragg] and Atlanta." Rosecrans, "Campaign for Chattanooga," 132.

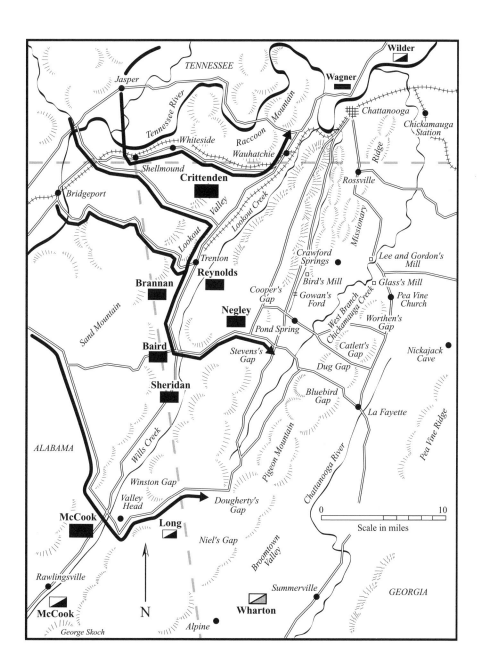

Wilder

Wagner

Jasper

TENNESSEE

Chattanooga

Chickamauga
Station

Whiteside

Raccoon Mountain

Wauhatchie

Tennessee River

Shellmound

Crittenden

Rossville

Bridgeport

Lookout Creek

Lookout Valley

Missionary Ridge

*Crawford
Springs*

Lee and Gordon's
Mill

Trenton

Bird's Mill

Glass's Mill

Reynolds

*Cooper's
Gap*

*Gowan's
Ford*

*Pea Vine
Church*

Brannan

Negley

*West Branch
Chickamauga Creek*

*Worthen's
Gap*

Pond Spring

*Nickajack
Cave*

Baird

Sand Mountain

*Stevens's
Gap*

*Catlett's
Gap*

Dug Gap

Sheridan

*Bluebird
Gap*

La Fayette

Pea Vine Ridge

Wills Creek

Pigeon Mountain

Chattanooga River

ALABAMA

Winston Gap

*Valley
Head*

*Dougherty's
Gap*

0   10

Scale in miles

McCook

Long

Niel's Gap

Broomtown Valley

Rawlingsville

N

Summerville

GEORGIA

McCook

Wharton

Alpine

George Skoch

Rome, Georgia. If the Confederates strongly contested the gaps, the Federals would be caught in the rugged mountains and faced with a logistical nightmare.

Rosecrans planned for all of the corps to be in position by midnight of September 4, but the schedule proved too ambitious. The XIV Corps fell two days behind. "Roads horrible. The crossing of Raccoon Mountain fully as bad as anything we have had," complained Reynolds. Capt. Alfred Hough, a Negley aide, gave a similar account: "Our division was all of one day and night in ascending the Mountain, not more than two miles certainly. . . . This ascent was finally made though we lost some wagons and several fine artillery horses, which dropped dead in the road." Huge rocks embedded in the middle of the road made the path, according to a correspondent, "very steep, and outrageously rough." Wood's division remained at Shellmound three days (September 2–5), waiting for the supply wagons to come up. Crittenden's wagons did not complete the crossing until the fifth. McCook had his own problems. On the night of the fifth, Sheridan's division remained at Trenton, having been blocked by Negley's wagons. Johnson's and Davis's divisions arrived at Winston's "Gap," only to find that it was no gap at all, only a horrid bridle path leading to the summit of the Lookout Mountain range. The men literally carried the wagons by hand by passing fence rails through the wheels from side to side, with three men on each.[29]

The scene in the valley below awed John Beatty: "The moon shone brightly, and many campfires glimmered in the valley and along the side of the mountain." The plateau, however, offered only "a few poorly cultivated cornfields, with here and there a cabin." Captain Hough found the inhabitants "very few and with few exceptions very ignorant[.] most of the men are in the army, or hidden in the mountains, afraid to go to the army and equally afraid of the Yankees. Our movement over here has very much surprised them, they did not see how we could cross the river after they burnt the bridge." Capt. Henry Richards of the 93d Ohio contemptuously related, "The inhabitants of these mountain regions seem very ignorant, especially the women, who all chew tobacco and dip snuff." Writing from Alabama, Capt. Phillip Welshimer of McCook's corps noted: "This is a rough country. I do not like it but these mountains are filled with Union people."[30]

On September 6, pursuant to orders from army headquarters, Crittenden directed Wood to make a reconnaissance along the railroad to Chattanooga to the

29. OR, 30(3):341, 344–45, 346, 347, 348, 368; Athearn, Soldier in the West, 133–34; New York Tribune, Sept. 18, 1863; F. W. Perry, "Toilsome March of the Fourteenth Corps over the Mountains," National Tribune, June 28, 1883; Horace Fisher, "Alexander McD. McCook," Boston Transcript, June 13, 1903, in folder 12, Alexander McCook Papers, McCook Family Papers, LC.

30. Beatty, Citizen Soldier, 328–29; Athearn, Soldier in the West, 136; Letters of Captain Henry Richards, 18–19; Welshimer to wife, Sept. 5, 1863, Phillip Welshimer Letters, 21st Illinois File, CCNMP.

base of Lookout Mountain. Not desiring to expose his division by marching up Lookout Valley, where his flanks and rear would be exposed, Wood ignored the order on the rather flimsy pretext that Crittenden "fixed no hour for the movement." Indeed, he pulled his division back two miles, which he reported with the rather interesting statement, "I shifted my position to the rear." When Crittenden sent two staff officers under the pretext of "exploring the road to your [Wood's] headquarters," the profane and outspoken division commander, feeling spied upon, exploded. "Neither of [them] has one-tenth of my military experience, nor a tenth of my military education," he railed. When told that the order for the reconnaissance came from Rosecrans, Wood unflinchingly wrote, "I cannot believe that General Rosecrans desires such a blind adherence to the mere letter of his order." Under pressure, Wood perfunctorily advanced Harker's brigade to Lookout Creek the next day.

Rosecrans proved to be in a foul mood over the matter. First, Crittenden had failed to endorse the order as prescribed under regulations. "I acknowledge the correctness of the reproof, and it shall not occur again, be I well or ill, sleepy or wide awake, in or out of bed," Crittenden answered. Second, Wood's lengthy epistle, in which he accused Crittenden of slandering him, irked Rosecrans. Garfield replied: "The general commanding directs me to say that he sees nothing in the endorsement of General Crittenden . . . which warrants your complaint. The general commanding was disappointed that your reconnaissance was not made earlier, and he still is uninformed of the place where you found the enemy, the strength of the force you encountered, and the distance to which you pushed your reconnaissance." Even in an officer corps brimming with egos, Wood stood apart. It was his first reproach of the campaign; it would not be his last.[31]

Stanley's recalcitrance also annoyed Rosecrans. Realizing that Forrest and possibly a portion of Wheeler's cavalry remained near Chattanooga, on September 6 the army commander directed the cavalry chief to go for the jugular and strike the Western and Atlantic Railroad between Resaca and Dalton. To his chagrin Rosecrans learned that the troopers had not been issued crowbars and clawhooks to rip up tracks or explosives to blow bridges. Nor did Stanley, suffering from dysentery, reveal any zeal for the mission. Although only two small Rebel cavalry divisions occupied the valley below Lookout Mountain—Wharton's to the south and Martin's to the north at La Fayette, a fact known by Stanley—he considered his approximately seventy-eight hundred troopers too few for so deep a penetration. He was told to try anyway. Yet for two days (September 6–8) he remained with McCook's infantry

31. *OR*, 30(1):602, 30(3):414–16, 419–25, 455–58.

at Winston, shoeing his horses and waiting for his wagons to come up. Rosecrans fumed, "your command has been a mere picket guard for our advance."[32]

The general had reason to be testy. With his army widely scattered and facing the thousand-foot-high Lookout Mountain range, scout reports arrived stating that Bragg had been heavily reinforced by Buckner and Johnston, the last estimated at twenty thousand men, for a possible stand south of Chattanooga. (Reports of enemy activity north of the city were dismissed as feints.) In response to a letter from Halleck, Rosecrans gave a rather alarming answer: "You have been often and fully advised that the nature of the country makes it impossible for this army to prevent Johnston from combining with Bragg. . . . This has doubtless been done, and Buckner, Johnston, and Bragg are all near Chattanooga. . . . Your apprehensions are just."[33]

By the evening of the eighth, all three corps had taken position: the XXI at Wauhatchie; the XIV at Trenton, with Negley's division atop Lookout Mountain and in possession of Stevens's and Cooper's Gaps; and the XX, with Stanley's cavalry, at Winston's Gap. Throughout the afternoon, thanks to Wilder's scouts, reports claimed that Bragg had evacuated Chattanooga, a fact confirmed by 8:30 P.M. Rosecrans's objective was no longer the city, however, but that which had eluded him back in July—the destruction of the Rebel army. McCook and Stanley were immediately ordered to ascertain the direction of the fleeing enemy and Crittenden to be prepared to occupy the city. Orders directed Thomas to report to headquarters and to hold his command "in readiness to move at once." Col. Smith D. Atkins, commanding the 92d Illinois Mounted Infantry, happened by headquarters at midnight and found Rosecrans brimming with confidence. Virtually lost in the exuberance was a line from Negley's 7:20 P.M. dispatch: "I have several confirmations of the report that Johnston is in command and brought with him upwards of 10,000 troops."[34]

32. OR, 30(1):52, 53, 891, 30(3):467–68, 53(3): 346, 375, 379, 431, 432, 607. Wrote Brigadier General Crook: "The officers were all together when General Stanley received a letter from General Rosecrans, accusing him unmercifully of procrastination, unnecessary delays, a want of appreciation of the situation, etc. . . . General Stanley was taken sick. In fact, he was sick then." Schmitt, General George Crook, 104.

33. OR, 53(3):381, 389, 393, 397, 398, 406–7, 418.

34. OR, 53(1):246, 53(3):408–9, 443, 444–45, 446, 449, 459–60, 481; Beatty, Citizen Soldier, 329–30; Remarks by Smith D. Atkins, Late Colonel of the Ninety-Second Illinois Volunteer Infantry (Mounted) (N.p., 1909), 100. Rosecrans's capture of Chattanooga may not have been so fully appreciated in Washington. On September 11 John Hay recorded: "R—— won a great and bloodless victory at Chattanooga which he had no business to win. The day that the enemy ran, he sent a mutinous message to H—— [Halleck] complaining of the very things that have secured us the victories, foreshadowing only danger or defeat." Hay, Letters of John Hay and Extracts from Diary, 3 vols. (reprint, New York: Gordian, 1969), 1:101–2.

So far, so good. Rosecrans had brilliantly and bloodlessly maneuvered Bragg out of Chattanooga. The next move would decide his career. Unfortunately, he had lost the Army of Tennessee. He hoped that the Confederates were retreating due south to Rome; if so, he had them. Crittenden could pursue from the north from Chattanooga, with McCook on the other end moving into Bloomtown Valley, blocking the escape route south. Thomas, in the center, could advance through the gaps into McLemore's Cove and pass through Dug and Catlett's Gaps over Pigeon Mountain, which would lead directly across the Confederate line of retreat. If Bragg fell back southeast along the Western and Atlantic Railroad, Rosecrans would face a more complex dilemma, for the Rebels would surely block the gaps of Taylor's Ridge and Rocky Face Ridge. Nonetheless, with luck and skill (and few at this stage would argue that Rosecrans did not possess both), the Confederates might have their flank and/or rear mauled. Whether or not Bragg was actually retreating or simply regrouping to the south received little thought, at least not on the night of the eighth.[35]

Rosecrans's other possibility was to prudently halt at Chattanooga, secure his lines of communication, and resupply his army for the next target—Atlanta. That is precisely what the conservative Thomas counseled ("to get a good ready"), or so he claimed in postwar years. Such a move would have subjected Rosecrans to the ire of the War Department, however, for repeating the Tullahoma campaign. Bragg might also have turned and occupied the heights above Chattanooga (as he subsequently did), trapping Rosecrans in the city. If, however, Rosecrans allowed a demoralized Confederate army to simply slip through his fingers, he most certainly would have been compared to Maj. Gen. George Meade, who "allowed" Lee's army to escape after Gettysburg. The victory is not always given to the methodical but sometimes the audacious.[36]

Historians enamored by the Thomas mystique have nonetheless used this as a springboard to suggest that the Virginian was alarmed about the plan of pursuit and proceeded only under protest. Absolutely no evidence suggests that the corps commander hesitated to proceed or that he sounded reports of foreboding. That Thomas would have adopted Rosecrans's aggressiveness had he been in command is unlikely; the suggestion that he smelled a trap and foresaw disaster is baseless.[37]

---

35. Woodworth, *Six Armies in Tennessee,* 62–63; Lamers, *Edge of Glory,* 308–9.

36. Van Horne, *Thomas,* 104–6; Cleaves, *Rock of Chickamauga,* 179; Piatt, *Thomas,* 366; Lamers, *Edge of Glory,* 308–9; *OR,* 30(1):184, 186. A news clipping in the Rosecrans Papers mentions that Thomas was not for proceeding. Rosecrans agreed but said that he was under pressure from the government. Someone—perhaps Rosecrans—wrote across the article, "Absolutely without foundation." Article 4, "Chickamauga—The Fight in the Valley of the River of Death," n.d., William S. Rosecrans Papers, UCLA.

37. Glenn Tucker, *Chickamauga: Bloody Battle in the West* (reprint, Dayton: Morningside, 1976), 62; Buell, *Warrior Generals,* 259; Cozzens, *This Terrible Sound,* 68; McKinney, *Education in Violence,* 224–27.

A flurry of activity occurred at general headquarters throughout the morning of September 9. Halleck was notified that "the enemy have decided not to fight at Chattanooga." At 10:00 A.M. Rosecrans ordered a general pursuit of the enemy, with McCook advancing to Alpine, Thomas passing through McLemore's Cove and over Pigeon Mountain at La Fayette, and Crittenden, after detaching Wagner's brigade to occupy Chattanooga, to Ringgold. A loyalist citizen claimed that Bragg's demoralized army was in full retreat to Rome. Captain Porter expressed the exuberance of the army staff: "The Rebel army is retreating through Georgia, and we are following as fast as we can drag our artillery."[38]

Armed with orders from Rosecrans that his 92d Illinois Mounted Infantry should be the first to enter Chattanooga, Colonel Atkins drove his four hundred men hard that morning. Thomas Wood, who had other plans, refused to clear his infantry from the road. Shown Rosecrans's order, the general openly cursed but reluctantly allowed the Illinoisans to pass. Just as Atkins was about to enter the city, Wood galloped up with Brigadier General Wagner and his brigade colors, ordering the colonel not to enter the city but to ride instead to Rossville. It was too late. Atkins had sent a detail ahead, and the Stars and Stripes even then waved atop the Crutchfield house. That evening Rosecrans telegraphed Halleck: "Chattanooga is ours without a struggle, and East Tennessee is free. Our move on the enemy's flank and rear progresses, while the tail of his retreating column will not escape unmolested."[39]

Not until the early afternoon of September 9 did Negley's division of the XIV Corps concentrate at the east end of Stevens's Gap, with skirmishers advanced into McLemore's Cove to Bailey's Crossroads. Although there appeared to be only a single enemy cavalry regiment ahead, citizens told of "three or four divisions" on the far side of Pigeon Mountain. One citizen, however, told quite a different story, one that the Federals wanted to hear. Having traveled from Ringgold through La Fayette, he saw nothing but signs of a general retreat to Dalton. Indeed, he saw only two or three regiments at La Fayette. The Union trap was closing.[40]

On the morning of the tenth, Negley's division traversed the narrow country road leading into McLemore's Cove, the picturesque six-to-nine-mile-wide inlet between Lookout Mountain and Pigeon Mountain bisected by the East Branch of Chickamauga Creek. It was six and a half miles from Stevens's Gap to Dug Gap, through which he would pass to La Fayette and pounce upon whatever Confederate force he found. Confident that the Rebels had been cleared from McLemore's Cove,

38. *OR*, 30(3):479, 481, 482, 483; Porter to mother, Sept. 13, 1863, Horace Porter Letters, LC.
39. Cozzens, *This Terrible Sound*, 61–64; *OR*, 30(1):482, 479, 629.
40. *OR*, 30(3):484, 485–86.

the Pennsylvanian rode at the head of the column with his staff. Before clearing the cedar thickets between Bailey's Crossroads and the Davis plantation, the cluster of officers suddenly came under fire. The lead regiment, the 78th Pennsylvania, immediately advanced skirmishers. The bluecoats made steady progress to the Widow Davis house, where on a knob to the east they saw, a thousand yards ahead, Rebels busily obstructing Dug Gap.[41]

An early report arrived of Confederate activity at La Fayette, but the forces seemed to have moved south toward Rome. In a note to Baird, a day's march to the rear, Negley apprised him of the situation: "All the information I have from other sources confirms the report that there is not more than a brigade of cavalry at La Fayette. But I would suggest general, that you push forward your division within supporting distance." By that evening, however, reports indicated a superior enemy force at Dug Gap and an enemy division approaching through Catlett's Gap, three miles to the northeast, in a pincers movement. A captured lieutenant of the 32d Mississippi boasted to Negley that if he continued to advance he would "get severely whipped." Nonetheless, when Negley wrote a 9:30 P.M. dispatch to Baird, he did not appear alarmed. Although "somewhat advanced and exposed to a flank approach," his position was still "a favorable one to fight the enemy, providing your division is within supporting distance."[42]

Interestingly, Negley's journal entry of September 10 does not square with this dispatch. The journal gives much more specific information—the approach of D. H. Hill's corps of three divisions at Dug Gap and Simon Buckner's corps of two divisions, along with Forrest's cavalry division, at Catlett's Gap. None of this appeared in the 9:30 dispatch, even though it should have been known by that time. "I felt confident the enemy proposed to attack me in the morning with a superior force," Negley wrote in his journal, yet no such alarm was expressed to Baird. Indeed, if he felt threatened, why did he not withdraw to Bailey's Crossroads that night rather than wait for Baird to close up? It would appear that Negley added to his journal in the light of subsequent events.[43]

The modern consensus that Thomas "smelled danger all along" is a myth. The corps commander, back at Stevens's Gap on the night of the tenth, acted prudently by ordering Baird to close up on Negley during the night and for Reynolds's and Brannan's divisions to pass through Cooper's Gap at daylight and come up on Baird's left. The Virginian remained confident that the enemy would be driven "be-

41. Cozzens, *This Terrible Sound*, 68–69; Athearn, *Soldier in the West*, 138–39; *OR*, 30(3):484, 510–11; Jacob Adams Diary, Sept. 11, 1863, 21st Ohio File, CCNMP.

42. *OR*, 30(3):509; Athearn, *Soldier in the West*, 138–39.

43. *OR*, 30(1):326, 30(3):509–10. Jim Ogden, historian at the Chickamauga National Military Park, concurs with my conclusion.

yond Pigeon Ridge by tomorrow night [the eleventh]." Clearly, he had no indica-
tion as of 9:00 P.M. that Negley might be in danger.[44]

Rosecrans remained noticeably agitated; first Stanley dragging his feet, now
Thomas. Wrote an aide to the corps commander: "The general commanding . . . is
disappointed to learn that his forces move tomorrow morning instead of having
moved this morning, as they should have done, this delay imperiling both extremes
of the army. Your movement on La Fayette should be made with the utmost
promptness. . . . Your advance ought to have threatened La Fayette yesterday eve-
ning." Never had Thomas, the revered senior adviser of the army, been so rebuked.
Further echoing these sentiments was Garfield, who wrote to Crittenden at mid-
night: "There have been several rumors within the last two days that General Bragg
had moved out with the design to fight us between this [Chattanooga] and LaFay-
ette. These rumors . . . are hardly worth a moment's consideration. They should be
treated with total indifference if General Thomas' corps had reached LaFayette this
morning, as it was expected to, but in all possibility has not."[45]

An aggravated Thomas gave immediate response. Had Negley proceeded into La
Fayette on the tenth, he "would have suffered very severely" since the Confederates,
it was now known, had concentrated in force around the town. "If I had had Wil-
der's brigade," he tersely concluded, "I am satisfied LaFayette would have been in
our possession now, as with it I could have prevented the enemy from blockading
this road." Thomas overstated the case, but his point could not have been missed—
the one at fault was Rosecrans, not him.[46]

It took six hours for Negley's 9:30 P.M. message of the tenth to get back to
Thomas at Stevens's Gap. The Virginian showed no undue concern about the divi-
sion's advanced position, however, confident that the balance of the XIV Corps was
rapidly moving up in support. Indeed, Thomas saw the opportunity of flanking the
Confederates emerging from Catlett's Gap. "I will send Generals Reynolds and
Brannan, by the Cooper's Gap road, to move upon the flank of the enemy at Mor-
gan's Mill," he notified the division commander at 3:25 A.M. on the eleventh. Negley
held his position and awaited reinforcements.[47]

Neither Thomas nor Negley appreciated the seriousness of the situation. Al-
though Baird's weary troops (Scribner's and Starkweather's brigades) arrived at the
Widow Davis house at 8:30 A.M. on the eleventh, thus increasing the Federal
strength to over nine thousand, Thomas's other two divisions, with the exception

44. *OR*, 30(3):510–11.
45. Ibid., 511, 517.
46. Ibid., 534.
47. Ibid., 534–35.

of Turchin's brigade (two thousand strong), which formed in line on the left at 10:00 A.M., were still on the other side of Lookout Mountain. By midmorning, scouts brought Negley alarming news: the Rebels, Maj. Gen. Patrick Cleburne's division of five thousand men moving up Dug Gap and Maj. Gen. Thomas Hindman's corps of fifteen thousand troops approaching from Catlett's Gap, were closing in fast, the latter only two miles from Negley's left. At last understanding the gravity of his situation, Negley began a skillful withdrawal, unlimbering ten guns on a commanding ridge behind the John Davis house. Negley sustained about 150 casualties, but boasted an aide, "we did not lose a wagon, horse or gun."[48]

In the middle of the near fatal McLemore's Cove trap came the farcical episode of Col. Benjamin Scribner, commanding one of Baird's brigades. Stricken with an attack of hay fever, he wore a pair of dark goggles to protect his eyes from the sun and dust. His horse suddenly walked into a hornet's nest, and in the bucking that followed, the colonel lost his goggles. Realizing that he was useless without them, Scribner stopped his men from firing and had them search the bushes. The goggles were soon recovered, "to my great relief," he recalled.[49]

At 4:00 A.M. on the twelfth, Thomas, now fully alerted to the danger ahead, notified Rosecrans that Negley had been attacked "with an overwhelming force" and had fallen back to Stevens's Gap. To his staff the Virginian could not hide his dismay: "Nothing but stupendous blunders on the part of Bragg can save our army from total defeat. I have ordered Negley to fall back from McLemore's Cove, and I believe we may be able to save this corps. But Bragg is also in a position to strike McCook and Crittenden before they have a chance to extradite themselves." As for Rosecrans, he dismissed Thomas's warning in caustic language. Wrote Garfield: "Your desperate dispatches of 10:30 last night and 4 this morning have been received. After maturely weighing the notes, the General Commanding is induced to think that General Negley withdrew more through prudence than compulsion. He trusts his loss is not serious."[50]

✱   ✱   ✱

48. *OR*, 30(1):247, 270, 327–28; Beatty, *Citizen Soldier*, 330–31; Athearn, *Soldier in the West*, 139–40. For estimates of the numbers involved, see *OR*, 30(1):289, 308, 30(2):158, 297, 306, 365, 419.

49. Scribner, *How Soldiers Were Made*, 140–41.

50. *OR*, 30(3):564–65, 566; Tucker, *Chickamauga*, 71. Although historians have long maintained that Bragg missed an excellent opportunity to destroy two Federal divisions in McLemore's Cove on September 10–11, I remain skeptical. It would have been a running fight, and Negley might have lost his train of 400 wagons, but there is no evidence to suggest that, with skillful delaying tactics along Chickamauga Creek (which, in fact, did occur), the Federals could not simply have withdrawn to Stevens's Gap. Had the Rebels pursued, the next day their own right flank would have been endangered via Cooper's Gap, as well as their rear at La Fayette, from the advance of the XXI Corps.

On the morning of September 11, still believing Bragg to be in retreat, Rosecrans sent Crittenden in pursuit. The XXI Corps, minus one brigade held at Chattanooga and one at Rossville, proceeded out the Ringgold Road—a logical choice, but as matters developed, one that sent seven brigades, plus Wilder's and Minty's mounted brigades, on a wild-goose chase. Meanwhile, Colonel Harker left a regiment and battery at Rossville and scouted toward Lee and Gordon's Mill, driving back squads of cavalry before him.[51]

By midafternoon Rosecrans had at long last begun to heed Thomas's warnings of a sizable Rebel concentration on the east side of Pigeon Mountain and began recalling the XXI Corps toward the La Fayette Road in a measured, though not yet frantic, attempt to connect his left and center wings. Even before receiving the change of orders, Crittenden realized that there was nothing in his front but Rebel cavalry, which could be dangerous nonetheless. Gray troopers made a bold dash upon Cruft's brigade of Palmer's division near Pea Vine Ridge, capturing fifty-eight bluecoats of the 1st Kentucky without firing a shot. With Wagner's brigade at Chattanooga and Harker's scouting up the Rossville Road, Wood marched with his remaining brigade to link up with the latter at Lee and Gordon's Mill, which he accomplished by 8:30 P.M. Enemy campfires, supposedly those of two of Forrest's brigades, could clearly be seen on the eastern bank of Chickamauga Creek.[52]

Although Rosecrans would note in his afteraction report that "it became a matter of life and death" to concentrate his army, the facts suggest that he remained ambiguous at this stage. At 10:00 P.M. on the eleventh, the army commander wrote a dispatch to McCook stating that the "weight of evidence" indicated that the Confederates had concentrated at La Fayette. He merely suggested that McCook close up on Thomas. Rosecrans hesitated to withdraw the XX Corps from the vicinity of the Summerville Road, believing that Bragg might yet escape to Rome. During this time, Charles A. Dana, former newspaperman and now assistant to Secretary of War Stanton, arrived at army headquarters. He was a de facto spy for Stanton, a fact fully appreciated by officers and journalists, who variously referred to him as "a loathsome pimp" and "a spy upon rival generals." He insisted that as late as the twelfth, Rosecrans remained convinced that Bragg "was merely making a show of the offensive to check pursuit, and that he would make his escape to Rome as soon as he found our army concentrated."[53]

51. OR, 30(1):53, 603, 683, 30(3):532–33, 538, 543, 544, 546, 547, 554, 564–65; Cozzens, This Terrible Sound, 76–77.

52. OR, 30(1):604, 628, 630, 683, 684–85; George Palmer, Conscientious Turncoat, 114; John Palmer, Personal Recollections, 172.

53. OR, 30(1):54, 30(3):541; Dana characterizations quoted in Cozzens, This Terrible Sound, 80; Charles A. Dana, Recollections of the Civil War (New York: D. Appleton, 1898), 108–9.

Although largely out of touch with Rosecrans and Thomas on the eleventh, Mc-
Cook, at Alpine and probing with cavalry toward Summerville, likewise recognized
potential trouble. Throughout the day, reports filtered in of a large Confederate
concentration at La Fayette (where Thomas was supposed to be) and Trion Factory,
five and a half miles from Summerville, the last (in truth a false report) supposed
to be Leonidas Polk's corps. McCook could "scarcely believe this [concentration],
yet all the cavalry we have driven from this vicinity runs in that [La Fayette] direc-
tion." Later that night an officer of the 1st Alabama Cavalry, captured near Summer-
ville, revealed disturbing news: Bragg had concentrated to turn on Rosecrans's
scattered army. "Up to that moment we believed the enemy to be east of us retreat-
ing toward Reseca," admitted a staff officer.[54]

McCook had to make a decision. Blocked by the Confederates at La Fayette, he
could not juncture with Thomas via Broomtown Valley. Indeed, if he continued
advancing up the valley, he might walk into a trap. Sheridan, whose division
camped several miles north of the parent corps, also became jittery. "This is all
wrong. We have no business here, we ought to be in Chattanooga," he confided to
Col. Luther Bradley. A local citizen under the general's employ made his way
through enemy lines, arriving at division headquarters on the eleventh. He told of
a large Confederate army at La Fayette preparing to attack.[55]

Despite the accelerating crisis, little movement occurred on the twelfth beyond
calling up Steedman's division of Granger's Reserve Corps from Bridgeport to Chat-
tanooga. Crittenden marched Van Cleve's and Palmer's divisions west toward Lee
and Gordon's Mills, their left flank covered by Wilder's brigade, which had a sharp
engagement at Leet's Tanyard, losing thirty men (the enemy, fifty). Fortunately, but
unknown to Crittenden, the Confederates bungled a planned attack upon Palmer's
division near Pea Vine Church that, if properly executed, could have mauled, if not
destroyed, it. Thomas used the day to form a defensive position at Stevens's and
Cooper's Gaps. Rosecrans continued to express irritation with his senior corps com-
mander due to Thomas's lack of information regarding his position and that of the
enemy. McCook, "not desirous of fighting Bragg's whole army," remained huddled
around Alpine, keeping his wagon train, for the time being, three and a half miles
from the eastern rim of Lookout Mountain.[56]

Throughout the day Crittenden, naively out of touch with the precariousness of
his position, continued to believe that Bragg was trying to escape. At 1:00 A.M. he

54. OR, 30(3):538–39, 540, 541, 542–43; Fisher, Staff Officer's Story, 79–80.

55. Luther Bradley Reminiscences, Luther Bradley File, CCNMP, 13; Sheridan, Memoirs, 1:275–76;
OR, 30(1):54, 486, 30(3):542–43.

56. OR, 30(3):563–71; Cozzens, This Terrible Sound, 79; Van Horne, Army of the Cumberland, 1:325;
John Palmer, Personal Recollections, 568–69.

notified army headquarters, "My only hope, or rather my great hope, is that General Thomas or General McCook may be able to hit them a side lick." At 9:45 that night, not fifteen minutes after Garfield wrote the corps commander a warning that "there is no longer doubt that the enemy is in heavy force in the neighborhood of La Fayette, and there is far more probability of his attacking you than that he is running," Crittenden sounded a very different note. "It has always been the plan of the enemy to make stubborn defenses on a retreat, and I do not yet believe that there is a strong force of infantry in the vicinity of La Fayette," he noted. Wood, who by now detested his superior, strongly disagreed.[57]

A crisis loomed throughout the thirteenth. "A battle is imminent," Garfield confided in a letter. "I believe the enemy now intends to fight us. He has a large force and the advantage in position. Unless we can outmaneuver him we shall be in a perilous situation." Early that morning Crittenden advanced Van Cleve, with one brigade, toward La Fayette, ignorant that two enemy corps lay in wait. The vigorous advance dissuaded Lieutenant General Polk from attacking, and he even called for reinforcements. At noon Rosecrans frantically began drawing his wings upon the center. He ordered Crittenden to leave Wood's two brigades at Lee and Gordon's Mill, the only Federal force on the main road back to Chattanooga. If attacked, Wood would fall back upon Rossville, where Granger's six thousand troops would be arriving. Meanwhile, Crittenden would march Palmer's and Van Cleve's divisions west of Chickamauga Creek and up the Cove Road to juncture with Thomas at Bailey's Crossroads.[58]

At 3:00 P.M. McCook, still dawdling near Alpine, received Rosecrans's order (through Thomas) to leave one division with the wagon train and proceed with the other two in support of the XIV Corps. Two hours later he received a second dispatch, this one from Garfield, with instructions to join Thomas at Stevens's Gap. Assuming (correctly) that Thomas did not have full possession of the cove, McCook believed his only option was to return to Winston's Gap, recross Lookout Mountain, proceed up Will's Valley, and approach Stevens's Gap from the west. He knew of a more direct route to Stevens's Gap, a road atop Lookout Mountain that led from Dougherty's Gap to Bailey's Crossroads, but considered it impassable. Early on the fourteenth, as the weary troops of the XX Corps retraced the torturous road over Lookout Mountain, McCook received another dispatch from Garfield. He expressed "regret" that such a roundabout route had been taken rather than the direct route atop Lookout Mountain. Garfield insisted that the Rebels did not possess Dug

57. *OR*, 30(1):575, 30(3):577–78, 580–81.

58. Williams, *Wild Life of the Army*, 295; *OR*, 30(1):604–5, 630, 30(3):602; Van Horne, *Army of the Cumberland*, 1:325–26.

Gap and that McCook should turn about and take the shorter road. Even though McCook could not possibly have been more than three or four hours into his march, he erupted. "By his [Thomas's] approval I am on this route. I will be pained to take my troops over the route again; they certainly would feel as if I were trifling with them. I will suspend the movement until I hear from you." Rosecrans backed down and allowed him to proceed, but valuable time was lost. Being told of a good mountain road that ran from Valley Head direct to Stevens's Gap, McCook now drove his infantry hard, from twenty to twenty-six miles a day. George Crook, who had by now replaced the ailing David Stanley, withdrew the cavalry to Alpine, with little to show for their weeklong effort except jaded horses.[59]

Due to a garbled staff officer's dispatch, Van Cleve's and Palmer's divisions made slight progress on the fourteenth. McCook remained far from Stevens's Gap, and Thomas made little movement either that day or during the fifteenth. Nonetheless, on the night of the fourteenth, Dana echoed the confidence at army headquarters by notifying Stanton that the geographic difficulties had been "substantially overcome" and that the army was "in the best possible condition."[60]

Early in the campaign Rosecrans became aware of the transfer of Confederate troops to Bragg. These included Buckner's corps from East Tennessee, estimated at ten thousand, and some if not all of Johnston's force in Mississippi, possibly twenty thousand men, including perhaps Maj. Gen. W. W. Loring's division (the last untrue). This gave Bragg an estimated sixty thousand troops—virtual parity with the Army of the Cumberland's sixty-two thousand. Although Rosecrans had expressed early concerns about the possibility of Lee sending troops west from the Army of Northern Virginia, Halleck put his mind at ease. Rumors of large troop transfer were not uncommon; indeed, Halleck suspected that Bragg might be reinforcing

59. *OR*, 30(1):187, 486, 892, 918, 30(3):599, 603, 628, 629; Cope, *Fifteenth Ohio*, 307; Carter, *First Regiment of Tennessee Volunteer Cavalry*, 89–90. Lytle was left at Dougherty's Gap with two brigades. The criticism of McCook is that, through negligence, he did not know that a direct road existed from Dougherty's to Stevens's Gap. See Cozzens, *This Terrible Sound*, 87–88. McCook entered in his journal, "It was my desire to join General Thomas by the Mountain road via Stevens' Gap, but not having any guide, all the citizens concurring that no such road existed . . . , I determined to join him by that [alternative] route." *OR*, 30(1):486. Yet McCook's 5:00 P.M. message on the thirteenth seems at variance. He acknowledged the existence of "the bad road from Dougherty's Gap over the spurs to Stevens' Gap" but suggested that it was too rough to pursue. *OR*, 30(3):599. The road in question can be seen in the *Atlas to Accompany the Official Records*, plate XLVIII, map 1. The road divided a mile and a half above Dougherty's Gap, one branch going to the Widow Davis house and the other to Bailey's Crossroads. It seems strange that Rosecrans would know about the road atop the mountain and not McCook.

60. *OR*, 30(1):54–55, 187, 486, 605, 802–803, 30(3):631, 632, 634, 645, 646, 650; Van Horne, *Army of the Cumberland*, 1:327; Noe, *Southern Boy in Blue*, 192.

Lee. Thus, when the *New York Tribune* of September 9 ran a story detailing the transfer of James Longstreet's corps to Bragg, the news received little attention in the War Department.[61]

By the morning of September 14, Halleck confirmed the startling truth. Longstreet had undeniably departed Virginia and was already in North Carolina. By the afternoon of the fifteenth, the general in chief had heard enough. An urgent dispatch was sent to Rosecrans: "From information received here today, it is very probable that all three divisions of Lee's army have been sent to re-enforce Bragg. All available forces of the Departments of the Ohio and Cumberland should be brought to the front to meet the enemy. Sherman [Vicksburg] and Hurlbut [Memphis] will bring re-enforcements to the Tennessee river as rapidly as possible."[62]

In postwar years Rosecrans would bitterly complain that he had received no reinforcements, yet he was in large part to blame for his present dilemma. When he had earlier requested the XXIII Corps to cover his left, he expressed no urgency; indeed, he assured Halleck that he was "sufficiently strong." Now that the seriousness of the situation had become undeniable, it might be (depending upon Longstreet's present location, which no one knew) too late for reinforcements to affect the upcoming battle. All prisoner and civilian reports indicated that Longstreet had already arrived in Georgia with twenty thousand troops, elevating Bragg's strength to a dangerous eighty thousand men. Given the changing picture, Rosecrans could, and perhaps should, have withdrawn the XXI Corps to Chattanooga and marched the XIV and XX Corps back across the Tennessee River, using Lookout Mountain as a shield. Scholars would long debate Rosecrans's disastrous tactical mistake during the Battle of Chickamauga, overlooking the more obvious fact that he did not have to fight a battle at all. He could have gone on the defensive, concentrated at Chattanooga, and awaited reinforcements. Yet the army commander listened to Crittenden, who disbelieved the Longstreet story and remained fixated on a Confederate retreat.[63]

On September 13 Halleck ordered Burnside to push forward all infantry to Chattanooga. The IX Corps, having returned from Mississippi and now in eastern Kentucky, was also ordered to Knoxville, though attrition and sickness had reduced its effective strength to only six thousand men. That Burnside did not respond to Halleck's urgent order is attributable to several factors. First, he had intelligence that Lt. Gen. Richard Ewell's corps of Lee's army might make a move on East Tennessee,

61. *OR*, 30(1):186, 30(3):321, 361, 530, 561, 644, 681; *Cincinnati Gazette*, Sept. 25, 1863; *New York Tribune*, Sept. 9, 1863.

62. *OR*, 30(1):35–36.

63. Rosecrans, "Campaign for Chattanooga," 132; *OR*, 30(3):666, 671, 685, 687.

though the War Department assured him that such was not the case. (Of course, Halleck had made the same claim of Longstreet's corps.) Second, ever since taking Knoxville, Burnside could think of little but his retirement. Third, he had no desire to serve under Rosecrans. He told Maj. Gen. George L. Hartsuff, his nominal second in command, that his commission predated Rosecrans's by three days and that there would be confusion over who commanded. "Let me go. I don't rank him," Hartsuff promptly replied, but Burnside insisted that there was insufficient time. The department commander clearly understood that in the event of a juncture, Rosecrans would command, and he had no desire to be humbled again by becoming a de facto corps commander under a junior. In later years Burnside wrote of his aversion "to doing what would in any way weaken our hold in east Tennessee," a decision that properly rested with the War Department, not him. In short, Halleck did not issue a peremptory order, so Burnside chose to do nothing.[64]

Realistically, how many troops could have been sent had all parties acted more promptly? At the very least, Burnside could have dispatched his two largest divisions, the First and Third, totaling 15,500 infantry. This would have left two small infantry divisions, the IX Corps, and a mounted infantry brigade, totaling over 16,000 troops, in upper East Tennessee. The problem is that, given railroad transportation of only five engines and twenty cars (barely enough to keep the troops supplied, much less transport them) and bridges that would have to be constructed, it would take a minimum of eight days to forward 12,000 troops, ten for 20,000. This meant that by the time Knoxville and the Cumberland Gap had been secured, there would still have been insufficient time to affect the upcoming battle. Considering that the Confederates got an entire corps from Virginia within ten days, however, it would seem that some of Burnside's troops could have made it to Chattanooga in time. Even if Hartsuff had been successful in getting Brig. Gen. Milo Hascall's Third Division, 7,000 strong, to Rosecrans, it is problematical that the outcome of the battle would have changed. Nonetheless, an effort should have been made.[65]

64. *OR*, 30(3):523, 717–18, 731, 746; Tucker, *Chickamauga*, 58. Interestingly, Bruce Catton sympathetically supported Burnside. *Grant Takes Command* (Boston: Little, Brown, 1968), 48. The *Cincinnati Enquirer* of October 2, 1863, concluded, "General Halleck declined to order the movement, limiting himself to suggesting, it being contrary to the usual habit of the General-in-Chief of the Army to commit himself by positive orders."

65. *OR*, 30(3):639, 717–18, 743; Roger Pickenpaugh, *Rescue by Rail: Troop Transfer and the Civil War in the West, 1863* (Lincoln: University of Nebraska Press, 1998), 4. Glenn Tucker noted that one of Burnside's brigades marched the sixty miles from Knoxville to Cumberland Gap in fifty-two hours. *Chickamauga*, 57. Applying the same speed, he claims that Burnside could have reached Rosecrans in seven or eight days, September 14 or 15, in advance of the Battle of Chickamauga. This assumes, of course, that Burnside would have departed virtually on the heels of the capture of Knoxville. If he had, in fact, de-

Getting rapid reinforcements from Sherman and Hurlbut would be impossible. By committing troops to the trans-Mississippi after the fall of Vicksburg, the War Department had effectively blocked the Army of the Tennessee as a manpower source for Rosecrans. Since the Mississippi and Ohio Rivers remained low, the troops from Vicksburg would have to be transported to Memphis and thence by rail to just past Corinth. From there they would have to march the final leg to Chattanooga. Besides, Halleck had concerns that Bragg might turn Rosecrans's right and sidestep into northern Alabama, meaning that a blocking force had to be in place. This became moot, however, for when an order went to Grant for immediate reinforcements for Rosecrans, the dispatch somehow got sidetracked and did not arrive until September 22.[66]

Thus, no one was coming to the aid of the Army of the Cumberland. Who was to blame—Halleck, Rosecrans, Burnside? One thing is certain. If the Federal reinforcements that arrived a month after Chickamauga had been on the battlefield, the results might have been very different.

Trouble brewed back at Rossville, and this time it had nothing to do with the Rebels. Gordon Granger had become irked that scores of men from Col. Daniel McCook's Second Brigade had been allowed to forage contrary to orders. Two hundred were brought in and, in an act reminiscent of Bull Nelson, he ordered that each be given forty lashes. So enraged were McCook's men that they sent a five-man delegation to the general asking him to rescind the order; they too were arrested. By now the entire brigade had become near mutinous. McCook warned Granger that there might be trouble, to which he replied: "Let them come. I will flog the whole division." The colonel quickly snapped back: "If the Second Brigade once gets started, all Hell can't stop it." Presently, a soldier presented himself with an ultimatum: Granger had ten minutes to release the prisoners. When the time passed and no action came, an angry mob marched on the general's headquarters. Seeing this, he released the bound soldiers, all the while cursing everyone.[67]

Finally getting his mind back on the war, Granger, on September 15, sent a dispatch to Rosecrans warning him about the army's left flank. He had received information that two Rebel divisions had marched through Graysville toward Ringgold to join four mounted brigades already at that place. Granger suspected that it might be the rear of Buckner's corps passing down from East Tennessee. Strangely, the

parted on the morning of the fourteenth, the day he received Halleck's order, he still would not have arrived in time for the battle, even using Tucker's math.

66. *OR*, 30(3):592, 594, 596, 655, 693, 720–21, 736, 840–41.

67. Cozzens, *This Terrible Sound*, 93–94; Levi Adolphus Ross Journal, Sept. 17, 1863, 86th Illinois File, CCNMP; W. G. Putney Memoir, I, 2d Illinois Battery File, CCNMP, 36.

news that the Confederates, in corps strength, were only nine miles from Ringgold failed to raise Rosecrans's eyebrows. Beyond sending Robert Minty's cavalry brigade to screen Granger, he did nothing. "The rebels seem disposed to make a stand in the valley," he replied late the next afternoon.[68]

Rosecrans, ailing but still maintaining an exhaustive schedule, moved his headquarters to the Gordon-Lee mansion on Wednesday morning, September 16. Throughout the day he remained ignorant of the threat to his left at Lee and Gordon's Mill ("Bragg is gone. Where to we do not know," Palmer conceded that day) and continued his northeast slide along the west bank of Chickamauga Creek. The XIV Corps was ordered to concentrate on Crittenden's right, between Gowan's Ford and Bird's Mill, but Thomas (correctly, though to Rosecrans's dismay) postponed the move for twenty-four hours, giving McCook more time to close. Since Bragg no longer faced a threat south of La Fayette, he could have hurled his army against Crittenden that day with devastating effect or crossed above Lee and Gordon's, thus driving a wedge across the two parallel roads that ran east of Missionary Ridge and back to Chattanooga, the La Fayette and Dry Valley Roads, which in that vicinity were only three-fourths of a mile apart. When Crittenden received a warning from Minty about a Rebel threat in his front, he gave a curt response: "All this [activity] would indicate infantry, which the Major General commanding cannot believe in." Later in the day, when the 4th U.S. Cavalry brought in twenty-three prisoners with blankets slung over their shoulders (clearly infantry), Crittenden dismissed them as stragglers.[69]

On the seventeenth Rosecrans at long last began to have suspicions that the enemy might be massing on his left. Minty, whose cavalry covered the army's northern flank at Reed's Bridge on Chickamauga Creek four and a half miles northeast of Lee and Gordon's Mill, had no doubt. That morning he rode to XXI Corps headquarters to warn Crittenden about the threat, only to be sloughed off. Later in the day the colonel again reported to Crittenden, this time at army headquarters and in the presence of Rosecrans. When told that deserters had revealed the presence of

---

68. *OR*, 30(2):651.

69. *Cincinnati Enquirer*, Sept. 19 [written Sept. 17], 1863; George Palmer, *Conscientious Turncoat*, 114; *OR*, 30(1):605, 895, 30(3):668–70, 699; "Remarks of Major General R. H. G. Minty at the Dedication of the Monument Erected to the Fourth Michigan Cavalry at Reed's Bridge," in *History of the Michigan Organizations at Chickamauga and Missionary Ridge, 1863* (Lansing: Robert Smith, 1899), 276. Such a move on the part of Bragg would not necessarily have spelled doom for Rosecrans. He could have withdrawn his army back up the cove and marched over to the west side of Missionary Ridge. Short of Burnside arriving in Chattanooga in the meantime, however, the city probably would have been lost to the Confederates, assuredly resulting in demands for Rosecrans's removal.

Longstreet's corps, the Kentuckian scoffed, "Longstreet is in Virginia." "Pardon me, General Crittenden," Minty tartly replied, "Longstreet, with a considerable force of the Army of Northern Virginia, is now at or near Ringgold." Glancing at the army commander, Crittenden exclaimed, "General Rosecrans, I will guarantee, with my corps, to whip every rebel within twenty miles of us."[70]

Realizing by late afternoon that the Rebels were indeed concentrating on his left (the signal station atop Lookout Mountain had observed columns of dust), but still fearing for his center in the cove, Rosecrans slightly shifted his line northeast; it was not enough. Palmer's division of the XXI Corps advanced to Glass's Mill, making room for the XIV Corps ("we got into confusion with some of Crittenden's forces, which began to move out just as we came up," complained one of Thomas's cannoneers), which extended the line southwest along Chickamauga Creek. The XX Corps finally entered the cove, Johnson's division having marched a torturous twenty-five miles over rugged terrain that day. The cavalry took the direct road into the cove, from Dougherty's Gap to Bluebird Gap. The Confederates made slight demonstrations in front of Sheridan's division from the direction of La Fayette.[71]

The developing news that day again came from Granger, who marched Steedman with a reinforced brigade and a battery out the old Federal Road on a reconnaissance toward Ringgold. Crossing the Red House Bridge over Chickamauga Creek six and a half miles north of Reed's Bridge, the troops marched to within a mile of the town, where they suddenly encountered the Rebels in division strength, including (unknown to Steedman) two brigades from Johnston in Mississippi and one from Lee's army in Virginia. The Federals withdrew six miles to Pea Vine Creek. Having been warned for two days of a substantial enemy force seven miles above Lee and Gordon's Mill, Rosecrans belatedly dispatched Wilder's mounted infantry to Alexander's Bridge on Chickamauga Creek in the three-mile gap between Minty and Crittenden's left.[72]

Rosecrans did not realize just how close he had come to having his flank rolled

70. OR, 30(1):925, 30(3):668; "Remarks of Major General R. H. G. Minty," 276. On the late afternoon of the fifteenth, Dana confided to Stanton, "Reports that Longstreet has reached Atlanta begin to come in from various sources." Despite Minty's certainty, it must be mentioned that a letter and diary, both written by members of the 4th Michigan Cavalry, one of Minty's outfits, made no mention of any sizable infantry force. Robert Burns to brother, Sept. 17, 1863, Robert Burns Letters, Minnesota Historical Society, St. Paul; Henry Albert Potter Diary, Sept. 16, 17, 1863, BHLUM. Indeed, Burns wrote: "I think they [Rebels] are all moving south, as fast as they can, leaving behind a force of their cavalry to cover their movements."

71. OR, 30(1):189, 248, 487, 605, 892, 898, 899 30(3):703–5, 708, 710–11; Eben P. Sturges Diary, Sept. 17, 1863, M, 1st Ohio Battery File, CCNMP; Sheridan, Memoirs, 1:149; Van Horne, Army of the Cumberland, 1:328–29.

72. OR, 30(1):445–46, 925; Cozzens, This Terrible Sound, 96, Woodworth, Chickamauga, 6.

up. Bragg's plan for the day included a demonstration with one cavalry and two infantry divisions (Polk's corps) against Crittenden's corps at Lee and Gordon's Mill and Crawfish Springs, while the bulk of his force, four divisions (W. H. T. Walker's and Buckner's corps) and Forrest's cavalry, crossed the creek at the fords and bridges to the north; Brig. Gen. Bushrod Johnson's division at Ringgold would cross at Reed's Bridge. True to Bragg's form and Rosecrans's good fortune, the Confederate commander again vacillated. This gave time for Wilder's brigade to block Alexander's Bridge, but unless Rosecrans acted quickly, there would be no reason why Bragg could not implement the same plan the next day. Indeed, that is precisely what he planned.[73]

Rosecrans's plan to capture Bragg's army in the hills of northern Georgia failed in both conception and execution. First, the risks of dispersing his army over forty miles outweighed the benefits. Even if Bragg had been blocked at La Fayette from the north, west, and south, he still could have easily escaped east over Taylor's Ridge through Ship's Gap, less than six miles distant. Additionally, the plan left Rosecrans vulnerable on his flanks. Only inept Confederate leadership spared Crittenden's corps from probable disaster. Concentration took much longer than Rosecrans could possibly have supposed, a criticism heaped upon Alexander McCook but more properly placed on the army commander.

Why did Rosecrans abandon his Buell-esque methodical planning? The answer typically given is that pressure from the War Department had been so great in the previous months that it forced him into unnecessary risks to avoid further criticisms. More to the point, Rosecrans became enamored with his own success. He ignored vital intelligence and relied upon Thomas L. Crittenden, who told him what he wanted to hear. Wrote Sheridan years later, "I have always fancied that the evacuation [of Chattanooga] made Rosecrans over confident, and led him to think that he could force Bragg south as far as Rome."[74]

Throughout the early morning hours of September 18, McCook's corps continued to close up to the north. About 1:00 A.M., in Lytle's brigade, a lone baritone broke the night's silence by singing "John Brown's Body." When it came to the chorus, the entire brigade spontaneously joined in.[75]

73. Cozzens, *This Terrible Sound,* 97, 102–3.

74. Sheridan, *Memoirs,* 1:156–57. Herman Hattaway and Archer Jones declared that Rosecrans had "headstrongly rushed forward as if he had defeated the enemy in battle and had it on the run. Nothing could have been further from the case." *How the North Won,* 448.

75. Alfred Pirtle, "Lytle's Last Sacrifice," typescript, FC.

17

Fatal Decision
The Battle of Chickamauga

FOR TWO WEEKS the opposing western armies danced around each other in the mountains of North Georgia. On the frost-covered morning of September 19, they finally joined in a two-day combat of huge proportions along Chickamauga Creek. Even with inferior numbers, it was a battle that Rosecrans should have won.

Despite skirmishing in front of Wood's division at Lee and Gordon's Mill (a feint by Polk's corps), all evidence by late morning of September 18 indicated a Confederate turning movement to the north. In an effort to extend his left, Rosecrans ordered Van Cleve's division at Crawfish Springs to pass behind Wood and form on his left.[1]

Meanwhile, Minty's and Wilder's horsemen held the line at Reed's and Alexander's Bridges respectively against a Rebel force of unknown but obviously large size. Throughout the late morning and afternoon, Minty's 973 troopers performed a commendable tiered withdrawal before Bushrod Johnson's division of 3,600 infantry. By 3:00 P.M., however, the Confederates had swept across Reed's Bridge, forcing Minty to withdraw down the Brotherton Road to Lee and Gordon's. To the southwest Wilder's horsemen, with their rapid-fire Spencers, held up Brig. Gen. Edward Walthall's division, inflicting over a hundred casualties before Wilder pulled out. At 5:00 P.M. Minty reported to Wood that the Rebels had crossed to the west bank of Chickamauga Creek. "Well, come along we'll drive them back to their own side," he answered with a swagger. In the dusk Wood rode ahead of Wilder's line. His bravado nearly cost him his life as Confederates in the thickets quickly fired upon him.[2]

1. *OR*, 30(1):109, 110, 605, 803. In his afteraction report Rosecrans stated that both Van Cleve's and Palmer's divisions were to march behind Wood and form on his left. The order that went out from headquarters was at variance with this statement. See ibid., 55, 110. Sometime during the night the matter was cleared up, however, for by the early morning of the nineteenth, Palmer had formed on Crittenden's left. See ibid., 249.

2. Ibid., 109, 113, 447, 466, 30(2):452, 471–72; Skinner, *Pennsylvania at Chickamauga*, 303, 309; Vale, *Minty and the Cavalry*, 226; Lawrence D. Schiller, "A Taste of Northern Steel: The Evolution of Federal Cavalry Tactics, 1861–1865," *N&S* 2 (Jan. 1999): 44–45, 80–82; *History of the Michigan Organizations at Chickamauga and Missionary Ridge*, 278; Baumgartner, *Blue Lighting*, 122–24.

Writing years later, Rosecrans stated that Bragg was clearly attempting to get between his left wing and Chattanooga and that he "had no time to waste." Throughout the afternoon of the eighteenth, however, the Ohio general fretted over Confederate activity to the south at Crawfish Springs (Polk's feint), and he did not commit until midafternoon. That night he ordered Palmer's division to leapfrog over Wood and Van Cleve, placing him on Crittenden's left. Leaving Negley's division to replace Palmer, Thomas would pass with the other divisions of the XIV Corps behind Crittenden and form to the north along the La Fayette Road. McCook's XX Corps would then close up on Negley, with Mitchell's cavalry on the right flank. Orders to begin the movement did not arrive until 5:00 P.M., and due to garbled instructions, General McCook started late. It would be a long night.[3]

Now began a series of blunders that squandered still more time on a night in which hours would be precious. At 5:00 P.M. Negley, with his division, arrived at Crawfish Springs to relieve Palmer. Palmer was not present, however, and Brigadier General Hazen and Col. Sidney Post refused to budge their brigades, not having received written orders. A frustrated Negley went in search of Thomas. He finally found him, along with an embarrassed Palmer. Rosecrans fumed as he scribbled written orders, later declaring that Hazen had held up the entire movement four hours over a technicality. With Negley finally out of the way, the XIV Corps began its march north. Long halts had to be taken in order for skirmishers to scour the woods to the front and right. At the pace of a quarter-mile an hour, could Thomas, never known for his speed, be in position by dawn?[4]

As dawn streaked over the field on September 19, Col. Dan McCook, brother to the XX Corps commander, was ecstatic. His and Colonel Mitchell's brigades from the Reserve Corps had arrived at Reed's Bridge at 11:00 P.M. the previous night. Although not finding Minty, they did pick up a few Rebel stragglers. From their interrogation McCook concluded that a Confederate brigade (Evander McNair's) had become isolated on the west bank. Hurriedly, he sent the 69th Ohio to burn Reed's

---

3. Rosecrans, "Campaign for Chattanooga," 132; *OR*, 30(1):55, 108, 109, 111–12, 248. Van Horne claimed that the slowness of the maneuver throughout the afternoon was due to caution, "though it was well known that the enemy had forces far beyond Wood's position." *Army of the Cumberland*, 1:331. I contend that the issues were not so clearly understood, nor was there any mention of the leapfrog maneuver until after Thomas arrived at Crawfish Springs. I place that time at five o'clock, Cleaves at six o'clock. *Rock of Chickamauga*, 156.

4. *OR*, 30(1):328, 336–37; Beatty, *Citizen Soldier*, 332; Rosecrans, "Mistakes by Grant," 587–88; Athearn, *Soldier in the West*, 332; John Palmer, *Personal Recollections*, 174–75; *Cincinnati Daily Gazette*, Sept. 25, 1863; *Minnesota in the Civil and Indiana Wars, 1861–1865* (St. Paul: Pioneer, 1890), 97; Frederick W. Kiel, *Thirty-Fifth Ohio* (Fort Wayne: Archer, House, 1894), 131.

Bridge, blocking the Rebels' escape. Years after the war the veterans of the 69th insisted that they completed the task; they did not. As McCook's and Mitchell's brigades were forming at 6:00 A.M., a messenger suddenly galloped up with a dispatch. Written by Rosecrans to Granger, it read: "Withdraw McCook and Mitchell if not already too late." A bewildered McCook could make no sense of it. What he did not know was that the "brigade" in his front was actually a division, and there were by now two others just like it across Chickamauga Creek at Alexander's Bridge.

As McCook and Mitchell talked, Baird's and Brannan's divisions of the XIV Corps began to arrive. It seemed that "Old Slow Trot" could move fast when needed. Colonel McCook explained his dilemma to Thomas, imploring him to override Rosecrans's order and allow him to bag his enemy brigade. The Virginian refused but, buying into the story, sent one of his own brigades, Col. John Croxton's of Brannan's division, to finish the job. McCook was livid. Encountering the young Croxton, he railed that he had "just plucked from his shoulder a star," then murmured to a staff officer that Croxton would "get the coveted prize [brigadier's star]."[5]

At 7:30 A.M. Croxton's men filed out a dirt path between the Reed's Bridge Road and Brotherton Road, thereby setting in motion an irrevocable chain of events. Cautiously forming line of battle, the troops emerged from the thick woods at Jay's Mill, where they encountered Rebels—not infantry but dismounted cavalry—a brigade of Nathan Bedford Forrest's division. The far right flank of Bragg's army had unwittingly been uncovered. The skirmishing expanded as Col. Ferdinand Van Derveer's brigade, advancing along the Reed's Bridge Road, encountered a second of Forrest's brigades. A half-hour firefight broke out in which the 35th Ohio lost sixty killed and wounded, but the Rebels were eventually driven back toward the creek.[6]

At nine o'clock a Confederate brigade, not dismounted cavalry but veteran infantry (Col. Claudius Wilson's Georgia brigade), suddenly came crashing out of the thickets from seemingly nowhere, crossed the Brotherton Road, and smashed into Croxton's right flank. More concerned about this new thrust, the colonel changed front, almost at right angles with the original line. He then sent a wry dispatch to

5. "Opened the Battle," *National Tribune*, Jan. 5, 1905; "Burning Reed's Bridge," *National Tribune*, Mar. 26, 1896; "The Part Taken by the 69th Ohio and McCook's Brigade," *National Tribune*, July 3, 1890; "Reed's Bridge: The 69th Ohio Did Burn It and Opened the Battle of Chickamauga," *National Tribune*, Dec. 10, 1914; "Burning Reed's Bridge," *National Tribune*, Dec. 10, 1914; Cozzens, *This Terrible Sound*, 122–23; OR, 30(1):66, 113, 116, 120, 121, 249, 860, 871, 30(3):743; J. T. Woods, *Steedman and His Men at Chickamauga* (Toledo: Blade Printing, 1876), 20–21. McCook's and Mitchell's brigades marched back north toward the junction of the Cleveland and Ringgold Roads. OR, 30(1):860. Dan McCook pointedly neglected to report his desire for a morning attack.

6. Shaw, *Tenth Regiment Indiana Volunteer Infantry*, 229; OR, 30(1):401, 408, 418, 428, 432, 434, 437.

Thomas asking which of the four or five brigades in his front he was supposed to capture. Brannan committed his final brigade, but it had not yet arrived when, at ten o'clock, Van Derveer was struck on his left by another enemy brigade (Matthew Ector's Texans). The Rebels advanced several lines deep on the double-quick. The bluecoats quickly formed an obtuse angle and unleashed a murderous fire, with the four Napoleon guns of Battery I, 4th U.S. Artillery, delivering double charges of canister at forty yards. Decimated, the Southerners withdrew by 10:30.[7]

Thomas, hearing the din of battle, committed Baird's First Division. The troops advanced up the Brotherton Road, Colonel Edward King's regular brigade on the left, Colonel Benjamin Scribner's on the right, and Brigadier General Starkweather's in reserve. Although Scribner's men got lost in the thickets, King's and Starkweather's veterans assisted in repulsing Wilson's and Ector's shattered brigades, which withdrew shortly after eleven o'clock. Thomas's two divisions (11,000 strong) had thus handily repulsed a like number of Rebel divisions (6,200 bayonets), backed by cavalry (1,500). Indeed, only confusion in the thickets prevented Baird's division from annihilating Wilson's Georgians.[8]

Both sides now seemed content to disengage and regroup. Baird paused, his right flank (the wayward Scribner's brigade) near Winfrey field. "They can't fight us; the bloody First [Brigade] is too much for them," laughed Col. Oscar Moore of the 33d Ohio. Within minutes, a fresh Confederate division (Brig. Gen. St. John Liddell's, thirty-six hundred strong) burst from the woods and attacked with terrible force. Although heavily outnumbered, the Rebels struck Baird's unconnected brigades successively and in flank, disintegrating the entire division, the cursing of Starkweather notwithstanding. The vaunted regulars ran pell mell for four hundred yards. As they passed through the ranks of Van Derveer's and Connell's brigades, those troops rose and unleashed a galling fire, staggering the pursuing Rebels. It was the charge of the 9th Ohio, however, that sent them reeling. The five hundred Cincinnati Germans came screaming through the thickets, the colonel swearing in two languages, chasing the grays for a quarter mile before being called back.[9]

7. *OR*, 30(1):400, 408, 416, 418, 422, 428–29; Tucker, *Chickamauga*, 130.

8. *OR*, 30(1):275, 293, 295, 297, 299–300, 304, 305; Scribner, *How Soldiers Were Made*, 143–44; Janet B. Hewett et al., eds., *Supplement to the Official Records of the Civil War*, 94 vols. (Wilmington, N.C.: Broadfoot, 1994–), 5:660. For troop-strength estimates, see *OR*, 24(3):958, 30(1):289, 308, 315, 412, 418, 427, 30(2):254. Forrest's strength estimate based upon a total strength of 3,500 less one-fourth to hold horses.

9. *OR*, 30(1):290, 293, 295, 299, 300, 309, 318–19, 324; Cozzens, *This Terrible Sound*, 143 (Colonel Moore quote), 147–48; Scribner, *How Soldiers Were Made*, 146–48; Woodworth, *Chickamauga*, 18; *Minnesota in the Civil and Indian Wars*, 98; Phisterer, *Association of Survivors, Regular Brigade*, 61; Carpenter to parents, Sept. 29, 1863, Arthur B. Carpenter Letters, Yale University, New Haven, Conn.; Henry Haymond to Father, Sept. 24, 1863, 18th U.S. File, CCNMP; S. A. Sweetser to John Mitchell, Oct. 15, 1863, John Mitchell Letters, 1st Wisconsin File, CCNMP.

* * *

Far to the south at Crawfish Springs, the sound of battle on the army's left could be clearly heard at army headquarters. The armies had obviously joined, with Thomas heavily engaged. Yet when Thomas requested Palmer's division to close up on his right, Rosecrans hesitated. He dismissed as mere rumor the mention of a sizable Confederate force at Alexander's Bridge. By midmorning he finally understood the demonstration at Crawfish Springs to be only a feint. At 10:15 A.M. Rosecrans ordered Palmer's division to Thomas, and he also directed McCook to start Johnson's and Davis's divisions in that direction. This left only two divisions at Crawfish Springs—Negley's of the XIV Corps and Sheridan's of the XX. A dispatch went to Reynolds's division, still an hour and a half from the battlefield, to press on. At eleven o'clock Crittenden, with Rosecrans's approval, committed Van Cleve's division to Thomas, leaving only Wood's division at Lee and Gordon's Mill. Four divisions, some twenty-two thousand men, were thus racing to Thomas's aid. Dressed in black pants with the legs stuffed in his boots, white vest, and dark blue coat, Rosecrans, chomping on an unlit cigar, appeared to one reporter as distant that morning. He rode rapidly north with his staff, establishing headquarters at the Widow Glenn house.[10]

Two fresh divisions arrived, both of which came under Thomas's command, but neither one of which belonged to his corps—Richard Johnson's of the XX at noon and John Palmer's of the XXI at 12:30. Johnson advanced east between the Alexander's Bridge and Brotherton Roads, with Palmer on his right along the latter. Wishing to avoid a repeat of what happened to Baird, Rosecrans ordered Palmer to advance in echelon. If the Southerners repeated their morning tactics, Palmer should be in position to meet them head on.[11]

The two divisions, 10,500 strong, advanced at an opportune time. Maj. Gen. Frank Cheatham's division of 6,000 Tennesseans, coming up from Dalton's Ford,

10. *OR*, 30(1):56, 76, 126, 487, 534–35; *New York Herald*, Sept. 27, 1863; *Cincinnati Daily Commercial*, Sept. 28, 1863; Glenn, *Chickamauga*, 139; John Sanderson Letter Diary, Sept. 19, 1863, John Sanderson Letters, OHS; Dana, *Recollections*, 111–12.

11. *OR*, 30(1):535; Cozzens, *This Terrible Sound*, 154; John Palmer, *Personal Recollections*, 176; Athearn, *Soldier in the West*, 147; Steven E. Woodworth, *A Deep Steady Thunder: The Battle of Chickamauga* (Fort Worth: Ryan Place, 1996), 39; Woodworth, crediting Rosecrans's order to advance in echelon, has stated, "Rosecrans has received little credit for his conduct of the battle of Chickamauga, but he deserves credit for this stage of the fight." *Chickamauga*, 22. Andrew Haughton points out, however, that part of the Confederate success in the morning, despite inferiority of numbers, was that their brigades advanced on an extended front with a small reserve, whereas most Federal brigades moved two regiments in front and two in reserve, thus shortening their front and making it susceptible to overlapping. *Training, Tactics, and Leadership in the Confederate Army of Tennessee* (London: Frank Cass, 2000), 124.

moved into the void directly in their path. Almost immediately the lines collided. Johnson's division, on the left, met with early success. After a forty-minute firefight, August Willich's brigade, spearheaded by the 89th Illinois, made a spectacular bayonet charge that swept the Southerners for a mile. On the right Palmer confronted the brunt of Cheatham's division. The near impenetrable thickets broke the Confederate formation apart before it even reached Palmer's right and center, and it was handily repulsed.[12]

A haphazard state of command existed by the time Reynolds's division arrived at the Poe house. Thomas vaguely instructed the division commander to march to the sound of the battle. Unaware that the Federals were winning in the thickets west of the La Fayette Road, the corps commander expressed doubt about holding his position. Reynolds's two brigades eased forward and relieved two of Palmer's, which had depleted their ammunition. Bending around the Brotherton Road, the Federal line now began to snake south down the La Fayette Road as Van Cleve's two brigades (a third remained at Lee and Gordon's) came into position at one o'clock. Samuel Beatty's brigade went clawing into the woods, striking Cheatham's far right flank and capturing a battery.[13]

Overall, the Confederate army outnumbered Rosecrans's, but the celerity with which Rosecrans fed the fight gave him the edge. This was particularly seen in the action against Cheatham, where eventually two and a half times the Tennessean's strength was thrown against him, shattering his division. By early afternoon the Federals were not just holding their own, they were winning.

Rosecrans now attempted to turn Bragg's left, toward what end is not exactly known. Either he naively believed that he faced the entire enemy army and could encircle it on the west bank or he was attempting to divide the Confederates and prevent reinforcements coming up from the south. The task went to Jefferson C. Davis, whose two-brigade division (a third brigade remained with the army's wagon train) arrived at 1:30. The problem is that Davis did not even know where the Union line ended, much less the Confederate. He thus marched his troops to the Viniard farm, where they crossed the La Fayette Road at a log schoolhouse at 2:00 P.M., unaware that a half-mile gap existed between his left and Van Cleve's right. "We were told that the enemy was in our front," recalled Carlin. "We could not see them. Trees and thick underbrush were all that could be seen by my men. But we plunged

12. OR, 30(1):535, 538–39, 543, 718, 780, 786, 792, 799, 30(2):82, 30(3):276; John Palmer, *Personal Recollections,* 176; Woodworth, *A Deep Steady Thunder,* 41.

13. OR, 30(1):440, 473, 803, 808, 811; "Statement of General J. J. Reynolds in Regard to What Occurred When He Came onto the Field near the Poe House," Joseph Reynolds File, CCNMP; Noe, *Southern Boy in Blue,* 196–98; Woodworth, *A Deep Steady Thunder,* 42. Col. Sidney Barnes's brigade of Van Cleve's division remained at Lee and Gordon's Mill. See OR, 30(1):838.

in to find without waiting to find out where the enemy's line was; that was our order—to go in."[14]

As fighting raged in the tangled forest, reducing visibility at times to twenty yards, Crittenden, who had arrived on the scene and taken command of the center, called up Col. Sidney Barnes's brigade and Wood's division from Lee and Gordon's Mill. The corps commander sent his chief of staff, Lt. Col. Lyne Starling, to Wood with a suggestion that he veer off on the Alexander's Bridge Road and take the Rebels in flank. Crittenden later lamented that he had not issued an order, but "the commanding general condemned the movement when I informed him that I suggested it to General Wood."[15]

The fighting continued to rage, with Crittenden's sector being invaded by the Confederate divisions of John Bell Hood from Virginia, Bushrod Johnson from Mississippi, and William Preston from East Tennessee. The situation became desperate at 3:30, when the Confederates swept around Davis's unprotected left. Eventually, the entire division broke and fled back across the Viniard farm. Crittenden greatly exposed himself in attempting to rally the troops. Carlin was fired on by his own men in the 21st Illinois as he attempted to halt them, and Colonel Heg fell mortally wounded while attempting to rally his brigade. Rosecrans's own headquarters came under fire. Wilder, his brigade in reserve on the edge of west Viniard field, recalled how the fleeing bluecoats "reached our works and poured over them like sheep in a panic." Wilder's Spencers, backed by Lilly's four guns belching out over two hundred rounds of canister (double shot), unleashed an unrelenting wall of flame that struck down scores and drove the Rebels back, saving the Union center.[16]

Rosecrans threw nearly everything he had into the fight. By midafternoon he had ordered Sheridan's division to leave one brigade at Lee and Gordon's Mill and race his other two to the battlefield in support of Davis. Col. Luther Bradley's Illinois brigade arrived at five o'clock, in time to assist in repulsing the Confederate attack at the Viniard field. By midafternoon the Brotherton farm had become the Union center, with the divisions of Van Cleve, Reynolds, and Palmer. The Confederates came dangerously close to breaking this line late in the afternoon but were checked by Thomas's timely reinforcement of Croxton's brigade and by four batteries (twenty guns) collected by Hazen near Poe field. There were "but about two minutes to make these dispositions before the blow came," Hazen wrote, and "for two

14. *OR*, 30(1):498, 516; Cozzens, *This Terrible Sound*, 198; Girardi and Hughes, *Memoirs of Brigadier General William Passmore Carlin*, 99.

15. *OR*, 30(1):608.

16. Ibid., 448, 467, 499, 517, 529, 533, 608, 987; Wilder quoted in Cozzens, *This Terrible Sound*, 220; Girardi and Hughes, *Memoirs of Brigadier General William Passmore Carlin*, 100; Baumgartner, *Blue Lighting*, 131–32.

or three minutes all the guns fired at point blank as rapidly as possible." An hour later Johnson's and Baird's wearied and depleted divisions on the left, which had fallen back and regrouped by order of Thomas, were struck by a fresh Confederate division (Cleburne's), with inconclusive results.[17]

Rosecrans's vague plan to turn the enemy left lost its best chance when he failed to support Crittenden's suggestion to send Wood's division down the Brotherton Road to flank the Confederates. Indeed, Crittenden started both Palmer's and Van Cleve's divisions to the battlefield on his own responsibility and before Rosecrans gave his approval. Had this not been done, it is highly possible that Thomas would have been cut off from the rest of the army, for both divisions became engaged almost immediately upon arrival. Crittenden received prior approval before starting Wood's division, but the idea came from him, not Rosecrans. The army commander exercised little control throughout the afternoon and mainly watched as his divisions, responding to the heaviest firing, disappeared one by one into near impenetrable thickets. Indeed, he pathetically relied upon the Widow Glenn to assist in fixing troop locations by listening to the din of battle, a scene that disgusted one reporter. When a captured Confederate boy was brought in and identified himself as one of Longstreet's troops, Rosecrans flew into a rage, insisting that it could not be so and frightening the lad into silence.[18]

The generals began to bicker under the stress. After supper the indelicate Palmer, in a temperamental mood, rode to army headquarters. When told he could see neither Rosecrans nor Crittenden, he indiscreetly blurted to Dana, "I have no hesitation in saying to you, Mr. Dana, that this battle has been lost because we had no supreme head to the army on the field to direct it." At some point Rosecrans could not resist pedantically lecturing Hazen for his dilatory action of the day before, stating, "You greatly detained the movements of the two corps and greatly imperiled the safety of another." According to Hazen, he spoke "in a tone and a spirit I never before listened to."[19]

Nevertheless, by the time Rosecrans telegraphed Halleck and Lincoln at 8:00 P.M., he sensed a victory. About eleven o'clock the army commander summoned his generals to a council of war, as he had done at Stones River, with ten or twelve reporting. Already the night had grown chilly, and the officers gathered around

17. *OR,* 30(1):77, 129, 133, 579; Sheridan, *Memoirs,* 1:150; James R. Furqueron, "The Best Hated Man in the Army," *N&S* 4 (Mar. 2001): 32; Woodworth, *Chickamauga,* 28–33; Woodworth, *A Deep Steady Thunder,* 52–57; *OR,* 30(1):250, 762, 768, 778, 779, 801.

18. *OR,* 30(1):987, 993, 1000; Shanks, *Personal Recollections,* 266; Atkins, *Chickamauga,* 10.

19. Shanks, *Personal Recollections,* 267; John Palmer, *Personal Recollections,* 180; Lamers, *Edge of Glory,* 334.

campfires outside. A thorough discussion of the day's battle ensued. Sheridan recalled that a somber mood prevailed, notwithstanding that the Rebel attacks had been repulsed. All present believed (from prisoner interrogation) that the Army of the Cumberland was heavily outnumbered. An exhausted Thomas dozed through much of the meeting, only occasionally opening his eyes to say, "I would strengthen the left." The conference adjourned well past midnight, McCook honoring Rosecrans's request to entertain the officers with a parting song.[20]

Thomas stated the obvious; the lifeline to Chattanooga had to be maintained. Unfortunately, the massive Crawfish Springs tent-hospital complex, with seven of the army's ten divisional hospitals, remained on the right. As the battle raged farther and farther north, the complex should have been moved back toward McFarland's Gap and in the rear of Snodgrass Hill. The six thousand or so Federal casualties included forty-five hundred wounded, the majority being sent south to Crawfish Springs.[21]

Hoping that Brig. Gen. Robert Mitchell's cavalry division, now reduced to 2,726 troopers, would move up to Glass's Mill in time to protect the vulnerable Crawfish Springs hospitals, Rosecrans abandoned Lee and Gordon's Mill and constricted his line to put most of his muscle on the left (six divisions), with McCook on the right (two divisions), and Crittenden (two divisions) in reserve. Two problems thus resulted. First, McCook, with five brigades, held the one-mile-long right; it was not enough. Davis's division was down to only fourteen hundred bayonets. Second, Thomas's position formed a large backward "C" facing the east side of Kelly field, with the divisions of Baird, Johnson, Palmer, and Reynolds. Brannan's division on his right bent parallel and west of the La Fayette Road, with Negley on his right. At 2:00 A.M. Thomas discovered that his left did not extend to the Reed's Bridge Road–La Fayette Road intersection as he thought. Rather than drawing on his own reserves, he requested, and was promised, Negley's division. McCook would have to stretch to close the gap.[22]

Even though Minty, operating on the left flank, reported all clear, Rosecrans re-

20. OR, 30(1):135, 136, 966; Dana, Recollections, 113–14; Gates P. Thurston, "Chickamauga," Southern Bivouac 6 (Dec. 1886): 409; Sheridan, Memoirs, 1:151. One source indicated that Crittenden, McCook, and Sheridan were not pleased with the meeting. W. H. Newlin, The Preacher Regiment: A History of the Seventy-Third Regiment of Illinois Infantry Volunteers (N.p.: privately printed, 1890), 228.

Thomas's postwar defenders claimed that he suggested pulling the right back to the eastern spurs of Missionary Ridge, the line thus facing south. The Union line would then resemble a shepherd's staff, with Thomas holding the crook. Van Horne, Thomas, 129. Like many of the claims made by Thomas's apologists, there is no contemporary evidence to support it. The general never claimed such in his after-action report.

21. Duncan, Medical Department, 286–95.

22. OR, 30(1):57, 69, 75, 137–38, 251, 488, 609, 952, 30(3):740.

mained nervous that the Rebels might bypass Thomas and attempt a wide flanking movement north at the Red House Bridge. Granger's three brigades were thus kept at Rossville. Meanwhile, Spears's East Tennessee brigade of the Reserve Corps arrived at Chattanooga, further augmenting the garrison.[23]

Following an uneasy night, Rosecrans held mass early on September 20. In his usual manic state, he rode off quickly, without either eating or drinking. In a dense fog and eerie silence, the general made his morning inspection of the lines. Glaring problems soon became apparent. McCook, who had wrongly posted his divisions, was ordered to move Sheridan closer to the Widow Glenn's house, with Davis's division adjusted more to the left but still in support. Sheridan thus continued to fret over the "considerable interval," actually a gaping hole, on his left. Rosecrans directed Crittenden's two divisions more to the left.[24]

The more urgent problem lay with Thomas. At 6:30 A.M. he sent a frantic dispatch to Rosecrans stating that the Confederates had already begun moving in his direction and that Negley's promised division had never arrived on his left. A Negley staff officer acknowledged the order had been received during the night, but that Negley's relief, Wood's division of the reserve, had not yet arrived. Rosecrans immediately ordered the Pennsylvanian to march to the left, with Thomas sending an aide, Capt. J. P. Willard, as a guide. The entire blunder could easily have been rectified by sending Wood's division to Thomas rather than Negley. Promptly obeying orders, Negley marched his reserve brigade, John Beatty's, forward and began withdrawing his two front-line brigades, even though their skirmishers were already engaged west of the Brotherton field. Rosecrans rode up at an opportune moment and canceled the order, admitting that he "spoke a little sharply." Negley should have sent his reserve brigade only and waited to be relieved by Wood before pulling out of line, Rosecrans declared, never addressing the obvious question of why Wood, rather than Negley, had not been sent from the outset.[25]

23. *OR,* 30(1):69, 139, 854, 858, 30(3):741. As late as 8:00 A.M. on the twentieth, Thomas fretted that the Confederate objective might be Rossville.

24. Cozzens, *This Terrible Sound,* 310; Sanderson Letter Diary, Sept. 21, 1863; *OR,* 30(1):58; Sheridan, *Memoirs,* 1:151.

25. *OR,* 30(1):69, 70, 338, 355, 1015; Athearn, *Soldier in the West,* 148. Cozzens suggested that "Thomas was thinking only of himself: he wanted Negley because he was accustomed to working with him and because he wanted to reunite his corps." *This Terrible Sound,* 312. His conclusion that "Negley had not reported because he had not been ordered to do so" does not seem to be substantiated by Captain Hough's letters. Ibid., 311. John Palmer later wrote that if the Rebels had attacked promptly at daylight, "the battle would not have lasted an hour; we would have gone to Chattanooga on the run." *Personal Recollections,* 181. Woodworth concluded, "So intense was Rosecrans's anxiety to hold his left that day, that he would refuse virtually nothing he [Thomas] asked." *A Deep Steady Thunder,* 66.

Further exacerbating the debacle, Wood apparently never received orders to relieve Negley. Captain Willard, hoping to expedite matters, rode over to Wood and asked him if he had not been directed to relieve Negley. "I am ordered to post my troops on this ridge," he answered. "Sir," pleaded Willard, "General Rosecrans promised to send one of the divisions of General Crittenden's corps to relieve General Negley that he might go to the relief of General Thomas' left." Wood did not budge. Willard reported to Rosecrans, who promptly sent his trusted aide, Captain Thoms, to order Wood forward. The general moved, but not far enough, occupying the place of Negley's now departed reserve brigade.

When Rosecrans found him at 9:00 A.M. a third of a mile from the battle line, Wood stated that he understood that he was to support Negley, not relieve him. The army commander erupted. "What is the meaning of this, sir?" he shouted. "You have disobeyed my specific orders. By your damnable negligence you are endangering the safety of the entire army, and, by God, I will not tolerate it. Move your division at once, as I have instructed, or the consequences will not be pleasant for yourself." Wood, who turned white with rage, was speechless. When he finally got his troops on the front line, Negley discovered that Wood's two brigades were not enough to fill the space being vacated. Negley, stricken for the past eight days with severe diarrhea and bowel inflammation and not wishing to be reprimanded again, hesitated to send his last brigade off, thus hopelessly dividing his division. The complete breakdown of command ultimately rested with Rosecrans, who appeared to be losing control.[26]

The army commander now unleashed his well-known temper on Alexander McCook. Riding to the south, he found the right wing stretched dangerously thin with a gap on his left. Rosecrans, in the presence of Dana, severely rebuked the corps commander. It was his parting words that proved most stinging: "It is indispensable to close to the left; we cannot afford to have another Stones River," a not-so-veiled reference to McCook's rout in that battle.[27]

As Rosecrans repositioned Van Cleve's division and a brigade of Wood's, Thomas grew increasingly jittery about his dangling left. He, of course, could have dispatched his two reserve brigades, Willich's and Grose's, toward the Reed's Bridge Road. He still would have held ten regiments in reserve. Instead, when the van of

---

26. OR, 30(1):355–56, 1014–15; Cist, Army of the Cumberland, 219; Edwin V. Westrate, Those Fated Generals (New York: Knight, 1936), 222–23; Rosecrans, "Chattanooga Campaign," National Tribune, Mar. 6, 1882; Welsh, Medical Histories, 240. In postwar years Rosecrans said that his actual words were, "By no means, you are to replace Negley's division on the line, and I want you to do it as soon as the Lord will let you." See Cozzens, This Terrible Sound, 314.

27. Dana, Recollections, 114–15; Cist, Army of the Cumberland, 202; Rosecrans, "Chattanooga Campaign."

Negley's division, John Beatty's brigade, arrived, he immediately sent it forward a half mile to the McDonald house despite the brigadier's protest.[28]

About 9:30 the Rebels at long last attacked, having given Rosecrans a marvelous gift of three and a half hours of undisturbed daylight to strengthen his lines. The onslaught came precisely where Rosecrans and Thomas had suspected. The Confederates of John Breckinridge's division emerged from the woods with a vengeance, easily brushing aside Beatty's isolated brigade at the McDonald house. Having overlapped the Yankee flank, two Rebel brigades wheeled south astride the La Fayette Road.[29]

While no Federal troops were positioned to check Breckinridge's two brigades, the Rebels could not advance until the left of the Kelly field salient had been crushed. A near suicidal assault by Breckinridge's third brigade (Benjamin Helm's) butted against Scribner's brigade, supported by enfilade fire from King's regulars. In less than an hour, the Federals mowed down 30 percent of Helm's fourteen hundred men, with some of the Rebels throwing down their arms and jumping over the barricades for safety. Cleburne's division later attacked the southernmost part of the salient, losing over thirteen hundred of forty-seven hundred men. Hazen's brigade, one of several that opposed Cleburne, lost a mere thirteen men; the slight barricades had made the difference. Even if the Confederate attacks had been coordinated, it would have been extremely difficult to break such a compact, well-manned line backed by four batteries.[30]

Not realizing that Brannan's division had already been committed on the right of the salient, Thomas ordered it to the left. Brannan rode over to Reynolds, his senior, and showed him the order. Since both divisions were now already slightly engaged, Reynolds insisted that he could not pull his troops out of line. "Oh!" said Brannan, "I am not going [to], but who will take the responsibility if there should be a hereafter to this apparent disobedience of orders, for that is what it amounts to?" "Of course, I will take the responsibility," replied Reynolds. "You send word to Thomas what the state of affairs is here and we need have no anxiety as to any 'hereafter' to your not moving now." Brannan did, however, send his reserve brigade, Van Derveer's to Thomas.[31]

---

28. *OR,* 30(1):489, 803; Van Horne, *Army of the Cumberland,* 1:344; Beatty, *Citizen Soldier,* 334–35. See Cozzens, *This Terrible Sound,* 322 (map). Counting Grose's and Willich's brigades, Thomas held eighteen regiments in reserve. This amounted to over 50 percent of his force in the Kelly field sector. Rather than dip into them, however, he made repeated calls for more reinforcements.

29. *OR,* 30(1):368; Van Horne, *Army of the Cumberland,* 1:345; Woodworth, *A Deep Steady Thunder,* 69.

30. Woodworth, *Chickamauga,* 48–56; Woodworth, *A Deep Steady Thunder,* 69–70; William C. Davis, *Breckinridge: Statesman, Soldier, Symbol* (Baton Rouge: Louisiana State University Press, 1974), 374; Scribner, *How Soldiers Were Made,* 155; Woodworth, *Six Armies in Tennessee,* 111.

31. Reynolds, "An Incident of the Second Day at Chickamauga," Joseph Reynolds File, CCNMP.

At 10:45, before reinforcements had arrived, Breckinridge's two brigades at the McDonald house began their march south down the La Fayette Road, Daniel Adams's brigade to the west and Marcellus Stovall's to the east. Stovall's 897 Rebels struck the northern portion of Thomas's salient, stampeding the regulars and Col. Joseph Dodge's brigades, the last firing only a single volley before breaking, as well as Grose's brigade, which marched into northern Kelly field in support. It proved the most pathetic Union showing of the day. The Confederates penetrated four hundred yards into the rear of the salient.[32]

Reinforcements were on the way—Van Derveer's brigade, the 15th and 49th Ohio of Willich's brigade, and the 5th Kentucky from Col. William Berry's (Philemon Baldwin's former) brigade, advancing east of the road, and Col. Timothy Stanley's brigade of Negley's division, backed by the remnants of Beatty's brigade, west of the road. As Van Derveer's troops shoved through their fleeing comrades running south, the 9th Ohio, without orders, made one of their now famed bayonet charges. "Don't let the 9th Ohio charge alone!" yelled a sergeant of the 2d Minnesota, prompting that regiment to join in. Adams's brigade was likewise checked to the west.[33]

Although the situation had been contained within a half hour, a dismayed Thomas, perhaps understandably given the disastrous results should the La Fayette Road be cut, continued his requests for more reinforcements. The Virginian now had thirteen brigades in or near the Kelly field salient to oppose six. To be sure, Thomas could not have known comparative strengths, and indeed, more Confederates were on the way—Walker's Reserve Corps with five brigades. Even though Thomas should have been able to contain them with his present force, a rattled Rosecrans, spurred by Thomas's solicitations, ordered two more divisions, Van Cleve's and Sheridan's, to his support. The result was not only an organizational mess and the confused movement of many units, but also the further weakening of the center and right. Only seven infantry brigades extended south of the salient along the La Fayette Road, with Wilder's horsemen covering the flank.[34]

According to the council of war the previous evening, Brannan's division of the

32. Cozzens, This Terrible Sound, 367–68.

33. Woodworth, A Deep Steady Thunder, 71–73; sergeant quoted in Cozzens, This Terrible Sound, 335; Cope, Fifteenth Ohio, 312; Grebner, "We Were the Ninth," 143; Kiene, Civil War Diary, 18.

34. Steven Woodworth is also critical of Thomas's performance, calling him "obsessed." Given the redeployment of so many brigades to the left, "Thomas's success was not too surprising." Six Armies in Tennessee, 107, 113. Albert Castel is more sympathetic to Thomas and Rosecrans at this point. Since from all indications this appeared to be the main Confederate attack, and since Rosecrans had uncommitted troops, he had little choice but to support Thomas's request, he asserts. Castel, phone conversation with author, Sept. 14, 2000.

XIV Corps was not to be placed in line but act as a reserve for Thomas. The Virginian now sent his nephew-aide, Capt. Sanford Kellogg, with a second call to bring up the division, unaware that one of its brigades was already on the way and that Brannan remained in line with his other two. (It is probable that Brannan's 10:00 A.M. message informing Thomas of his disposition had not arrived by the time Kellogg was dispatched.) Brannan rode over to Reynolds. "I am again ordered to the left with my command. Do you think you can maintain your position without me? Kellogg is here and says the call is urgent." Reynolds replied: "Well, perhaps Thomas needs you more than I do, and I believe I can hold my own here. So go along and good luck to you." Before the division moved out, however, Thomas, apparently receiving Brannan's earlier message that he was in line, canceled the order, a fact not immediately known to Kellogg. A misunderstanding of disastrous proportions was in the making.[35]

Kellogg reported Thomas's initial request to Rosecrans at 10:30. "Yes; tell him [Thomas] to dispose of Brannan, who has only one brigade [two] in line and to hold his position, and we will reinforce him, if need be, with all the right," the general replied. Ignoring chain of command, as he frequently had done at Stones River, Rosecrans turned to Major Bond and said: "If Brannan goes out, Wood must fill his place. Write him that the commanding general directs him to close to the left on Reynolds and support him." Bond's 10:45 dispatch read, "The general commanding directs that you close upon Reynolds as fast as possible and support him." The major has been criticized for leaving out the words "to the left" and thus writing an order that contradicted itself. Wood could not "close upon" (a lateral maneuver) and "support" (move behind) at the same time. It must be stated, however, that Rosecrans admitted using both terms in his spoken order. Additionally, he did not read the written order before it was sent.[36]

As a backup, Rosecrans instructed Lieutenant Colonel Starling to deliver the same message to Wood orally, and Starling clearly understood the words "to the left." Since there was no firing on Reynolds's front and there seemed no need for support, Starling looked puzzled. Garfield thus explained that when Brannan moved out of line, Wood would fill the vacancy. Unfortunately, neither staff officer challenged the mutually exclusive terms "close upon" and "support." When Wood received the spoken order and told Starling that Brannan was still in line and that no vacancy existed, the officer answered: "Then there is no order, for that was the object of it." Starling then reported the conversation to Rosecrans.[37]

35. Reynolds, "Incident of the Second Day"; *OR*, 30(1):979; Cozzens, *This Terrible Sound*, 360–61.

36. Rosecrans, "Campaign for Chattanooga," 133; *OR*, 30(1):59, 635. Henry Cist branded Bond as inexperienced, while Emerson Opdycke labeled Bond's order a "blunder." Cist, *Army of the Cumberland*, 220; Opdycke, "Notes on the Chickamauga Campaign," in *B&L*, 3:670.

37. *OR*, 30(1):983–84.

Wood had several options. He could have followed Starling's advice (put in writing if necessary) and ignore the order. Or he could have sent Starling the one-third mile back to Rosecrans to ask for clarification. He could have split the difference and begun a minimal withdrawal of troops while sending Starling for confirmation and giving Davis a chance to close up on his right. He could also have sent Starling to Brannan to ask why he was still in line. Yet Wood had been severely dressed down earlier that morning for not obeying orders and moving fast enough. Since the message appeared urgent, and since he did not wish to be on the receiving end of Rosecrans's temper again, he chose to do none of the above.

He had yet another option, however, and one strangely overlooked by historians. Since McCook was reportedly beside him, he could have deferred to the corps commander's guidance as the senior officer (as Brannan had earlier done with Reynolds). Wood instead told McCook that he would pull his two brigades and Barnes's brigade of Van Cleve's division out of line, pass in the rear of Brannan, and form behind Reynolds. According to one source, Wood said, "Mack, I'll move out by the right flank and rear to hide my move from the enemy." McCook answered, "No, Tom, just march out by the left flank, and I'll order Jeff [Davis] to close your gap." McCook later denied this, saying that, "much to my surprise," Wood pulled out of line. Either Wood or McCook (probably the latter) was lying to cover himself. Crittenden, only a hundred yards in the rear, was also notified of Wood's plans.[38]

Regardless, Wood began pulling his division out of line on the double-quick, even though his skirmishers were sharply engaged, thus leaving a sizable gap in the Union line. Perhaps he had another motive in mind. Upon his return to Rosecrans, the orderly who delivered the dispatch noted that "General Wood on receipt of the order remarked that he 'was glad the order was in writing, as it was a good thing to have for future reference.'" He then carefully placed it in his notebook. Some said that he also waved it before his staff and declared, "Gentlemen, I hold the fatal order of the day in my hand and would not part with it for five thousand dollars." Blinded by hatred, Wood interpreted the order literally and began pulling three brigades out of line to fill a gap that did not exist, thus creating an actual gap.[39]

38. Ibid., 490, 635, 944, 984; William J. Richards, "Rosecrans and the Chickamauga Campaign," in *MOLLUS, Indiana* (reprint, Wilmington, N.C.: Broadfoot, 1993), 475. Rosecrans declared that if there was no interval to close, it was Wood's "plain duty as a division commander" to report the fact. *OR*, 30(1):1017. Col. Smith Atkins of Wilder's brigade later stated that he warned McCook of a "heavy column" of the enemy in his front but that he refused to listen. Tucker, *Chickamauga*, 290.

39. Alexander D. Bache to Rosecrans, Jan. 12, 1864, William S. Rosecrans Papers, UCLA; Cist, *Army of the Cumberland*, 220; Cozzens, *This Terrible Sound*, 363; *OR*, 30(1):941. For yet another and even more damning version of Wood's comments, see Westrate, *Those Fated Generals*, 224. Among other things, Wood is quoted as saying savagely: "I shall obey my orders. General Rosecrans will never have another opportunity to speak to me as he did this morning. I have my order here—in writing; and I couldn't think of disobeying an order in writing—not when it comes from General Rosecrans." Glenn Tucker

In attempting to fix blame, historians have overlooked the obvious. Rosecrans had lost control of his army. He and Thomas were clearly overfeeding the left, thus setting up inevitable gaps. Had Rosecrans's orders been carried through, Thomas would have had every division in the army except Brannan's, and one brigade each of Van Cleve's, Wood's, and Davis's, seven brigades in all. It was precisely what Bragg had hoped for. At eleven o'clock every Union division on the right was in motion—Wood marching behind Brannan, Davis moving up to fill the gap, and Sheridan double-quicking to reinforce Thomas. McCook was in no position to respond quickly. Had he or Crittenden stopped Wood's fatal move, a gap would not have existed. Had Rosecrans personally gone to Wood, a gap would not have existed. But a six-hundred-yard gap did exist; disaster loomed.[40]

Attempting to fill the void left by Wood, Davis's division began sliding north. His lead brigade had filed behind the vacated wood-rail breastworks when, at 11:10, a stunning event occurred. Longstreet launched a massive twenty-three-thousand-man assault force, three of his six divisions marching down the Brotherton Road directly toward the gap now being filled. Davis never stood a chance—"it was a continuous line of battle nearly surrounding me." His fourteen hundred men were almost effortlessly swept away, as was Wood's trailing brigade and the right of Brannan's division. Colonel Croxton's brigade, backed by Battery C, 1st Ohio Light Artillery, momentarily held by facing south and fighting with all they had ("We mowed them down in windrows," wrote a cannoneer), but it too eventually broke under the gray tidal wave. By 11:30 Maj. Caleb Bates, a McCook aide, returned from Wilder's brigade on the flank. In horror he saw the Federal line "broken and falling back fast."[41]

Chaos reigned at army headquarters, four hundred yards southwest of the Dyer house. A thunderous din of battle and steady flow of fugitives gave grim evidence that something had gone terribly wrong. "Our men are giving way yonder!" cried an aide. Rosecrans could not believe his eyes and instinctively crossed himself. Capts. Horace Porter and James P. Drouillard futilely attempted to check some of the stragglers; one threatened to bayonet Porter, though the young officer refused to budge. Shells began exploding in the vicinity, and James St. Clair Morton, stand-

---

supported Wood, while William Lamers, not surprisingly, supported Rosecrans. Albert Castel believed that Rosecrans would have won the battle "if not for a petty-minded subordinate who put personal resentment ahead of military duty." Tucker, *Chickamauga*, 255–56; Lamers, *Edge of Glory*, 344–45; Castel, "Why the North Won and the South Lost," *Civil War Times Illustrated* 39 (May 2000): 60.

40. Lamers, *Edge of Glory*, 345; Woodworth, *Six Armies in Tennessee*, 103.

41. *OR*, 30(1):402, 417, 423–26, 499–500, 516, 517, 522, 525, 532, 534, 657, 664, 667, 673, 933, 952; Sherman Hendricks, "Chickamauga: The Part Taken in the Great Battle by Battery C, 1st Ohio L.A.," *National Tribune*, July 2, 1891; Girardi and Hughes, *Memoirs of Brigadier General William Passmore Carlin*, 103.

ing next to Rosecrans, suddenly had his coat torn by a bullet. Rosecrans and his staff hurriedly mounted and escaped behind a hill.[42]

Only two options remained to check the onslaught. Maj. John Mendenhall had earlier collected Van Cleve's three batteries (sixteen guns) along the western edge of Dyer field since the thickly wooded terrain had prevented their use. Three additional batteries now gathered, bringing the number of guns to twenty-nine. When the breakthrough occurred, Crittenden uttered, "We will go to the batteries and we will yet drive these fellows back and hold them in check." For half an hour artillery blasted out a wall of flame, keeping five of Longstreet's brigades at bay. It seemed as though Mendenhall was on the verge of pulling off another Stones River miracle. But with no infantry support save the seventy or so men collected by Van Cleve, horses began to fall by the dozen to small-arms fire. When Lt. Harry Cushing, commanding the regular-army battery, told Crittenden he was preparing to limber up, the corps commander snapped, "You are not to retire at all, but hold your position." To stay meant annihilation, however, and eventually the artillerists made their escape, leaving behind a staggering seventeen pieces.[43]

The fate of the Union right now rested with Sheridan's forty-three hundred men. Forty minutes earlier (10:30) Rosecrans had ordered that division to the left. Fortunately, as matters developed, Sheridan did not receive the order until 10:55 and had barely started his march when Longstreet struck. McCook, who had been a nonentity in the battle thus far, now gave his first and only order; it proved a bad one. From a relatively good position on a hillside, he ordered Bernard Laiboldt's brigade to charge the six-thousand-man assault column (Thomas Hindman's division) sweeping past the Glenn-Kelly Road. Meeting Rosecrans, McCook naively uttered that Laiboldt "would soon set the matter to rights." Instead, the colonel was predictably overwhelmed. Sheridan's other two brigades fared no better. Lytle shouted, "Boys, if we whip them today, we will eat our Christmas dinner at home." A bullet shortly afterward struck him, leaving him mortally wounded. Sheridan's wrecked division joined the swarming masses fleeing toward the Dry Valley Road, ignoring Rosecrans's pleas to "Form a line! Don't fall back! Make a stand here! Hold this ridge for General Sheridan's sake." Captain Gates P. Thurston encountered the swearing Sheridan; "General Phil was furious," he recalled.[44]

---

42. Dana, *Recollections*, 115–16; *OR*, 30(1):979; Porter to sister, Oct. 3, 1863, Horace Porter Letters, LC; Sanderson Letter Diary, Sept. 21, 1863.

43. *OR*, 30(1):610–11, 622–23, 667, 975–76, 984, 991, 1002; Woodworth, *Chickamauga*, 70–71; Cozzens, *This Terrible Sound*, 401.

44. *OR*, 30(1):937–38, 939, 940–41, 942, 943, 945, 968; Lytle quoted in Cozzens, *This Terrible Sound*, 386; Austin E. Stebbins, "A Daring Movement," *National Tribune*, Oct. 19, 1899; Tucker, *Chickamauga*, 293–95; Sheridan, *Memoirs*, 1:152; Gates P. Thurston, "The Crisis at Chickamauga," in *B&L*, 3:665.

By noon Rosecrans, Crittenden, and McCook had all gotten swept up in the wreckage of the army clogging the Dry Valley Road. Col. John Parkhurst, the army's provost, had gathered up a thousand stragglers and, seeing Crittenden, asked him to take command of them; the general rode on. Rosecrans intended to rejoin Thomas but found the way blocked. Along with Garfield, Bond, and a few others of his staff, the dazed army commander made for McFarland's Gap and Rossville. At the latter he encountered Negley's rabble, who claimed the division had been "knocked all to pieces." Since Negley was supposed to be on Thomas's left, Rosecrans suspected that the entire army had been defeated. He sent the chief of staff south to communicate with the Virginian, if alive, while he headed for Chattanooga. It would be the commanding general's final mistake of the day.[45]

With Mendenhall's guns gone, Evander Law's Confederate brigade attempted to exploit the breakthrough by marching north up the Dyer field, where they could advance in the rear of Thomas's salient. Checking their advance was Charles Harker's brigade, Wood by his side, at the intersection of the Glenn-Kelly and Vittetoe Roads. The 64th and 125th Ohio raked the Confederate flank, while Harker boldly counterattacked with the 3d Kentucky and 65th Ohio, sending the Rebels fleeing; thereafter Colonel Opdycke's 125th would carry the sobriquet "Opdycke's Tigers." The success proved momentary as additional enemy brigades sent Harker's men reeling back a half mile to Snodgrass Hill.[46]

The Federals used the Wood-Harker stand to consolidate their position on Horseshoe Ridge. There a rag-tag line of four thousand men formed about 12:45 P.M., composed of some of Thomas's reserve units from the Kelly field sector and refugees from the center, all under Brannan's command. Harker's battered brigade took up a new position on a spur of the ridge in Snodgrass field. Thomas, electrifying the troops with his presence, established his afternoon headquarters not far from

---

Captain Thurston found one of Wilder's regiments, the 39th Indiana Mounted Infantry, and ordered it to attack dismounted with their carbines, striking the Rebel flank, then only 300–400 yards distant. They succeeded in capturing 200 prisoners before being forced to flee, "with the rebels in full sight trying to overtake us." "Statement of General G. P. Thurston in Relation to the Battle of Chickamauga," File 55, Box 1, Ser. 8, CCNMP.

45. *OR*, 30(1):59–60, 611, 984–85; Buell, *Warrior Generals*, 266–67; Cist, *Army of the Cumberland*, 212, 224–25; Rosecrans, "Campaign for Chattanooga," 132. Cox, *Military Reminiscences*, 2:10; Swedberg, *Three Years with the 92d Illinois*, 125. Rosecrans did send a dispatch to Sidney Post's brigade at Stevens's Gap to hurriedly get the commissary train into Chattanooga. Concerning Rosecrans's ride back to Chattanooga, Cozzens concluded that he was "teetering on the edge of nervous collapse." *This Terrible Sound*, 405.

46. *OR*, 30(1):635–37, 640, 694, 704; Cozzens, *This Terrible Sound*, 408–10; Charles Clark, *Opdycke's Tigers, 125th O.V.I., a History of the Regiment and the Campaigns and Battles of the Army of the Cumberland* (Columbus, Ohio: Spahr and Glenn, 1895), 107–10.

the Snodgrass house. "This hill must be held and I trust you to do it," he told Harker. "We will hold it or die here," came the reply. When Brannan sent a courier with news that his ammunition was running low, Thomas calmly replied, "Tell General Brannan that his is my old [First] division and that they will hold their position."[47]

Forming in the half-mile-wide gap between Wood and Brannan was Negley, with sixteen guns and Col. William Sirwell's brigade minus the 21st Ohio (seven companies armed with Colt's revolving rifles), sent to bolster Brannan's right. Negley did not stay long. Having been warned (wrongly) of Rebel cavalry in his rear, he became nervous for the safety of his guns. He sent an aide, Lt. William H. Moody, for reinforcements. In time Moody returned with Rosecrans's response: "It is too late. I cannot help him." Negley decided to pull out, taking not only his guns and the balance of Sirwell's brigade but also a hodgepodge of units that joined the column—perhaps fifteen hundred badly needed infantrymen. Wood and Brannan would never forgive him.[48]

Beginning at one o'clock, the Confederates made repeated and savage assaults against Horseshoe Ridge, but the Federals stood firm. The anchor proved to be Thomas, the "Rock of Chickamauga" as he would henceforth be known. His controlled poise and determination to hold the high ground kept a defeat from turning into a disaster. A departing staff officer, fearful that the Horseshoe Ridge line would not hold, asked, "General, after delivering your order, where shall I report to you?" "Here, Sir, here," he snapped. Thomas's magnificent afternoon performance barely made up for his mistakes of the morning.[49]

47. OR, 30(1):370, 403, 424–25, 638, 701, 704–5, 708, 830–31, 1008; Beatty, Citizen Soldier, 340; Van Horne, Army of the Cumberland, 1:352; Cozzens, This Terrible Sound, 422; McKinney, Education in Violence, 251.

48. OR, 30(1):330, 331, 338, 339, 360–61, 410, 1012, 1013, 1016, 1018, 1023, 1026, 1030, 1041, 1045, 1047, 1050; Silas S. Canfield, History of the Twenty-First Regiment Ohio Volunteer Infantry (Toledo: Vrooman, Anderson, and Bateman, 1893), 142–43; Athearn, Soldier in the West, 148–49. The artillery under Negley's direction included two six-gun batteries, G and M, 1st Ohio Light Artillery, and a section each of Bridge's Illinois battery and Battery I, 4th U.S. Artillery.

49. Thomas quoted in Cozzens, This Terrible Sound, 453. Thomas's mistakes were threefold: First, his repeated calls for help caused Rosecrans to overcommit to the left, helping set up a disaster in the center; second, the failure to use his own reserves more effectively; third, his early morning request for Negley's division, which he knew to be in line, rather than accepting a reserve division to extend his left. Had Thomas not held, it would have been difficult for the exhausted Confederates to break through a defensive line at McFarland's Gap. They clearly would have mauled the Federal rear, however, and ended up capturing many more soldiers and guns than they subsequently did.

Thomas Connelly argued that the Federal stand at Horseshoe Ridge succeeded not only due to Federal tenacity but also to Rebel tactical ineptitude. "Obviously, Longstreet could have controlled McFarland's Gap even if he had not carried the Snodgrass Hill position. By 1 P.M., the Federal right was in

By 1:45 the Rebels had come dangerously close to sweeping around the 21st Ohio, the far right regiment on the ridge. At this juncture, dust swirls could be seen coming from the Federal rear. Thomas strained to see if it was friend or foe. A staff officer returned with the glad news that it was Gordon Granger with Steedman's thirty-nine-hundred-man division. The former was short-tempered, crude, and at times a sadist, the latter an addict to drink, women, cursing, and cards. Whatever their faults, they were a welcome sight, and Thomas stoically greeted Granger, "I am very glad to see you, General."[50]

Granger had in fact not been ordered to Thomas, Rosecrans seemingly forgetting about the one-division reserve at Rossville. Granger could clearly hear the battle rolling south, however, and at noon, in a classic example of battlefield initiative, he left Dan McCook's brigade and started to the battlefield with Steedman's division. He easily brushed aside Forrest's cavalry at the Cloud house—"They are nothing but rag-a-muffin cavalry," he contemptuously barked. Thomas committed the fresh troops on Brannan's right at the opportune moment. Granger asked Steedman if he could do anything for him in the event of his death. "Wall, general, I don't know of what you can do for me except, by Gawd, to see that those damned reporters spell my name with two ees." In a fierce twenty-minute conflict, in which Steedman seized the colors of a regiment and personally led the charge, the Federals beat back Bushrod Johnson's division, losing perhaps six hundred men in the process. Thomas conceded to Granger, "Fifteen minutes more, General, might have been too late." Atop Snodgrass Hill Colonel Opdycke yelled, "I am willing to die for my country right here and I hope you will all be with me." He later boasted to his wife that only one man from his 125th Ohio fled.[51]

As the fighting raged along the Horseshoe Ridge–Snodgrass Hill line, the divisions of Baird, Johnson, Palmer, and Reynolds held fast in the Kelly field sector, with Palmer sending Hazen's brigade to reinforce Thomas. Rumors circulated that Rosecrans and all the corps commanders had been killed or captured. An unnamed division commander approached Palmer about the possibility of pulling out. "I had

flight on the Dry Valley Road. Had a strong Confederate force pursued, McFarland's Gap could have been seized, and the only remaining line of retreat for the remnants of Rosecrans' army would have entailed moving northward in the face of Bragg's army to reach Rossville Gap." *Autumn of Glory,* 224.

50. Shanks, *Personal Recollections,* 68–69, 268, 271, 276, 279; Cozzens, *This Terrible Sound,* 440; Woodworth, *Chickamauga,* 77–78; Joseph S. Fullerton, "Reinforcing Thomas at Chickamauga," in *B&L,* 3:667.

51. *OR,* 30(1):854, 860, 871; Fullerton, "Reinforcing Thomas," 666–67; Woodworth, *A Deep Steady Thunder,* 94–95; Cist, *Army of the Cumberland,* 451–52; Cozzens, *This Terrible Sound,* 441–42, 451–52; Mary Ann Steedman Wanatick, "Major General James Blair Steedman" (master's thesis, University of Toledo, 1988), 22; "Gen. Steedman: His Brilliant Services at Chickamauga," *National Tribune,* Aug. 4, 1887; Opdycke to wife, Sept. 28, 1863, Folder 9, Box 2, Emerson Opdycke Letters, OHS.

rather be killed, and be damned, than be damned by the country for leaving the battlefield under such circumstances," he grimly answered. Capt. William R. Lowe, a staff officer, also claimed that Baird was approached about a withdrawal. "No, we have repulsed the enemy in two attacks; he will probably try it again, and then the jig will be up with him," he replied.[52]

About four o'clock Garfield, accompanied by a few orderlies and staff officers, arrived at Thomas's Snodgrass Hill headquarters. Back at Rossville, Rosecrans had ordered his chief of staff there while he went to Chattanooga to direct operations; the reverse should have happened. Garfield brought little news to Thomas beyond confirming the now self-evident fact that a significant part of the army had been routed. Being apprised of the situation, Garfield sent Rosecrans a dispatch stating that the men were fighting better than he had ever seen and that he hoped that Thomas could hold until night. "Granger thinks we can defeat them badly tomorrow if all our forces come in. I think you had better come to Rossville tonight and bring ammunition," he concluded. Barely had the courier departed when, at 4:30, a telegraph from Rosecrans was handed to Thomas ordering his withdrawal. The Virginian vacillated, preferring to hold until night. Yet casualties had been terrific, Brig. Gen. Walter Whitaker having been shot, along with every member of his staff save one, and 950 of his 2,800 men killed or wounded. Even with the additional ninety-five thousand rounds brought by Granger, his men had less than ten rounds each. Thomas had no choice.[53]

An intense, but as matters developed moot, conference took place at that time at the McFarland house with Generals Davis, Sheridan, Negley, and staff officers Capt. Gates Thurston and Lieutenant Colonel Ducat. Thurston had just returned from a meeting with Thomas, and he had an order for the generals to return and assist the beleaguered corps commander. Davis, full of fight, did an about face with the 10th Ohio and marched back down the Dry Valley Road. Sheridan, arguing that the Rebel artillery now dominated the road, marched to Rossville and then doubled back to the battlefield by the most secure route. Thomas had begun his withdrawal by the time both Davis and Sheridan arrived. Thomas's defenders would unjustly take Sheridan to task for deserting the field.[54]

52. John Palmer, *Personal Recollections*, 183–84; John A. Baird Jr., "'For Gallant and Meritorious Service': Major General Absolam Baird," *Civil War Times Illustrated* 15 (June 1976): 45–46.

53. James R. Gilmore, "Garfield's Ride at Chickamauga," *McClure's Magazine* 5 (1895): 358; Cist, *Army of the Cumberland*, 225; OR, 30(1):253, 254, 856, 860; Rosecrans, "Campaign for Chattanooga," 134; *Cincinnati Enquirer*, Oct. 3, 1863; Cozzens, *This Terrible Sound*, 476–77.

54. OR, 30(1):331, 339, 375, 500–501, 505, 581, 1022–23, 1036; H. V. Boynton, "The Chickamauga Campaign," *MASS*, 7:366; Morris, *Sheridan*, 135; Thurston, "Chickamauga," 415. Negley, apparently feeling nervous about quitting the field, attempted to go back, but he could not get through. Therefore, he returned with Sheridan.

Thomas began a withdrawal by divisions at 5:00 P.M., beginning with the Kelly field sector. Reynolds's division, a strong line of skirmishers being left in the breastworks, pulled out first. A fierce charge by Willich's brigade easily brushed aside Liddell's division, blocking the La Fayette Road, and earned it the name "Iron Brigade of the Army of the Cumberland." Palmer withdrew next toward McFarland's Gap, with Cruft's brigade marching out as if on dress parade. By the time Johnson's and Baird's divisions began their withdrawal, the Confederates renewed their assault. Johnson's division escaped relatively intact, but Baird's men got caught in a melee, Scribner's brigade being particularly chewed up, losing over four hundred men prisoners.[55]

As Thomas departed he placed Granger in charge, but Granger himself left shortly thereafter. By 6:00 P.M. Steedman's troops began their withdrawal under heavy pressure. Hazen disengaged at seven o'clock, followed by Harker. Incredibly, the 89th Ohio and 22d Michigan were ordered back in line by a staff officer, as was the valiant 21st Ohio by an officer wearing large, colored glasses that appeared to be goggles—probably Col. H. V. Boynton. Over six hundred men subsequently fell prisoner. Granger failed to inform Brannan of Steedman's withdrawal, and as the Rebels appeared on his right and rear, Brannan re-fused his right, beating them back. The fighting then sputtered out as darkness descended.[56]

Charles Dana's 4:00 P.M. telegram to Washington told of a disastrous rout. "Chickamauga is as fatal a name in our history as Bull Run," he related. Federal casualties had not been less than twenty thousand, with all of the wounded left behind, and many cannon were lost. Four hours later, as news of Thomas's stand began to trickle in, Dana tempered his story. Only two divisions (Davis's and Sheridan's) had been routed, with two others (Van Cleve's and Negley's) only temporarily disordered. Thomas held firm with the balance of the army. "Some gentlemen of Rosecrans' staff say Chickamauga is not very much worse than was Murfreesboro," he concluded, adding that Davis and Sheridan had rallied and marched back to the battlefield.[57]

To be sure, the last message did not convey the magnitude of what had befallen the army, but there was a note of truth in it. Probably 55 percent of the army had

55. *OR*, 30(1):171, 279, 288, 289, 312–13, 475, 535–36, 544–45, 556, 715; Cozzens, *This Terrible Sound*, 492–93; Boynton, "Chickamauga Campaign," 363; John Palmer, *Personal Recollections*, 184–85; Van Horne, *Army of the Cumberland*, 1:355–56; Scribner, *How Soldiers Were Made*, 159–60.

56. Boynton, "Chickamauga Campaign," 365–66; Cozzens, This *Terrible Sound*, 486–87, 612–13 n. 33; *OR*, 30(1):172, 856, 860; Tucker, *Chickamauga*, 368–69; William G. Robertson, *The Battle of Chickamauga* (Philadelphia: Eastern National Park and Monument Association, 1995), 50.

57. *OR*, 30(1):192–94.

held, even amid disaster. If Wood's division had not left a gap in the line, it is very possible that Longstreet's attack would have been beaten back. Even if the center and right had been pierced, a secondary line at Horseshoe Ridge could have held, making the battle a tactical draw, similar to Stones River. Even with all of Rosecrans's blunders, the battle was salvageable.

But Wood did open a gap and Rosecrans, back in Chattanooga, did not immediately know about Thomas's valiant stand. A staff officer found the broken army commander at midnight. He looked "worn and exhausted and was laboring under excitement," noted Captain Hough. "He heard my statement but in doing so showed want under adverse circumstances. He was evidently crushed under the weight of his disaster." As the captain departed, he looked back to see the general on his knees before his priest, weeping and seeking solace.[58]

Back at Rossville all was chaos as Thomas's wearied troops straggled into town. "At this hour of the night (eleven to twelve o'clock) the army is simply a mob. There appears to be neither organization nor discipline," noted John Beatty. "The various commands are mixed up in what seems to be inextricable confusion. Were a division of the enemy to pounce down upon us between this and morning, I fear the Army of the Cumberland would be blotted out." Captain Hough concurred: "I truly believe that a charge of one regiment of cavalry suddenly made would have routed the whole mass, but thanks to General Thomas they were kept too busily occupied for any such movement." James Chapin of the 39th Indiana felt "almost heart sick to see the army in such a state."[59]

Even by 1863 standards, the North was sobered by the carnage. The army counted a staggering 16,170 casualties (1,957 killed, 9,765 wounded, and 4,757 missing), the XIV Corps bearing the brunt (6,114). Included among the total were 1,002 officers. It was a high cost, to be sure, especially considering that Rosecrans had barely over 58,000 effectives of all arms on the field, yet compared to Stones River, where his 41,400 effectives suffered losses of nearly 13,000, not inordinately so. Fortunately, the Crawfish Springs hospitals, for the most part, were able to evacuate unmolested, leaving behind perhaps 600 wounded. The loss in ordnance proved high, though not irreplaceable for the Northern industrial complex: thirty-six field guns; twenty caissons; 8,008 rifled muskets; 442 carbines, Colt's rifles, and Spencer rifles; 410 revolvers; and 5,834 sets of accouterments. Expended or lost ammunition included a huge 2,801,232 small-arms rounds and 9,875 artillery rounds.[60]

58. Athearn, Soldier in the West, 150–52.

59. Beatty, Citizen Soldier, 345; Athearn, Soldier in the West, 345; Reynolds and Hikele, "With the Army of the Cumberland in the Chickamauga Campaign," 236 (entry for Sept. 20, 1863).

60. OR, 30(1):169–79, 233; Cincinnati Enquirer, Oct. 20, 1863; Duncan, Medical Department, 298–300.

Everything seemed to be in Bragg's favor. Thomas hung on by a thread at Rossville. The number of Rebels, according to Dana's army headquarters sources, topped seventy thousand—twice that of the Federals. Rosecrans, who had plunged into defeatism, was uncertain if Chattanooga could be held. September 20–21, 1863, would be the darkest night in the army's history.

18

The Removal
Purge and Reorganization

THE ARMY OF THE Cumberland remained in severe straits throughout late September, brought about more by strategic bungling than by Rebel force. During October, Rosecrans's erratic behavior—confident one moment, hopeless the next—coupled with quarreling and reprisals within the officer corps, led to the army's second internal crisis, this one more serious than the Buell crisis of the previous year. The result would be the purge or de facto demotion of one army, three corps, and three division commanders, affecting six major generals and one brigadier.

Matters remained grim on September 21. Although subject to being turned via Mc-Farland Gap, the Rossville position was never truly tested. Based upon faulty intelligence and minor skirmishing, the advance line withdrew to Chattanooga that night. Historians would blame Rosecrans for this impulsive order, but the recommendation had come from Thomas. A reporter claimed that as Rosecrans began drafting the withdrawal order, Granger snapped: "Oh, that's all nonsense, general! Send Thomas an order to retire. He knows what he is about as well as you do." Rosecrans tore up the paper and silently obeyed. Realizing the mistake by 9:00 P.M., Rosecrans attempted to remand the order, but the retreat had already begun.[1]

By 7:00 A.M. the next morning, the army had taken up a perimeter position, with McCook on the right, Thomas in the center, and Crittenden on the left. The infantry began hastily digging rude earthworks, which stretched from Citico Creek to the Tennessee River near the mouth of Chattanooga Creek, a distance of six miles. Mitchell's cavalry, meanwhile, rounded up hundreds of runaways who had gotten to the north bank of the Tennessee River. Rosecrans estimated his effective infantry and artillery at thirty-five thousand (unknown to him, only four thousand fewer than the Confederates), but Dana feared less. Ten days' rations remained, which

---

1. *OR*, 30(1):150–52, 155–58, 254–55; Wiley Sword, *Mountains Touched with Fire: Chattanooga Besieged, 1863* (New York: St. Martin's, 1995), 38–39. Sword harshly criticized Rosecrans for the decision and credited Thomas for seeing what others could not.

could be stretched to twenty, as well as sufficient ammunition for two days' fighting. Fortunately, a fifty-wagon reserve ammunition train arrived from Bridgeport. Brigadier General Johnson later wrote that a council of war was held to determine whether or not to hold the city or occupy the bluffs of the north bank. Some counseled holding, others not. Dana telegraphed that the army commander contemplated the evacuation of the city, the only move that would truly turn the late battle from a defeat into a disaster, but he decided to stay in Chattanooga, vowing to fight it out.[2]

Despite Rosecrans's newfound determination, Garfield's letter to his wife on the morning of September 23 reflected continued gloom at army headquarters. "Burnside will not reach us for six days," he lamented. "We must therefore save ourselves if [be] saved at all. I expect the battle will be renewed this morning and with fury. If calamity befal[l]s us you may be sure we shall sell ourselves as dearly as possible. . . . The country will triumph if we do not." By early afternoon the enemy could be seen occupying Missionary Ridge and investing the outer perimeter, the trenches at places being only yards apart. An Illinois soldier revealed in a letter, "We are expecting a fourth of July today in the way of fire works." By late afternoon, however, the anticipated attack still had not come. The men nonetheless continued "digging away as though our lives depended upon it."[3]

That day Rosecrans made his most egregious postbattle error. Fearing his lone brigade atop Lookout Mountain, Brigadier General Spears's East Tennesseans, would become isolated and captured, he ordered its withdrawal at night, Granger's disapproval to the contrary. Although correct in his assessment, Rosecrans should have been willing to give the Tennesseans the post of honor and, if need be, sacrifice the brigade, which had rations through October 10. If so, some of his subsequent logistical crisis could have been averted. The problem was that the Memphis and Charleston Railroad, the south bank Bridgeport wagon road, and the main channel of the Tennessee River all passed at the base of the mountain. If the Confederates possessed the summit, they could (and promptly did) go for the jugular by planting batteries, effectively shutting down the gorge. Officials estimated that two hundred tons of supplies could come by river alone, the daily equivalent of twenty-six railroad cars. The river gauge remained so low throughout late September that the army's single supply ship could not navigate, but several flats were available, and the wagon trail through Lookout Valley was far preferable to the one on the north

---

2. *OR*, 30(1):158, 196–97, 198, 255, 30(2):25, 30(3):805, 30(4):12–13; William F. Smith, "An Historical Sketch of the Military Operations around Chattanooga," *MASS*, 8:155.

3. Williams, *Wild Life of the Army*, 297; *OR*, 30(1):198; Richard Johnson, "Battle above the Clouds," *National Tribune*, Jan. 30, 1896; Gates, *Rough Side of War*, 88.

bank. Dana fumed that Rosecrans, who could be as obstinate as he could be irreso-
lute, "pettishly rejected all arguments."[4]

It soon became evident that the Confederates could not get in the city, and the
Federals dared not leave it—stalemate. "The rebels seem to show no disposition to
make an attack on us and we are beginning to apprehend the troubles and uncom-
fortable necessities of a long siege," diarist Marcus Woodcock noted on September
27. Two days later Colonel Sherman, writing to his father, remarked, "Everything
looked blue for a while, but from that the men have recovered, and every day shows
the works rising under their hands." Nonetheless, he admitted, Chickamauga had
"partially taken the conceit out of the Army of the Cumberland."[5]

"Old Rosy" attempted to bolster morale by personally visiting the regiments and
speaking with the troops. Everywhere the men gathered about him and cheered; he
shined. "He was everywhere greeted with cheers," related Sanderson. Typically, he
told the joke of the troops reserving their fire until the Rebels closed their range so
that they could have what the Irishman had in his pocket—a hole. His forced buoy-
ancy proved transparent to some. "When he reached my brigade, he seemed almost
overcome with emotion and leaned forward from his horse as if intending to em-
brace me," observed Colonel Carlin. "I felt as deeply as he did the disappointment
that then filled his heart, and for him personally I felt the deepest sympathy."[6]

General Palmer had problems of his own. He had emerged unscathed from
Chickamauga, but a sniper's bullet struck him in the left hip while he inspected the
lines one day. He did not appear to be in any initial pain, and the incident even

4. Sword, *Mountains Touched with Fire*, 41; *OR*, 30(1):214–15, 30(3):890, 30(4):65, 101–2; Thomas L.
Livermore, "The Siege and Relief of Chattanooga," *MASS*, 8:294, 297; Dana, *Recollections*, 118. Brigadier
General William F. Smith concluded that it would have been impossible to hold Lookout Mountain in
the long term. To hold the plateau and mountain pass at Trenton, 8,000 men would have been required.
The road leading to the mountain from Chattanooga was two miles south of the city's defense line.
Smith, "Operations around Chattanooga," 156. A small steamboat was being prepared at Bridgeport but
would not be operational until October 21. For a description, see Grant, *Memoirs*, 411. Livermore figured
that Rosecrans's six-mile line averaged 6,300 men per mile, compared to the Confederates' 5,996 men
per each of their seven miles. He claimed that Rosecrans could have stretched his line to cover Lookout
Mountain and still have more men per mile than the Confederates at Vicksburg, who held out for six
weeks of siege. "Siege and Relief of Chattanooga," 285–86.

5. Noe, *Southern Boy in Blue*, 220; Aldrich, *Quest for a Star*, 63.

6. Noe, *Southern Boy in Blue*, 220; John Sanderson Letter Diary, Sept. 22, 1863, John Sanderson Let-
ters, OHS; Richard Mann, comp., "The Journal of First Lieutenant Robert S. Dilworth, Company I, 21st
Ohio Volunteer Infantry," Sept. 24, 1863, typescript, OHS; Gates, *Rough Side of War*, 89; Girardi and
Hughes, *Memoirs of Brigadier General William Passmore Carlin*, 108–9. Rosecrans continued his erratic
work hours, rarely going to bed before 2:00 or 3:00 A.M. He got up at 10:00 A.M., ate breakfast at eleven
o'clock or noon, then worked until 3:00 or 4:00 P.M., when he had lunch. After that he typically rode
out of town on inspection tours. Sanderson Letter Diary, Sept. 27, 1863.

incurred laughter from fellow officers. On October 2 he optimistically wrote his wife that he would be on his horse in a few days; he miscalculated. The pain increased for a week, and he could only sleep on one side. Palmer eventually had to take a brief leave of absence.[7]

The army required a huge resupply of quartermaster stores, including forty-five thousand coats and seventy-five thousand pairs of shoes, only a fraction of which could be obtained. On September 28 a shipment that originated in Louisville passed through Nashville on the way to the army. It included twenty-four thousand shirts, five thousand blankets, twenty-six thousand pairs of socks, and five thousand axes. The Army of the Cumberland also required 768 wagons, only 135 of which were immediately available in Nashville. The quartermaster shops in that city pledged to repair forty to fifty vehicles per week from a stock of 400 unserviceable wagons.[8]

Matters soon worsened. On September 30 word arrived at army headquarters of a large enemy cavalry force under Wheeler, estimated at ten thousand (actually about five thousand), that had crossed upriver near Washington. Rosecrans immediately did as he should have, that is, telegraph Burnside to close up on his left flank. Predictably, the Department of the Ohio commander failed him. Realizing the vulnerability of his supply route in the Sequatchie Valley, Rosecrans ordered Crook's cavalry division (Minty's and Long's brigades comprising two thousand sabers and the Chicago Board of Trade Battery) and Wilder's brigade (reduced by one-quarter due to poor horses) into the valley. Additionally, McCook proceeded with three regiments from the Bridgeport vicinity.

The gray horsemen were one step ahead. On October 1 fifteen hundred men split off from the main column and descended into the valley, swooping down on thirty-four wagons south of Dunlap the next day. Proceeding on to Anderson's Cross-roads, they encountered the commissary and baggage trains of Baird's and Sheridan's divisions (Negley's train made it over Walden's Ridge just in time) and the ammunition train of the XIV Corps. Easily scattering the 21st Kentucky and the small cavalry guard, the Rebels torched 350 army wagons, plus 40 sutlers' wagons, and carried away eighteen hundred mules, though in the two-day rear-guard fighting that ensued, eight hundred of the beasts were retaken. Smoldering wagons and the carcasses of dead animals stretched for miles. The next day the other enemy column struck McMinnville, capturing the 4th Tennessee Infantry (U.S.) and sacking the town.[9]

7. John Palmer, *Personal Recollections*, 197–98; George Palmer, *Conscientious Turncoat*, 197–98.

8. Lenette Sengel Taylor, "'The Supply for Tomorrow Must Not Fail': A Union Quartermaster's Civil War" (Ph.D. diss., Kent State University, 2001), 256–57, 260.

9. Starr, *Union Cavalry*, 3:292–300; *OR*, 30(1):205, 30(2):723, 30(4):23–24, 38, 44–45, 59, 67–68, 102. The Union cavalry got its revenge at Farmington, west of Shelbyville, on October 7. Wheeler's command was defeated, much of it captured, and the balance chased back into northern Alabama.

Rosecrans unleashed a salvo at Burnside: "I know that your failure to close your troops down to our left has cost 500 wagons loaded with essentials, and the post of McMinnville, and Heaven only knows where the mischief will end. I presume the Louisville & Nashville road and all your trains and communication to Kentucky are aimed at, but possibly my cavalry may stop it by the pursuit in which I hoped part of yours would join, while the remainder watched the river between us. If you don't unite with us soon, you will be responsible for another catastrophe, I fear." There would be no reply.[10]

Afterward, conditions rapidly deteriorated. Rations were reduced to three-quarters, though some troops had already been on half rations for several days. All unnecessary horses and mules, including one-third of the artillery horses, moved to Bridgeport. Brig. Gen. William F. "Baldy" Smith, the army's new chief engineer, as talented as he was openly opinionated, arrived from the East and, upon examining affairs, unsuccessfully attempted to convince Rosecrans that the army simply could not exist unless the river was opened. Convinced that there was "no use in arguing the question with a positive man," Smith went to work on the fortifications.[11]

The seventy-five hundred wounded in the city had to be removed. Some three thousand walking wounded, including some malingerers, reached Bridgeport on foot. Within a few days, steamers arrived at Kelly's Ford, ten miles below the city, and the more seriously wounded were taken to Bridgeport. By the end of October, fifteen hundred sick and wounded still remained in Chattanooga. A hospital established on Stringer's Ridge helped accommodate them.[12]

With the Confederates continuing an annoying, though largely ineffective, shelling from Lookout Mountain, the only supply routes (or escape routes, if it came to that) remaining were Haley's Trace, which hugged the river at the northern tip of Raccoon Mountain, and the sixty-mile-long Bridgeport wagon road that intersected at Anderson's Crossroads, the very one that had been recently raided. To prevent further incursions a garrison force of three regiments and an artillery section, eleven hundred men, was placed at the crossroads and fortified. Crews went to work improving the nearly impassable road over Walden's Ridge, the eastern descent of which proved especially treacherous. "It was a rickety, insecure, makeshift of a road and was so narrow that only in places could two teams pass each other," described an officer. Since the road could tolerate only one-way traffic, a new roundabout outbound road had to be built for the returning empty wagons.[13]

Both of the army's flanks remained vulnerable. An escaped slave who had been

10. OR, 30(1):210, 30(4):114, 231.

11. OR, 30(4):36, 64, 102; Herbert M. Schiller, ed., Autobiography of Major General William F. Smith, 1861–1864 (Dayton: Morningside, 1990), 72.

12. Duncan, Medical Department, 301, 306; OR, 31(1):244–45.

13. OR, 30(4):85, 86; James Lee McDonough, Chattanooga—A Death Grip on the Confederacy (Knoxville: University of Tennessee Press, 1984), 47–48; Gates, Rough Side of War, 106–7.

with Forrest overheard the Southern general say that he would soon undertake a raid into Middle Tennessee. Granger had a mere eleven hundred troops of his Reserve Corps, thinly stretched from Murfreesboro to Stevenson, to defend the region; only 115 men guarded the vital eleven-hundred-foot Cowan tunnel. Bragg could also move against Bridgeport and Stevenson (held by a 2,800-man brigade) and interpose himself between Chattanooga and Nashville.[14]

One person who clearly realized the army's dangerous predicament was Dana, who, though vilified by officers and modern historians for his not-so-veiled clandestine messages to Washington, usually represented the voice of reason (but admittedly prejudiced and occasionally bent toward exaggeration). Although convinced that Chattanooga could not be taken and that the Rebels had been equally, if not more, damaged at Chickamauga, Dana warned authorities that the clock was ticking. Heavy and immediate reinforcements had to be sent if the town was to be held. As for Rosecrans, Dana reported that he was a broken, indecisive man who pathetically clung to useless officers such as McCook, Crittenden, Stanley, and Negley. Someone in Washington paid attention.[15]

Just past midnight of September 21, Lincoln hastened to the telegraph office in the War Department, a short walk from the White House, to wire Rosecrans words of encouragement: "Be of good cheer," and, "We have unabated confidence in you." At dawn the president entered John Hay's bedroom and spoke with candor. "Well, Rosecrans has been whipped. I have feared it for several days. I believe I feel trouble in the air before it comes. Rosecrans says we have met with a serious disaster—extent not ascertained. Burnside, instead of obeying orders which were given him on the fourteenth, and going to Rosecrans, has gone upon a foolish affair to Jonesboro, to capture a party of guerrillas."[16]

The next day, not having heard from Rosecrans in thirty-six hours, Lincoln again shuffled over to the telegraph office. "Please relieve my anxiety as to position and condition of your army up to the latest moment," he pleaded. When a response came, it was not what he wanted to hear. "General Burnside will be too late to help us. We are about 30,000 brave and determined men; but our fate is in the hands of God, in whom I hope." An earlier message received by Halleck appeared more encouraging—the disaster was "not as great as anticipated," and "if re-enforcements come up soon everything will come out right."[17]

Stanton had made up his mind: Rosecrans had to go. On Wednesday night, Sep-

14. *OR*, 30(3):816, 832.
15. *OR*, 30(1):197–98, 199, 204.
16. Ibid., 146; Hay, *Letters*, 2:92.
17. Bates, *Lincoln in the Telegraph Office*, 163; *OR*, 30(1):160–61.

tember 23, a dispatch clicked over the wire at the telegraph office detailing the reasons for failure at Chickamauga. "I know the reasons well enough. Rosecrans ran away from his fighting men and did not stop for 13 miles," the secretary of war blurted. A moment later he added: "No, they need not shuffle it off on McCook. He is not much of a soldier. I was never in favor of him for a Major Genl. But he is not accountable for this business. He & Crittenden both made pretty good time away from the fight to Chattanooga, but Rosecrans beat them both."[18]

The secretary was not alone. Earlier in the day Lincoln had read Rosecrans's dispatch to Secretary of State William Seward and Secretary of the Navy Gideon Welles. "The president has clearly lost confidence [in Rosecrans]," Welles concluded. Seward believed that the general should be relieved, though the navy secretary questioned if there was anyone suitable who would be the equal of Thomas. Attorney General Montgomery Blair and Secretary of the Treasury Chase continued to back Rosecrans, the last blaming Halleck for "doing nothing" while the Rebels concentrated, but cabinet support for the army commander clearly waned.[19]

Late that evening, after Lincoln had retired, the president was abruptly awakened by Hay; Stanton wished to see him at the War Department. It did not sound good; never before had Stanton awakened him. Present at the impromptu conference were Stanton, Halleck, Chase, Seward, and Peter H. Watson and James A. Hardie, both of the War Department. The secretary of war began by asking Halleck how long it would take Burnside to get to Chattanooga. He calculated that twelve thousand men could arrive in eight days, twenty thousand in ten. "After Burnside begins to arrive the pinch will be over," Lincoln commented. Stanton then made a startling proposal—to send thirty thousand troops from the Army of the Potomac. "[Meade's] great numbers where they are, are useless. In five days 30,000 could be sent to Rosecrans." Lincoln, taken aback, caustically answered, "I will bet that if the order is given tonight, the troops could not get to Washington in five days." The secretary wanted to try this—if not thirty thousand, at least twenty thousand. Halleck remained skeptical, stating that it would take forty days to move the troops west, but Chase and Seward backed Stanton. Daniel C. McCallum, superintendent of military railroads, was summoned and asked his opinion. After scribbling some figures, he concluded the troops could arrive in seven days. "Good! I told you so," exclaimed Stanton. "Go ahead; begin now." Orders would soon be cut for the transfer of the XI and XII Corps to Tennessee.[20]

18. Dennett, *Lincoln and the Civil War*, 93.

19. Gideon Welles, *Diary of Gideon Welles*, 3 vols. (Boston: Houghton Mifflin, 1911), 1:447; Document "B," William S. Rosecrans Papers, UCLA.

20. Dennett, *Lincoln and the Civil War*, 93; Donald, *Inside Lincoln's Cabinet*, 201–3; Pickenpaugh, *Rescue by Rail*, 5–7. Rosecrans received word of the reinforcement on September 24. *OR*, 31(1):812–13. In response to Stanton's dispatch of September 23, Brigadier General Boyle in Louisville replied the next day that the Louisville and Nashville could transport 3,000–4,000 troops per day. *OR*, 29(1):147, 149.

Meanwhile, Lincoln sent clear orders to Burnside to hasten to Chattanooga without a moment's delay. "Am sending now every man that can be spared to aid Rosecrans," the Ohio department commander replied, but nothing happened. Lincoln resorted to useless nagging. "I telegraphed him fifteen times to [reinforce Rosecrans], and the President [likewise] three or four times," Halleck noted. The real outrage regarding Burnside is that he was not promptly relieved of command. The dilatory general insisted that the reinforcement of Rosecrans would mean the evacuation of East Tennessee. Eventually, Lincoln became convinced that Bragg would pin Rosecrans down and go after Burnside, and thus he allowed the Army of the Ohio to remain at Knoxville.[21]

The supply situation deteriorated on October 7, when Rebel sharpshooters, hiding in the woods and among the rocks on the northern end of Raccoon Mountain, suddenly opened fire on the engineer party repairing Haley's Trace, dropping five men and a dozen mules. The next day a wagon train came under fire at Little Suck Creek, leaving five men and a score of mules dead or wounded. Rosecrans sent seventy of his own sharpshooters with Spencers and a 12-pounder Napoleon to dislodge the marksmen, but to no avail. With Haley's Trace dominated by sniper fire for four miles, nothing could be done but close it down. This left only the torturous road over Walden's Ridge as the Federals' only operational supply line into Chattanooga.[22]

By October 1 the newspapers claimed that William T. Sherman's relief column from Mississippi had arrived at Chattanooga. In truth, the three divisions of the XV Corps and one of the XVII, seventeen thousand troops in all, stretched from Corinth to south of Memphis, with the most optimistic arrival date being the thirteenth. The list of annoyances included a Mississippi River so low that locals declared it a record, a shortage of fuel, damage to the Memphis and Charleston Railroad, and a Confederate force composed of Loring's infantry division and four cavalry brigades moving toward Corinth in an apparent effort to make a dash at the track and interrupt the movement.[23]

Meanwhile, the transfer of the eastern troops, under Maj. Gen. Joseph Hooker, proceeded on schedule. Taking a crazy-quilt network of railroads through Maryland, West Virginia, Ohio, Indiana, Kentucky, and Tennessee, the twenty-three thousand troops and seven batteries completed the 1,159-mile journey in eight days, most of them arriving within the seven days promised by McCallum. The 570 wag-

21. *OR*, 30(1):146, 155, 30(3):904–5; Woodworth, *Six Armies in Tennessee*, 136; Basler, *Collected Works of Abraham Lincoln*, 6:481, 510–11.

22. Sword, *Mountains Touched with Fire*, 116–18; Livermore, "Siege and Relief of Chattanooga," 287, 291, 294, 296–97.

23. *OR*, 30(4):3, 4, 5, 29, 30, 50, 52, 73, 77, 98, 99; John Sanderson Letter Diary, Sept. 27, 1863, John Sanderson Letters, OHS.

ons, 150 ambulances, and three thousand horses and mules took longer. On October 3 Hooker established his headquarters at Stevenson, Alabama. To his chagrin he was ordered to stop his troops along the railroad. He had barely enough rations to feed his own army, but Chattanooga could not accommodate more troops until secure communications could be reestablished.[24]

Although two small, temporary trestle bridges for wagon traffic initially spanned the Tennessee River, high water swept one away, and the other was removed to save the lumber. Supplies crossed by means of a flatboat and a repaired steamer, the *Paint Rock*. Meanwhile, a battalion of Michigan engineers went to work preparing pontoons. Utilizing an old engine that had been found, a sawmill was placed in operation, cutting timber found in town and logs obtained from across the river and floated downstream. Couriers on horseback brought in supplies of nails, and cotton served as caulking material. By mid-October one pontoon bridge had been constructed, with a second being prepared.[25]

Rosecrans later claimed that he had a plan to extradite the army; indeed, it was the same idea ultimately used by his successor—the opening of the "Cracker Line" via Brown's Ferry. Rosecrans did have a plan, but it was not nearly so creative. He desired to slowly move Hooker's corps into Lookout Valley, opening up river traffic as they advanced. He soon canceled the operation, but it most likely would not have worked anyway. The Confederates could simply have moved in force against Hooker's infantry, with the immobile Army of the Cumberland unable to assist their comrades. Rosecrans also toyed with repairing the Jasper Railroad spur along the north bank. He planned to use the pontoon train then under construction at the mouth of Chattanooga Creek, not at Brown's Ferry, the clear idea being to communicate with Hooker as he advanced into Lookout Valley. The span would have soon been made untenable by Confederate artillery atop Lookout Mountain. Rosecrans also discussed the possibility of retaking Lookout Mountain, which would have taken weeks to implement, at a time when his supplies had dwindled to days. In sum, the general had no viable plan.[26]

24. Pickenpaugh, *Rescue by Rail*, 73, 77, 84, 95, 101, 110–11, 121, 130, 142; Woodworth, *Six Armies in Tennessee*, 137–38; OR, 31(1):684.

25. Smith, "Operations around Chattanooga," 162–63, 180.

26. Ibid., 162, 169, 177–82; Schiller, *Autobiography of Major General William F. Smith*, 75 n. 39; Rosecrans, "Mistakes of Grant," 594, 597; William G. Le Duc, "The Little Steamboat That Opened the 'Cracker Line,'" in *B&L*, 3:676. Henry V. Boynton, an engineer on Rosecrans's staff and eventual superintendent of the Chickamauga-Chattanooga National Military Park, gave Rosecrans credit for the Brown's Ferry idea, stating that the location had been known by the general. William F. Smith angrily insisted that Rosecrans was oblivious to its importance and that he conceived the idea. All of the evidence supports Smith.

* * *

Rain poured, at times unrelentingly, throughout the first two weeks in October, adding a gloominess to the mountain surroundings. The trenches filled with a foot and a half of water, with no means of draining except bailing. Even more serious was the condition of the Bridgeport Road, which degenerated into a ribbon of mud, slowing the shipment of supplies to a trickle. Exhausted mules were mired belly deep in mud, and no whipping would induce them to move. The Sequatchie River became so swollen that the returning wagons got stranded between Walden's Ridge and the river, five hundred teams stacking up with no forage. By the sixteenth returning wagons had to be double teamed to get over the mountain. Two days later Dana telegraphed, "Our condition and prospects grow worse and worse." At that time a one-way trip required eight days. The army could not hold out another week. If a supply line was quickly reopened, he revealed, the army might get off with the loss of a staggering twelve thousand animals.[27]

Morale plummeted as the suffering became immense. Described Colonel Sherman: "The present ration issued officers and men alike is a half pound of hard bread, a quarter ration of sugar, a quarter ration coffee, and a full ration of salted fresh beef—only about a third [of the] ration allowed by law. It is piteous to see the men half fed and half clothed, with keen appetites and no way to satisfy the cravings of the stomach. Officers are no better fed." The men working on the fortifications frequently yelled out "Crackers!" as officers walked past. An Indiana diarist noted, "The rations I drew today were one cracker and a half, one spoonful of coffee, and a little piece of meat for two days." Writing to his wife on October 24, Capt. Daniel O'Leary of the 15th Kentucky concluded: "This state of affairs cannot last much longer. If we do not succeed in opening rail communication we will either have to suffer or evacuate."[28]

Rosecrans planned to bring Hooker's corps forward, gain the passes of Raccoon Mountain, and march past Shellmound and Wauhatchie to within five miles of Lookout Mountain. Even though the river was now navigable, the single transport boat under construction at Bridgeport had not been completed. Too, the rain that raised the river gauge transformed the south-bank wagon road into impassable mud. Since Hooker's transportation had not yet arrived, Rosecrans had no choice but to continue waiting.[29]

27. *OR*, 30(1):214, 216, 217, 218, 219, 220. The number of lost horses apparently did not exceed 10,000. See *OR*, 31(1):29.

28. Aldrich, *Quest for a Star*, 68; *OR*, 30(1):167–68; Peter Cozzens, *The Shipwreck of Their Hopes: The Battles for Chattanooga* (Urbana: University of Illinois Press, 1994), 22; Daniel O'Leary to wife, Oct. 24, 1863, 15th Kentucky File, KMNMP.

29. *OR*, 30(1):216, 218, 30(4):413; Schiller, *Autobiography of Major General William F. Smith*, 73.

* * *

The largest battle in the West had been fought, leaving four divisions of the Army of the Cumberland stampeded. Recriminations were not long in coming, the initial targets being Alexander McCook and Thomas L. Crittenden. Both corps commanders had quit the field and fled to Chattanooga, creating intense animosity on the part of many of their officers—Palmer, Sheridan, Johnson, Hazen, Wood, and Davis among them. "Old Gut" McCook mustered little sympathy, his corps now having been routed at Perryville, Stones River, and Chickamauga. While Rosecrans made one of his stump speeches to the troops, a soldier asked if McCook would be retained. "Yes," came the answer. "Then the right will be licked again," the soldier shouted. Because of his amicable personality, there was less enmity against Crittenden, but Dana pointed out that the Kentuckian paid little attention to detail and never rode his lines.[30]

News correspondent Henry Villard called upon McCook the evening of October 9 and found Crittenden with him. The reporter observed both to be in a "bitter and depressed state of mind," irritated at calls for their removal and wishing to tell their side of the story. McCook pointed to the 10:30 A.M. dispatch of September 20 ordering him to report to army headquarters. Incredibly ignoring the army disaster that occurred in the meantime, he felt "complete justification" for following Rosecrans to Chattanooga. Crittenden's equally weak excuse claimed that he had no command and no orders and therefore felt "duty bound" to report to the army commander in Chattanooga. Even as they talked, Nashville newspapers three days old arrived, detailing a September 28 War Department order relieving both men of command and directing them to report to Indianapolis for a court of inquiry. They departed the next day after issuing pathetic farewell addresses. Both officers blamed reporters, McCook bitterly referring to the "news scribblers" who had defamed his troops. The generals would eventually be exonerated, but their military careers were finished.[31]

Colonel Opdycke, who had stood firm on Snodgrass Hill, expressed good riddance to both. "McCook is more to blame than Crittenden, because he has always failed, and he left his troops before Crittenden. Then, too, he is full of the loftiest pretensions." As for Crittenden, he "has just enough sense to keep still, say nothing, and do little. His troops have made him." One of those soldiers, however, Kentuckian Marcus Woodcock, felt "truly sorry that Gen. Crittenden was about to leave for I had ever considered him a brave and efficient officer." There was more involved. "We feared that if this [inquiry] mania did sweep over us that we would lose 'Rosy'

---

30. *OR*, 30(1):201–2, 204; Dana, *Recollections*, 122–24.

31. Villard, *Memoirs*, 2:186–89; Andrews, *North Reports the Civil War*, 470. The Kentucky legislature, for what it was worth, promptly passed a resolution of support for native son Crittenden. *OR*, 31(1):18–19.

in the operation and 'who could succeed him?' was the question that always fol-
lowed." After McCook departed, "many dark hints were whispered about the camp
that Gen. Rosecrans would come in for his share of censure."[32]

Next in the purge came James Negley, whom Wood and Brannan bitterly de-
nounced for leaving them stranded on Horseshoe Ridge, the former labeling him a
"damned poltroon." John Beatty took supper with Negley on the afternoon of Octo-
ber 4 and found him utterly whipped. Rosecrans dismissed the charges of miscon-
duct but sent Negley home on a thirty-day medical leave in the hopes that a court
of inquiry would clear his name. On his last night with the army, the Pennsylvanian
had a few officers over for drinks; some got drunk. He was eventually exonerated,
with the court denouncing Wood's baseless allegations, but like McCook and Crit-
tenden, Negley's career was over. "Poor Negley too was in all the newspapers. He
could not stand fire at Chickamauga. Lost his presence of mind and the battlefield
lost his presence. He has gone home in disgrace," summarized Palmer to his wife.
Thomas later expressed his disappointment to Captain Hough. "Negley had been
such a reliable man before, and always had such a good Division, and kept it so well
in hand, that [I] could not understand how he could have failed [me] on that day."[33]

The September 28 order relieving Crittenden and McCook also announced the
merger of the XX and XXI Corps into the new IV Corps, to be commanded by
Gordon Granger. The order, first seen in Chattanooga on October 5 in a Nashville
paper, resulted in a total restructuring of virtually every division and brigade. Six
divisions became three, and twelve brigades (including the regular brigade) became
six "demi-brigades," an awkward invention of Granger. Steedman's division of the
reserve was also divided, one brigade going to the IV Corps and the other to the
XIV Corps, the infantry thus being evenly divided, with twenty thousand men in
each corps. The new structure, though necessitated because of so many skeleton
regiments, was universally despised, officers and men alike believing it to be a pun-
ishment for Chickamauga. "It is bad to break up a brigade, of so old and well tryed
[sic] troops. We were sorry to part with our old commanders. We have been to-
gether so long, and have shared the hardships," a member of the 34th Illinois com-
mented. On a practical level, dozens of regiments now had to move camp. Also,
several batteries, essentially without horses, were sent back to Nashville and placed
in the artillery reserve.[34]

32. Opdycke to wife, Oct. 14, 1863, Folder 9, Box 2, Emerson Opdycke Papers, OHS; Noe, *Southern
Boy in Blue,* 225–26. See also Morse, *Diaries and Letters of Bliss Morse,* 86–87.

33. Beatty, *Citizen Soldier,* 349; Villard, *Memoirs,* 2:191–92; *OR,* 30(1):207, 1018, 1005–53; Mann, "Jour-
nal of First Lieutenant Robert S. Dilworth," 18; Athearn, *Soldier in the West,* 155; *New York Herald,* Oct.
24, 1863.

34. *OR,* 30(1):211, 30(4):209–13, 31(1):684; Dana, *Recollections,* 126; Sheridan, *Memoirs,* 1:162; *New York
Tribune,* Oct. 24, 1863; Morse, *Diaries and Letters of Bliss Morse,* 89; DeWayne Kellogg Diary, Oct. 17, 1863,
34th Illinois File, CCNMP.

The new structure left an excess of four division commanders. Negley accounted for one slot, leaving three. Horatio Van Cleve was the first to go, due to partial blindness, infirmity, and complaints from his fellow officers of confusion of mind. He was appointed to the post of Murfreesboro. "To assign him to the command of that place retired him virtually from command. Poor old fellow he is too old to be in the field," Brigadier General Johnson remarked to his wife. Baldy Smith talked John Brannan into accepting the position of army artillery chief, a good move for the newly organized long arm, the batteries at long last being placed at the division level. As army chief of staff, James Garfield was now out and Joseph Reynolds in, representing a marked improvement.[35]

The late battle had reduced the number of brigade commanders by four—two, Colonels Baldwin and King, being killed, and two, Brigadier General Lytle and Colonel Heg, mortally wounded. A few others, being superseded by seniors, went back to their regiments, a disgruntled Colonel Scriber among them. The new consolidation left most brigades with from six to nine regiments, typically averaging two thousand to twenty-two hundred troops. Colonel Sherman disgustedly concluded, "Ohio and the regular officers run this army, and there is not much chance for volunteer officers of other states getting any advancements."[36]

The administration might well have removed Rosecrans from command in late September but for the upcoming gubernatorial and congressional races, especially in Ohio. There the Republican candidate, John Brough, faced the "King of the Copperheads," the vehemently antiwar Democrat Clement Vallandigham. Only months earlier Rosecrans, by Lincoln's order, had turned Vallandigham over to the Rebels, but he had gotten back into the North. The outcome of the Ohio race would have national implications, perhaps serving as a barometer for Lincoln's own 1864 reelection bid. Considering Rosecrans's strong Ohio contacts, especially in Cincinnati (where his brother was Catholic bishop), the administration would run a risk to move against the War Democrat general, fearing a political backlash. On October 9, Ohioans went to the polls and gave the Republicans a smashing victory. "Glory to God in the highest. Ohio has saved the Nation!" Lincoln exclaimed. The Army of the Cumberland had done its part. Of the 9,675 votes cast from thirty-seven regiments and six batteries, Brough received all but 252 ballots; the 59th Ohio, from

35. Johnson to wife, Dec. 7, 1863, Richard W. Johnson File, CCNMP; Welsh, *Medical Histories*, 351; *OR*, 30(1):203, 213, 250; Noe, *Southern Boy in Blue*, 226; Schiller, *Autobiography of Major General William F. Smith*, 72. For comments on Brannan's appointment, see *New York Herald*, Oct. 29, 1863. Sanderson considered Reynolds an "excellent selection and decided improvement on Garfield." Sanderson Letter Diary, Oct. 15, 1863.

36. Scribner, *How Soldiers Were Made*, 169; *OR*, 30(1):213; Girardi and Hughes, *Memoirs of Brigadier General William Passmore Carlin*, 110; Aldrich, *Quest for a Star*, 66.

Vallandigham's district, cast 70 of the 252. The 10th Ohio, a Cincinnati Irish Catholic regiment expected to strongly support the antiwar candidate, gave him only 12 of its 208 votes cast. The 6th Ohio cast all of its 206 votes, save 1, for Brough. Colonel Opdycke crowed to his wife that the 19th Ohio went solid for the Republican. "This is especially noteworthy as its former colonel and lieutenant colonel, also its present colonel, major, and a large number of its officers were Democrats of the [John] Breckinridge school!" But with the victory won, Rosecrans lost his leverage.[37]

Some Democratic soldiers silently grumbled that Rosecrans had stacked the deck. "There are about one-half of the troops in this department who would vote the democratic ticket if they could only get a Democratic paper occasionally. But the pleasure is denied them, for what reason I cannot say, unless it is for political interest," a soldier wrote privately. Even the Republican-influenced *Cincinnati Commercial* conceded that Democratic politicians had not been allowed south of Nashville to ensure the distribution of Democratic ballots. Rosecrans did not wish "missionaries" to reach Ohio soldiers, the paper declared, adding that he told someone returning from that state that Brough would have won by a wider margin "had not Vallandigham's friends over yonder killed two or three thousand Ohio voters the other day at Chickamauga."[38]

Rosecrans's dispatches continued to croak with pessimism, unwittingly substantiating Dana's portrait of ineptitude. "Our future is not bright," the general flatly stated on the sixteenth. Dana too continued his bleak dispatches, insisting that Rosecrans remained "insensible to the impending danger, and dawdles with trifles in a manner which can scarcely be imagined." Precious time had been lost because of "our dazed and mazy commander. . . . I never saw anything which seemed so lamentable and hopeless. Nothing can prevent the retreat of the army from this place within a fortnight." Two days later Dana questioned the army commander's sanity, declaring him an imbecile. Stanton erupted. "The tycoon of the War Department is on the war path, his hands are red and smoking with the scalping of Rosey," Hay revealed to a friend.[39]

That evening, October 16, the cabinet met in closed session. Not surprisingly,

37. Lamers, *Edge of Glory*, 380; Keller, "Diary of Albion W. Tourgée," 128; Hannaford, *Story of a Regiment*, 481–82; John C. Waugh, *Reelecting Lincoln: The Battle for the 1864 Presidency* (New York: Crown, 1997), 14–15; *New York Tribune*, Oct. 29, 1863; Opdycke to wife, Oct. 14, 1863, Opdycke Letters, OHS. See also George Botkin to friend, Sept. 22, 1863, Sidney Botkin Papers, OHS; Charles E. Willett, ed., *A Union Soldier Returns South: The Civil War Letters and Diary of Alfred C. Willett, 113th Ohio Volunteer Infantry* (Johnson City, Tenn.: Overmountain, 1994), 13; and Sanderson Letter Diary, Oct. 17, 1863. Opdycke noted that the vote was low because of so many underage boys and foreigners in the Ohio ranks who could not vote.

38. Arnold Shankman, "Soldier Votes and Clement L. Vallandigham in the 1863 Ohio Gubernatorial Election," *Ohio History* 82 (1974): 95, 101.

39. *OR*, 30(1):218–19, 221; Hays to Miles, Oct. 24, 1863, John Hay Letters, LC.

Grant's name came up, though not as a replacement for Rosecrans as widely rumored. The issue of a supreme western commander had been previously discussed. The inability to rapidly reinforce the Army of the Cumberland had confirmed the administration's belief that an overall commander was needed. All three western departments—Cumberland, Ohio, and Tennessee—would be merged into a new superdepartment fashioned the Military Division of the Mississippi and placed under the Illinois general's command. Two sets of orders were drawn up, essentially the same except for one item. One retained Rosecrans as commander of the Army of the Cumberland, the other superseded him with George Thomas. The decision would be Grant's.[40]

While some writers have portrayed Lincoln as waffling on the removal issue, the decision to hand it off to Grant clearly had political overtones. Administration officials believed that Chase would "try to make capital out of the Rosecrans business." Indeed, on October 24 the president informed John Hay that Rosecrans was completely broken and acted "confused and stunned like a duck hit in the head," hardly the words of indecisiveness. When Wisconsin senator James R. Doolittle inquired about the removal, Lincoln quickly passed off to Grant, saying that he had done so at the general's request. The president clearly gave his consent for the removal, later confiding to Gilmore: "I couldn't do anything but remove him. We could not have held Chattanooga three days longer if he had not been removed."[41]

The precise role of Garfield in the removal became an issue of postwar recrimination. In 1882 Dana claimed that the chief of staff had written a damaging letter to Chase in October 1863 urging the army commander's removal. (Dana later backed down and said that the letter did not mention removal but was nonetheless critical.) The letter, eventually shown to Lincoln, became the proverbial straw that broke the camel's back. The story, adamantly denied by Garfield, seemed to be substantiated in 1895, when J. A. Gilmore wrote on the subject. He met with Chase on Christmas Day, 1863, at which time the Treasury secretary told him of the letter and its effect upon a subsequent cabinet meeting. A postwar affidavit by Montgomery Blair, a Rosecrans supporter, confirmed that the Garfield letter had indeed been read before the cabinet.[42]

The matter was purportedly resolved when John W. Shuckers, Chase's secretary, wrote that the letter in question was not written in October 1863 but the previous

40. *OR*, 30(1):404.

41. Cozzens, *This Terrible Sound*, 527; Dennett, *Lincoln and the Civil War*, 106, 110; Lamers, *Edge of Glory*, 407.

42. Document "B," Rosecrans Papers; James R. Gilmore, "Why Rosecrans Was Removed," *Atlanta Constitution*, Dec. 22, 1895; Theodore C. Smith, *The Life and Letters of James Abram Garfield* (New Haven: Yale University Press, 1925), 862–71.

July 27, before the Battle of Chickamauga. The missive merely expressed Garfield's frustration over his commander's slowness to move. But how could such a letter have affected the October 16 cabinet meeting? Did Garfield write a defaming letter in October? The truth will never be known. The subsequent postwar publication of the July 27 letter, though absolving Garfield of asking for Rosecrans's removal, nonetheless infuriated the general and convinced him of his chief of staff's duplicity. Had he known of such treachery, Rosecrans wrote, a court-martial would have resulted.[43]

Although the orders to Grant gave discretion, Stanton decided to travel west and personally present them so that there would be no foul ups. Even before the meeting between him and the Illinois general occurred, the secretary informed Governor Morton that Rosecrans was to be removed. Along with Governor Brough, Stanton boarded Grant's train at Indianapolis on October 18. Never having met the general, the secretary mistook a surgeon for him and began heartily shaking hands, exclaiming: "How do you do General Grant? I recognize you from your pictures." He was quickly introduced to the smiling general. On their way to Louisville, the two discussed Grant's orders.[44]

Stanton had no cause for concern. While Grant distrusted Thomas, he detested Rosecrans. Officially, Stanton noted, Grant rejected the Cumberland commander because he "would not obey orders." In truth, a long history between the two made the decision inevitable. Historian Leslie Gordon has accounted for their failed relationship as "a mixture of personality clashes, bad timing, bad press (for Grant), and poor communication." On the evening of the nineteenth, Grant drew up General Orders No. 1, relieving Rosecrans from command. Later that evening one of Dana's exaggerated telegrams arrived, implying that matters had so badly deteriorated that Chattanooga might be evacuated. Grant immediately sent a dispatch assuming command and instructing Thomas to hold "at all hazards."[45]

Monday morning, October 19, Rosecrans rode out for his daily inspection tour, leaving Granger in charge, an odd selection given that Thomas ranked him by five

43. Smith, *Life and Letters of James Abram Garfield*, 872–73.

44. Lamers, *Edge of Glory*, 397; John Y. Simon, ed., *The Papers of Ulysses S. Grant*, 22 vols. (Carbondale: Southern Illinois University Press, 1967–), 9:281; James H. Wilson, *Under the Old Flag: Recollections of Military Operations in the War for the Union, the Spanish War, the Boxer Rebellion, Etc.*, 2 vols. (reprint, Westport, Conn.: Greenwood, 1971), 1:259–60.

45. Simon, *Papers of Ulysses S. Grant*, 9:256, 298 n.; Lamers, *Edge of Glory*, 407; OR, 30(1):221, 30(4):479; Leslie Gordon, "The Failed Relationship of William S. Rosecrans and Grant," in *Grant's Lieutenants: From Cairo to Vicksburg*, ed. Steven E. Woodworth (Lawrence: University Press of Kansas, 2001), 127.

months. When the order relieving Rosecrans arrived, Granger read it and placed it on the general's desk. Later he discreetly showed it to Maj. Gen. Daniel Butterfield, Hooker's chief of staff, swearing him to secrecy. "Rosecrans is out on a tour of inspection. He doesn't know this himself." When the army commander returned later that evening, Granger pulled Reynolds over to the side and whispered: "The old man has been relieved. Thomas is in command."[46]

Rosecrans appeared to be in a good mood as he returned to headquarters around 6:00 P.M., joking about the recent elections. He "laughed and talked with those who came in and had faces as if they were mourning the death of a near kin." Reading the order, the Ohio general immediately summoned Thomas. It was the moment the Virginian had dreaded. For weeks his name had been floated as a replacement. Baldy Smith had even confided to his wife in early October, "We shall have a change of commanders, and General Thomas is to be the man." When questioned about the possibility, Dana wrote Stanton: "He refused [command] before [in 1862] because a battle was imminent and he was unacquainted with the combinations. No such reason now exists, and I presume that he would accept." On September 30 Stanton replied: "If Hooker's command can get safely through, all the Army of the Cumberland can need will be a competent commander. The merit of General Thomas and the debt of gratitude the nation owes to his valor and skill are fully appreciated here, and I wish you to tell him so. It was not my fault that he was not in command months ago." Concerned about the perception of political intrigue, Thomas rejected the possibility of replacing Rosecrans and asked Dana to suppress such thoughts to the secretary. Dana did not, only saying in his October 4 dispatch, "General Thomas desires me to say to you that he is deeply obliged to you for good opinion." Thomas even went to Rosecrans personally and pledged his loyalty, warning him about "the traitors from Washington [Dana] now in camp."[47]

Thomas now read the order giving him command, "turning pale and drawing his breath harder as he proceeded," Rosecrans later described. "General, you remember what I told you some two weeks ago," the Virginian began. Rosecrans interrupted: "George, but we are in the face of the enemy. No one but you can safely take my place now; and for our country's sake you *must* do it. Don't fear; no cloud of doubt will even come into my mind as to your fidelity to friendship and honor."[48]

Despite Thomas's anger from the outset that Rosecrans had gotten the Cumberland department, that their relations in the days prior to the recent battle had been

46. Cozzens, *This Terrible Sword,* 527–28; Lamers, *Edge of Glory,* 391–92.

47. Buell, *Warrior Generals,* 275; Lamers, *Edge of Glory,* 386; *Society of the Army of the Cumberland, 1879 Reunion* (Cincinnati: Robert Clarke, 1880), 176.

48. Lamers, *Edge of Glory,* 392.

strained, and that he must have been outraged that Rosecrans fled the field of Chickamauga, Thomas was clearly embarrassed at his ascent to command. He and Buell had never had a relationship, but it was quite different with Rosecrans, their friendship dating back to West Point. There was, however, a deeper issue. Thomas was a man of great personal pride and professionalism and, perhaps to a fault, shunned political influence. (Thomas Buell, one of Thomas's most ardent modern supporters, has been critical of the general's naïveté on this point—"A general in high command could not stay aloof from politics; for a civil war is the most political of all wars.") Additionally, Thomas was miffed at Grant's "at all hazards" dispatch and quickly replied, "We will hold the town till we starve."[49]

A bitter but composed Rosecrans quietly announced that he would be departing at 5:00 A.M. the next morning, confiding to Thomas, "I can't bear to meet my troops." He wrote a brief farewell speech to be read in his absence, but most of the night was spent conferring with Thomas on operational matters. Early on the twentieth, in the company of his aides Captains Thoms and Bond and his personal chaplain, Fr. Patrick Treacy, "Old Rosy" departed for Cincinnati. One of Hooker's soldiers saw him as his train passed through Murfreesboro. The general wore a blue overcoat and had pulled a white wool hat over his eyes. "He was either tired with riding all night or he had something on his mind for he appeared almost *sad* as he looked vacantly out the window without seeming to see anything that was passing," Harvey Reid wrote his father. Rosecrans had opened the way for ultimate victory in the West, yet it was not enough. In the end it may not have been the War Department but Rosecrans's own regrettable personal habits that became his undoing.[50]

News of Rosecrans's departure swept the officer corps, evoking mixed emotions. "A bomb-shell fell amongst us today in the shape of an order from the War Department removing Rosecrans," Palmer revealed to his wife. "He fell a victim of his own weakness and for want of courage to fight his own battles, fell ingloriously and without dignity. He has not deceived me as to his capacity nor did his fall surprise me except that it came a little sooner than I expected." Palmer did express sympathy for the commanding general being betrayed by some professing to be his friend, a veiled reference to Garfield, whom Palmer detested. Thomas, however, he found to be "an honorable, upright man."[51]

Captain Hough, on Negley's staff, casually wrote his wife on the twentieth: "We

49. Buell, *Warrior Generals,* 275; Rosecrans, "Mistakes of Grant," 595–96; Van Horne, *Thomas,* 156.

50. Sanderson Letter Diary, Oct. 20, 1863; *OR,* 30(1):478; Lamers, *Edge of Glory,* 395, 450; Frank L. Byrne, ed., *The View from Headquarters: Civil War Letters of Harvey Reid* (Madison: State Historical Society of Wisconsin, 1965), 101.

51. George Palmer, *Conscientious Turncoat,* 120–21.

are undergoing a change of Commanders to-day, Genl Rosecrans goes I don't know where, and Genl Thomas takes command. The change somewhat astonished the Army, but I cannot say that I was surprised. It has been evident to me for a long time that Genl Thomas would eventually command this Army. Anyhow, the efficacy of the Army will not be injured by the change."[52]

Colonel Sherman surmised that Rosecrans "was getting too popular with his army and the masses of the north" and that he had "been too successful in handling this difficult Department to suit old Brains [Halleck] and, therefore he and the Secretary of War determined upon his removal whenever there was a shadow they could use against him." The blow was softened only by the appointment of Thomas, who was "universally respected and esteemed throughout this Department."[53]

"What the effect of this removal will be upon the morale of this army, I know full well. . . . Tomorrow when it becomes known, we shall have a gloomy, desolate and sad day," Colonel Sanderson believed. He was wrong. Oddly, the response among the soldiers "created very little surprise, and no feeling of either joy or sorrow—none that was perceptible to me, at least. The army seemed totally apathetic on the subject," observed Cincinnati reporter Joseph McCullagh. The letters and diaries bear out his conclusion. Rumors that made their way into the press, though outrageously false, claimed that Rosecrans had been a drunkard and an opium eater. John Shank of the 125th Illinois perhaps represented many when he wrote: "I feel sorry for Rosecrans, and I think the country will generally be disappointed. Thomas, I believe, however to be his superior[,] and in reality no injury will result from the change." Writing bluntly to his mother, James Wier expressed, "I think the government is right in removing Rosecrans and McCook and Crittenden for the army came the nighest being destroyed of any since the war began." There were, of course, dissenting voices. "We were not very well pleased with Rosecrans' displacement, as he enjoyed the perfect confidence of all. Gen. Thomas, however, is a brick," a trooper in the 15th Pennsylvania Cavalry related to his aunt.[54]

On October 22 Grant, on crutches and wearing an open coat with no rank showing, and Rosecrans met at Stevenson, Alabama. In surely one of the most humiliating scenes in his career, the Ohio general boarded Grant's rail car and had a

52. Athearn, *Soldier in the West,* 155.
53. Aldrich, *Quest for a Star,* 78.
54. Sanderson Letter Diary, Oct. 20, 1863; *Cincinnati Daily Commercial,* Nov. 3, 1863; Andrews, *North Reports the Civil War,* 471; Edna J. Shank Hunter, ed., *One Flag, One Country, and Thirteen Greenbacks a Month: Letters from a Civil War Private and His Colonel* (San Diego: Hunter, 1980), 128; Wier to mother, Nov. 17, 1863, James K. Wier Letters, 25th Illinois File, CCNMP. Typical was the response of Albion Tourgée, who noted Rosecrans's removal but made no comment. Keller, "Diary of Albion W. Tourgée," 113; Susan Colton Wilson, ed., *Column South: With the Fifteenth Pennsylvania Cavalry* (Flagstaff: J. F. Colton, 1960), 147.

interview. The meeting proved polite and brief, though "they were far from sympathetic with each other," a staff officer observed. Grant would later write that Rosecrans "made some excellent suggestions as to what should be done," adding caustically, "my only wonder was that he had not carried them out."[55]

With Thomas elevated to army command, Palmer, who intensely disliked Granger and did not wish to serve under him, was suddenly notified that he had been given the XIV Corps. Thomas apparently had a hand in the matter. Johnson and Baird, both West Pointers, expressed disgust that they had been superseded by a volunteer officer. Baird became such a constant critic that Palmer unsuccessfully asked for his removal; ironically, in postwar years the two became warm friends. Even Dana believed that Palmer was "hardly equal to this new position." Rousseau, who returned to the army in late September, was egregiously taken aback to hear about the appointment. Being Palmer's senior in rank ("and this grinds him," wrote John Beatty), Rousseau not only failed to get the corps but also lost his own division to his temporary successor, Baird, and instead received the nominal command of the District of Tennessee. Dana, who viewed the Kentuckian as "an ass of eminent gifts," humorously informed Stanton that Rousseau had earlier revealed that he really did not wish to be considered for army command. Replacing Palmer at division command would be Charles Cruft, one of the army's ablest brigadiers.[56]

David Stanley briefly returned to his cavalry corps until a de facto demotion on November 20 and to command an infantry division (Cruft's former) in the IV Corps. The general, a bitter alcoholic who held a low opinion of most officers and one whom Thomas considered a worthless drunk, dismissed the change by saying that he was relieved—"It [cavalry service] was most unsatisfactory and annoying." Brigadier General Mitchell, still suffering from bouts of asthma, returned from chasing Wheeler on October 14, declaring to Garfield, "I am as near a dead man on horse back as you ever saw." He was soon relieved of duty and replaced by the senior officer of the First Cavalry Division, Col. Edward McCook.[57]

*   *   *

55. Grant, *Memoirs*, 2:410; K. Jack Bauer, ed., *Soldiering: The Civil War Diary of Rice C. Buell, 123rd New York Volunteer Infantry* (San Rafael, Calif.: Presidio, 1977), 96; Edward G. Longacre, *From Union Stars to Top Hat: A Biography of the Extraordinary General James Harrison Wilson* (Harrisburg, Pa.: Stackpole, 1972), 88. Rosecrans later bristled at Grant's sarcastic comment, denouncing it as either "stupidity or malice," for every effort was being made to bridge the river. Rosecrans, "Mistakes of Grant," 596. If Rosecrans's idea was to cross at Chattanooga Creek rather than Brown's Ferry, however, as the evidence seems to indicate, it is difficult to see how it would have worked, being under the very muzzles of Confederate guns atop Lookout Mountain.

56. John Palmer, *Personal Recollections*, 191, 198–99; *OR*, 30(1):220, 30(3):818–19, 31(1):842, 31(2):54–55. Dana's choice for IV Corps command was Reynolds. *OR*, 31(1):69.

57. Stanley, *Personal Memoirs*, 158–59; *OR*, 30(1):220, 30(2):62, 63, 30(3):204; Starr, *Union Cavalry*, 3:303; Welsh, *Medical Histories*, 233.

With the departure of Rosecrans and the purge of certain high-ranking generals, the Army of the Cumberland completed its third phase. No longer would Kentuckians dominate the officer corps. In addition, the surface rapport among officers self-destructed in accusations and jealousies. It remained for George Thomas to shape the restructured and humbled army.

PART 6

THE EMERGENCE OF THOMAS

19

Chattanooga
Thomas Takes Command

FORTY-SEVEN-YEAR-OLD, RED-HEADED George H. Thomas, the fifth commander of the Army of the Cumberland, established his headquarters in an unassuming one-story frame house on Walnut near Fourth Street in Chattanooga. When Thomas, at age twenty, was clerking in a Virginia law office, his congressman, who had heard good things about Thomas, sought him out as a possible candidate for West Point. He subsequently agreed and was accepted, rooming with an eighteen-year-old Ohio plebe, William T. Sherman. Thomas later served in the Seminole and Mexican Wars, receiving two brevets in the former, and after fifteen years' service in the artillery, in 1855 he became junior major in the 2d U.S. Cavalry, an outfit that fought Comanches along the Texas frontier. Thomas married Frances Kellogg of Troy, New York, a thirty-one-year-old spinster five years his senior; they would have no children. Exactly why he chose the North over his native Virginia is not known—his pro-Southern sisters (who suggested that he change his last name) insisted that he came under the influence of Frances. She adamantly denied this, claiming that her husband never discussed the issue with anyone, herself included. The answer may be in Thomas's childhood, where he found an association with blacks, playing with slave children and at night teaching them, against his father's will, what he had learned in school that day. He retained this affinity as an adult.

Thomas exhibited slavish work habits and was methodical to a fault; he even assigned seats to staff officers at dinner. Although commonly believed to possess a stoic personality (he once said that he taught himself "not to feel"), he could in fact become quite prickly and moody. Generally, however, colleagues knew him as soft spoken and reserved. Thomas was a private man who concealed his inner feelings; his wartime letters to his wife would be destroyed. Unlike Rosecrans, he showed little interest in religion and harbored a disdain for politics. John Beatty noted that he "puts on less style" than the other generals. Colonel Opdycke expressed "profound confidence in Thomas, not that he is brilliant, but he is firm, solid." In battle he was unflappable.

His organization and training of the First Division revealed his administrative ability. Thomas, when pressed, could also fight; he had shown that at Mill Springs and Chickamauga. Nonetheless, he did not participate at Shiloh or Perryville, and despite some historians' insistence that he saved the day at Stones River, his precise contribution, beyond general overseer, is difficult to discern in contemporary evidence. (The "hero," if any, seems to have been Sheridan.) He was on record as supporting Rosecrans in his six months' inaction after Stones River. Thomas's constant requests for reinforcements on the second day at Chickamauga helped contribute to the disaster that occurred. He had saved the army, however, and that is all that the troops and a thankful nation cared about. His contemporaries knew him as "Slow Trott," an old nickname related to his riding skills but one that now referred to his perceived tactical slowness. "Old Pap," as the troops fondly referred to him, was thus solidly competent but not brilliant. Clearly, no one else in the army approached his revered status.[1]

Thomas understood that Grant's selection of him over Rosecrans did not necessarily represent a vote of confidence; Grant simply distrusted Rosecrans more. The genesis of his less-than-enthusiastic estimation of Thomas is difficult to determine. Neither general enumerated their differences in postwar years. Brigadier General Reynolds, Thomas's new chief of staff and also a friend of Grant, later recounted: "The only thing Grant ever had against Thomas was that Thomas was slow. And it's the God of Almighty truth he *was* slow." It has been suggested that the Virginian simply lacked Sherman's aggressive style, which meshed so well with Grant's. Steven Woodworth has concluded that Thomas resented and perhaps envied Grant's new position, a conclusion that, though likely true, does not explain the history behind their cold relationship. Another historian has even implausibly conjectured that

1. For comments on Thomas's red hair, see Julia A. Drake, comp., *The Mail Goes Through; or the Civil War Letters of George Drake* (San Angelo, Tex.: Anchor, 1964), 67; McKinney, *Education in Violence*, 82–83, 89–90; Cleaves, *Rock of Chickamauga*, 8, 21, 28–31, 45, 49, 50–51, 59–61, 64, 71; Warner, *Generals in Blue*, 50, 665; John Scully to wife, Jan. 5, 1862, John W. Scully Letters, Duke University, Durham, N.C.; Richard Johnson, "Recollections of Distinguished Generals in the Civil War," *National Tribune*, Aug. 15, 1895; Shanks, *Personal Recollections*, 71–72; O. O. Howard, "A Sketch of the Life of General George H. Thomas," in *MOLLUS, New York*, 4 vols. (reprint, Wilmington, N.C.: Broadfoot, 1993), 1:287, 301; George Palmer, *Conscientious Turncoat*, 121; John Sanderson Letter Diary, Oct. 20, 1863, John Sanderson Letters, OHS; Opdycke to wife, Sept. 28, Oct. 25, Nov. 16, 1863, Folder 9, Box 2, Emerson Opdycke Letters, OHS. I concur with Albert Castel that Thomas was the North's second-leading general, but I view him as a distant second. "Why the North Won and the South Lost," 59–60. As far as Thomas's role at Stones River, the two leading books on the subject (McDonough, *Stones River*, and Cozzens, *No Better Place to Die*) barely mention him as a factor in the battle. For Thomas's comments on religion, see Piatt, *Thomas*, 359–60.

At Thomas's death, Major General Oliver O. Howard sent a note to Thomas's sister in Southampton, Virginia, highly complimentary of her brother. She curtly replied, "In answer to your inquiry respecting the character of the late General Thomas, I can only inform you that he was as all other boys are well born and well reared."

Grant scorned an old back injury Thomas suffered and associated it with "sluggish-ness in making war," a rather interesting conclusion since in October 1863 Grant himself was still on a crutch and a cane from his previous horsing accident. The answer may not be so shrouded. After Shiloh, when Grant was "promoted" to sec-ond in command, a de facto demotion, Thomas temporarily received the command of the Army of the Tennessee. It is highly possible that Grant always harbored the suspicion that Thomas had something to do with the switch.[2]

Grant and his staff arrived at army headquarters on the rainy evening of October 23 after a grueling two-day ride. Although advised that the general was on his way, no one suspected that he would arrive so soon, given the miserable weather and his injured leg. In a now famous scene, Maj. James Wilson, a Grant aide, wrote that he came into army headquarters to find Grant on one side of the room and Thomas on the other, both looking "glum and ill at ease." Wilson called attention to the fact that Grant was wet and needed a change of clothing and some food. "Can't you officers attend to these matters for him?" he asked, thus belatedly stirring Thomas into action. Although invited to step into the next room and change, Grant de-clined. The two staffs, mirroring the relationship between the generals, never estab-lished cordial relations, though Wilson insisted that Grant's men were more conciliatory than Thomas's. Colonel Sanderson was certainly unimpressed with the new department commander. "If he [Grant] be a great man, his looks are very de-ceptive." He radiated "nothing but mediocrity," and "most of the officers and men feel cool, doubtful, and distrusting."[3]

Grant listened intently as Baldy Smith presented his idea (sanctioned by Thomas) of opening a supply line that would avoid the Rebel artillery atop Lookout Mountain and the gauntlet of sharpshooters at the Raccoon Mountain bend in the Tennessee River, the so-called Suck. He proposed capturing and constructing a pon-toon bridge at Brown's Ferry, on the west side of Moccasin Point some two and a half miles from Lookout Mountain, screened by intervening mountains. Supplies could thus be transported by river to Kelley's Ferry, hauled by wagon through a

2. Sword, *Mountains Touched with Fire*, 161; Steven Woodworth, *This Grand Spectacle: The Battle of Chattanooga* (Abilene: McWhiney Foundation, 1999), 29; Buell, *Warrior Generals*, 34–35. See also Coz-zens, *Shipwreck of Their Hopes*, 46. In October 1863 neither Grant nor Thomas had ever personally met Lincoln; Grant would later do so.

3. Wilson, *Under the Old Flag*, 1:268–69, 273–74; Grant, *Memoirs*, 411; Horace Porter, *Campaigning with Grant* (New York: Century, 1897), 1–4; Jean Edward Smith, *Grant* (New York: Simon and Schuster, 2001), 266. Some writers suggest that Thomas was simply preoccupied and that the incident has been exaggerated. I view it as another example of Thomas's passive-aggressive nature. Thomas Buell dismisses the incident, stating that no other evidence than Wilson's account mentions it. *Warrior Generals*, 463. Porter, however, who was apparently present and an admirer of Thomas, also mentioned the event.

pass in Raccoon Mountain to Brown's Ferry, and then on to the pontoon bridge at Chattanooga. The present supply route would thus be cut in half, with the possibility of both wagon and river traffic from Bridgeport. While establishing a beachhead at Brown's Ferry (known to be held by about a thousand Rebel infantry), Hooker would march with his corps along the railroad into Lookout Valley, eventually communicating with the Brown's Ferry position. Although ridiculed by some of Thomas's generals, the plan was solid and could have been implemented under Rosecrans. The next day, October 24, Grant made a brief inspection and gave his approval.[4]

Hazen's brigade was selected to make the assault on the early morning of October 27. The troops, commanded by Col. Timothy Stanley, boarded fifty pontoons, each capable of holding 25 men in addition to the crew, and two flats, carrying 40 and 75 men each—a total of 1,365 men and 100 crewmen. The boats pushed off at 3:00 A.M. and quietly steered (no oars were needed) the nine miles downriver, the men lying flat so as not to present a silhouette, especially as they rounded Moccasin Bend. Some wag remarked that he was reminded of a painting he had seen of George Washington (apparently crossing the Delaware), prompting much laughter. "Shut up you damn fools—do you think this is a regatta?" shouted an officer, prompting immediate silence. Despite tense moments (a signal torch was seen flashing against the sky on Lookout Mountain), the dawn assault went off without a hitch, the Confederates being caught unprepared and easily chased off. After establishing a beachhead, Turchin's brigade and the remaining 750 men of Hazen's brigade, all hiding in the woods out of sight on the east bank, were ferried over, raising the total Federal strength to 4,000. By 3:00 P.M. a pontoon bridge had been completed and three batteries under Major Mendenhall crossed. "The question of supplies may now be regarded as settled," Grant telegraphed Halleck that evening.[5]

Grant's statement notwithstanding, it would be weeks more before the issue of supplies was totally resolved. On October 31 the IV and XIV Corps counted 38,361 "fighting men present," with 7,830 "other men present," an aggregate of 46,200. Beyond stockpiling rations and a resupply of clothing and shoes, a huge issue of quartermaster stores was needed.[6]

4. Schiller, *Autobiography of Major General William F. Smith*, 75–76; Smith, "Operations around Chattanooga," 168–70; Wilson, *Under the Old Flag*, 1:277; *OR*, 31(1):70; Grant, *Memoirs*, 411; Joseph S. Fullerton, "The Army of the Cumberland at Chattanooga," in *B&L*, 3:720.

5. *OR*, 31(1):40, 41, 52, 54, 56, 77–80, 82, 84–86, 89, 31(2):28; Hannaford, *Story of a Regiment*, 487–88; Thomas, *Thomas*, 413; Fullerton, "Army of the Cumberland at Chattanooga," 720; Catton, *Grant Takes Command*, 51; George B. Turner to mother, Nov. 1, 1863, George B. Turner Letters, OHS; *Letters of Captain Henry Richards*, 155; Arnold Brandley, "The Cracker Line," *National Tribune*, May 28, 1885; Hazen, *Narrative*, 163.

6. Monthly Inspection Report, Oct. 31, 1863, Monthly Inspections Reports Received, 1863–65, Entry 1058, Vol. 243, RG 393, Pt. 1, NA.

IV AND XIV CORPS, OCTOBER 31, 1863

Item	On Hand	Needed
Knapsacks	15,274	9,172
Haversacks	21,795	8,250
Canteens	20,420	7,656
Hospital Tents	48	48
Shelter Tents	16,672	8,712
Axes	1,132	2,005
Shovels	144	212
Spades	933	1,329
Camp Kettles	3,063	2,125
Wagons	1,117	113
Ambulances	197	7

The next phase of the operation involved the newly arrived Hooker, who proved to be as troublesome as the Rebels. "Fighting Joe," a nickname that annoyed the general, could be vain, self-seeking, and overtly opinionated, but he retained the support of the Radical Republicans. Due to recriminations over his defeat at Chancellorsville, Hooker detested the two corps commanders under him, Maj. Gens. Oliver O. Howard and Henry B. Slocum, and they in turn him. Indeed, Slocum would have resigned rather than further serve under Hooker, but he was detached with a division to guard the Nashville and Chattanooga Railroad. Brig. Gen. John Geary, commanding a division in the XII Corps, did not like what he found in Tennessee. "I cannot tell you how I will like it in the West, but 'as far as I have got' I don't like it very well," he wrote his wife. "There seems to be considerable lack of brains among some of the commanding officers about whom we read so much. The system of the Great Army of the Potomac is entirely wanting here." The officers of the eastern corps were thus strife-ridden and disgruntled.[7]

Although Grant and Hooker had been friends years earlier, in their present circumstance friction occurred almost immediately. Back on October 21, as Grant's train stopped at Stevenson on the way to Chattanooga, a Hooker staff officer entered and asked if Grant would not like to call upon the general, who was not feeling well. John Rawlins, a Grant staff officer, blurted: "General Grant himself is not very well and will not leave his car tonight. He expects General Hooker and all other generals who have business with him to call at once, as he will start overland to

---

7. Castel, *Decision in the West*, 95–97; William A. Blair, ed., *A Politician Goes to War: The Civil War Letters of John White Geary* (University Park: Pennsylvania State University Press, 1995), 120.

Chattanooga early tomorrow morning." Grant added, "If General Hooker wishes to see me he will find me on this train." Hooker immediately broke all speed records in making an appearance, but Grant declined his offer of lodging, instead continuing to Bridgeport, where he pointedly stayed with Howard.[8]

On October 24 Hooker received his marching orders. On the twenty-seventh he would cross at Bridgeport without wagons with Howard's XI Corps and Geary's division of the XII Corps, in all ten thousand infantry, and advance along the south bank of the Tennessee River by way of Wauhatchie to link up at Brown's Ferry. Palmer, with two brigades of the XIV Corps, would proceed downriver by a back road along the north bank until at Whiteside's, where he would cross and hold the road in Hooker's rear. The column moved out as scheduled at 6:30 A.M., with no indication of enemy resistance. Hooker was, according to Dana, "in an unfortunate state of mind for one who has to cooperate, fault finding, criticizing, dissatisfied . . . , truculent toward the plan he is now to execute." His complaints, though several, came down to one—he did not desire a direct march into Lookout Valley for fear of an attack. Hooker later wrote to Chase: "I regarded it [maneuver] precisely as I did sending my Corps across the Antietam Creek to attack the whole rebel army. I could not know if I was advancing against a mouse or an elephant."[9]

Hooker's column, reduced to a mere 6,800 men after deductions to guard the rear, reached Whiteside's after 8:00 P.M. The march resumed the next day with only minor skirmishing. Howard's corps completed the juncture at 5:00 P.M., with Geary's undersized 1,500-man division encamping three miles away at Wauhatchie. Hazen's men enthusiastically greeted the easterners. "Our joy was almost uncontrollable on seeing these veterans coming to our relief," an Ohioan jotted in his diary. A New Yorker, however, saw the westerners as "a nondescript lot." Hooker took up an incredibly haphazard position that night, ignoring Hazen's pleas to consolidate his line. At midnight Longstreet, in a botched effort, attacked Geary's isolated division with a single brigade, the Federals sustaining 216 casualties to the Confederates' 356. Had Southern ineptitude not excelled Hooker's, Geary's men surely would have been captured. Despite the close call, the "Cracker Line," as it became known, was now secure.[10]

8. Wilson, *Under the Old Flag*, 1:264; O. O. Howard, "Grant at Chattanooga," in *MOLLUS, New York*, 1:246–47; John A. Carpenter, *Sword and Olive Branch: Oliver Otis Howard* (Pittsburgh: University of Pittsburgh Press, 1964), 247, 257.

9. *OR*, 31(1):43–44, 46–47, 72; Grant, *Memoirs*, 417. Palmer's troops would cross by moving the Shellmound pontoon bridge to Rankin's Ferry. *OR*, 31(1):73; Hooker to Chase, Nov. 3, 1863, in Niven, *Chase Papers*, 4:172.

10. Cozzens, *Shipwreck of Their Hopes*, 72–100; John D. Innskeep Diary, Nov. 6, 1863, OHS; New Yorker quoted in John E. Clark Jr., *Railroads in the Civil War: The Impact of Management on Victory and Defeat* (Baton Rouge: Louisiana State University Press, 2001), 205, 208.

Supplies came overland and by means of two small steamers, the *Paint Rock* in Chattanooga and the *Chattanooga* at Bridgeport. On October 29 the latter made her maiden voyage, towing two barges with thirty-four thousand rations to Rankin's Ferry. After a return trip to reload that night, the *Chattanooga* again proceeded upriver with two barges, in all some forty thousand rations and thirty-nine thousand pounds of forage. The boat made slow progress against the rapid current, yet desperation pushed the crew forward—the garrison had only four boxes of hardtack remaining. The word of her landing spread rapidly, and soon cheers could be heard: "The Cracker line open. Full rations, boys! Three cheers for the Cracker line." The next night, about midnight, the *Paint Rock* unloaded two hundred tons at Kelly's Ferry. On November 2–3 a total of a quarter-million rations were landed.[11]

By early November sixty freight cars a day arrived at Bridgeport, with an increase to seventy expected soon. Grant required only thirty-five carloads daily to feed the Army of the Cumberland, meaning that ordnance, quartermaster, and medical stores could be obtained too. The steamboats went directly to Brown's Ferry by this time, cutting out eight miles of wagon trail but slowing up the boats because of the strong upriver currents around the Suck. A third old steamboat at Chattanooga only awaited new engine parts from Nashville to be made operational. But all did not go as planned. The pontoon bridges sometimes broke (apparently caused by the Rebels floating down large logs), and the steamboats came up with light loads due to inadequate stockpiling at Stevenson. Derailments due to worn tracks became a common occurrence. "Rations very scarce. Having a hungry time of it, going without days at a time," Pvt. George A. Cummins of the 36th Illinois noted on November 4. Geary wrote to his wife on the eighth: "The situation of the Army of the Cumberland has been, and still is, very precarious for want of subsistence and forage. The men being upon half-rations, and many of the horses are without anything."[12]

Although it would take time to replenish horses and stockpile supplies, and Sherman's army was still two weeks away, Grant would not wait to take the offensive. Aware (from prisoners and scouts) that Bragg had detached Longstreet's corps and five thousand cavalry under Wheeler to swing around the army's left flank and move on Knoxville, he had increasing pressure from Washington to relieve Burnside—a rather ironic turn of events given the latter's lethargy toward Rosecrans's similar plight. This left, according to Grant, but thirty thousand Rebels before Chattanooga; Thomas more correctly believed forty thousand. Baldy Smith suggested a

11. Le Duc, "Steamboat That Opened the 'Cracker Line,'" 678; *OR*, 31(1):67, 31(2):55.

12. *OR*, 31(2):54–56, 61; George A. Cummins Diary, Nov. 4, 1863, ILSHL; Blair, *Politician Goes to War*, 136.

368 DAYS OF GLORY

demonstration against the northern end of Missionary Ridge, threatening Bragg's right and getting him to recall Longstreet. What Grant ordered was a full-scale attack that would occupy the ridge and even penetrate the enemy's communications between Cleveland, Tennessee, and Dalton, Georgia. Thomas balked, desiring instead an advance on Lookout Mountain from the rear, say Cooper's Gap, but Grant would not budge: "for the sake of Burnside the attack must be made at once." To Thomas's claim that he could not move his artillery, Grant merely suggested that he strip mules and horses from wagons, ambulances, and officers.[13]

Back at army headquarters, Smith discovered that the order had "staggered Thomas." "You must get that order for an advance countermanded; I shall lose my army," he pleaded to Smith, virtually conceding that an intermediary was needed for communication. The engineer suggested an upriver reconnaissance to see how far Bragg's right extended. The result, probably predetermined by the officers before the trip even began, proved no surprise—Bragg's line stretched too far north, thus jeopardizing the attacking column's communication with Chattanooga. That night both officers, along with Dana, returned to Grant in the hopes of his revoking the order. The concept was correct, they affirmed, but the attack must be made by the Army of the Tennessee. Grant canceled the assault, but a dispatch to Halleck two weeks later revealed his agitation with Thomas: "I have never felt such restlessness before as I have at the fixed and immovable condition of the Army of the Cumberland."[14]

Grant, unquestionably feeling pressure from Washington and perhaps perceiving himself as the savior of the West, had badly miscalculated. The attack would have failed unless it was possible for four divisions, without artillery, to accomplish what six with artillery could not achieve eighteen days later. Perhaps more than anything, the incident underscored the at-best formal relationship between Grant and Thomas. It was not an open breach; indeed, there were generals' gatherings at Grant's headquarters in which even Thomas, according to Wilson, "unbent and told his reminiscences with wit and good feeling." An occasional relaxed evening could still not veil the lack of warmth between the generals.[15]

13. Schiller, *Autobiography of Major General William F. Smith*, 78; Van Horne, *Army of the Cumberland*, 1:409; Grant, *Memoirs*, 425; *OR*, 31(1):58–59. Longstreet initially got no farther than Loudon but still threatened Burnside.

14. William F. Smith, "Comments on General Grant's 'Chattanooga,'" in *B&L*, 3:716; Smith, "Operations around Chattanooga," 193–94; McDonough, *Chattanooga*, 107.

15. Wilson, *Under the Old Flag*, 1:280. There are several recent biographies of Grant, the best being by Brooks Simpson, who concedes the strained relations between Grant and Thomas. *Ulysses S. Grant: Triumph over Adversity, 1822–1865* (New York: Houghton Mifflin, 2000), 232–33, 494 n. 43. Simpson does, however, question Smith's efforts to disavow any role in the attack order. Thomas Buell asserted that when Grant wrote his *Memoirs*, "the story became embellished to the effect that Thomas and his sick artillery horses had scotched a perfectly good idea." *Warrior Generals*, 464.

* * *

"Major General and Brigadier General stars are getting to be as plentiful as corporals chevrons," thought Major Connolly, adding, "I am afraid that's one trouble with our army just now—we have too many Brigadier stars and not enough of the other kind of 'Stars' that fights and lives on 'hard tack' at $13 a month." Marcus Woodcock thought little about the goings on at army headquarters and worried more about the shortage of wood, nearly every stick having been consumed before winter.[16]

Grant, meanwhile, developed his plans, clearly giving the Army of the Cumberland a supportive role. The main assault would be made by Sherman's veterans, who still lagged behind due to bad weather and horrid roads. Once atop the northern flank of Missionary Ridge, Sherman would be in a position to sweep south along the crest and also continue to Chickamauga Station, thus severing Bragg's supply line and driving a wedge between him and Longstreet. On the right Hooker, with a mixed command, would hold Lookout Valley and attack Lookout Mountain, driving to Rossville. As for Thomas, he would carry the ridge in the center, but as Smith wrote, an assault before either flank was turned "was never seriously contemplated." Indeed, Thomas's was a "secondary plan" meant for "following up the successes [on the flanks.]"[17]

Apparently concerned about Moccasin Bend separating his right from Hooker's left, Thomas still preferred a major strike against Lookout Mountain first. Grant, perceiving the mountain as having "no special advantage to us now," continued to ignore him. Clearly, Grant's close friend Sherman was "in" and Thomas increasingly "out," but the problem went deeper than that. The department commander held a prejudice in favor of his old army and a certain disdain for the Army of the Cumberland. Indeed, he would later quietly reveal to Sherman that he "feared they could not be got out of their trenches to assume the offensive."[18]

Sherman arrived in advance of his army on the evening of November 14. Grant and Thomas received him well, the former even joking with "Cump." Back in 1842–43, while at Fort Moultrie, Thomas and Sherman were part of an eleven-officer eating mess that, ironically, included Bragg. The lighthearted reunion could hardly veil Sherman's deep grief over the death of his nine-year-old son, Willie, who had died of fever six weeks earlier. At Bridgeport Sherman had written his wife, Ellen, "I cannot banish from my mind Poor Willy." Grant and Sherman shared a bottle, the former imbibing freely, according to Smith.[19]

16. Connolly, *Three Years in the Army of the Cumberland*, 133; Noe, *Southern Boy in Blue*, 228–29.

17. *OR*, 31(2):30–31, 314; Smith, "Comments on General Grant's 'Chattanooga,' " 717.

18. McDonough, *Chattanooga*, 109–10; Grant, *Memoirs*, 427; Sherman, *Memoirs*, 1:362.

19. Howard, "Grant at Chattanooga," 248; Hirshson, *White Tecumseh*, 165–66, 168. For the issues regarding Grant's possible intoxication during this time, see Simpson, *Ulysses S. Grant*, 236, 494–95 n. 51. Simpson dismisses the mixed evidence as much to do about nothing.

The next morning Thomas, Sherman, Smith, and Brannan, in company with staff officers, crossed the pontoon bridge and rode in back of the hills four miles, then dismounted and ascended a height that overlooked the mouth of Chickamauga Creek. Smith and Sherman crept uncomfortably close to the riverbank (Confederate pickets could easily be heard conversing on the opposite shore), where the engineer pointed to Tunnel Hill, the intended target. Examining the terrain with his field glass for a half hour, Sherman confidently declared that he could take it.[20]

As the officers returned, Sherman inquired of Thomas if he had seen or had any communication with their old messmate Bragg. The Virginian bristled: "Damn him, I'll be even with him yet." When asked what the problem was, Thomas explained that sometime earlier he had attempted to send a letter through the lines by flag of truce, trusting that his old acquaintance Bragg would agree. What he instead received was an endorsement on the letter that read: "Respectfully returned to Genl. Thomas. Genl. Bragg declines to have any intercourse with a man who has betrayed his state." Sherman noted that Thomas flared as he related the story and muttered many threats about what he intended to do.[21]

The attack, scheduled for November 20, did not take place. The fault was Halleck's, who ordered the Army of the Tennessee to repair the Memphis and Charleston as it advanced, and Sherman's, who unnecessarily slowed his column by mixing wagons with the infantry rather than having them follow in the rear. It was, therefore, decided to move Howard's corps (which was to participate in the attack with Sherman) into Chattanooga on the twentieth rather than follow in the rear of the Army of the Tennessee. The movement was momentarily foiled by Thomas's prearrangement with Smith for the use of the pontoon. Historian Wiley Sword has suggested that, irritated with his friend Sherman, Grant instead "increasingly turned his wrath on a favorite target, George H. Thomas and the Army of the Cumberland." Yet another problem occurred on the twenty-second, when Confederate rafts and debris sent downriver broke the Brown's Ferry pontoon bridge. And with Longstreet inching closer to Knoxville, Burnside was becoming panicked. Yet Grant had to postpone the attack on Bragg two more times until the twenty-third. Finally, Sherman's weary soldiers dragged in, greeted by "a hearty welcome from the Army of the Cumberland," described one of Hazen's men. "They were no paper collar soldiers."[22]

20. Schiller, *Autobiography of Major General William F. Smith,* 79; Sherman, *Memoirs,* 1:362–63.

21. Cleaves, *Rock of Chickamauga,* 192.

22. Woodworth, *Six Armies in Tennessee,* 169–70; Sword, *Mountains Touched with Fire,* 160–62; Cozzens, *Shipwreck of Their Hopes,* 123. Dana reported to Washington, "Grant says the blunder is his; that he should have given Sherman explicit orders to leave his wagons behind; but I know that no one was so much astonished as Grant on learning that they had not been left, even without such orders." *OR,*

Even now Grant did not possess the overwhelming host so often depicted by historians. On November 20 the "present for duty" strength of the infantry and artillery (there was little or no cavalry available at Chattanooga) was 63,614 (Thomas, 36,176; Hooker, 10,636; Sherman, 16,802), with 212 guns, a large percentage of which remained immobile. Opposing them would not be the 30,000 Rebels Grant suspected but nearly 45,000, with over 100 guns. Operating on the offensive, with terrain features clearly favoring the defender, further closed the numerical advantage for Grant.[23]

On November 22 Wood began to detect movement across the valley in his front. Jefferson C. Davis also reported that the enemy camps on his right appeared to be deserted. This intelligence, coupled with stories from Confederate deserters, indicated that Bragg might be withdrawing. Grant had to act quickly lest Longstreet be reinforced. The task of uncovering the enemy's intentions went to Thomas.[24]

What Grant got was not an intended reconnaissance but an overblown assault against Orchard Knob, an almost isolated hundred-foot-high hill twelve hundred yards in advance of the Union works and about halfway to the base of Missionary Ridge. In Thomas's overacted debut, he ordered Wood's division to assault the knob, supported on the right, along the Moore Road, by Sheridan's division and on the left by Howard's XI Corps—some twenty-five thousand Yankees marching out as if on parade, with flags snapping in the autumn wind and drums beating. The Confederates, apparently thinking the hoopla to be a grand review, took no action. At 1:30 the advance sounded, with Wood's eight thousand bluecoats easily driving the two Alabama regiments facing them back to their main line. The Federals sustained 190 casualties but captured 174 Rebel prisoners. Grant, Thomas, Dana, Hooker, Granger, and Howard, all watching from the parapet of Fort Wood, realized that they had gotten more than expected. Wood was merely to feel the line, not capture it. Quickly consulting with Thomas, Grant gave his order: "Intrench them and send up support." Howard's easterners on the left badly stumbled as they advanced against minor opposition, giving Granger an opportunity to poke fun at the

---

31(2):64. Wilson noted that if Grant and Sherman had not been warm friends, Grant's annoyance would surely have led to "sharp criticism and censure."

23. *OR*, 31(2):12–13; Livermore, *Numbers and Losses*, 106–7. Livermore, usually so accurate in his numbers, simply erred on his projection of the Union army. The actual total of the combined armies was 68,753 (not 63,010) before deductions, which he places (and I accept) as 5,139. Thomas Connelly, who often played loose with numbers, suggested that 90,000 Federals faced a paltry 36,000 Rebels, thus adding to the myth. *Autumn of Glory*, 262, 263.

24. Thomas J. Wood, "The Battle of Missionary Ridge," in *MOLLUS, Ohio*, 9 vols. (reprint, Wilmington, N.C.: Broadfoot, 1991), 4:26–27; *OR*, 31(2):32, 40, 64, 100, 102.

corps commander. More importantly, Grant had the information he needed—Bragg had gone nowhere.[25]

The Orchard Knob sideshow would, of course, pale next to Grant's planned assault, if it ever occurred, being postponed yet another day to November 24. Before Sherman's trailing division could cross the Brown's Ferry pontoons, the bridge snapped, leaving it stranded. The assault would thus be made by three divisions of the Army of the Tennessee, two from the Army of the Potomac, and one (Davis's) from the Army of the Cumberland—in all some twenty-five thousand men. A last-minute change also occurred on the right. Grant, much to Thomas's and Hooker's delight, the latter grousing for days over his non-role, decided upon a full-scale attack on Lookout Mountain. Operating in that sector were three divisions, one from each army. This left Thomas, still in a supporting role, in the center, with the divisions of Baird, Sheridan, Wood, and Johnson.[26]

The long-anticipated attack finally began to unfold in the predawn hours of November 24. Initially using 116 pontoons to effect a beachhead with two divisions on the south bank of the Tennessee River at Chickamauga Creek, the repaired steamer *Dunbar* later brought up Sherman's third division. Davis's and Howard's troops arrived throughout the day, the former by pontoon bridge and the latter by direct march from Chattanooga. By 3:30 Sherman was astride the northern tip of Missionary Ridge, having encountered little opposition. With only one hour remaining to the brief autumn afternoon, the general decided to prepare defensive positions and finish the job the next day. It was a reasonable decision but, as events developed, a wrong one.[27]

On the right the slightly rainy, unusually foggy morning shrouded Hooker's movement against the western slope and nose of Lookout Mountain. The three divisions blindly began their ascent. As the fog lifted in the afternoon, the troops of the Army of the Cumberland, watching from the safety of the valley, strained to see the

25. Wood, "Battle of Missionary Ridge," in *MOLLUS*, 29; Howard, "Grant at Chattanooga," 212; Fullerton, "Army of the Cumberland at Chattanooga," 721; Grant, *Memoirs*, 434; Sheridan, *Memoirs*, 1:166; Montgomery Meigs, "Journal of the Battle of Chattanooga," Nov. 23, 1863, Montgomery Meigs Papers, LC; *OR*, 31(2):24, 251, 254–56, 359. The Orchard Knob engagement caused Bragg to recall two divisions on the way to reinforce Longstreet, though most of one had already departed.

26. Cozzens, *Shipwreck of Their Hopes*, 144; Woodworth, *This Grand Spectacle*, 48. Thomas Buell cited Grant's *Papers* (9:411–12) as evidence that Sherman and Thomas had equal roles in the attack. "This refutes most theories that Thomas was given a minor role because Grant did not trust the Army of the Cumberland," he wrote. *Warrior Generals*, 464. The letter in question, however, stated that Thomas was "to co-operate with Sherman" and then "form a junction with Sherman." The juncture would not occur, however, until Sherman had taken the northern end of the ridge. I would thus need more evidence to concur with Buell's contention.

27. Woodworth, *This Grand Spectacle*, 48–52.

"Battle above the Clouds," which, despite its spectacular nature, was really more of an extended skirmish. Although 10,000 Federals opposed 7,000 Confederates, making the outcome far from a certainty, the Rebels were badly scattered. "We fancied at times we could catch glimpses of dark lines fighting their way up the mountain side, but we could not be positive," Marcus Woodcock wrote in his diary that night. The echoes of cheering finally indicated that Hooker had control, if not complete possession, of the mountain. Casualties totaled 480 for Hooker, the Confederates 1,251, mostly prisoners.[28]

At 2:00 P.M. Carlin's brigade reinforced the right. Hooker, who even amid the rain appeared "faultlessly clean and neat," ordered the troops to report to Geary. Encountering the vain division commander and former Kansas governor, Carlin later wrote: "He seemed disposed to give me his military history as soon as I met him. . . . He told me he was the only Federal general who had ever beaten Stonewall Jackson." Geary then barked to his staff, "If any officer of my staff falls asleep tonight, I'll brain him, by the Eternal!"[29]

The haze burned off early on November 25, revealing a clear autumn day and an even more beautiful sight—the Stars and Stripes flying atop Lookout Mountain. Sherman began brisk skirmishing about 7:00 A.M., but the main attack did not begin until about 10:30. Throughout the morning and early afternoon, repeated savage attacks were made against Tunnel Hill, but the vaunted heroes of Vicksburg, Grant's own, recoiled time and again under galling Confederate fire. Eventually, Sherman threw all six divisions into the fray and was even offered a seventh (Baird's), though he turned it down. Believing (falsely) that the Rebels were heavily reinforcing their right, Sherman, at 12:45, tersely signaled Grant, "Where is Thomas?" Grant, realizing that he had to do something, determined to create a diversion. Since Hooker's troops were slowed in crossing Chattanooga Creek, the theater commander turned to Thomas.[30]

Grant and the Cumberland commander had been standing atop Orchard Knob, watching the day's events unfold. Only a mile from Missionary Ridge and within easy 3-inch- or Parrott-rifle range, the officers sloughed off the clear danger. Sometime between 2:00 and 2:30 P.M., Grant approached Wood, standing nearby, and remarked that Sherman appeared to be "having a hard time, and it seems as if we

28. For concise accounts of the Battle of Lookout Mountain, see Cozzens, *Shipwreck of Their Hopes*, 159–98; Sword, *Mountains Touched with Fire*, 203–21; McDonough, *Chattanooga*, 129–42; and Noe, *Southern Boy in Blue*, 233.

29. Girardi and Hughes, *Memoirs of Brigadier General William Passmore Carlin*, 113–14. That night the Confederate division on Lookout Mountain quietly withdrew to Missionary Ridge.

30. McDonough, *Chattanooga*, 143–60; Woodworth, *This Grand Spectacle*, 76–79; OR, 31(2):41, 115.

ought to help him." If Wood and Sheridan could advance to the base of the ridge, it might take the pressure off Sherman. "If you order it, we will try it," the division commander answered.[31]

Grant walked back to Thomas, who maintained his sullen mood. The two talked, Wood admitting that he could not hear what was being said. He assumed that Thomas at this point convinced Grant to add Johnson's and Baird's divisions to the assault, the last having returned from the left. Thomas clearly did not agree with an assault on the Rebel center. Smith ventured that he desired to give Hooker more time to get in position and roll up the Confederate left on Missionary Ridge, thus making an assault on the center unnecessary. His reservations probably went deeper than that. Only days earlier he had written Rosecrans, "If we can hold out for a month longer, our position will be entirely secure." Thomas, so effective on the defensive, showed little stomach for the offensive.[32]

Having given the attack order, Grant quietly walked away. For a half hour Thomas continued to peer at the ridge and do nothing (yet another example of his passive-aggressive behavior), to the utter annoyance of Grant and his staff. Adding to his irritation was Granger, who acted like an overgrown boy, fiddling with and personally sighting the field guns of Bridge's Illinois battery. About three o'clock Grant could take no more. "General Thomas order Granger to turn that battery over to its commander and take command of his corps. And now order your troops to advance and take the enemy's first line of rifle pits." Showing his disapproval by not answering, Thomas walked over to Granger and snapped, "Pay more attention to your corps, sir!"

The minutes ticked away, but still no movement occurred. Walking over to Wood, Grant demanded to know why his troops had not gotten into line. Wood answered that he had received no orders. Turning to Thomas, Grant peevishly inquired: "General Thomas, why are these troops not advancing?" "I don't know. General Granger has been instructed to move them forward." Incredibly, Granger had wandered back over to the artillery pieces and was again sighting guns. Grant erupted: "General Granger. Why are your men waiting?" "I have no orders to advance," came the reply. Grant, pushed to the brink, barked, "If you will leave that battery to its captain, and take command of your corps, it will be better for all of us." The general made all haste to mount up and ride off.[33]

31. Sword, *Mountains Touched with Fire*, 262; Wood, "Battle of Missionary Ridge," in *MOLLUS*, 47–49; Thomas J. Wood, "The Battle of Missionary Ridge: Reflections by Gen. Thomas J. Wood," *New York Times*, July 16, 1876.

32. Wood, "Battle of Missionary Ridge," *New York Times;* Simpson, *Ulysses S. Grant*, 237.

33. Wilson, *Under the Old Flag*, 1:297–98; Benjamin P. Thomas, ed., *Three Years with Grant, as Recalled by War Correspondent Sylvanus Cadwallader* (reprint, New York: Knopf, 1955), 153–54; Hazen, *Narrative*, 174. Dana, in his telegram to Washington, blamed the delay on Granger's "sighting a battery." See *OR*, 31(2):68.

Granger having related the advance order to Wood, staff officers now dashed off to the other division commanders. Some twenty-three thousand veterans soon marched into line formation, skirmishers in front with double rows of infantry behind, with Baird on the left and, in succession, Wood, Sheridan, and Johnson. The Cumberlanders faced the most daunting prospect in the army's two-and-a-half-year history. The ridge was a mile in their front, some five hundred to seven hundred yards of which would be across open plain. At least thirty-two cannon had been counted dotting the crest. Once the base of the ridge had been taken, the bluecoats would have to endure the enemy raining down a severe fire upon them from the heights above. As Sheridan rode up and down his line, an artillery round landed uncomfortably close. "That's damned unkind. Here's to you, General Bragg," the general shouted, holding up a whiskey flask. A private in the ranks watched in disgust: "I only wished he would quit his foolishness, for it was drawing Rebel cannon shot down on us."[34]

About 3:40 six artillery shots rang out from Orchard Knob, the signal to begin the advance. As he stepped out, Colonel Carlin glanced to his left. "It seemed to be two miles in length, and without a crook or curve in it. Every man seemed to have the same step. The national flag of each regiment was fluttering in the breeze and bathed in the sunlight." A Michigan cannoneer, watching from a rear position, marveled, "It was the grandest sight I ever witnessed in my life."[35]

As the blue line swept onto the open plain, it came under the massed fire of some sixty guns on the crest. Artillery from Forts Wood and Negley and Orchard Knob quickly responded. The ineffectiveness of the Rebel fire soon became evident, the shells typically bursting early in the air or burrowing in the ground before exploding. Indeed, the barrage did little to blunt or even slow the attackers. One officer noted that fatigue took a far heavier toll among his men than the enemy artillery. Soon the Federals gained the base of the ridge, and the Rebels stampeded up the slope.[36]

With the Federals in possession of the rifle pits, confusion reigned. Brigade and regimental commanders, who knew virtually nothing of the plan, shouted garbled and contradictory orders. Some of the men by instinct, some burning with revenge, and others simply not understanding the order to stop began clawing up the mountain. Some of Sheridan's soldiers were recalled, only to be sent up a second time. Hazen later

34. Wood, "Battle of Missionary Ridge," in *MOLLUS,* 35; Smith, "Operations around Chattanooga," 215–16; Absalom Baird, "Correspondence Relating to Chickamauga and Chattanooga," *MASS,* 8:250; McDonough, *Chattanooga,* 168; Sword, *Mountains Touched with Fire,* 269. A somewhat different version of the Sheridan story is told in Fullerton, "Army of the Cumberland at Chattanooga," 725.

35. Girardi and Hughes, *Memoirs of Brigadier General William Passmore Carlin,* 116; Genco, *To the Sounds of Musketry,* 131.

36. *OR,* 31(2):79, 199, 230, 234, 238, 287, 288, 310, 313, 525, 530, 544.

reported, "Giving the men five minutes to breathe, and receiving no orders, I gave the word forward, which was eagerly obeyed." Carlin admitted that he went because he "saw the troops on my left going up." Slowly, in a broken-V line formation, the Federals ascended the slope, taking every advantage of the natural cover.[37]

Grant watched in shock. Turning to Thomas, who stood by his side, he angrily said: "Thomas, who ordered those men up that ridge?" Responding in his typically quiet manner, he answered: "I don't know; I did not. Did you order them up Granger?" "No," replied the corps commander, "they started up without orders. When those fellows get started all hell can't stop them." Grant muttered that someone would suffer if it did not go well. Granger told Col. Joseph S. Fullerton, his chief of staff, to ride out to Wood and ask if he gave the advance order and, if he could take the ridge, to push on. Capt. William Avery went with the identical message to Sheridan. Wood declared: "I didn't order them up; they started on their own account, and they are going up, too! Tell Granger if we are supported we will take and hold the ridge!" Sheridan gave a similar answer: "I didn't order them up, but we are going to take the ridge!"[38]

And take the ridge they did. The Confederate line melted under the unrelenting blue wave. Seeing his men surge forward, Phil Sheridan tossed aside his cape and ran among his men still lingering back in the breastworks: "Boys, we are going to take that ridge. Forward and help your comrades!" Wood's men (the general himself confessing that he "was simply one of the boys on that occasion") first pierced the line. The entire Rebel position a mile south of Tunnel Hill was eventually routed, the enemy running pell mell down the reverse slope. When the color bearer of the 24th Wisconsin fell, the eighteen-year-old adjutant "immediately took [the colors] and carried them up the balance of the way," he wrote his father, even though "a whole dose of canister went through [the flag,] tearing it in a frightful manner." The young man's name was Lt. Arthur MacArthur Jr. (father of famed general Douglas MacArthur), and for his bravery he would receive the Medal of Honor. By nightfall Hooker's men finally pressed north up the ridge, collapsing an enemy division.

Bragg lost 2,500 killed and wounded, 6,100 prisoners, and thirty-nine guns captured. Union casualties for the two-day battle totaled 5,824. Granger rode along the ridge, joking: "I will have you all court-martialed! You were ordered to take the works at the foot of the hill, and you have taken those at the top!" Old Glory atop Missionary Ridge represented the crowning achievement of the Army of the Cumberland. Relegated to a supporting role, the Cumberlanders had instead won the

37. McDonough, *Chattanooga*, 175–79; Cozzens, *Shipwreck of Their Hopes*, 272–81; Woodworth, *This Grand Spectacle*, 91–93; Girardi and Hughes, *Memoirs of Brigadier General William Passmore Carlin*, 115.

38. Fullerton, "Army of the Cumberland at Chattanooga," 725.

battle. "There was many cheers given when the Old Flag was planted on top of the Ridge," wrote an artilleryman. "Chickamauga has been avenged," concluded Frank Phelp of the 10th Wisconsin.[39]

Historians have long argued that Grant's lack of an immediate pursuit marred the army's stupendous victory, but insufficient time remained to accomplish much that day. Granger suggested a pursuit, but Grant hesitated, planning instead to immediately relieve Burnside, with Granger spearheading the move. By the time he changed his mind, night had set in. Later that evening a disgusted Sheridan found his superior asleep in Bragg's bed. The corps commander reluctantly relented to Sheridan's badgering and consented to a limited pursuit, though no farther than the crossing of Chickamauga Creek. Sherman pressed ahead on the twenty-sixth, but Thomas got off to a slow start. When Hooker's "Potomacs," as they were called, finally caught up with the Rebel rear guard at Ringgold Gap on the twenty-seventh, they got their nose bloodied, losing 507 men. The Chattanooga campaign had concluded.[40]

Hooker and his officers harbored a grudge. In conversation Butterfield was heard to say: "If Thomas's staff had only had the proper snap in them we would have captured six thousand more prisoners than we did. It was with difficulty, and only after persistent talk that I got the pontoons ordered out, and then you know the officer left them at Rossville and came forward himself, and thus we had a long delay at the creek, and could not get the artillery across."[41]

The Army of the Cumberland had sustained light casualties in the campaign by 1863 standards: 415 killed, 2,834 wounded, and 20 missing, a total of 3,269. (The Confederates suffered losses of over 8,400 men, including over 6,100 prisoners and thirty-nine field guns.) Thomas eventually had his dead gathered and interred on an appropriate hill. When asked by a chaplain if they should be grouped by states, the general hesitated and then answered: "No, no. Mix them up. Mix them up. I am tired of states' rights."[42]

*   *   *

39. *OR,* 31(1):99–100, 553–54; Fullerton, "Army of the Cumberland at Chattanooga," 726; Wood, "Battle of Missionary Ridge," in *MOLLUS,* 37–46; Bennett and Haigh, *Thirty-Sixth Regiment Illinois Volunteers,* 528; MacArthur quoted in Sword, *Mountains Touched with Fire,* 302; Genco, *To the Sound of Musketry,* 131; Frank Phelps to "Dear Friend," Dec. 2, 1863, Frank Phelps Letters, USAMHI.

40. *OR,* 31(2):122, 326; Grant, *Memoirs,* 455, 456. For opposing views concerning Grant's role in the pursuit of Bragg, see Cozzens, *Shipwreck of Their Hopes,* 349–52; and Simpson, *Ulysses S. Grant,* 242, 496 n. 69.

41. William G. Le Duc, *Recollections of a Civil War Quartermaster* (St. Paul: North Central, 1963), 120.

42. Buell, *Warrior Generals,* 294.

Grant now turned his attention to Burnside, who with about fourteen thousand troops, was being invested in Knoxville by Longstreet, with an equal (though believed significantly larger) number. The theater commander wrote an order at 1:00 P.M. on November 27 (though not received by Thomas until 7:00 P.M.), placing Granger in charge of a relief column of twenty-five thousand troops. Leaving on an inspection tour to Graysville, Grant returned on the night of the twenty-ninth only to find that Thomas had still not started the column (nor did Granger want to go, "he having decided for himself that it was a very bad move to make," wrote Grant). When he finally did move, Granger dawdled and complained, causing Grant to lose "all faith in his energy and capacity to manage an expedition of the importance of this one." The commanding general replaced him with Sherman. At the sight of the Federal reinforcements, Longstreet broke off the siege and returned to Virginia.[43]

Granger remained in Knoxville, where he continued to make a fool of himself. On Christmas Day, while obviously intoxicated, he sent a telegram to Grant, apparently meant as a joke: "We are in Knoxville and will hold it till hell freezes over." Grant was not amused, either at the humor or at the fact that Granger was not in pursuit of Longstreet. He had him transferred out of the department that winter.[44]

Following Missionary Ridge, Lincoln, still recovering from a mild form of small pox, expressed his heartfelt thanks to Grant, despite Dana's follow-up dispatch that "neither Grant nor Thomas intended it [the attack]." The president, who only days earlier had been "a little despondent ab[ou]t Grant," according to Hay, "took heart again" at his success. On December 7, upon learning that Sherman had reached Knoxville, the president again wired his "profoundest gratitude." The previous evening he had uttered, "Can anyone doubt, if Grant were here in command [Virginia], that he would catch him [Longstreet]?" Although Lincoln was not ready yet to transfer the general from the West, Grant clearly had the eye of the administration.[45]

Brig. Gen. Alpheus Williams, commanding one of Hooker's divisions, hoped that he would get a furlough and be home at Christmas. Yet, he related to his wife, Thomas "is one of those officers who never leaves himself and thinks nobody else should." In the camp of the 105th Ohio, Bliss Morse settled down on Christmas Day to a meal of hard bread, coffee, and bacon.[46]

43. Grant, *Memoirs*, 452–54; *OR*, 31(2):35, 36, 40, 47, 49, 139, 271, 279, 280, 288.

44. Wilson, *Under the Old Flag*, 1:304–7.

45. *OR*, 31(2):69; Benjamin P. Thomas, *Abraham Lincoln* (New York: Alfred A. Knopf, 1952), 403–4; Simpson, *Ulysses S. Grant*, 246.

46. Milo M. Quaife, ed., *From the Cannon's Mouth: The Civil War Letters of General Alpheus Williams* (Detroit: Wayne State University Press, 1959), 270; Morse, *Diaries and Letters of Bliss Morse*, 100.

20

The Army Remodeled
Winter at Chattanooga

FOR THE EAST TENNESSEE relief column, a bitterly cold New Year's Day came and went with depressingly little fanfare. According to John Beatty, murders and robberies in that mountainous area were as commonplace "as marriages in Ohio, and excite about as little attention." The tents would not arrive until the end of January 1864, so ponchos remained the only protection from weather. Wood's and Sheridan's men wore out their shoes in hard marching, with six hundred of the latter division protecting their feet with a sort of moccasin made from blankets. Yet at the end of the month, Little Phil proudly reported that almost all of his veterans with expiring enlistments had reenlisted. Colonel Sherman nonetheless wrote bluntly: "On half rations; no shoes, hats, shirts, socks, pants, or coats; without tents or blankets; the earth frozen six inches deep and covered with snow—that sums up in brief the comforts of the men who were at Chickamauga and Missionary Ridge, and no prospect of relief. Is loyal East Tennessee worth the sacrifice? I say No, and the prayer of every man and officer of the 4th Corps is that we may be ordered back to Chattanooga."[1]

Back in Chattanooga, six trains, each with a dozen cars, now arrived daily. "Everything is quiet here, but Chattanooga is much more lively than it was before the cars ran through," Major Connolly informed his wife. The government sent fifteen hundred civilian mechanics from the East to repair the railroad to Knoxville and another three hundred to four hundred to work on bridges and the steamboats of the Army of the Cumberland. Thomas still complained that too many of his troops had been diverted for repair duty. By February 12 the track as far as Loudon had been opened, with four steamboats also churning the river between that place and Bridgeport. It would nonetheless be the middle of spring before vegetables arrived. Despite a bleak winter and supply problems, the Rebels clearly had it worse—1,048 deserters turned themselves in during January, with another 110 on February 2 alone.[2]

---

1. Rowell, *Yankee Cavalrymen,* 165; Newlin, *Preacher Regiment,* 286; Beatty, *Citizen Soldier,* 368; Sheridan, *Memoirs,* 1:179, 183; *OR,* 32(2):484; *New York Tribune,* Jan. 11, 1864; Aldrich, *Quest for a Soldier,* 98.

2. Morse, *Diaries and Letters of Bliss Morse,* 110; Angle, *Three Years in the Army of the Cumberland,* 166; *New York Tribune,* Jan. 25, Feb. 9, 1864; *OR,* 32(2):437–38, 38(2):23, 148.

A number of soldiers (at least those who reenlisted for the duration of the war) received four-hundred-dollar bounties and thirty-day furloughs and went home that winter. Some regiments returned with several hundred recruits, men who wanted to avoid the stigma of being conscripted. Only those outfits with three-fourths reenlistments were allowed to retain their original organization. A disappointing 26,838 men would eventually "veteranize" in the IV and XIV Corps and the two Potomac corps—8,000 from Ohio, 4,700 from Indiana, a shockingly low 3,000 from Illinois, a predictably low 2,000 from Kentucky, 1,780 from Michigan, 2,600 from Pennsylvania, 1,300 from New York, and the balance from eastern states in Hooker's corps. These "re-upped" veterans could now wear red, white, and blue chevrons on the lower part of their sleeves. In the 52d Ohio, for example, 418 of 440 men reenlisted. The recruits, plus an influx of conscripts, helped fill the ranks of many depleted units. The thousands who opted not to reenlist were dubbed "stoten-bottles," a term not meant as derogatory. Yet it was the veterans who provided the hardcore fighting edge of the army and without whom the upcoming campaign would be nearly impossible.[3]

Thomas continued to peeve Grant that winter with huge requisitions. On February 5 Lt. Col. Langdon C. Easton, chief quartermaster of the Army of the Cumberland, submitted the needs of the department: 9,000–10,000 cavalry horses, 3,500 artillery horses, 3,000 sets of harness, 3,000 six-mule wagons, 170 ambulances, 45 medicine wagons, 23,200 mules, and 950 horses for ambulances. These requests were in addition to the 2,700 wagons, 450 ambulances, 13,466 mules, 3,174 draft horses, and 16,748 sets of harnesses already on hand. Grant, clearly annoyed by the requests, replied that it was more than was needed in all four of his departments. An exasperated Charles Thomas, assistant chief quartermaster in Washington, queried: "Is the Army of the Cumberland to be doubled in size? . . . To supply 3,000 more wagons in any short time will be difficult. Are they really necessary?"[4]

Brig. Gen. James H. Wilson, chief of the cavalry bureau, discovered in an inspection that February that, at least in terms of the cavalry mounts, the requisition was only slightly exaggerated. In short, Thomas's cavalry corps approached collapse. To

---

3. New York Tribune, Dec. 21, 1863, Mar. 11, 1864; Morse, Diaries and Letters of Bliss Morse, 105, 110, 111; OR, 32(3):25; Army of the Cumberland Memorandum Book, May 31, 1864, Box 11, George Thomas Papers, Misc. Papers, 1861–62, Generals' Papers, RG 94, NA; Castel, Decision in the West, 10–12; Bennett and Haigh, Thirty-Sixth Regiment Illinois Volunteers, 549; Chicago Tribune, Jan. 24, 29, 1864; Robert A. Driver and Gloria S. Driver, eds., Letters Home by Jacob Early (Privately printed, 1992), 216.

4. Special Requisition, Jan. 18, 1864; L. C. Easton to J. L. Donaldson, Feb. 2, 5, 1864; Easton to Meigs, Feb. 5, 1864; L. C. Easton, Estimates of Means of Transportation for the Army of the Cumberland, Feb. 6, 1864; and Charles Thomas to Brig. Gen. A. Allen, Feb. 10, 1864, Correspondence Relating to the Transportation of the Army of the Cumberland, Entry 937, RG 393, NA; OR, 32(2):436, 351–52.

get the nineteen veteran regiments and five mounted infantry regiments back in condition would require 6,000–9,000 horses. The 7th Pennsylvania Cavalry, which had been recruited up to a huge (by 1864 standards) eleven hundred troopers, especially needed animals, "as it is one of the best regiments in the service." Wilson felt it imperative to remount Thomas's cavalry, giving it priority over that of the Army of the Ohio. Meanwhile, some firepower was added with the addition of seven hundred Spencer carbines going to the 2d and 4th Michigan Cavalry and six hundred to the 4th U.S. Cavalry.[5]

The problems related to the First Brigade, First Cavalry Division, camped at "Howard House, Tennessee," on February 15 were indicative of the whole. The three regiments, the 2d Michigan, 7th Pennsylvania, and 1st East Tennessee, counted 1,161 horses, 298 of which were unserviceable. Requisitions had been placed for an additional 1,350 mounts. "The horses of the brigade are all very much jaded out, not by hard marching so much as by foraging," concluded the inspector. "They having to go from three to fifteen miles for forage and then many times coming in with over half rations and that in sacks carried on the horses in front of the trooper, causing almost inevitably the horses to have sore backs rendering them worthless until recruited up. The brigade at present has not over one half horses enough to mount duty men." On another issue, boots "in many instances [are] so bad as to allow the men's bare feet exposed to the ground and cold weather." Of the 1,000 saddles in use, 105 were unserviceable, and a complete resupply of halters, curry combs, saddle blankets, and brushes was needed.[6]

General Sherman soon returned to his old department, where the majority of his army remained, to clear out the remaining Rebels in Mississippi, ten thousand infantry and six thousand cavalry known to be concentrated at Canton and Brandon. His twenty-one-thousand-man column departed Vicksburg on February 3, pushing the defenders past Jackson. He arrived at Meridian on the fourteenth, which he found deserted, the Confederates having withdrawn into Alabama. Sherman thought about pursuing them, but Sooy Smith's seven thousand cavalry from Memphis had not linked up as planned—nor would they. Smith encountered Nathan Bedford Forrest along the way, and though having half Smith's numbers, he sent the Northern force reeling back to Memphis. Sherman torched Meridian and then conducted a slow retreat back to Vicksburg, destroying 115 miles of track in the process.[7]

5. *OR*, 32(3):255–57.
6. Summary of Inspection Report, Feb. 15, 1864, First Brigade, First Cavalry Division, Monthly Inspection Reports Received, 1863–65, Entry 1058, RG 393, Pt. 1.
7. Grant, *Memoirs*, 463; Marszalek, *Sherman*, 253–54; Hirshson, *White Tecumseh*, 183–84.

In order to prevent Joseph Johnston, who had replaced Bragg in command of the Army of Tennessee, from sending reinforcements into Alabama (which in fact he did) and to ascertain enemy strength, Grant ordered a reconnaissance in force against the Rebel stronghold at Dalton. John Palmer would lead the expedition, Thomas having been stricken with a painful case of neuralgia. The XIV Corps arrived at Ringgold on the twenty-third, forcing advanced enemy pickets at Tunnel Hill to withdraw. Palmer notified Grant that evening that he would venture toward Dalton if Stanley's division at Cleveland, under the temporary command of Brigadier General Cruft, would move down the railroad to cover his left. As requested, the division, spearheaded by Eli Long's cavalry brigade, got into position by the morning of the twenty-fifth.

Palmer found Johnston's mountain den fronted by formidable Rocky Face Ridge, stretching north to south for nearly twenty-three miles. He ordered Johnson's and Davis's divisions to attack Buzzard's Roost Gap, the opening through which the railroad ran. Baird's thirty-five hundred men meanwhile moved to the left, north of the gap. Extensive skirmishing lasted throughout the day on both Palmer's front, supported by Battery H, 4th U.S. Artillery, and the 5th Indiana Artillery, and Baird's line. The Confederates clearly remained in force—forty thousand infantry and ten thousand cavalry, according to the best estimates. Seeing no reason to continue the unequal contest, Thomas, who by this time had arrived on the field, ordered a withdrawal, having sustained 345 casualties. Col. Geza Mihalotzy of the Chicago 24th Illinois had been wounded four previous times, but his luck ran out here; he fell mortally wounded. The dry leaves and pine cones lying along the mountain slopes caught fire, spreading a choking smoke and inhibiting the withdrawal.[8]

The expedition accomplished little since Sherman had chosen not to advance into Alabama. One sidelight, however, would have future implications. Col. Thomas Harrison's 39th Indiana Mounted Infantry, scouting five miles south of Buzzard's Roost Gap, actually entered Dug Gap, a manmade pass, driving away the small infantry picket post and repulsing a subsequent attack by a cavalry regiment. A single regiment, of course, even a very good one like Harrison's, could obviously not cut the Western and Atlantic Railroad and threaten Johnston from the rear. In hearing the report, however, Thomas nonetheless became intrigued that Johnston had been so easily caught off guard. He began developing an idea for future operations.[9]

* * *

8. John Palmer, *Personal Recollections,* 199–200; *OR,* 32(1):422–27, 443–44, 452–57, 32(2):435, 458–59, 461, 480, 482, 32(3):90; Athearn, *Soldier in the West,* 177; *Chicago Tribune,* Mar. 3, 1864.

9. Castel, *Decision in the West,* 54.

By late February Grant, ill and tanked with enough quinine "to make my head buz," had grown weary of the continued talk of his presidential aspirations, which were nonexistent. Word soon arrived that Lincoln had nominated him to the new rank of lieutenant general. In early March he reported to Washington, where he met the president for the first time. In a private meeting in the East Room of the White House, Lincoln informed Grant that he would assume command of all Union armies. In a subsequent inspection of the Army of the Potomac, the new general in chief made a good impression upon Meade and others, though several old friends could not resist commenting smilingly, "You have not yet met Bobby Lee."[10]

Grant returned to Nashville to confer with Sherman, who arrived on March 17. Announcing that he had decided to accompany the Army of the Potomac, Grant appointed his trusted subordinate as his successor in the West. It seems clear that he never seriously considered Thomas for the job. In a dinner meeting with Andrew Carnegie back in Virginia, the industrialist had asked: "I suppose you will place Thomas in command in the West?" "No," Grant answered, "Sherman is the man for chief command. Thomas would be the first to say so." From Nashville the two generals took a train to Cincinnati, discussing a master strategy along the way. There would be a coordinated offensive in the spring, Grant in Virginia and Sherman in Georgia. "This was the plan. No routes prescribed," Sherman wrote.[11]

Historians have almost uniformly taken the position that, given Sherman's close ties to Grant, his selection over Thomas was inevitable but unjustified based upon the facts. "On the basis of his record, Sherman did not merit such a promotion, certainly not ahead of Thomas," concluded Richard McMurry. Sherman had failed in Kentucky in 1861, at Chickasaw Bayou in 1862, and at Missionary Ridge in 1863. Thomas, though, had saved the army's flank at Mill Springs in 1861 and the army itself at Chickamauga in 1863. Only his own rejection had kept him from army command over a year earlier.[12]

Precisely how Thomas felt about Sherman's appointment is not known; he never publicly commented and left no personal papers. The assumption has long been that he was quietly embittered and angry. Such may not have been the case. Only months earlier, when his name had been rumored to succeed George Meade as commander of the Army of the Potomac, Thomas had made it clear that he wanted nothing to do with it. He wrote Garfield (the one promoting the idea) on December

10. Simpson, *Ulysses S. Grant*, 258–64.

11. Castel, *Decision in the West*, 67–68; Carnegie quoted in McKinney, *Education in Violence*, 313; Joseph T. Glatthaar, *Partners in Command: The Relationships between Leaders in the Civil War* (New York: Free Press, 1994), 156.

12. Buell, *Warrior Generals*, 295; Richard McMurry, *Atlanta 1864: Last Chance for the Confederacy* (Lincoln: University of Nebraska Press, 2000), 19–20.

17, 1863: "You have disturbed me greatly with the intimation that the command of the Army of the Potomac may be offered to me. It is a position to which I am not the least adapted, and putting my own reputation entirely aside I sincerely hope that I at least may not be victimized by being placed in a position where I would be utterly powerless to do good or contribute in the least toward the suppression of the Rebellion. The pressure always brought to bear against the commander of the Army of the Potomac would destroy me in a week without having advanced the cause in the least. Much against my wishes I was placed in command of this army." It was not Thomas's nature to play coy or to posture, and he had previously shown a reluctance to assume ultimate command. Whether or not he would have felt the same way about supreme western command is not known. Even if he did not desire the position, it may not necessarily follow that he relished being under Sherman, whom he certainly viewed as out of his depth at best and a failed commander at worst. Additionally, Sherman had been his junior, the exact situation that had so irked Thomas about Rosecrans's assumption of command.[13]

When Sherman first met Thomas in Chattanooga after the appointment, the Virginian revealed no outward resentment; Thomas's passive-aggressive nature toward superiors was more subtle. When one of Sherman's staff officers asked if there was any truth to the rumors that Thomas was disgruntled, Sherman answered: "Not a bit of it. It don't make any difference which of us commands the army. I would obey Tom's orders tomorrow as readily and cheerfully as he does mine. But I think I can give the army a little more impetus than Tom can." Sherman added that Thomas knew "how to pull with me, tho' he don't pull in the same way."[14]

Being from Virginia and having no political base, in addition to shunning army politics, Thomas had no advocates who might come to his defense or advance his name for promotion. The notable exception proved to be Andrew Johnson, who wrote Lincoln that the placement of Sherman over Thomas "will produce disappointment in the public mind and impair the public service." The western press remained silent on the subject.[15]

Resolving Hooker's anomalous command of two corps proved to be the first order of business. During Grant's tenure in command, there had been talk about consolidating the XI and XII Corps, though the general had been more inclined to recruit them up to strength. As for Hooker, Grant wanted him out, perhaps transferred to an administrative position. Hooker, well aware of his declining status, wrote Stanton: "I find I am regarded with a great deal of jealousy by those filling

13. Buell, *Warrior Generals*, 295. Writes McMurry: "As a human being and as a very competent army officer, Thomas resented Grant's decision and the situation in which it placed him. As a practical man, a patriot, and a good soldier, he silently accepted the new arrangement." *Atlanta 1864*, 20.

14. Castel, *Decision in the West*, 85–86; McKinney, *Education in Violence*, 313.

15. Graf, Haskins, and Bergeron, *Papers of Andrew Johnson*, 6:652.

high places here, but of the balance of the army I have no cause to complain. I can survive if they can." From the outset he believed that the Missionary Ridge plan had been designed "to shut me out of the fight, Grant's object being to give the eclat to his old army [the Army of the Tennessee]."[16]

Sherman did not have to take his cues from Grant; his own distaste for Hooker went back to their California days in the 1850s. Hooker, who incurred gambling debts and speculated in land, never repaid money borrowed from Sherman. Following Missionary Ridge, Fighting Joe went on the attack. In a letter to Chase, he contemptuously denounced Sherman's recent unsuccessful attack at Tunnel Hill. "Sherman is an active, energetic officer, but in judgment is as infirm as Burnside. He will never be successful. Please remember what I tell you." Hooker's biographer has implied that Thomas and Hooker, both on the outs with the Grant-Sherman team, warmed to each other. There is no real substantiating evidence beyond the fact that Thomas suggested that Hooker take his old XIV Corps. (Palmer had submitted his resignation to run in the Illinois gubernatorial race.)[17]

Sherman instead chose to consolidate the two corps into the new XX Corps, with Hooker at its head, and placed it in the Army of the Cumberland as a third corps. This would give Hooker a clear subordinate role under Thomas, but he was reportedly pleased with the arrangement. To a friend he immodestly wrote: "You must know that I am regarded with more jealousy in this new sphere of operation than I ever was in the East. It is not without reason for it is as certain as any future event can be that I shall be regarded as the best soldier in this Army if I am not now, provided we have a few opportunities to establish our relative merits. An effort will be made to prevent this but the result will likely be as futile as the last one."[18]

In order to separate Hooker and Slocum, the latter was sent to command the District of Vicksburg. Hooker also wanted to be rid of three of his division commanders—Carl Schurz, Adolph von Steinwehr, and Alpheus Williams—and eventually gave two of his three divisions to Geary and Butterfield. Thomas conceded that he was not impressed with Schurz and would not be sorry to see him go. Schurz and von Steinwehr soon departed, though Williams remained.[19]

16. *OR*, 32(2):313–15, 467–69, 32(3):364–66.

17. Walter H. Hebert, *Fighting Joe Hooker* (Indianapolis: Bobbs-Merrill, 1944), 39–41, 266–67, 269; Hirshson, *White Tecumseh*, 221; *OR*, 32(3):377; George Palmer, *Conscientious Turncoat*, 133–35, 137, 139–40. In the first draft of his memoirs, Sherman wrote that Hooker believed Thomas to be jealous of him. He later removed these words. Hirshson, *White Tecumseh*, 381–82.

18. Hebert, *Fighting Joe Hooker*, 269, 271; *OR*, 32(3):364–66; Castel, *Decision in the West*, 96–97. Included in the reorganized XX Corps was John Coburn's brigade, captured ten months earlier at Thompson's Station. The troops had been exchanged and on garrison duty for some months. Welcher and Ligget, *Coburn's Brigade*, 100–101, 107–8, 158, 160.

19. *OR*, 32(3):292, 341.

Sherman next went after the profane and hard-drinking Granger, who so irritated him with his grousing and lethargy in chasing Longstreet past Knoxville that he determined to be rid of him. An incident around Christmas 1863 did not help Granger's stock. The IV Corps commander, then in Nashville, had Sherman and Grant to dinner at the home of his Southern mother-in-law, at which time the woman angrily denounced Sherman for his supposed foraging on the route to Knoxville. The general bristled and retorted: "Madame, my soldiers have to subsist even if the whole country must be ruined to maintain them. . . . War is cruelty. There is no use trying to reform it; the crueler it is the sooner it will be over." Granger preempted the inevitable by requesting a leave of absence.[20]

Command of the IV Corps went to one-armed, thirty-nine-year-old Oliver O. Howard. His transfer from the XI Corps was clearly meant to get him out from under Hooker, but he had performed poorly back east. A devout Methodist (he had considered going into the ministry after West Point) and a strict teetotaler, officers referred to him as the "Christian soldier," the men as "Old Prayer Book." He squirmed and blushed when anyone cursed, which caused the religiously indifferent Sherman to mischievously break out into profanity when he walked in the room. "Well, the Christian soldier business is all right in its place. But he needn't put on airs when we are among ourselves," Sherman once snipped. Howard, thrilled to receive the new command, confided to his wife that he felt emancipated from both Hooker and his old XI Corps, having lost confidence in both. "I like the 4th Corps. It is much larger than any command I have ever had."[21]

It had been rumored that Sheridan would take Granger's place with the IV Corps, but on March 23, 1864, he received orders to report to Washington; Grant had tapped him as the new cavalry chief of the Army of the Potomac. Having com-

20. Sherman, *Memoirs*, 1:368, 2:8; Grenville M. Dodge, *Personal Recollections of President Abraham Lincoln, General Ulysses S. Grant, and General William T. Sherman* (Council Bluffs, Iowa: Monarch, 1914), 139–42. Thereafter, Granger bounced around to insignificant commands.

21. Oliver O. Howard, *Autobiography of Oliver O. Howard, Major General United States Army*, 2 vols. (New York: Baker and Taylor, 1908), 1:499; Frederick Bancroft and William A. Dunning, eds., *The Reminiscences of Carl Schurz*, 3 vols. (New York: McClure, 1908), 3:78–79; Castel, *Decision in the West*, 97–98; Sherman to Howard, Dec. 18, 1863, Apr. 5, 1864, Oliver O. Howard Papers, Bowdoin College, Brunswick, Maine; *OR*, 32(3):258.

Lyman S. Widney noted that "the hardest sinner in our ranks respected him [Howard]." Widney Diary, June 27, 1864, KNBP. A Michigan soldier also expressed his admiration: "[Howard] is the only Major General I have ever seen on his knees in prayer. He frequently attends the soldier's religious meetings and prays and speaks like everyone else." "Civil War Letters," *Michigan History Magazine* 1 (Oct. 1917): 13. It should also be mentioned that Sherman later reproached Brigadier General Wood for attempting to entice Howard to drink: "Wood, let Howard alone! I want one officer who don't drink." Howard, *Autobiography*, 1:537.

manded his division for a year and a half, Sheridan did not trust his emotions, so he planned to leave quietly and without fanfare. Word leaked out, however, and the entire division turned out on the hillsides of East Tennessee to bid him farewell. "I regretted deeply leaving such soldiers," he admitted. Succeeding him would be forty-one-year-old Brig. Gen. John Newton of the Army of the Potomac. An able brigadier, the Virginia-born Newton had led the I Corps at Gettysburg after the death of Maj. Gen. John F. Reynolds. The transfer was not intended as an east-west swap; the I Corps had been broken up and Newton needed a command.[22]

Changes also occurred in the cavalry, with the addition of a third division, to be commanded by the reckless twenty-eight-year-old Brig. Gen. Judson "Kill Cavalry" Kilpatrick, a reject from the Army of the Potomac. An officer described him as "the most vain, conceited, egotistical little popinjay I ever saw. He is a very ungraceful rider, looking more like a monkey than a man on horseback." The riding problem actually related to his kidneys (sometimes he urinated too much, sometimes not enough), which often gave him severe back pains.[23]

Predictably, easterners taking top spots did not set well with the western armies. "I cannot say that I am very favorably impressed with [Newton]," wrote Colonel Sherman. "The changes thus made in our Corps and our Division, bringing strangers amongst us, is not to our liking. I do not know as we have any choice in the matter; we certainly have not been consulted as to whether we would prefer our old and loved commanders with whom we have fought and endured to those [of whom] we know naught. . . . Our likes and wishes we cannot help."[24]

Hazen, one of those blocked for promotion, believed that officers from Virginia, such as Newton, should have been given posts in rear positions and that divisions should be reserved for those within the corps who had proven themselves on the battlefield. Discounting easterners such as Newton and Brannan; those from Rosecrans's army from Mississippi, such as Sheridan, Palmer, Cruft and Davis; and those from the old Army of Kentucky, such as Baird, only one general from within the Army of the Cumberland, Horatio Van Cleve, had received either a division or corps command since the fall of 1862. Somewhat reversing the trend was the assignment of Brig. Gen. William T. Ward of Kentucky, who had commanded various posts throughout the war, to command a brigade in the Third Division of the XX Corps. An Illinois soldier held a decidedly negative view of his new brigadier, describing him as "a regular old Falstaff [a drunken Shakespearean character] whose sheer de-

---

22. Sheridan, *Memoirs*, 1:183–85; Morris, *Sheridan*, 152; Warner, *Generals in Blue*, 344–45; *OR*, 32(3):292.

23. Quoted in Evans, *Sherman's Horsemen*, 382–84.

24. Aldrich, *Quest for a Star*, 108.

light is to swill whiskey, etc. No one respects him and all unite in hoping that he will soon be removed." A Hoosier denounced Ward as "the poorest excuse for a Genl I ever saw, he keeps eternally drunk and has no confidence placed in him either by superiors or inferiors."[25]

Steedman, despite his heroic stand at Chickamauga, did not have his promotion confirmed by the Senate until the spring of 1864. His conservative views on emancipation, expressed in several articles, may have played a role. He would remain in rear-echelon positions, bitter at his lack of recognition.[26]

Regarding the XIV Corps, Thomas wrote Sherman in early April: "I have said nothing to Palmer [whose political aspirations had not panned out], but I do not think he would object to take a division under Buell, and if Buell comes and would be willing to do duty under me I would be very glad to give him the Fourteenth Corps. . . . If you could give [Richard] Johnson a command in Kentucky, at Louisville, for instance, I think he would be satisfied and Palmer would take his division. Should Buell not come or be willing to take that command, I prefer to have Palmer remain." Palmer, as it turned out, had privately confided his doubts to Thomas about his ability at corps command. Sherman, believing the political general to be in over his head, proved surprisingly receptive to the Buell suggestion, turning a blind eye to the complications of having two failed army commanders (Buell and Hooker) serving under him. It proved moot, however, since neither Washington officials nor Buell himself agreed.[27]

In early February a veteran brigadier, John Beatty, resigned in order to tend the family's bank in Cardington, Ohio, giving his brother an opportunity to serve in the army. Succeeding him would be the senior colonel in the brigade, twenty-five-year-old John G. Mitchell, making him the youngest brigade commander in the Army of the Cumberland.[28]

Changes also occurred in the army staff. With the transfer of Joseph Reynolds to command Federal forces at New Orleans, Thomas got Brig. Gen. William D. Whipple, an officer who had served in sundry administrative posts back east, as his chief of staff. Not in good health, Whipple contracted a severe case of neuralgia jaw pain in January 1864, which he blamed on his Cincinnati dentist, or "butcher," as he referred to him. (Whipple came dangerously close to being struck by a shell frag-

25. Hazen, *Narrative*, 245; Warner, *Generals in Blue*, 538; Jennifer Cain Bohrnstedt, ed., *Soldiering with Sherman: Civil War Letters of George F. Cram* (DeKalb: Northern Illinois University Press, 2000), 89; Lorna Lutes Sylvester, ed., "'Gone for a Soldier:' The Civil War Letters of Charles Harding Cox," *Indiana Magazine of History* 68 (1972): 198.

26. *OR*, 32(3):221, 292, 312–14; Engle, *Buell*, 339–40; Sherman, *Memoirs*, 2:5–7.

27. McKinney, *Education in Violence*, 277; Warner, *Generals in Blue*, 473, 662.

28. *New York Tribune*, Feb. 12, 1864; Warner, *Generals in Blue*, 28, 328.

ment during the February reconnaissance to Dalton.) Thomas also lost Horace Porter as his chief of ordnance, Grant transferring him to Virginia. Lieutenant Colonel Ducat, a leftover from Rosecrans's staff and a mediocre officer at best, resigned. John Mendenhall, promoted to lieutenant colonel, became the army inspector general. Thomas did retain his three longtime aides, Oscar Mack, John P. Willard (a distant relative of Mrs. Thomas), and nephew Sanford Kellogg.[29]

Sherman continued the same distant relationship with Thomas begun by Grant. The new department commander took personal control of the railroads when Maj. Gen. John Logan, temporarily commanding the Army of the Tennessee, complained of Thomas's prejudice toward his army. One historian has suggested that the armies, like their commanders, differed greatly. Hazen noted that "jealousies, dislike and dissensions were developing in the Army of the Cumberland while they were nearly unknown in the Army of the Tennessee." In terms of drill and discipline, however, Thomas's army so surpassed Sherman's "as scarcely to admit of comparison." Hair below the shoulder, unheard of in the Army of the Cumberland, became commonplace in the Army of the Tennessee. While all of Thomas's division and corps commanders, save Palmer, had graduated from West Point, Sherman's old army had no professionals in those positions. As a result, an intense democracy, even feistiness, existed in the Army of the Tennessee.[30]

Thomas's chief engineer, W. E. Merrill, oversaw the development of a new canvas pontoon boat. Equipped with hinges, the boats could fold back upon themselves, making them small enough to transport on regular army wagons. Each corps carried a train sufficient to bridge a nine-hundred-foot-wide river. The lead division on the march, assisted by engineers, would have the responsibility of assembling the span. Merrill also worked on map improvements. Capt. William L. Margedant, borrowed from an Ohio regiment, invented a field reproduction process for maps, meaning that even brigadiers had the latest sketches.[31]

Thomas's biographers have asserted that Sherman relied upon the infrastructure of the Army of the Cumberland. To be sure, Sherman used Thomas's intelligence-gathering network and topographical and engineer staffs. Regarding the railroads, Thomas had utilized the services of Col. Daniel McCallum, a railroad genius, replac-

29. Warner, *Generals in Blue*, 555; Porter, *Campaigning with Grant*, 12–13; *OR*, 32(2):57–58, 488. Reynolds departed the army on December 5, 1863. *New York Tribune*, Dec. 16, 1863; *Chicago Tribune*, Mar. 3, 1864; McKinney, *Education in Violence*, 472; Welsh, *Medical Histories*, 366–67.

30. Lewis, *Sherman*, 347–48; *OR*, 32(3):490, 522. Thomas stiffly wrote Logan: "I regret very much that you did not communicate with me on this subject [Army of Tennessee prejudice] before reporting it to the major general commanding the Military Division of Mississippi." Ibid.

31. W. E. Merrill, "The Engineer Service in the Army of the Cumberland," in Van Horne, *Army of the Cumberland*, 2:439–58.

390 DAYS OF GLORY

ing the generally inept John B. Anderson, department superintendent of railroads. Yet many problems remained when Sherman assumed command, including accusations by both the Tennessee and Ohio army commanders of favoritism toward the Cumberland army. Sherman clearly took railroad organization beyond Thomas's earlier efforts. In an April 2 meeting in Nashville, in which the Virginian was not present, Sherman completely reorganized his rail transportation. He accomplished more with the same equipment simply by cracking down on civilian traffic and freight, no longer feeding eight thousand Southern civilians, and by moving cattle and horses overland rather than by rail, the last saving ten cars per day. Sherman also obtained additional locomotives and cars, something that Thomas's badgering of Anderson had been unable to accomplish. If Thomas got the trains moving, it was Sherman who enabled the army to get beyond a hand-to-mouth existence to stockpiling.[32]

On Thursday, March 10, Thomas rode to his Chattanooga front lines, finding all quiet. Two divisions of the IV Corps remained in East Tennessee, with Stanley's division five miles in advance of Cleveland. The Army of the Cumberland had regained considerable strength as furloughed veterans and new recruits, many of them having to march from Nashville due to the jammed rail system, now returned at the rate of two thousand per day. The reenlistment process continued smoothly, despite the fact that Capt. John H. Young, the army's chief mustering officer, had begun his annual drinking binge. A late March snow, followed by gusty winds and rain, ended the warm spell. Rebel deserters continued to come into the Federal lines at the rate of twenty-five per day.[33]

All was not army monotony, though. Geary wrote his wife on March 19: "On Tuesday [the fifteenth] I was one of a special dinnery-party at Maj. Genl Hooker's Hd. Qrs. at Wauhatchie. The party consisted of Maj. Gens. Thomas, Howard & Hooker, Brig. Gens. Whipple, Brannan, Elliott, Steinweir, Ward, & Geary together with sundry Colonels and Captains. The Dinner was a good one, for a camp getting up. The party was pleasant and refreshing from the monotony of a soldier's life."[34]

By the end of the month, the army had swollen to 56,500 infantry "present for duty," distributed about 20,000 each in the XIV and XX Corps and 16,500 in the IV Corps. The cavalry branch had been resurrected to an impressive 14,000 troopers. Two brigades, one each of engineers and pioneers, plus an independent engineer

32. McKinney, *Education in Violence*, 309, 316–17, 318, 320–21. The assertion that Sherman relied "on Thomas for staff work" is unsubstantiated. See R. Steven Jones, *The Right Hand of Command: Use and Disuse of Personal Staffs in the Civil War* (Harrisburg: Stackpole, 2000), 159–68.

33. McKinney, *Education in Violence*, 308, 316; *New York Tribune*, Mar. 25, 1864; Athearn, *Soldier in the West*, 182–83, 191; *Chicago Tribune*, Mar. 15, Apr. 5, 1864.

34. Blair, *Politician Goes to War*, 158.

regiment, totaled an additional 3,400 men, bringing total army strength to near 74,000 and 126 guns. It was larger by far than the other components of Sherman's army group, the Army of the Tennessee, now under Maj. Gen. James McPherson, with 24,500 troops and 96 guns; and the reorganized Army of the Ohio (minus the IX Corps, sent back to Virginia), now under Maj. Gen. John M. Schofield, with only 11,000 infantry and 28 guns.[35]

The problem with Sherman's organizational arrangement, according to Richard McMurry, was that "the Army of the Cumberland proved too large for rapid movement, and the other two armies often proved too weak to accomplish their missions." In postwar years Schofield wrote that Thomas did not want to relinquish any of his troops. McMurry has argued that the XX Corps had no historic relationship to the Army of the Cumberland, and all or some of the troops should have been transferred to McPherson or Schofield. But since Hooker outranked both McPherson and Schofield, he would have been loath to work with them, much less under them. The same would have been true of Palmer, who outranked Schofield.[36]

Thomas's westerners certainly did not receive Hooker's "New England Yankee peddlers" with open arms. John King of the 92d Illinois Mounted Infantry wrote bluntly:

Hooker's corps was composed of New England regiments, or "downeast Yankees." These men all had their peculiarities, which, of course, differed from Westerners and Southerners. Every man seemed to be in a trade, a sutler, or tinker of some kind. Nearly every man had a little box, bag, or basket in which he had something to sell, or took to fix something with. Every man would have a consignment of some kind of goods such as could pass through the mails. On one or two occasions, the 92nd rode through the camps of Hooker's corps, composed as it was of these genuine Yankee "soldier boys," the road was lined on either side with them, and every man appeared to have something in his hands or hanging on his arms to sell. It seemed as though the whole corps was made up of peddlers ready to cheat the South of their Confederacy. Their goods consisted of pens, penholders, tobacco, tobacco pouches, diaries, rings, watches, toothbrushes, combs, watch chains, jackknives—in fact, every trinket known to the small Yankee trade.[37]

Routine camp life continued in April. Orson Brainard of the 51st Ohio noted that a soldier found guilty of desertion had his head shaved, was fined over eleven months' pay, and then drummed out with the brigade formed in a square—"he bore it like a man," the Ohioan wrote. As the month wore on, troops began the serious business

35. *OR*, 32(2):207–11, 32(3):90.
36. McMurry, *Atlanta 1864*, 34–35.
37. Swedberg, *Three Years with the 92d Illinois*, 205–6.

of target practice—five rounds daily. "I can hit the targaret [sic] about 3 times out of five at 150 yards," he boasted.[38]

Thomas fretted over news leaks, both from correspondents and from his own division commanders, who could not resist talking to reporters. He was also peeved at Baird, who "let it get out all over camp" that the Federal signal corps had broken the Rebel flag code being used on Tunnel Hill.[39]

By mid-April, reports filtered in from Rebel deserters that Johnston had sent William Hardee's corps to Lee in Virginia. These types of stories were not unusual, but given the recent history of troop transfers on both sides, Sherman had to take them seriously. Thomas reassured him that his best scout, in addition to spies who visited Dalton on a weekly basis, confirmed that Johnston, with his estimated forty thousand troops, had gone nowhere. Wheeler had two cavalry brigades advanced, one at Tunnel Hill and another at Varnell's Station. A sizable cavalry force also scouted Nickajack Gap below Ringgold. There the pickets had closed to within a mile, with neither side crowding the other.[40]

Montgomery Meigs, meanwhile, continued his search for additional mules for the Army of the Cumberland, with five hundred teams promised from Missouri and a thousand from Camp Nelson. The quartermaster general nevertheless declared that Thomas must shrink his train, telling him that Grant in Virginia had recently reduced thirty-five thousand men to a mere six hundred wagons. Thomas reportedly never came into compliance. Sherman would later write: "Most of the general officers, except Thomas, followed my [austere] example strictly; but he had a regular headquarters-camp. I frequently called his attention to the orders on this subject, rather jestingly than seriously. He would break out against his officers for having such luxuries, but, needing a tent himself, and being good-natured and slow to act, he never enforced my orders perfectly. In addition to his regular wagon-train, he had a big wagon which could be converted into an office, and this we used to call 'Thomas's circus.' "[41]

An inspection of the XX Corps on the twenty-third, followed by a sham battle

38. Orson Brainard to father, Apr. 10, 25, 1864, in Wilfred W. Black, ed., "Orson Brainard: A Soldier in the Ranks," *Ohio History* 76 (1967): 62.

39. *OR*, 32(3):341.

40. Ibid., 411, 412; *New York Tribune*, Apr. 4, 1862.

41. *OR*, 32(3):423, 454–55; Sherman, *Memoirs*, 2:22. Despite Sherman's postwar jab at Thomas, records indicate that the Army of the Cumberland was lean on transportation. The entire IV Corps traveled with only six hospital wagons, and regiments were allotted only ammunition wagons and ambulances. The IV Corps train on May 5 comprised only 233 commissary wagons (sufficient for two days' rations). Other forage wagons and a thirty-wagon reserve medical train traveled in the rear. *OR*, 38(1):218, 518, 840; Surgeon General's Office, *Medical and Surgical History*, 1(2):299.

five days later, brought out the top brass, Thomas, Hooker, and Howard among them. In the ranks of the Third Division was George F. Cram of the 105th Illinois, who held his own opinions about what he viewed. "With regard to Hooker, everybody loves him and to see him as he rides along our lines is only to like him more each time," he wrote his mother. As for the Cumberland army commander, he continued: "I do not like the appearance of Thomas so well as Hooker or Howard. He is a sort of burly looking man and my convictions are that he passes [sic] more of brute courage than military skill, however, I may be wrong."[42]

42. Bohrnstedt, *Soldiering with Sherman,* 88–89.

21

The Atlanta Campaign
"A Spirit of Jealousy"

MILD, SPRINGLIKE, but unusually dry weather ushered in May, as Sherman made final arrangements to advance his armies. The soldiers stripped down to light marching order, leaving behind all cooking utensils except coffeepots, frying pans, and an occasional camp kettle. Major Connolly, writing to his wife, seemed resigned to the coming operations: "My goodness! I do dread starting out in the dust and hot sun, after such a long period of ease, but the rebels must be whipped, and since we can't do it sitting in the house, I suppose we must content ourselves with going after them."[1]

The original campaign plan envisioned by Sherman was a wide sweep southwest of Dalton to Rome by McPherson's Army of the Tennessee. When it became apparent that two divisions of the XVII Corps would not arrive in time to participate, Sherman realized that McPherson's remaining five divisions of twenty-three thousand troops would be insufficient to operate so far from his main force. Nonetheless, he maintained the concept of using his cherished old command as the pivotal army of the campaign, while the Army of the Cumberland served in a support role.[2]

The strategic plan eventually developed was in fact not Sherman's but Thomas's, the Virginian conceiving the idea during his February Dalton reconnaissance. He proposed to use Taylor's Ridge as a screen and march his entire army through Snake Creek Gap, thirteen miles south of Dalton, to Resaca, where the Western and Atlanta Railroad would be cut. All the while McPherson and Schofield would keep Johnston occupied by demonstrations against Rocky Face Ridge to the west and Crow Valley to the north. Having turned his position, Johnston would either have to fight or escape east into barren country. Sherman accepted the plan, though with one main revision: the flanking column would be the Army of the Tennessee.

But Sherman, who never gave Thomas his due credit for the concept, had made a

1. George E. Cooper, "Report on the Operations of the Medical Department of the Army of the Cumberland through Georgia, in the Summer of 1864," in Surgeon General's Office, *Medical and Surgical History*, 1(2):299; Angle, *Three Years in the Army of the Cumberland*, 203; Widney to parents, May 1, 1864, Lyman S. Widney Letters, KNBP.
2. McMurry, *Atlanta 1864*, 57; Castel, *Decision in the West*, 121.

major error, according to historian Albert Castel. He should have adopted Thomas's original plan or, if intent upon using the Army of the Tennessee, a variation of it—namely, to reinforce McPherson with one of Thomas's corps, which ultimately he did, but too late. Scholars have lined up on both sides of the issue, Richard McMurry concurring that Sherman had chosen to send "a relatively weak column to Snake Creek Gap" and John Marszalek questioning whether or not Thomas's large force would "have moved that resolutely."[3]

Several points are salient. First, whether good or bad, Thomas's bold plan revealed that he was not simply a defensive general; he was coming of age. Second, whether or not his original plan would have worked is a nonhistorical question, but an interesting comparison can be made with the Tullahoma campaign. In that instance Thomas seized Hoover's Gap but then squandered his success and subsequently stalled, thus giving the Confederates time to withdraw to Tullahoma. If Thomas performed sluggishly with one corps, would he have acted more boldly with three? Third, what was the evolving relationship between Sherman and Thomas? Not long before the campaign commenced, Thomas Ewing wrote Sherman that he should have replaced Thomas for his perceived delay in attacking Missionary Ridge. Sherman, in his response, set the record straight that Grant had directed affairs. Regarding Thomas, he wrote: "If we were to dispose of such men as Thomas summarily who would take his place? We are not masters as Napoleon was. He [Napoleon] could make & unmake on the spot. We must take the tools provided us, and in the order prescribed by Rank of which the Law judges." Hardly a ringing endorsement of Thomas, Sherman's statement reveals more a respect of his seniority and the lack of a realistic alternative. Finally, this would not be the last time Sherman would show preferential treatment toward the Army of the Tennessee. Indeed, McMurry refers to the "Halleck-Grant-Sherman Army of the Tennessee clique that dominated the Union military establishment after early 1864."[4]

3. Castel, *Decision in the West*, 121–23, 181–82; McMurry, *Atlanta 1864*, 65; John F. Marszalek, "Sherman Called It the Way He Saw It," *Civil War History* 40 (1994): 75. For Castel's assessment of B. H. Liddell-Hart's negative view of Thomas's plan, see *Decision in the West*, 567–68.

4. Brooks D. Simpson and Jean V. Berlin, eds., *Sherman's Civil War: Selected Correspondence of William T. Sherman, 1860–1865* (Chapel Hill: University of North Carolina Press, 1999), 630–31; McMurry, *Atlanta 1864*, 33. Marszalek maintains that Sherman liked "Thomas personally and respected him. Thomas was indeed slow moving in personality and cautious in military action. This attribute was neither good nor bad; it simply was. At times it drove Sherman crazy, but he also recognized it as making Thomas so tenacious a defender." "Sherman Called It," 75.

I tend more toward the views of Albert Castel and Michael Fellman. Indeed, beyond minor anecdotal information (calling each other Tom and Cump), there is little to suggest the close friendship (during the Civil War years) between the two officers that has traditionally been claimed. Maybe Sherman had something to do with overriding the War Department's 1861 decision to replace Thomas with Mitchel,

Departing Cleveland, Tennessee, at 5:00 A.M., the IV Corps, spearheaded by Wood's division, arrived at Catoosa Springs, Georgia, by midmorning. In its heyday tourists flocked to the mineral springs and its nearby three-story hotel, now an abandoned Confederate hospital and in a dilapidated state. To the west Palmer's corps, accompanied by Thomas, marched into Ringgold, and to Palmer's right Hooker's corps passed the old Chickamauga battlefield and Leet's Tanyard. The men expressed revulsion and anger at seeing the half-buried remains of their fallen comrades. "The bodies of many a soldier lay scattered over the field. Some of the graves are so shallow that their feet and heads can be seen entirely bare. Twas a horrible sight," Cpl. Joseph W. Ely of the 19th Michigan related to his parents.[5]

Thomas's army remained essentially stationary throughout May 5 and 6: Howard in position at Catoosa Springs, Palmer at Ringgold, and Hooker at Pleasant Grove, Leet's, and Pea Vine Church, three, six, and eight miles southwest of Ringgold respectively. The Army of the Tennessee, a day behind schedule, arrived at Lee and Gordon's Mill, and the Army of the Ohio anchored the left at Red Clay. Sherman's plans for the seventh called for Thomas to advance and take Tunnel Hill—Palmer from the front and Howard from the flank—while Hooker continued his southward slide along the western foot of Taylor's Ridge.[6]

At daybreak on May 7, the troops of Davis's division, Dan McCook's brigade in the lead, advanced toward Tunnel Hill. In brief skirmishing that "did not amount to much," the Federals easily dispersed a small contingent of gray cavalry. That afternoon the XIV Corps occupied the Western and Atlantic Railroad tunnel (fortunately still intact), and Stanley's and Wood's divisions of the IV Corps the ridge to its left. The XX Corps passed through Nickajack Pass of Taylor's Ridge, "a rough

---

maybe he did not. I strongly suspect that Sherman perceived Thomas to be irked about his ascendancy to command. I also suspect that his views of the Virginian were influenced by Grant during their time together in Chattanooga. In short, Thomas was too slow and traditionalist and Sherman too prejudiced about the Army of the Tennessee for these totally opposite personalities (Sherman impatient and Thomas deliberate, according to Fellman) to probably have much more than a superficial mutual respect.

Fellman concluded that Sherman admired Thomas's bravery but became "annoyed at his ponderous and tentative approach to combat. In his turn, Thomas was aware of the feelings of his superiors [Sherman and Grant], and he was dubious of Sherman's talents." These tensions "re-asserted themselves as post Civil War feuds," especially in the Army of the Cumberland and Army of the Tennessee association meetings. *Citizen Sherman: A Life of William Tecumseh Sherman* (New York: Random House, 1995), 323–28. For the traditional view of the Sherman-Thomas relationship, see Cox, *Military Reminiscences*, 2:205.

5. *OR*, 38(1):840, 38(4):27–29; Bennett and Haigh, *Thirty-Sixth Regiment Illinois Volunteers*, 576; Sherman, *Memoirs*, 2:31; Terry L. Jones, " 'The Flash of Their Guns Was a Sure Sign': The 19th Michigan as Infantry in the Atlanta Campaign," in *The Campaign for Atlanta and Sherman's March to the Sea*, ed. Theodore P. Savas and David A. Woodbury (Campbell, Calif.: Savas Woodbury, 1992), 135; Wilson Hobbs to wife, May 4, 1864, Wilson Hobbs Letters, INHS; Rowell, *Yankee Artillerymen*, 192.

6. *OR*, 38(4):35, 36, 43, 44, 45.

and dangerous pass over a pretty sharp mountain," according to Brigadier General Williams, whose division marched into Trickum Post Office that morning, with Sherman and Thomas arriving there at noon. Butterfield and Geary deployed to the right, encountering only a few cavalry pickets. Kilpatrick's cavalry took post at Gordon's Springs in order to communicate with the Army of the Tennessee, expected at Villanow the next day.[7]

Ahead of them, the men of the IV and XIV Corps peered at the six-hundred-foot-high Rocky Face Ridge. The rock wall along the top of its western slope made it easy to see how it got its name. That night Cpl. Joseph Van Nest, whose 101st Ohio encamped on the summit of the tunnel, noticed the sea of Federal campfires in his rear and the campfires of the enemy in his front, making it seem as though he was in the midst "of a stupendous camp" and presenting a scene "beyond description."[8]

Thomas's role on the eighth was diversionary: amuse the enemy and probe for weaknesses as McPherson continued his flanking march. Toward that end, Harker's brigade of Newton's division clawed its way to the northern tip of Rocky Face Ridge and proceeded south astride the narrow crest. The 125th Ohio gained a foothold by early afternoon, and after two hours of fighting, advanced three-fourths of a mile, the enemy steadily resisting behind boulders and inflicting losses of five killed and nineteen wounded. The XXIII Corps extended the line eastward across Crow Valley.[9]

That afternoon Thomas demonstrated against the Rebel front, advancing Wood's division of the IV Corps, Davis's of the XIV, and Butterfield's of the XX, each with a line of skirmishers, against Rocky Face Ridge and Buzzard Roost Gap, now made impassable due to the damming of Mill Creek by the Confederates. Although making no serious headway beyond driving the Rebel pickets back to their entrenchments, Thomas accomplished his mission of keeping Johnston occupied.[10]

Meanwhile, six miles to the south, Geary's division of the XX Corps was ordered to attack Dug Gap—primarily a feint but offering a significant advantage if successful. A thousand Rebels held the gap, far fewer than Geary's forty-five hundred Yankees, but the treacherous ascent to the summit more than offset the numerical disparity. Beginning at 3:00 P.M., Col. Adolphus Bushbeck's and Col. Charles Candy's brigades, the 119th New York preceding them as skirmishers, scaled the ridge,

7. *OR*, 38(1):140, 188, 240, 842, 38(4):56–57; Stewart, *Dan McCook's Regiment*, 98; Quaife, *From the Cannon's Mouth*, 306; *New York Tribune*, May 16, 1864.

8. Van Nest quoted in Larry M. Strayer and Richard A. Baumgartner, comps., *Echoes of Battle: The Atlanta Campaign* (Huntington, W.Va.: Blue Acorn, 1991), 65.

9. *OR*, 38(1):140, 292, 352, 367, 368; Clark, *Opdycke's Tigers*, 367–68; Gates, *Rough Side of War*, 193; *New York Tribune*, May 16, 1864; Tapp and Klotter, *Tuttle*, 177–78.

10. *OR*, 38(1):140, 220, 481, 844, 38(4):70; Van Horne, *Army of the Cumberland*, 2:48.

only to be beaten back in three desperate assaults. The 33d New Jersey reached the summit a half-mile to the south, but it too had to ultimately withdraw. Geary lost 357 casualties, the Confederates about 20. Although the maneuver was tactically a failure, Geary received word later in the evening that McPherson had taken possession of Snake Creek Gap.[11]

The fact that the Rebels around Dalton had used almost no artillery throughout the day concerned Sherman. "I fear Johnston is annoying us with small detachments, whilst he will be about Resaca in force," he wrote Thomas that night. More demonstrations were planned for the next day, especially Schofield pressing the enemy in Crow Valley.[12]

Minor skirmishing, accompanied by an hour and a half of sporadic artillery fire, occupied the morning of May 9. Strong probes were later made along the line. As Harker's brigade continued its advance astride the ridge, Col. Alexander McIlvaine of the 64th Ohio muttered, "Well, I must get out of this, I am getting demoralized." The Rebels put up particularly stubborn resistance against Harker. "Numbers of my men were pushed off of rocks and fell six to ten feet," Colonel Opdycke reported, his 125th Ohio losing twenty-five casualties in the fighting. In front of Buzzard Roost Gap, as Howard made preparations for an assault, a sniper's bullet suddenly zipped through the back of his coat without wounding him. Stanley advanced the 96th Illinois and 84th Indiana against the gap, only to be driven back by a severe fire, losing about sixty men. From all evidence the enemy remained in force at Dalton.[13]

On the morning of the tenth, Sherman learned to his dismay that McPherson, though securing Snake Creek Gap, had found Resaca occupied in division strength. (Confederate reinforcements from Mobile had made a timely arrival.) Sherman's great flanking effort had failed, and he was now forced to adopt a new plan. Through Thomas's urging, Sherman determined to heavily reinforce McPherson and possibly salvage the original plan. Leaving the IV Corps and two cavalry divisions north of Dalton, he proceeded to remove the balance of the Army of the Cumberland and the XXIII Corps south to join McPherson. Yet he moved too slowly, and Johnston belatedly rushed with his army to Resaca, where other reinforcements from Mississippi joined him. On the morning of the thirteenth, Howard's IV Corps marched into Dalton.[14]

Johnston's three infantry corps occupied an entrenched position that roughly

11. *OR*, 38(2):114–17, 38(4):70, 76, 79; Castel, *Decision in the West*, 132–34.

12. *OR*, 38(4):71; Van Horne, *Army of the Cumberland*, 2:49.

13. *OR*, 38(1):89, 220, 368, 847; Strayer and Baumgartner, *Echoes of Battle: Atlanta*, 71, 73; Howard, *Autobiography*, 1:506; Cope, *Fifteenth Ohio*, 430.

14. Castel, *Decision in the West*, 142–43, 149–50; Howard, *Autobiography*, 1:510; Aldrich, *Quest for a Star*, 113; Cope, *Fifteenth Ohio*, 432.

resembled a large shepherd's crook, with the end of the crook resting on the Connasauga River. The three-mile-long "staff" ran southeast toward Resaca, eventually connecting with the Oostanaula River. When it became clear that Johnston would not retreat, the Federals took up corresponding positions, with the Army of the Tennessee on the right; the XX and XIV Corps in the center, deploying in the wooded hills bordering Camp Creek (the staff); and the XXIII Corps partially covering the crook. The IV Corps would complete the formation on the far left upon its arrival, though the Rebel rear guard slowed it considerably. Thomas suggested a flanking maneuver by the Army of the Tennessee, reinforced by the XX Corps, across the Oostanaula via Lay's Ferry. Sherman again accepted the concept but not the combination; he used a single division of the XVI Corps.[15]

On the morning of the fourteenth, Sherman ordered a wheeling movement by Johnson's and Baird's divisions of the XIV Corps and two divisions of the XXIII Corps against the Confederate right-center. Johnson's assault collapsed when Carlin's brigade made initial contact and fell back under heavy fire. Turchin's brigade of Baird's division, "not understanding the nature of the [pivot] movement," stood fast as a brigade of Brig. Gen. Henry Judah's division of the XXIII Corps collided with and even passed through their ranks. The fighting sputtered out by midafternoon, having accomplished little.[16]

By noon of the fourteenth, Wood's and Stanley's divisions of the IV Corps had arrived and deployed on Schofield's right. Realizing Stanley's left was in the air, Johnston savagely attacked at 5:00 P.M. with Stevenson's division. "Shouting like devils," the grays swept Cruft's and Whitaker's brigades from the field. A disaster was averted only by the determined stand of the 5th Indiana Artillery, the six guns staggering the entire Rebel division. The timely arrival of Williams's division of the XX Corps (pulled out of the center and sent to the left by Thomas) routed the attackers and regained the lost ground.[17]

Throughout the night, Hooker's entire corps redeployed to the left of Howard. At noon on the fifteenth, Geary's and Williams's divisions attacked Johnston's right

15. *OR,* 38(4):160–61. McMurry concluded that by ignoring Thomas's advice to send a strong column south of the Oostanaula, Sherman missed a second opportunity to win "a great, if not complete, success." *Atlanta 1864,* 73–74. Yet without the presence of the XX Corps (which Thomas had recommended to be a part of the flanking column), the Federal left wing might well have been rolled up on May 14. This attack occurred *before* the Federal crossing.

16. *OR,* 38(1):528–29, 735, 758–59; Girardi and Hughes, *Memoirs of Brigadier General William Passmore Carlin,* 125.

17. *OR,* 38(1):190–91, 220–21, 231, 257–58; Philip L. Secrist, *The Battle of Resaca* (Macon, Ga.: Mercer University Press, 1998), 33–37; Quaife, *From the Cannon's Mouth,* 308; John O. Holzhueter, ed., "William Wallace's Civil War Letters: The Atlanta Campaign," *Wisconsin Magazine of History* 57 (winter 1973–74): 95.

(the end of the crook). Although the main Confederate line easily repulsed the assault, inflicting 1,229 casualties, several regiments, led by 70th Indiana colonel Benjamin Harrison, a future president of the United States, did manage to overrun the uncompleted dirt fort of a Georgia battery, capturing all four 12-pounder Napoleons. That night the Yankees dug out a section of the fort and pulled the guns to safety with ropes.[18]

A successful downriver crossing of the Oostanaula caused Johnston to evacuate Resaca on the sixteenth. The Rebels continued their retreat, enabling Sherman to secure a crossing of the Etowah River by May 20. The army now rested briefly and preparations were made for the next phase. "Johnsons [sic] retreat from Resaca, leaving his dead and wounded in our hands, shows that he was whipped. His retreat from this place [Cassville] after fortifying it very strongly, shows that he is afraid to risk another engagement," Col. James R. Robinson, commanding one of Hooker's brigades, wrote a friend.[19]

Once across the Oostanaula, Thomas marched the bulk of his army (Davis's division had been detached to capture Rome) south on two roads that converged outside of Adairsville, with McPherson's army eight miles to the west. Most of May 17 was spent in annoying and time-consuming rear-guard actions mounted by Confederate cavalry. When the van of the IV Corps, Col. Francis Sherman's brigade, encountered stiff resistance outside of Adairsville, Howard could hardly believe it. "Your brigade must move forward," he notified the colonel. When it became apparent, however, that the enemy had prepared some sort of demonstration in force, Howard, at 4:00 P.M., deployed his corps. With his army strung out for miles, Thomas ordered no action until daylight. During the night, the Southerners withdrew.[20]

Following the railroad due south, Sherman entered Kingston without opposition on the morning of the nineteenth. The IV Corps, plus Baird's division, marched east along the railroad to Cassville while McPherson's army and Johnson's division proceeded south to the Etowah River, seizing Gillem's Bridge. The XX and XXIII Corps, meanwhile, approached Cassville from the north along the direct road from Adairsville. Hood's corps lay in ambush to pounce upon the column. The trap was sprung, however, when McCook's and Brig. Gen. George Stoneman's cavalry divisions accidentally collided with the Rebel infantry east of town. Johnston pulled

---

18. OR, 38(1):118–19, 121, 141, 190–91, 322–24, 340–41; Secrist, Battle of Resaca, 47–57; Welcher and Ligget, Coburn's Brigade, 171–75; Robert L. Kilpatrick, "The Fifth Ohio Infantry at Resaca," in The Atlanta Papers, comp. Sydney C. Kerksis (Dayton: Morningside, 1980), 355–60; Jones, "Flash of Their Guns," 141–42; Reyburn and Wilson, "Jottings from Dixie," 214–16.

19. Robinson quoted in McMurry, Atlanta 1864, 84.

20. McKinney, Education in Violence, 327–28; Castel, Decision in the West, 193–94.

back and took up a new position, one that quickly proved untenable to a forty-gun Union crossfire from north, northeast, and southwest of Cassville at 5:30. During the early morning hours of the twentieth, the Confederates withdrew across the Etowah River.[21]

A series of tactical blunders now occurred that, besides inflicting heavy losses on the Army of the Cumberland, led to intra-army bickering as well as a further widening of the developing breach between Sherman and the Cumberland's high command.

On May 23 Sherman thrust his army well west of the railroad toward Dallas, with an ultimate view of turning Marietta. McPherson would approach Dallas from the west, Thomas from the northwest, with Schofield and the cavalry protecting the left flank. Sherman anticipated little resistance, but Johnston quickly anticipated the move and shifted accordingly. On the afternoon of the twenty-fourth, McCook's cavalry brought in a Rebel courier who revealed that the entire Confederate army was headed for Dallas. Although this should have signaled to Sherman that his plan had been uncovered, he remained remarkably optimistic.[22]

On the morning of the twenty-fifth, the Army of the Cumberland continued its march west on four separate roads. Geary's division of the XX Corps tramped down the Burnt Hickory Road toward the crossroads at the New Hope Methodist Church. Encountering unexpected resistance several miles out, Geary's troops, now five miles in advance of the column, captured several prisoners who revealed that the thickets ahead concealed Hood's entire corps, which blocked their path. As Geary frantically prepared makeshift defenses, a stunned Hooker hurriedly ordered up Williams's and Butterfield's divisions. Thomas, who was present, sent Lieutenant Colonel Mendenhall and later Capt. Henry Stone to "hurry up the Fourth Corps." The staff officers found Howard at 1:50 and 2:20 P.M. respectively, explaining the crisis. Despite the urgency, Howard's troops marched at a deliberate pace, the general not wanting to "use them up." On the way back to Thomas, Stone encountered an impatient Sherman wanting to know why the column had stalled. When told of Geary's dilemma and that Williams's division would soon be up, the general testily replied: "Let Williams go in anywhere as soon as he gets up. I don't see what they are waiting for in front now. There haven't been twenty rebels there today."[23]

21. Castel, *Decision in the West*, 202–6.

22. Ibid., 218–19. Stephen Davis states that the intelligence that Hood was in his front "seemed not to have registered with Sherman." *Atlanta Will Fall: Sherman, Joe Johnston, and the Yankee Heavy Battalions* (Wilmington, Del., Scholarly Resources, 2001), 61.

23. Van Horne, *Army of the Cumberland*, 2:75; *OR*, 38(1):192, 193, 862, 38(2):123; Henry Stone, "Part II: From the Oostanaula to the Chattahoochee," in *The Atlanta Papers,* comp. Sydney C. Kerksis (Dayton: Morningside, 1980), 407–9.

By late afternoon the balance of the XX Corps arrived near the crossroads and deployed for an attack, pursuant to Sherman's orders. The in-depth formation was designed for penetration, with Williams's division in column of brigades, Geary in his rear, and Butterfield in reserve. At five o'clock Hooker's veterans advanced a mile and a half through thick underbrush until encountering the main enemy line along a low ridge. Opposing them would be all or parts of four brigades of Alexander Stewart's division, about 4,000 troops to oppose probably 11,000 in the two attacking divisions. Yet the enemy was dug in and backed by sixteen guns, and the "stacked" formation of the Federals allowed for a very narrow front. Fierce fighting ensued in first dusk, then darkness, and then a heavy thunderstorm, with the bluecoats being predictably repulsed, with a loss of 1,554 men (including three colonels killed or mortally wounded) to Stewart's 300–400.[24]

A disgusted Sherman always maintained that if an attack had been launched earlier (presumably by Geary's lone and unsupported division), the crossroads would have been easily cleared and the road to Marietta open. It is true that the Confederates had been given more time to entrench, but Hood's corps had been in position since morning—hardly Sherman's "twenty or so" Rebels. Although he channeled his criticisms toward Hooker, they were actually aimed at Thomas, who had been beside the corps commander the entire day.[25]

May 27 found Sherman's army in three clusters: the Army of the Tennessee and Davis's division of the XIV Corps, rejoined from its Rome foray, on the right in front of Dallas; the Army of the Cumberland (minus Baird's division, guarding the wagons) around New Hope Church; and the XXIII Corps on the left, astride Possum Creek. Sherman determined to flank the Rebel right and drive a wedge between it and the railroad. He ordered Howard to select one of his IV Corps divisions and march it northeast, passing behind the XXIII Corps.[26]

Remarkably, Howard chose Wood's division, already in the trenches, to be withdrawn and replaced by Stanley's, then in reserve. Wood, perhaps with the specter of Chickamauga still in his mind, protested, but to no avail. This time the Federals were lucky, and the exchange of units occurred uneventfully. The IV Corps commander later confided to Hazen that he had selected Wood because his troops held the greatest possibility for success.[27]

Thomas now ordered Palmer to send Johnson's division of the XIV Corps to the left in support of Howard (who commanded the assault) and Wood, thus effectively

24. OR, 38(1):66, 143, 38(2):30, 123; Quaife, From the Cannon's Mouth, 312; Van Horne, Army of the Cumberland, 2:81.

25. Sherman, Memoirs, 2:44; OR, 38(3):761, 843.

26. McMurry, Atlanta 1864, 89–90.

27. Hazen, Narrative, 256; Castel, Decision in the West, 229.

leaving him with no command. The short-tempered political general exploded and promptly requested to be relieved. Since Howard's move left would leave "two of his [Howard's] divisions without a commander, and me without a duty or a man beyond my escort," the only motive for this arrangement, he concluded, "is that you [Thomas] believe me unfit for a command." Thomas placated him, but Palmer was beginning to be more trouble than he was worth.[28]

Beginning at 11:00 A.M., Wood's men, followed by Johnson's, stumbled through about three miles of thickets so dense that a compass had to be used to determine their direction. "No person can appreciate the difficulty in moving over this ground unless he can see it," Howard informed Thomas at 4:35, adding that he was "now turning the enemy's right flank, I think." What Howard did not know was that the enemy had discovered his move almost from the outset and had extended their right throughout the afternoon. Wood's bluecoats would soon be encountering head-on the trans-Mississippians of Patrick Cleburne's division.[29]

The attack occurred about 4:30 in the vicinity of Pickett's Mill along Little Pumpkinvine Creek. "Are the orders still to attack?" Wood asked. Howard answered simply: "Attack." "We will put in Hazen, and see what success he has," Wood replied. To his dismay Hazen suddenly realized that he was going in alone. Incredibly, just as his 1,500 veterans marched off, Sherman determined to cancel the attack, but the word came too late. Clawing through undergrowth, the brigade came upon an open field with dead timber, where for the first time, the enemy's works could be seen. The Federals immediately came under a heavy fire that shredded their ranks, leaving 467 of their number dead or wounded within forty-five minutes. Hazen sent back several requests for reinforcements, but none arrived. Several soldiers, thinking that the men might yet rally, came up to the brigadier and asked, "General, where is your brigade?" With tears in his eyes he answered, "Brigade, hell, I have none."[30]

As the survivors fell back (three hundred hid in a depression in no man's land), Howard committed Col. John Gibson's brigade to the meat grinder. Gibson's men butted against the same earthworks that had stopped Hazen in his tracks, and they now shared his fate. Howard excitedly told a staff officer to go forward and tell the men to hold and he would get reinforcements up on the flanks. Just then a shell exploded nearby, a fragment striking his left boot. "I am afraid to look down! I am afraid to look down!" the one-armed general shouted. The officer assured him that his leg remained intact. His foot had been badly bruised, however, and he had to

28. *OR*, 38(4):324.

29. *OR*, 38(1):377, 865, 38(4):325; Hazen, *Narrative*, 257.

30. *OR*, 38(1):866; Howard, *Autobiography*, 1:553; Hazen, *Narrative*, 256–58; Strayer and Baumgartner, *Echoes of Battle: Atlanta*, 115–16.

wear a slipper for several days. Incredibly, the same fragment struck Brigadier General Johnson, breaking two ribs on his right side and causing him to temporarily turn over command of his division to David H. King.[31]

About six o'clock Howard received Sherman's orders to cancel the attack, one that had already cost 1,148 men. Wood was instructed to send in Col. Frederick Knefler's brigade to buy time while the Federals constructed their own log barricades. As the two sides exchange shots in the night, Hiram Granbury's Texas brigade suddenly charged, overrunning Knefler's position, sending his men reeling into the darkness, and inflicting an additional 250 casualties, mainly in taking prisoners. In two days of hard fighting, the Army of the Cumberland had lost 3,000 casualties, leaving three divisions weakened.[32]

Having failed in his attempt to turn Johnston's line, and with the campaign settling into routine trench warfare, Sherman now returned to the railroad. Throughout the first three weeks in June, it rained almost daily, further adding to the misery. One thing was for certain, rank was not royalty in the Army of the Cumberland. "The ground is saturated from surface to center and the roads, of course, 'awful.' It is so cold I have on my winter coat. . . . All of us have to take to the deeply saturated ground and as our bedding consists of blankets with now and then a buffalo robe you can fancy we sleep rather moist," Brigadier General Williams described to his daughter. In Davis's division Capt. James Burkhalter of the 86th Illinois jotted in his journal on the tenth that, just as dinner had been prepared, "one of the most tremendous rain showers that I ever saw then ensued. The water literally fell in torrents for about an hour and of course extinguished all our little fires, so that we could not make our coffee." Nonetheless, Col. Oscar F. Harman felt upbeat as he wrote, "We may have to do some fighting before we get to Atlanta, but think not much, for there is only a river [Chattahoochee] to cross, and when we get over it, the enemy will run."[33]

Johnston occupied the heights around Marietta, with Sherman taking his time to follow (the destroyed Etowah River bridge would not be completed until the eleventh). At Ackworth the 9,000-man XVI Corps of the Army of the Tennessee linked up. That number, added to the ten Cumberland regiments (5,000 men) that re-

31. Hazen, *Narrative*, 258; Howard quoted in Castel, *Decision in the West*, 238–39; Girardi and Hughes, *Memoirs of Brigadier General William Passmore Carlin*, 126; Welsh, *Medical Histories*, 184; *New York Tribune*, June 10, 1864.

32. Castel, *Decision in the West*, 239–41. The Confederates lost about 500 men at Pickett's Mill.

33. Quaife, *From the Cannon's Mouth*, 315; "Captain Burkhalter's Georgia War," in *Voices of the Prairie Land*, ed. Martin Litvin, 2 vols. (Galesburg, Ill.: Mother Bickerdyke Historical Collection, 1972), 2:492; Hunter, *One Flag, One Country*, 184.

turned from veteran furlough in May, more than offset the losses up to that time. By mid-June Johnston had withdrawn to what would become known as the Second Kennesaw Line, extending ten miles from Brushy Mountain on the right and Lost Mountain on the left. On the fifteenth Stanley's division occupied the abandoned Confederate position at Pine Mountain. Hooker pushed an afternoon attack with Geary's and Butterfield's divisions against an enemy salient at Gilgal Church, losing over 600 men to the Confederates' 230. Nonetheless, Johnston abandoned the Lost Mountain position and formed a new line running north to south behind Mud Creek.[34]

On the morning of June 17, the XX and XXIII Corps, on the right, advanced down the Sandtown Road, opposed only by cavalry. Hooker deployed his escort company as skirmishers, and Williams recounted to his daughter a resulting humorous scene: "Suddenly we saw, half a mile or more on our right, a great cloud of Rebel cavalry flying in disorder to the rear. There must have been a brigade of them and every man was kicking and spurring for dear life. Many horses were riderless. We opened on them with artillery, which greatly increased the disorder. It was laughable to see Hooker's excitement. 'Williams,' he would cry out, 'see them run. They are thicker than flies on a Mexican ranch. See them go,' and we all shouted, to the astonishment of our troops who had not gone up. In truth our line of skirmishers that morning had [been] . . . about fifteen poorly armed cavalry!"[35]

In the center the IV Corps stalled. Sherman had ordered Thomas to march at daylight, yet at 9:30 A.M. he found Stanley and Wood quarreling about who should lead. Sherman exploded in anger, cursing and saying things that he later admitted he should not have said, "but I got them started," he informed Grant. At ten o'clock Wood received orders to attack the enemy's earthworks (the entrenched skirmish line of W. H. T. Walker's Georgia division), located in a forest fronted by an open field. What occurred was not an assault but long-range skirmishing, which continued throughout the afternoon. At 6:30, amid a downpour, Thomas finally brought up artillery, pulverizing the enemy works in a half-hour bombardment, whereupon Wood's division charged and occupied the now-abandoned trenches. Sherman related his displeasure to both Thomas and Howard, noting that "the troops seem timid in these dense forests of stumbling on a hidden breastwork." The troops had good reason to hesitate; this was the same division that had been bloodied at Pickett's Mill.[36]

34. McMurry, *Atlanta 1864*, 93–94, 102–3; Stone, "From the Oostanaula to the Chattahoochee"; Castel, *Decision in the West*, 264–65; Davis, *Atlanta Will Fall*, 78–79. The Army of the Cumberland sustained 6,856 casualties during May, more than the combined losses it suffered at Shiloh and Perryville. Sherman, *Memoirs*, 2:47, 51.

35. Quaife, *From the Cannon's Mouth*, 321.

36. *OR*, 38(1):149, 197, 38(4):507–8; Van Horne, *Army of the Cumberland*, 2:87.

Back at his headquarters at Big Shanty that evening, Sherman vented to Grant in an unofficial letter. He criticized McPherson for not capturing Resaca outright as well as two of his cavalry commanders, the "over-cautious" Brig. Gen. Kenner Gerrard and the "lazy" George Stoneman (Army of the Ohio), both of whom had squandered opportunities to get in Johnston's rear. But he reserved his greatest salvo for Thomas:

> My chief source of trouble is the Army of the Cumberland, which is dreadfully slow. A fresh furrow in a plowed field will stop the whole column, and all begin to entrench. I have again and again tried to impress upon Thomas that we must assail and not defend; we are the offensive, and yet it seems the whole Army of the Cumberland is so habituated to be on the defensive that, from its commander down to the lowest private, I cannot get it out of their heads. . . . This slowness has cost me the loss of two splendid opportunities which never recur in war. At Dallas [New Hope Church] there was a delay of four hours to get ready to advance, when we first met Johnston's head of column, and that four hours enabled him to throw up works to cover the head of his column, and he extended the works about as fast as we deployed. Also here I broke one of his lines [the First Kennesaw Line], and had we followed it up as I ordered at daylight, there was nothing between us and the railroad back of Marietta.

Sherman then brought up the issue of baggage, which continued to irk him. "I came out without tents and ordered all to do likewise, yet Thomas has a headquarters camp on the style of Halleck at Corinth; every aide and orderly with a wall tent, and a baggage train big enough for a division. He promised to send it all back, but the truth is everybody there is allowed to do as he pleases, and they still think and act as though the railroad and all its facilities were theirs."[37]

Sherman erred in blaming Thomas for the May 25 incident, though his frustration over the June 17 debacle was understandable. The group commander had earlier touted that he would be at the Chattahoochee River by the end of May. Nearly three weeks behind schedule and with no end in sight, he nervously scribbled his ungraceful and somewhat inaccurate letter. The issue of transportation had been a recurring irritant to Sherman, each time Thomas promising to get the matter in hand. In a characteristic passive-aggressive gesture, however, the Virginian stubbornly held on to his eleven Sibley tents. Sherman once reined in at a cluster of tents and asked, "Whose quarters are these?" "General Thomas's, general." Sherman

37. OR, 38(4):507–8.

quipped: "Oh yes, Thomastown—Thomastown, a very pretty place, appears to be growing rapidly." He conveniently neglected to mention to Grant, however, that his Spartan headquarters transportation proved so sparse that Thomas, early in the campaign, had loaned him some wall tents.[38]

The next incident of note, and one that exacerbated the already abysmal relationship between Sherman and Hooker, occurred on the twenty-second. The Confederates had withdrawn to their Third Kennesaw Line, anchored on the north by Big Kennesaw and Little Kennesaw Mountains. The Federals took a corresponding parallel position running north to south, with McPherson on the left, Thomas in the center, and Schofield on the right. (While getting his brigade into position, Brigadier General Carlin, puffing on a pipe, suddenly had a shell explode not ten yards from him, inflicting on him a temporary concussion.)[39]

The XX Corps served as the right of the Army of the Cumberland, astride and to the north of the Powder Springs Road about a mile from the Kolb Farm. Hascall's and Cox's divisions of the XXIII Corps came in line south of the road on Hooker's right. Learning (from prisoners) that Hardee's and Hood's corps had massed in their front, the Federals immediately prepared for an attack. In response to a message from Hooker that "the whole rebel army lies between my immediate front and Marietta," Thomas hastened to the scene. He found the situation under control and disregarded his corps commander's alarmist note.

About 5:00 P.M. two divisions of Hood's corps attacked, only to be met by a wall of flame from Williams's and Hascall's divisions. Williams admitted, "after the first half hour [my] men considered the whole affair great sport. They would call out to the Rebels who had taken shelter in the woods and in the deep ravines in our front, 'Come up here Johnny Reb. Here is a weak place!' 'Come up and take this battery; we are Hooker's paper collar boys.'" When the smoke cleared, 1,100 Rebels lay strewn about, many huddled in a creek ravine where they had sought shelter, compared to 230 Yankees. David Nichol, a gunner in Knap's Pennsylvania Battery, recorded in his diary: "We had quite an exciting time, worked the guns as fast as we were able. There must have been a Corps of Rebels."[40]

Hooker sent a message to Sherman at 5:30 (not received until 9:30) stating: "We have repulsed two heavy attacks and feel confident, our only apprehension being

38. McKinney, *Education in Violence*, 331, 336; Cleaves, *Rock of Chickamauga*, 219.

39. Girardi and Hughes, *Memoirs of Brigadier General William Passmore Carlin*, 127–28.

40. Castel, *Decision in the West*, 291–95; Quaife, *From the Cannon's Mouth*, 327–29, 333–34; Davis, *Atlanta Will Fall*, 82; Van Horne, *Army of the Cumberland*, 2:92; James P. Brady, comp., *Hurrah for the Artillery! Knap's Independent Battery "E," Pennsylvania Light Artillery* (Gettysburg: Thomas, 1992), 354. Thomas moved quickly to support Hooker, sending the reserve regiments of the IV Corps and eventually replacing Butterfield's division with Stanley's, the former division moving to Williams's rear.

our extreme right flank. Three entire corps are in front of us." Could Hooker's flank be in the air? How could three Rebel corps (all that Johnston had) have assaulted? After several tense hours, the truth became known. Hooker (at least Williams's division) had been savagely attacked by a single Rebel corps, but Hascall's division was (and had been all along) on his right and had measurably assisted in the repulse. The next morning Sherman appeared on the scene and angrily (according to Schofield) dressed down Hooker. This caused the "jealous" former Potomac commander to "sulk," wrote Sherman. For Hooker it proved to be the beginning of the end. The evidence seems to substantiate that the corps commander became overly excited—"stampeded," according to Thomas. His poorly worded message at best led to a misunderstanding and at worst attempted to claim singular credit for the victory.[41]

Sherman was growing increasingly weary of flanking. When, on June 24, Schofield informed him that the grays had extended their trenches farther than he could safely get around, the group commander caustically remarked: "I suppose the enemy, with his smaller force, intends to surround us." Sherman made plans (contemplated for over a week) for a direct assault on the Rebel center; perhaps the Confederates had extended their lines so far that weaknesses existed there. He ordered demonstrations for the next two days in hopes that Johnston would reinforce his left. The attack, scheduled for 8:00 A.M. on the twenty-seventh, called for McPherson to feign from the north but attack a point south of Little Kennesaw (McPherson chose south of Pigeon Hill), while Thomas, about a mile south, would assault the sector fronting the IV Corps, the specific point "to be selected by himself."[42]

Thomas, receiving the order on the twenty-fifth, lamented to Whipple, "This is too bad." "Why don't you send a written protest against the assault?" the adjutant questioned. In a resigned tone the Virginian said: "I have protested so often against such things that if I protest again Sherman will think I don't want to fight. But he knows my views."[43]

Thomas met in consultation with Palmer and Howard. The Cumberland high command had clearly become estranged from Sherman. He pointedly had not conversed with Thomas about the attack. Perhaps the Virginian was more resigned than

41. *OR*, 38(4):558–60; Sherman, *Memoirs*, 2:57–59; John M. Schofield, *Forty-Six Years in the Army* (New York: Century, 1897), 133–36. Castel and McMurry both defended Hooker. McMurry argued, among other things, that "our extreme right flank" in Hooker's message clearly meant the right flank of the army group, not just his own corps. See Castel, *Decision in the West*, 297–99; and McMurry, *Atlanta 1864*, 106–7. I view this argument as hindsight. Sherman's misreading was understandable.

42. *OR*, 38(4):492, 582, 588. Schofield was initially to be a part of the attack, but Sherman later canceled his participation.

43. *Society of the Army of the Cumberland, 24th Reunion*, 118.

irritated about being ignored; all his ideas to date had been rebuffed. Palmer, however, sent a defiant letter of complaint about the order, or so he stated in postwar years. Thomas spent half a day inspecting the ground, at times venturing beyond his pickets. He finally selected a sector south of the Dallas Road. Davis's division of the IV Corps would attack a salient six hundred yards distant (Cheatham's Hill), and Newton's division of the XIV Corps would strike the line just to the north of it. During the early morning hours of the twenty-seventh, as word of the impending attack became known, Captain Burkhalter of the 86th Illinois wrote: "So much for the foolish dream of our soldiers who thought that our few days in reserve presaged a new status as a pet brigade. Pet my foot. Rested for the slaughter would be more like it. The stupidity of this order is enough to paralyze me."[44]

A fifteen-minute artillery barrage opened at 8:00 A.M. but accomplished little more than alerting the enemy of the coming assault. At nine o'clock, an hour behind schedule, the bluecoats emerged from the wooded area that had hidden their activity and advanced into a no man's land bristling with abatis. The assault was made in a narrow "stacked" formation (one regiment behind another). Brigadier General Newton's men, smashing against Cleburne's parapets, came under a murderous fire. "Men were falling down all around but we pressed forward. The rebels had pointed stakes driven in the ground in front of the works and our men were shot down while trying to pull them out," recorded a member of the 26th Ohio. A Hoosier noted, "The enemy reserved their artillery fire till the 40th [Indiana] advanced to within a short distance of their works, had raised the yell, and were moving forward on the double quick, when they opened a withering fire of grape and canister." Brigadier General Harker, who had a premonition of his own death, fell mortally wounded. Davis's men butted against Frank Cheatham's salient and were stopped cold, the front ranks being literally swept away. Soldiers pleaded with Col. Dan McCook to protect himself. "God damn you, attend to your own business," he snapped, whereupon a bullet popped his chest, and he fell mortally wounded.[45]

The fighting had been as intense as it had been futile. Sherman claimed 3,000

44. Howard, *Autobiography*, 1:582; John Palmer, *Personal Recollections*, 205; Henry Stone, "Part IV: Strategy of the Campaign," in *The Atlanta Papers*, comp. Sydney C. Kerksis (Dayton: Morningside, 1980), 150; *OR*, 38(4):602–3; "Captain Burkhalter's Georgia War," 497.

45. Howard, *Autobiography*, 1:582; Richard A. Baumgartner and Larry M. Strayer, comps., *Kennesaw Mountain, June 1864: Bitter Standoff at the Gibraltar of Georgia* (Huntington, W.Va.: Blue Acorn, 1998), 126–35, 138–64; *OR*, 38(1):295–96, 319–20, 370–71, 887–88; Phillip Sidney Post Letters, KC; F. B. James, "McCook's Brigade at the Assault upon Kennesaw Mountain, Georgia, June 27, 1864," in *The Atlanta Papers*, comp. Sydney C. Kerksis (Dayton: Morningside, 1980), 255–70; John Palmer, *Personal Recollections*, 205–6; Col. Allen L. Fahnestock Diary, June 27, 1864, KNBP; Janet Correll Ellison, ed., *On to Atlanta: The Civil War Diaries of John Hill Ferguson, Illinois Tenth Regiment of Volunteers* (Lincoln: University of Nebraska Press, 2001), 54.

casualties, two-thirds of whom (2,078 to be precise) came from the Army of the Cumberland, including the two mortally wounded brigade commanders. Although small by 1864 standards, the defeat left the army embittered. "It has been a bloody day & with all our loss did not gain a *single* thing nor (probably) killed one man among the enemy," Capt. Alexander Ayers angrily wrote. When Sherman appeared at IV Corps headquarters, Newton, furious over the loss of Harker, stormed up to him and defiantly barked, "Well this is a damned appropriate culmination of one month's blundering." Sherman gave no response. That evening Palmer wrote his wife: "You will probably hear that the 14th corps was badly repulsed. The correspondents will mention my reversals cheerfully. It will be popular with the regulars [professionals] to exaggerate the repulse of any body of troops commanded by me."[46]

In response to Sherman's 2:45 P.M. dispatch asking whether or not the attack should continue, Thomas answered, "We have already lost heavily today without gaining any material advantage; one or two more such assaults would use up this army." Later that evening Sherman inquired if the Cumberland commander would be willing to attempt a flanking movement. His biting response could not have been missed: "What force do you think of moving with? If with the greater part of the army, I think it decidedly better than butting against breastworks twelve feet thick and strongly abatised." Sherman planned to again leave the railroad, using the Army of the Tennessee (his "whip-lash," as he referred to it) as the main flanking column. In his reply to Thomas, Sherman used some sarcasm of his own. "Go where we may we will find the breastworks and the abatis, unless we move more rapidly than we have heretofore."[47]

After resting and consolidating his armies for several days, Sherman proceeded to the Chattahoochee River. July 4 would have gone unnoticed but for the martial music that awoke the troops that morning. "It was perfectly splendid to hear all the bands of the Army of the Cumberland playing along the whole line," New Yorker Edwin Weller wrote.[48]

That day Sherman paid Howard, whose corps had become stalled, a visit. Believing that the Confederates could not possibly have taken another position north of the Chattahoochee, Sherman blurted, "Howard, you are mistaken; there is no force in your front; they are laughing at you!" "Well, general, let us see," he answered. He turned to Stanley and said, "General, double your skirmishers and press them." The

46. Castel, *Decision in the West*, 319–20; Stanley, *Personal Memoirs*, 174; George Palmer, *Conscientious Turncoat*, 144. Johnston lost 700 men in the attack.

47. *OR*, 38(4):607, 609–10; Castel, *Decision in the West*, 322.

48. William Walton, ed., *A Civil War Courtship: The Letters of Edwin Weller from Antietam to Atlanta* (Garden City, N.Y.: Doubleday, 1980), 94.

initial Confederate picket line was quickly overrun and a number of prisoners taken, but the main enemy line soon opened with a crossfire of hidden artillery, forcing a retreat. Acknowledging that Howard had been correct, Sherman abruptly rode off.[49]

The next day, from a high bluff overlooking the river, Sherman and Thomas gazed in silence at the spires of Atlanta in the distance. Sherman stepped nervously about, analyzing where he could best cross, but Thomas stood "with no trace of excitement," according to Major Connolly. Turning to Baird, the Virginian said quietly, "Send up a couple of guns and we'll throw some shells over there," pointing to a heavily timbered area across the river. Thomas confided to Sherman that he "dreaded it [the crossing] more than any one thing ahead."[50]

During this period, Thomas again demonstrated his stoic demeanor. He, along with some staff officers, rode to a vacant log cabin near the Chattahoochee, the horses being kept in a depression in the rear. Snipers suddenly opened fire, and since there were many openings between the logs, some of the bullets entered the building. The officers immediately exited and ran to their horses, but Thomas walked slowly back. He stopped at a gate in the rear, faced about, looked defiantly in the direction of the shooting, and then continued calmly to his horse, all the while bullets zipping past him.[51]

At 8:00 P.M. on the evening of July 7, the batteries of the IV Corps at Isham's Ford opened a thunderous half-hour barrage across the Chattahoochee, expending four hundred rounds. It turned out to be a diversion for the real crossing upriver by cavalry and the XXIII Corps at Soap Creek and Roswell. On the night of July 9–10, the Confederates withdrew to the south bank. Sherman subsequently crossed his army: the XXIII Corps at Phillips's and Isham's Ferries, the Army of the Tennessee at Roswell, the IV Corps at Power's Ferry, and the XIV and XX Corps at Pace's Ferry.

Sherman began a right-wheel movement, with McPherson, followed by Schofield, swinging far to the east to strike the Georgia Railroad beyond Decatur. On the eighteenth, amid a downpour, Thomas more directly approached Atlanta, with Palmer's corps toward Peachtree Creek and Howard's toward Buckhead, two miles

49. Oliver O. Howard, "The Struggle for Atlanta," in *B&L*, 3:311, 313. See also Glenn W. Sunderland, *Five Days to Glory* (New York: A. S. Barnes, 1970), 150–51.

50. Angle, *Three Years in the Army of the Cumberland*, 234; Sherman to Philemon Ewing, July 13, 1864, in Simpson and Berlin, *Sherman's Civil War*, 667.

51. *Chicago Tribune*, July 21, 1864; Van Horne, *Army of the Cumberland*, 2:110–12; McMurry, *Atlanta 1864*, 146–47; Howard, *Autobiography*, 1:607; Castel, *Decision in the West*, 369–71; McKinney, *Education in Violence*, 345. Thomas correctly suspected that the main portion of the Confederate army fronted him, not McPherson. Considering his limited knowledge of Rebel dispositions at noon on June 20, when he wrote the dispatch, one must conclude that Thomas simply outguessed Sherman. *OR*, 38(5):196.

from the creek. The next afternoon Wood's division constructed a bridge and forced a crossing at the creek. Some distance to the left, Stanley, encountering stiff resistance, crossed the north fork of the creek. On the right Geary's division secured a bridgehead. Davis forded Col. William S. Dilworth's brigade, which quickly came under attack by Rebels in brigade strength, losing 245 men. Davis forded his Third Brigade in support, thus ending the action. A member of the 85th Illinois wrote his parents that "Col. Dilworth came to our regiment and saw how badly they were cut up. He sat down and cried like a child." That night Baird's division crossed. Aware that a gap of several miles had developed between Thomas and the other two armies, Sherman ordered Howard to take two divisions (Stanley's and Wood's) and close up on Schofield. This still left an interval of nearly two miles, with Thomas's left on the Buckhead Road. "We must not mind the gap. We must act independently," Thomas related to Howard. By noon of July 20, seven divisions had deployed on the south bank of Peachtree Creek, though not in a continuous line. Thomas himself was on the far left with Newton's division, his left in the air.[52]

John Newton marched his command down Peach Tree Road, and three-fourths of a mile on his left, across Tanyard Branch, Geary's division occupied Collier Ridge. Hooker would not advance his entire corps until Palmer covered his right. Palmer demurred, insisting that Hooker move first. (In addition, Palmer had been told that John Bell Hood now commanded the Confederate army, a man described to him as a desperate gambler.) The bickering continued throughout midafternoon. At 3:30, when Thomas informed Hooker that Palmer awaited his advance, the former Potomac commander gave a sharp reply: "General Palmer's extreme left connects with [my right], but his right falls away to the rear and affords me little or no protection. Major General Palmer can scarcely understand where my line is—or his own, if he makes that statement."[53]

Newton's and Geary's divisions, meanwhile, cautiously advanced over rugged ground cut by ravines. Three prisoners brought to Adolphus Williams related that the Rebels were not in force, and Williams himself admitted that "Not a man of theirs was to be seen or heard in any direction." Thomas brought up some artillery, and the troops in places began making makeshift logworks, with here and there cleared fields of fire, mainly on Hooker's front. Yet with the division between them (Ward's) and the one to Geary's right (Williams's) recessed a third of a mile, Newton and Geary remained dangerously exposed.[54]

52. Van Horne, *Army of the Cumberland*, 2:110–12; McMurry, *Atlanta*, 146–47; Howard, *Autobiography*, 1:607; Castel, *Decision in the West*, 369–71; Hughes and Whitney, *Jefferson Davis in Blue*, 265–66.

53. *OR*, 38(2):138; John Palmer, *Personal Recollections*, 207–8.

54. *OR*, 38(2).138, 38(5):199; Van Horne, *Army of the Cumberland*, 2:112–13.

About 4:00 P.M. Lt. Stephen Pierson, adjutant of the 33d New Jersey of Geary's division, rode to the left of his regiment, then on picket duty. Suddenly, he beheld "a beautiful sight. Down through the great, open fields they were coming, thousands of them, men in gray, by brigade front, flags flying. . . . I stopped but a few minutes to take it all in, and then rode back to report." On Newton's front a skirmisher of the 26th Ohio came running pell mell toward the main line, shouting: "Here they come boys! By God, a million of them!"[55]

Palmer's information was correct: Hood had indeed replaced Joe Johnston and was now hurling two of his corps against Thomas. Sherman's support/pivot army had suddenly become the focal point of attack. Three Rebel divisions slammed Newton on front and both flanks. (Colonel Opdycke related several days later that he had seen Newton "very tipsy" and that his division had succeeded "in spite of him.") His men barely had time to jump behind their half-completed barricades. Luther Bradley's brigade, backed by six guns, easily repulsed the division (William Bate's) on the left, which barely penetrated the thick undergrowth, and Nathan Kimball's and John Blake's brigades the division (Walker's) in front. This was Thomas's kind of battle. It was he who had positioned the guns as well as a hodge-podge battalion composed of the pioneers of Kimball's brigade and some of the straggling skirmishers who had fallen back on the initial onslaught. After twenty minutes the Rebels fell back in confusion, keeping up a desultory fire. Kimball then changed front at right angles to engage the division (George Maney's) on his right. As the Confederates began to swarm into the six-hundred-yard interval on Newton's right, Ward charged his skirmish line (the 22d Wisconsin and 136th New York) into the hole. They held long enough for his entire division to rush ahead. "Meeting my line of battle seemed to completely addle their brains," boasted Ward, who on this day, fortunately, was sober.[56]

Geary, whose division held Collier Ridge from Tanyard Branch to the Howell Mill Road, noted, "Pouring out from the woods they advanced in immense brown and gray masses (not lines), with flags and banners, many of them new and beauti-

55. Stephen Pierson, "From Chattanooga to Atlanta in 1864—A Personal Reminiscence," *Proceedings of the New Jersey Historical Society* 16 (1931): 344–45; Strayer and Baumgartner, *Echoes of Battle: Atlanta,* 250.

56. *OR*, 38(1):297–98, 38(2):327–28; *Chicago Tribune*, July 27, 1864; Howard, "Struggle for Atlanta," 314; Van Horne, *Army of the Cumberland*, 2:114; Castel, *Decision in the West*, 376–77; *New York Tribune*, July 27, 1864. Thomas Livermore states that the Confederates had about 20,000 men, minus Cleburne's and Bate's divisions, the former not engaged and the last only slightly. *Numbers and Losses*, 122. Probably not half that number actually pulled trigger. The attack was originally planned for 1:00 P.M. Most historians claim that if it had been made on time, Thomas stood to be defeated. I disagree. Virtually all of his army was across even then, and the likelihood is that the results would have been about the same.

ful, while their general and staff officers were in plain view, with drawn sabers flash-
ing in the light, galloping here and there as they urged their troops on to the
charge." The general charged front to the right with almost his entire command,
leaving only five regiments and his artillery, Aleshire's, Bundy's, and Sloan's batter-
ies, on the original line. To the west Williams's division advanced on the double-
quick—Joseph Knipe's brigade on the right, James Robinson's on the left, and
Thomas Ruger's in reserve. His troops came under heavy fire, with Williams send-
ing the 27th Indiana to reinforce Knipe's right. The fighting soon spread to Anson
McCook's brigade of Johnson's division.[57]

For two hours the fighting raged, much of it in the open, with the Federals repul-
sing the attackers at all points. Sherman might, and often did, complain about the
Army of the Cumberland's offensive capability, but its defensive prowess was be-
yond dispute. The XX Corps sustained nearly 1,700 casualties (Williams, 627; Ward,
561; and Geary, 476), with Newton suffering only 102. The single brigade of the XIV
Corps engaged lost 80–100 troops, bringing total losses to about 1,900 men, or 10
percent of those engaged. By contrast, the Confederates lost 2,500 soldiers, a stagger-
ing 25 percent of those engaged. The next day, July 23, a Federal yelled across the
line, "Johnny, how many men have you got left over there?" Came the reply, "About
two more killings."[58]

Sherman, who did not even know about the battle until midnight, when he re-
ceived a message from Thomas, visited the battlefield the next day. By now he
loathed Hooker for his supposed missed opportunity at New Hope Church, an un-
dignified panic that led to misinformation at Kolb's Farm, and widening the admin-
istrative gap between his corps and the balance of Thomas's army to effect an
independent command. When told by Hooker of his casualties, Sherman, according
to staff officer Henry Stone, "in the most flippant and unfeeling manner, snapped
out, 'Oh, most of 'em will be back in a day or two,'" implying that his men had
fled.[59]

During the morning of the twenty-first, Thomas advanced his line, the enemy
having withdrawn into the city defenses during the night. The three Union armies
now reconnected in a continuous line, with the XIV Corps west of the Western and
Atlanta Railroad, the XX Corps from the railroad to the Buckhead Road, and the
IV Corps from the road to Schofield's right. Brig. Gen. Edward McCook's cavalry

57. OR, 38(2):33–34, 136–40; Van Horne, Army of the Cumberland, 2:114–15; Geary to wife, July 24,
1864, John Geary Letters, Atlanta Historical Society; Quaife, From the Cannon's Mouth, 335–36, 339; Chi-
cago Tribune, July 27, 1864; Jenny O'Leary and Harvey H. Jackson, eds., "The Civil War Letters of Captain
Daniel O'Leary," The Register of the Kentucky Historical Society 77 (summer 1979): 173.
58. Castel, Decision in the West, 380–81; Butler to parents, July 31, 1864, in Butler, Letters Home, 140.
59. Henry Stone, "Siege and Capture of Atlanta," MASS, 8:119.

covered Thomas's right along Proctor's Creek. "Everything seems remarkable quiet. It is the oppinion here that both parties are buirrying their dead under a flag of truce," 10th Illinois member John Ferguson wrote in his diary.[60]

Hood had not yet shot his bolt. On July 22 he did as Sherman had expected two days earlier, that is, attacked McPherson and Schofield east of Atlanta. "A great battle was raging on the extreme left. We could hear the continuous roar, and see the smoke hovering about the treetops," Sergeant Major Widney remarked in his diary that day. Although achieving momentary success, the Rebels were eventually beaten back, with a loss of 5,500 men, compared to 3,500 Federals, including General Mc-Pherson, killed when he accidentally rode into a party of Confederates. Sherman now shifted his army by leapfrog movements west of the city in order to reach the railroads below Atlanta. Hood again attacked the Army of the Tennessee on the twenty-eighth at Ezra Church, being repulsed with a loss of 3,000 men, compared to 632 Federals.[61]

By the end of July, Thomas had lost 16,357 casualties in his infantry and artillery (equivalent to Chickamauga), or 30 percent, thus reducing his army to 40,000 infantry and artillery. By comparison, the Army of the Tennessee had suffered 8,066 casualties, or 25 percent. Despite Sherman's repeated attempts to marginalize both Thomas and his army, they had borne themselves well on the field of battle. Sherman nonetheless continued his blatant bias toward his favorite army. During the Battle of Atlanta, he rejected Howard's suggestion that he use his and Schofield's forces to counterattack the Rebel left, possibly cutting it off from the city. "Let the Army of the Tennessee fight it out!" Sherman exclaimed. He later justified his decision by claiming that "if any assistance were rendered by either of the armies, the Army of the Tennessee would be jealous." Because of this attitude, concluded historian Castel, Sherman rejected any attempt by Thomas to enter the city from the north during the battle, thus casually dismissing an opportunity of possibly gaining a major offensive victory.[62]

The issue of preferential treatment again arose on August 12. Sherman had been misinformed that John Brannan had refused the use of a newly arrived 20-pounder Parrott rifle for the Army of the Tennessee. Touchy and overprotective, Sherman lashed out at the general's "spirit of jealousy," an offense of which he himself was guilty. The matter was eventually resolved, but the incident proved symptomatic of the larger and continuing problem of Sherman's prejudice.[63]

60. Van Horne, *Army of the Cumberland*, 2:117; Ellison, *On to Atlanta*, 66.
61. McMurry, *Atlanta 1864*, 153–57; Lyman S. Widney Diary, July 22, 1864, KNBP.
62. Castel, *Decision in the West*, 414.
63. *OR*, 38(5):470–73.

22

Command Fracture
The Grand Old Army Divides

BEGINNING IN LATE JUNE and extending through early August, a series of command changes occurred in the Army of the Cumberland that would affect all three corps commanders, four division commanders, and several leaders at the brigade level. Unfortunately, few of the original army's officer base benefited.

Several turnovers at the brigade level occurred during June. Brigadier General Whitaker, known as much for his alcoholism as his bravery, had a shell burst near his head at Resaca, resulting in deafness in his left ear. He was now stricken with dysentery and forced to take a leave of absence. Samuel Beatty and Charles Cruft also took sick leaves, the last suffering from a severe fever. Later George D. Wagner, down with dysentery, took a furlough.[1]

Later that month Major General Butterfield took permanent leave of absence due to a severe case of diarrhea, though rumors wrongly claimed that his departure hinged on recent poor performance. Alpheus Williams quietly wrote: "He says [he is] sick, but I think he was disgusted and tired. . . . Butterfield was a much more honorable officer than Geary, but he 'hankered' after the newspaper fame, and was uneasy that as a major general he had a subordinate command to others he ranked." Brigadier General Ward assumed command of the Third Division, XX Corps, much to the dismay of his men. "Ward is one of those home made Brigadiers appointed during the early part of the war because he had some political influence in Kentucky," wrote Harvey Reid. He conceded that he might be a good general "when he is sober, but that is a circumstance that has not occurred within the memory 'of the oldest inhabitant.'" A Hoosier added that Ward "is the poorest excuse for a Genl I ever saw, he keeps eternally *drunk* and has no confidence placed in him either by his superiors or inferiors." In the pursuit south of Marietta, the XX Corps encountered resistance and was ordered to halt. Ward nonetheless continued to march his division a mile in advance of the corps until Hooker rode up and angrily de-

---

1. Welsh, *Medical Histories,* 25, 86, 367, 356; Cozzens, *This Terrible Sound,* 448.

manded, "Are you drunk or are you crazy, or are you a fool?" It turned out to be the former.[2]

A second medical leave occurred when, on July 14, Turchin suffered sunstroke, with an accompanying violent headache. He received a furlough the next day to go to Chicago. The rumor mill circulated that his leave meant that he would receive a division; as usual, the rumors were wrong. The brigadier later resigned due to poor health. The senior colonel of the brigade, Moses Walker, succeeded him.[3]

Finding a replacement for McPherson as head of the Army of the Tennessee in late July became a prime concern. The issue of succession, according to the *Chicago Tribune* correspondent who followed the XX Corps, was "already mooted. Maj. Gen. Hooker is the ranking officer in Sherman's army, and could best fill the vacancy; though he would scarcely like to accept the position unless he can take his corps with him, and this feeling is strongly reciprocated by the corps, which holds him in the high estimation. . . . 'Uncle Joe' is the man for our money *every time*."[4]

John Logan temporarily commanded the Army of the Tennessee, but Thomas harbored a grudge against him because that officer had complained directly to Sherman about Thomas's perceived mishandling of the railroads back at Chattanooga. "If there was ever a man on earth whom Thomas hated, it was Logan," Sherman would later write. In postwar years Sherman related an incident at Wood's headquarters, where he found Thomas, who expressed his dissatisfaction. "If he [Logan] had an army I'm afraid he would edge over on both sides and annoy Schofield and me. Even as a corps commander he is given to edging out beyond his jurisdiction." It would appear that Thomas did protest the appointment of Logan, though postwar accounts left by Sherman (including the scene at Wood's headquarters and an account of Thomas threatening to quit) have been questioned by historian Albert Castel. Although Sherman may have used Thomas's opposition, he probably never intended to select Logan, a fact hinted in his *Memoirs*. Thomas supported Oliver Howard, who was subsequently offered the command. When the IV Corps commander called attention to Hooker's seniority, Sherman snapped, "Hooker has not the moral qualities that I want—not those adequate to command; but if you don't want promotion, there are plenty who do." Howard quickly accepted.[5]

2. Welsh, *Medical Histories*, 50; *OR*, 38(5):246; Quaife, *From the Cannon's Mouth*, 331; Byrne, *View from Headquarters*, 165; Sylvester, " 'Gone for a Soldier,' " 198; William M. Anderson, *They Died to Make Men Free: A History of the 19th Michigan in the Civil War* (Berrien Springs, Mich.: Hardscrabble, 1980), 218; Castel, *Decision in the West*, 331. Crittenden was offered Butterfield's division but declined. *OR*, 38(5):3.

3. Welsh, *Medical Histories*, 342–43; *Chicago Tribune*, July 27, 1864.

4. *Chicago Tribune*, Aug. 2, 1864.

5. For a summary of the Sherman-Logan-Thomas controversy, see Castel, *Decision in the West*, 611. Castel concluded that Sherman attempted to deflect postwar criticism of his failure to select Logan by

Given Sherman's distaste for Hooker, his selection of Howard was predictable. Indeed, Daniel Butterfield had warned Hooker back on June 12 about indiscreetly talking around his staff, who in turn whispered "Hooker's opinions." If he persisted, Butterfield wrote, he would be accused of undercutting Sherman in order to obtain army command. "You never were, nor never will be a politic man—of that I am well aware—but you must be more guarded."[6]

Upon hearing of Howard's appointment to command the Army of the Tennessee, Hooker angrily submitted his resignation—"Justice and self-respect alike require my removal from an army in which rank and service are ignored." In his letter to Halleck, now chief of staff of the Union armies, Sherman wrote bluntly: "General Hooker is offended because he thinks he is entitled to the command. I must be honest and say he is not qualified or suited to it. He talks of quitting. . . . I shall not object. He is not indispensable to our success." Two days later he added in a letter home: "[Hooker] is envious, imperious and [a] braggert. Self prevailed with him and knowing him intimately I honestly preferred Howard." Adding insult to injury, Sherman selected Henry Slocum, Hooker's archenemy, to command the XX Corps. Alpheus Williams, the senior division commander in the corps, expressed resignation: "I am satisfied with my old division and I have long given up all hope of promotion from the present powers."[7]

Hooker, true to form, left in style. He "rode around the lines to bid good-bye to the soldiers of the Corps. He was received with great enthusiasm, though any noisy demonstration was forbidden as it would attract the enemy's fire." Two regiments of wagon guards lined the road as he rode away, and "he seemed much affected by the parting." Harvey Reid added, however, that it was well known throughout the corps that Hooker was "almost a drunkard." Nonetheless, another soldier noted, "Uncle Joe Hooker has left us—relieved at his own request—never has the loss of a Comdr cast such a gloom over troops as now hang over the XX Corps and the rest of the army, at his departure."[8]

"putting the blame on Thomas, who was not alive to contradict him." A full account of the scene at Wood's headquarters can be read in McKinney, *Education in Violence*, 352. See also Marszalek, *Sherman*, 279; Oliver O. Howard, "The Battles around Atlanta," *Atlantic Monthly* 38 (Oct. 1876): 395; and Sherman, *Memoirs*, 2:85, 86. The appointments were subject to the approval of the president, but Howard's, as well as all subsequent recommendations, were granted.

6. Julia L. Butterfield, ed., *A Biographical Memorial of General Daniel Butterfield* (New York: Grafton, 1903), 146–48.

7. *OR*, 38(5):272, 273; Sherman quoted in Hebert, *Fighting Joe Hooker*, 286; Quaife, *From the Cannon's Mouth*, 338, 341. Alpheus Williams noted that when Slocum arrived, "he seemed to fear that I would be greatly disappointed in not getting command of the corps." The *Chicago Tribune* of August 31, 1864, declared: "Gen. Howard's appointment comes from Washington. Hooker never has been a favorite of Grant's."

8. Byrne, *View from Headquarters*, 175–76; Sylvester, "'Gone for a Soldier,'" 213. Hooker's drinking habits were also well known in the Army of the Potomac.

Despite Stanley's reported inertness back at Chattanooga, he now received the IV Corps command by Thomas's recommendation. Capt. Jay Butler noted to his parents: "Gen'l Stanley has taken the corps, and I don't believe there is a general in the army thought any more of by his troops than General Stanley was by his division. In passing some of our boys the other day, one says to the other, 'I wonder what time it is.' The Gen'l stops, takes out his watch, gives the desired information, and passes on. He is not too high up to notice any soldier, and in time of need, he is cool and cautious, and in the advance—a splendid soldier and perfect gentleman."[9]

Succeeding him at First Division command was Brig. Gen. Nathan Kimball, a recent arrival to the Cumberland army. He had served back east and participated in the Battles of Antietam and Fredericksburg, receiving a severe groin wound at the latter. He continued to struggle with pain long after he transferred to the Army of the Tennessee during the Vicksburg campaign.[10]

The next incident occurred on July 28. On that day Sherman ordered Davis's division to Turner's Ferry, the extreme Federal right, in support of Howard's Army of the Tennessee. Davis, stricken with chronic jaundice and running a fever, had turned command over to Brig. Gen. James D. Morgan. When the Confederates attacked Howard at Ezra Church, Sherman saw an opportunity to assault their flank, yet Morgan was nowhere to be found. There were actually two roads to Turner's Ferry, and having neither map nor guide, Morgan took the wrong one. Unaware of this, an "anxious and impatient" Sherman rode over to XIV Corps headquarters, where he found Palmer on the front porch of a house. He ripped into the corps commander, claiming that he had written a misleading order to Morgan. Palmer insisted that he had given the order "precisely as Sherman had issued it." Cump chewed his cigar and paced. "I wish to God Davis was in command of his division today," he finally blurted. The general, in his sickbed, overheard the conversation through an open window. Determined to please, he got dressed, came outside, and mounted his horse, whereupon he fainted, being caught by his staff members. Palmer, irked that Davis's division was routinely being detached from his corps, complained to Thomas, "This is the fourth order from the headquarters of the military division [Sherman] imposing special duties upon Davis' division away from his corps." The day's debacle added to Palmer's already simmering anger.[11]

On August 4–5 Sherman ordered the XXIII and XIV Corps to move against the railroad between Atlanta and West Point. He specifically chose the XIV Corps because it had "fewer hard knocks than any other corps in the whole army, and I was anxious to give it a chance." Precisely who was senior, Schofield or Palmer, proved

9. Butler to parents, July 29, 1864, in Butler, *Letters Home*, 137.
10. Warner, *Generals in Blue*, 267–68; Welsh, *Medical Histories*, 194–95.
11. Hughes and Whitney, *Jefferson Davis in Blue*, 267–69; OR, 38(1):635, 651, 38(5):279, 311.

somewhat murky, for both received commissions as major generals on the same day. Sherman, due to several technical reasons, declared (and a court later concurred) Schofield the senior officer. Palmer disagreed and stubbornly refused to receive orders from him. An irritated Sherman notified Palmer: "The Sandtown road and the railroad, if possible, must be gained tomorrow [the fifth] if it costs half you command. I regard the loss of time this afternoon as equal to the loss of 2,000 men." The maddening delay continued the next day, during which time the XIV Corps made little progress. "From what I saw myself there was a manifest determination not to move toward the enemy," Sherman informed Thomas, prompting the Cumberland commander to defend his old corps ("Thomas pets," as they were known), "It has always been prompt in executing any work given it heretofore." When Palmer declared his intention to resign, Sherman wrote him: "If you think of resigning it is probably better it should be now. . . . To be honest, I must say that the operations [of the XIV Corps] . . . yesterday and today have not been satisfactory." An angry Palmer thus departed the army, much to Sherman's relief.[12]

None regretted the departure. "We all expect some work out of the old 14th Corps now that Palmer does not command it," Opdycke related. Major Connolly candidly wrote his wife that if either Palmer or Schofield were killed, "the army would go along just the same." He expressed disgust at the petty bickering in high places. "I feel quite certain that if our Generals hadn't fallen to quarreling among themselves, Atlanta would have been ours. I'm glad I'm not a General to be quarreling with my companions about questions of rank, like a bunch of children quarreling about their painted toys. We will get Atlanta some day though, in spite of our family broils."[13]

The ranking division commander in the corps was Richard Johnson, but Sherman queried Thomas: "Will General Johnson be any better than General Palmer? I would prefer to move a rock than to move that corps. On the defensive it would be splendid, but for offensive it is of no use. It must have a head that will give it life and impulse. . . . If an enemy can be seen by a spy-glass the whole corps is halted and entrenched for a siege." Sherman's sarcastic exaggeration and implied criticism of the Cumberland army's leadership must have rankled Thomas, but he gave no reply. Jefferson C. Davis was preferable to Johnson, but he remained sick. Again, Sherman ranted: "That is the largest corps we have, and thus far [it] has not sustained heavy losses in this campaign. It moves slowly or reluctantly and there is something wrong." The next day, August 6, after witnessing Johnson in temporary

12. *OR*, 38(5):378–85; Sherman, *Memoirs*, 2:99; John Palmer, *Personal Recollections*, 210–11; George Palmer, *Conscientious Turncoat*, 155–58. Sherman was correct in his assertion. The IV Corps had sustained 32 percent casualties up to that time; the XX Corps, 34 percent; and the XIV Corps, 20 percent.

13. Opdycke to wife, Aug. 13, 1864, Emerson Opdycke Letters, OHS; Angle, *Three Years in the Army of the Cumberland*, 252.

command, Sherman concluded that the general lacked "the ability or vigor" necessary for the position. Thomas wanted Davis, and if not him, Brannan.[14]

As the command vacuum persisted, Johnson remained in charge of the XIV Corps and Morgan of the Second (Davis's) Division. Johnson still resisted advancing past Utoy Creek on August 7; a decision had to be made. Davis was tapped for corps command, though he continued sick through August 23. In order to resolve the seniority issue, Johnson was transferred to a cavalry command in Nashville. William Carlin, presently on a leave of absence to get married, received command of the First Division. Carlin's and Davis's mutual hatred was no secret, and conflict between the two would again erupt.[15]

In mid-August an opening occurred in the Second Division, XV Corps, Army of the Tennessee, with the sudden departure of Brig. Gen. Morgan L. Smith due to an old wound sustained during the Vicksburg campaign. The division went to a Cumberland officer—William B. Hazen. "Hazen seems cheerful[;] says he can have a division in the Army of [the] Tennessee[;] at any time he will go over there and in a Corps where he would rank all but its present commander. I think he ought to go, for he has commanded a brigade until he is tired of it. . . . [Robert] Kimberly told me that H[azen] did not care much for his brigade," Opdycke confided. It was probably the most deserved promotion that summer. At last an officer-hero from the old Ohio army core had received advancement—ironically, in another army.[16]

Following Union cavalry raids and the siege of Atlanta, both of which failed to break the backbone of Confederate resistance, Sherman again resorted to a wheeling movement against the railroads south of the city. Leaving Slocum's XX Corps to protect the Chattahoochee River bridge, the balance of the army quietly evacuated their trenches and swung west of Atlanta. Two of Howard's corps arrived at Fairburn, along the Atlanta and West Point Railroad, at noon on August 28. Several hours later the IV and XIV Corps marched into Red Oak five miles to the northeast, also along the railroad. The twenty-ninth was spent in wrecking thirteen miles of track at and between the towns, a waste of time as it turned out since the Atlanta and West Point was virtually nonoperational at the time.[17]

14. *OR*, 38(5):369, 371, 392, 393. After the war Sherman openly wrote what he must have then thought, that is, that the XIV Corps "had imbibed somewhat his [Thomas's] personal character . . . nothing hasty or rash, but always safe, 'slow, and sure.'" *Memoirs*, 2:101. It was his veiled way of saying that the corps, like Thomas, had no offensive edge.

15. Sherman, *Memoirs*, 2:100–101; Girardi and Hughes, *Memoirs of Brigadier General William Passmore Carlin*, 129, 132, 271; Warner, *Generals in Blue*, 334–35.

16. Warner, *Generals in Blue*, 460; Hazen, *Narrative*, 278; Opdycke to wife, Aug. 14, 1864, Opdycke Letters.

17. Castel, *Decision in the West*, 486, 489, 503; McMurry, *Atlanta 1864*, 170–73.

On the thirtieth Thomas, with the IV and XIV Corps, reached Couch's house at the northern end of the Flint River, about six miles northwest of Jonesboro, and went into camp. That evening Kimball's and Newton's divisions of the IV Corps noticed activity in their front. At sunset the 36th Illinois of Newton's division saw a considerable column of troops moving northeast of their position, while Colonel Opdycke heard the movement of artillery six hundred yards distant. It could have been Schofield's corps moving up on the left flank, though Newton noted, "I incline to think it was not." Col. Sidney Post, commanding Hazen's old brigade, reported, "a large force of the enemy, with artillery and [wagon] trains, moved past our position in a southerly direction." What Newton's and Post's men had uncovered was the passage of Hardee's corps toward Jonesboro.[18]

On the morning of the thirty-first, the Federals clearly spotted dust clouds— probably S. D. Lee's corps, also on its way to Jonesboro. According to Lieutenant Colonel Fullerton, Thomas pleaded with Sherman to attack the enemy in flank. Sherman, however, concerned about his old army, the lead elements of which were already on the east bank of the Flint River within a half-mile of Jonesboro, "would not allow Thomas to move out of position from which he could quickly go to its support." Thus, Sherman rejected Thomas's fourth tactical suggestion of the campaign and allowed two Confederate corps to pass unscathed under Thomas's nose.[19]

By then one corps and elements of two others of the Army of the Tennessee had taken up a defensive position on a ridge near Jonesboro, with skirmishers approaching to within a quarter mile of the town. Howard notified Sherman that the Rebels were "shoving troops down here with great rapidity." That afternoon the Confederates attacked, 20,000 of them, but the bungled, half-hearted assault was repulsed with murderous losses—2,200 Confederates compared to 172 Federals.[20]

Stanley's corps arrived at Rough and Ready on the Macon and Western Railroad that day, forming a junction with the XXIII Corps, and took up an entrenched position facing south. The leading elements of Baird's division of Davis's XIV Corps reached the railroad four miles north of Jonesboro. Late in the afternoon Carlin's (Davis's old) division was ordered to Howard's assistance at Jonesboro, though it did not arrive until after the battle had been completed. The next day, September 1, Sherman planned for Stanley's and Schofield's corps to work south from Rough and Ready, wrecking the track as they advanced, while Baird's and Morgan's divisions moved north, doing the same.[21]

18. *OR*, 38(1):213, 428, 38(5):711.

19. *OR*, 38(1):428; Fullerton quoted in Cleaves, *Rock of Chickamauga*, 238. Some units of J. D. Cox's division of the XXIII Corps, on Thomas's left, did make contact, causing the Confederates to divert east.

20. Castel, *Decision in the West*, 494–95, 497, 503.

21. Van Horne, *Army of the Cumberland*, 2:142.

But Thomas saw an opportunity to capture the two enemy corps. At 7:00 P.M. he wrote Sherman what would be his fifth tactical suggestion of the campaign. The IV and XXIII Corps could work their way down the Macon and Western, destroying it as they advanced, until they met the XIV Corps. The two Cumberland units could then swing southwest and then east to Lovejoy's Station, south of Jonesboro, thus cutting off any Rebel retreat to Macon. At 9:00 P.M. Sherman, as usual, rejected the idea. "Inasmuch as I have already given orders to Schofield, based on the idea that he and Stanley move down the railroad, breaking it till they come to Baird and Davis [Morgan], near Jonesborough, I think we had better adhere to that plan till we develop the first step in the enemy's game, after he knows we are between him and Atlanta. My own impression is that Hardee will try to join Hood in Atlanta," a rather far-fetched idea, given the wrecked condition of the sole remaining railroad.[22]

Like all of Thomas's ideas, this one aimed at decisiveness. Although praised by modern historians, there are reasons why it probably would not have succeeded even had Sherman approved. Perhaps Thomas could have marched his two corps the eighteen miles to Lovejoy's (passing through Fayetteville) and been astride the railroad by the night of September 1, though it is conceivable that the Confederates would have detected the movement and beat him there. On the night of the thirty-first, however, while Thomas would be marching, Lee's corps was recalled to Atlanta and departed east to McDonough. Had Hardee discovered the blocking force to the south (he had scouts in Fayetteville), he clearly would have done the same, escaping east through McDonough on the night of the first. Additionally, the absence of the two Cumberland corps at Jonesboro on September 1 would have dramatically affected the outcome of what was an undisputed, if incomplete, victory against Hardee's lone corps. Thus, the plan to "crush Confederate military power in the West once and for all" probably would have fallen far short of expectations.[23]

Sherman's true blunder for September 1 was not in rejecting Thomas's plan but in having the IV and XXIII Corps spend the entire day (6:00 A.M. to 4:00 P.M.) destroying the Macon and Western. "Thanks to Sherman's foolish compulsion to destroy a railroad the Confederates could no longer use, the Yankees wasted the entire morning of September 1," concluded McMurry. True enough, but Thomas's plan had called for at least a portion of the day to be spent doing the same thing.[24]

Throughout the afternoon of the first, Davis's XIV Corps maintained contact

22. *OR*, 38(5):718–19.

23. McMurry, *Atlanta 1864*, 173–74. If Sherman wanted to block the southern escape route, all he had to do was advance one of Howard's corps south of Hardee's left flank and get astride the railroad. Sherman belatedly used the XVII Corps to demonstrate against the Confederate left on September 1, but it barely got across the Flint River before night.

24. Ibid., 174; *OR*, 38(5):261, 277, 284, 299, 322, 339, 366.

with Howard's left, with Carlin's and Baird's divisions approaching from the north and Morgan's from the northwest. Learning that only Hardee's corps remained at Jonesboro, Sherman (through Thomas) directed Stanley's corps forward at once, thus giving the Federals an outrageous five to one advantage. The XIV took an excessively long time preparing for an assault, prompting Sherman to write Thomas, "we must risk everything rather than dilly-dally about." To Halleck he later wrote: "I expected Thomas to be ready by 11 A.M. . . . A part of my army is too slow," a clear reference to the XIV Corps. At 4:00 P.M. Davis's command, in two lines, at last attacked. Baird personally led the one brigade of his division (Col. George P. Este's) that was engaged. He apparently did so because Davis had made "an insulting remark about Este," or so Baird wrote Palmer several days after the battle. His horse was shot from under him, sending Baird head over heels, but he quickly jumped to his feet and ran alongside the men. For his bravery Baird would, years later, receive the Medal of Honor. So withering was the fire on Este's front that two color bearers of the 74th Indiana fell as well as three each in the 14th Ohio and 30th Ohio.

After an hour's hard fighting, Morgan's division broke the Confederate angle, capturing 880 men of Cleburne's division and eight guns. A jubilant Sherman shouted, "They're rolling 'em up like a sheet of paper!" He directed Stanley, opposite the Confederate far right, to go for the jugular and attack their flank and rear. Confronted by only a single Rebel brigade, Stanley could hardly have failed. Yet he made only a feeble advance, and night soon stopped that. Stanley explained that it was five o'clock before Grose's and Kirby's brigades broke through the thickets, and then they could not penetrate the Confederate obstructions. By the time Newton's division found the enemy's flank, it proved too late to accomplish anything. The XIV Corps incurred 1,272 casualties. Total Union losses tallied at about 1,400 men, the same as the Rebels. The bluecoats overran eight guns, four of which had been taken from Loomis's battery at Chickamauga. That night Hardee escaped south to Lovejoy's Station.[25]

25. William R. Scaife, *The Campaign for Atlanta* (Atlanta: privately printed, 1985), 111–12; *OR*, 38(1):514; Simpson and Berlin, *Sherman's Civil War*, 699; *New York Tribune*, Sept. 19, 1864; Hughes and Whitney, *Jefferson Davis in Blue*, 280–85; Angle, *Three Years in the Army of the Cumberland*, 258; Lee H. Rudisille, "The Charge at Jonesboro: The Magnificent Charge by Este's Brigade," *National Tribune*, Aug. 5, 1909; *History and Tour of the Atlanta Campaign* (Columbus, Ohio: Blue and Gray Enterprises, 1996), 294, 297; *New York Tribune*, Sept. 8, 15, 1864. Castel offered an interesting assessment of a comment made in Sherman's *Memoirs*. Sherman claimed that he finally sent Thomas to hurry on the IV Corps, and "this is the only time in the campaign I can recall seeing General Thomas himself urge his horse into a gallop." Castel concluded that the event never happened and was but "another example of his [Sherman's] persistent disparaging of Thomas as being chronically slow and plodding." *Decision in the West*, 570–71. Yet Howard, a Thomas ally, also made mention of the incident. See Cleaves, *Rock of Chickamauga*, 239.

Ignoring the fact that the Army of the Tennessee sat mostly idle throughout the day and that hours had been wasted by the IV Corps in destroying the railroad, Sherman believed that Stanley had squandered what would have been a decisive victory. He thus wrote to Thomas that evening: "I regret to learn that General Stanley remained today for hours on the railroad awaiting orders, when he heard firing heavy to his front and right. I may be in error, but such is reported to me by Captain [Joseph] Audenried and Captain [Orlando] Poe. I knew you had given him orders, and think we should not overlook it." He concluded by adding that if Stanley "lost a minute of time when he should have been in action, I beg you not to overlook it." The next day Sherman saw Stanley and accused him of losing a great chance to bag Hardee's corps. "If I did so, Sir, it was owing to your orders," he retorted.[26]

That night Sherman, restless and impatient, could not sleep. About midnight he heard "heavy firing and saw a large fire in the direction of Atlanta." Carlin recalled that the explosions "continued almost incessantly for an hour or longer. At times the roar would rise step by step to almost deafening volume, and then subside into silence." Two possibilities came to mind: either the Confederates had blown their own ammunition supplies or Slocum had become embroiled in a battle to the north. Early on the third Sherman received a dispatch from Slocum stating that Hood had evacuated Atlanta and that he had entered the city unopposed. Before he shared the news with the army, Sherman notified Thomas, who soon came to his headquarters to verify the information. In a rare display of emotion, he snapped his fingers, whistled, and almost danced. The men expressed elation. "The long agony is over, and Atlanta is ours! The army is frantic with exultation, and the rebel army is scattered over the country," Major Connolly wrote.[27]

Early on the previous day, the enemy having retreated south from Jonesboro, Sherman went in pursuit, the IV Corps east of the Macon and Western Railroad and the Army of the Tennessee west of it. By noon the Yankees encountered the enemy a mile north of Lovejoy's Station, "briskly fortifying across the road and railroad." Howard planned to keep the Rebels preoccupied while Stanley maneuvered around their right. Unfortunately, Stanley's men encountered difficult ground, cut by ravines and marshes. As at Jonesboro the flanking column did not deploy until late—6:00 P.M. to be precise. While Wood was engaged in selecting a point of attack, a sniper struck him in the left foot, the same one as hit at Stones River. Although not leaving the field, he used crutches for the next six months and had to be transported in an ambulance. Sherman subsequently canceled the attack order

26. *OR*, 38(5):746; Stanley, *Personal Memoirs*, 182–83.

27. Sherman, *Memoirs*, 2:108–9; Girardi and Hughes, *Memoirs of Brigadier General William Passmore Carlin*, 136; Angle, *Three Years in the Army of the Cumberland*, 256–57.

for Howard, but not for Stanley. Apparently, the army commander thought that a flank attack alone would do the job. It did not. After he had taken an advanced line of trenches, capturing a few dozen prisoners in the process, a murderous artillery fire (the IV Corps artillery had not yet come up to provide counter fire) forced Stanley back. On the fifth the armies were recalled to Atlanta; the campaign had concluded.[28]

The Army of the Cumberland, though relegated to a supporting role, had served as Sherman's warhorse. The army was perceived as too ponderous for rapid flank maneuvers, but Sherman used the army as his sledgehammer in direct assaults at Resaca, New Hope Church, Pickett's Mill, Gilgal Church, Kennesaw Mountain, and Jonesboro. On two occasions, at Kolb's Farm and Peachtree Creek, the Confederates chose to attack the pivot rather than the "whip-lash." Prior to August 31 the army sustained in the infantry and artillery 3,009 killed, 15,456 wounded, and 1,775 missing, a total of 20,240 casualties. From September 1 to 15, the army reported an additional 2,567 casualties, for a grand total of 22,807, proportionally as many as the vaunted Army of the Tennessee.[29]

Sherman clearly respected Thomas for his knowledge and solid war record, but their tactical and personal styles differed radically, the notable exception being their mutual lack of a killer instinct. On September 4, in a dispatch to Halleck, Sherman characterized the Virginian as "slow, but true as steel." On five occasions Thomas had made tactical suggestions that were rejected: (1) to use the Army of the Cumberland as the flank army at Snake Creek Gap; (2) to use the XX Corps to reinforce the Army of the Tennessee in crossing the Oostanaula; (3) to outflank the Confederate position at Kennesaw Mountain on their right; (4) to attack the Confederates in flank at Rough and Ready, though this is not verified in contemporary evidence;

28. OR, 38(1):215–16, 218, 228, 261–62, 384; Welsh, Medical Histories, 377. Castel's assertion that Sherman punitively ordered Stanley forward out of bitterness over his performance the day before strikes me as a stretch. See Decision in the West, 531.

29. OR, 38(5):791–94. McMurry asserted that even though Sherman eventually won the Atlanta Campaign, Thomas "would have secured the victory there sooner and at far less overall cost to the nation." He based this on the fact that Sherman "almost totally lacked the killer instinct," that "he had little taste for battle," and that he "chose to allow the enemy force to march away to fight again another day," an "inconceivable" action that Thomas would not have allowed. Thomas, of course, did allow the enemy to escape at Mill Springs, though it could be argued that he had matured during the intervening two and a half years. As regards the present campaign, however, he had even less taste for battle than Sherman. As a strategist, Thomas was essentially a maneuverer whose flanking ideas were designed either to capture the Confederate army or, presumably, to place the enemy in a position to cut their way out, leaving the Federals to operate on the defensive, a tactic with which he ultimately felt more comfortable. Richard McMurry, The Fourth Battle of Winchester: Toward a New Civil War Paradigm (Kent, Ohio: Kent State University Press, 2002), 104–5.

and (5) to send the Army of the Cumberland on a flank march to Lovejoy's Station to block the Confederate escape route. Whether or not any of the ideas would have worked, they clearly revealed Thomas as more than a plodding and uncreative defensive general.[30]

The campaign had reduced Thomas's army to forty thousand effectives in infantry and artillery, and not surprisingly, it had taken its toll on their appearance. To the question "Is hair kept short and beard neatly trimmed," an inspector of the IV Corps on September 20 answered candidly: "Generally it is not." Singled out in this respect was Samuel Beatty's brigade. In the First Brigade, Second Division, XIV Corps, the officers received low marks for not wearing the prescribed uniform, and the troops did not keep their hair properly cut. The Second and Third Brigades of that division were also cited for their dirty personal appearance.[31]

By late August interest heightened in the upcoming fall presidential election. The badly fractured Democratic Party, widely perceived as the peace party, would hold its convention in Chicago at the end of the month. "The soldiers are looking with some anxiety as to what course the opposition [Democrats] propose taking in the Presidential election," William Robinson of the 34th Illinois candidly wrote. "The question seems to be narrowed to that of Peace or war, and though we have faith in the loyalty of the masses at home, yet there appears to be great danger of counter revolution in some parts of the North." Described William Wallace of the 3d Wisconsin to his wife: "We are all anxious to hear who will be the nominee of the Chicago Convention; two months more and we will know who will be our roolers for the next four years. I hope it will be the incumbent. A large majority will vote for Mr. Lincoln in the army, but some will vote for almost any man so that peace may be brought about and get out of the army. Such men is not worth much in a fight."[32]

Many perceived Lincoln's popularity to be on the decline. A Connecticut soldier in the XX Corps expressed "fear that our want [of] decided victories will have a tendency to encourage the enemies of the Administration and possibly defeat Uncle Abe, though I can't hardly believe it yet." Harvey Reid of the same corps wrote his father on August 9: "The fear is pretty generally expressed in the army that he [Lincoln] will not be elected, if McClellan, or someone else who can command a portion of the *conservative* Republican vote, is nominated at Chicago. I wait with considerable anxiety for the decision of that Convention." He continued on the twenty-sixth:

30. McMurry, *Atlanta 1864*, 196.

31. Monthly Inspection Reports Received, Sept. 20, 1864, Entry 1058, Vol. 240, RG 393, Pt. 1, NA.

32. Robinson quoted in James Lee McDonough and James Pickett Jones, *War So Terrible: Sherman and Atlanta* (New York: W. W. Norton, 1987), 283; Holzhueter, "William Wallace's Civil War Letters," 107.

"I know that Mr. Lincoln is becoming almost daily unpopular, and I earnestly hope that the Chicago Convention will nominate some honest, patriotic, energetic man who can in some degree alleviate the bitterness of this cursed party strife, that has brought our country to the verge of ruin." He quietly expressed his preference for either Grant or Sherman.[33]

The results of the Chicago Convention did not reach the Army of the Cumberland until September 5. While McClellan, the party nominee, held deep inroads into the Army of the Potomac, he attracted little attention in the West. Indeed, given the Democratic platform (declaring the war a failure), and that McClellan's nomination "was made unanimous on the motion of the Traitor Vallandigham is more than the admirers of little 'Mac' can stand and I can assure you that 'Mac' has lost thousands of votes within three weeks," concluded one Cumberland soldier. Alfred Hough concurred: "McClellan is fast losing what friends he had in the army, and I have no doubt Lincoln will have a large majority of the army vote." Even a New Yorker in the XX Corps declared: "McClellan is naught here in the army. It is all old Abe." On September 21 Chesley Morman, while admitting that there were only a few McClellan supporters in his camp, remained concerned that "there is very little interest in politics in the men in our Brigade, though Illinois men ought to be partisans of an Illinois [Lincoln] candidate." George Drake of the 5th Illinois wrote on the twenty-second: "There is several of the Democrats in our company that say they will not support Mac if he runs on the [Democratic] platform." Writing to his parents on November 3, New Yorker John Gourlie, formerly a McClellan supporter, revealed that he was now a "Lincoln man to the backbone."[34]

While thirteen states had passed laws allowing soldiers in the field a proxy vote, in five others (notably Illinois and Indiana in the West), the troops remained disenfranchised. Lincoln, urged on by Governor Morton, wrote Sherman after the fall of Atlanta, requesting but not ordering that Hoosiers be allowed to return home to vote, which they were. Exactly how the fall of Atlanta influenced the presidential election has been debated, but the Army of the Cumberland did its part in reelecting Lincoln, giving him a commanding 87 percent of their vote.[35]

33. James A. Padgett, ed., "With Sherman through Georgia and the Carolinas: Letters of a Federal Soldier," *Georgia Historical Quarterly* 32 (1948): 307; Byrne, *View from Headquarters*, 178–79, 181.

34. Cope, *Fifteenth Ohio*, 560; soldier quoted in Waugh, *Reelecting Lincoln*, 342; Athearn, *Soldier in the West*, 218; Drake, *Mail Goes Through*, 115; Gates, *Rough Side of War*, 282; Gourlie quoted in Anne J. Bailey, *The Chessboard of War: Sherman and Hood in the Autumn Campaigns of 1864* (Lincoln: University of Nebraska Press, 2000), 11.

35. Waugh, *Reelecting Lincoln*, 340–41. The vote estimate is based upon 3,266 known votes of sixteen regiments in the IV and XIV Corps. Of that number, 3,266 voted for Lincoln and 503 for McClellan. See Joseph T. Glatthaar, *The March to the Sea and Beyond: Sherman's Troops in the Savannah and Carolinas*

* * *

Matters calmed after the fall of Atlanta, as Sherman's army regrouped in and around the environs of the city. There was even talk on Thomas's staff that the general had sent for his wife. "He has not seen her since the war commenced, and can't find time to go and see her," noted an officer.[36]

It was not to be. By September 20 Hood's army at Lovejoy's Station and Forrest's cavalry, estimated at ten thousand (actually forty-five hundred), in Tennessee were on the prowl. Thomas, sent to deal with the communications in Tennessee, arrived in Chattanooga on the twenty-ninth, establishing his headquarters at the Crutchfield house. Two divisions, one each from the IV and XIV Corps, also arrived. Thomas went on to Nashville, where he directed seemingly futile operations to bag the elusive Forrest. Hood's army, meanwhile, crossed the Chattahoochee and struck the Western and Atlantic, capturing several small garrisons and destroying eight miles of track, repairs requiring six miles of iron and thirty-five thousand replacement ties. Hood then veered west, bypassing Rome on October 10. By the eighteenth the Army of the Cumberland, minus the XX Corps, still in Atlanta, had massed near Summerville, Georgia, to the left and east of the Army of the Tennessee. Thomas began to deploy his forces so as to prevent Hood from crossing the Tennessee River, "and while I hold him in front, Sherman will attack him in the rear."[37]

But Sherman had other plans. Colonel Fullerton, in postwar years, would claim that the idea for the famed "March to the Sea" came from Thomas, who proposed to release the thirty thousand Federal prisoners at Andersonville, Georgia, and then move on to the coast. Like many claims of Thomas's supporters, there is no contemporary evidence to substantiate it. Indeed, as early as September 4, Sherman had mentioned a march to Macon and Savannah. Sherman nonetheless later admitted that "in 1862 every soldier of Gen. Buell's fifty thousand not only conceived the idea, but absolutely undertook it. Every officer of the Army of the Cumberland, before the XX Corps joined it, 'conceived the idea' of 'cutting their way to the sea,' and it was common talk around the campfires of the West."[38]

Campaign (New York: New York University Press, 1985), 200–202. To Glatthaar's regiments I have added a brigade total mentioned in Angle, *Three Years in the Army of the Cumberland,* 292. For my views on the influence of the fall of Atlanta upon the 1864 election, see Larry J. Daniel, "The South Almost Won by Not Losing: A Rebuttal," *N&S* 1 (Feb. 1998): 44–61. See also McMurry, *Atlanta 1864,* 204–8.

36. As quoted in McKinney, *Education in Violence,* 370. Actually, Thomas had been with his wife back in September 1861, making a full three-year absence.

37. Cleaves, *Rock of Chickamauga,* 243–44; OR, 39(1):581, 39(3):175, 325, 347.

38. "Sherman's Famous March to the Sea," *New York Times,* Dec. 28, 1894; Sherman quoted in Hirshson, *White Tecumseh,* 249. Fullerton claimed that Sherman's proposal to march on Columbus, Mississippi, can be found in OR, 38(5). The document in question is clearly found elsewhere and says something very different from what Fullerton suggested. See OR, 39(3):377–78.

Sherman revealed his plan to Thomas on October 20. He had no intention of chasing Hood, "for he can twist and turn like a fox and wear out an army in pursuit." He instead would give Thomas the IV and XXIII Corps, and with them the responsibility of dealing with Hood, while, with the balance of the army, some sixty-two thousand troops, Sherman would proceed to Savannah and then through the Carolinas, leaving "a trail that will be recognized for fifty years hence." Grant initially balked at the idea, but he eventually consented.[39]

By separating the IV and XIV Corps, Sherman had undermined the historic cohesion of the Army of the Cumberland; indeed, as a distinct army, it no longer existed. Thomas requested the return of his old corps, but to no avail. "It is too compact and reliable a corps for me to leave behind," Sherman answered. Although not inevitable, the move was certainly foreseeable. When Sherman operated south of Atlanta, he had left the XX Corps north of the city and used the XXIII Corps as a de facto wing of the Cumberland army. On one occasion, as previously mentioned, Schofield had even commanded the XIV Corps, as well as his own, in a joint operation. It had by now become commonplace for an officer of rank to receive promotion by transfer to another army. Even Thomas made no strong protest against the loss of the XIV Corps; he filed no complaint to his friend Halleck. Perhaps the war had simply entered a new phase, with ad hoc, conglomerate armies, such as now commanded by Thomas and Sherman, being the order of the day. Yet it seemed an inglorious end for the grand old army.[40]

There was an alternative—exchange the XIV Corps for the XXIII Corps. According to the returns, doing so would have reduced Sherman's marching force by only twenty-five hundred infantry and artillery. With the loss of veteran regiments in the XXIII Corps, the difference between the two units might have climbed to four thousand men. Nonetheless, had such an exchange maintained the historical unity of his coveted Army of the Tennessee, would not Sherman have done it? But the issue had been decided, and the corps that Sherman had cursed for the past three months he would not now relinquish. The XIV and XX Corps would become the "Army of Georgia" under Slocum. The XIV, with the acorn as its corps badge, the symbol of the stability of the oak, and the oldest of the army's corps, would henceforth fight on separate fields from the IV Corps.[41]

Perhaps eager to regain independent command, Thomas too easily acquiesced to Sherman's division of the forces. Although Sherman claimed to leave Thomas

---

39. Cleave, *Rock of Chickamauga*, 245. Thomas would also receive two divisions of the XVI Corps, then in Missouri, and a considerable amount of cavalry.

40. McKinney, *Education in Violence*, 376–77.

41. The exchange of the XIV and XXIII Corps might have resulted in as much as a 6,000-man reduction to Sherman, as Schofield later claimed that his corps was down to 8,000 men.

forty-nine thousand infantry and seventy-seven hundred mounted and ten thousand dismounted cavalry, the numbers in fact were not so large (he overestimated the IV and XXIII Corps by five thousand men, and there were never more than twelve thousand cavalry) and the forces were widely scattered. This was an insufficient force to confront a Rebel army estimated at forty thousand men, plus ten thousand cavalry under Forrest (numbers also inflated as it turned out.) On October 21, however, Thomas related to Halleck: "I feel confident that I can defend the line of Tennessee with the force General Sherman proposes to leave with me. . . . I shall be able to send General Sherman all the cavalry he needs and still have a good force left." A month later he would be claiming that he could not attack Hood for want of cavalry. When ordered to send home the Illinois troops to vote in the presidential election, Thomas refused, sending only those unfit for duty. Given Sherman's feeble opposition in his March to the Sea, the XIV Corps, rather than the XXIII, should have been sent to Tennessee.[42]

42. *OR,* 39(2):389. Thomas Buell has offered rare criticism of Thomas at this point, stating that he "miscalculated" and promised "too much with too little." *Warrior Generals,* 380–83.

Epilogue

WHILE SHERMAN'S COLUMNS tramped through Georgia, Hood kept his army, now reduced to 30,600 men, on the move. He crossed the Tennessee River at Tuscumbia, Alabama, and raided into Tennessee. The IV and XXIII Corps finally concentrated at Franklin, their flanks firmly anchored on the Harpeth River, and watched as the Rebels approached. Shortly after noon on November 30, two of Hood's corps arrived. At 4:00 P.M. a frontal assault of 18,000 Rebels advanced astride the Columbia Pike, their hundred banners snapping in the warm autumn breeze. Two brigades of the IV Corps, foolishly positioned a half mile in advance of the Union line, were routed. The Confederates penetrated to the edge of town before a Union counterattack hurled them back. Although left in possession of the battlefield, Hood's army had been wrecked, losing a staggering 6,700 men to the Federals 2,300, General Stanley among the wounded of the latter. The Federals fell back to Nashville.[1]

Despite the hard-fought Federal victory, Grant and Sherman remained perturbed. "Why he [Thomas] did not turn on Hood at Franklin, after checking and discomforting him, surpasses my understanding. I know full well that General Thomas is slow in mind and in action, but he is judicious and brave, and the troops feel great confidence in him. I still hope he will out-maneuver and destroy Hood," Sherman summarized. A week and a half into December, after the Federal army at Nashville had increased to sixty thousand, Grant applied great pressure for an immediate offensive. When no action was forthcoming, he considered replacing Thomas with either Schofield or John Logan. On the seventh Secretary of War Stanton wrote Grant that if Thomas planned to wait on his cavalry to get ready, "Gabriel will be blowing his last horn." The next day Grant noted to Halleck, "There is no better man to repel an attack than Thomas, but I fear he is too cautious to ever take the initiative." The next day he sternly wrote the Virginian, "It seemed to me that you have been slow, and I had no explanation of affairs to convince me otherwise." Thomas called the general in chief's hand: "If you should deem it necessary to relieve me I shall submit without a murmur." To some officers Thomas mused about

---

1. Castel, *Decision in the West*, 556–57.

Grant's foolish order to attack at Chattanooga in the fall of 1863 before the Army of the Tennessee had come up.[2]

The issue soon came to a head. In a two-day battle waged on December 15–16, Thomas, in a spectacular "right hook" assault, overran Hood's entrenched troops at Nashville, routing them and sending them fleeing. By the time Hood returned to the Tennessee River, he had only twenty thousand men remaining. The Army of Tennessee had been effectively eliminated from the war. Yet Thomas halted to refit the army rather than continue a relentless pursuit, again evoking the anger of Grant. "His pursuit of Hood indicated a sluggishness that satisfied me he would never do to conduct one of your campaigns," Grant confided to Sherman. Thomas's army was eventually dispersed to other sectors.[3]

Nonetheless, on Christmas Eve, Thomas received a telegram from Stanton informing him that the president had submitted his nomination as major general in the U.S. Army to the Senate. At his Pulaski, Tennessee, headquarters, when he received the message, Thomas turned to his chief surgeon, George E. Cooper, handed him the telegram, and asked: "What do you think of that?" Reading it, Cooper replied: "It is better late than never." Thomas testily responded: "It is better late than never but it is too late to be appreciated. I earned this at Chattanooga." He was wrong; he had earned it at Chickamauga.[4]

On May 9, 1865, Thomas held a spectacular review; his farewell to the IV Corps. He took his place in a stand constructed outside the city. Leading the march was David Stanley, having recovered from his Franklin wound. In the ranks were such officers as Thomas Wood, who was with the original Ohio army; Emerson Opdycke; and Charles Harker. Perhaps they, and the troops who marched with them, thought back to the immortal charge up Missionary Ridge—the pinnacle of the Army of the

2. *OR*, 44:728, 45(2):17, 55, 97, 115; Simon, *Papers of Ulysses S. Grant*, 13:77, 83, 87, 107; Bailey, *Chessboard of War*, 141, 143, 152, 159; Buell, *Warrior Generals*, 399.

3. Van Horne, *Thomas*, 361. During the Gulf War, Gen. Norman Schwarzkopf stated that his military hero was Sherman. John Hubbell at Kent State University has pointed out, however, that the coalition plan of battle was actually Thomas's battle plan for the second day at Nashville. The plan, of course, was in reverse—a left hook rather than a right hook—but otherwise identical. Perhaps also the condition of the Confederates and that of the Iraqis was comparable. John Hubbell, conversation with the author.

4. Cleaves, *Rock of Chickamauga*, 273–75. An officer later related to Montgomery Meigs: "He [Thomas] feels very sore at the rumored intentions to relieve him and the major generalcy does not cicatrize the wound. You know Thomas is morbidly sensitive and it cut him to the heart to think that it was contemplated to remove him. He does not blame the Secretary, for he said Mr. Stanton was a fair and just man." The implication was that he blamed Halleck and Grant. On the issue of Thomas's potential removal, Halleck had written to Grant on December 8: "No one here, I think, will interfere. The responsibility, however, will be yours, as no one here, so far as I am informed, wishes Genl Thomas' removal."

Cumberland's glory. But there were other episodes as well: the murder of a corps commander in Louisville; the secret meeting of some officers of the First Division to wrestle command from Don Carlos Buell; the rout of the army's right wing on a bitter-cold morning at Stones River; the army's polarization over the issue of emancipation; the disastrous collapse of the battle line on a hot September afternoon at Chickamauga; a bloodstained battlefield fronting Cheatham's Hill at Kennesaw Mountain. No matter—in the army's postwar society meetings, the war years would be remembered as the days of glory.[5]

5. McKinney, *Education in Violence*, 444–45; Cleaves, *Rock of Chickamauga*, 283–84.

ORDERS OF BATTLE

BATTLE OF MILL SPRINGS
January 18, 1862

First Division, Brig. Gen. George H. Thomas
Second Brigade, Col. Mahlon D. Manson: 10th Ind., 4th Ky., 10th Ky., 14th Ohio
Third Brigade, Col. Robert L. McCook: 2d Minn., 9th Ohio
Twelfth Brigade, Brig. Gen. Samuel P. Carter: 12th Ky., 1st East Tenn., 2d East Tenn., 1st Ky. Cav.
Artillery: Btry. B, Btry. C, 1st Ohio; 9th Ohio Btry.
Camp Guard: Michigan Engineers (3 cos.), 38th Ohio (1 co.)

Brig. Gen. Albin Schoepf joined on the evening of the battle with the 17th, 31st, and 38th Ohio.

BATTLE OF SHILOH
April 6–7, 1862

ARMY OF THE OHIO
Maj. Gen. Don Carlos Buell

First Division, Brig. Gen. George H. Thomas
First Brigade, Brig. Gen. Albin Schoepf: 17th Ohio, 31st Ohio, 38th Ohio, 12th Ky.
Second Brigade, Brig. Gen. Speed S. Fry: 4th Ky., 10th Ky., 14th Ohio, 10th Ind.
Third Brigade, Col. Robert L. McCook: 18th U.S., 2d Minn., 9th Ohio, 35th Ohio
Artillery: 4th Mich. Btry.; Btry. C, 1st Ohio; Btry. I, 4th U.S.

Second Division, Brig. Gen. Alexander McD. McCook
Fourth Brigade, Brig. Gen. Lovell H. Rousseau: 1st Ohio; 5th Ky.; 6th Ind.; 1st Bn., 15th U.S.; 1st Bn., 16th U.S.; 1st Bn., 19th U.S.
Fifth Brigade, Col. E. N. Kirk: 29th Ind., 30th Ind., 34th Ill., 77th Pa.

Sixth Brigade, Brig. Gen. Richard W. Johnson: 15th Ohio, 49th Ohio, 32d Ind., 39th Ind.
Artillery: Btry. H, 5th U.S.; Goodspeed's Ohio Btry., Stone's Ky. Btry.
Cavalry: 2d Ky.

Third Division, Brig. Gen. Ormsby M. Mitchel
Eighth Brigade, Col. John B. Turchin: 19th Ill., 24th Ill., 37th Ind., 18th Ohio
Ninth Brigade, Col. Joshua H. Sill: 2d Ohio, 21st Ohio, 33d Ohio, 10th Wis.
Seventeenth Brigade, Col. W. H. Lytle: 3d Ohio, 10th Ohio, 15th Ky., 42d Ind.
Artillery: Simonson's Ind. Btry., Loomis's Mich. Btry., Edgarton's Ohio Btry.
Cavalry: 4th Ohio

Fourth Division, Brig. Gen. William Nelson
Tenth Brigade, Col. Jacob Ammen: 6th Ohio, 24th Ohio, 17th Ky., 36th Ind.
Nineteenth Brigade, Col. William B. Hazen: 41st Ohio, 9th Ind., 6th Ky., 27th Ky.
Twenty-Second Brigade, Col. Sanders D. Bruce: 1st Ky., 2d Ky., 20th Ky., 31st Ind.
Artillery: 7th Ind. Btry.; 10th Ind. Btry.; Btry. D, 1st Ohio
Cavalry: 2d Ind.

Fifth Division, Brig. Gen. Thomas L. Crittenden
Eleventh Brigade, Brig. Gen. J. T. Boyle: 19th Ohio, 59th Ohio, 9th Ky., 13th Ky., 21st Ky.
Fourteenth Brigade, Col. William Sooy Smith: 11th Ky., 26th Ky., 13th Ohio
Artillery: Btry. H/M, 4th U.S.; Btry. G, 1st Ohio
Cavalry: 3d Ky.

Sixth Division, Brig. Gen. Thomas J. Wood
Fifteenth Brigade, Col. Milo S. Hascall: 17th Ind., 58th Ind., 13th Mich., 26th Ohio
Twentieth Brigade, Col. Charles G. Harker: 64th Ohio, 65th Ohio, 51st Ind., 13th Mich.
Twenty-First Brigade, Col. George D. Wagner: 15th Ind., 40th Ind., 57th Ind., 24th Ky.
Artillery: 5th Ohio Btry., 6th Ind. Btry., 10th Ind. Btry.
Cavalry: 3d Ohio

Seventh Division, Brig. Gen. George W. Morgan
Twenty-First Brigade, Brig. Gen. Samuel P. Carter: 1st East Tenn., 2d East Tenn., 7th Ky., 49th Ind.
Twenty-Fifth Brigade, Brig. Gen. J. G. Spears: 3d East Tenn., 4th East Tenn., 5th East Tenn., 6th East Tenn.
Twenty-Sixth Brigade, Col. John F. DeCourcy: 22d Ky., 16th Ohio, 42d Ohio
Twenty-Seventh Brigade, Brig. Gen. Absalom Baird: 33d Ind., 14th Ky., 19th Ky.
Artillery: 7th Mich. Btry., 9th Ohio Btry., 1st Wis. Btry.
Cavalry: 1st Ky. Bn.
Unassigned: 18th Ky., 4th Ind. Btry., 11th Ind. Btry., 12th Ind. Btry., Bradley's Ohio Btry., Drury's Wis. Btry.

BATTLE OF PERRYVILLE
October 8, 1862

ARMY OF THE OHIO
Maj. Gen. Don Carlos Buell
Maj. Gen. George H. Thomas

I Corps
Maj. Gen. Alexander McD. McCook

Third Division, Brig. Gen. Lovell H. Rousseau
Ninth Brigade, Col. Leonard A. Harris: 38th Ind., 2d Ohio, 33d Ohio, 94th Ohio, 10th Wis., 5th Ind. Btry.
Seventeenth Brigade, Col. William H. Lytle: 42d Ind., 88th Ind., 15th Ky., 3d Ohio, 10th Ohio, 1st Mich. Btry.
Twenty-Eighth Brigade, Col. John C. Starkweather: 24th Ill., 79th Pa., 1st Wis., 21st Wis., 4th Ind. Light Btry., 1st Ky. Btry.

Unattached: 2d Ky. Cav. (6 cos.), 1st Mich. Engineers (3 cos.)

Tenth Division, Brig. Gen. James K. Jackson
Thirty-Eighth Brigade, Brig. Gen. William R. Terrill: 80th Ill., 123d Ill., detachments (7th Ky.—1 co.; 32d Ky.—1 co.; 3d Tenn.—1 co.), Parson's Btry.
Thirty-Fourth Brigade, Col. George Webster: 80th Ind., 50th Ohio, 98th Ohio, 121st Ohio, 19th Ind. Btry.

II Corps
Maj. Gen. Thomas L. Crittenden

Fourth Division, Brig. Gen. William S. Smith
Tenth Brigade, Col. William Grose: 84th Ill.; 36th Ind.; 23d Ky.; 6th Ohio; 24th Ohio; Btry. H, Btry. M, 4th U.S. Art.
Twenty-Second Brigade, Brig. Gen. Charles Cruft: 31st Ind.; 1st Ky.; 2d Ky.; 28th Ky.; 90th Ohio; Btry. B, 1st Ohio Art.
Cavalry: 2d Ky. (4 cos.)

Fifth Division, Brig. Gen. Horatio P. Van Cleve
Eleventh Brigade, Col. Samuel Beatty: 79th Ind., 9th Ky., 13th Ky., 19th Ohio, 59th Ohio
Fourteenth Brigade, Col. Pierce B. Hawkins: 44th Ind.; 86th Ind.; 11th Ky.; 26th Ky.; 13th Ohio; Btry. B, 26th Pa. Art.
Twenty-Third Brigade, Col. Stanley Matthews: 35th Ind., 8th Ky., 21st Ky., 51st Ohio, 99th Ohio, 3d Wis. Btry.

Sixth Division, Brig. Gen. Thomas J. Wood
Fifteenth Brigade, Brig. Gen. Milo S. Hascall: 100th Ill., 17th Ind., 58th Ind., 3d Ky., 26th Ohio, 8th Ind. Btry.
Twentieth Brigade, Col. Charles G. Harker: 51st Ind., 73d Ind., 13th Mich., 64th Ohio, 65th Ohio, 6th Ohio Btry.
Twenty-First Brigade, Col. George D. Wagner: 15th Ind., 40th Ind., 57th Ind., 24th Ky., 97th Ohio, 10th Ind. Btry.
First Cavalry Brigade, Col. Edward D. McCook: 2d Ind.; 1st Ky.; 3d Ky.; 7th Pa. (1 bn.); Btry. M, 4th U.S. Art. (1 sec.)
Unattached: 1st Mich. Engineers (4 cos.), 1st Ohio Cav. (4 cos.), 3d Ohio Cav. (4 cos.)

III CORPS

Maj. Gen. (Acting) Charles C. Gilbert

First Division, Brig. Gen. Albin Schoepf
First Brigade, Col. Moses B. Walker: 82d Ind., 12th Ky., 17th Ohio, 31st Ohio, 38th Ohio
Second Brigade, Brig. Gen. Speed S. Fry: 10th Ind., 74th Ind., 4th Ky., 10th Ky., 14th Ohio
Third Brigade, Brig. Gen. James B. Steedman: 87th Ind., 2d Minn., 9th Ohio, 35th Ohio, 18th U.S.
Artillery: 4th Mich. Btry.; Btry. C, 1st Ohio; Btry. I, 4th U.S.
Cavalry: 1st Ohio (6 cos.)

Ninth Division, Brig. Gen. Robert B. Mitchell
Thirtieth Brigade, Col. Michael Gooding: 74th Ill., 75th Ill., 22d Ind., 5th Wis. Btry.
Thirty-First Brigade, Col. William P. Carlin: 21st Ill., 38th Ill., 101st Ohio, 15th Wis., 2d Minn. Btry.
Thirty-Second Brigade, Col. William W. Caldwell: 25th Ill., 35th Ill., 81st Ind., 8th Kan. Bn., 8th Wis. Btry.
Cavalry: 36th Ill. (1 co.)

Eleventh Division, Brig. Gen. Philip H. Sheridan
Thirty-Fifth Brigade, Lt. Col. Bernard Laiboldt: 85th Ill., 86th Ill., 125th Ill., 52d Ohio
Thirty-Seventh Brigade, Col. Nicholas Greusel: 36th Ill., 88th Ill., 21st Mich., 24th Wis.
Artillery: Btry. I, 2d Ill.; Btry. G, 1st Mo.
Third Cavalry Brigade, Brig. Gen. (Acting) Ebenezer Gay: 9th Ky. (8 cos.), 2d Mich., 9th Pa., 2d Minn. Btry. (1 sec.)

BATTLE OF CHICKAMAUGA
September 19–20, 1863

ARMY OF THE CUMBERLAND
Maj. Gen. William S. Rosecrans

Department Headquarters: 1st Bn. Ohio Sharpshooters, 10th Ohio (provost guard), 15th Pa. Cav. (escort)

XIV Corps
Maj. Gen. George H. Thomas
Corps Headquarters: 9th Mich. (provost guard), 1st Ohio Cav. (1 co.)

First Division, Brig. Gen. Absalom Baird
First Brigade, Col. Benjamin F. Scribner: 38th Ind., 2d Ohio, 33d Ohio, 94th Ohio, 10th Wis.
Second Brigade, Brig. Gen. John C. Starkweather: 1st Wis., 21st Wis., 24th Ill., 79th Pa.
Third Brigade, Brig. Gen. John H. King: 1st Bn., 15th U.S.; 1st Bn., 16th U.S.; 1st Bn., 18th U.S.; 2d Bn., 18th U.S.; 1st Bn., 19th U.S.
Artillery: Btry. A, 1st Mich.; 4th Ind. Btry.; Btry. H, 5th U.S.

Second Division, Maj. Gen. James S. Negley
First Brigade, Brig. Gen. John Beatty: 42d Ind., 88th Ind., 104th Ill., 15th Ky., 3d Ohio*
Second Brigade, Col. Timothy R. Stanley: 18th Ohio, 69th Ohio,* 19th Ill., 11th Mich.
Third Brigade, Col. William Sirwell: 78th Pa., 21st Ohio, 74th Ohio, 37th Ind.
Artillery: Bridge's Ill. Btry.; Btry. G, Btry. M, 1st Ohio

Third Division, Brig. Gen. John M. Brannan
First Brigade, Col. John M. Connell: 17th Ohio, 31st Ohio, 38th Ohio,* 82d Ind.
Second Brigade, Col. John T. Croxton: 4th Ky., 10th Ky., 10th Ind., 74th Ind., 14th Ohio
Third Brigade, Col. Ferdinand Van Derveer: 9th Ohio, 35th Ohio, 2d Minn., 87th Ind.
Artillery: Btry. D, 1st Mich.; Btry. C, 1st Ohio; Btry. I, 4th U.S.

Fourth Division, Maj. Gen. Joseph J. Reynolds
First Brigade, Col. John T. Wilder: (Detached on mounted duty) 17th Ind., 72d Ind., 92d Ill., 98th Ill., 123d Ill.
Second Brigade, Col. Edward A. King: 68th Ind., 75th Ind., 101st Ind., 80th Ill.*
Third Brigade, Brig. Gen. John B. Turchin: 11th Ohio, 36th Ohio, 89th Ohio, 92d Ohio, 18th Ky.
Artillery: 18th Ind. Btry., 19th Ind. Btry., 21st Ind. Btry.

XX Corps
Maj. Gen. Alexander McD. McCook
Escort: 2d Ky. Cav. (1 co.)

First Division, Brig. Gen. Jefferson C. Davis
First Brigade, Col. Phillip Sidney Post: 22d Ind., 59th Ill., 74th Ill., 75th Ill.
Second Brigade, Brig. Gen. William P. Carlin: 21st Ill., 38th Ill., 81st Ind., 101st Ohio

Third Brigade, Col. Hans C. Heg: 15th Wis., 25th Ill., 35th Ill., 8th Kans.
Artillery: 5th Wis. Btry.; 2d Minn. Btry.; 8th Wis. Btry.

Second Division, Brig. Gen. Richard W. Johnson
First Brigade, Brig. Gen. August Willich: 49th Ohio, 39th Ind. (detached and mounted), 3d Ind., 15th Ohio
Second Brigade, Col. Joseph B. Dodge: 77th Pa., 29th Ind., 30th Ind., 79th Ill.
Third Brigade, Col. Philemon P. Baldwin: 6th Ind., 1st Ohio, 93d Ohio, 5th Ky.
Artillery: Btry. A, 1st Ohio; 20th Ohio Btry.; 5th Ind. Btry.

Third Division, Maj. Gen. Philip H. Sheridan
First Brigade, Brig. Gen. William H. Lytle: 36th Ill., 85th Ill., 24th Wis., 21st Mich.
Second Brigade, Col. Bernard Laiboldt: 2d Mo., 15th Mo., 44th Ill., 73d Ill.
Third Brigade, Col. Luther P. Bradley: 22d Ill., 27th Ill., 42d Ill., 51st Ill.
Artillery: 11th Ind. Btry.; Btry. G, 1st Mo.; Btry. C, 1st Ill.

XXI Corps
Maj. Gen. Thomas L. Crittenden

First Division, Brig. Gen. Thomas J. Wood
First Brigade, Col. George P. Buell: 26th Ohio, 58th Ind., 13th Mich., 100th Ill.
Second Brigade,* Brig. Gen. George D. Wagner: 15th Ind., 40th Ind., 51st Ind., 57th Ind., 97th Ohio
Third Brigade, Col. Charles G. Harker: 3d Ky., 64th Ohio, 65th Ohio, 125th Ohio, 73d Ind.*
Artillery: 8th Ind. Btry., 10th Ind. Btry.,* 6th Ohio Btry.

Second Division, Maj. Gen. John M. Palmer
First Brigade, Brig. Gen. Charles Cruft: 1st Ky., 2d Ky., 31st Ind., 90th Ohio
Second Brigade, Brig. Gen. William B. Hazen: 41st Ohio, 124th Ohio, 6th Ky., 9th Ind.
Third Brigade, Col. William Grose: 36th Ind., 24th Ohio, 6th Ohio, 23d Ky., 84th Ill.
Artillery: Btry. B, Btry. F, 1st Ohio; Btry. H, Btry. M, 4th U.S.

Third Division, Brig. Gen. Horatio Van Cleve
First Brigade, Brig. Gen. Samuel Beatty: 9th Ky., 17th Ky., 19th Ohio, 79th Ind.
Second Brigade, Col. George F. Dick: 44th Ind., 86th Ind., 13th Ohio, 59th Ohio
Third Brigade, Col. Sidney M. Barnes: 51st Ohio, 99th Ohio, 35th Ind., 8th Ky., 21st Ky.*
Artillery: 7th Ind. Btry., 26th Pa. Btry., 3d Wis. Btry.

Reserve Corps
Maj. Gen. Gordon Granger**

First Division, James B. Steedman
First Brigade, Brig. Gen. Walter C. Whitaker: 40th Ohio, 89th Ohio, 84th Ind., 96th Ill., 115th Ill., 22d Mich., 18th Ohio Btry.

Second Brigade, Col. John G. Mitchell: 98th Ohio; 113th Ohio; 121st Ohio; 78th Ill.; Btry. M, 1st Ill. Art.

Second Division
Second Brigade, Col. Daniel McCook: 85th Ill.; 86th Ill.; 125th Ill.; 52d Ohio; 69th Ohio; Btry. I, 2d Ill. Art.

Cavalry Corps
Brig. Gen. Robert B. Mitchell

First Division, Col. Edward M. McCook
First Brigade, Col. Archibald P. Campbell: 2d Mich., 9th Pa., 1st East Tenn.
Second Brigade, Col. Daniel M. Ray: 2d Ind.; 4th Ind.; 2d Tenn.; 1st Wis.; Btry. D, 1st Ohio Light (1 sec.)
Third Brigade, Col. Louis D. Watkins: 4th Ky., 5th Ky., 6th Ky.

Second Division, Brig. Gen. George Crook
First Brigade, Col. Robert H. G. Minty: 3d Ind. (1 bn.), 4th Mich., 7th Pa., 4th U.S.
Second Brigade, Col. Eli Long: 2d Ky., 1st Ohio, 3d Ohio, 4th Ohio
Artillery: Chicago Board of Trade Btry.

*Not engaged in battle.

**Reserve Corps comprised three divisions, but only three brigades participated in the battle.

CHATTANOOGA CAMPAIGN

ARMY OF THE CUMBERLAND
Maj. Gen. George H. Thomas
Department Headquarters: 1st Ohio Sharpshooters, 10th Ohio

IV Corps
Maj. Gen. Gordon Granger

First Division, Brig. Gen. Charles Cruft
Second Brigade, Brig. Gen. Walter C. Whitaker: 96th Ill., 35th Ind., 8th Ky., 40th Ohio, 51st Ohio, 99th Ohio
Third Brigade, Col. William Grose: 59th Ill., 75th Ill., 84th Ill., 9th Ind., 36th Ind., 24th Ohio

Second Division, Maj. Gen. Philip Sheridan
First Brigade, Col. Francis T. Sherman: 36th Ill., 44th Ill., 73d Ill., 74th Ill., 88th Ill., 22d Ind., 2d Mo., 15th Mo., 24th Wis.

Second Brigade, Brig. Gen. George D. Wagner: 100th Ill., 15th Ind., 40th Ind., 51st Ind., 57th Ind., 58th Ind., 26th Ohio, 97th Ohio
Third Brigade, Col. Charles G. Harker: 22d Ill., 27th Ill., 42d Ill., 51st Ill., 79th Ill., 3d Ky., 64th Ohio, 65th Ohio, 125th Ohio
Artillery: Btry. M, 1st Ill.; 10th Ind. Btry.; Btry. G, 1st Mo.; Btry. I, 1st Ohio; Btry. G, 4th U.S.; Btry. H, 5th U.S.

Third Division, Brig. Gen. Thomas J. Wood
First Brigade, Brig. Gen. August Willich: 25th Ill., 35th Ill., 89th Ill., 32d Ind., 68th Ind., 8th Kans., 15th Ohio, 49th Ohio, 15th Wis.
Second Brigade, Brig. Gen. William B. Hazen: 6th Ind., 5th Ky., 6th Ky., 23d Ky., 1st Ohio, 6th Ohio, 41st Ohio, 93d Ohio, 124th Ohio
Third Brigade, Brig. Gen. Samuel Beatty: 79th Ind., 86th Ind., 9th Ky., 17th Ky., 13th Ohio, 19th Ohio, 59th Ohio
Artillery: Bridge's Ill. Btry.; 6th Ohio Btry.; 20th Ohio Btry.; Btry. B, Pa. Light

XI Army Corps
Maj. Gen. Oliver O. Howard
Corps Headquarters: Independent Company, 8th N.Y.

Second Division, Brig. Gen. Adolph von Steinwehr
First Brigade, Col. Adolphus Bushbeck: 33d N.J., 134th N.Y., 154th N.Y., 27th Pa., 73d Pa.
Second Brigade, Col. Orland Smith: 33d Mass., 136th N.Y., 55th Ohio, 73d Ohio

Third Division, Maj. Gen. Carl Schurz
First Brigade, Brig. Gen. Hector Tyndale: 101st Ill., 45th N.Y., 143d N.Y., 61st Ohio, 82d Ohio
Second Brigade, Col. Wladimir Krzyzanowski: 58th N.Y., 119th N.Y., 141st N.Y., 26th Wis.
Third Brigade, Col. Frederick Hecker: 80th Ill., 82d Ill., 68th N.Y., 75th Pa.
Artillery: Btry. I, 1st N.Y.; 13th N.Y. Btry.; Btry. I, Btry. K, 1st Ohio; Btry. G, 4th U.S.

XII Corps

Second Division, Brig. Gen. John W. Geary
First Brigade, Col. Charles Candy: 5th Ohio, 7th Ohio, 29th Ohio, 66th Ohio, 28th Pa., 147th Pa.
Second Brigade, Col. George A. Cobham Jr.: 29th Pa., 109th Pa., 111th Pa.
Third Brigade, Maj. Gen. George Sears Greene: 60th N.Y., 78th N.Y., 102d N.Y., 137th N.Y., 149th N.Y.
Artillery: Btry. E, Pa. Light; Btry. K, 5th U.S.

XIV Corps
Maj. Gen. John M. Palmer
Escort: 1st Ohio Cav.

First Division, Brig. Gen. Richard W. Johnson
First Brigade, Brig. Gen. William P. Carlin: 104th Ill., 38th Ind., 42d Ind., 88th Ind., 2d Ohio, 33d Ohio, 94th Ohio, 10th Wis.
Second Brigade, Col. Marshall F. Moore: 19th Ill.; 11th Mich.; 69th Ohio; 1st Bn., 2d Bn., 15th U.S.; 1st Bn., 2d Bn., 16th U.S.; 1st Bn., 19th U.S.
Third Brigade, Brig. Gen. John C. Starkweather: 24th Ill., 37th Ind., 21st Ohio, 74th Ohio, 78th Pa., 79th Pa., 1st Wis., 21st Wis.
Artillery: Btry. C, 1st Ill.; Btry. A, 1st Mich.; Btry. H, 5th U.S.

Second Division, Brig. Gen. Jefferson C. Davis
First Brigade, Brig. Gen. James D. Morgan: 10th Ill., 16th Ill., 60th Ill., 21st Ky., 10th Mich., 14th Mich.
Second Brigade, Brig. Gen. John Beatty: 34th Ill., 78th Ill., 3d Ohio, 98th Ohio, 108th Ohio, 113th Ohio, 121st Ohio
Third Brigade, Col. Daniel McCook: 85th Ill., 86th Ill., 110th Ill., 125th Ill., 52d Ohio
Artillery: Btry. I, 2d Ill.; 2d Minn. Btry.; 5th Wis. Btry.

Third Division, Brig. Gen. Absalom Baird
First Brigade, Brig. Gen. John B. Turchin: 82d Ind., 11th Ohio, 17th Ohio, 31st Ohio, 36th Ohio, 89th Ohio, 92d Ohio
Second Brigade, Col. Ferdinand Van Derveer: 75th Ind., 87th Ind., 101st Ind., 2d Minn., 9th Ohio, 35th Ohio, 105th Ohio
Third Brigade, Col. Edward H. Phelps: 10th Ind., 74th Ind., 4th Ky., 10th Ky., 18th Ky., 14th Ohio, 38th Ohio
Artillery: 7th Ind. Btry.; 19th Ind. Btry.; Btry. I, 4th U.S.

ATLANTA CAMPAIGN
April 30, 1864

ARMY OF THE CUMBERLAND
Maj. Gen. George H. Thomas

IV Corps
Maj. Gen. Oliver O. Howard

First Division, Maj. Gen. David S. Stanley
First Brigade, Brig. Gen. Charles Cruft: 21st Ill., 38th Ill., 31st Ind., 81st Ind., 1st Ky., 2d Ky., 90th Ohio, 101st Ohio
Second Brigade, Brig. Gen. Walter C. Whitaker: 96th Ill., 115th Ill., 35th Ind., 84th Ind., 21st Ky., 40th Ohio, 51st Ohio, 99th Ohio

Third Brigade, Col. William Grose: 59th Ill., 75th Ill., 80th Ill., 84th Ill., 9th Ind., 30th Ind., 36th Ind., 77th Pa.
Artillery: 5th Ind. Btry.; Btry. B, Pa. Light

Second Division, Brig. Gen. John Newton

First Brigade, Col. Frances T. Sherman: 36th Ill., 44th Ill., 73d Ill., 74th Ill., 88th Ill., 2d Mo., 15th Mo.
Second Brigade, Brig. Gen. George D. Wagner: 100th Ill., 40th Ind., 57th Ind., 58th Ind., 26th Ohio, 97th Ohio
Third Brigade, Brig. Gen. Charles G. Harker: 22d Ill., 27th Ill., 42d Ill., 51st Ill., 79th Ill., 3d Ky., 64th Ohio, 65th Ohio, 125th Ohio
Artillery: Btry. M, 1st Ill.; Btry. A, 1st Ohio
Unattached: 24th Wis.

Third Division, Brig. Gen. Thomas J. Wood

First Brigade, Col. William H. Gibson: 25th Ill., 35th Ill., 89th Ill., 32d Ind., 8th Kans., 15th Ohio, 49th Ohio, 15th Wis.
Second Brigade, Brig. Gen. William B. Hazen: 6th Ind., 5th Ky., 6th Ky., 23d Ky., 1st Ohio, 6th Ohio, 41st Ohio, 93d Ohio, 124th Ohio
Third Brigade, Brig. Gen. Samuel Beatty: 79th Ind., 86th Ind., 9th Ky., 17th Ky., 13th Ohio, 19th Ohio, 59th Ohio
Artillery: Bridge's Ill. Btry., 6th Ohio Btry.

XIV Corps
Maj. Gen. John M. Palmer

First Division, Brig. Gen. Richard W. Johnson

First Brigade, Brig. Gen. William P. Carlin: 104th Ill., 38th Ind., 42d Ind., 88th Ind., 2d Ohio, 33d Ohio, 94th Ohio, 10th Wis., 15th Ky.
Second Brigade, Brig. Gen. John H. King: 19th Ill.; 11th Mich.; 69th Ohio; 1st Bn., 2d Bn., 15th U.S.; 1st Bn., 2d Bn., 16th U.S.; 1st Bn., 2d Bn., 18th U.S.; 1st Bn., 19th U.S.
Third Brigade, Col. James M. Neibling: 24th Ill., 37th Ind., 21st Ohio, 74th Ohio, 78th Pa., 79th Ind., 1st Wis., 21st Wis.
Artillery: Btry. C, 1st Ill.; Btry. I, 1st Ohio

Second Division, Brig. Gen. Jefferson C. Davis

First Brigade, Brig. Gen. James D. Morgan: 10th Ill., 16th Ill., 60th Ill., 10th Mich., 14th Mich.
Second Brigade, Col. John G. Mitchell: 34th Ill., 78th Ill., 98th Ohio, 108th Ohio, 113th Ohio, 121st Ohio
Third Brigade, Col. Daniel McCook: 85th Ill., 86th Ill., 110th Ill., 125th Ill., 22d Ind., 52d Ohio
Artillery: Btry. I, 2d Ill.; 5th Wis. Btry.

Third Division, Brig. Gen. Absalom Baird
First Brigade, Brig. Gen. John B. Turchin: 82d Ind., 11th Ohio, 17th Ohio, 31st Ohio, 89th Ohio, 92d Ohio
Second Brigade, Col. Ferdinand Van Derveer: 75th Ind., 87th Ind., 101st Ind., 2d Minn., 9th Ohio, 35th Ohio, 105th Ohio
Third Brigade, Col. George P. Este: 10th Ind., 74th Ind., 4th Ky., 10th Ky., 18th Ky., 14th Ohio, 38th Ohio
Artillery: 7th Ind. Btry., 19th Ind. Btry.

XX Corps
Maj. Gen. Joseph Hooker

First Division, Brig. Gen. Alpheus S. Williams
First Brigade, Brig. Gen. Joseph F. Knipe: 5th Conn., 3d Md., 123d N.Y., 141st N.Y., 46th Pa.
Second Brigade, Brig. Gen. Thomas H. Ruger: 27th Ind., 2d Mass., 13th N.J., 107th N.Y., 150th N.Y., 3d Wis.
Third Brigade, Brig. Gen. Hector Tyndale: 82d Ill., 101st Ill., 45th N.Y., 143d N.Y., 61st Ohio, 82d Ohio
Artillery: Btry. I, Btry. M, 1st N.Y.

Second Division, Brig. Gen. John W. Geary
First Brigade, Col. Charles Candy: 5th Ohio, 7th Ohio, 29th Ohio, 66th Ohio, 28th Pa., 147th Pa.
Second Brigade, Col. Adolphus Bushbeck: 33d N.J., 119th N.Y., 134th N.Y., 154th N.Y., 27th Pa., 73d Pa., 109th Pa. (detachment)
Third Brigade, Col. David Ireland: 60th N.Y., 78th N.Y., 102d N.Y., 137th N.Y., 149th N.Y., 29th Pa., 111th Pa.
Artillery: 13th N.Y. Btry.; Btry. E, Pa. Light

Third Division, Maj. Gen. Daniel Butterfield
First Brigade, Brig. Gen. William T. Ward: 102d Ill., 105th Ill., 129th Ill., 70th Ind., 79th Ohio
Second Brigade, Col. Samuel Ross: 20th Conn., 85th Ind., 19th Mich., 22d Wis.
Third Brigade, Col. James Wood Jr.: 33d Mass., 136th N.Y., 55th Ohio, 73d Ohio, 26th Wis.
Artillery: Btry. I, 1st Mich.; Btry. C, 1st Ohio

Cavalry Corps
Brig. Gen. Washington L. Elliott

First Division, Col. Edward M. McCook
First Brigade, Col. Joseph B. Dorr: 8th Iowa, 2d Mich., 9th Pa., 1st Tenn.
Second Brigade, Col. Oscar H. LaGrange: 2d Ind., 4th Ind., 1st Wis.

Third Brigade, Col. Louis D. Watkins: 4th Ky., 6th Ky., 7th Ky.
Artillery: 18th Ind. Btry.

Second Division, Brig. Gen. Kenner Garrand
First Brigade, Col. Robert H. Minty: 4th Mich., 7th Pa., 4th U.S.
Second Brigade, Col. Eli Long: 1st Ohio, 3d Ohio, 4th Ohio
Third Brigade (mounted infantry), Col. John T. Wilder: 98th Ill., 123d Ill., 17th Ind., 73d Ind.
Artillery: Chicago Board of Trade Btry.

Third Division, Brig. Gen. Judson Kilpatrick
First Brigade, Col. William W. Lowe: 3d Ind., 5th Iowa, 9th Pa.
Second Brigade, Col. Charles C. Smith: 8th Ind., 2d Ky., 10th Ohio
Third Brigade, Col. Eli H. Murray: 92d Ill. Mt. Inf., 3d Ky., 5th Ky.
Artillery: 10th Wis. Btry.

Unattached
Provost: 9th Mich.
Pontoniers: 58th Ind.
Ammunition Train Guard: 1st Bn. Ohio Sharpshooters

BIBLIOGRAPHY

PRIMARY SOURCES

MANUSCRIPTS

Bentley Historical Library, University of Michigan, Ann Arbor
Benjamin Boadner Letters
Morris E. Pitch Papers
Henry Albert Potter Diary

Chicago Historical Society, Chicago
Speed Fry Letter
William Lytle Family Papers

Chickamauga-Chattanooga National Military Park, Chickamauga, Georgia
Jacob Ammen Diary, 21st Ohio File
Luther Bradley File
DeWayne Kellogg Letters, 34th Illinois File
Gerald J. Miller, "Middletown Yank's Journey to War and Back," 25th Illinois File
William S. Mitchell Letters, 1st Wisconsin File
W. G. Putney Memoir, Battery I, 2d Illinois Artillery File
Joseph Reynolds File
Levi Adolphus Ross Journal, 86th Illinois File
Hiram Strong Letters, 93d Ohio File
Eben P. Sturges Diary, Battery M, 1st Ohio Battery File
Statement of General G. P. Thurston in Relation to the Battle of Chickamauga, Box 1, File 55, Ser. 8
Phillip Welshimer Letters, 21st Illinois File
James K. Wier Letters, 25th Illinois File

Cincinnati Historical Society
Jacob Ammen Papers
Stanley Matthews Letters

Duke University, Durham, North Carolina
John W. Scully Letters
James H. Wiswell Letters

Filson Club, Louisville, Kentucky
Don Carlos Buell Papers
Thomas L. Crittenden Papers
James F. Mohr Letters
Alfred Pirtle, "Lytle's Last Sacrifice" (typescript)

Illinois State Historical Library, Springfield
George A. Cummins Diary
Thomas Frazee Letters
Frederick Marion Letters
John Palmer Papers

Indiana Historical Society, Indianapolis
William W. Blair Letters
Jefferson C. Davis Papers
Alva Griest Diary
Perry Hall Diary
Thomas Harrison Letters
William Hobbs Letters
R. S. Lackey Letters
Winfield Scott Miller Letters
Oliver P. Morton Dispatch Book
Thomas Small Diary
Joseph T. Smith Letter
William N. Steele Letters
Archibald Stinson Diary and Letters

Kennesaw National Military Park, Kennesaw, Georgia
Lucius F. Brown Letters
Allen L. Fahnestock Diary
Daniel O'Leary Letters
Lyman S. Widney Diary and Letters

Knox College, Galesburg, Illinois
Phillip Sidney Post Diary

Library of Congress, Washington, D.C.
Harold Bartlett Diary
A. S. Bloomfield Letters
Charles Buford Letters
Joseph Warren Keifer Papers
Alexander McCook Papers, McCook Family Papers

Montgomery Meigs Papers
Horace Porter Letters
Almon F. Rockwell Diary
Edwin M. Stanton Papers

National Archives, Washington, D.C.
"Cavalry Returns, December 23, 1862, Department of the Cumberland," Entry 1062, Record Group 393
"Consolidated Semi-Monthly Report of Batteries, December 15, 1862," Entry 1062, Record Group 393
"Consolidated Semi-Monthly Report of Wings and Divisions, XIV Army Corps, December 12, 1862," Entry 1061, Record Group 393
Correspondence Relating to the Transportation of the Army of the Cumberland, Entry 937, Record Group 393
Correspondence with Units Relating to Inspection Reports, Entry 1054, Record Group 393
Daily Summaries of the News Reaching the Headquarters of Gen. W. S. Rosecrans, 1863–64, Entry 986, Record Group 393
General Orders, Department of the Ohio, by Command of Don Carlos Buell, Adjutant General's Office, Record Group 94
Generals' Papers, Don Carlos Buell, June–August 1862, Entry 159, Record Group 94
Letters and Telegrams Sent, December 1861–May 1862, Generals' Papers, Don Carlos Buell, Entry 159, Record Group 94
Letters Received, January–November 1862, Department of the Cumberland, Record Group 393
Monthly Inspection Reports Received, 1863–65, Entry 1058, Record Group 393, Pt. 1
Register of Inspection Reports, Entry 1057, Vol. 139, Record Group 393, Pt. 1
"Rough Draft of a History of the Department of the Cumberland with Accompanying Notes and Consolidated Strength Reports, November 1861–June 1865," Record Group 393
Telegrams Received, December 1861–January 1862, Department of the Ohio, Record Group 393
Telegrams Sent and Received, October 1862–January 1865, Department of the Cumberland, Entry 916, Record Group 393
George Thomas Papers, Miscellaneous Papers, 1861–62, Generals' Papers, Record Group 94

Ohio Historical Society, Columbus
Sidney Botkin Papers
Gov. Dennison's Military Correspondence Letter Book, August–November 1861
John D. Innskeep Diary
George W. Landrum Letters
Richard Mann, comp., "The Journal of First Lieutenant Robert S. Dilworth, Company I, 21st Ohio Volunteer Infantry" (typescript)
Emerson Opdycke Letters

Henry M. Osborn Diary
John Sanderson Letter Diary, John Sanderson Letters
State of Ohio, Quartermaster General's Department, Ordnance and Ordnance Stores, 1860–61
George B. Turner Letters

Perryville Battlefield State Historical Park, Perryville, Kentucky
"The Fight for Starkweather's Hill," Post No. 7
Charles C. Gilbert File
James Jackson File

Shiloh National Military Park, Shiloh, Tennessee
Horace N. Fisher, "Memorandum of September 5, 1904, Buell's Army at Shiloh, April 6 and 7, 1862"

Stones River National Battlefield Park, Murfreesboro, Tennessee
Azra Bartholomew Letters, 21st Michigan File
W. W. Blair Letters, 58th Indiana File
A. S. Bloomfield Letters, Battery A, 1st Ohio Artillery File
Walter S. Burns, 21st Ohio File
J. B. Dodge, "What I Saw at Stones River," 30th Indiana File
William E. Eamers Letters
John C. Leanard Letters, 21st Ohio File
Henry Potter Letters, 4th Michigan Cavalry File
George B. Ridenour Letters, 6th Ohio File
Hiram Russell Letters, 21st Wisconsin File
George W. Sinclair Letters, 89th Illinois File
Samuel Welch, "A Sketch of the Movements of the Fifty-First Ohio Volunteer Infantry," 51st Ohio File
Lyman S. Widney Diary and Letters, 34th Illinois File

U.S. Army Military History Institute, Carlisle Barracks, Pennsylvania
William B. Hazen Papers
Eli Long Papers, Civil War Miscellaneous Collection
Frank Phelps Letters

University of California, Los Angeles
William S. Rosecrans Papers

Western Reserve Historical Society, Cleveland, Ohio
James Barnett Papers
John Henry Otto Memoirs
Alexander Varian Letters

Yale University, New Haven, Connecticut
Arthur B. Carpenter Letters

OFFICIAL DOCUMENTS

Agriculture of the U.S. in 1860: Compiled from the Original Returns of the Eighth Census, under the Direction of the Secretary of the Interior. Washington, D.C.: Government Printing Office, 1864.

Atlas to Accompany the Official Records of the Union and Confederate Armies. Washington, D.C.: Government Printing Office, 1891–95.

Heitman, Francis B. *Historical Register and Dictionary of the United States Army, from Its Organization, September 29, 1789, to March 2, 1903.* 2 vols. Washington, D.C.: Government Printing Office, 1903.

Hewett, Janet B., et al., eds. *Supplement to the Official Records of the Union and Confederate Armies.* 94 vols. Wilmington, N.C.: Broadfoot, 1994–.

Manufacturers of the United States in 1860; Compiled from the Original Returns of the Eighth Census, under the Direction of the Secretary of the Interior. Washington, D.C.: Government Printing Office, 1865.

Reece, J. N. *Report of the Adjutant General of the State of Illinois.* 2 vols. Springfield: Phillips Brothers, 1900.

Report of the Adjutant General of the State of Indiana. 2 vols. Indianapolis: Alexander H. Corner, 1869.

U.S. Surgeon General's Office. *The Medical and Surgical History of the War of the Rebellion, 1861–1865.* 3 vols. in 6 pts. Washington, D.C.: Government Printing Office, 1870–88.

U.S. War Department. *The War of the Rebellion: A Compilation of the Official Records of the Union and Confederate Armies.* 128 vols. Washington, D.C., 1880–1902.

White, Robert H., ed. *Messages of the Governors of Tennessee, 1857–1868.* 6 vols. Nashville, 1952–63.

NEWSPAPERS

Chicago Tribune
Cincinnati Commercial
Cincinnati Daily Times
Cincinnati Enquirer
Cleveland Plain Dealer
Indianapolis Daily Journal
Louisville Courier Journal
Louisville Daily Democrat
Louisville Daily Journal
Mobile Advertiser and Register
National Intelligencer
New York Herald
New York Times

New York Tribune
(Columbus) Ohio Statesman
Richmond Examiner

BOOKS

Albertson, Joan W. *Letters Home to Minnesota.* Spokane, Wash.: P. D. Enterprises, 1993.

Aldrich, C. Knight, ed. *Quest for a Star: The Civil War Letters and Diaries of Colonel Francis T. Sherman of the 88th Illinois.* Knoxville: University of Tennessee Press, 1999.

Ambrose, Stephen E., ed. *A Wisconsin Boy in Dixie: The Selected Letters of James K. Newton.* Madison: University of Wisconsin Press, 1961.

Anderson, Isabel, ed. *The Letters and Journal of General Nicholas Longworth Anderson.* New York: Fleming H. Revell, 1942.

Angle, Paul M., ed. *Three Years in the Army of the Cumberland.* Bloomington: Indiana University Press, 1959.

The Army Reunion: Reports of the Meetings of the Society of the Army of the Cumberland, Fifth Reunion. Cincinnati: Robert Clark, 1871.

Athearn, Robert G., ed. *Soldier in the West: The Civil War Letters of Alfred Lacey Hough.* Philadelphia: University of Pennsylvania Press, 1957.

Bancroft, Frederick, and William A. Dunning, eds. *The Reminiscences of Carl Schurz.* 3 vols. New York: McClure, 1908.

Bascom, Elizabeth E. P., ed. *"Dear Lizzie."* Privately printed, n.d.

Basler, Roy P., ed. *The Collected Works of Abraham Lincoln.* 9 vols. New Brunswick, N.J.: Rutgers University Press, 1953–55.

Bates, David Homer. *Lincoln in the Telegraph Office: Recollections of the States Military Telegraph Corps during the Civil War.* Reprint, Lincoln: University of Nebraska Press, 1995.

Bauer, K. Jack, ed. *Soldiering: The Civil War Diary of Rice C. Buell, 123rd New York Volunteer Infantry.* San Rafael, Calif.: Presidio, 1977.

Baumgartner, Richard A., and Larry M. Strayer, comps. *Kennesaw Mountain, June 1864: Bitter Standoff at the Gibraltar of Georgia.* Huntington, W.Va.: Blue Acorn, 1998.

Beatty, John. *The Citizen Soldier.* Cincinnati: Wilstach, Baldwin, 1879.

Bennett, Charles. *Historical Sketches of the Ninth Michigan Infantry (General Thomas Headquarters Guard) with an Account of the Battle of Murfreesboro, Tennessee, Sunday, July 13, 1862.* Coldwater, Mich.: Daily Courier, 1913.

Bennett, L. G., and William M. Haigh. *History of the Thirty-Sixth Regiment Illinois Volunteers, during the War of the Rebellion.* Aurora, Ill.: Knickerbocker and Hodder, 1876.

Berkley, John L., ed. *In Defense of This Flag: The Civil War Diary of Pvt. Ormond Hupp, 5th Indiana Light Artillery.* Fredonia, N.Y.: N.p., 1992.

Bickham, William. *Rosecrans' Campaign with the Fourteenth Army Corps, or the Army of the Cumberland: A Narrative of Personal Observations.* Cincinnati: Moore, Wilstach, Keys, 1863.

Bircher, William. *A Drummer Boy's Diary: Comprising Four Years of Service with the Second Regiment Minnesota Veteran Volunteers, 1861 to 1865.* St. Paul: St. Paul Book and Stationery, 1889.

Blackburn, John. *A Hundred Miles, a Hundred Heartbreaks.* Fordsville, Ky.: Nicholstone Book Bindery, 1972.

Blair, William A., ed. *A Politician Goes to War: The Civil War Letters of John White Geary.* University Park: Pennsylvania State University Press, 1995.

Blegen, Theodore C., ed. *The Civil War Letters of Colonel Hans Christian Heg.* Northfield, Minn.: Minnesota-Norwegian American Historical Association, 1936.

Bohrnstedt, Jennifer Cain, ed. *Soldiering with Sherman: Civil War Letters of George F. Cram.* DeKalb: Northern Illinois University Press, 2000.

Bond, Otto F., ed. *Under the Flag of the Nation: Diaries and Letters of a Yankee Volunteer in the Civil War.* Columbus: Ohio State University Press, 1961.

Brady, James P., comp. *Hurrah for the Artillery! Knap's Independent Battery "E," Pennsylvania Light Artillery.* Gettysburg: Thomas, 1992.

Butler, Watson Hubbard, comp. *Letters Home: Jay Caldwell Butler.* Privately printed, 1930.

Butterfield, Julia L., ed. *A Biographical Memorial of General Daniel Butterfield.* New York: Grafton, 1903.

Byrne, Frank L., ed. *The View from Headquarters: Civil War Letters of Harvey Reid.* Madison: State Historical Society of Wisconsin, 1965.

Canfield, Silas S. *History of the Twenty-First Regiment Ohio Volunteer Infantry.* Toledo: Vrooman, Anderson, and Bateman, 1893.

Carter, Ruth C., ed. *For Honor, Glory, and Union: The Mexican and Civil War Letters of Brig. Gen. William Haines Lytle.* Lexington: University Press of Kentucky, 1999.

Carter, W. R. *History of the First Regiment of Tennessee Volunteer Cavalry in the Great War of the Rebellion.* Knoxville: Gaut-Ogden, 1902.

Chamberlain, Dick, and Judy Chamberlain, eds. *Civil War Letters of an Ohio Soldier: S. O. Chamberlain and the 49th Ohio Volunteer Infantry.* (Flournoy, Calif.: Walker Lithograph, 1990.

Clark, Charles. *Opdycke's Tigers, 125th O.V.I., a History of the Regiment and the Campaigns and Battles of the Army of the Cumberland.* Columbus, Ohio: Spahr and Glenn, 1895.

Connolly, James A. *Three Years in the Army of the Cumberland: The Letters and Diary of Major James A. Connolly.* Bloomington: Indiana University Press, 1959.

Cope, Alexis. *The Fifteenth Ohio Volunteers and Its Campaigns, War of 1861–1865.* Columbus, Ohio: Press of Edward T. Miller, 1916.

Cox, Jacob D. *Military Reminiscences of the Civil War.* 2 vols. New York: Charles Scribner's Sons, 1900.

Crofts, Thomas, ed. *History of the Service of the Third Ohio Veteran Volunteer Cavalry.* Reprint, Huntington, W.Va.: Blue Acorn, 1997.

Crummer, Clayton E., ed. *By the Dim and Flaring Lamps: The Civil War Diaries of Samuel McIlvaine.* Monroe, N.Y.: Library Research Associates, 1990.

Curry, W. L. *Four Years in the Saddle.* Reprint, Jonesboro, Ga.: Freedom Hill, 1984.

Dana, Charles A. *Recollections of the Civil War.* New York: D. Appleton, 1898.

Davidson, Henry M. *History of Battery A, First Regiment of Ohio Vol. Light Artillery.* Milwaukee: Daily Wisconsin Printing House, 1865.

Day, Lewis. *Story of the One Hundred and First Ohio Infantry.* Cleveland: W. M. Bayne, 1894.

Dennett, Tyler, ed. *Lincoln and the Civil War: In the Diaries and Letters of John Hay.* Reprint, New York: Da Capo, 1988.

DeRosier, Arthur H. Jr., ed. *Through the South with a Union Soldier.* Johnson City: Research Planning Center, East Tennessee State University, 1969.

Dodge, Grenville M. *Personal Recollections of President Abraham Lincoln, General Ulysses S. Grant, and General William T. Sherman.* Council Bluffs, Iowa: Monarch, 1914.

Dodge, William Sumner. *History of the Old Second Division, Army of the Cumberland.* Chicago: Church and Goodman, 1864.

Donald, David, ed. *Inside Lincoln's Cabinet: The Civil War Diaries of Salmon P. Chase.* Reprint, New York: Kraus, 1970.

Doyle, Julie A.; John David Smith; and Richard McMurry, eds. *The Wilderness of War: The Civil War Letters of George W. Squier, Hoosier Volunteer.* Knoxville: University of Tennessee Press, 1998.

Drake, Julia A., comp. *The Mail Goes Through; or the Civil War Letters of George Drake.* San Angelo, Tex.: Anchor, 1964.

Driver, Robert A., and Gloria S. Driver, eds. *Letters Home by Jacob Early.* Privately printed, 1992.

Duncan, Louis C. *The Medical Department of the United States Army in the Civil War.* Reprint, Gaithersburg, Md.: Olde Soldier, 1987.

Dunlap, Leslie W., ed. *"Your Affectionate Husband, J. F. Culver": Letters Written during the Civil War.* Iowa City: Friends of the University of Iowa Libraries, 1978.

Ellison, Janet Correll, ed. *On to Atlanta: The Civil War Diaries of John Hill Ferguson, Illinois Tenth Regiment of Volunteers.* Lincoln: University of Nebraska Press, 2001.

Excursion Made by the Executive and Legislatures of the States of Kentucky and Tennessee to the State of Ohio, January 1860. Cincinnati: Robert Clarke, 1860.

Federico, Bianca M., ed. *Civil War: The Letters of John Holbrook Morse, 1861–1864.* Washington, D.C.: privately printed, 1975.

Fisher, Cecil H., ed. *A Staff Officer's Story: The Personal Experiences of Colonel Horace Newton Fisher in the Civil War.* Boston: Todd, 1960.

Fitch, John. *Annals of the Army of the Cumberland.* Philadelphia: J. P. Lippincott, 1883.

Fitch, Michael H. *Echoes of the Civil War.* New York: R. F. Fenno, 1905.

Fry, James B. *Operations of the Army under Buell: From June 10th to October 30th, 1862, and the "Buell Commission."* New York: Van Nostrand, 1884.

Gates, Arnold, ed. *The Rough Side of War: The Civil War Journal of Chesley A. Mosman, 1st Lieutenant, Company D, 59th Illinois Volunteer Infantry Regiment.* Garden City, N.Y.: Basin, 1987.

Genco, James G., ed. *To the Sound of Musketry and Tap of the Drum.* Detroit: Detroit Book, 1990.

Gilmore, James. R. *Personal Recollections of Abraham Lincoln and the Civil War.* Boston: L. C. Page, 1898.

Girardi, Robert I., and Nathaniel C. Hughes, eds. *The Memoirs of Brigadier General William Passmore Carlin, U.S.A.* Lincoln: University of Nebraska Press, 1999.

Graf, Leroy P.; Ralph W. Haskins; and Paul H. Bergeron, eds. *The Papers of Andrew Johnson.* 13 vols. Knoxville: University of Tennessee Press, 1979.

Grant, Ulysses S. *Personal Memoirs of U. S. Grant.* Reprint, 2 volumes in 1, New York: Library of America, 1990.

Grose, William. *The Story of the Marches, Battles and Incidents of the Thirty-Sixth Regiment Indiana Volunteer Infantry.* New Castle, Ind.: Courier, 1891.

Hannaford, Edwin. *Story of a Regiment: A History of the Campaigns and Association in the Field of the Sixth Regiment Ohio Volunteer Infantry.* Cincinnati: privately printed, 1868.

Hartpence, William R. *History of the Fifty-First Indiana Veteran Volunteer Infantry.* Cincinnati: Robert Clarke, 1894.

Harwell, Richard B., ed. *Union Reader.* Secaucus, N.J.: Blue and Grey, 1958.

Hay, John. *Letters of John Hay and Extracts from Diary.* 3 vols. Reprint, New York: Gordian, 1969.

Haynie, J. Henry. *The Nineteenth Illinois.* Chicago: M. A. Donohue, 1912.

Hazen, W. B. *A Narrative of Military Service.* Boston: Ticknor, 1885.

Hinman, Wilbur F. *The Story of the Sherman Brigade: The Camp, the Bivouac, the Battle, and How 'the Boys' Lived and Died during Four Years of Active Field Service.* Alliance, Ohio: privately printed, 1897.

Hinsdale, Mary L., ed. *Garfield-Hinsdale Letters: Correspondence between James Abram Garfield and Burke Aaron Hinsdale.* Reprint, New York: Kraus, 1969.

History of the Michigan Organizations at Chickamauga and Missionary Ridge, 1863. Lansing: Robert Smith, 1899.

History of the Seventy-Ninth Regiment Indiana Volunteer Infantry in the Civil War of Eighteen Sixty-One in the United States. Indianapolis: Hollenbeck, 1899.

Horrall, Spillard. *History of the Forty-Second Indiana Volunteer Infantry.* Chicago: Horrall, 1892.

Howard, Oliver O. *Autobiography of Oliver O. Howard, Major General United States Army.* 2 vols. New York: Baker and Taylor, 1908.

Hume, Thomas William. *The Loyal Mountaineers of East Tennessee.* Knoxville: Ogden Brothers, 1888.

Hunter, Edna J. Shank, ed. *One Flag, One Country, and Thirteen Greenbacks a Month: Letters from a Civil War Private and His Colonel.* San Diego: Hunter, 1980.

Jewell, William R., ed. *History of the 72d Indiana Volunteer Infantry of the Mounted Lighting Brigade.* Lafayette, Ind.: S. Vater, 1882.

Johnson, Richard W. *A Soldier's Reminiscences.* Philadelphia: J. B. Lippincott, 1886.

Keil, F. W. *Thirty-Fifth Ohio: A Narrative of Service from August 1861–1864.* Fort Wayne: Archer, Housh, 1894.

Kiene, Ralph E., Jr., ed. *A Civil War Diary: The Journal of Francis A. Kiene, 1861–1865.* N.p.: privately printed, 1974.

Kimberly, Robert L., and Ephraim S. Holloway. *The Forty-First Ohio Veteran Volunteer Infantry.* Cleveland: W. R. Smellie, 1897.

Lathrop, David. *The History of the Fifty-Ninth Regiment Illinois Volunteers.* Indianapolis: Hall and Hutchinson, 1865.

Letters of Captain Henry Richards of the Ninety-Third Ohio Infantry. Cincinnati: Wrightson, 1883.

Marshall, Carrington T., and Leon C. Marshall, eds. *Civil War Journal of John Wesley Marshall.* Privately printed, 1958.

Mathis, Frank Furlong, ed. *Incidents and Experiences in the Life of Thomas W. Parsons, from 1826 to 1900.* Frankfort: University Press of Kentucky, 1975.

McBride, John R. *History of the Thirty-Third Indiana Veteran Volunteer Infantry.* Indianapolis: William B. Burford, 1900.

McClellan, George B. *McClellan's Own Story.* New York: Charles La Webster, 1887.

McCutchan, Kenneth P., ed. *"Dearest Lizzie": The Civil War as Seen through the Eyes of Lieutenant Colonel James Maynard Shanklin.* Evansville, Ind.: Friends of Willard Library Press, 1908.

Minnesota Board of Commissioners. *Minnesota in the Civil and Indiana Wars, 1861–1865.* St. Paul: Pioneer, 1890.

Mitchell, John. *In Memoriam: Twenty-Fourth Wisconsin Infantry.* N.p., 1906.

Morse, Loren J. *Civil War Diaries and Letters of Bliss Morse.* Wagoner, Okla.: privately printed, 1985.

Newlin, W. H. *The Preacher Regiment: A History of the Seventy-Third Regiment of Illinois Infantry Volunteers.* N.p.: privately printed, 1890.

Nicolay, John G. *The Outbreak of Rebellion.* Reprint, New York: Jack Brussel, n.d.

Nicolay, John G., and John Hay. *Abraham Lincoln: A History.* 10 vols. New York: Century, 1917.

Niven, John, ed. *The Salmon P. Chase Papers.* 4 vols. Kent, Ohio: Kent State University Press, 1993–97.

Noe, Kenneth W., ed. *A Southern Boy in Blue: The Memoir of Marcus Woodcock, 9th Kentucky Infantry (U.S.A.).* Knoxville: University of Tennessee Press, 1996.

Osheskie, Edward S. *Civil War Echoes.* N.p., n.d.

Palmer, John M. *Personal Recollections of John M. Palmer: The Story of an Earnest Life.* Cincinnati: Robert Clarke, 1901.

Payne, Edwin W. *History of the Thirty-Fourth Regiment of Illinois Volunteer Infantry.* Clinton, Iowa: Allen, 1902.

Pennsylvania Battlefield Commission. *The Seventy-Seventh Pennsylvania at Shiloh.* Harrisburg, Pa., 1909.

Phisterer, Frederick. *Association of Survivors, Regular Brigade, Fourteenth Corps, Army of the Cumberland.* N.p., n.d.

Porter, Horace. *Campaigning with Grant.* New York: Century, 1897.

Quaife, Milo M., ed. *From the Cannon's Mouth: The Civil War Letters of General Alpheus Williams.* Detroit: Wayne State University Press, 1959.

Reid, Harvey. *The View from Headquarters: Civil War Letters of Harvey Reid.* Edited by Frank L. Byrne. Madison: State Historical Society of Wisconsin, 1965.

Remarks by Smith D. Atkins, Late Colonel of the Ninety-Second Illinois Volunteer Infantry (Mounted). N.p., 1909.

Rerick, John H. *Forty-Fourth Indiana Volunteer Infantry.* LaGrange, Ind.: privately printed, 1880.

Reyburn, Phillip J., and Terry L. Wilson, eds. *"Jottings from Dixie": The Civil War Dispatches of Sergeant Major Stephen F. Fleharty, U.S.A.* Baton Rouge: Louisiana State University Press, 1999.

Richards, Henry. *Letters of Captain Henry Richards of the Ninety-Third Ohio Infantry.* Cincinnati: Wrightson, 1883.

Rosecrans, William S. *Letter from General Rosecrans to the Democracy of Indiana.* Philadelphia: Union League, 1863.

———. *The Patriot Soldier and Hero: General Rosecrans to the Legislatures of Ohio and Indiana.* Loyal Publication Society, 1863.

———. *A Savory Dish for Loyal Men.* Philadelphia: For Gratuitous Distribution, 1863.

Schiller, Herbert M., ed. *Autobiography of Major General William F. Smith, 1861–1864.* Dayton: Morningside, 1990.

Schmitt, Martin F., ed. *General George Crook: His Autobiography.* Norman: University of Oklahoma Press, 1960.

Schofield, John M. *Forty-Six Years in the Army.* New York: Century, 1897.

Scribner, Benjamin F. *How Soldiers Were Made, Or the War as I Saw It.* New Albany, Ind.: Chicago, Donohue, and Henneberry, 1887.

Shanks, William F. G. *Personal Recollections of Distinguished Generals.* New York: Harper and Brothers, 1866.

Shaw, James B. *History of the Tenth Regiment Indiana Volunteer Infantry.* Lafayette, Ind.: Burt-Haywood, 1912.

Sheridan, Philip H. *Personal Memoirs of P. H. Sheridan.* 2 vols. New York: Charles L. Webster, 1888.

Sherman, William T. *Memoirs of William T. Sherman.* 2 vols. Reprint, in 1 vol., New York: Da Capo, 1984.

Simmons, Louis A. *The History of the 84th Ill. Vols.* Macomb, Ill.: Hampton Brothers, 1866.

Simon, John Y., ed. *The Papers of Ulysses S. Grant.* 22 vols. Carbondale: Southern Illinois University Press, 1967–.

Simpson, Brooks D., and Jean V. Berlin, eds. *Sherman's Civil War: Selected Correspondence of William T. Sherman, 1860–1865.* Chapel Hill: University of North Carolina Press, 1999.

Sligh, Charles R. *History of the Service of the First Regiment Michigan Engineers and Mechanics during the Civil War, 1861–1865.* Grand Rapids: White, 1921.

Smith, W. D. *The Battle of Stones River, Tennessee, December 31, 1862–January 2, 1863.* N.p., n.d.

Snetsinger, Robert J. *Kiss Clara for Me: The Story of Joseph Whitney and His Family: Early Days in the Midwest and Soldiering in the American Civil War.* State College, Penn.: Coronation, 1969.

Society of the Army of the Cumberland, Eighth Reunion, 1874. Cincinnati: Robert Clarke, 1875.

Society of the Army of the Cumberland, 1879 Reunion. Cincinnati: Robert Clarke, 1880.

Society of the Army of the Cumberland, 22nd Reunion, 1891. Cincinnati: Robert Clarke, 1892.

Society of the Army of the Cumberland, 23rd Reunion, September 1892. Cincinnati: Robert Clarke, 1892.

Society of the Army of the Cumberland, 24th Reunion, 1893. Cincinnati: Robert Clarke, 1894.

Society of the Army of the Cumberland 31st Reunion, 1903. Cincinnati: Robert Clarke, 1904.

Speed, Thomas. *The Union Cause in Kentucky, 1860–1865.* New York: Knickerbocker, 1907.

Stanley, David. *Personal Memoirs of Major-General D. S. Stanley, U.S.A.* Cambridge, Mass.: Harvard University Press, 1917.

Stevenson, Alexander F. *The Battle of Stone's River near Murfreesboro', Tenn., December 30, 1862, to January 3, 1863.* Reprint, Dayton: Morningside, 1983.

Stormont, Gilbert R. *History of the 58th Regiment Indiana Vol. Inf.* Princeton, N.J.: Press of the Clarion, 1895.

Strayer, Larry M., and Richard A. Baumgartner, comps. *Echoes of Battle: The Atlanta Campaign.* Huntington, W.Va.: Blue Acorn, 1991.

Sunderland, Glenn W. *Five Days to Glory.* New York: A. S. Barnes, 1970.

Swedberg, Claire E., ed. *Three Years with the 92d Illinois: The Civil War Diary of John M. King.* Mechanicsburg, Pa.: Stackpole, 1999.

Tapp, Hambleton, and James C. Klotter, eds. *The Union, the Civil War, and John W. Tuttle: A Kentucky Captain's Account.* Frankfort: n.p., 1980.

Tarrant, E. *The Wild Riders of the First Kentucky Cavalry.* Louisville: R. H. Carothers, 1894.

Thatcher, Marshall P. *A Hundred Battles in the West.* Detroit: privately printed, 1884.

Thomas, Benjamin P., ed. *Three Years with Grant, as Recalled by War Correspondent Sylvanus Cadwallader.* Reprint, New York: Knopf, 1955.

Tourgée, Albion W. *Story of a Thousand, Being a Story of the Service of the 105th Ohio Volunteer Infantry, in the War for the Union from August 21, 1862, to June 6, 1865.* Buffalo: S. McGerald and Son, 1896.

Troutman, Richard L. *The Heavens Are Weeping: The Diaries of George Richard Browder, 1852–1886.* Grand Rapids: Londervan, 1987.

Truxall, Aida Craig, ed. *"Respects to All": Letters of Two Pennsylvania Boys in the War of the Rebellion.* Pittsburgh: University of Pittsburgh Press, 1962.

Vale, Joseph G. *Minty and the Cavalry Campaigns in the Western Armies.* Harrisburg, Pa.: Edwin K. Meyers, 1886.

Villard, Henry. *Memoirs of Henry Villard: Journalist and Financer, 1835–1900.* 2 vols. Boston: Houghton, Mifflin, 1904.

Waddle, Angus L. *Three Years in the Army of the Ohio and Cumberland.* Chillicothe, Ohio: Scioto Gazette Book and Job Office, 1889.

Walton, Clyde C., ed. *Behind the Guns: The History of Battery I, 2nd Regiment, Illinois Light Artillery.* Carbondale: Southern Illinois University Press, 1965.

Walton, William, ed. *A Civil War Courtship: The Letters of Edwin Weller from Antietam to Atlanta.* Garden City, N.Y.: Doubleday, 1980.

Weber, Daniel B., ed. *The Diary of Ira Gillaspie of the Eleventh Michigan Infantry.* Mount Pleasant: Central Michigan University Press, 1965.

Welles, Gideon. *Diary of Gideon Welles.* 3 vols. Boston: Houghton Mifflin, 1911.

Wiley, Robert. *The Iron 44th.* N.p., n.d.

Willett, Charles E., ed. *A Union Soldier Returns South: The Civil War Letters and Diary of Alfred C. Willett, 113th Ohio Volunteer Infantry.* Johnson City, Tenn.: Overmountain, 1994.

Williams, Frederick D., ed. *The Wild Life of the Army: Civil War Letters of James A. Garfield.* East Lansing: Michigan State University Press, 1964.

Wilson, James H. *Under the Old Flag: Recollections of Military Operations in the War for the Union, the Spanish War, the Boxer Rebellion, Etc.* 2 vols. Reprint, Westport, Conn.: Greenwood, 1971.

Wilson, Susan Colton, ed. *Column South: With the Fifteenth Pennsylvania Cavalry.* Flagstaff: J. F. Colton, 1960.

Woodruff, George H. *Fifteen Years Ago; or, the Patriotism of Will County.* Joliet, Ill.: Joliet Republican and Job Steam Printing House, 1876.

Wright, T. J. *History of the Eighth Kentucky Vol. Inf. during Its Three Years Campaigns Embracing Organization, Marches, Skirmishes, and Battles of the Command, with Much of the History of the Old Reliable Third Brigade, Commanded by Hon. Stanley Matthews, and Containing Many Interesting Incidents of Army Life.* St. Joseph, Mo.: St. Joseph Steam Printing, 1880.

ARTICLES

"Account by a Participant." In *The Rebellion Record,* edited by Frank Moore. New York: G. P. Putnam, 1862.

Baird, Absalom. "Correspondence Relating to Chickamauga and Chattanooga." In *Papers of the Military Historical Society of Massachusetts,* 14 vols., 8:249–71. Boston: Military Historical Society of Massachusetts, 1910.

Barnhart, John D. "A Hoosier Invades the Confederacy: Letters and Diaries of Leroy S. Mayfield." *Indiana Magazine of History* 39 (1943): 144–91.

Bates, Joshua H. "Ohio's Preparations for the War." In *Military Order of the Loyal Legion of the United States, Ohio,* 9 vols., 1:128–41. Reprint, Wilmington, N.C.: Broadfoot, 1991.

Benjamin, Charles F. "Hooker's Appointment and Removal." In *Battles and Leaders of the Civil War,* 4 vols., edited by Robert U. Johnson and Clarence C. Buel, 3:239–43. Reprint, New York, 1956.

Boynton, H. V. "The Chickamauga Campaign." In *Papers of the Military Historical Society of Massachusetts,* 14 vols., 7:321–72. Boston: Military Historical Society of Massachusetts, 1910.

Brandley, Arnold. "The Cracker Line." *National Tribune,* May 28, 1885.

Bright, Thomas R. "Yankee in Arms: The Civil War as a Personal Experience." *Civil War History* 19 (September 1973): 197–281.

Buell, Don Carlos. "East Tennessee and the Campaign of Perryville." In *Battles and Leaders of the Civil War,* 4 vols., edited by Robert U. Johnson and Clarence C. Buel, 3:31–51. Reprint, New York, 1956.

———. "Major General W. T. Sherman and the Spring Campaign of 1862 in the West." *Historical Magazine* 8 (August 1870): 74–82.

———. "Operations in North Alabama." In *Battles and Leaders of the Civil War,* 4 vols., edited by Robert U. Johnson and Clarence C. Buel, 2:701–8. Reprint, New York, 1956.

———. "Shiloh Reviewed." In *Battles and Leaders of the Civil War,* 4 vols., edited by Robert U. Johnson and Clarence C. Buel, 1:487–536. Reprint, New York, 1956.

"Burning Reed's Bridge." *National Tribune,* March 26, 1896.

"Burning Reed's Bridge." *National Tribune,* December 10, 1914.

"Captain Burkhalter's Georgia War." In *Voices of the Prairie Land,* 2 vols., ed. Martin Litvin. Galesburg, Ill.: Mother Bickerdyke Historical Collection, 1972.

Carman, Henry ed. "Diary of Amos Glover." *The Ohio State Archeological and Historical Quarterly* 44 (April 1935): 258–72.

Castle, Henry A. "Sheridan with the Army of the Cumberland." In *Military Order of the Loyal Legion of the United States, District of Columbia,* 4 vols., 2:161–83. Reprint, Wilmington, N.C.: Broadfoot, 1993.

"Chickamauga." *National Tribune,* December 28, 1893.

"Civil War Letters." *Michigan History Magazine* 1 (October 1917): 3–18.

Cox, Jacob D. "McClellan in West Virginia." In *Battles and Leaders of the Civil War,* 4 vols., edited by Robert U. Johnson and Clarence C. Buel, 1:126–48. Reprint, New York, 1956.

———."War Preparations in the North." In *Battles and Leaders of the Civil War,* 4 vols., edited by Robert U. Johnson and Clarence C. Buel, 1:84–98. Reprint, New York, 1956.

Crittenden, Thomas L. "The Union Left at Stone's River." In *Battles and Leaders of the Civil War,* 4 vols., edited by Robert U. Johnson and Clarence C. Buel, 3:632–34. Reprint, New York, 1956.

Dillon, William D., ed. "The Civil War Letters of Enos Barret Lewis, 101st Ohio Volunteer Infantry—Part 2." *Northwest Ohio Quarterly* 57 (summer 1985): 83–100.

Ecelbarger, Gary L., ed. "Shiloh." *Civil War Times Illustrated* (April 1995): 50, 66–69.

Ferguson, Edward. "The Army of the Cumberland under Buell." In *Military Order of the Loyal Legion of the United States, Wisconsin,* 4 vols., 1:424–32. Reprint, Wilmington, N.C.: Broadfoot, 1993.

Freeman, Henry V. "Some Battle Recollections of Stones River." In *Military Order of the Loyal Legion of the United States, Illinois,* 8 vols., 3:227–46. Reprint, Wilmington, N.C.: Broadfoot, 1993.

Frémont, John C. "In Command of Missouri." In *Battles and Leaders of the Civil War,* 4 vols., edited by Robert U. Johnson and Clarence C. Buel, 1:278–88. Reprint, New York, 1956.

Fullerton, Joseph S. "The Army of the Cumberland at Chattanooga." In *Battles and Leaders of the Civil War,* 4 vols., edited by Robert U. Johnson and Clarence C. Buel, 3:719–26. Reprint, New York, 1956.

———. "Reinforcing Thomas at Chickamauga." In *Battles and Leaders of the Civil War,* 4 vols., edited by Robert U. Johnson and Clarence C. Buel, 3:665–67. Reprint, New York, 1956.

Funk, Arville L., ed. "A Hoosier Regiment at Stone's River: An Account by Lt. Colonel Daniel F. Griffen." *Filson Club Historical Quarterly* 37 (January 1963): 24–28.

"General W. H. Lytle." *National Tribune,* July 15, 1883.

"Gen. Steedman: His Brilliant Services at Chickamauga." *National Tribune,* August 4, 1887.

Gilbert, Charles C. "Bragg's Invasion of Kentucky." *Southern Bivouac* 1 (August 1885): 217–22; (September 1885): 296–301; (November 1885): 336–42.

———. "On the Field of Perryville." In *Battles and Leaders of the Civil War,* 4 vols., edited by Robert U. Johnson and Clarence C. Buel, 3:52–59. Reprint, New York, 1956.

Gilmore, James R. "Garfield's Ride at Chickamauga." *McClure's Magazine* 5 (1895): 357–68.

Grant, Ulysses S. "The Battle of Shiloh." In *Battles and Leaders of the Civil War,* 4 vols., edited by Robert U. Johnson and Clarence C. Buel, 1:465–86. Reprint, New York, 1956.

Guerrant, Edward O. "Marshall and Garfield in Eastern Kentucky." In *Battles and Leaders of the Civil War,* 4 vols., edited by Robert U. Johnson and Clarence C. Buel, 1:393–97. Reprint, New York, 1956.

Hascall, Milo S. "Personal Recollections and Experiences Concerning the Battle of Stones River." In *Military Order of the Loyal Legion of the United States, Illinois,* 8 vols., 4:148–70. Reprint, Wilmington, N.C.: Broadfoot, 1993.

Hendricks, Sherman. "Chickamauga: The Part Taken in the Great Battle by Battery C, 1st Ohio L.A." *National Tribune,* July 2, 1891.

Holzhueter, John O., ed. "William Wallace's Civil War Letters: The Atlanta Campaign." *Wisconsin Magazine of History* 57 (winter 1973–74): 28–59.

Hosea, Lewis. "The Regular Brigade of the Army of the Cumberland." In *Military Order of the Loyal Legion of the United States, Ohio,* 9 vols., 5:328–60. Reprint, Wilmington, N.C.: Broadfoot, 1991.

———. "The Second Day at Shiloh." In *Military Order of the Loyal Legion of the United States, Ohio,* 9 vols., 6:195–218. Reprint, Wilmington, N.C.: Broadfoot, 1991.

Howard, O. O. "The Battles around Atlanta." *Atlantic Monthly* 37 (October 1876): 385–99, 559–67.

———. "Grant at Chattanooga." In *Military Order of the Loyal Legion of the United States, New York,* 4 vols., 1:244–57. Reprint, Wilmington, N.C.: Broadfoot, 1993.

———. "A Sketch of the Life of George H. Thomas." In *Military Order of the Loyal Legion of the United States, New York,* 4 vols., 1:285–302. Reprint, Wilmington, N.C.: Broadfoot, 1993.

Hubbard, Paul, and Christine Lewis, eds. "Give Yourself No Trouble about Me: The Shiloh Letters of George W. Lennard." *Indiana Magazine of History* 76 (March 1980): 21–53.

James, F. B. "McCook's Brigade at the Assault upon Kennesaw Mountain, Georgia, June 27, 1864." In *The Atlanta Papers,* compiled by Sydney C. Kerksis, 255–70. Dayton: Morningside, 1980.

———. "Perryville and the Kentucky Campaign of 1862." In *Military Order of the Loyal Legion of the United States, Ohio,* 9 vols., 5:130–66. Reprint, Wilmington, N.C.: Broadfoot, 1991.

Johnson, Richard. "Battle above the Clouds." *National Tribune,* January 30, 1896.

———. "Recollections of Distinguished Generals in the Civil War." *National Tribune,* August 15, 1895.

Johnstone, Alexander S. "Scenes at Shiloh." In *Camp-Fire Sketches and Battle-Field Echoes,* ed. W. C. King and W. P. Derby, 49–51. Cleveland: N. G. Hamilton, 1888.

Jones, Frank J. "Personal Recollections of Some of the Generals in Our Army during the War." In vol. 6 of *Military Order of the Loyal Legion of the United States, Ohio.* Reprint, Wilmington, N.C.: Broadfoot, 1991.

Kaiser, Leo M., ed. "Civil War Letters of Charles W. Carr of the 21st Wisconsin Volunteers." *Wisconsin Magazine of History* 43 (summer 1960): 264–72.

Keller, Dean H. "A Civil War Diary of Albion W. Tourgée." *Ohio History* 74 (spring 1965): 99–131.

Kelly, R. M. "Holding Kentucky for the Union." In *Battles and Leaders of the Civil War,* 4 vols., edited by Robert U. Johnson and Clarence C. Buel, 1:373–92. Reprint, New York, 1956.

Kemper, A. C. "General W. H. Lytle." *National Tribune,* July 15, 1883.

Kerr, Charles D. "An Episode in the Kentucky Campaign of Generals Buell and Bragg." In *Military Order of the Loyal Legion of the United States, Minnesota.* 6 vols., 2:266–80. Reprint, Wilmington, N.C.: Broadfoot, 1992.

Kilpatrick, Robert L. "The Fifth Ohio Infantry at Resaca." In *The Atlanta Papers,* compiled by Sydney C. Kerksis, 355–60. Dayton: Morningside, 1980.

Kniffen, Gilbert C. "Army of the Cumberland at Stone River." In *Military Order of the Loyal Legion of the United States, District of Columbia,* 4 vols., 3:411–32. Reprint, Wilmington, N.C.: Broadfoot, 1993.

———. "The Battle of Stone's River." In *Battles and Leaders of the Civil War,* 4 vols., edited by Robert U. Johnson and Clarence C. Buel, 3:613–32. Reprint, New York, 1956.

———. "The Life and Services of Major General George H. Thomas." In *Military Order of the Loyal Legion of the United States, District of Columbia,* 4 vols., 2:13–31. Reprint, Wilmington, N.C.: Broadfoot, 1993.

Le Duc, William G. "The Little Steamboat That Opened the 'Cracker Line.'" In *Battles and Leaders of the Civil War,* 4 vols., edited by Robert U. Johnson and Clarence C. Buel, 3:676–78. Reprint, New York, 1956.

Livermore, Thomas L. "The Siege and Relief of Chattanooga." In *Papers of the Military Historical Society of Massachusetts,* 14 vols., 8:273–339. Boston: Military Historical Society of Massachusetts, 1910.

McCandless, Perry, ed. "Civil War Journal of Stephen Keyes Fletcher." *Indiana Magazine of History* 54 (June 1958): 141–90.

McCook, D. "The Second Day at Shiloh." *Harper's New Monthly Magazine* 28 (1863–64): 828–33.

McDowell, William P. "The 15th Kentucky." *Southern Bivouac* 5 (1886): 246–53.

Morgan, George W. "Cumberland Gap." In *Battles and Leaders of the Civil War,* 4 vols., edited by Robert U. Johnson and Clarence C. Buel, 3:62–69. Reprint, New York, 1956.

Norris, James D., and James K. Martin, eds. "Three Civil War Letters of James A. Garfield." *Ohio History* 74 (autumn 1965): 247–52.

"Old Rosy." *National Tribune,* May 26, 1887.

O'Leary, Jenny, and Harvey H. Jackson, eds. "The Civil War Letters of Captain Daniel O'Leary." *The Register of the Kentucky Historical Society* 77 (summer 1979): 157–85.

Opdycke, Emerson. "Notes on the Chickamauga Campaign." In *Battles and Leaders of the Civil War*, 4 vols., edited by Robert U. Johnson and Clarence C. Buel, 3:668–71. Reprint, New York, 1956.

"Open the Battle." *National Tribune*, January 5, 1905.

Otis, Ephraim A. "General George H. Thomas." In *Military Order of the Loyal Legion of the United States, Illinois*, 8 vols., 1:395–425. Reprint, Wilmington, N.C.: Broadfoot, 1993.

———. "The Murfreesboro Campaign." In *Papers of the Military Historical Society of Massachusetts*, 14 vols., 7:293–320. Boston: Military Historical Society of Massachusetts, 1910.

———. "Recollections of the Kentucky Campaign of 1862." In *Papers of the Military Historical Society of Massachusetts*, 14 vols., 7:229–53. Boston: Military Historical Society of Massachusetts, 1910.

Padgett, James A., ed. "With Sherman through Georgia and the Carolinas: Letters of a Federal Soldier." *Georgia Historical Quarterly* 32 (1948): 284–322.

"The Part Taken by the 69th Ohio and McCook's Brigade." *National Tribune*, July 3, 1890.

Perry, F. W. "Toilsome March of the Fourteenth Corps over the Mountains." *National Tribune*, June 28, 1883.

Pierson, Stephen. "From Chattanooga to Atlanta in 1864—A Personal Reminiscence." *Proceedings of the New Jersey Historical Society* 16 (1931).

"Reed's Bridge: The 69th Ohio Did Burn It and Opened the Battle of Chickamauga." *National Tribune*, December 10, 1914.

Reynolds, Donald E., and Max Hikele, eds. "With the Army of the Cumberland in the Chickamauga Campaign: The Diary of James W. Chapin, Thirty-Ninth Indiana Volunteers." *Georgia Historical Quarterly* 59 (summer 1975): 223–42.

Richards, William J. "Rosecrans and the Chickamauga Campaign." In *Military Order of the Loyal Legion of the United States, Indiana*, 465–75. Reprint, Wilmington, N.C.: Broadfoot, 1991.

Rosecrans, William S. "The Campaign for Chattanooga." *Century Magazine* (May 1887): 129–35.

———. "The Mistakes of Grant." *North American Review* (December 1885): 580–99.

———. "Rosecrans on Chattanooga." *National Tribune*, March 25, 1882.

———. "Tullahoma Campaign." *National Tribune*, March 11, 1882.

Rudisille, Lee H. "The Charge at Jonesboro: The Magnificent Charge by Este's Brigade." *National Tribune*, August 5, 1909.

Shanks, William F. G. "Recollections of General Rousseau." *Harper's Magazine* 30 (November 1865): 762–68.

Smith, Jacob H. "Personal Reminiscences—Battle of Shiloh." In *War Papers, Michigan Commandery, Military Order of the Loyal Legion of the United States*, 8–15. N.p., 1894.

Smith, William F. "Comments on General Grant's 'Chattanooga.'" In *Battles and Leaders of the Civil War*, 4 vols., edited by Robert U. Johnson and Clarence C. Buel, 3:714–17. Reprint, New York, 1956.

———. "An Historical Sketch of the Military Operations around Chattanooga." In *Papers of the Military Historical Society of Massachusetts*, 14 vols., 8:149–246. Boston: Military Historical Society of Massachusetts, 1910.

"Statement of Major General Buell in Review of the Evidence before the Military Commission." Cincinnati: n.p., 1863.

Steahlin, George. "Stanley's Cavalry: Colonel Minty's Sabre Brigade at Guy's Gap." *National Tribune,* May 27, 1882.

Stebbins, Austin E. "A Daring Movement." *National Tribune,* October 19, 1899.

Stewart, James E. "Fighting Them Over." *National Tribune,* February 19, 1885.

Stone, Henry. "The Operations of General Buell in Kentucky and Tennessee." In *Papers of the Military Historical Society of Massachusetts,* 14 vols., 7:255–91. Boston: Military Historical Society of Massachusetts, 1910.

Sylvester, Lorna Lutes, ed. " 'Gone for a Soldier:' The Civil War Letters of Charles Harding Cox." *Indiana Magazine of History* 68 (1972): 181–239.

Tapp, Hambleton, ed. "The Battle of Perryville, October 8, 1862, as Described in the Diary of Captain Robert B. Taylor," *Register of the Kentucky Historical Society* 60 (October 1962): 255–92.

Tatum, Margaret Black, ed. "Please Send Stamps: The Civil War Letters of William Allen Clark." *Indiana Magazine of History* 91 (March 1995): 81–108.

Thurston, Gates P. "Chickamauga." *Southern Bivouac* 6 (December 1886): 406–15.

Torkelson, Anthony R., ed. "A Norwegian in Blue: Letters of Iver Torkelson, 15th Wisconsin." *Military Images* 9 (January–February 1988): 6–13.

"War in the West." *National Tribune,* June 14, 1883.

"With an Artilleryman at Stones River." *Civil War Times Illustrated* 2 (February 1964): 41.

Wood, Thomas J. "The Battle of Missionary Ridge." In *Military Order of the Loyal Legion of the United States, Ohio,* 9 vols., 4:22–51. Reprint, Wilmington, N.C.: Broadfoot, 1991.

Woodward, James H. "Gen. A. McD. McCook at Stone River." In *Military Order of the Loyal Legion of the United States, California/Oregon,* 154–58. Reprint, Wilmington, N.C.: Broadfoot, 1991.

Wright, J. Montgomery. "Notes of a Staff-Officer at Perryville." In *Battles and Leaders of the Civil War,* 4 vols., edited by Robert U. Johnson and Clarence C. Buel, 3:60–61. Reprint, New York, 1956.

Yaryan, John Lee. "Stone River." In *Military Order of the Loyal Legion of the United States, Indiana,* 157–77. Reprint, Wilmington, N.C.: Broadfoot, 1991.

SECONDARY SOURCES

BOOKS

Ambrose, Stephen. *Halleck: Lincoln's Chief of Staff.* Baton Rouge: Louisiana State University Press, 1962.

Anderson, William M. *They Died to Make Men Free: A History of the 19th Michigan in the Civil War.* Berrien Springs, Mich.: Hardscrabble, 1980.

Andrews, J. Cutler. *The North Reports the Civil War.* Reprint, Pittsburgh: University of Pittsburgh Press, 1985.

Bailey, Anne J. *The Chessboard of War: Sherman and Hood in the Autumn Campaigns of 1864.* Lincoln: University of Nebraska Press, 2000.

Baumgartner, Richard A. *Blue Lightning: Wilder's Mounted Infantry Brigade in the Battle of Chickamauga.* Huntington, W.Va.: Blue Acorn, 1997.

Baumgartner, Richard A., and Larry M. Strayer. *Echoes of Battle: The Struggle for Chattanooga.* Huntington, W. Va.: Blue Acorn, 1996.

Bingham, Barry. *City of Conflict: Louisville in the Civil War.* Louisville: Louisville Civil War Round Table, 1962.

Bradley, Michael R. *Tullahoma: The 1863 Campaign for the Control of Middle Tennessee.* Shippensburg, Pa.: Burd Street, 2000.

Brown, Kent Masterson, ed. *The Civil War in Kentucky: Battle for the Bluegrass State.* Mason City, Iowa: Savas, 2000.

Buell, Thomas B. *The Warrior Generals: Combat Leadership in the Civil War.* New York: Crown, 1997.

Burton, William L. *Melting Pot Soldiers: The Union's Ethnic Regiments.* Ames: Iowa State University Press, 1988.

Caldwell, Robert G. *James A. Garfield: Party Chieftain.* Hamden, Conn.: Archon, 1965.

Carpenter, John A. *Sword and Olive Branch: Oliver Otis Howard.* Pittsburgh: University of Pittsburgh Press, 1964.

Castel, Albert. *Decision in the West: The Atlanta Campaign of 1864.* Lawrence: University Press of Kansas, 1992.

Catton, Bruce. *Grant Moves South.* Boston: Little, Brown, 1960.

———. *Grant Takes Command.* Boston: Little, Brown, 1968.

Cist, Henry M. *Army of the Cumberland.* Reprint, Wilmington, N.C.: Broadfoot, 1989.

Clark, John E. Jr. *Railroads in the Civil War: The Impact of Management on Victory and Defeat.* Baton Rouge: Louisiana State University Press, 2001.

Cleaves, Freeman. *Rock of Chickamauga: The Life of General George H. Thomas.* Norman: University of Oklahoma Press, 1948.

Connelly, Thomas L. *Army of the Heartland: The Army of Tennessee, 1861–1862.* Baton Rouge: Louisiana State University Press, 1967.

———. *Autumn of Glory: The Army of Tennessee, 1862–1865.* Baton Rouge: Louisiana State University Press, 1971.

Cooling, Benjamin Franklin. *Fort Donelson's Legacy: War and Society in Kentucky and Tennessee, 1862–1863.* Knoxville: University of Tennessee Press, 1997.

Coulter, E. Merton. *The Civil War and Readjustment in Kentucky.* Chapel Hill: University of North Carolina Press, 1926.

Cozzens, Peter. *No Better Place to Die: The Battle of Stones River.* Urbana: University of Illinois Press, 1990.

———. *The Shipwreck of Their Hopes: The Battles for Chattanooga.* Urbana: University of Illinois Press, 1994.

———. *This Terrible Sound: The Battle of Chickamauga.* Urbana: University of Illinois Press, 1992.

Current, Richard N. *Lincoln's Loyalists: Union Soldiers from the Confederacy.* Boston: Northeastern University Press, 1992.

Daniel, Larry J. *Shiloh: The Battle That Changed the Civil War.* New York: Simon and Schuster, 1977.

Daniel, Larry J., and Lynn N. Bock. *Island No. 10: Struggle for the Mississippi Valley.* Tuscaloosa: University of Alabama Press, 1996.

Davis, Stephen. *Atlanta Will Fall: Sherman, Joe Johnston, and the Yankee Heavy Battalions.* Wilmington, Del., Scholarly Resources, 2001.

Davis, William C. *Breckinridge: Statesman, Soldier, Symbol.* Baton Rouge: Louisiana State University Press, 1974.

———. *The Orphan Brigade: The Kentucky Confederates Who Couldn't Go Home.* New York, 1980.

Dell, Christopher. *Lincoln and the War Democrats.* Cranbury, N.J.: Associated University Presses, 1975.

Donald, David. *Lincoln.* New York: Simon and Schuster, 1995.

Duncan, Louis C. *The Medical Department of the United States Army in the Civil War.* Reprint, Gaithersburg, Md.: Olde Soldier, 1987.

Dunnavant, Robert. *Decatur, Alabama: Yankee Foothold in Dixie, 1861–1865.* Athens, Ala.: Pea Ridge, 1995.

Dyer, Frederick H. *A Compendium of the War of the Rebellion.* 3 vols. Reprint, New York: Thomas Yoseloff, 1959.

Eddy, T. M. *The Patriotism of Illinois.* 2 vols. Chicago: Clarke, 1865.

Engle, Stephen D. *Don Carlos Buell: Most Promising of All.* Chapel Hill: University of North Carolina Press, 1999.

Evans, David. *Sherman's Horsemen: Union Cavalry Operations in the Atlanta Campaign.* Bloomington: Indiana University Press, 1996.

Faust, Patricia L., ed. *Historical Times Illustrated Encyclopedia of the Civil War.* New York: Harper and Row, 1986.

Fellman, Michael. *Citizen Sherman: A Life of William Tecumseh Sherman.* New York: Random House, 1995.

Fisher, Noel C. *War at Every Door: Partisan Politics and Guerilla Violence in East Tennessee, 1860–1869.* Chapel Hill: University of North Carolina Press, 1997.

Fitch, Michael H. *The Chattanooga Campaign.* Madison: Wisconsin Historical Commission, 1911.

Foote, Shelby. *The Civil War: A Narrative.* 3 vols. New York: Random House, 1958.

Foulke, William D. *Life of Oliver P. Morton.* Indianapolis: Bowen-Merrill, 1899.

Garesché, Louis. *Biography of Lieut. Col. Julius P. Garesche.* Philadelphia: J. P. Lippincott, 1887.

Glatthaar, Joseph T. *The March to the Sea and Beyond: Sherman's Troops in the Savannah and Carolinas Campaign.* New York: New York University Press, 1985.

———. *Partners in Command: The Relationships between Leaders in the Civil War.* New York: Free Press, 1994.

Gleason, Chester F. *One Moment of Glory in the Civil War: When Cincinnati Was Defended from the Hills of Northern Kentucky.* Newport, Ky.: Otto Printing, 1965.

Grebner, Constantine. *"We Were the Ninth": A History of the Ninth Regiment, Ohio Volunteer Infantry, Apr. 17, 1861, to June 7, 1864.* Reprint, Kent, Ohio: Kent State University Press, 1987.

Greene, W. P. *The Greene River Country from Bowling Green to Evansville.* Evansville, Ind.: J. S. Reilly, 1898.

Griess, Thomas E., ed. *American Civil War.* Wayne, N.J.: Avery, 1987.

Grimsley, Mark. *The Hard Hand of War: Union Military Policy toward Southern Civilians, 1861–1865.* New York: Cambridge University Press, 1995.

Hafendorfer, Kenneth. *Mill Springs: Campaign and Battle of Mill Springs, Kentucky.* Louisville: KH Press, 2001.

———. *Perryville: Battle for Kentucky.* Owensburg, Ky.: McDowell, 1981.

———. *They Died by Twos and Tens: The Confederate Cavalry in the Kentucky Campaign of 1862.* Louisville: KH Press, 1995.

Hagerman, Edward. *The American Civil War and the Origins of Modern Warfare: Ideas, Organization, and Field Command.* Bloomington: Indiana University Press, 1988.

Hallock, Judith. *Braxton Bragg and Confederate Defeat.* Tuscaloosa: University of Alabama Press, 1991.

Harrison, Lowell H. *The Civil War in Kentucky.* Lexington: University Press of Kentucky, 1975.

Hattaway, Herman, and Archer Jones. *How the North Won.* Urbana: University of Illinois Press, 1983.

Haughton, Andrew. *Training, Tactics, and Leadership in the Confederate Army of Tennessee.* London: Frank Cass, 2000.

Haven, Thomas T. *Forty-Eight Days: The 105th Ohio Volunteer Infantry, Camp Cleveland, Ohio to Perryville, Kentucky.* Vista, Calif.: n.p., 1997.

Headley, P. C. *The Patriot Boy; or the Life and Career of Major-General Ormsby Mitchel.* New York: William H. Appleton, 1865.

Hebert, Walter H. *Fighting Joe Hooker.* Indianapolis: Bobbs-Merrill, 1944.

Hess, Earl J. *Banners to the Breeze: The Kentucky Campaign, Corinth, and Stones River.* Lincoln: University of Nebraska Press, 2000.

Hicken, Victor *Illinois in the Civil War.* Urbana: University of Illinois Press, 1966.

Hirshson, Stanley P. *The White Tecumseh: A Biography of General William T. Sherman.* New York: John Wiley and Sons, 1997.

History and Tour of the Atlanta Campaign. Columbus, Ohio: Blue and Gray Enterprises, 1996.

Howe, Henry. *Historical Collections of Ohio.* 3 vols. Cincinnati: Henry Howe and Son, 1891.

Hughes, Nathaniel Cheairs Jr., and Gordon D. Whitney. *Jefferson Davis in Blue: The Life of Sherman's Relentless Warrior.* Baton Rouge: Louisiana State University Press, 2002.

Hughes, Susan Lyons. *Camp Dick Robinson: Holding Kentucky for the Union.* Frankfort: Kentucky Historical Society, 1990.

Hume, Thomas William. *The Loyal Mountaineers of East Tennessee.* Knoxville: Ogden Brothers, 1888.

Johnson, J. Stoddard. *Memorial History of Louisville: From Its Settlement to the Year 1896.* 2 vols. Chicago: American Biographical Publishing, 1896.

Jones, Archer. *Civil War Command and Strategy: The Process of Victory and Defeat.* New York: Free Press, 1992.

Jones, R. Steven. *The Right Hand of Command: Use and Disuse of Personal Staffs in the Civil War.* Harrisburg: Stackpole, 2000.

Kamm, Samuel H. *The Civil War Career of Thomas A. Scott.* Philadelphia: University of Pennsylvania Press, 1940.

Kleber, John E., ed. *The Kentucky Encyclopedia.* Lexington: University Press of Kentucky, 1992.

Klein, Maury. *History of the Louisville and Nashville Railroad.* New York: Macmillan, 1972.

Klement, Frank L. *The Copperheads of the Middle West.* Chicago: University of Chicago Press, 1960.

Lambert, D. Warner. *When the Ripe Pears Fall: The Battle of Richmond, Kentucky.* Richmond, Ky.: Madison County Historical Society, 1995.

Lamers, William M. *Edge of Glory: A Biography of General William S. Rosecrans, U.S.A.* New York: Harcourt, Brace, and World, 1961.

Lewis, Lloyd. *Sherman: Fighting Prophet.* New York: Harcourt Brace, 1932.

Liddell-Hart, B. H. *Sherman: Soldier, Realist, American.* Reprint, New York: Frederick A. Praeger, 1958.

Livermore, Thomas L. *Numbers and Losses in the Civil War in America: 1861–1865.* Reprint, Bloomington: Indiana University Press, 1957.

Logsdon, David R., ed. *Eyewitnesses at the Battle of Stones River.* Nashville: n.p., 1989.

Longacre, Edward G. *From Union Stars to Top Hat: A Biography of the Extraordinary General James Harrison Wilson.* Harrisburg, Pa.: Stackpole, 1972.

Lonn, Ella. *Foreigners in the Union Army and Navy.* Baton Rouge: Louisiana State University Press, 1951.

Love, William DeLoss. *Wisconsin in the War of the Rebellion: A History of All Regiments and Batteries.* Chicago: Church and Goodmen, 1866.

Marszalek, John F. *Sherman: A Soldier's Passion for Order.* New York: Free Press, 1993.

———. *Sherman's Other War: The General and the Civil War Press.* Memphis: Memphis State University Press, 1981.

McDonough, James Lee. *Chattanooga—A Death Grip on the Confederacy.* Knoxville: University of Tennessee Press, 1984.

———. *Stones River: Bloody River in Tennessee.* Knoxville: University of Tennessee Press, 1980.

———. *War in Kentucky: From Shiloh to Perryville.* Knoxville: University of Tennessee Press, 1994.

McKinney, Francis F. *Education in Violence: The Life of George H. Thomas and the History of the Army of the Cumberland.* Detroit: Wayne State University Press, 1961.

McMurry, Richard. *Atlanta 1864: Last Chance for the Confederacy.* Lincoln: University of Nebraska Press, 2000.

———. *The Fourth Battle of Winchester: Toward a New Civil War Paradigm.* Kent, Ohio: Kent State University Press, 2002.

———. *John Bell Hood and the War for Southern Independence.* Lexington: University Press of Kentucky, 1982.

———. *Virginia Military Institute Alumni in the Civil War.* Lynchburg: VMI, 1990.

McPherson, James M. *Battle Cry of Freedom: The Civil War Era.* New York: Oxford University Press, 1988.

McWhiney, Grady. *Braxton Bragg and Confederate Defeat.* Tuscaloosa: University of Alabama Press, 1969.

Merideth, Roy. *Storm over Sumter: The Opening Engagement of the Civil War.* New York: Simon and Schuster, 1957.

Merrill, Catherine. *The Soldiers of Indiana in the War for the Union.* Indianapolis: Merrill, 1866.

Merrill, James E. *William Tecumseh Sherman.* New York: Rand McNally, 1971.

Miller, Francis T., ed. *The Photographic History of the Civil War.* 10 vols. New York, 1911.

Miller, Randall M., and John Davis Smith. *Dictionary of Afro-American Slavery.* Westport, Conn.: Praeger, 1997.

Mitchel, F. A. *Ormsby Macknight Mitchel: Astronomer and General, a Biographical Narrative.* Boston: Houghton, Mifflin, 1887.

Morris, Roy, Jr. *Sheridan: The Life and Wars of General Phil Sheridan.* Reprint, New York: Vintage, 1992.

Myers, Raymond E. *The Zollie Tree.* Louisville: Filson Club, 1964.

Nevins, Allan. *Ordeal for the Union.* 4 vols. Reprint, New York: Macmillan, 1992.

Noe, Kenneth W. *Perryville: The Grand Havoc of War.* Lexington: University Press of Kentucky, 2001.

Overmyer, Jack K. *A Stupendous Effort: The 87th Indiana in the War of the Rebellion.* Bloomington: Indiana University Press, 1997.

Palmer, George Thomas. *A Conscientious Turncoat: The Story of John M. Palmer, 1817–1900.* New Haven: Yale University Press, 1941.

Piatt, Don. *General George H. Thomas: A Critical Biography.* Cincinnati: Robert Clarke, 1893.

Pickenpaugh, Roger. *Rescue by Rail: Troop Transfer and the Civil War in the West, 1863.* Lincoln: University of Nebraska Press, 1998.

Plum, William R. *The Military Telegraph during the Civil War in the United States.* 2 vols. Chicago: Jansen, McClung, 1882.

Prokopowicz, Gerald G. *All for the Regiment: The Army of the Ohio, 1861–1862.* Chapel Hill: University of North Carolina Press, 2001.

Rawley, James A. *The Politics of Union: Northern Politics during the Civil War.* Lincoln: University of Nebraska Press, 1974.

Reid, Richard J. *The Army That Buell Built.* Fordsville, Ky.: Wendell Sandefur, 1994.

Reid, Whitelaw. *Ohio in the War: Her Statesmen, Generals, and Soldiers.* 2 vols. Columbus, Ohio: Electric, 1893.

Reinhart, Joseph R. *A History of the 6th Kentucky Volunteer Infantry U.S.* Louisville: Beargrass, 2000.

Robertson, William G. *The Battle of Chickamauga.* Philadelphia: Eastern National Park and Monument Association, 1995.

Rothrock, Mary U., ed. *The French Broad-Holston Country: A History of Knox County, Tennessee.* Knoxville: East Tennessee Historical Society, 1946.

Rowell, John W. *Yankee Artillerymen: Through the Civil War with Eli Lilly's Indiana Battery.* Knoxville: University of Tennessee Press, 1975.

———. *Yankee Cavalrymen: Through the Civil War with the Ninth Pennsylvania Cavalry.* Knoxville: University of Tennessee Press, 1971.

Royster, Charles. *The Destructive War: William Tecumseh Sherman, Stonewall Jackson, and the Americans.* New York: Alfred A. Knopf, 1991.

Sandburg, Carl. *Abraham Lincoln: The War Years.* 4 vols. New York: Harcourt, Brace, 1939.

Scaife, William R. *The Campaign for Atlanta.* Atlanta: privately printed, 1985.

Sears, Stephen W. *George B. McClellan: The Young Napoleon.* New York: Ticknor and Fields, 1988.

Secrist, Phillip L. *The Battle of Resaca.* Macon, 1998.

Simpson, Brooks. *Ulysses S. Grant: Triumph over Adversity, 1822–1865.* New York: Houghton Mifflin, 2000.

Skinner, George W. *Pennsylvania at Chickamauga and Chattanooga.* Harrisburg, Pa.: William Stanley Ray, 1900.

Sloan, Mary Rahn. *History of Camp Dennison, 1796–1956.* Cincinnati: Joseph Berning, 1956.

Smith, Jean Edward. *Grant.* New York: Simon and Schuster, 2001.

Smith, Theodore C. *The Life and Letters of James Abram Garfield.* New Haven: Yale University Press, 1925.

Starr, Louis M. *Bohemian Brigade: Civil War Newsmen in Action.* Madison: University of Wisconsin Press, 1987.

Starr, Stephen Z. *The Union Cavalry in the Civil War.* 3 vols. Baton Rouge: Louisiana State University Press, 1985.

Sullivan, James R. *Chickamauga and Chattanooga Battlefields.* Washington, D.C.: National Park Service, 1956.

Sword, Wiley. *Mountains Touched with Fire: Chattanooga Besieged, 1863.* New York: St. Martin's, 1995.

Temple, Oliver P. *East Tennessee and the Civil War.* Cincinnati: Robert Clarke, 1899.

Thomas, Benjamin P., and Harold M. Hyman. *Stanton: The Life and Times of Lincoln's Secretary of War.* New York: Knopf, 1962.

Thornbrough, Emma Lou. *Indiana in the Civil War Era, 1850–1880.* Indianapolis: Indiana Historical Bureau and Indiana Historical Society, 1965.

Townsend, William. *Lincoln and the Bluegrass: Slavery and Civil War in Kentucky.* Lexington: University Press of Kentucky, 1955.

Tredway, G. R. *Democratic Opposition to the Lincoln Administration in Indiana.* Indianapolis: Indiana Historical Society, 1973.

Trefousse, Hans L. *Andrew Johnson: A Biography.* New York: W. W. Norton, 1989.

Tucker, Glenn. *Chickamauga: Bloody Battle in the West.* Reprint, Dayton: Morningside, 1976.

Van Horne, Thomas B. *History of the Army of the Cumberland: Its Organization, Campaigns, and Battles,* 2 vols. Reprint, Wilmington, N.C.: Broadfoot, 1988.

———. *The Life of Major General George H. Thomas.* New York: Charles Scribner's Sons, 1882.

Van Tassell, David D., ed. *The Encyclopedia of Cleveland History.* Bloomington: Indiana University Press, 1996.

Warner, Ezra J. *Generals in Blue: Lives of the Union Commanders.* Baton Rouge: Louisiana State University Press, 1964.

Waugh, John C. *Reelecting Lincoln: The Battle for the 1864 Presidency.* New York: Crown, 1997.

Weigley, Russell F. *A Great Civil War: A Military and Political History, 1861–1865.* Bloomington: University of Indiana Press, 2000.

Welcher, Frank J., and Larry G. Ligget. *Coburn's Brigade.* Carmel, Ind.: Guild Press of Indiana, 1999.

Welsh, Jack D. *Medical Histories of Union Generals.* Kent, Ohio: Kent State University Press, 1996.

Westrate, Edwin V. *Those Fated Generals.* New York: Knight, 1936.

Williams, Kenneth P. *Grant Rises in the West: The First Year of the War, 1861–1862.* Reprint, Lincoln: University of Nebraska Press, 1997.

———. *Lincoln Finds a General: A Military Study of the Civil War.* 5 vols. New York: Macmillan, 1949–58.

Williams, Samuel C. *General John T. Wilder.* Bloomington: Indiana University Press, 1936.

Williams, T. Harry. *Lincoln and the Radicals.* Madison: University of Wisconsin Press, 1941.

Woods, J. T. *Steedman and His Men at Chickamauga.* Toledo: Blade Printing, 1876.

Woodworth, Steven. *Chickamauga: A Battlefield Guide.* Lawrence: University Press of Kansas, 1999.

———. *A Deep Steady Thunder: The Battle of Chickamauga.* Fort Worth: Ryan Place, 1996.

———. *Jefferson Davis and His Generals.* Lawrence: University Press of Kansas, 1990.

———. *Six Armies in Tennessee: The Chickamauga and Chattanooga Campaigns.* Lincoln: University of Nebraska Press, 1998.

———. *This Grand Spectacle: The Battle of Chattanooga.* Abilene: McWhiney Foundation, 1999.

ARTICLES

Baird, John A., Jr. "'For Gallant and Meritorious Service': Major General Absolam Baird." *Civil War Times Illustrated* 15 (June 1976): 45–46.

Bates, Joshua H. "Ohio's Preparations for the War." In *Military Order of the Loyal Legion of the United States, Ohio.* 9 vols., 1:128–41. Reprint, Wilmington, N.C.: Broadfoot, 1991.

"The Battle of Perryville." *Blue and Gray Magazine* 1 (October–November 1983): 21–39.

Bearss, Edwin C. "Cavalry Operations in the Battle of Stones River." *Tennessee Historical Quarterly* 19 (March 1960): 23–53.

———. "General Bragg Abandons Kentucky." *Register of the Kentucky Historical Society* 59 (July 1961): 217–44.

————. "Stones River: The Artillery Fight at 4:45 P.M., January 2, 1863." *Civil War Times Illustrated* 2 (February 1964): 12–13.

Becker, Carl M. "Miles Greenwood." In *Ohio Leaders in the Civil War,* edited by Kenneth W. Wheeler. Columbus: Ohio State University Press, 1968.

Bright, Thomas R. "Yankee in Arms: The Civil War as a Personal Experience." *Civil War History* 19 (Sept. 1973).

Castel, Albert. "The War Moves West." In *Shadows of the Storm,* 5 vols., edited by William C. Davis, 1:264–78. Garden City, N.Y.: Doubleday, 1981.

————. "Why the North Won and the South Lost." *Civil War Times Illustrated* 39 (May 2000): 56–60.

Coleman, J. Winston, Jr. "Old Kentucky Iron Furnaces." *The Filson Club Historical Quarterly* 31 (July 1957): 227–42.

East, Ernest E. "Lincoln's Russian General." *Journal of the Illinois State Historical Society* 52 (spring 1959): 106–22.

Ecelbarger, Gary L., ed. "Shiloh." *Civil War Times Illustrated* (April 1995): 50, 66–69.

Ellis, A. M. "Major General William Nelson." *Kentucky Historical Society Register* 7 (May 1906): 56–64.

Engle, Stephen D. "Don Carlos Buell: Military Philosophy and Command Problems in the West." *Civil War History* 41 (June 1995): 89–115.

Farrelly, David G. "John Marshall Harlan and the Union Cause in Kentucky in 1861." *Filson Club Historical Quarterly* 37 (January 1963): 5–23.

Fish, Carl Russell "The Decision of the Ohio Valley." In *American Historical Association, Annual Report of 1910,* 155–64. N.p., 1910.

Fisher, Noel C. "Groping toward Victory: Ohio's Administration of the Civil War." *Ohio History* 105 (winter–spring 1996): 25–45.

Furqueron, James R. "The Best Hated Man in the Army." *North and South* 4 (March 2001): 24–34.

————. "A Fight Soon or a Footrace: The Tullahoma Campaign." *North and South* 1 (January 1998): 28–38, 82–89.

Griese, Arthur A. "A Louisville Tragedy—1862." *Filson Club Historical Quarterly* 26 (April 1952): 133–54.

Jenkins, Kirk C. "A Shooting at the Galt House: The Death of General William Nelson." *Civil War History* 43 (June 1997): 101–18.

Jones, Terry L. "'The Flash of Their Guns Was a Sure Sign': The 19th Michigan as Infantry in the Atlanta Campaign." In *The Campaign for Atlanta and Sherman's March to the Sea,* edited by Theodore P. Savas and David A. Woodbury, 134–67. Campbell, Calif.: Savas Woodbury, 1992.

Lang, Wendell W., Jr. "Corps Badges of the Civil War." *Military Images* 8 (November–December 1986).

Madden, David. "Union Resistance to Confederate Occupation: The Bridge Burners of East Tennessee." *East Tennessee Historical Society's Publication* 53 (1981): 23–39.

Marszalek, John F. "Sherman Called It the Way He Saw It." *Civil War History* 40 (1994): 72–78.

McKinney, Francis F. "The First Regiment of Michigan Engineers and Mechanics." *Michigan Alumnus Quarterly Review* 62 (1956): 140–44.

McMurtry, Gerald. "Zollicoffer—Battle of Mill Springs." *Filson Club Historical Quarterly* 29 (October 1955): 303–19.

Miller, E. Eugene. "The Contribution of German Immigrants to the Union Cause in the Civil War in Kentucky." *Filson Club Historical Quarterly* 64 (October 1990): 462–78.

Morris, Roy, Jr. "The Sack of Athens." *Civil War Times Illustrated* 24 (February 1986): 26–32.

Noe, Kenneth W. "Grand Havoc: The Climatic Battle of Perryville." In *The Civil War in Kentucky: Battle for the Bluegrass State,* edited by Kent Masterson Brown, 175–220. Mason City, Iowa: Savas, 2000.

Oyes, Matthew. "The Mobilization of the Ohio Militia in the Civil War." *Ohio History* 98 (summer–autumn 1989): 147–74.

Pabst, Lawrence B. "The Sack and Occupation of Athens, Alabama." *Bulletin of the North Alabama Historical Association* 4 (1959): 18–20.

Poulter, Keith. "But Then Again . . . ." *North and South* 1 (January 1998): 36–38, 82–83.

Prokopowicz, Gerald A. "Tactical Stalemate: The Battle of Stones River." *North and South* 2 (September 1999): 10–21, 24–27.

Sanders, Stuart W. "Buckeye Warriors at Perryville." *American's Civil War* (January 2001): 41–44.

Schiller, Laurence D. "A Taste of Northern Steel: The Evolution of Federal Cavalry Tactics, 1861–1865." *North and South* 2 (January 1999): 44–45, 80–82.

———. "Two Tales of Tennessee: The Ups and Downs of Cavalry Command." *North and South* 4 (April 2001): 78–86.

Shankman, Arnold. "Soldier Votes and Clement L. Vallandigham in the 1863 Ohio Gubernatorial Election." *Ohio History* 82 (1974): 88–104.

Shinman, Phillip L. "Engineering and Command: The Case of General William S. Rosecrans 1862–1863" In *The Art of Command in the Civil War,* edited by Steven F. Woodworth, 84–117. Lincoln: University of Nebraska Press, 1998.

Simon, John Y. "Lincoln, Grant, and Kentucky in 1861." In *The Civil War in Kentucky: Battle for the Bluegrass State,* edited by Kent Masterson Brown, 1–21. Mason City, Iowa: Savas, 2000.

Stampp, Kenneth M. "Kentucky's Influence upon Indiana in the Crisis of 1861." *Indiana Magazine of History* 39 (September 1943): 263–76.

Starr, Stephen Z. "Camp Dennison, 1861–1865." *Bulletin of the Historical and Philosophical Society of Ohio* 18 (July 1960): 167–90.

Stevenson, Daniel "General Nelson, Kentucky, and Lincoln Guns." *Magazine of American History* 10 (August 1883): 115–39.

Tucker, Glenn. "George H. Thomas—A Personality Profile." *Civil War Times Illustrated* 5 (April 1966).

Wittle, Carl. "The Ninth Ohio Volunteers." *Ohio Archaeological and Historical Publications* 35 (1927): 408–13.

Woodworth, Steven E. "Braxton Bragg and the Tullahoma Campaign." In *The Art of Command in the Civil War,* 157–82. Lincoln: University of Nebraska Press, 1998.

DISSERTATIONS AND THESES

Chumney, J. R. "Don Carlos Buell: Gentleman General." Ph.D. diss., Rice University, 1964.

Prokopowicz, Gerald. "All for the Regiment: Unit Cohesion and Tactical Stalemate in the Army of the Ohio, 1861–1862." Ph.D. diss., Harvard University, 1994.

Swittik, Matthew C. "Loomis Battery: First Michigan Artillery, 1859–1865." Master's thesis, Wayne State University, 1975.

Taylor, Lenette Sengel. "'The Supply for Tomorrow Must Not Fail': A Union Quartermaster's Civil War." Ph.D. diss., Kent State University, 2001.

Wanatick, Mary Ann Steedman. "Major General James Blair Steedman." Master's thesis, University of Toledo, 1988.

INDEX